WORKING AMERICANS

1880–2010

Volume XI:
Inventors & Entrepreneurs

WORKING AMERICANS
1880–2010

Volume XI:
Inventors & Entrepreneurs

by Scott Derks

A Universal Reference Book

PUBLISHER:	Leslie Mackenzie
EDITORIAL DIRECTOR:	Laura Mars
EDITORIAL ASSISTANT:	Diana Delgado
PRODUCTION MANAGER:	Kristen Thatcher
MARKETING DIRECTOR:	Jessica Moody
AUTHOR:	Scott Derks
CONTRIBUTORS:	Jael Bridgemahon, Jimmy Copening, Roy Eargle, Jim Reindollar, Tony Smith
COPY EDITOR:	Elaine Alibrandi
COMPOSITION:	Computer Composition of Canada Inc.

Grey House Publishing, Inc.
4919 Route 22
Amenia, NY 12501
518.789.8700
FAX 845.373.6390
www.greyhouse.com
e-mail: books@greyhouse.com

While every effort has been made to ensure the reliability of the information presented in this publication, Grey House Publishing neither guarantees the accuracy of the data contained herein nor assumes any responsibility for errors, omissions or discrepancies. Grey House accepts no payment for listing; inclusion in the publication of any organization, agency, institution, publication, service or individual does not imply endorsement of the editors or publisher.

Errors brought to the attention of the publisher and verified to the satisfaction of the publisher will be corrected in future editions.

Publisher's Cataloging-In-Publication Data

Derks, Scott.
  Working Americans 1880-2010 / by Scott Derks.
  v. : ill. ; cm.
Title varies.
"A universal reference book."
Includes bibliographical references and indexes.
Contents: v. 1. The working class—v.2. The middle class—v.3. The upper class—v.4. Their children.—v.5. At war.— v.6. Women at work—v.7. Social movements—v.8. Immigrants—v.9. Revolutionary war to civil war—v.10. Sports & recreation.—v.11. Inventors & Entrepreneurs.
  ISBN: 1-891482-81-5 (v.1)
  ISBN: 1-891482-72-6 (v.2)
  ISBN: 1-930956-38-X (v.3)
  ISBN: 1-930956-35-5 (v.4)
  ISBN: 1-59327-024-1 (v.5)
  ISBN: 1-59237-063-Z (v.6)
  ISBN: 1-59237-101-9 (v.7)
  ISBN: 978-1-59237-197-6 (v.8)
  ISBN 13: 1-978-1-59237-101-3 (v.9)
  ISBN: 1-59237-441-7 (v. 10)
  ISBN: 1-59237-565-3 (v. 11)

1. Working class—United States—History. 2. Labor—United States—History. 3. Occupation—United States—History.
4. Social classes—United States—History. 5. Immigrants—Employment—United States—History. 6. United States—Economic conditions. 1. Title.
HD 8066   .D47 2000
305.5/0973/0904

Printed in the USA

ISBN 10: 1-59237-565-3

DEDICATION

May this book embrace the American spirit that unleashed its inventors and entrepreneurs, especially Keith Wakeman, Ross Consaul, Kenny Jarrett, and Roy and Dotty Eargle.

TABLE OF CONTENTS

1930 – 1939 INTRODUCTION

1940 – 1949 INTRODUCTION

1950 – 1959 INTRODUCTION

1960 – 1969 INTRODUCTION

1970 – 1979 INTRODUCTION

1980 — 1989 INTRODUCTION

1990 — 1999 INTRODUCTION

2000 — 2010 INTRODUCTION

PREFACE

This book is the eleventh in a series examining the social and economic lives of working Americans. In this volume, the focus is on inventors and entrepreneurs whose work and inspirations are the foundation of the American economic success story. Without their willingness to take risks, the American story would be radically different and far less robust. Some of these entrepreneurs and inventors were also granted fame and fortune, others simply liked the process of making something new, making something better, or creating opportunity from a concept. Their stories include an immigrant machinist whose inventive ways revolutionized shoemaking, a book peddler who organized the distribution of U.S. Grant's autobiography in Ohio, the inventors of the cash register, vacuum cleaner and even street car bumpers. Along the way we encounter a woman whose artistry and imagination birthed the Campbell Kids, we witness the multi-decade journey of the zipper for market acceptance, a legal stock manipulation, the invention of the French fry, the role of mechanical glassblowers in the expansion of electric light, patent fights over FM radio, and the struggle to make hydrogen fuel cells economically viable. In all, there are 36 stories about real struggles in the search for the American dream.

In this volume of the *Working Americans* series, little effort has been expended to distinguish inventors from entrepreneurs. In many cases, these roles are blended, often enriching the grit of the tale, but not always to the financial benefit of the inventor. As will become obvious, inventing and then commercializing an idea are separate activities and skills requiring enormous dedication, imagination and luck. As in previous volumes, all the profiles are modeled on real people and events, with some details added based on the statistics, the popularity of an idea, or writings of the time. Unlike most previous volumes, the need to identify by name the inventors of certain products overrode the historical pattern of these books using no factual names. Therefore, the majority of individuals profiled in this volume include their real names. They are:

Jan Matzeliger (1886), James "Jake" Ritty (1895), Milton S. Hershey (1907), Henry Wood (1908), James Murray Spangler (1911), Grace Wiederseim (1917), Madam C.J. Walker (1919), Gideon Sundback (1926), George Mecherle (1931), Donald Davis (1935), Herbert Thomas Kalmus (1939), William J. Woods (1940), Lt. (Dr.) Mary Sears (1945), Percy Lebraon Spencer (1947), Edwin Howard Armstrong (1954), Jack Simplot (1955), Jack Kilby (1959), Norton Simon (1965), Dr. Harry Coover (1967), Benjamin Eisenstadt (1969), Roy and Dotty Eargle (1975), Bette Nesmith Graham (1976), Stephen Hassenfeld (1984), James Kennedy Jarrett (1986), Bill Reindollar (1989), Jerry D. Neal (1995), Maurice Jennings (1996), Rey Banatao (2008), William Thomas Davis (2009), and Gorm Bressner (2010).

Every effort has been made to profile accurately the individual's expertise, as well as home and work experiences. To ensure that the profiles reflect the mood of each decade and the feelings of the subjects, letters, biographies, interviews, high school annuals, and magazine articles were consulted and used. In some cases, the people profiled represent national trends and feelings, but mostly they represent themselves. Ultimately, it is the working Americans and their activities—along with their investment, spending decisions, passions and jobs—that shape the society and economy of the United States.

About the *Working Americans* Series

The first three volumes of *Working Americans: 1880-1999* explore the economic lives and loves of working-class, middle-class and upper-class Americans through the eyes and wallets of more than 100 families. Employing pictures, stories, statistics and advertisements of the period, these intimate profiles study their jobs, wages, family life, expenditures and hobbies throughout the decades. Although separated by levels of wealth, each volume also captures the struggles and joys of a shifting American economy and the transformation they brought to communities and families in the workplace, regardless of economic status. The fourth volume, *Their Children*, builds upon the social and economic issues explored previously by examining the lives of children across the entire spectrum of economic status. Issues addressed include parents, child labor, education, peer pressure, food, fads and fun. *Volume V: Americans at War* explores the life-changing elements of war and discusses how enlisted personnel, officers and civilians handle the stress, exhilaration, boredom and brutality of America's various wars, conflicts and incursions. *Volume VI: Women at Work* celebrates the contributions of women, chronicling both their progress and roadblocks along the way, highlighting the critical role of women in the front lines of change.

Working Americans VII: Social Movements explores the various ways American men and women feel called upon to challenge accepted conventions, whether the issue is cigarette smoking in 1901 or challenging the construction of a massive hydroelectric dam in 1956. *Working Americans VIII: Immigrants* examines the lives of first- and second-generation immigrants with a focus on their journey to America, their search for identity and their emotions experienced in the new land. *Working Americans IX: The Revolutionary War to the Civil War* steps back in time to chronicle the lives of 36 families from the 1770s to the 1860s, detailing their troubles and triumphs, whether they were farmers, postal clerks, whiskey merchants, lawyers or cabinetmakers. *Working Americans X: Sports & Recreation* tackles the diverse and ever-changing world of competitive sports in America from the viewpoint of the professional, the amateur and the spectator. Along the way, we meet Olympic swimmers, basketball players who rarely play, boxers with extraordinary stamina, weightlifters of unbelievable determination and weekend athletes thrilled by the opportunity to be in the open air.

Each of these 11 volumes—embracing the lives of more than 365 families throughout American history—strives to tell a story, a simple story of struggling, hoping and enduring. And if I've learned anything in the last 12 years of writing these books, it is that the American spirit lives on, maintains its free will, and endeavors to meet the challenges of the day. This spirit is alive and well, and still lives in America.

Scott Derks

INTRODUCTION

Working Americans 1880-2010 Volume XI: Inventors & Entrepreneurs is the eleventh volume in the *Working Americans* series. Like its predecessors, this work profiles the lives of Americans—how they lived, how they worked, how they thought—decade by decade. Earlier volumes focus on economic status or social issues. More recent volumes focus on a specific group of Americans—like immigrants in *Volume VIII* and athletes in *Volume X*. This volume highlights American ingenuity—men and women with a mission. They are the folks who struggled to reach for the American dream with new inventions, improved products, or perseverance, plain and simple.

Praise for earlier volumes—

"this volume engages and informs, contributing significantly and meaningfully to the historiography of the working class in America...a compelling and well-organized contribution for those interested in social history and the complexities of working Americans."

Library Journal

"... the Working Americans *approach to social history is interesting and each volume is worth exploring ..."*
"these interesting, unique compilations of economic and social facts, figures, and graphs...support multiple research needs [and] will engage and enlighten patrons in high school, public, and academic library collections."

Booklist

"[the author] adds to the genre of social history known as 'history from the bottom up'
...Recommended for all colleges and university library collections."

Choice

"the volume succeeds at presenting various cultural, regional, economic and age-related points of view... [it is] visually appealing [and] certainly a worthwhile purchase..."

Feminist Collections

"... promises to enhance our understanding of the growth and development of the working class over more than a century.' It capably fulfills this promise... recommended for all types of libraries. "

ARBA

All eleven volumes, regardless of economic status, time period, or specific focus, offer a unique, almost uncanny, look at those Americans whose talents, desires, motivations, struggles, and values shaped—and continue to shape—this nation. Without exception, the 365 individuals profiled in the eleven volumes of this *Working Americans* series are working toward their version of the American dream.

Volume XI: Inventors & Entrepreneurs takes you:
- To Hershey, PA, where Milton Hershey perfected his recipe for milk chocolate in 1907;
- Onto the drawing table of Grace Wiederseim, creator, in 1917, of the still recognizable Campbell Kids;
- To NYC's Wall Street in 1928, where Joseph Ridgeway experienced the highs and lows of a stock pool manager;
- Behind the scenes of the U.S. Navy in Falmouth, MA, where Lt. Mary Sears overcame prejudices in 1945 that still exist 55 years later;
- Into a 1954 courtroom where FM radio inventor Edwin Armstrong was left so depressed over the legal battle in which RCA claimed ownership of his designs and patents, that he claimed his own life;
- To Los Angeles, CA, where, in 1967, Dr. Harry Coover discovered Super Glue by accident—a substance that literally stopped the bleeding;
- Inside a bottle of Liquid Paper, invented in 1976 by Bette Graham, who grew tired of fixing her mistakes by retyping entire pages;
- To Jackson, SC in 1986, where soybean farmer James Jarrett built rifles so accurate that customers waited up to 12 months to own one;
- To the shores of the Pacific Ocean in 2008, where young Ray Banatao and his brother launched a greener surfboard.

Arranged in 12 chapters, this newest *Working Americans* includes three **Profiles** per chapter for a total of 36. Each profile offers personal insight using *Life at Home*, *Life at Work* and *Life in the Community* categories. These personal topics are followed by historical and economic data of the time. **Historical Snapshots** chronicle major milestones. Various **Innovation** charts list products and ideas born is a specific year. **Timelines** include *Chocolate Making, Refrigeration, Business Machines* and *Fast Food Restaurants*. A variety of **News Features** puts the subject's life and work in context of the day. These common elements, as well as specialized data, such as **Selected Prices**, in currency of the time, punctuate each chapter and act as statistical comparisons between decades. The 36 men and women profiled in this volume represent all regions of the country, and a wide variety of age and ethnicity. The Table of Contents provides a detailed list.

Like the other ten volumes in this series, *Working Americans 1880-2010 Volume XI: Inventors & Entrepreneurs* is a compilation of original research (personal diaries and family histories) plus printed material (government statistics, commercial advertisements, and news features). The text, in easy-to-read bulleted format, is supported with hundreds of graphics, such as photos, advertisements, pages from printed material, letters, and documents.

All eleven *Working Americans* volumes are "point in time" books, designed to illustrate the reality of that particular time. Some Americans portrayed in this 11th volume realized the American dream and some did not. Many of their stories continue.

ACKNOWLEDGMENTS

This 11th volume of the *Working Americans* series is an especially satisfying book because of the courageous people it profiles. Ours is an innovative culture whose lifeblood is fueled by men and women willing to work for years—at little or no pay—to see the fulfillment of a dream. Innovation always comes at a price but is not always rewarded in recognition or money. For this volume several veterans of the *Working Americans* series gathered to do research and tell stories about America's inventors and entrepreneurs. My appreciation and graditude goes to Jim Reindollar, Jimmy Copening, Tony Smith, Roy Eargle and Laura Mars, while Bill Davis, Katie Barnes, Brian Cendrowski, Linda Kusse-Wolfe and Holly H. Zimmer all provided special assistance. Special thanks goes to Elaine "Brandy" Alibrandi for cracking her grammatical whip on legions of misbehaving adverbs, wayward pronouns and the always sneaky verbs. May all your nouns and verbs be in agreement and your prepositions restrained.

1880-1899

The last two decades of the nineteenth century danced in the reflected glow of the Gilded Age, when the wealth of a tiny percentage of Americans knew no bounds. It was a time of vast, accumulated wealth and an abundance of emerging technology —all racing to keep up with the restless spirit of the American people. The rapid expansion of railroads opened up the nation to new industries, new markets and the formation of monopolistic trusts that catapulted a handful of corporations into positions of unprecedented power and wealth. This expanding technology also triggered the movement of workers from farm to factory, the rapid expansion of wage labor, reinvigorated entrepreneurs nationwide, and the explosive growth of cities. Farmers, merchants and small-town artisans found themselves increasingly dependent on regional and national market forces. The shift in the concentrations of power was unprecedented in American history. At the same time, professionally trained workers were reshaping America's economy alongside business managers or entrepreneurs eager to capture their piece of the American pie. It was an economy on a roll with few rudders or regulations.

Across America the economy—along with its work force—was running away from the land. Before the Civil War, the United States was overwhelmingly an agricultural nation. By the end of the century, non-agricultural occupations employed nearly two thirds of the workers. As important, two of every three Americans came to rely on wages instead of self-employment as farmers or artisans. At the same time, industrial growth began to center around cities, where wealth accumulated for a few who understood how to harness and use railroads, create new consumer markets, and manage a ready supply of cheap, trainable labor.

Jobs offering steady wages and the promise of a better life for workers' children, drew people from the farms into the cities, which grew at twice the rate of the nation as a whole. A modern, industrially-based work force emerged from the traditional farmlands led by men skilled at managing others and the complicated flow of materials required to keep a factory operating. This led to an increasing demand for attorneys, bankers and physicians to handle the complexity of the emerging urban economy. In 1890, newspaper editor Horace Greeley remarked, "We cannot all live in cities, yet nearly all seem determined to do so."

The new cities of America were home to great wealth and poverty—both produced by the massive migrations and influx of immigrants willing to work at any price. It was a time symbolized by Andrew Carnegie's steel mills, John D. Rockefeller's organization of the Standard Oil monopoly, and the manufacture of Alexander Graham Bell's wonderful invention, the telephone. By 1894, the United States had become the world's leading industrial power, producing more than England, France and Germany—its three largest competitors—combined. For much of this period, the nation's industrial energy focused on the need for railroads requiring large quantities of labor, iron, steel, stone, and lumber. In 1883, nine tenths of the nation's entire production of steel went into rails. The most important invention of the period—in an era of tremendous change and innovation—may have been the Bessemer converter, which transformed pig iron into steel at a relatively low cost, increasing steel output 10 times from 1877 to 1892.

The greatest economic event during the last two decades of the nineteenth century was the great wave of immigration that swept America. It is believed to be the largest worldwide population movement in human history, bringing more than 10 million people to the United States to fill the expanding need for workers. Scandinavia, Italy, and China sent scores of eager workers, normally men, to fill the expanding labor needs of the United States. To attract this much-needed labor force, railroad and steamship companies advertised throughout Europe and China the glories of American life. To an economically depressed world, it was a welcome call.

The national wealth in 1890 was $65 billion; nearly $40 billion was invested in land and buildings, $9 billion in railroads, and $4 billion in manufacturing and mining. By 1890, 25 percent of the world's output of coal was mined in the United States. Annual production of crude petroleum went from 500,000 barrels in 1860 to 63.6 million in 1900. This was more than the wealth of Great Britain, Russia, and Germany put together.

Despite all the signs of economic growth and prosperity, America's late-nineteenth-century economy was profoundly unstable. Industrial expansion was undercut by a depression from 1882 to 1885, followed in 1893 by a five-year-long economic collapse that devastated rural and urban communities across America. As a result, job security for workers just climbing onto the industrial stage was often fleeting. Few wage-earners found full-time work for the entire year. The unevenness in the economy was caused both by the level of change underway and irresponsible speculation, but more generally to the stubborn adherence of the federal government to a highly inflexible gold standard as the basis of value for currency.

Between the very wealthy and the very poor emerged a new middle stratum, whose appearance was one of the distinctive features of late-nineteenth-century America. The new middle class fueled the purchase of one million light bulbs a year by 1890, even though the first electric light was only 11 years old. It was the middle class also that flocked to buy Royal Baking Powder, (which was easier to use and faster than yeast) and supported the emergence and spread of department stores that were sprouting up across the nation.

1882 News Feature

"Remarkable Developments in Oil," *Scientific American*, July 22, 1882:

The history of the oil trade in this country does not furnish a parallel to the effect of recent developments. The result of the penetration of a certain rock 1,600 feet below the surface, in the wilderness of Warren County, Pennsylvania, has been to form anew the map of the oil regions, to depreciate the value of oil above ground (30,000,000 barrels) 30 cents per barrel, for a total shrinkage of $9,000,000, and to enrich a few and impoverish many. The history of well "646" would read like a romance, but the reality of its effect upon the trade is grim and matter-of-fact to the last degree. On the 1st of April last, crude oil was selling at 80 cents per barrel. The producers had good grounds for encouragement in the general situation. Consumption was increasing, and one of the old producing regions (Bradford) was rapidly declining. Its young rival (Richburg, New York) had reached its highest point, and everything in reason pointed to "dollar oil." Meanwhile, a patient and disappointed driller was nearing the end of his cable and his credit, in the dense hemlock forest of Cherry Grove Township, Warren County, six miles from any oil well, four miles from the nearest gas well, and two miles from a "dry hole." At 1,612 feet, the sand pump brought up that which threw the owners of the well into a fever of excitement. They suspended all operations, boarded up and locked the derrick, and employed a patrol of armed men to keep out every intruder. Every available acre of land in the vicinity was quietly bought up by the few favored ones, and on May 18 the owners were ready to start the drill into the oil rock. In the interval, the fame of the "Mystery, No. 646" had traveled throughout the region. Producers in general regarded the whole affair as a deep laid plot, but were uneasy nevertheless, and oil had dropped to 73 cents. Since the "Mystery" had exerted an influence on the market, 10,000,000 barrels had been sold "short," and every producer heartily wished "646" in Jericho. On the date named, fires were lighted and the drill started in the bottom of the well. By the time the soft, pebble-filled rock had been pierced eight feet, the oil was flowing from the top of the well, through two, two-inch pipes, at the rate of 1,400 barrels per day, and the entire trade was, for the time, paralyzed. Today this well is rated at 800 barrels, and, since May 18, a 3,000-, a 2,500-, and a 2,000-barrel well have each been added their production to the original "Mystery"; a town has grown up in the hemlock forest, and a score more drills are nearing the same long-neglected storehouse. The price of oil has reached 52 cents, and the older oil regions are being depopulated to fill the new field with excited multitudes. One thousand dollars an acre and half the oil is the price for all land on the "45 degree line" along which the larger wells have so far been developed. Garfield City is today the Mecca of the oil producer, and is as strange a creation itself as can be noted in the entire oil country.

1885 Profile

After a youth spent on a farm and some years in the Union Army, Buck Blanchard wanted to direct his own success by becoming an entrepreneur, selling books and making profits from the sales of other "canvassers."

Life at Home

- Buck Blanchard met his first traveling salesman when he was eight years old.
- The peddler was from Connecticut, a distant, almost unimaginable place for a boy living in rural Ohio in 1841.
- The hawker was impressive in his speech, his dress and the way he displayed the "highest value" mantel clock he had brought, even though most farmhouse wives never knew they needed one until the salesman arrived.
- While strolling together on the quarter-mile run up to the farmhouse, the man asked Buck about that year's crops, the number of brothers and sisters he had, the foods his mother liked to cook and what church they all attended.
- Buck was delighted by all the attention.
- Buck's father was not happy to see the peddler.
- Previous waves of Yankees salesmen had left farmers with mediocre goods, merchants unhappy about lost sales and housewives suddenly discontented by the stinginess of their husbands.
- This was especially true if the area had been worked by a traveling lightning rod salesman, who often frightened farmers into signing contracts filled with hidden costs or additional fees.
- Buck's newfound friend had concerns of his own—Ohio farm wives were well known for their bargaining skills.
- Bartering was a respected skill in a nation without a uniform currency in which three-quarters of its population were farmers and dependent on bargaining to obtain everything from soap to wagon wheels.

Buck Blanchard was a traveling book salesman.

- Each peddler had to calculate the exchange rates of Ohio bank-issued funds, the appropriate value of six large eggs (were they offered as part of the settlement) and the possibility of selling the clock he had on hand later in the year when the harvest was past and farmers were feeling more prosperous.
- Clock peddlers, who charged $10 or more for their goods, preferred bank notes or coins—commodities which were in short supply in most farmhouses.
- Buck was fascinated with how the peddler talked his normally stubborn father into leaving his plow and listening to a lengthy spiel, before walking to the farmhouse to see how a "genuine Eli Terry" clock looked on the mantel.
- Along the way, the salesman called each of the children by name, as though he were a visiting uncle, mused about the rumored rise in wheat prices and praised God for the moral leadership provided by the Methodist church where the family worshipped.
- He even mentioned the intentions of their nearest neighbor to buy a clock "not nearly so fine as this one."
- In the end, the salesman asked Buck's parents to do him a favor: keep the clock for a month so "I don't have to tote it" around Ohio.
- When he returned 26 days later, Buck's family had received so many compliments on being sophisticated clock owners, they begged the peddler to let them buy it.

Buck did not want to grow up to be a farmer.

- The experience left Buck dazzled by the power of words and the opportunity to be an entrepreneur free from the seasonal burdens imposed by plowing, planting and picking, all integral to farm life.
- When Buck joined the Union Army in 1862, the clock still stood as one of his mother's most prized possessions, even though it had stopped working years before.
- Buck was 30 years old when he joined the army in hopes that he could leave small-town Ohio behind; his dream was to study the way the military distributed supplies so he could be a regional mercantile man when the war ended.

- After two years of service in the Quartermaster Corps, he knew a lot about mud, blood, standing around on idle days and working like a demon on busy ones.

- He also learned to love the pomp and ceremony of the military, with all its glitz and glamour, even though General Ulysses S. Grant disappointed Buck with his perennial rumpled look.

- Buck and the general were both in Nashville, Tennessee, in the spring of 1864, when General Grant was asked to assume command of all the Union armies.

- After the war with the South, Buck had little interest in commanders, commands or being commanded.

- He also had less interest in being a farmer; after discovering how big the nation really was, he was convinced that being an entrepreneur was his destiny.

- So Buck rented an apartment in Columbus, Ohio, and then took to the road to claim his fortune selling Bibles, *Webster's American Spelling Book* and the *Farmer's Almanac*.

After the war, Buck took to the road selling books.

- For special customers he carried scandalous titles such as *Fanny Hill* or *Memoirs of a Woman of Pleasure*, and read everything he could find on salesmanship including the satirical *The Clockmaker; or, The Sayings and Doings of Samuel Slick, of Slickville*.

- A dozen magazine and book subscription houses, most headquartered in Hartford, Connecticut, employed as many as 50,000 part-time agents per year, including disabled soldiers, retired ministers and children.

- Book peddlers hawked 600-page volumes detailing the events of the Civil War, natural history, and life in Central America.

- Most agents had to purchase the books at discount and pay their own expenses, and were responsible for tracking down customers to collect payments.

- Contract agents were forbidden from selling any copies to store owners.

- Instructions in the "canvassing kit" included a sales handbook, advice for overcoming objections, calling cards, weekly report forms, posters, and methods for closing the sale.
- American industry also provided new products to the traveling salesman: a new pie crimper, an improved apple peeler, darning machine or a patented farm gate.
- But Buck carefully avoided selling patent medicines, composed of curative spices liberally endowed with alcohol.
- During his first year on the road, he met a patent medicine man whose face was mangled and arm broken by a gang of dissatisfied customers.
- It was a lesson he never forgot.

Life at Work

- Buck Blanchard's big break came in 1885 when he put his Union soldier uniform back on and became a regional distributor for the *Personal Memoirs of U. S. Grant.*
- Now 52 years old, Buck was weary of the road but still enthusiastic about becoming rich as a peddler, or "canvasser," the term he now preferred.
- During the past decade, some 53,000 salesmen had taken to the roads, often with overlapping circuits or territories.
- Buck's plan was to manage a dozen or so salespeople in the Ohio-Indiana area and receive a percentage of their sales.

Mark Twain formed his own publishing company.

  - He knew that the secret of success was the ability to arouse interest in the "mystery" of the book, not the book itself; he had even sold books to people who couldn't read but wanted the prestige of a bound volume in the parlor.
  - Plus, he could become an entrepreneur in partnership with author Mark Twain and General Ulysses S. Grant.
  - Former General and President Grant had started writing his memoirs in the summer of 1884 after learning he had cancer.
  - As a result of a financial reversal, Grant was bankrupt and announced plans to finish the two-volume project in less than a year.
  - He was desperate to avoid leaving his family destitute at his death.
  - Mark Twain, eager to earn more money from his own projects and profit from the works of others, had recently formed his own publishing company.
  - When he learned that Grant agreed to publish with the well-established Century Company but had failed to come to terms, he went to see the ailing general.
  - He knew that Grant's brokerage company, Grant and Ward, had declared bankruptcy after Grant's partner Ferdinand Ward had engaged in fraud and left the former president nearly broke.
  - Twain persuaded Grant to sign with his new publishing company by promising him an astounding 70 percent of the profits, even though the book was still unfinished.
- While the ailing Grant handwrote his massive two-volume autobiography, with little assistance, Twain's company secured agents in cities throughout the nation.

- Of particular interest were the 80,000 Grand Army Veterans, viewed as the perfect sales force, all eager to make money retelling the heroic battles that they had waged two decades earlier.
- As Grant frantically worked on his memoirs, sometimes compiling up to 10,000 words a day, the nation became excited.
- In total, 10,000 canvassers fanned out over the countryside, all carefully drilled in the principles set forth in a little manual, *How to Introduce the Personal Memoirs of U.S. Grant*.
- It contained necessary arguments to help the agent deliver an effective spiel: introduce yourself by name, shake hands, keep the prospectus concealed from view in a special pocket on the inside of your coat.
- Buck fully understood this was the opportunity for which he had been waiting his entire life.
- If he could manage a dozen salespeople across Ohio, he could make a killing.
- The entire nation knew that General Grant had been forestalling his own death for months, simply to complete the memoir.
- Newspapers across the country had shown dramatic photographs of Grant's heroic exertion to complete the book that every American should read.
- Besides, Grant's two green and gold volumes would serve as the perfect accent for the marble-top center table in every civilized home, and would be a fitting companion for the family Bible.
- Buck had little trouble recruiting a dozen men, eager to once again wear their soldier's uniform for the purpose of making money.
- They came from all corners of the state and possessed widely varying experience regarding sales.

Stories about the Civil War helped to sell Personal Memoirs of U.S. Grant.

- At their first meeting, Buck talked about the glorious battles of the Civil War described in the book, became animated and incredulous that people would deny themselves the pleasure of this tome, and lectured "more orders are lost because the agent does not hang on long enough than any other one cause."

- Carefully, Buck told them that each volume would contain a facsimile of the gold medal presented by Congress to General Grant in 1863 in honor of his successes.
- Then he showed them where to find within the 600 large octavo pages a fine steel portrait of the general made from a daguerreotype taken when he was 21 years of age, plus more than a dozen maps and a steel engraving of his birthplace.
- He taught them how to provide answers when customers said, "I can't afford a $3.50 book right now," by offering delayed payments "when times are better."
- Prospects were to be told the book was a great investment whose value would grow over time.
- "Get the prospect seated—a tree stump or fancy chair, it doesn't matter— where you can put the book right in their lap but make sure you turn the pages and keep talking," Buck instructed, based on the recommendations of the company manual.
- Buck told his sales force never to use the word "dollars"—"three fifty is fine"—and that he expected them to make 20 exhibitions daily in towns and 15 in the country.
- He also provided financial incentives for one-third of all sales to include leather-bound volumes whose prices ranged from $4.50 to $12.50.
- For the first three weeks, Buck traveled the state, making calls with his peddlers and offering them tips on how to close deals.
- After that, he simply waited each week for the letters to arrive, accounting for the number of sales in each region of the state.
- Within 60 days, more than 1,000 books had been sold in Ohio, and more than 100,000 nationwide.
- The autobiography was a huge success, and women were delighted that the Grants would be well provided for upon the general's passing.
- Buck was enormously pleased that 80 percent of the sales force met their quota and that 35 percent exceeded expectations, thereby earning a bonus.
- The top salesman sold more than 800 books, collected 95 percent of the money owed on the books, and made more than $600 in four months.
- Buck's personal take after six months was equally impressive: $2,357 for directing the team salesmen—an entrepreneur at last with new plans for the future.

Columbus, Ohio.

Life in the Community: Columbus, Ohio

- The selection of Columbus as the capital of Ohio was the result of compromise, geography and deal-making.
- After Ohio achieved statehood in 1803, political infighting among Ohio's more prominent leaders caused the state capital to be moved from Chillicothe to Zanesville and back again.
- The state legislature finally decided that a new capital city, located in the center of the state, was a necessary compromise.
- Several small towns and villages petitioned the legislature for the honor of becoming the state capital, but ultimately a coalition of land speculators made the most attractive offer.
- Named in honor of Christopher Columbus, the capital city was founded on February 14, 1812.
- Although plagued by outbreaks of cholera, the town began to boom after the National Road reached Columbus from Baltimore in 1831, which complemented the city's new link to the Ohio and Erie Canal.
- A wave of immigrants from Europe brought significant numbers of Irish and German workers to the area.

Irish and German immigrants worked the land in Ohio.

- With a population of only 3,500, Columbus was officially chartered as a city on March 3, 1834.

- By 1850, the Columbus and Xenia Railroad became the first railroad to enter the city, followed by the Cleveland, Columbus and Cincinnati Railroad in 1851.
- By 1875, Columbus was served by eight railroads.
- On January 7, 1857, the Ohio Statehouse finally opened to the public after 18 years of construction.
- During the Civil War, Columbus was a major base for the volunteer Union Army that housed 26,000 troops and held up to 9,000 Confederate prisoners of war at Camp Chase.
- By virtue of the Morrill Land-Grant Colleges Act, the Ohio Agricultural and Mechanical College was founded in 1870 on the former estate of William and Hannah Neil.
- By the 1880s, Columbus became known as the "Buggy Capital of the World," thanks to the presence of some two dozen buggy factories, notably the Columbus Buggy Company, which was founded in 1875 by C.D. Firestone.
- The Columbus Consolidated Brewing Company also rose to prominence during this time, and it may have achieved even greater success were it not for the influence of the Anti-Saloon League, based in neighboring Westerville.
- In the steel industry, a forward-thinking man named Samuel P. Bush presided over the Buckeye Steel Castings Company.
- Columbus was also a popular location for the organization of labor.
- In 1886, Samuel Gompers founded the American Federation of Labor in Druid's Hall on South Fourth Street.

HISTORICAL SNAPSHOT
1885

- The first successful appendectomy was performed by Dr. William W. Grant
- L. A. Thompson patented the roller coaster

CHESTER A. ARTHUR.
PRESIDENT OF THE UNITED STATES.

- President Chester A. Arthur dedicated the Washington Monument
- A subsidiary of the American Bell Telephone Company, American Telephone & Telegraph (AT&T), was incorporated in New York
- W. S. Gilbert and Arthur Sullivan's *The Mikado* opened at the Savoy Theatre
- The Prussian government expelled all ethnic Poles and Jews who did not have German citizenship
- Gottlieb Daimler was granted a German patent for his single-cylinder water-cooled engine
- *Good Housekeeping* magazine began publication
- The Statue of Liberty arrived in New York Harbor

- Louis Pasteur successfully tested his vaccine against rabies on a patient bitten by a rabid dog
- Sarah E. Goode was the first female African-American to apply for and receive a patent, for the hideaway bed
- The Rock Springs Massacre in Wyoming involved 150 white miners who attacked their Chinese coworkers, killing 28 and wounding 15
- A train wreck involving the P.T. Barnum Circus killed the giant elephant Jumbo
- The Georgia Institute of Technology was established in Atlanta as the Georgia School of Technology
- The drink Dr Pepper was served for the first time
- The first skyscraper, boasting 10 floors and known as the Home Insurance Building, was built in Chicago
- Bicycle Playing Cards were first produced

Selected Prices

Bicycle Skirt $2.50
Civil War Picture Book $7.50
Corset $3.00
Ladies' Home Journal $1.00
Music Box $2.50
Parasol $0.50
Sewing Machine $9.00
Suspenders $0.05
Whisk Broom Holder $0.20
Woman's Storm Cape $8.25

1885 Innovations

- An **automobile** powered by a four-stroke cycle gasoline engine was built in Mannheim, Germany, by Karl Benz, whose company, Benz & Cie., was granted a patent for it. Production of the Benz Patent Motorwagen began in 1888. About 25 Benz vehicles were sold between 1888 and 1893.

- The first self-powered **machine gun** was invented by Sir Hiram Maxim. The "Maxim gun" used the recoil power of the previously fired bullet to reload, enabling a much higher rate of fire than earlier designs such as the Nordenfelt and Gatling weapons. Maxim also introduced the use of water cooling utilizing a water jacket around the barrel to reduce overheating. Heavy guns based on the Maxim, such as the Vickers machine gun, were joined by many other weapons such as the Hotchkiss machine gun, which mostly had their start in the early twentieth century.

- The first internal combustion petroleum fueled **motorcycle** was built by the German inventors Gottlieb Daimler and Wilhelm Maybach. It was designed as an expedient testbed for their new engine and not as a prototype vehicle.

- John Kemp Starley came out with the first commercially successful **safety bicycle** named the Rover. A big improvement on the previous penny-farthing design, the safety bike had a chain drive that multiplied the revolutions of the pedals. This allowed for much smaller wheels, and replaced the need for the large, directly pedaled front wheel of the penny-farthing. With the center of gravity low and between the wheels, rather than high and over the front hub, the safety greatly reduced the danger of a long fall over the handlebars. This made braking more effective and cycling became extremely popular, especially among women.

The Maxim gun.

Clockmaker; or, The Sayings and Doings of Samuel Slick, of Slickville, 1835:

The house of every substantial farmer had three substantial ornaments: a wooden clock, a tin reflector, and a Polyglot Bible. How is it that an American can sell his wares, at whatever price he pleases, where a Bluenose would fail to make a sale at all? I will inquire of the clockmaker the secret of his success.

"What a pity it is, Mr. Slick"—for such was his name—"what a pity it is," said I, "that you who are so successful in teaching these people (in Nova Scotia) the value of a clock, could not also teach them the value of time."

"I guess," said he, "they have got that ring to grow on their horns yet, which every four-year-old has in our country; we reckon hours and minutes to the dollars and cents. They do nothing in these parts but eat, drink, smoke, sleep, ride about, lounge at taverns, make speeches at temperance meetings, and talk about 'House of Assembly.'..."

"But how is it," said I, "that you manage to sell such an immense number of clocks, which certainly cannot be called necessary articles, among the people with whom there seems to be so greater scarcity of money?" Mr. Slick paused, as if considering the propriety of answering the question, and looking me in the face, said in a confidential tone, "Why, I don't care if I do tell you, the market is flooded, and I shall quit this circuit. It is done by knowledge of soft sawder in human nature.' But here is Deacon Flint's," said he; "I have but one clock left, and I guess I will sell it to him."

At the gate of the most comfortable-looking farmhouse stood Parson Flint, a respectable man, who had understood the value of time better than most of his neighbors, if one might judge from the appearance of everything about him. After the usual salutation, an invitation to "alight" was accepted by Mr. Slick, who said he wished to take leave of Mrs. Flint before he left Colchester.

We had hardly entered the house before the clockmaker pointed to the view from the window, and, addressing himself to me, said, "if I was to tell them in Connecticut there was such a farm as this way down east here in Nova Scotia, they wouldn't believe me. Why, there ain't such a location in all New England. The Deacon has 100 acres of dyke."

"Seventy," said the Deacon, "only seventy."

"Well, seventy; but then there is the fine deep bottom; why I could run a ramrod into it."

"Interval, we call it," said the Deacon, who though evidently pleased at this eulogium, seemed to wish the experiment of the ramrod to be tried in the right place.

"Well, interval, if you please—though Professor Eleazer Cumstick, in his work on Ohio, calls them bottoms—is just as good as dyke. Then there is the water privilege, three or $4,000, twice as good as what Gov. Cass paid fifteen thousand dollars for. I wonder, Deacon, you don't put up a carding mill on it, and same works with a turning lathe, shingle machine, circular saw, grind bark, and...."

"Too old!" said the Deacon, "too old for all those speculations."

continued

***Clockmaker; or, The Sayings and Doings of Samuel Slick,
of Slickville, 1835: (continued)***

"Old!" repeated the clockmaker, "not you; why you are worth half a dozen of the young men we see nowadays; you are young enough to have"—here you said something in a lower tone of voice, which I did not distinctly hear; but whatever it was, the Deacon was pleased; he smiled, and said he could not think of such things now.

The Precision
of Performance

of the **Full Ruby Jeweled Elgin Watch** is the marvel of the mechanical world—a lifetime of service in every watch.

Made in different sizes.

At all dealers, in cases to suit the purse and taste of the buyer.

An **Elgin Watch** always has the word "Elgin" engraved on the works—fully guaranteed.

Design Copyrighted 1897.

Manual: How to Introduce the
Personal Memoirs of U.S. Grant, 1885:

Canvassing in Towns

Make a thorough canvas. See every family from whom there is a possibility of obtaining an order, on each street before leaving it, even if you have to call several times at some residences. It is not policy to canvas one whole side of a street before canvassing the other; you should canvas one side of the street until you reach a crossing, then cross over and canvas the other side. The object in doing this is to keep within the influence of your names. Only a systematic, careful canvas pays and permits the agent to canvas a long time in a place.

What Door to Enter

Always go in at the front door; it shows that you have respect for yourself and your business. Entering back or kitchen doors advertises a salesman's work as fit only for the less honorable parts of the house. Advertise your work as fit for the sitting room, library, or the parlor, by seeking to enter and sit there; show that you are a gentleman, and at home in the most honorable part of the house.

While on the steps of the house, soliciting admission, keep the hat on the head, merely touching it to the lady, until invited to cross the threshold. Upon entering the house, remove your hat as soon as you are inside. Be very easy and agreeable in your manners, but do not go to the extreme of making yourself too agreeable.

How to Leave the House

In leaving the house, be careful not to turn your back to the family; retire sideways, keeping your eye on the good people, and let your last glance be full of sunshine.

Salesmen did not receive an order by saying "good day" and immediately turning their backs to the family. This will never do. It is not retreating in good order, with colors flying. The proper way is to retire backwards or sideways saying: "I think you will yet conclude to order a copy, and when you do, you can drop me a line in the post office." While doing this, shower smiles on the people as bountiful as though you had received an order for 10 copies—then walk off treading the ground as though victory sat enthroned upon your brow; to do this will require much effort on your part at first, but practice will make perfect, and it must be done. Though some hours, or even days, may prove financially fruitless, yet time will show all to be well at the close of the week, if you push steadily on.

"Recent Inventions," *Scientific American*, July 22, 1882:

Improved Button: Mr. William H. Ward, of Topeka, Kansas, has patented an improved button. This button consists of a fastening made of a strip of thin flexible metal having angular slots cut in one end and rolled into a cylindrical shape, an eyelet in which the fastening is secured, and a back. The back is a central perforation through which the high eyelet and clasp are passed and secured by spreading their inner ends. The face of the button is secured in the back in the usual manner, and is constructed with a depression which fits into the end of the eyelet and fastening, and assists in forming a firm and compact button. The eyelet forming the stem of the button is made so as to allow the face of the button to rotate. Mr. Ward has also recently patented improved pliers for attaching the buttons to garments.

Spark Arrester: An efficient and durable spark arrester, that is easily attached to and detached from the smokestack of a locomotive, has recently been patented by Mr. John L. Kantner, of South Easton, Pennsylvania. Inside the smokestack is placed a concavo-convex grate, formed of parallel bars attached at their ends to a rim. This grate fits into the outer part of an outer rim, and has guide pins which enter vertical slots in the rim. The rim is fitted into the smokestack and rests against the rim of the lower grate.... With this construction, the incandescent pieces that are carried up the smokestack will be broken, by striking against the grate bars, into such small pieces as to be rendered incapable of doing damage.

Show Card Holder: A novel device for holding price and show cards has recently been patented by Mr. Will. C. Rood, of Quincy, Illinois. A frame is provided on its front side, at its lower age and ends, with grooved flanges, behind which a sign or show card can be passed and retained. At the rear side, near its bottom edge, the frame has a socket for receiving the upper end of the standard, the lower end of which fits in an aperture in the top of the base. At the upper edge of the rear side, a ring is attached by which the frame may be suspended from a nail.

"Phantom Lights at Sea," *Scientific American*, July 22, 1882:

Fulton Market fish dealer gives the following explanation of some of the strange lights, phantom vessels, and other mysterious appearances that puzzle seamen:

"Two years ago I went menhaden fishing, and one day as we were going up the Sound, one of the hands said he hoped we are not going off the Point, meaning Montauk. I asked him why. He seemed kind of offish, but at last he let out that he had seen ships sailing about in the dead of night in a dead calm. I laughed at him, but two nights later we came to anchor at Gardiner's Bay, and it is a hot night we stretched out on deck. In the middle of the night I was awakened by someone giving me a tremendous jerk, and when I found myself on my feet, my mate, shaking like a leaf, was pointing over the rail. I looked, and sure enough, there was a big schooner about an eighth of a mile away, bearing down on us. There wasn't a breath of wind in the bay, but on she came at a 10-knot rate, headed right for us. 'Sing out to the skipper,' I said. 'It's no use,' said my mate, hanging on to me. 'It's no vessel.' But there she was, within 100 yards of us. Shaking him off, I swung into the rigging, and yelled 'Schooner ahoy!' And shouted to her to bear away, but in a second the white sails were right aboard of us. I yelled to the hands, and made ready to jump, when, like a flash, she disappeared, and the skipper came on deck with all hands and wanted to know if we had the jimjams. I'd have sworn that I had seen the *Flying Dutchman* but for one thing. We saw the same thing about a week afterwards. The light passed around us and went up the bay. I got out the men and seine [a large net] and followed in the path of the phantom schooner, and as sure as you are alive, we made the greatest single haul of menhaden on record. The light, to my mind, was nothing more or less than the phosphorescence that hovered over the big shoal. The oil from so many millions of fish moving along was enough to produce a light; but you will find men all along the shores of Long Island who believe there is a regular phantom craft that comes in on and off—similar to a coaster in the spirit trade. I saw an account of something like this in the Portland papers sometime after, and I thought it was very remarkable; for wherever you find menhaden you may look for queer lights on the water—phantom ships and the like."

"Men who began life as bargaining for small wares will invariably become sharpers. The commanding aim of every such man will soon be to make a good bargain, and he will soon speedily consider every gainful bargain as a good one. The tricks of fraud will assume in his mind the same place which commercial skill and an honorable system of dealing hold in the mind of merchant."
—Timothy Dwight, president of Yale College

"Lee's Surrender at Appomattox Court House," *Personal Memoirs of U.S. Grant, Volume II*, 1886:

I had known General Lee in the old army, and had served with him in the Mexican War; but did not suppose, owing to the difference in our age and rank, that he would remember me, while I would more naturally remember him distinctly, because he was the chief of staff of General Scott in the Mexican War. When I had left camp that morning I had not expected so soon the result that was then taking place, and consequently was in rough garb. I was without a sword, as I usually was when on horseback on the field, and wore a soldier's blouse for a coat, with the shoulder straps of my rank to indicate to the army who I was. When I went into the house I found General Lee. We greeted each other, and after shaking hands, took our seats. I had my staff with me, a good portion of whom were in the room during the whole of the interview. What General Lee's feelings were I do not know. As he was a man of much dignity, with an impassible face, it was impossible to say whether he felt inwardly glad that the end had finally come, or felt sad over the result, and was too manly to show it. Whatever his feelings, they were entirely concealed from my observation; but my own feelings, which had been quite jubilant on the receipt of his letter, were sad and depressed. I felt like anything rather than rejoicing at the downfall of a foe who had fought so long and valiantly, and had suffered so much for a cause, though that cause was, I believe, one of the worst for which a people ever fought, and one for which there was the least excuse. I do not question, however, the sincerity of the great mass of those who were opposed to us. General Lee was dressed in a full uniform which was entirely new, and was wearing a sword of considerable value, very likely the sword which had been presented by the State of Virginia; at all events, it was an entirely different sword from the one that would ordinarily be worn in the field. In my rough traveling suit, the uniform of a private with the straps of a lieutenant-general, I must have contrasted very strangely with a man so handsomely dressed, six feet high and of faultless form. But this was not a matter that I thought of until afterwards. We soon fell into a conversation about old army times. He remarked that he remembered me very well in the old army; and I told him that as a matter of course I remembered him perfectly, but from the difference in our rank and years (there being about sixteen years' difference in our ages), I had thought it very likely that I had not attracted his attention sufficiently to be remembered by him after such a long interval. Our conversation grew so pleasant that I almost forgot the object of our meeting. After the conversation had run on in this style for some time, General Lee called my attention to the object of our meeting, and said that he had asked for this interview for the purpose of getting from me the terms I proposed to give his army. I said that I meant merely that his army should lay down their arms, not to take them up again during the continuance of the war unless duly and properly exchanged. He said that he had so understood my letter. Then we gradually fell off again into conversation about matters foreign to the subject which had brought us together. This continued for some little time, when General Lee again interrupted the course of the conversation by suggesting that the terms I proposed to give his army ought to be written out.

1886 Profile

Shoe manufacturing would never be the same after Jan Matzeliger, the son of a Dutch engineer, invented a machine that would attach the shoe's upper to the sole, and revolutionize the shoe-making industry.

Life at Home

- Jan Ernst Matzeliger's inventive mind did not create the modern shoe; he simply made it affordable.
- Born in the Dutch colony of Dutch Guiana, or Surinam, in 1852, Jan was the son of a Dutch engineer who headed the government's machine works in the capital city.
- Because most of the colony was located at or below sea level, the Dutch, with the labor provided by some 300,000 West African slaves, had built numerous dikes and seawalls to reclaim the land from the sea.
- Jan's mother was a slave on one of the 800 sugar plantations stretched across the island.
- Ethnically and culturally diverse families were common in Surinam, where slaves outnumbered the white Dutch settlers 14 to one.
- But Jan never saw his mother after his earliest years and spent most of his youth with his father and paternal aunt in Paramaribo.
- When he was 10 years old his father entered him in a machine apprentice program.
- There he learned to cut and shape metal on a fast-moving lathe and how to manipulate other power-operated machines.
- At age 19, Jan followed the lure of the sea, serving two years as a merchant seaman before coming ashore in Philadelphia.
- There he found his options limited by his Dutch-African heritage, as well as his inability to speak more than a few words of English.
- Unfortunately, the Panic of 1873, one of the worst depressions in United States history, was also underway.

Jan Matzeliger's invention revolutionized the shoe making industry.

- The economic downturn was triggered by the overbuilding of railroads and speculation in the bonds that underwrote their construction.
- Nearly 90 railroad companies disappeared; more than 18,000 other businesses dependent on the railroads went bankrupt.
- Unemployment surged to 14 percent.
- Initially, Jan managed only to find a string of unfulfilling odd jobs, despite being a skilled machinist, before becoming an apprentice at a shoemaking shop.
- The shoe factory was stocked with the revolutionary McKay stitching machines that helped bring automation to the shoe-making industry.
- A McKay was capable of sewing the outer soles of shoes to the inner soles; previously, this time-consuming operation was done by hand.
- After attending a Philadelphia exhibition that showcased Lynn, Massachusetts, as the shoe-making center of America, Jan decided to move there to pursue his dream of being an inventor.

McKay stitching machine.

Life at Work

- By the time Jan Matzeliger was 26, he left Philadelphia for Lynn, Massachusetts, the shoe-making capital the world.
- Although he arrived in Lynn with few possessions, Jan had carefully charted the course he would take to realize his ambitions.
- First, he found a job operating a McKay stitching machine for the M. H. Harney Company and rented a room at the West Lynn Mission on Charles Street in the area of town populated by African-Americans.
- To get on the fast track to citizenship, Jan enrolled in night school to learn English.

Jan enrolled in night school to learn English.

- He also purchased a set of books called *Popular Educator* and a five-volume series called *Science for All* to further improve himself.
- Jan then used a second-hand set of drafting instruments to draw out his mechanical innovations every night after the grind of 10-hour work days in the shoe factory.
- For pleasure, Jan painted landscapes on dishes, oils on canvas, watercolors on paper, and made toys for children.
- Driven to excel, he spent the majority of his earnings on materials for his projects, often while neglecting basic creature comforts.
- Sometimes he denied himself proper warmth during the New England winters, proper rest and nourishment; cornmeal mush was his standard meal.
- Even with the labor-saving innovations like the McKay, the shoe industry was still far from being fully mechanized in the 1880s.
- The process of fastening the shoe upper to the inner sole or "lasting" was an intricate process which defied the most exhaustive attempts at mechanization.
- As a result, the men who did this work, known as lasters, were the most skillful and best paid workers in the shoe industry; their detail-oriented step in the making of shoes had to be done completely by hand.

Attaching the shoe upper to the inner sole was one of the few steps not automated.

- But because most of the steps that led up to this crucial phase were mechanized and "lasting" was not, hundreds of nearly completed shoes often piled up while waiting for the laster to do his work.
- An experienced laster could process 50 or 60 pairs of shoes per day.
- Gordon McKay, who manufactured the stitching machine, had spent $120,000 in a fruitless attempt to build a machine that could form, shape, tug, pleat, hold and tack like a human laster.

For his invention, Jan needed precision parts manufactured in a professional machine shop.

- Realizing his need for more working space and access to machine tools, Jan parlayed his mechanical aptitude into a job with Beal Brothers Shoe Company, where he was given access to both space and tools.
- He scoured junkyards and factory dumps for discarded levers, pulleys, gears and cams which he reworked to his specifications.
- After two years of solitary work, he created a crude working prototype which he filed for a patent on January 24, 1882.
- The resulting 15-page text and drawings was so complex, an inspector from the U.S. Patent Office personally visited Jan to have him explain the invention.
- At this point, financing became a serious issue.
- In order to produce a model that would work under demanding factory conditions, Jan needed precision parts manufactured in a professional machine shop.
- Obtaining the necessary capital meant giving up the rights to a portion of the future profits; this was simply the first step in the long process of getting a patent.
- Thanks to his reputation as a skilled machinist, Jan obtained the financial backing he needed from Charles H. Delnow and Melville S. Nichols in return for two-thirds of all eventual profits—a substantial price to pay to see his dream fulfilled.
- His lasting machine patent was issued on March 20, 1883, with Delnow and Nichols listed as assignees.

- Jan's experimental machine took three years of hard work, soaring excitement, and deep despair to complete.
- Some days he was unsure if he would ever be successful.
- Jan demonstrated his machine on May 29, 1885.
- The device flawlessly fashioned 75 pairs of shoes that day—indistinguishable from handmade shoes—and produced them five times faster than a human laster could.
- A hand operation that previously required highly paid, skilled workers five to six minutes per shoe could now be done in one minute.
- And Jan's invention could handle all shoe styles, including women's pointed-toe shoes made of various grades of leather.
- The impossible had become a reality.
- Once a worker placed an insole and upper on Jan's last machine, it drove a tack, turned the shoe, pleated the leather, drove another tack, then turned the shoe—until the process was completed.
- In 1886 Jan sold the consolidated hand method lasting machine company all rights to his patents for more than $15,000 in stock.
- As use of the lasting machine spread, the price of shoes fell rapidly—from an average $6.00 a pair to $3.00.
- Advertisements sprouted in newspapers across the nation touting $3.00 shoes; entire companies sprang up to meet the demand for less expensive shoes.
- With his newfound wealth, Jan bought a house, on the same street as his commercial backers, and rented the house to the couple with whom he had boarded for years.

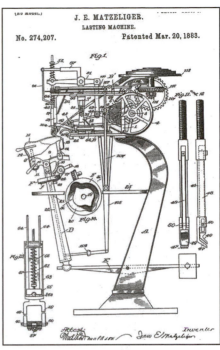

Jan's new machine.

Life in the Community: Paramaribo, Surinam, and Philadelphia, Pennsylvania

- Surinam, the Dutch colony where Jan Matzeliger was born, was settled by men and women from Holland's most prominent families.

The Matzeliger family in Surinam.

- Built from bricks that had been carried as ballast in the hulls of sailing ships and topped by red tile roofs, the homes in Paramaribo resembled gingerbread houses.
- In fact, if not for the orange trees, royal palms, and tamarinds which lined the streets and walkways, the city looked like a piece of Amsterdam transported to the New World.
- The river docks where Jan and the other boys of Paramaribo played were filled with merchant steamships from all over the world.
- The Dutch were proud of their reputation as formidable seamen, and Jan was no different from the average young Dutchman in this respect.
- In 1871 he sailed with the Dutch East India Company for two years before landing in Philadelphia.

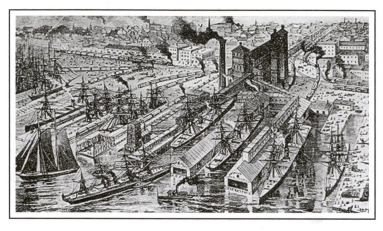

Philadelphia, Pennsylvania.

- In the 1870s Philadelphia was a black cultural center with a black-owned and operated hospital, black newspapers, and was the home of the largest contingent of black entrepreneurs in the world.
- Although Philadelphia was a leading manufacturing city, Jan found his career path handicapped by his Dutch African heritage and his limited understanding of racial interaction in America.
- The black population of Philadelphia was 4 percent, the largest of any major northern city, but Jan formed no close relationships because of the cultural differences with African-Americans with whom he lived.
- Also, the panic of 1873 and the five-year depression that followed increased black unemployment in Philadelphia to 70 percent by 1876.
- Between 1873 and 1876, 18,000 businesses failed and half a million workers lost their jobs in one of the worst financial disasters in American history.
- Frederick Douglass, the most influential black man in America and a former resident of Lynn, Massachusetts, spoke at the 1876 Centennial exhibition held in Philadelphia, which showcased Lynn as the shoe capital of the world.
- After he moved to Lynn, Jan was refused membership in three local churches, the Episcopal, Roman Catholic and Unitarian; he never forgot the slights.
- He never attempted to join the only black church in town, the African Methodist Episcopal church which represented an African-American culture he did not understand or relate to.

HISTORICAL SNAPSHOT
1886

- A general strike that escalated into the Haymarket Riot built momentum toward the eight-hour workday in the U.S.
- Emil Berliner began his work that resulted in the invention of the gramophone
- Pharmacist Dr. John Stith Pemberton invented a carbonated beverage that would be named Coca-Cola and began advertising his product in the *Atlanta Journal*
- In the case of *Santa Clara County v. Southern Pacific Railroad,* the U.S. Supreme Court ruled that corporations have the same rights as living persons
- *The Strange Case of Dr Jekyll and Mr. Hyde* was first published
- Karl Benz patented the first successful gasoline-driven automobile, the Benz Patent Motorwagen, which was built in 1885

- The first trainload of oranges was shipped from Los Angeles to the East over the transcontinental railroad
- President Grover Cleveland married Frances Folsom in the White House, becoming the only president to wed in the executive mansion

- The American Federation of Labor (AFL) was formed by 26 craft unions led by Samuel Gompers
- The first U.S.-based nurses' magazine, *The Nightingale,* was published in New York City
- Charles Hall filed a patent for his process of turning aluminum oxide into molten aluminum
- After almost 30 years of conflict, Apache leader Geronimo surrendered with his last band of warriors to General Nelson Miles at Skeleton Canyon in Arizona
- William Stanley, Jr. created the first practical alternating current transformer device, known as the induction coil
- President Grover Cleveland dedicated the Statue of Liberty in New York Harbor
- Heinrich Hertz verified the existence of electromagnetic waves
- Scotch whisky distiller William Grant & Sons was founded

Selected Prices

Babies' Shoes $0.15
Baking Powder $0.20
Buggy Carriage $135.00
Coffee, Pound $0.25
Dental Fees, Gold Filling $1.00
Horse's Hoof Ointment, Jar $1.00
Men's Lace Shoes $0.98
Violin $5.00
Women's Button Shoes $1.50
Women's Lace Shoes $0.63

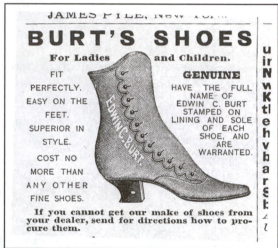

1886 Innovations

- **Dishwashers**, descended from the 1886 invention of Josephine Cochrane, were unveiled at the 1893 Chicago World's Fair. The granddaughter of John Fitch, the inventor of the steamboat, Cochrane invented the dishwasher because her servants were chipping her fine china.

- The foundation for **radio broadcasts** was established during the 1860s, when Scottish physicist, James Clerk Maxwell predicted the existence of radio waves; then in 1886, German physicist Heinrich Rudolph Hertz demonstrated that rapid variations of electric current could be projected into space in the form of radio waves similar to those of light and heat.

- The development of **advertising branding** began in the shoe industry when 17-year-old John H. Hanan went into partnership with his father and insisted that all their shoes be stamped Hanan, paving the way for national trade-marked shoes. James Means, William L. Douglas. and J. P. Lewis then pioneered the concept, selling men's shoes for $3.00 to $3.50 per pair in newspaper advertisements across the country.

"Wages of Cloak-Models," *Waterloo Courier* (Iowa), July 28, 1886:

A cloak manufacturer downtown was asked by a reporter what he paid his models. He said: "That all depends on their shape, symmetry and adaptability to the business. That woman who is a good height, weighs about 150 pounds, has a bust measure 36 inches or a little over, is perfect in form, receives $15 a week to stand up from nine o'clock in the morning until six in the afternoon trying on cloaks. She is receiving the highest price and is our star model. She is always in demand and has to do more, perhaps, than the others. Ten dollars is about the average price per cloak model. Some belong to the fitting and others to the cutting department, and of course the prices vary: eight dollars is a fair price, and a few get under that per week."

"Base-Ball," *Waterloo Courier* (Iowa), July 28, 1886:

In contrast to the base-ball world of long ago with that of to-day is very striking, and some idea of the stronghold this sport has taken in the popular mind is gained from the fact that the quantity of base-balls manufactured last year numbered between seven and eight million. Of this number, less than four thousand were used by the three leading professional clubs. The manufacturer of this enormous number of balls forms no small industry, and is the means of furnishing employment to many in Boston, New York, and several other principal cities. Philadelphia and Chicago, however, are generally admitted as being the great centers of this industry, and it is estimated that fully two-thirds of all the balls used are manufactured at these two places.

"A Pair of Shoes," *The Marion Daily Star* (Ohio), January 15, 1885:

A great naturalist said, "Show me a scale, I'll draw you the fish." Had he been a shoemaker he might have said, "Show me a shoe, I'll tell you the wearer." The sandal of the Arab, the tiny shoe of the high-bred woman of China, the wooden dancing shoe of the Dutch, the high-heeled court slipper or the wearable walking shoes of the English and Americans proclaim their nationality to the tyro. An amateur might not readily recognize the characteristics of different districts within a single nation, but the practiced designer must know that in the United States, for instance, the Northerner want his shoes comfortable, neat and stylish; a Southerner asks for something fancy-pants; the agricultural West demands solidity, fullness and an article stout enough to break the land for a coming population.

"A pair of shoes" is one of the most typical products of modern industry. To make them, the animal kingdom contributes from the herds roaming on Western plains or South American pampas or from the barnyard near at home; the vegetable, from dotted groves of hemlock and oak, or from the great forest still left to us. Great textile manufacturers supply cloth and thread: mines, furnaces, and forges combine to furnish nail or wire. A hundred machines have been invented, one of which has changed the whole course of a great industry and produced large cities. Through scores of processes, the 44 pieces of a pair of shoes requires to bring them together the co-operation of 50 men, women and children; the division of labor is pursued to the utmost, demanded in turn for its successful maintenance the dispersion of products the world over until, as a result, you, well-shod reader, can buy for $3.00 what would have cost your forefather $6.00.

As the reader buys a pair of shoes, his next pair may at the same moment be dodging the lasso of the "cowboy" on some faraway plain or perhaps be in the process of slaughter in Chicago. The perishable beef promptly reaches the market, and one day soon you dine from a fat, juicy roast, little thinking as you smack your lips after a dinner that the fine, pliable skin which once protected the delicate morsel may sometime contribute to your outward comfort. Stranger things have happened. The skins or hides meantime are salted, and the buyer of salted hides sends part of them, say, to Peabody, Mass., to be tanned for upper leather, and the rest to central New York to be tanned for sole leather.

"Shoes for Comfort," *The New York Times*, October 8, 1886:

Now that the elevated railways have reduced their rates to five cents, and have become so crowded that some people do not like to ride on them, there is nothing so desirable as an easy and neat shoe. No matter how well a person is dressed, his costume is not complete without good shoes, and if he wants to be sure of getting these, he should go to A. J. Cammeyer's, where he will find all kinds of foot clothing without the trouble of going further to hunt for it. He cannot miss Cammeyer's if he walks along 6th Ave. in the neighborhood of 14th St. because he will be sure to see the windows of the store at 6th Ave. and 12th St. These windows are an exhibition in themselves, and anyone who takes a stroll near the store is sure to be attracted by the crowd he will find gazing into the windows. He will go and take a look himself and will be treated to a perfect panorama of shoes of all kinds, from the daintiest slipper that ever graced a feminine foot up to the stoutest boot that ever crushed the flagstones of the city's streets.

Inside the store will be found crowded at all times with ladies and gentlemen, for it has departments for both. And the crowds that may be seen there do not represent the store's full trade, for a large business is done in orders sent by mail. Persons living out of town can send for a catalogue and directions for measuring their own feet, and so have their shoes sent to them without the trouble of coming to town. Mr. Cammeyer deals largely in hand-sewn welt shoes, which are soft and flexible and have no roughness inside. They do not cost the buyer any more than machine-made shoes.

"FOR THE FARMER. A Substitute for Cedar Wood Wanted to Support Barbed Wire in Farm Fences," *The Stevens Point Daily Journal*, Stevens Point, Wisconsin, July 5, 1884:

THE MATTER OF FENCE-POSTS. It seems certain that steel or iron barbed wire will in the future supersede boards for making farm fences. The objections to it are few and are gradually diminishing as animals become accustomed to it. The advantages of it are many. It is cheap, easy to transport, durable, and convenient to put in position. Prairie fires do not burn it and violent winds do not blow it down.... It is easily removed if it is no longer wanted in the place where it was first erected. Barbed wire has obviously "come to stay." It is likely that it will be improved and cheapened, but it is not likely that it will go out of use. There is now an excellent opportunity for inventive talent to find a substitute for the ordinary material for farm fence-posts. Cedar is fast becoming scarce and high.... A vast amount of cedar blocks are now used for paving the streets.... There are few or no cedar trees within easy reach of the territory that is now being settled up. Chestnut, which furnishes the best substitute for cedar, does not grow to any considerable extent in the west....

Much has been written during the past few years on the advantages of employing living trees for supporting boards or wire employed for fencing. The appearance of a farm is greatly improved by having it surrounded by stately trees. If these trees could be used for the purpose of supporting fence-wire, they would be both useful and ornamental. Great trouble, however, has been found in attaching wire to them. As the trunks expand they grow over the wire, cause it to rust, and finally to break.... A correspondent of an eastern paper suggests boring holes through the trunks of trees and passing the wires through them.... A better plan would seem to be to put a piece of iron tubing, like a gas pipe, through the augur hole. This would exclude the air and allow an opportunity to stretch the wire when it became necessary, or to remove it altogether. In some of the eastern states, granite fence-posts have been in use for more than a century.

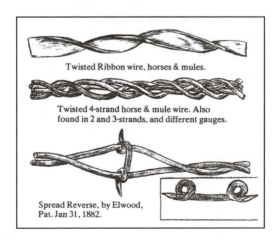

Twisted Ribbon wire, horses & mules.

Twisted 4-strand horse & mule wire. Also found in 2 and 3-strands, and different gauges.

Spread Reverse, by Elwood, Pat. Jan 31, 1882.

"The Barbed Wire Monopoly," *Waterloo Courier*, (Iowa), April 20, 1881:

It is probably safe to say that no invention or device was ever introduced to the American people which has been of greater value to the farming community, especially on the timberless plains of the west, than that of barbed wire for fencing purposes.... It requires only one post where the other kind of a fence requires three. It is not easily thrown down by cattle...and in every way it is cheaper and more convenient than any other fence made. These features have led to the using of immense quantities of this wire by the farmers. It is estimated that a tin of the wire will make two miles of three-strand fence, and in 1880 there were 40,000 tons of barbed wire manufactured in the United States—equal to 80,000 miles of fence. These figures will give some idea of the immense industry the manufacture of this wire has grown to be. But along with the benefits of this invention has developed one of the most gigantic of monopolies, a brief history of which is as follows:

The original utilization of the idea of putting spikes on the top of a board or fence...was seized upon by someone and a patent obtained, and in a short time other patents were issued upon improvements in the barb. In the meantime, the original patent, and some of the subsequent ones, were purchased by a manufacturing firm in Massachusetts. They surrendered the original patent and some of the others, and had them reissued as one patent. Shortly afterwards, other parties obtained patents for various devices, and a lively war among the patentees resulted. Suits were then begun by the holders of the original patent.... In December last, the suit was decided by Judge Blodgett, in Chicago, favorable to the claimants. In deciding the case, the Judge said:

"As to the question of patentability, a device to be patented must, of course, be the result of inventive genius, and not a mere mechanical adaptation of old things to new uses. It was, however, exceedingly difficult to draw the dividing line between the two.... It required invention to devise and produce a barbed wire which could be used for fences. In the absence of any other test, courts had assumed that the fact of the acceptance of a new device or combination by the public, and putting it into extensive use, was evidence that it was the product of invention. In other words, utility was suggestive of originality."

Of course this is subject to appeal, but pending the appeal, the manufacturers, who are enjoined, must continue to pay the royalty demanded by the successful contestants. A few figures will show what a large sum these royalties amount to. On the 40,000 tons manufactured last year, the royalty demanded was $60 per ton, or $2,400,000, on the amount manufactured during the year.

1895 Profile

Saloon-owner James "Jake" Ritty, tired of being robbed by employees dipping into the cash drawer, or pocketing customers' money for themselves, decided to create a machine that prevented such thefts from happening and thus, the origin of the National Cash Register Company.

Life at Home

- It was retirement day for James "Jake" Ritty, and it felt like a life well lived.
- His restaurant, Ritty's Pony House, had been visited by the world's most famous actors and athletes, he had been a supportive member of the Dayton, Ohio, community, and he was an inventor.
- Even the success of the National Cash Register Company did not diminish his contentment—he had been paid well for his idea even though others had profited more from it.
- History would record that he was the inventor of the cash register.
- Born in 1836 in Dayton, Ohio, the son of French immigrants Dr. Leger and Mary Ritty, Jake briefly attended medical school and was listed as a physician in the 1860 Census.
- When the Civil War broke out in 1861, 25-year-old Jake enlisted in the 4th Ohio Cavalry, where he was promoted from first lieutenant to captain during his three years of service.
- Jake called himself a "Dealer in Pure Whiskeys, Fine Wines, and Cigars" when he opened his first saloon in 1871.
- The Pony House first opened its doors in 1882, when beer was a nickel a stein and $0.15 a bucket.
- The building on South Jefferson Street where the Pony House was established had previously been a school for teaching French and English to young ladies.

Jake Ritty invented the cash register.

- To make the saloon attractive and unique, Jake commissioned woodcarvers from the Barney and Smith Car Company to convert 5,400 pounds of Honduras mahogany into a huge bar.
- The result was a wooden bar both tall and wide, a style reminiscent of the interior of a passenger rail car; the initials JR were carved into the center peak and the left and right sections.
- To accompany the drinks, a free lunch was open to all, consisting of boiled eggs, sardines, blind robins (smoked herring), cold meats, pigs' feet, pickles, pretzels, crackers and bread.
- It wasn't the only free lunch.

Company cash boxes invited stealing.

- Despite a booming business, the Pony House was losing money every year into the pockets of cashiers and bartenders who took the customers' dinner and bar payments, but did not deposit them into the company cash box.
- Jake had no way to determine how much he was losing or how to stop the thefts.
- It was a problem that plagued every merchant—how to keep your profits from walking out the door in the pants of your employees.
- In 1878, while on a steamboat trip to Europe, Jake became intrigued by a mechanism that counted the number of times the ship's propeller went around.
- A number of recent inventions, such as the screw propeller and the triple expansion engine, had recently made transoceanic shipping economically viable, ushering in an era of cheap and safe travel and trade around the world.
- Jake wondered if something like this could be made to record the cash transactions in his restaurant and saloon.
- When he returned to Dayton, Jake and his brother, a skilled mechanic, began designing a device for counting cash.
- The first two attempts were dismal failures.
- Their third design operated by pressing a key that represented a specific amount of money.
- It recorded the amount of each transaction.
- They had invented a way to reconcile the nightly cash with the sales receipts to keep everyone honest.
- Jake was delighted.
- Both the honest and dishonest cashiers disliked this intrusion into "their" affairs.
- Jake and his brother called the design, patented in 1879, "Ritty's Incorruptible Cashier."
- It consisted of two rows of keys attached to a dial that looked like a large clock face which together kept a running total of the amount deposited.
- A bell—later advertised as the "bell heard round the world"—rang when the register was opened.

- It also had a total adder that summed all the cash values for the keys pressed during the day.
- The 22 x 14 x 20 inch machine looked like a clock mounted on a board.
- To the Ritty brothers, it looked like the way to make a fortune.
- But the patent was simply a right to do business, not a ticket to success.

Ritty's incorruptible cashier.

Life at Work

- James "Jake" Ritty, upon reflection, was unprepared for the amount of work required to set up a manufacturing plant and sell his new invention, the cash register.
- Restaurants and bars he understood; manufacturing and distribution of a product as heavy as a cash register were a different proposition.
- Four long, frustrating years after they received a patent in 1883, Jake and his brother started the National Manufacturing Company with high expectations.
- They quickly discovered that businessmen were reluctant to buy expensive machines that they had never needed before.
- And Jake didn't have time to manufacture his machine, travel from place to place to sell his invention, and continue to run his saloon.
- Jake and his brother sold the patent to a group of Ohio investors, including John Henry Patterson, who believed they could fulfill Jake's dream of commercializing his invention and also making a fortune.
- The investor group paid $6,500 for the rights to the "Incorruptible Cashier."
- Soon thereafter, Patterson bought out the other investors and changed the firm's name to the National Cash Register Company.
- John Patterson had also grown up in Dayton, Ohio, where he attended public schools and worked in his father's saw and gristmills.

Dayton, Ohio.

- Patterson graduated from Dartmouth College in 1867, and worked as a collector of tolls on the Miami and Erie Canal for three years before entering the coal industry, where he served as manager of the Southern Ohio Coal and Iron Company.
- His coal distribution business had been losing revenues to pilfering, so he bought two of the cash registers, sight unseen.
- Within six months, he reduced his debt from $16,000 to $3,000 and became convinced that every businessman needed a cash register.
- After Patterson bought the patent rights to Ritty's invention, he improved its operation by adding spare rolls to reconcile the day's transactions in each price range.
- This was accomplished by building a hole puncher into each cash register that created holes to represent the amount of the purchase.
- If the paper had two holes punched in the dollars column, for example, and 50 holes punched in the cents column, the total would be $2.50.
- At the end of a transaction, a bell rang on the cash register and recorded the amount received on a large dial on the front of the machine.
- At the end of the day, the merchant could add up the holes and, therefore, his daily cash.
- As head of the National Cash Register Company (NCR), Patterson quickly expanded the factory's workforce and the number of salesmen.
- He also persuaded salesmen who sold registers part-time to become full-fledged national agents and devote all of their energy to his product.
- Under his system, agents were shipped cash-rich consignments with a retail price of $150 to $200.
- Salesmen were entitled to a 50 percent discount on the purchase price, and many became wealthy overnight.
- During its first decade of operation, NCR produced 16,000 registers and brought dozens of lawsuits against its competitors.
  - As department stores proliferated and retailers nationwide recognized the value of a good on-site accounting system, 86 companies began manufacturing different types of cash registers.
  - In 1888, NCR had agents working in 34 U.S. cities from Pensacola, Florida, to Portland, Oregon.
  - Patterson also dreamed of creating an international sales organization such as the Singer Manufacturing Company did with its sewing machines.
  - Since other organizations such as McCormick and Kodak had proven that Europeans would buy American goods, Patterson wanted to add NCR to that list.
  - In 1893, the company sold 100 registers per month in Germany.
  - By 1895, 23 percent of total sales were made outside the United States and Canada, with Great Britain representing 9 percent and South Africa 2 percent.
  - Early advertisements shouted in bold headlines "Stop the Leaks" and showed shop owners how they were being ruined by clerks who stole from an unmonitored cash drawer.
  - NCR even hired detectives to watch as unsupervised employees pilfered from their employers and thus created testimonials for the NCR machine.

National Cash Register's improved model.

- NCR also used advertisements to highlight an owner's fear of losing profits from sloppy record-keeping.
- By 1895, one-fourth of the company's registers were in saloons, 17 percent sold to general merchants and 11 percent to drugstores.

Life in the Community: Dayton, Ohio

- Dayton, Ohio, was not only a manufacturing center for cash registers: it was an employee laboratory.
- Dayton was home to a wide variety of manufacturing firms, including the National Cash Register Company, most interested in ways to reduce the cost of making its product in a era when extensive efforts were underway to accurately measure productivity.
- The National Cash Register Company experimented with its lighting and discovered that improved, brightly lit factories resulted in better productivity.
- NCR also provided its workers a cafeteria, hospital, library and recreational facility to reward loyalty.
- The company showed movies and hosted lectures for employees during lunchtime—all innovations for a city known for its manufacturing skills.
- After Ohio became a state in 1803, Dayton became the seat of Montgomery County, but growth was slow until the War of 1812.
- During the 1812 Second War of Independence, Dayton served as a mobilization point for American attacks on Canada and against British troops in the northwestern part of the United States.
- After the war, a tobacco factory, two banks, textile mills, and several other businesses were begun.
- With the completion of the Miami and Erie Canal in 1829, Dayton was linked to Cincinnati, promoting growth.
- Nine turnpikes connected Dayton to other areas of the state.
- By the 1840s, Dayton was one of the largest and wealthiest communities in Ohio.
- By the late 1800s, the community supported a growing publishing industry, offering publications that focused either on religious issues such as *Christian World*, *Young Catholic Messenger*, *Ohio Bible Teacher*, or agricultural interests such as *Farmer's Home*, The *Ohio Swine Journal*, and The *Ohio Poultry Journal*.
- There were also German newspapers for the area's German settlers.
- A number of companies manufactured farm implements, including the Buckeye Mower and Reaper Company.

National Cash Register Company.

HISTORICAL SNAPSHOT
1895

- Mintonette, later known as volleyball, was created by William G. Morgan in Holyoke, Massachusetts
- Oscar Wilde's last play, *The Importance of Being Earnest*, was first shown at St. James's Theatre in London

- The Treaty of Shimonoseki was signed between China and Japan, marking the end of the first Sino-Japanese War
- The U.S. Supreme Court ruled that the federal government had the right to regulate interstate commerce, legalizing the military suppression of the Pullman Strike.
- American frontier murderer and outlaw John Wesley Hardin was killed by an off-duty policeman in a saloon in El Paso, Texas
- The first professional American football game was played in Latrobe, Pennsylvania, between the Latrobe YMCA and the Jeannette Athletic Club
- Rudyard Kipling published the story "Mowgli Leaves the Jungle Forever" in Cosmopolitan illustrated magazine
- George B. Selden was granted the first U.S. patent for an automobile
- Wilhelm Röntgen discovered a type of radiation later known as x-rays
- Oscar Hammerstein opened the Olympia Theatre, the first theatre to be built in New York City's Times Square district
- Alfred Nobel signed his last will and testament, setting aside his estate to establish the Nobel Prize after his death
- Two hundred African-Americans left from Savannah, Georgia, headed for Liberia
- The United States received the first shipment of canned pineapple from Hawaii
- George Brownell patented a machine to make paper twine
- The Anti-Saloon League of America was formed in Washington D.C.
- Frederick Blaisdell patented the pencil
- George Washington Vanderbilt II officially opened his "Biltmore House" on Christmas in Asheville, North Carolina
- Auguste and Louis Lumière displayed their first moving picture film in Paris
- The London School of Economics and Political Science was founded in England
- W. E. B. Du Bois became the first African-American to receive a Ph.D. from Harvard University
- The gold reserve of the U.S. Treasury was saved when J. P. Morgan and the Rothschilds loaned $65 million worth of gold to the U.S. Government

Selected Prices

Business Cards, One Dozen	$0.05
Demorest's Monthly Magazine, per Year	$3.00
Fire Insurance, $500.00, per Year	$4.75
Hair Wave	$12.00
Horse Boarding Fee, Monthly	$8.00
Japanese Fan	$0.02
Lactated Baby Food	$0.25
Men's Silk Walking Costume	$16.84
Saloon for Sale, San Francisco	$650.00
Song Sheet	$0.30

Advertisement, The Limitations of the Cash Drawer, created by the National Cash Register Company, 1892:

I am the oldest criminal in history.

I have acted in my present capacity for many thousands of years.

I have been trusted with millions of dollars.

I have lost a great deal of this money.

I have constantly held temptation before those who have come in contact with me.

I have placed a burden upon the strong, and broken down the weak.

I have caused the downfall of many honest and ambitious young people.

I have ruined many business men who deserved success.

I have betrayed the trust of those who have depended upon me.

I am a thing of the past, a dead issue.

I am a failure.

I am the Open Cash Drawer.

"We were obliged to be away from the store most of the time so we employed a superintendent. At the end of three years, although we had sold annually about $50,000 worth of goods on which there was a large margin, we found ourselves worse off than nothing. We were in debt, and we could not account for it, because we lost nothing by bad debt and no goods had been stolen. But one day I found several bread tickets lying around loose, and discovered that our oldest clerk was favoring his friends by selling below the regular prices. Another day I noticed a certain credit customer buying groceries. At night, on looking over the blotter, I found that the clerk had forgotten to make any entry of it. This set me to thinking that the goods might often go out of the store in this way—without our ever getting a cent for them. One day we received a circular from someone in Dayton, Ohio, advertising a machine which recorded money and sales in retail stores. The price was $100. We telegraphed for two of them, and when we saw them we were astonished at the cost. They were made mostly of wood, had no cash drawer, and were very crude. But we put them in the store, and, in spite of their deficiencies, at the end of 12 months we cleared $6,000."

—John Patterson, President of the National Cash Register Company

"Electro-Plating," *The Youth's Companion*, February 19, 1891:

Whenever a current of electricity passes through a liquid which contains metallic salt in solution, the metal of the salt would be deposited upon the place where the current leaves the liquid. The ends of the wires which bring and carry away the current are called electrodes. The electrode which is connected with the zinc and the battery is the one which receives the deposit.

This principle lies at the foundation in the process of electro-plating, by means of which any cheap sheet metal is covered with a thin coating of a dearer metal.

To experiment with electro-plating you will need three things—a battery, a plating bath and a means of cleaning the article which is to be plated.

For a battery, three cells of any of the batteries hitherto described will suffice. Connect the zinc of No. 1 to the copper or carbon of No. 2, the zinc of No. 2 to the carbon of No. 3 and the remaining terminals of No. 1 and No. 3 are connected with the bath.

As a receptacle for the solution, use a pint bowl—a cheap finger bowl, or bread and milk bowl with wide bottom, will do. Across the top of this, place two bright copper or brass wires, an eighth of an inch in diameter. Connect the ends of these with a terminal of the battery.

To plate with copper, fill the bowl with a solution made by dissolving two ounces of blue vitriol in a pint of boiling water.

To plate with silver, use a solution of 70 grains each silver cyanide and potassium cyanide in a little less than a pint of water. These salts are poisonous, and the hand should not be brought to the mouth after handling them.

Upon the wire, which is connected with the zinc of the battery, hang, by means of an S-shaped hook of bright copper wire, the article to be plated. Upon the other wire suspend in the same manner a piece of sheet copper, about the same size as the article.

In order that the article may receive an even coating of metal, it must be thoroughly cleaned.... After this it should not be touched by the hands, but must be handled with tissue paper. The perspiration from the hands would prevent the deposit from adhering. In some cases it is necessary to dip the article, for a few minutes, in nitric acid, and then thoroughly rinse with water.

After the articles have received a sufficiently thick coating, they may be removed from the bath and washed in an abundance of water. The copper needs no further attention; but silver-plated articles appear dull, and will need to be polished. This can be done with a chamois skin and any ordinary polishing powder.

"An Ermine by Flash-Light," *The Youth's Companion,*
February 19, 1891:

A subscriber has recently sent us a photograph of a very large and beautiful ermine, in its white winter pelage, taken under somewhat peculiar circumstances.

Our correspondence family consists of two daughters, young ladies, 16 and 18 years of age, who last summer became much interested in photography. Their home is in one of the extreme Northern states of the country, where they have a farm, and what is more to the point of our story, a large hennery.

One morning about the middle of December, it was discovered that three fine "Plymouth Rock" chickens lay on the floor beneath their roost, dead—the brain of each having been very cleverly and cleanly removed through a small hole near the base of the skull.

Immediately on observing this peculiarity in the marauder's manner of attack, our friend fancied that a weasel had levied upon him, but after noting the distance which the animal had been obliged to leap, laterally, to reach the roost, he came to the conclusion that it could hardly have been a common weasel, and must have been the weasel's larger and less frequently seen congener, the stoat, or ermine.

He understood the habits of this little epicure among the mustelidae sufficiently well to note that it would, in all probability, return for the brains of three more chickens the following night, and continue the process indefinitely, unless its career was summarily cut short.

The hennery building is a large one, not easily closed to the entry of so small and insidious a robber, and he could think of no better way of procedure than to post himself, with a bull's-eye lantern and a small shot-gun, just within the doorway, leading from a passage into the hennery, at about level with the chicken roost.

Sitting quietly here, he thought, at first sounds of commotion from the chickens, he might be able to turn the line relied upon the rooster, and shoot the ferocious little disturber.

They had no sooner broached this plan at the breakfast table, than his daughters proposed an amendment.

"Let us watch with you!" they exclaimed, "With our camera and flashlight, we'll get a picture of the rascal! We will flash the lights and get a photograph, and you may do the shooting. We will see whether you can shoot quicker than we can take a picture!"

As they were quite enthusiastic, the plan was adopted. During the day the camera was prepared for instantaneous photography, also the little alcohol lamp along with the rubber bulb for puffing a pinch of magnesia powder into the flame, to produce the kind of light necessary for securing a picture. The camera was focused as accurately as possible, in advance, and all made ready for quick work.

The party began the vigil at nine in the evening, well wrapped in blankets and robes, for the mercury was almost down to zero.

continued

"An Ermine by Flash-Light," *The Youth's Companion, (continued)*

They had long to wait. It was after one o'clock in the morning before the ermine was heard, effecting an entrance at a small crevice beneath the eaves of the building.

A minute or two later, they heard it leap down upon the roost. A sudden outcry from one of the fowls succeeded, immediately. One of the girls then flashed the lights; then they all plainly saw the white, slim creature on the back of one of the speckled chickens, in the very act of turning his neck to bite into the brain.

A perfect picture was secured. And, meantime, paterfamilias blazed away with his gun, and riddled both the ermine and the chicken with shot. He was too late to get his part of the performance into the photograph.

Put a Kodak In your Pocket.

The Folding Pocket Kodak is only 1¼ inches in thickness, so shaped as to slip readily into the pocket and so light as to be no trouble when there, yet is capable of making pictures 2¼ x 3¼ inches of the finest quality.

Uses our light-proof film cartridges and

LOADS IN DAYLIGHT.

Price Folding Pocket Kodak, with achromatic lens, - $10.00
Light-proof Film Cartridge, 12 exposures 2¼ x 3¼, - .40

KODAKS $5.00 to $25.

Catalogues free at agencies or by mail.

No Camera is a KODAK unless manufactured by the Eastman Kodak Co.

EASTMAN KODAK CO.
ROCHESTER, N. Y.

There are Times and Seasons for Most Things but the

Premo Camera

ha no limitations as to time, place or range of work. Summer or winter, indoors or out of doors, town or country, it is equally effective and satisfactory. Send for samples of its work to

The Rochester Optical Co.
ROCHESTER, N.Y.

"New Information Notes," *Self Culture, A Magazine of Knowledge,* April, 1897:

A fruitful cause of collisions at sea during fogs is to be found in the difficulty experienced in locating the position of all foghorns, sirens and other such sonorous signals. One of the devices lately brought out for removing this danger consists of two microphones, one in the bow and the other in the stern of the vessel. The bow microphone is connected with the telephone placed at the right ear, and the stern microphone with another at the left ear of the operator, who otherwise is isolated from the sound of the signal. Taking the speed of the sound and the time it takes to travel the length of the ship, the observer can estimate the direction of the fog signal. When both sounds are simultaneous, the signal is at right angles to the vessel.

****

Superintendent Knoll, at the Hudson Street Hospital, New York City, recently completed an x-ray photograph clearly outlining the brachial artery of the right arm of an adult. This is said to be the first time such a feat has been accomplished. The patient was 60 years old and had been suffering from an affection of the arm. The physicians were unable to tell exactly what was the matter. The photograph clearly shows deposits of lime salts in the blood, which has hardened the artery. The treatment of the case was governed accordingly.

****

What is the most expensive product of the world? It is charcoal thread (filament de charbon), which is employed for incandescent lamps. It is, for the most part, manufactured at Paris and comes from the hands of an artist who desires his name to remain unknown in order to better protect the secret of manufacture. It is by the gramme (15½ grains) that this product is sold at wholesale. In reducing its price to the basis of pounds, it is easily found out that the filaments for the lamps of 20 candles are worth $8,000 per pound, and for lamps of 30 candles they are worth $12,000 per pound.

****

In an article entitled "Made in Japan," a contemporary describes how manufacturing nations have always encroached upon each other's domains. The Dutch, importing English clay, made good profit out of imitations of Chinese porcelain, and after a while the Dutch product became firmly established in the markets of the world as Delft ware. English potters copied the Dutch pattern, sold it a good deal cheaper, and the North of England became the headquarters for Delft china. Lately the Japanese, having acquainted themselves with the patterns best liked in England, encroach upon the domain long monopolized by the English potter. The Japanese product is much finer and stronger, and above all much cheaper than the best English ware, and thus Japan is providing the markets with goods which were originally regarded as a Chinese monopoly.

Circular Letter
The National Cash Register Company
Dayton, Ohio, U.S.A.,
February 4, 1892

To All Managers:

We send you under separate cover devices for beating the Simplex Cash Register which consists of a lead bullet with a common horse hair attached. We want you to have your agents call on the parties who are using the Simplex Register, in your territory, and explain how easy it is to beat them. (But do not show them how to do it.)

You can easily ask the proprietor to step away about 20 feet from the machine, and then, by concealing the bullet in your hand, register any amount you want by simply dropping the bullet in the small hole directly under the amount you wish to register.

In all cases, be sure and withdraw the bullet from the machine at the same time that you open the cash drawer (that is, providing you can get the combination of the lock), which can be easily done.

Of course, if you do not want to open the cash drawer, you can step away from the machine and the proprietor (unless he has an eagle eye) cannot discover the horse hair protruding from the machine. Be particularly careful to cut the horse hair off so that it will protrude only about one inch from the opening. We think agents will have little trouble in using the above simple device effectively and impressing users that they have a machine which can easily be beaten and is worthless.

Kindly let us know what success you have in using the above device.

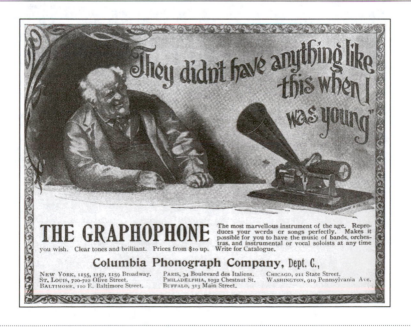

1900-1909

The first decade of the twentieth century was marked by dramatic innovation and keen-eyed energy as America's men and women competed to invent a better automobile, mass market soft drinks or configure the right land deal that would propel them into the millionaire's mansions so frequently described by the press. At the same time, the number of inventions and changes spawned by the expanded use of electricity was nothing short of revolutionary. Factories converted to the new energy force, staying open longer. A bottle-making machine patented in 1903 virtually eliminated the hand-blowing of glass bottles; another innovation mechanized the production of window glass. A rotating kiln manufactured in 1899 supplied large quantities of cheap, standardized cement, just in time for a nation ready to leave behind the bicycle fad and fall madly in love with the automobile. Thanks to this spirit of innovation and experimentation, the United States led the world in productivity, exceeding the vast empires of France and Britain combined.

In the eyes of the world, America was the land of opportunity. Millions of immigrants flooded to the United States, often finding work in the new factories of the New World—many managed by the men who came two generations before from countries like England or Germany or Wales. When Theodore Roosevelt proudly proclaimed in 1902, "The typical American is accumulating money more rapidly than any other man on earth," he described accurately both the joy of newcomers and the prosperity of the emerging middle class. Elevated by their education, profession, inventiveness, or capital, the managerial class found numerous opportunities to flourish in the rapidly changing world of a new economy.

At the beginning of the century, the 1900 U.S. population, comprising 45 states, stood at 76 million, an increase of 21 percent since 1890; 10.6 million residents were foreign-born and more were coming every day. The number of immigrants in the first decade of the twentieth century was double the number for the previous decade, exceeding one million annually in four of the ten years, the highest level in U.S. history. Business and industry were convinced that unrestricted immigration was the fuel that drove the growth of American industry. Labor was equally certain that the influx of foreigners continually undermined the economic status of native workers and kept wages low.

The change in productivity and consumerism came with a price: the character of American life. Manufacturing plants drew people from the country into the cities. The traditional farm patterns were disrupted by the lure of urban life. Ministers complained that lifelong churchgoers who moved to the city often found less time and fewer social pressures to attend worship regularly. Between 1900 and 1920, urban population increased by 80 percent compared to just over 12 percent from rural areas. During the same time, the non-farming work force went from 783,000 to 2.2 million. Unlike farmers, these workers drew a regular paycheck, and spent it.

With this movement of people, technology, and ideas, nationalism took on a new meaning in America. Railroad expansion in the middle of the nineteenth century had made it possible to move goods quickly and efficiently throughout the country. As a result, commerce, which had been based largely on local production of goods for local consumption, found new markets. Ambitious merchants expanded their businesses by appealing to broader markets.

In 1900, American claimed 58 businesses with more than one retail outlet called "chain stores"; by 1910, that number had more than tripled, and by 1920, the total had risen to 808. The number of clothing chains alone rose from seven to 125 during the period. Department stores such as R.H. Macy in New York and Marshall Field in Chicago offered vast arrays of merchandise along with free services and the opportunity to "shop" without purchasing. Ready-made clothing drove down prices, but also promoted fashion booms that reduced the class distinctions in dress. In rural America, the mail order catalogs of Sears, Roebuck and Company reached deep into the pocket of the common man and made dreaming and consuming more feasible.

All was not well, however. A brew of labor struggles, political unrest, and tragic factory accidents demonstrated the excesses of industrial capitalism so worshipped in the Gilded Age. The labor-reform movements of the 1880s and 1890s culminated in the newly formed American Federation of Labor as the chief labor advocate. By 1904, 18 years after it was founded, the AFL claimed 1.676 million of 2.07 million total union members nationwide. The reforms of the labor movement called for an eight-hour workday, child-labor regulation, and cooperatives of owners and workers. The progressive bent of the times also focused attention on factory safety, tainted food and drugs, political corruption, and unchecked economic monopolies. At the same time, progress was not being made by all. For black Americans, many of the gains of reconstruction were being wiped away by regressive Jim Crow laws, particularly in the South. Cherished voting privileges were being systematically taken away. When President Roosevelt asked renowned black educator Booker T. Washington to dine at the White House, the invitation sparked deadly riots. Although less visible, the systematic repression of the Chinese was well under way on the West Coast.

The decade ushered in the opening of the first movie theater, located in Pittsburgh, in 1905. Vaudeville prospered, travelling circuses seemed to be everywhere, and America was crazy for any type of contest, whether it was "cute baby" judging or hootchy-kootchy belly dancing. The decade marked the first baseball World Series, Scholastic Aptitude Tests, the subway , and Albert Einstein's new theories concerning the cosmos. At the same time, the $1 Browning Box camera from Eastman Kodak made photography available to the masses.

1900 Profile

After the frustration of designing a sewing pin that she discovered had been patented before she was born, Marguerite Globman decided to invent something totally different that would save lives—a streetcar fender.

Life at Home

- Marguerite Globman was beside herself with anger.
- It was bad enough that she had to acknowledge that she was wrong, but to realize that her insufferable aunt might be right was downright infuriating.
- Five years earlier, in a moment of exuberance Marguerite had announced to the world that she had invented a streetcar fender capable of preventing hundreds of deaths in New York City when pedestrians were hit by the electric cars.
- Her aunt Sarah had told her to get a patent—then she could talk.
- But when the newspaper reporter arrived to talk about her invention, he was so nice, she had no choice but to tell her story.
- Now, every time she turned around, someone was claiming credit for her streetcar fender; some were even making money off her idea.
- Worst of all, daily she had to hear Aunt Sarah remind her of her impetuous foible and what it had cost the family.
- Her brother, who had assisted in the invention, insisted that "no one stole anything; the idea was in the air, catchable by anyone and everyone."
- Besides, a similar basket-like fender, created in San Francisco in 1894, was used by the pair as a prototype to design their own New York City version.

Marguerite Globman invented a streetcar fender.

Better dressmaking pins were Marguerite's first invention.

- Still, she stood by what she had said in the paper, "My faith in it has not been shaken, and until every car in the United States is using a fender different from mine I shall not give up hope."
- Now 25 years old, Marguerite still lived with her family on 63rd St. where she was born and raised by first-generation German immigrants.
- Like many Jewish immigrants, her father started as a merchant—a peddler of kitchen goods—but had managed in America so well he now operated his own women's clothing store.
- Marguerite spent most of her time caring for her invalid mother and advising her father on the latest "young" taste in high-fashion gowns, the latest trends in shirtwaist garments, and any fashion fads regarding the current bicycle phenomenon.
- Marguerite's first invention grew out of her knowledge of clothing—an improvement on the straight pin, used so prodigiously in sewing.
- "I was sewing one day and a pin I was using annoyed me by slipping out," Marguerite explained.
- So she thought to herself, "What a good thing it would be if there were only pins that would always stay firmly in place."
- One reason dresses fit badly was pin slippage during the trying-on process and thus the stitches were taken in the wrong place.
- "I decided to invent something that would be a blessing to dressmakers," Marguerite said.
- So she carefully observed her pins, noticing that when there were waves or corrugations just below the head, the possibility of slipping was reduced.
- "I sent a model into Washington, and they sent me back the description of the pin exactly like mine which had been patented before I was born."
- The pin invention had never been put on the market.
- "The only thing that inventor did with his patent was to keep me from getting mine."
- After that she was determined to invent something else.
- Her grandfather had been an inventor and her mother had shown herself, despite being an invalid, to be an excellent businesswomen.
- Marguerite said, "One of my brothers was around a great many places, and I said to him one day to keep a good lookout, and if you see anything that is needed anywhere, come home and tell me and I will invent it."
- Then one day he came home and suggested that Marguerite invent a streetcar fender; "He thought those were needed more than anything else—fenders that would safely catch people and prevent them from being struck by the wheels of the streetcar."
- With the help of her other brother, she began work immediately and explored various ideas for more than a year.

Marguerite's well-traveled brother suggested the need for streetcar fenders.

Life at Work

- Marguerite Globman's design for a streetcar fender first captured public attention when she appeared before the Board of Aldermen at their fender-inspection meeting.
- There she demonstrated a scale model of her idea that was capable of collecting a small sandbag with its fender.
- While readily acknowledging that she had never had any interest in or knowledge of mechanical affairs, Marguerite, along with her scale model, made quite an impression.
- She and her brother had spent more than a year drawing probable car fenders on paper in search of ways to reduce the rising number of fatalities on the crowded streets of New York.
- Everyone fully understood how angry the public was concerning streetcar accidents; newspapers carried stories almost daily on tragic deaths.
- More than 300 people had died from streetcar accidents that year alone.
- Although Marguerite and her brother understood little about mechanics, they were able to draw their idea well enough to submit a patent application.
- "We never made any special study of cars," Marguerite told the Board of Aldermen. "I used to stand on a corner and watch the trolleys go around the corner, and I stooped down and looked under the car to see just how they worked."
- She used an umbrella to mark the distance from the inside of the trolley car track to the top of the pavement.
- "I don't know if people thought I was crazy but I didn't care."
- Marguerite told the Aldermen, "Our fender is the only one exhibited that follows the track going around a curve. That is a necessary point, I think."

Streetcar fatalities were commonplace in New York City.

- The fender also was designed to be adjustable so that it was used to project several feet as desired by circumstance.
- The small demonstration model she brought to the meeting showed how the fender would pick up obstructions on any track.
- The committee was impressed by her ingenuity and initiative, even though her patent application had yet to be approved.
- "A great many people tried to discourage me," Marguerite told the newspaper. "People who have invented different things themselves with which they have not been successful. But as I said I shall not be discouraged or lose faith in my fender until there is actually no hope for it."
- Since the 1880s, many would-be inventors had been attempting to improve upon the electric trolley car system.

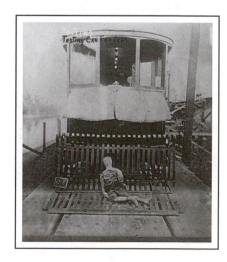

Marguerite created a working model of her fender.

- With the rise of factories and a flood of immigrants, America's cities were growing very rapidly and no one was sure whether electricity or compressed air was the real answer to the city transportation dilemma.
- Compressed air, which could be generated at central stations by means of water turbines or steam engines, could be distributed great distances, making it attractive to design engineers.
- In 1889, Washington, DC—in an attempt to avoid overhead electrical lines—experimented with a compressed air-powered trolley car system whose theoretical potential vastly outstripped the working model.
- In places like Wichita, Kansas, the city fathers were engaged in heated arguments between those who wanted the proposed Arkansas River bridge to be wide enough to carry the streetcar tracks, and those who claimed the streetcars would frighten the horses.
- Among the half million-plus patents that had been issued since the Patent Act of 1836, several had transformed the age: Charles Goodyear's 1839 patent for the vulcanization of rubber, Elias Howe's patent for the sewing machine in 1846, Alexander Graham Bell's 1876 patent for the telephone, and Thomas Edison's 1880 patent for the carbon filament that served as the cornerstone of the electrical lighting system.
- Each patent had been a catalyst to tremendous change because an inventive idea had found the capital needed to produce it and the marketing thrust to make it popular.
- Each patent had made its inventors wealthy.
- But most of the thousands of patents granted annually were simply minor modifications to existing ideas; some were impractical, irrelevant and unnecessary.

Life in the Community: New York City

- In the 1880s, when horse-drawn trolleys provided the main form of transportation in New York City, pedestrians literally watched their step.
  - Horses could produce 20 to 30 pounds of manure a day.
  - Multiply that by a couple of thousand horses, and electric streetcars became a welcome change for walker and rider alike.
  - By the 1890s, electric streetcars had replaced horse-drawn vehicles.
  - Ironically, paved streets came about late in the nineteenth century at the urging of bicyclists.
  - In early 1900, Mayor Van Wyck of New York broke ground for the New York subway tunnel that would link Manhattan and Brooklyn to provide transportation in a crowded city and encourage immigrants to settle more broadly throughout the boroughs.
  - During the nineteenth century, New York had grown from an oversized seaport town into a giant industrial and commercial metropolis: the largest city in the United States and the second-largest in the world.

New Yorkers waiting for the streetcar.

- In the course of the city's metamorphosis from town to metropolis, the native-born business elite who had controlled New York's politics since the American Revolution surrendered power to new political leaders drawn from the immigrant groups, particularly the Irish, who swelled the city's population in the first half of the century.

- Through Tammany Hall, as their seat of power, these new leaders gave the city a government that served a broad spectrum of special interests.

- Tammany quickly became a byword for bossism, corruption, payroll padding, and favoritism.

- By the turn of the century, New York had become too large and complex a city to allow for this state of affairs.

- The city required efficient and active government and officials whose first concern was not political patronage but rather the provision of urgently needed public works and services.

- When the business elite attempted to regain control of the city, public transportation was a priority.

- The increase in New York's population, particularly from 1860-1900, was largely fueled by immigration from the poorest rural areas of Southern, Central, and Eastern Europe.

- The new immigrants customarily settled and tried to remain in the overcrowded areas of the Lower East Side of Manhattan, where they lived in densely packed ghettoes.

- The solution, business leaders believed, was to focus on rapid transit that would disperse the immigrant population to the relatively undeveloped northern part of the city.

- In these surroundings, the immigrants would slowly become more like New Yorkers and reject corrupt city politics.

Immigrants arriving in New York.

HISTORICAL SNAPSHOT
1900

- The *Encyclopedia Britannica* advertised itself as "a million-dollar library for $25"
- The American League of Professional Baseball Clubs was organized in Philadelphia, Pennsylvania, with eight founding teams
- Dwight F. Davis created the tennis Davis Cup
- The first electric bus began operations in NYC

- John Hay announced the Open Door Policy to promote trade with China
- Dr. Henry A. Rowland of Johns Hopkins University discovered the cause of Earth's magnetism
- U.S. cruisers were sent to Central America to protect American interests in a dispute between Nicaragua and Costa Rica
- Popular songs included, "Rosie, You Are My Rosie," "He Was a Married Man," "I'm a Respectable Working Girl," "Strike Up the Band (Here Comes a Sailor)" and "You Can't Keep a Good Man Down"
- Botanist Hugo de Vries rediscovered Mendel's laws of heredity
- The Gold Standard Act was ratified, placing U S currency on the gold standard
- NYC Mayor Van Wyck broke ground for a new underground "Rapid Transit Railroad" to link Manhattan and Brooklyn
- Hawaii officially became a U.S. territory

- Published books included *Sister Carrie* by Theodore Dreiser, *Lord Jim* by Joseph Conrad, and *The Wonderful Wizard of Oz*, by L. Frank Baum
- In the Philippine-American War, Filipino resistance fighters defeated a large American column in the Battle of Pulang Lupa
- The first automobile show in the United States was staged at New York City's Madison Square Garden
- The bison of the Western Plains were nearing extinction
- Women enjoyed suffrage in Colorado, Idaho, Utah, and Wyoming; 13 states voted against giving women the right to vote
- Incumbent William McKinley was reelected president by defeating Democratic challenger William Jennings Bryan
- Approximately 8,000 automobiles traveled on 144 miles of hard-surface road
- Louis's Lunch in New Haven, CT, made the first hamburger sandwich

Selected Prices

Coffee, 10 Pounds $2.10
Dance Lessons, Five $5.00
Floor Mop $0.10
Home Heater, Coal $9.55
Mattress $10.00
Sewing Machine $23.20
Shotgun $27.75
Tool Chest $5.40
Toothbrush $0.25
Violin $2.45

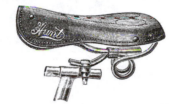

"Shirtwaist to Be Popular," *Indianapolis Journal,*
January 1, 1900:

The shirtwaist will be with us more than ever this summer. Women are wearing shirtwaists because they are comfortable, because they can be made to fit any form, because they are mannish. Sleeves will be smaller, but still not tight, according to A. T. Hearst, a dry goods salesman from New York. "The shirtwaist has come to stay."

FIGURE No. 278 R.—LADIES' BLOUSE-WAIST.—This illustrates Pattern
No. 8259 (copyright), price 1s. or 25 cents.
(For Description see Page 386.)

FIGURE No. 279 R.—LADIES' SHIRT-WAIST.—This illustrates Pattern
No. 8260 (copyright), price 1s. or 25 cents.
(For Description see this Page.)

"FOR SAVING LIFE, Another Fender Invented Which Fits Directly on to the Truck of the Streetcar," *San Francisco Call,*
May 26, 1895:

Frank Hoffman and John Dahl have invented a car-fender which seems to possess considerable merit. The arrangement has been submitted to the railroad companies, Model of a Streetcar Fender, who report that, although the invention is a good one, it is too expensive. The two inventors propose to take the fender before the Board of Supervisors.

The fender is designed to fit upon the car truck. It is made of iron throughout, and is so designed that when the front portion strikes an obstruction, two lids fall down, thus preventing the body passing under the wheels. The faster the car goes, it is claimed, the quicker will the obstruction be moved off the track. There is also provided an arrangement of wires, which is designed to prevent the body going over the truck.

"Revival of the Use of Compressed Air as a Motive Power," Dr. P. H. Van Der Weyde, *Manufacturer and Builder*, December 1894:

Lately an important problem has again been brought to public notice—namely, the propulsion of streetcars by means of compressed air, carried on the car itself.

The solution of the problem requires the execution of two kinds of contrivances—first, a reservoir strong enough to withstand considerable pressure, and, secondly, a motor machine to be put in operation by this pressure. The reservoir is by preference made in the form of cylinders, of say one or two feet in diameter, so that they can be placed under the seats of the car, and of a length sufficient to utilize all the space afforded. The motor is best placed under the floor of the car, now a common method in the electric trolley cars, while the regulating devices are on both platforms where the motorman performs his duty.

It is evident that this system offers particular advantages, especially by reason of its apparent simplicity. The cylinders containing the compressed air—the motive power—are charged at the station and need no further attention, as is the case with locomotive boilers, where the chances of safety depend on the engineer and stoker. All the heavy machinery used for the production of the primary power is stationary, and no power is wasted to move it about as in the case of the locomotive; the only weight to be transported is the motor and the cylinders containing the compressed air. Summing up the advantages, they are:

1. No dead weight of coal or fuel on board.
2. No dead weight of water, boiler, furnace, and other material which has to he stabilized: the real primary motor, which is a stationary structure of large dimensions, and therefore economical, as the economy increases at a very large ratio as the engines are increased in size.
3. The compression of air is going on continually in the reservoirs, and is always connected with the gauges, so as to insure safety.

The first application of this principle was seen some six or eight years ago at the Harlem station of the Second Avenue Railroad. It was intended for the propulsion of trains, and the compressed air reservoirs consisted of two huge cylinders placed horizontally, with a space between, through which the engineer could see the forward track while standing on the motor, and having the train of cars behind.

"An Improved Safety Fender for Trolley and Cable Cars," *Manufacturer and Builder*, February 1894:

The comparatively high rate of speed at which the trolley and cable cars are run in many cities and towns has been productive of a corresponding increase in the number of fatal and minor accidents. To such an extent, indeed, have accidents increased in some localities, that, by municipal action, the street railway companies have been compelled to adopt some form of safety fender to the front of these cars. The object in view in a device of this kind is to prevent the car wheels from passing over the body of a person accidentally run down, by some device which is designed either to push the body before it, or to cause it to be thrown sideways, free of the tracks. Many of the street railway companies have adopted the use of a fender, which, on the cars of all that we have thus far seen, is formed of a rigid framework of iron or steel, presenting in front either a fiat surface or one that is conical, after the pattern of the cow-catcher commonly used on locomotives of steam roads.

Devices of this description, to our mind, do not meet the requirements of the case. A rigid framework of this kind doubtless will effectually prevent the body of an unfortunate victim from being crushed and mangled by the wheels of the car, but the impact of an unyielding iron frame propelled at the rate of from six to nine miles an hour against a human body, will be sufficiently severe, in most cases, to inflict painful bruises, if not more serious injuries.

What is required, it appears to us, is some slightly forward-projecting framework of strong yet elastic construction, with its front edge carried sufficiently near the ground to strike any yielding obstruction, such as a human body, an elastic blow, that will neither inflict bruises nor break bones, and either to scoop up the body into a strong but elastic net, where it will be held safely until the car can be stopped, or to sweep it to one side free of the tracks.

Several devices have lately been invented which perform these operations in a satisfactory manner. One of the best of these is described and illustrated herewith.

The device in question originated with Dr. L. L. Seaman, of this city, who has been assisted in the practical development of the invention by Samuel A. Darrach. Its construction and mode of operation will be understood from the following account, reference being made to the two engravings shown in connection therewith:

The apparatus consists of a light framework of steel pipe, supporting a gang of flat steel springs arranged in the form of a scoop, which extends the full width of the front of the car. It is automatic in its action, and also under the control of the motor-man. The elasticity of the springs insures a yielding blow to any person who chances to come in contact with it—very different from that which would be struck by a rigidly constructed fender—and the springs themselves form an elastic seat upon which the individual may fall, and secure protection from striking any part of the front of the car.

continued

"An Improved Safety Fender for Trolley and Cable Cars," *Manufacturer and Builder*, February 1894: *(continued)*

If the individual is overtaken while lying upon the track, the spring seat, being hinged at the point of its attachment, glides over the body. The seat, also, is so balanced that a very slight weight rests on the person passing under it. This elevation of the spring seat over the body of the victim depresses a sort of spring shovel which extends the entire width of the track, and is located under the front of the car. This shovel has some peculiar features which facilitate its passage under the body of the victim. On falling, it is automatically locked, and its elasticity permits it to glide easily under any obstruction that may be on the track in front of it, and at the same time it adapts itself to any inequalities in the surface of the street.

The advantages of this combined apparatus are claimed to be as follows: It is automatic in its action and independent of the motor-man; it insures protection from a hard blow or concussion from the front end of the car; it does not throw the victim to either side of the track where he may be exposed to passing trucks or vehicles; it provides an elastic spring seat upon which a person struck may fall without injury; it also provides an elastic edge which glides along the surface of the ground and slides under any obstruction or person that may be lying upon the track, instead of grinding them between itself and the earth, as do many fenders in use at present.

A series of interesting practical tests of this device was made at Roseville, N.J., a few weeks ago on a trolley car of the New Jersey Traction Co., and appeared to those who witnessed it to be highly satisfactory. The tests consisted in running the car at a speed of six miles an hour toward a dummy propped up on the track. The practical operation of the forward fender was successfully demonstrated a number of times. Then the dummy was laid on the track; when the car met it, the forward fender glided easily over it, the scoop was instantly released, and the dummy was rolled over into it in a second.

After this, a young man stood up and laid down in front of the car, and the same tests were repeated with equal success. Finally, Mr. Darrach himself—quite an elderly gentleman—submitted to the tests, both standing up and lying down, with no worse results than to get a little snow on his clothes.

A modification of the above design is in the process of construction that will be adaptable to cars on which it is not desirable to have a fender project beyond the platform.

"The Great Cost of Cable Laying in New York Streets,"
Manufacturer and Builder, March 1894:

The chief reason why New York, aside from the difficulties of obtaining the necessary permits from the city authorities, was so far behind other cities in replacing horse-car lines by cable roads, was that here the cost of laying the cable was much more than in smaller cities. The expense of cutting a path through the network of pipes of every description in the New York streets frightened capital away. At Broadway and 14th Street there were no less than 32 different pipes belonging to more than a dozen different companies—gas, water, sewer, steam, pneumatic, electric, etc. All these companies had rights which the cable company was under bonds to respect. The work of getting the pipes out of the way had to be done without interfering with the service of each of these corporations. Sometimes days were wasted in trying to find the owners of pipes that had been abandoned, perhaps for years. Gas companies and steam companies had gone out of business, but had left their pipes to make the confusion under the pavements worse confounded. The enormous cost of this work explains the high price asked by some of the contractors for certain parts of the lines in New York city. Some blocks along the lower parts of the Bowery are said to have cost the contractors at the rate of $300,000 a mile.

"The Cable Costs Much Less to Run Than Horse Cars," *Manufacturer and Builder*, March 1894:

The first outlay for a cable plant is, of course, enormous as compared to a horse-car road, but the deterioration is insignificant. Steam engines and driving machinery last a lifetime, while the hard work required of a car-horse uses the animal up in less than five years. Another item of saving is in the wages of stablemen and hostlers. Wherever a machine can be made to do the work of a man there is a saving, and the force of men now required at the power houses of the Broadway road in New York City to run the machinery is only one-eighth of what it used to be when horses were used. Still another advantage is in the smaller quarters required. A building half the size of the old stables will contain the boilers and engines required for the cable. The enormous stables of the big horse-car lines have long been a menace to the city on account of the danger from fire, and a source of foul odors at all times. The carting through the streets of vast quantities of manure from the stables is also done away with.

There is also one advantage which the cable road has over horse-cars that few persons not familiar with the subject realize. Both cable roads and horse-car roads have to be prepared at all times to carry an exceptionally large number of passengers. During certain hours of the day the business requires four times as many cars as at other times; then upon occasions of public ceremony, parades, celebrations, etc., the whole force of cars may fall short. In order to be ready for such emergencies, both daily and occasional, the horse-car road has to keep in readiness a large number of horses, probably twice the number required for the average work of the road. And, of course, the car-horse costs as much to keep in idleness as when at work. With the cable roads, a greater demand means simply more steam, more coal to be shoveled into the furnaces.

"MR. MOORE'S ETHERIC LIGHT. The Young Newark Electrician's New and Successful Device," *The New York Times*, October 2, 1896:

Etheric lighting has long been the "philosopher's stone" of the electrician. The possibility of doing away with the inconvenience of the present electric-light system and the expensive gas tip has fascinated every electrical scientist in the world for many years.

Daniel McFarlan Moore, the electrician of Newark, N.J., claims to have solved this problem, and solved it in a simple, practicable way. By his method it is asserted that the largest building in New York can be lighted by power furnished by a machine that occupies just one cubic foot of space and weighs less than six pounds. The electric current necessary to run this machine need not exceed 100 volts.

Mr. Moore, who is only 29 years old, exhibited the first fruits of his experiments at the electrical exposition in this city last May. Only small vacuum tubes were lighted then, and they for but a few moments. Now he lights his laboratory, a room 60 feet long and 25 feet wide, throughout with tubes eight feet long and shuts off the light only when he has finished work. There is no heat whatever in the light.

A reporter for *The New York Times* saw Mr. Moore in his laboratory at Newark last night. He entered the laboratory in total darkness. "Touch this button," said the inventor. This was done, and immediately the large room was lighted by a soft, mellow light with a violet tinge. It came from large vacuum tubes suspended in the air, between which there was a small wire connection. The whole was attached to the small machine called the "rotator." Every object in the room was plainly made visible, and there was an entire absence of glare.

Mr. Moore had this to say: "The scheme of etheric lighting is very simple. It is nothing more or less than the vibrations of etheric atoms in a glass tube by means of an electric current. A perfect vacuum is impossible, but when we have exhausted as nearly as possible the air in a tube, the remaining atoms are more active, until as a result of many vibrations, the light is produced. The chief problem we had to contend with was to make a steady and uniform rate of vibrations. I had to abandon springs and adopt rotary lotion. This little machine I call the 'rotator' has solved that problem for me. This, in combination with some exceedingly important new electric principles, has enabled me to produce a light that far surpasses any light ever produced by artificial means."

1905 News Feature

"An Antitoxin for Laziness," *Scientific American*, April 8, 1905:

If the conclusions drawn from experiments detailed in a recent issue of the Muenchener Medicinische Wochenschrift (number 48, vol. 51) are substantiated, fatigue and exhaustion will be a thing of the past. To banish sleepiness, it will only be necessary to drink an antitoxin (a substance that renders a toxin of poison inactive), which will invigorate you, no matter how jaded you may be. Henceforth, such a thing as a somnolent policeman would be unknown on the force, and the speed of the messenger boys will only be comparable to that of the winged Mercury himself. Women who are fond of talking will be able to enjoy their gossiping proclivity to the full, and renew the flagging interest of the victims by an occasional hypodermic injection of new stimulant. Factory and office employees will lead a strenuous life indeed when the vigilant inspector makes the rounds with a syringe full of the new serum, so called after one of the fluid constituents of the blood from which it is derived. Indeed, when one comes to think of it, the application of this marvelous discovery would be almost illimitable. Race horses, sustained by the antitoxin, would be sure to win, armies enabled to endure forced marches in order to snatch victory from the jaws of defeat, and worshipers prevented from falling asleep in church during the dry sermon and suffering the consequent disgrace. Possibly at some time in the remote future, it will become customary to politely offer a fellow mortal a dose of antitoxin, whenever he yawns or exhibits any sign of weariness, much as a pinch of snuff was proffered, as a matter of course, in centuries past.

But, seriously, if we believe the eminent authority mentioned, Dr. Wolfgang Weichardt, of Berlin, has made a very important contribution to the science of physiology, a discovery that is destined not only to be of service to acrobats but in the treatment of neurasthenia, better known as nervous exhaustion, and the convalescence from acute diseases. Briefly, his experiments may be described as follows: A guinea pig was drawn backwards, on a rough carpet, by means of a string, until it no longer resisted interference with its motion and was totally exhausted. Stimulation was continued, by means of electricity, until the animal was in a state of autointoxication, that is to say, a condition of infection from the toxin or poison generated by itself. During the experiment the temperature of the guinea pig fell from 39.2 to 34.8

degrees, Celsius. When exhaustion could be carried no further, the animal was killed. Immediately after death, the toxin (or poison) was obtained from crushed muscles of the animal. When dried in a space exhausted of air, the toxin was found to consist of yellowish brown scales, that were not very stable and had to be kept in sealed glass tubes, preferably in liquid air. This toxin or poison, injected into other guinea pigs, reduced symptoms of exhaustion followed by death within 24 hours. The same poison could not be obtained from the muscles of non-exhausted animals.

Weichardt's antitoxin is produced very much like that of diphtheria, by injecting the toxin into the circulation of horses. When dried in a vacuum, the resulting scales—unlike those in the toxin—are permanent; in fact, the substance retains its activity even after months. It is readily taken up by the stomach, but generally injected under the skin by means of a hypodermic syringe. It was determined that 10 milligrammes of the toxin are neutralized (or rendered inactive) by 1/10 of a milligramme of the antitoxin. Small animals, into which the toxin was injected, remained in a perfectly normal condition and treated with the antitoxin, but succumbed to the poison when the antitoxin was not administered. After taking four doses of a quarter of a gramme of antitoxin, in pastilles, a young lady was able to lift two kilogrammes, 2,478 meters with the middle finger of her right hand, whereas she'd only been able to lift the same weight 1,533 meters alone. The ingestion of antitoxin did not produce any disturbance whatsoever; on the contrary, it was followed by increased vigor and energy. Dr. Weichardt's findings are based upon a large number of experiments.

1907 Profile

Milton S. Hershey had known the bitter taste of repeated bankruptcies before he at last tasted sweet success with his chocolate business.

Life at Home

- Long before he was known as the "chocolate man" who created an entire town in his image, Milton S. Hershey had often dined with failure.
- The son of an entrepreneur who constantly chased the newest idea—whether it was a farm equipment invention, oil exploration or trout farming—Milton grew up in Lancaster, Pennsylvania, plagued by intermittent poverty and a modicum of formal education.
- Surrounded by Mennonite farmers, he learned early the lessons of self-denial and modesty; playfulness was met with scorn.
- He lost his first job at 15 when he intentionally allowed his hat to fall into the printing press he was operating.
- His next job was at Joseph C. Royer's Ice Cream Parlor and Garden, the perfect place to meet pretty girls, ambitious men and prominent visitors.
- In 1872, even writer and entertainer Mark Twain came to town to perform at the Fulton Opera House.
- At Royer's, Milton learned to make boiled sugar candies to include taffies, rock candy, lemon drops and lollipops.
- There Milton learned that when sugar is added to water, the boiling point rises to 330°F and requires constant stirring.
- If the semi-solid sugar concoction was destined to be taffy, it would be cooled and then thrown onto hooks where it was pulled to make it soft and airy.
- He also learned his employer's philosophy of pleasing the customer—every time.
- These skills were tested for 18-year-old Milton when he opened his first business during the Philadelphia Exposition of 1876, an

Milton S. Hershey tasted sweet success with chocolate.

event that attracted 10 million visitors at $0.50 a ticket in a country of 46 million people.

- With the financial backing of his aunt, Milton opened a candy shop near the Centennial fair grounds, where he lured customers in by installing a pipe that carried the sweet aromas of his basement kitchen into the streets.
- When the 100-year celebration of America's founding was complete, Milton stayed in Philadelphia where business was good, but by 1880, his inexperience began to show, and even generous loans from his uncle could not rescue the failing candy store.
- So at 24 years old, Milton returned home after investing the first six years of his young life in a failed business.
- In Denver, he learned the secret of making caramels with vanilla, sugar and milk, a lesson he took to the tough streets of Chicago, where he and his father opened a caramel wholesale business that was short-lived.
- After seeking more funding in Lancaster, Pennsylvania, Milton struck out for New York City, where massive immigration was altering the city daily.
- While the wealthy built ever larger mansions, the rising middle class was eager to possess canned foods, Ivory Soap, Campbell Soup and Kodak cameras.
- Newly created East Coast department stores were experimenting with mass-market selling—high-volume sales at low prices—as they made their stores more attractive, filled with bright lights and friendly salespeople.

Milton opens his New York store.

- At the time Milton established his New York candy store, his competition comprised more than 50 candy wholesalers and hundreds of candy retailers.
- By 1884, Milton was making and selling candy seven days a week on 6th Avenue in the shadow of a new elevated railroad that ran to the city, showering the streets with cinders and ash.
- For two years he prospered.
- Then, in 1886, he was unable to pay a $10,000 debt on some cough drop-making equipment he had bought, and once again he returned to Lancaster, Pennsylvania, without a dime in his pocket.
- He was so broke he was forced to borrow money from friends so he could pay the railroad charges on the crates he had shipped home.
- Milton asked his uncle for one more loan, one more opportunity, but he turned him down.
- Milton returned to making candy on his own and selling it from a pushcart on the streets of Lancaster.
- But he had an idea: by increasing the amount of milk in caramel candy, he could reduce the stickiness and chewiness that bothered so many people.
- Fresh milk also made the candy taste healthy.
- Then, one day, opportunity appeared in the form of an English purchaser who admired Milton's caramels and wanted a big order.
- From there Milton's business took off.
- By the early 1890s, Milton's Lancaster Caramel Company occupied 450,000 square feet of factory space on Church Street in Lancaster.
- Cooking was done in enormous steam-heated kettles—some as big as barrels—where hundreds of pounds of sugar were mixed in each batch.
- Candy-making required precise applications of heat, ingredients, timing, and careful mixing; caramels required proper mixing and cooling.

- Texture could be fatally altered when certain ingredients were added to the boiling water.
- Milton's expertise made him rich and a leading citizen of Lancaster; Lancaster Caramel established factories in several states and sold millions of the soft candy annually.
- And his timing was superb.
- America was changing, displaying an eagerness to buy cheap, quality manufactured food goods of all sorts: Pillsbury flour, Log Cabin Syrup, Lipton Tea, Good and Plenty candy and Juicy Fruit gum.
- Companies, in general, were growing larger; the Pennsylvania Railroad alone employed 110,000 people.
- And the World's Columbian Exposition of 1893 in Chicago became the show-case to demonstrate the New World that America was becoming.

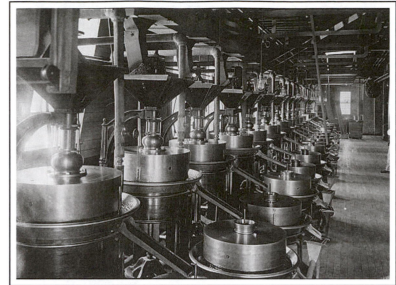

Hundreds of pounds of sugar were mixed daily.

- Built at a cost of $27 million, the buildings were spectacular; fountains shot water hundreds of feet into the air, while nearly 200,000 light bulbs lit the night sky.
- There Milton discovered his next career: chocolate.
- The caramel business was a fad; real money could be found in chocolate, and he began the transition by buying $20,000 worth of equipment, including the newly invented conches which mixed ingredients for hours on end.
- The new machinery once assembled would make 5,000 pounds of chocolate per day; Milton declared he wanted to be the largest chocolate maker in the world.

Life at Work

- Once Milton Hershey had demonstrated the money-making potential of turning sugar, flavorings and milk into sweet caramels in the early 1890s, competitors flooded to the opportunity.

Competition rose by the mid-1890s.

- By the mid-1890s, dozens of competitors offered caramel products, often with similar names and pricing.
- Consumer optimism was in the air, making investors eager to cash in on the emergence of consumer brands that might build a loyal following like Coca-Cola and Kodak.
- At the same time in Europe, affordable, mass-produced Swiss-made milk chocolate was making significant inroads in the candy market.

- The king of caramel had already convinced himself he needed to be in the chocolate business when his chief competitor offered to buy Lancaster Caramel, which boasted annual sales of $1 million a year.

- Where competitor Daniel LaFean only saw growth in the future, Milton, from his vantage point, saw only decline.
- LaFean first offered $500,000 for Lancaster Caramel, which was declined through Milton's attorney.
- The next offer was for $500,000 in cash and $500,000 in stock in the new company.
- This, too, was rejected.
- As the negotiations continued, Milton was prepared to accept $900,000 in cash and $100,000 in stock, becoming very agitated when his attorney turned down that opportunity also.
- The final agreement was $1 million in cash.
- Milton used the first $150,000 to negotiate the purchase of cocoa beans and sugar and launch the chocolate business—even though he had thus far been unsuccessful in producing a milk chocolate product comparable to that of the Swiss.

Chocolate bars were individually wrapped by hand.

- His initial foray into the chocolate business involved a hard candy chocolate, similar to what was already on the market.
- To differentiate the Hershey brand, Milton put his signature on the labels as his personal guarantee of quality.
- He also advertised heavily in journals read by candy retailers and distributed thousands of patriotic postcards which illustrated America's victory in the 1898 war with Spain and declared "Remember the Maine" alongside the Hershey chocolate name.
- Milton also bought an automobile, a Riker electric, to make deliveries and to attract attention.
- But Milton knew his fortune rested in his ability to reach that magic place where cost and quality converged.
- Restlessly he toured Europe, attempting to discover the secret of manufacturing milk chocolate, but a simple solution eluded him.

- The problem was fundamental: milk mostly consists of water, and chocolate contains a lot of oil in the form of cocoa butter—properties that do not mix well.
- Variations in the rate of heating, cooling, the quality of milk and the origin of the chocolate all made a difference.
- For years companies across Europe had been trying to replicate the Swiss formula for milk chocolate—a task made more difficult when the complications of commercial, large-scale production work were factored in.
- So while his hard chocolate company continued to grow—producing $620,000 in annual revenues in 1901—Milton experimented with a small team.
- They tinkered with vacuum pans and closed kettles, skim milk and cream, exploring when to boil and when to cool, 16 hours a day, every day.
- Work for the 18-man team led by Milton started at 4:30 a.m. when they milked 75 cows in preparation for the day's experiments.
- Sometimes they didn't stop work until the next morning; 16-hour days were not unusual.
- Experts were hired and fired; night watchmen patrolled the grounds to keep away spies.
- Finally, with the help of a longtime employee, Milton discovered that the secret of milk chocolate rested in gradual heating and cooling of the mixture.
- The result was a mild-tasting milk chocolate that not only melted smoothly in the mouth, it could be stored for months without spoiling.
- The employee received a $100 bonus for the innovation that would launch Hershey's chocolate.
- Success had only come after hundreds and hundreds of failed experiments.

Milton's research for milk chocolate began with the milk.

- By 1904, Milton was building his new milk chocolate business in the town of Hershey out on the rolling countryside.
- He was personally involved in everything: inspecting the tracks being laid for the trolley, supervising crews excavating sites for commercial buildings and inspecting the new homes being built for his workers.
- While consolidation had become the norm in America—1,800 companies in various industries had merged into fewer than 160 in the six years preceding 1904—Milton was determined to grow his business himself, one milk chocolate bar at a time.
- In 1904, 318 trusts, with capital of more than $7 billion, controlled 40 percent of U.S. manufacturing.
- To promote Hershey's chocolate, Milton hired dozens of salesmen to sell his product to retailers, including bowling alleys, tobacco shops, ice cream parlors, and general stores.
- During his first year of chocolate manufacturing in 1905, net sales were over $1 million and on par with another new national brand known as Jell-O.
- Then, in 1907, Hershey's chocolate introduced a small conical-shaped drop of chocolate called the "sweetheart."
- Soon renamed the Hershey Kiss, the foil-wrapped delight propelled sales to more than $2 million.
- Milton soon developed a business model that emphasized a limited number of high-quality, mass-produced products that could be sold for under a nickel.

Life in the Community: Hershey, Pennsylvania

- Milton Hershey built his dream town near his birthplace and named it after himself.
- The young entrepreneur who had traveled extensively in his effort to conquer the world of candy making envisioned a town suitable for his family, and for the people he considered family who worked in his factory.
- First in 1897, Milton acquired his family's original home, The Homestead farm, in a small community named Derry Church.

Hershey, Pennsylvania.

- The Pennsylvania countryside provided the pure milk and fresh water needed to make quality chocolate and The Homestead provided a hub for his new ventures.
- It didn't matter that Derry Church lacked the basic infrastructure to provide energy or transportation, that no population center rich with potential workers existed nearby and there were no library, shops, men's clubs, parks or theaters.
- Then, in 1903, he acquired 4,000 acres of rolling pasture and farmlands and work began for the factory to recover six acres itself.
- While all this work was underway, quarrymen were mining Milton's own land for limestone to be used on the outer walls while stone-crushing equipment was turning out gravel for roads.
- Milton hired architects to design and build homes, each individual and unique, for the chocolate-factory workers.
- He laid out avenues and named them after the places where cocoa was grown: Granada, Ceylon, Java, and Caracas.
- He mapped out parks that integrated a zoo, a carousel and even a miniature railroad, built a school named for President William McKinley, and public buildings tied to the same electrical system that operated the factory.
- Every effort was made to keep the newly formed community from overwhelming the natural beauty of the area.
- To supply the growing need for milk, Milton purchased dozens of nearby farms and contracted with the owners to continue living on the property as dairy farmers.
- Workers' homes offered electricity, indoor plumbing and central heating in contrast to the water pumps, gas lights and outhouses to which they were accustomed.
- Across America only 8 percent of homes were wired for electricity.
- The town itself was renamed Hershey following a community-wide contest that offered a $100 prize to the person who suggested the best name for the new town.
- Among the suggestions were Ideal, Majestic, Oasis, Zenith, and St. Milton.
- The winning entry was Hersheykoko, but the United States Post Office declared the name too commercial and not usable.
- The official name of the town was shortened to Hershey after Milton realized that it was the name suggested by more than 2,000 different contestants.

HISTORICAL SNAPSHOT
1907

- Robert Baden-Powell led the first Scout camp on Brownsea Island, England
- The passenger liner *RMS Lusitania* made its maiden voyage from Liverpool, England, to New York City
- Guglielmo Marconi initiated commercial transatlantic radio communications between his high-power long wave wireless telegraphy stations in Clifden, Ireland, and Glace Bay, Nova Scotia
- The *Diamond Sutra* of 868, the earliest example of block printing, was discovered
- The triode thermionic amplifier was invented by Lee DeForest, starting the development of electronics as a practical technology
- The Autochrome Lumière became the first commercial color photography process
- A. A. Michelson became the first American to win the Nobel Prize in physics for his optical precision instruments
- *Harper's Weekly* warned of "nickel madness" as millions of Americans flocked to the nickelodeons to see the latest picture shows
- A record 1.3 million immigrants arrived in the United States, prompting Congress to raise the head tax on immigration to $4 dollars a person
- More than 50 newspapers and periodicals were published in Yiddish in NYC alone
- Ringling Brothers bought out competitor Barnum & Bailey
- Pepsi-Cola sales topped 104,000 gallons, up from 8,000 four years earlier
- Rube Goldberg cartoons, self-threading sewing machines, Willy's Overland Motors, Neiman Marcus, Armstrong linoleum, and the spray paint gun all made their first appearance

- The Forest Preservation Act set aside 16 million acres in five states
- The Protestant Episcopal Convention condemned the removal of "In God We Trust" from new gold coins

Selected Prices

Baby Carriage $16.95
Bread Maker $3.25
Caster Oil Tablets, Box $0.10
Chicks, Each $0.15
Chocolate Bonbons, Pound..$1.35
Chocolate, One-Pound Box $0.60
Dental Filling...$1.00
Milk Cocoa, Pound $0.10
Motor Oil, Gallon...$0.60
Trunk $6.88

Chocolate Timeline

1657
London's first chocolate house opened.

1659
In France, David Chalious was granted a royal monopoly on the production and use of chocolate, including its medicinal properties.

1668
In Florence, Italy, the chocolate drink became popular with Florentines who could afford it.

1680
The French began major production of cocoa on the Caribbean island of Martinique.

1700–1720
In London, chocolate houses eclipsed coffeehouses and taverns as centers for amusement, business and political debate.

1727
A major blight devastated Trinidad's cacao plantations.

1746
The French attempted to break the Spanish dominance of cocoa production by bringing cacao to Bahia, in Brazil, which became a major cocoa-producing region by the end of the nineteenth century.

1765
Chocolate production began in North America, with the establishment of a cocoa bean grinding mill in Massachusetts.

1778
The Dutch brought cacao from the Philippines to Jakarta, where they established a facility that soon led to major production in the Dutch East Indies, later known as Indonesia and Malaysia.

1828
The Dutch chemist Conrad van *Houten* patented a technique for pressing most of the fat from roasted and crushed cocoa beans; the creation of "Dutch cocoa" permitted mass production of cheap chocolate.

1847
The English manufacturer J.S. Fry & Sons used cocoa powder to create the first successful mass-produced chocolate bar.

1853
The Cadbury family business became the purveyor of chocolate to Queen Victoria.

continued

Chocolate Timeline *(continued)*

1879

In Switzerland, the chemist Henri Nestlé and the chocolate manufacturer Daniel Peter discovered how to mix chocolate with milk—an objective that had frustrated chocolate aficionados for centuries.

The Swiss chocolate manufacturer Rudolphe Lindt invented the "conch," a machine for stone-grinding chocolate, producing a much finer-grained, more mellow chocolate.

1894

Milton Hershey, already the owner of a caramel candy business, founded the Hershey Chocolate Company in Pennsylvania.

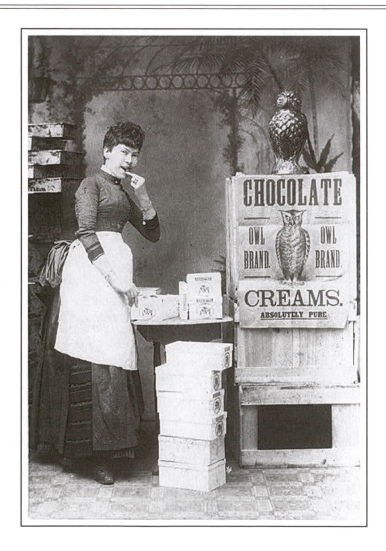

"Socket for Electric Lamps, Recently Patented Inventions,"
Scientific American, **April 8, 1905:**

J. A. Mebane, South Boston, Virginia: The object of the inventor is to provide an improved socket for incandescent lamps in which socket-screws are wholly dispensed with, the separate parts being adapted to be easily and quickly connected and disconnected and electrical connections being made in such a manner that the socket may be produced at much less cost than those of the usual construction. The casting of the socket is likewise so constructed that its two parts are held together detachably by means of a spring-clamp without aid of screws.

"The Development of Motor Traffic," *Scientific American*,
April 8, 1905:

Some interesting remarks were made by Mr. C. S. Rolls in the course of a paper on "The Development of Motor Traffic." After describing older types of vehicles, Mr. Rolls said it was not until 1894 that the development became rapid. In the Paris-Bordeaux race of 1895, the speed of 15 miles per hour was obtained, while in the Paris-Madrid race of last year the rate was nearly 70, and now a maximum speed of 100 miles has been reached. After the passage of the Light Locomotive Act, 1896, the manufacture of motor cars in Great Britain had shown remarkable growth. There are now at least 130 makers, but trade did not yet equal that of France, where the industry employed 200,000 men, and last year's exports amounted to about $5,000,000. England, however, produces more cars for heavy traffic. Last year, 6,133 light vehicles were imported, as against 3,747 in 1904, and the value of cars and parts imported during the year amounted to $10,000,000.

"Hershey Plans Orphanage," *Lebanon Daily News* (Pennsylvania),
June 22, 1906:

Milton S. Hershey, the millionaire chocolate manufacturer, of Derry Church, where a new industrial town and railway station, called Hershey, is being built, is said to contemplate the erection of an orphanage for homeless boys.

Mr. Hershey's plans are said to provide for a home for four or five hundred youths. It is to be an industrial orphanage, where not only food and shelter, but also education and training in the manual arts will be provided.

Plans have been drawn by an architect for the home, which will be located, if built, at a point near the model village in the Hershey Chocolate Works.

Speech, Working In a Silver Mine, by Mark Twain, 1872:

Whenever I had a lot of sand to shovel, I was so particular that I would sit down for an hour and a half and think about the best way to shovel that sand. And if I could not cipher it out in my mind just so, I would not go shoveling it around heedless. I would leave it alone till the next day.

As you know these women dress somberly and look much alike. On one side of the store was a row of large mirrors that extended down to the floor, and before I could wait on her she walked up to that part of the store. Seeing her reflection in the glass she exclaimed, "Ach, Fanny I didn't know you were in town, too!" She was amazed to learn that what she saw wasn't her friend Fanny, but her own reflection. I couldn't help laughing at her, and she laughed too after I explained it to her.

—Recollections of Amish a Woman in 1872, by Milton S. Hershey

1908 Profile

Henry Wood directed his entrepreneurial energies toward improving sales and profits in the family businesses—selling seeds to farmers and gardeners through a mail-order catalog.

Life at Home

- Henry W. Wood fell in love with growing plant seeds as a boy under the tutelage of his father, Timothy Ward Wood.
- Together they created one of the nation's largest seed and plant catalogue companies, based in Richmond, Virginia.
- Growing up, Henry had often heard his father's stories of the seed business in England—lessons his father had learned when he sold seeds to farmers in the British Isles.
- Realizing the huge potential in America, Henry's father Timothy left England for the United States and settled in Virginia in 1873 with plans to establish his business for the American agricultural market.
- On the Virginia farm, Henry grew up watching his father grow a variety of crops from the seeds he had brought with him from England.
- Adapting to the differences in climate and soil conditions, Timothy Wood became adept at cross-pollinating numerous types of plants to improve yield for the American climate.
- By the time he was in his teens, Henry and his brothers, William and Charles, could distinguish a wide array of plants, even by their classification in Latin.
- White clover was *Trifolium repens,* English winter vetch was *Vicia sativa* and Kentucky blue grass was *Poa pratensis.*
- By 1879, he and his two brothers joined their father and started business as seed merchants in Richmond.
- The company was called T. W. Wood, Seedman, and he sold his wide selection of seeds by catalogues shipped by mail.

Henry Wood gained success through mail-order catalogs.

- Dozens of competitors were battling for the seed catalogue business, offering customers seeds for growing annuals, perennials, ornamental grasses, fruits, and vegetables, and some catalogues even offered seed starter kits, garden tools and fertilizers.
- In all, more than 250 seed companies emerged from the nineteenth and early twentieth centuries, including the Park Seed Company, established in 1868; Burpee in 1876; Jung Seeds & Plants in 1907; and John Scheepers, Inc. in 1908.
- Due to the family's reputation and personal involvement with the Richmond Grain and Cotton Exchange, orders came quickly to the Wood business.
- Within a few years, as the operations grew and the number of employees tending to the nursery increased, T.W. Wood, Seedman was relocated to downtown Richmond.
- As the Woods' expertise grew, so did the company's sales pitch within the catalogue: "Without wishing to disparage other seedmen, I beg to say, that it shall ever be my endeavor to sell as good seed as can be obtained in this county, and at as reasonable a rate as first-class seed can be sold."
- One issue plaguing farmers was an inexpensive method to recover soil nutrients for crops.
- Thanks to extensive research, the family's seed business provided a solution—quality grass and clover seed.

T. W. Wood, Seedman was known for its grass and clover.

- Farmers used grass and clover with rich nutrients to plow into fields left undeveloped for crop rotation—a proven method without the expense of fertilizer.
- Quickly, T.W. Wood, Seedman became best known for its grass and clover products to redeem worn-out lands throughout the South.
- The T.W. Wood, Seedman catalogue listed 14 grasses and seven clovers based upon the soil conditions and uses.
- Tall meadow oat grass was popular for cattle to graze upon, while Timothy grass made the best hay.
- Also popular was the company's Fine Mix Lawn Grass that sold for $0.25 per pound, or $3.00 per bushel.
- At the same time, county agricultural agents, expounding upon the new scientific methods of agriculture reminded farmers, "It costs us as much to prepare the soil for poor seeds as it does for good ones."
- Studies showed that a 60-pound bushel of clover seeds, sold at a bargain price, contained as many as 59,000 weed seeds, dramatically increasing the labor costs of cheap seeds.
- Because of the convenience of ordering through the mail from the extensive T.W. Wood, Seedman catalogue, customers often included a few flower purchases with their grass orders.

- T.W. Wood also attracted orders from those in remote areas dissatisfied with the seed offerings or prices in their local country stores.
- Henry and his brothers encountered numerous penciled orders scribbled by semi-literate farmers that proved a challenge.
- Complaints typically followed, by farmers whose orders were not met properly.
- To remedy the mail problems, the company printed, "Orders should be legibly written in a list, and not mixed up in the body of your letter; this will avoid confusion and prevent mistakes."
- This helped slow the flow of complaints and the loss of money in reshipping seeds, thereby increasing the company's profits.
- After a few years, Henry's father changed the name of the company to T.W. Wood & Sons.

Life at Work

- Henry Wood believed advertising was essential to reach new customers unfamiliar with T.W. Wood & Sons.
- To drive sales, numerous advertisements were placed in trade publications, newspapers and college quarterlies.
- Henry realized they could sell not only to the farmers, but also to people interested in flowering plants.
- The family agreed to mail catalogues at no cost to anyone who wrote requesting one.
- More orders resulted, and soon the men had to open a second store at 1530 Main Street, as well as establish a warehouse on 14th Street along the James River next to Mayo's Bridge.
- The warehouse had a rail spur that went along the building and could load nine railcars at one time to ship goods throughout the South.
- The mail order catalogue business was so well known that customers visiting Richmond on business would visit T.W. Wood & Sons as well as the Confederate monuments.

The seed company warehouse.

- By 1889, the company ranked as one of the largest seed businesses in America.
- Taking the profits from the business, Henry's father bought a majority ownership in The Implement Company, located in Richmond.
- The acquired operation sold farm implements—such as plows, threshers, feed cutters and the sort.
- Experienced at shipping goods via mail, Henry marketed the farm equipment directly to agricultural retailers throughout the South.
- He mailed the company's small 22-page wholesale catalogue in envelopes that required the least postage.

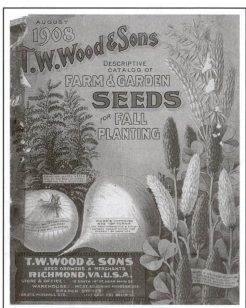

Mail order helped grow the business.

- The business offered 60 days' credit to approved customers, or two percent off for prompt cash payment within 10 days.
- Catalogue products included a Dixie boy, a one-horse plow that sold for $1.25, and Buckeye Wagons that were warranted for 12 months.
- At the same time, catalogue competitors were trying to distinguish themselves by giving vegetable and flower varieties names containing hyperbolic language such as "Mammoth," "Giant" or "Perfection."
- Catalogue covers became more elaborate, and companies devoted more space to illustrations, descriptions, testimonials, contests, special offers, and awards won at horticultural fairs or exhibitions.
- Catalogues catered to the widespread passion for flowers, and contained selections for gardeners of every taste.
- Those who wished to plant formal geometric bedding designs could find many dwarf varieties of brightly hued annuals and tropical plants with colorful foliage.
- Gardeners who preferred a nostalgic, neocolonial "grandmother's garden" could choose from a vast selection of poppies, hollyhocks, and climbing vines.
- Along with ornamental plantings, lawns became important for status-conscious suburbanites, especially after rotary push mowers came into widespread use.
- Grass seed was also in demand for tennis courts, croquet grounds, and parks.
- As business grew, it became challenging for all three brothers to run their two businesses.
- Arguments ensued, especially with Charles, the youngest.
- Soon it became clear that Charles wanted to go out on his own and start a new seed business in Louisville, Kentucky.
- With Charles departing, it was agreed that, although Henry was not as scientific as his father, he would run the two businesses and handle the majority of the business operations.
- Even though he ran the businesses for years, but his father never gave him sole authority.
- In addition to his personal interest in the greenhouse and nursery at the family home, Henry's father designed and built a number of machines.
- One of those machines was a turbine engine that utilized tidewater but was not developed.
- He did build and patent a swing churn for the dairy industry.
- It was a required product to sell in The Implement Company catalogue and had a prominent place on the back cover.
- Concerned with the plight of the farmer in the poor economy of the late nineteenth century, T.W. Wood also wrote a number of booklets promoting the free coinage of gold and silver during William Jennings Bryan's presidential campaign in 1896 and 1900.
- Over the years, Henry heard his father complain about unpaid debts owned to the seed business and firmly believed that free coinage put more money in circulation and solve the problems.
- Those matters took a backseat when his father fell ill and had to give up all business involvement.
- Under the advisement of a physician, he went to Europe for a few months in the summer of 1905 hoping the change of air and scenery would improve his heath.

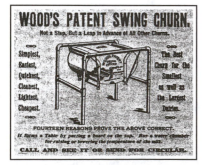

Henry's father received the patent for the swing churn.

- He did improve upon his return in September, but died a few weeks later in the family home in Forest Acres, just as the economy was beginning to grow.
- Within 12 months of his father's death, Henry experienced significant growth.
- The Implement Company saw increasing demand for farm equipment from across the South due to the scarcity of laborers.
- Farmers were willing to purchase more tools and labor-saving products because their workers were leaving for the cities to take factory jobs.

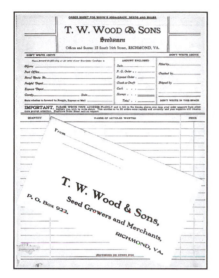

A perforated order sheet was included in the catalogue.

- Richmond's geographic location with the railroads and Henry's advertising efforts enabled him to sell his products as far as eastern Tennessee, northern Georgia and Florida.
- According to the city's *Times Dispatch,* "several million dollars' worth of agricultural implements" were sold out of Richmond, a 33 percent increase annually over the past several years.
- To continue the momentum, improvements were made in the catalogues for both The Implement Company and T.W. Wood & Sons, including photographs and drawings of various crops.
- Henry even added a perforated order sheet that was easy to complete and provided an addressed 6½ by 3½ envelope to the company's office in Richmond.
- Postage was a major issue.

- By 1907, the trademarked Wood's Evergreen Lawn Grass, developed by Henry's father, was covering the lawns along Richmond's Monument Avenue, and T.W. Wood & Sons became the largest seed house in the entire South.
- Utilizing the Richmond Chamber of Commerce, Henry Wood decided to expand his role to help promote the city and develop his business connections.
- He believed that if he helped grow the city's business community, it would help his companies.
- One strategy was to advertise to business visitors that the Richmond Chamber of Commerce would reimburse the amount of rail fare based upon the cost of purchases.
- Henry worked with the Massengale Advertising Agency on the promotion in a number of daily newspapers and weekly journals.
- Company representatives visiting the city on business had to register with the Richmond Chamber of Commerce upon arrival to take advantage of the offer.
- Registration provided new business contacts and steered prospective buyers to participating Chamber members' stores—including Henry's companies.
- The rail fare reimbursement strategy was a huge success.
- It was not long before Henry and his Chamber colleagues recognized a huge marketing potential—the 300th Anniversary of the Jamestown Settlement.

Henry used his success to help grow Richmond's business community.

- Henry volunteered his advertising expertise and developed a new marketing approach for this event.
- He quickly was appointed as Chairman of the Chamber's Advertising Committee.
- Working with five other business members, he created a 30-page booklet that promoted the commercial activity of the City of Richmond.
- Over the course of several weeks, he spent many late hours working on the promotional material for Richmond's business community.
- Bourbon and cigars were also a requirement for a number of these planning meetings.
- On one occasion, Henry reprimanded one of his Chamber partners for suggesting a "lighter beverage," Budweiser beer.
- He later learned that his colleague wished to limit his alcohol content for "religious" reasons.
- Within a few months, Henry and his team finished the booklet that discussed the city's cultural, social and educational advantages, as well as the tens of millions of dollars of industrial activity within the city.
- Thousands were distributed at the Jamestown Exhibition, especially to potential business candidates.
- Henry's team also did considerable advertising in magazines and publications for general circulation to promote the city.
- During the Exhibition, T.W. Wood & Sons was one of many companies displaying products and educating the population.
- At one point, Henry had to harshly address a representative whose publication was doing a fair amount of "muck-raking, pessimistic, destructive articles" on businesses.

- Henry believed that when one was not being positive or optimistic towards business, it undermined the public confidence in companies and could lead to an economic panic.
- Henry spent hours creating an impressive display on the various plants and seeds, including cowpeas, clover and grasses found throughout America.
- He also had an extensive variety of feed corn.
- Henry was particularly impressed with the types of agricultural practices conducted in India, Australia, and all parts of Europe.
- During the Jamestown Exhibition, thousands of people toured the numerous business displays and voted on the best exhibit to win a highly prized gold medal for Best Exhibition.
- Henry was shocked to learn that the public jury awarded T.W. Wood & Sons the gold metal, and that it was reported extensively in the Richmond newspaper.

Henry was interested in agriculture in other countries.

- It was Henry's first international award that he won on his own for the family company; he would display it proudly next to the gold medals his father won at the 1900 Paris Exposition and at the 1904 St. Louis Exhibition, where he had won the Grand Prize.
- With his role at the Richmond Chamber of Commerce and his success at the Jamestown Exhibition, Henry continued to develop relationships at major events—including the Virginia State Fair.
- There, hundreds of farmers from across the state arrived in Richmond by rail or wagon and listened to Henry discuss the benefits of various plants based upon soil conditions.
- Henry often used agricultural journal studies on the benefits of his various farm seeds, illustrating the number of ears of corn generated per stalk and the number of bushels expected per acre.
- It was also common to see The Implement Company exhibiting at the State Fair the large machinery available.
- One of the farmers' favorites was the Crown Drill with grass seed and fertilizer attachment.
- Often, many of these farmers visited Henry's store after selling their tobacco crops or other goods and made their pre-orders for next season.
- Then, late one summer's evening in 1908, calamity struck T.W. Wood & Sons when a fire wrecked the seed warehouse.
- Practically all of the city's fire crews arrived after midnight to fight the second-story fire and continued to douse streams of water on it for over two hours.
- After the blaze was extinguished, Henry and his workers sifted through the charred debris to determine the damages.
- He approximated at least $50,000 worth of damages to the entire building and that roughly $8,000 to $10,000 worth of field seed was damaged and covered by the insurance.
- The likely cause was a defective electrical wire used for lighting the interior.
- Even with the disaster, Henry could access surplus from his farms outside the city to meet his orders.
- The problem Henry's staff had to resolve was the records lost in the fire.

Timothy Ward Wood, Henry's father.

Life in the Community: Richmond, Virginia

- The migration of people into urban areas promoted the growth of the City of Richmond and increased its economic activity in the early part of the twentieth century.
- Since the Civil War, the city underwent an economic transformation from being the former capital of the Confederacy to a strong business community.
- The city's Chamber of Commerce estimated Richmond's population to be 110,000 in 1907, and 130,000 when one included the suburban sections.
- Over a four-year period, investments in buildings and equipment increased exponentially in the city by over 80 percent.
- In 1903, property tax valuation totaled $73,850,700, and by 1907 it was $134,707,103.
- Manufacturers represented a strong portion of Richmond's economic growth and represented over $56 million of the property value of the community.
- Many businesses took advantage of the six railway systems that brought Richmond in close connection with the rest of the United States.

Many families migrated from the country into the city.

- The systems included the Chesapeake & Ohio, whose rails led in three different directions, the Southern, and the Norfolk & Western lines.

The railroad connected Richmond with the rest of the country.

- With rail access, Richmond was only three hours and five minutes from Washington, D.C. and nine hours from New York City.
- Travel to Chicago took just over 20 hours.
- Two steamship lines—the Old Dominion and Virginia Navigation Company—took advantage of the city's port on the James River and was only 90 miles to the Atlantic Ocean.
- This enabled Richmond's citizens to easily access the world.
- Indicative of the community's high quality of life, Richmond possessed 18 parks that included fine views of the river, monuments, fountains, lakes, and carefully maintained flower beds.
- Such venues included Monument Avenue, where monuments were dedicated to President Jefferson Davis, General Robert E. Lee, and J.E.B. Stuart.
- Historical locations also included the home of John Marshall, a great Chief Justice of the United States, the White House of the Confederacy, and St John's Church, were Patrick Henry made his dramatic speech to the colonists before the American Revolution.
- Richmond leaders promoted the higher educational institutions in the city, which included two medical schools—the Medical College of Virginia and the University College of Medicine.
- Richmond College, founded in 1832, provided academic and law degrees for many of the city's ambitious young men.
- By 1907, the city proposed to develop the University of Richmond on the same plan of Oxford and Cambridge to provide a prestigious university for the city.
- The city even had Virginia Union University and Hartshorn Memorial College, which were connected to the public-school system for the higher education of blacks.
- Many of the visiting guests staying in Richmond came to the city to conduct business with the 250 manufacturing plants within the its borders.

- In 1908, the city claimed to lead the world in a number of industries ranging from boots to machine shops.
- However, Richmond was best known for tobacco.
- Many farmers and merchants delivered their tobacco leafs by water and rail to Richmond, where over 20 public and private warehouses could store over 80,000 hogsheads.
- With a large gathering of product gathered from across Virginia, North Carolina and South Carolina, Richmond sold over 60 million pounds annually to the world.
- Taking advantage of the high-quality tobacco, Richmond's manufacturers produced over 22 million pounds of tobacco products sold to the world's cigarette and cigar factories.
- The tobacco manufacturers were the community's largest industry segment in 1908 and represented over $6.5 million in investments in the city; the industry employed over 10,000 people.
- Over 33,000 people worked in manufacturing, from printing and publishing to the bottling of beer and mineral water.

Tobacco was a popular crop in Richmond.

Historical Snapshot
1908

- A long-distance radio message was sent from the Eiffel Tower for the first time
- The first around-the-world car race, the 1908 New York to Paris Race, began in New York City's Times Square and was won by George Schuster in Paris, France, after 169 days of travel
- At Ft. Myer, Virginia, Thomas Selfridge became the first person to die in an airplane crash; pilot Orville Wright was severely injured
- The first production of the Ford Model T automobile was built at the Piquette Plant in Detroit, Michigan and cost $825

- Western bandits Butch Cassidy and the Sundance Kid were killed in Bolivia after being surrounded by a large group of soldiers
- Cincinnati Mayor Mark Breith told his city council, "women are not physically fit to operate automobiles"
- At Masjed Soleyman in southwest Persia, the first major commercial oil strike in the Middle East was made; rights to the resource were acquired by the U K
- The first Gideon Bible was placed in a hotel room
- Albert Einstein presented his quantum theory of light

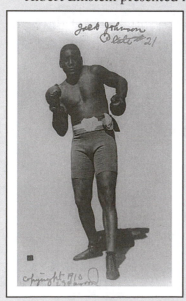

- In Sydney, Australia, Jack Johnson knocked out Tommy Burns in 14 rounds for the heavyweight boxing title and became first black heavyweight champion
- President Theodore Roosevelt visited Panama to inspect the canal, the first sitting president to travel abroad
- In Springfield, Illinois, several thousand white men went on a rampage in black residential areas
- The Supreme Court handed down prison sentences to American Federation of Labor officers Samuel Gompers, John Mitchell, and Frank Morrison for violating an injunction against a boycott of Buck's Stove and Range Company

Selected Prices

Carburetor...$18.00
Hotel Room, Chicago, The Plaza, per Day $2.50
Lawn Mower... $6.50
Motorcycle $275.00
Potatoes, Sack $2.50
Roses, 24 Plants.. $1.00
Seeds, Five Packages, Giant Sweet Peas................................ $0.10
Strawberries, Basket $0.15
Suitcase. Leather $3.00
Toffee, Four Pounds $1.60

Advertisement for T.W. Wood & Son's Lawn Grass, 1908 Fall Catalogue

Wood's Evergreen Lawn Grass

This will form a rich, deep green velvety lawn in a few weeks' time. It is composed of various grasses that grow and flourish during different months of the year, so that, with proper care and attention, a beautiful green lawn can be kept all year round. The grasses used have shown to succeed and do best in our southern soils and climate. Sow at the rate of 60 to 75 lbs per acre, or for small yards, one quart to 300 square feet. Price per qt. 25cts; if sent by mail, 30 cts; 4 lbs for $1.00; bushel of 20 lbs. $4.00; 100-lb lots and over 19 cts lb.

I sowed the Wood's Evergreen Law Grass I bought from you last fall on my yard, and I never dreamed that such a yard of grass could come so quick. I only wish everyone who wants to sow a yard could see it. No one that sees it believes it could only be nine months old. If I had to sow another yard, I would write to you to send me what you thought best to sow. I would feel sure that it was right. E.P. Cahill, Rockingham Co., N.C., June 6, 1907

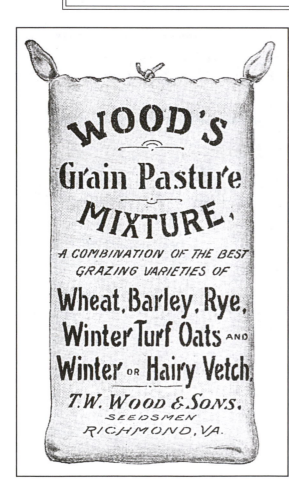

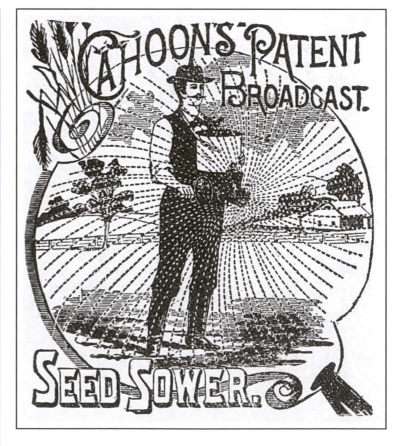

"Section for Prospective Manufacturers,"
1907 Booklet on Richmond, Virginia,
developed by the Richmond Chamber of Commerce

Although the desire to own and operate a manufacturing plant is a very general one, and no other commercial enterprise offers such large returns as a factory property located and systematically conducted, many are puzzled to know what line of manufacture to adopt, or at what place to locate.

RICHMOND'S GREAT NATURAL ADVANTAGE

There are two questions in connection with a project plant that demand thorough investigation, for the measure of success hangs largely upon the wisdom of the selection. A large manufacturer, with unlimited capital, can, by expensive advertising campaigns, surmount to some extent geographical disadvantages; but the manufacturer of moderate means, to make his success assured, must follow the line of least resistance; and, by the selection of his article of manufacture and the location of his plan, assemble on his behalf the greatest possible number of nature's auxiliaries.

INVESTIGATION OF THE MANUFACTURING OPPORTUNITIES INVITED

Careful investigation will result in the conviction that, since manufacturing in the South at large is practically in its infancy, no other section of the country offers the prospective manufacturer so many inviting opportunities; and, with its excellent railway facilities, with its good system of rail and water rates to and from all parts of the country, with its superb climatic conditions, with its proximity to an unlimited supply of raw materials, and with its reputation already established as a successful manufacturing point, no other city in the South offers so many circumstances that combine to make success easy for its own manufacturers as does Richmond. This latter statement is effectively confirmed by the unusual success of Richmond's two hundred and fifty (250) factories now in operation, a number of smaller but growing industries.

"The Implement Company at the State Fair," *The Richmond Times-Dispatch*, October 1907:

At the great State Fair, just closed, The Implement Company, whose stores are No. 1302 and 1304 East Main Street, had a strictly wire fence exhibit, and it was a beauty, a piece of perfection in model wire-fencing. The Implement Company are the agents for the American Steel and Wire Company.

Special agents of the company came from the factory to make an exhibit at the Fair, showing how wire fences should be built on every farm and everywhere else they are put in use. On the large space the Implement Company occupied on the Fair Grounds, there were erected fences of all sizes, shapes and styles. There were more than a dozen lines, run showing as many a different style of fences and also the most approved manner of setting posts and bracing them....

Educational Pamphlet, T.W. Wood, Seedman (1901):

Remarks on the Importance of Grass Culture

The Grasses are exceedingly valuable to mankind, for they nourish and sustain by far the greatest portion of the animals which minister to man's wants. And when our Creator said, "Let the earth bring forth grass," he bestowed one of the greatest blessings upon us, but, unwisely, our Southern farmers have too long considered grass as an enemy, and cultivated such crops as would most effectually destroy it: hence, the abundance of land which has been made poor, and the number of poor farmers. If these lands are to be redeemed, and the farmers made prosperous and happy, a reverse policy should be adopted, and the land put down in grass, to rest and recuperate, and thereby save the constant expense of implements and defective labor....

"Sailors and Negroes Clash, Authorities Have Great Difficulty in Preventing Lynching in Berkley," *The Richmond Times-Dispatch*, August 4, 1908:

NORFOLK, VA—August 3. There was a serious clash between negroes and United States sailors in Berkley and South Norfolk last night, and but for the timely arrival of the civil authorities, who took charge of three negroes, with whom the trouble originated, and gave them police protection, there might have been a loss of life. It is said that the sailors from the St. Helena, a naval training station a short distance away, had been taking corn from the farm land of the negroes. One of the negroes fired upon the sailors, but said he did so only to frighten them off. The seamen then drove the negroes, with their families, into the house on the place, and many shots, it is said, were fired into this. The police called upon the naval authorities for aid, and the negroes who were being attacked were finally gotten to the Berkley Ward Police Station.

Several hundred sailors assembled, and the police, hearing threats of lynching, hastened the negroes in a special car from Berkley across the river to the central police station in the city, where they still remain. The sailors assembling around Berkley Police Station openly threatened attack, and the naval authorities had to again send aid to disperse and run the enlisted men back to their station. When officers arrived at the farm house where the negroes were being attacked by the sailors, there were 300 enlisted naval men endeavoring to find some way of getting hold of the negroes. Many of these sailors had guns, ropes and missiles. The sailors threatened to burn the house, with the negroes therein, but the officers declared if the negroes were burned, the officers, too, would be burned.

The sailors charged that three of them had been held up and robbed by the negroes.

Advertisement, Rail Fare Reimbursements to Merchants:

The leading manufacturers and jobbers of Richmond have joined in an agreement that will greatly benefit merchants wishing to do their buying in person. Any Southern merchant whose purchases during his stay in Richmond are made from the firms composing this association will be refunded his railroad fare in whole or in part, according to amount of said purchases. Merchants taking advantage of this offer should register at the Chamber of Commerce promptly upon arrival in Richmond. Write the Chamber of Commerce for full particulars.

Speech, Optimism and Progress, by Henry Wood at the Richmond Chamber of Commerce:

The Chamber of Commerce stands for optimism and progress in all lines of our development, and it hopes to make such an impression upon this community in this direction that our people will always be in favor of measures which are calculated for the advancement and best development of our commercial, municipal and social life....

I believe firmly that the present administration of our government under President Taft is going to be one of the most successful and prosperous administrations we have ever experienced, and I believe that a good deal of it will be due to President Taft's announced belief in optimism, and his resultant temperament of cheerfulness, helpfulness and progressiveness....

Every thought, every act, and every impression influences the mind, consciously or unconsciously. Progressive thoughts and uplifting influences build up and strengthen; depressing influences weaken and destroy. How important it is for us to control our thoughts and actions aright, if we would build up both our success and happiness. Train your minds to think prosperous thoughts, success thoughts, and work industriously towards these ends, and success and prosperity are pretty apt to come to you.

Advertisement, Bell Telephone, Richmond, 1908:

The Bell Telephone: Its Uses and Abuses

When you buy a cigar, you don't expect the clerk to give one to the friend who accompanies you. You wouldn't think of taking a paper from a news stand without paying for it or tapping your neighbor's gas pipe and using gas through his meter.

But how about the telephone? If you are not a subscriber, you do not hesitate to use your friend's telephone, and you often step into a store and use the telephone without paying for it. If you are a subscriber you are doubtless accommodating and permit the general public to use your telephone as often as seems desirable.

Now, this is apparently a small matter, but it represents a big problem in telephone operating. It encourages useless and unnecessary telephone conversations. While people are using free the telephone for which you are paying, you wonder why your station is so often reported "busy" to people who are trying to reach you.

It's not the loss of money that disturbs us, because we would willingly stand a large expense to overcome the evil. It is the additional and unnecessary load placed upon our switchboards and the heavy burden thrust upon our operators. The effect is felt in the service—your service. And the whole responsibility is thrown back upon us by our subscribers.

Worse still, the STRONGEST KICKERS are people who are NOT subscribers, but who are using other people's telephones FREE OF COST.

With a little co-operation on your part we could correct service defects in this manner. We don't ask you to be discourteous to your friends and patrons, but we do want you to bear in mind that we are handling thousands of calls every day for which you are receiving NO RETURN and for which we are receiving no revenue. These calls are a heavy burden upon us, lessen the facility of the service, bring us no revenue, and cause both the company and its subscribers to suffer. We want you to know we are doing our part. Your co-operation will bring results beneficial to us both....

—Southern Bell Telephone & Telegraph Co. of Virginia

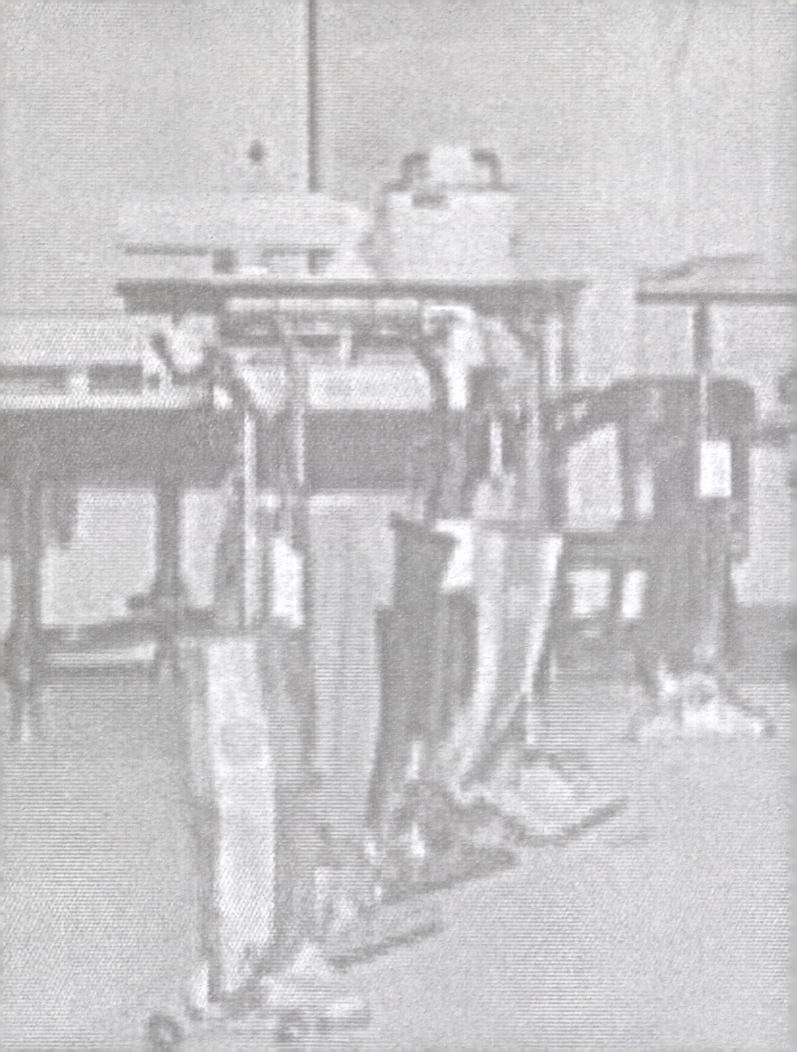

1910-1919

America was booming during the second decade of the century, and economic excitement was in the air. Anything seemed possible to inventive minds and entrepreneurs willing to risk everything for the opportunity of wealth. America's upper class now enjoyed the world's finest transportation—by train and automobile—and spent considerable time discovering new forms of entertainment. At the same time, an emerging middle class was showing that it was capable of carrying a greater load of managerial decisions, freeing factory owners and stockholders to travel, experiment, and study ways to cure the ills of the poor. Millions of dollars were poured into libraries, parks, and literacy classes designed to uplift the immigrant masses flooding to American shores. America was prospering and, at the same time, the country's elite were reevaluating America's role as an emerging world power which no longer had to look to Britain for approval.

During the decade, motorized tractors changed the lives of farmers, and electricity extended the day of urban dwellers. Powered trolley cars, vacuum cleaners, hair dryers, and electric ranges moved on the modern scene. Wireless communications bridged San Francisco to New York and New York to Paris; in 1915, the Bell system alone operated six million telephones, which were considered essential in most middle class homes as the decade drew to a close. As the sale of parlor pianos hit a new high, more than two billion copies of sheet music were sold as ragtime neared its peak. Thousands of Bibles were placed in hotel bedrooms by the Gideon Organization of Christian Commercial Travelers, reflecting both the emerging role of the traveling "drummer," or salesman, the evangelical nature of the Progressive Movement.

Immigration continued at a pace of one million annually in the first four years of the decade. Between 1910 and 1913, some 11 million immigrants—an all-time record—entered the United States. The wages of unskilled workers fell, but the number of jobs expanded dramatically. Manufacturing employment rose by 3.3 million, or close to six percent in a year during that period. At the same time, earnings of skilled workers rose substantially and resulted in a backlash focused on protecting American workers' jobs. As a result, a series of anti-immigration laws was passed culminating in 1917 with permanent bars to the free flow of immigrants into the United States. From the beginning of World War I until 1919, the number of new immigrants fell sharply while the war effort was demanding more and more workers. As a result, wages for low-skilled work rose rapidly, forcing the managerial class—often represented by the middle class—to find new and more streamlined ways to get the jobs done—often by employing less labor or more technology.

In the midst of these dynamics, the Progressive Movement, largely a product of the rising middle class, began to shape the decade, raising questions about work safety, the rights of individuals, the need for clean air and fewer work hours. It was the people's movement that grasped the immediate impact of linking the media to its cause. The results were significant and widespread. South Carolina prohibited the employment of children under 12 years in mines, factories, and textile mills; Delaware began to frame employer's liability laws; the direct election of U.S. Senators was approved; and nationwide communities argued loudly over the right and ability of women to vote and the need and lawfulness of alcohol consumption.

Yet in the midst of blazing prosperity, the nation was changing too rapidly for many—demographically, economically, and morally. Divorce was on the rise. One in 12 marriages ended in divorce in 1911, compared with one in 85 only six years earlier. The discovery of a quick treatment for syphilis was hailed as both a miracle and an enticement to sin. As the technology and sophistication of silent movies improved yearly, the Missouri Christian Endeavor Society tried to ban films that included any kissing. At the same time, the rapidly expanding economy, largely without government regulation, began producing marked inequities of wealth—affluence for the few and hardship for the many. The average salary of $750 a year was rising, but not fast enough for many.

But one of the biggest stories was America's unabashed love affair with the automobile. By 1916, the Model T cost less than half its 1908 price, and nearly everyone dreamed of owning a car. Movies were also maturing during the period, growing rapidly as an essential entertainment for the poor. Some 25 percent of the population, including many newly arrived immigrants, went weekly to the nickelodeon to marvel at the exploits of Charlie Chaplin, Mary Pickford, and Douglas Fairbanks, Sr.—each drawing big salaries in the silent days of movies.

The second half of the decade was marked by the Great War, later to be known as the First World War. Worldwide, it cost more than nine million lives and swept away four empires—the German, the Austro-Hungarian, the Russian, and the Ottoman—and with them the traditional aristocratic style of leadership in Europe. It bled the treasuries of Europe dry and brought the United States forward as the richest country in the world.

When the war broke out in Europe, American exports were required to support the Allied war effort, driving the well-oiled American industrial engine into high gear. Then, when America's intervention in 1917 required the drafting of two million men, women were given their first taste of economic independence. Millions stepped forward to produce the materials needed by a nation. As a result, when the men came back from Europe, America was a changed place for both the well-traveled soldier and the newly trained female worker. Each had acquired an expanded view of the world. Yet women possessed full suffrage in only Wyoming, Colorado, Utah, and Idaho.

The war forced Americans to confront one more important transformation. The United States had become a full participant in the world economy; tariffs on imported goods were reduced and exports reached all-time highs in 1919, further stimulating the American economy.

1911 Profile

James Murray Spangler's most important upright suction sweeper sale was to his first cousin, whose husband, William "Boss" Hoover, was intrigued by the new invention, patent number 889,823.

Life at Home
- James Murray Spangler loved to tinker.
- His first patent was issued for a grain harvester when he was 34, his second, for a hay rake and tedder, when he was 47.
- The company he formed to sell this second invention was unsuccessful.
- Three years later, his third patent was granted for a velocipede wagon.
- His fourth was for an upright vacuum cleaner created after he turned 60 years old.
- This last invention made him financially secure.
- At the time of this invention, James was working as a janitor at the Zollinger Department Store in downtown Canton, Ohio.
- While handling the messy cleanup with broom and carpet sweeper, he developed the idea for an upright vacuum cleaner.
- The tedious, daily labor of sweeping the dust and dirt aggravated James's asthmatic condition.
- Inspired by the mechanics of a rotary street sweeper, James decided to mount a sewing machine motor onto the carpet sweeper, where fan blades would blow dirt out of the rear of the cleaner and into a cloth bag to collect the dirt that was vacuumed up.
- Thus was born the electric carpet sweeper that he called a "suction sweeper."
- It was not the first vacuum cleaner, but it was certainly the first one practical for home use.
- One of 10 children, James was born in 1848, and grew up in Ohio.
- He collected his first business experience selling gentlemen's furnishings in Akron, Ohio.

James Spangler invented an upright vacuum.

- He had always been interested in mechanics, so in 1887 he created a new and useful improvement for grain harvester by removing the standard tailboard and installing a sliding tailboard to better regulate the width of the platform and permit the harvester to be adjusted for wheat stalks of different lengths.
- In 1893, James invented a combined hay rake and tedder in one machine, thereby providing more efficiency at a reduced cost.
- He was sure that farmers would readily see the wisdom of his work.
- However, raising capital was often difficult, running a successful, growing and profitable business even harder.
- Four years later, James was granted a patent on a velocipede wagon.
- This time he sold his invention and had the joy of seeing his creation do well in the marketplace for a time.

Life at Work

- James's upright suction sweeper basically consisted of an electric fan to generate suction, rotating brushes to loosen dirt, a pillowcase for a filter and a broomstick for a handle.
- James first tested his invention in 1907 and patented it after a number of modifications in 1908.

Housewives were impressed with the suction sweeper.

- Capitalized with $5,000 invested by a friend, he founded the Electric Suction Sweeper Company to manufacture his design.
- He was aided by his son, who helped him assemble the machines, and his daughter, who made the dust bags.
- James assembled just two to three machines a week.
- Even though he only made a couple per week, he quickly ran out of money.
- At the same time, his cousin's husband, William "Boss" Hoover, was looking to diversify out of the leather business.
- Automobiles, electric trolleys and other modern inventions were cutting into his profits; the market for horse collars and harnesses had peaked, he believed.
- He was ready to expand his product lines in a changing marketplace when he was introduced to the suction sweeper.
- He quickly came to believe that the electric suction sweeper would "sell itself if we can get the ladies to try it."
- So Boss Hoover formed a partnership with James to build the new device, bought the patent from James, but allowed him to share in the royalties.
- Hoover even set aside a corner of his North Canton factory for the production of sweepers, supervised by the inventor/janitor himself.
- After many months of experiments and numerous improvements, James Spangler and Boss Hoover introduced American housewives to the vacuum sucking cleaner by offering a 10-day free home trial, assuming, of course, the house had electricity.
- Less than 20 percent of American homes were wired for electricity, but the new energy source was spreading quickly.
- Small motors powered by electricity had entered the household market in 1891 when a rotary fan was introduced by the Westinghouse Electric & Manufacturing Company.

- Soon the power of the electric motor was being applied to washing machines, sewing machines, refrigerators, dishwashers, can openers, coffee grinders, eggbeaters, hair dryers and knife sharpeners.
- Advertisers stated, "Electric servants can be depended on to do the muscle part of washing, ironing, cleaning and sewing. Go to your leading electric shop to solve your servant problem."
- Using a network of local retailers to support its advertising campaign, Hoover developed a system of national retailers for the distribution of the vacuums.
- By the end of 1908, the company had sold 372 Model O's.
- By 1911, the company had gone international.
- The vacuum cleaner offered a respite from the annual ritual of spring cleaning in which all the furniture was removed from the house so that the carpets and rugs could be taken outside to be beaten clean.
- Various metal and wood and rug beaters were created for this unpleasant and exhausting task.
- Year-round indoor gas lighting and the smoke it emitted created a layer of dust that added an extra week's work to the average spring cleaning; open windows from spring to fall, most without screens, added their own complications.
- But as soon as mechanization took housewives one step toward less physical labor, Americans embarked on a newfound passion for greater hygiene and cleanliness.
- This obsession with microbes coincided with a trend toward houses possessing more light-admitting windows that highlighted any lingering dirt.
- Advertisements and medical pronouncements emphasized the dire dangers of household filth.
- Vacuum cleaner advertisements in particular portrayed the dangers that lurked in uncaptured dirt.
- Motherhood was hard work in 1907, the year the upright vacuum cleaner was invented.
- In fact, to make ends meet, most families needed several wage earners; married women often took in boarders, earned cash sewing at home or cleaning someone else's house.
- Only one American family out of 15 employed servants, despite a steady stream of immigrants eager for work.
- Keeping house was a full-time job.
- Cooking a meal on cast-iron or steel stove required constant attention; throughout the day a stove had to be continually fed with coal or wood consuming up to 50 pounds a day.
- Poultry and fish purchased live from the market had to be killed, plucked or scaled.
- Green coffee had to be roasted and ground.
- Soot and smoke from wood-burning stoves blackened the walls and dirtied draperies and carpets.
- Gas and kerosene lamps left smelly deposits of soot on the furniture and curtains.
- Laundry, one of the most detestable of household chores, often consumed most of Mondays and Tuesdays.

Boss Hoover partnered with James to build his new vacuum.

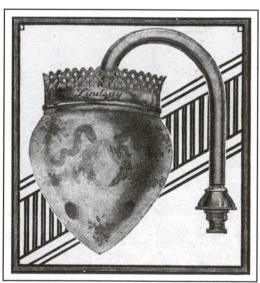

Electricity improved life and eased household chores.

Laundry often took days to complete.

- At the same time, processed foods were appearing, including canned pickles and sauerkraut from the H.J. Heinz Company and condensed soups from the Joseph Campbell Company.
- By the turn of the century, the carpet sweeper was commonly used, various forms of washing machines were being introduced, and by 1903 the electric iron was invented, followed by the first commercially successful electric toaster in 1909.

Life in the Community: Canton, Ohio

- Founded in 1805 on the West and Middle Branches of the Nimishillen Creek, Canton, Ohio, rapidly became a manufacturing center for farm implements.
- It was a natural way to support the blossoming agricultural activity of the state, whose bounty was attracting the construction of transportation canals and railroads.
- This industrial base attracted immigrants eager for work, particularly Italians, Greeks, Spaniards, Romanians and Russians.
- Steel became a major product of the area, thanks to a plentiful supply of water.
- In nearby North Canton, William H. "Boss" Hoover moved his tannery business in 1873 from the family farm east of town to the center of the village.
- There he ran a successful leather business before he branched into the manufacturing of vacuum cleaners.
- Beginning in 1901, Main Street was the location of the Interurban Line which ran between Canton and Akron.
- A decade later the street was paved in brick, and soon the streetcar lines were replaced by automobile traffic.

Automobile traffic was replacing streetcar lines.

HISTORICAL SNAPSHOT
1911

- Eugene B. Ely landed on the deck of the USS *Pennsylvania* stationed in San Francisco harbor, the first time an aircraft landed on a ship
- Glenn H. Curtiss flew the first successful seaplane
- The first installment of Frederick Winslow Taylor's monograph, *The Principles of Scientific Management*, appeared in *The American Magazine* to promote the efficiency movement
- International Women's Day was celebrated for the first time

- Denmark abolished the death penalty and flogging
- A fire at the Triangle Shirtwaist Factory in New York City killed 146 women workers
- The United States Army formally adopted the M1911 pistol as its standard sidearm, thus giving the gun its 1911 designation
- Mexican Revolutionary Pancho Villa launched an attack against government troops in Ciudad Juarez
- The U.S. Supreme Court declared Standard Oil to be an "unreasonable" monopoly under the Sherman Antitrust Act and ordered the company to be dissolved

continued

HISTORICAL SNAPSHOT *(continued)*
1911

- The first Indianapolis 500-mile auto race was won by Ray Harroun driving a Marmon "Wasp"
- Charles F. Kettering filed U.S. patent 1,150,523 for an electric starter for automobiles
- IBM was incorporated as the Computing Tabulating Recording Corporation (CTR) in New York
- Hiram Bingham rediscovered Machu Picchu
- The number of representatives in the U.S. House of Representatives was set at 435
- The *Mona Lisa* was stolen from the Louvre; it was found in Italy in 1913
- Orville Wright remained in the air nine minutes and 45 seconds in a glider at Kill Devil Hills, North Carolina, setting a new world record
- Chevrolet officially entered the automobile market to compete with the Ford Model T

Selected Prices

Apartment, Vacuum Cleaning System, Month......................$40.00
Campbell's Soup $0.10
Cleanser $0.10
Face Powder.. $0.50
Lamp Burner.. $0.04
Manure Spreader...$69.50
Rocking Chair.. $5.35
Transmission Grease, Five Pounds......................... $0.80
Vacuum Cleaner...$35.00
Wood Stain, Can... $0.50

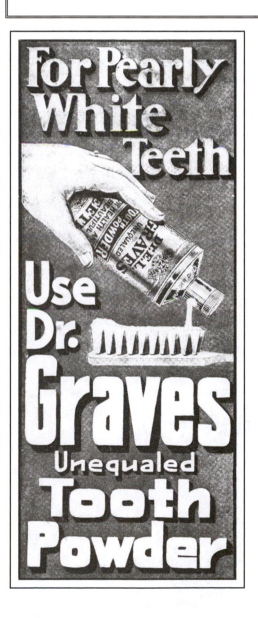

Artistic MISSION LAMP
$2.45

For Gas or Electricity

Other designs for oil

This lamp is made of Oak, finished in Weathered, Golden or Fumed. 19 inches high, with handsome 4-panel Art glass shade of amber or green and white, 12 inches square. Fully guaranteed. Price $2.45. Send for new catalog in colors showing designs of

Chandeliers, Portables and Domes

made of Oak, Mahogany, Maple, etc., finished to match any interior. Very beautiful and artistic. Never tarnish.

MARION MISSION FIXTURE CO., Dept. B11, Marion, Indiana

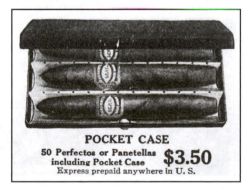

POCKET CASE

50 Perfectos or Panetellas including Pocket Case **$3.50**
Express prepaid anywhere in U. S.

Vacuum Cleaner Timeline

1869
In his Chicago basement, Ives W. McGaffey invented the "whirlwind," a hand-pumped, non-electric vacuum cleaner made of wood and canvas.

1901
British engineer Cecil Booth pioneered the concept of sucking dust using an electrical pump; the contraption weighed more than 100 pounds.

1905
Chapman Skinner in San Francisco created the first portable electric vacuum; it weighed 92 pounds and used a fan 18 inches in diameter to produce the sucking action.

1907
James Murray Spangler invented a portable electric upright vacuum cleaner that used a cloth bag to collect dust.

1910
The Hoover Vacuum Cleaner Company manufactured a vacuum cleaner that weighed only 10 pounds.

Advertisement, To the Ladies of Victoria, *The Victoria Daily Advocate* (Texas), October 19, 1909:

Having equipped our plant with the latest improved machinery, we are prepared to handle your family washing at 6c per pound. All flat pieces ironed, balance starched, ready for ironing. No worry about washday, no supplies to furnish. Just ring 104. We will call for and deliver. You can do up your bundle, weigh it, and you know what it costs. We will please or refund the price. Victoria Steam Laundry.

Advertisement, Would You Like to Know How the Vacuum Cleaner Works? *The New York Times*, **February 10, 1906:**

A wagon stands at the curb; we run a line of hose from the wagon to the room on any floor of your house.

On the end of the hose is attached a mouthpiece or "renovator." The pumps in the wagon create so strong a vacuum in the hose that every particle of dust which comes under the mouthpiece as it is moved along the carpet, or the walls, or furniture, is instantly drawn into the hose and then into a tank in the wagon. Not a particle of dust can escape.

When you clean with a broom or carpet sweeper, you get less than half the dust into the dust pan, and the rest floats in the air and lodges everywhere. When we clean with the vacuum cleaner, we get all the dust and carry it away. Vacuum Cleaner Company, 130 West 18th St., New York

Editorial, Edward William Bok, *Ladies' Home Journal*, **1899:**

Just as more and more is constantly expected of a man in business by reason of keener competition and wider markets, so housekeeping is getting to be more and more complicated as the condition of our social lives change. The introduction labor-saving devices does not simplify housekeeping any more than does the introduction of machinery simplify business. With easier and greater facilities, the demand becomes greater and responsibilities increase rather than decrease.

"The Patent Cycle," John Boyle, Jr., *The Magazine of Wall Street*, June 1913:

When an inventor has completed his invention and desires to protect the same by a patent, he usually secures the services of a patent solicitor, who prepares a specification and drawings of the invention. These papers, together with the first fee of $15, are filed in the Patent Office and are designated as applications for patents. On receipt of an application by the Patent Office, it is assigned to the examiner having in charge the art to which the invention relates, who examines the same to determine the scope of the invention which the inventor is entitled to claim. As a result of his examination, he hands down a decision on the application, setting forth any objections and citing prior anticipating patents.

The applicant for a patent is allowed by law one year in which to reply to any official action. This latitude can be taken advantage of to keep the application in the office until such time as is most opportune to take out the patent. The famous Selden automobile patent was filed in 1879, and was issued in 1895. Another Selden patent, an off-shoot of this same application of 1879, was issued in 1912, 33 years after the invention was first filed in the Patent Office. But in the case of the *U.S. v. American Bell Telephone* Co., which was a suit by the government to annul one of the telephone patents which had been pending in the Patent Office 14 years before issuing, the U.S. Supreme Court held that, inasmuch as the law expressly gave this latitude, it was perfectly legal for an applicant to avail himself of the same.

After varied correspondence between the office and the applicant on the question principally of the scope of the invention, it is finally decided to allow the application to go to patent. During all this correspondence, the applicant has been permitted one year in which to respond to official actions, although in the majority of cases the applicants do not avail themselves of this right. In fact, it might be said that it is only a small number of applicants that take the full legal limit of time in which to respond to official actions.

After the applicant has received notice of the allowance of his application for a patent, he has six months in which to pay the final fee of $20. Should he fail to pay the same within the prescribed time, the application becomes forfeited. But it is not dead yet, only sleeping, for he may renew this forfeited application at any time within two years from the date of the original allowance of the same. Upon payment of the final fee, the application goes to patent and bears a date of about a month later than the payment. These various and liberal time limits permitted applicants in the prosecution of their cases are brought out here to show the great elasticity of the system, and how it can be readily adapted to either hasten the issue of a patent during a period of prosperity, or delay the issue of the same during a period of depression.

Domestic Labor-Saving Invention Timeline

1844
Linus Yale of Springfield, Massachusetts, received a patent for a "Door Lock."

1846
Elias Howe, Jr. of Cambridge, Massachusetts, received the first American patent for a "Sewing Machine" that used a lock stitch.

1848
William C. Young of Baltimore, Maryland, received a patent for an "Ice Cream Freezer."

1850
Joel Houghton of Ogden, New York, received the first U.S. patent for a "Table Furniture Cleaning Machine" for washing dishes; it featured hand- turned beaters to move water against tableware set in a basket in a tub of hot water.

1851
Dr. John Gorrie of New Orleans, Louisiana, received a patent for an "Ice Machine" which he described as a "new and useful Machine for the Artificial Production of Ice and for general Refrigeratory Purposes."

Isaac M. Singer of New York, New York, received a patent for a "Sewing Machine" that featured a rocking double treadle; used a flying shuttle instead of a rotary shuttle with the needle mounted vertically and a presser foot to hold the cloth in place; Singer later introduced business innovations such as installment buying, after-sale servicing, and trade-in allowances.

1857
James T. Henry and William P. Campbell of Philadelphia, Pennsylvania, received a patent for a "Closet Cistern" described as "...combining the basin of a water closet with a valved chamber, cistern, and communicating pipes...that the soil may be readily and effectually disposed of, and all offensive smells obviated."

1858
Hamilton E. Smith of Philadelphia, Pennsylvania, received a U.S. patent for a "Washing Machine" that cycled reheated water and contained a reciprocating plunger and two horizontal diaphragms in the tub which moved vertically with the action of the plunger.

1859
George B. Simpson of Washington, DC, received a patent for an "Electrical Heating Apparatus" which generated heat by passing electricity through wire coils.

1866
Orrin L. Hopson and Eli J. Manville of Waterbury, Connecticut, and Herman P. Brooks of Wolcottville, Connecticut, received a patent for an "Improved Machine for Reducing Pointing Wires" and organized the Excelsior Needle Company.

continued

Domestic Labor-Saving Invention Timeline *(continued)*

1867

Sheldon B. Everitt of Ansonia, Connecticut, received a patent for a "Tea Kettle."

1868

Amariah M. Hills of Hockanum, Connecticut, received a patent for an "Improvement in Lawn-Mowers" described as a "device for mowing grass by hand, and is more especially designed for mowing lawns."

1869

Ives W. McGaffey of Chicago, Illinois, received a patent for a "Sweeping Machine" called the "whirlwind" vacuum cleaner; the first suction-type vacuum cleaner was a light, hand-powered device for surface cleaning consisting of a handle to turn a pulley which used a belt to drive a fan in a casing, thus producing a strong current of air, "controlled to take up dust and dirt, and carry the fine particles into a porous air-chamber, so constructed as to allow the air to escape while the dust is retained"; McGaffey started the American Carpet Cleaning Company.

Cornelius Swartwout of Troy, New York, patented a "Waffle Iron."

1871

Mary Florence Potts of Ottumwa, Iowa, received a patent for a "Sad Iron" with a detachable handle for pressing irons; it was widely manufactured and licensed in the U.S. and Europe with advertising featuring her picture.

1873

Josiah George Jennings, sanitary engineer from Palace Wharf, Stangate, England, received a patent for "Water Closets" in which the "pan discharges itself by a side opening into the upright limb of a siphon-trap."

Ludwig M. N. Wolf of Avon, Connecticut, received a patent for "Lamp-Brackets for Sewing Machines," which the Singer Sewing Machine Company introduced to meet the needs of those who wished to sew at night.

Anthony Iske of Lancaster, Pennsylvania, received the first U.S. patent for "Machines for Slicing Dried Beef."

1875

Francis Torrance, James W. Arrott, and John Fleming in Pittsburgh, Pennsylvania, formed the Standard Manufacturing Company, making cast-iron bathtubs, wash-stands and water closets.

1876

Melville R. Bissell of Grand Rapids, Michigan, received a U.S. patent for a "Carpet-Sweeper "; he was attempting to eradicate the effect on his wife's health of dust from packing materials at his crockery shop; hog bristles bound with string were dipped in hot pitch, inserted in brush rollers, and trimmed with scissors.

continued

Domestic Labor-Saving Invention Timeline *(continued)*

1879
Black American inventor Thomas Elkins of Albany, New York, received a patent for a "Refrigerating Apparatus" for "food or corpses," which provided a convenient container and method of chilling using the evaporation of water.

1881
John Reece of Boston, Massachusetts, received patent for a "Button Hole Sewing Machine."

1882
Henry W. Seely of New York received a patent for an "Electric Flat-Iron" that weighed almost 15 pounds.

1883
Thomas J. Clark and John K. Stewart developed hair and wool clipping machines for shearing sheep and grooming horses in Dundee, Illinois.

Jonas Cooper of Washington, DC, received a patent for a "Shutter and Fastening" for inside shutters.

1885
Rufus M. Eastman of Boston, Massachusetts, received a patent for a "Mixer for Cream, Eggs, and Liquors," or electric mixer.

1886
Josephine G. Cochran of Shelbyville, Illinois, received a patent for a "Dish Washing Machine."

1888
Edward Katzinger founded a commercial baking pan company in Chicago, Illinois, later registered as "ECKO."

1890
George K. Cooke of Jamaica, New York, received a patent for a "Gas-Burner" known as a "self-lighter," having a main and auxiliary jet.

Daniel Johnson received a patent for a "Grass-Receiver for Lawn-Mowers."

Daniel McCree of Chicago, Illinois, received a patent for a "Portable Fire-Escape."

1891
Cyrenus Wheeler, Jr. of Auburn, New York, received a patent for a "Clothes-Wringer."

1892
Sarah Boone of New Haven, Connecticut, received a patent for an "Ironing Board" for sleeves.

continued

Domestic Labor-Saving Invention Timeline *(continued)*

George T. Sampson of Dayton, Ohio, received a patent for a "Clothes Dryer."

1893
Lyde W. Benjamin of Boston, Massachusetts, received a patent for a "Broom Moistener and Bridle" that kept the broom moist while sweeping without being so wet as to drip but to prevent the dust from rising.

Black American inventor Fredrick J. Loudin of Revanna, Ohio, received a patent for a "Fastener for the Meeting-Rails of Sashes."

1894
Frederick J. Loudin of Ravenna, Ohio, received a patent for a "Key-Fastener" which prevented a burglar from disengaging the key from outside the door by inserting something through the keyhole.

Simeon Newsome of Detroit, Michigan, received a patent for an "Oil Heater or Cooker."

1895
Robert H. Gray of Lexington, Kentucky, received a patent for a "Cistern-Cleaner."

1899
Benjamin F. Jackson of Cambridge, Massachusetts, received a patent for a "Gas-Burner" in which air was supplied "under pressure and in which all parts of the burner-tube...got the same amount of air and consequently maintained an even combustion, thereby producing a more efficient burner and one having a longer life."

John Albert Burr of Agawam, Massachusetts, received a patent for a "Lawn-Mower."

Albert T. Marshall of Brockton, Massachusetts, received a patent for an "Automatic Refrigerating Apparatus" ("relates to the class of refrigerating-machines which ordinarily employ anhydrous ammonia as a refrigerating medium"): a household refrigerator.

John S. Thurman of St. Louis, Missouri, received a patent for a "Pneumatic Carpet-Renovator," a gasoline-powered, motor-driven vacuum cleaner drawn by horses door to door.

1901
Hubert Cecil Booth, a bridge engineer, developed first power-driven vacuum cleaner named "Puffing Billy."

continued

Domestic Labor-Saving Invention Timeline *(continued)*

1902
Willis Haviland Carrier, chief engineer of Buffalo Forge Company from 1902 to 1915, completed drawings recognized as the world's first scientific air conditioning system.

1906
Alfred C. Fuller, entrepreneur from Nova Scotia, founded the Fuller Brush Company.

1907
Maytag introduced the first wringer washing machine, "Pastime Washer."

1910
Louis H. Hamilton, Chester Beach, and Fred Osius formed Hamilton Beach Manufacturing Company to develop "universal" motor-driven appliances and introduced its first product: the electric hand-held massager.

William M. Frost of Eureka, Montana, received the first U.S. patent for an "Electric Insect Destroyer."

1911
Louis, Frederick, and Emory Upton founded Upton Machine Company in St. Joseph, Michigan, to produce an electric, motor-driven wringer washer; the company later became the Whirlpool Corporation.

"Housekeeping," Laura Clarke Rockwood, *The Craftsman Magazine*, 1907:

This mother of to-day hurries from kitchen to nursery and over the other parts of the house, performing as best she can the many home duties of our times. But she is so overwearied in the doing of it all that the deep well of mother love which should overflow, flooding the world with happiness and cheer, runs well nigh dry at times...there should be food kitchens easily accessible to every home where cooked foods can be bought cheaply because of consolidation, and delivered hot to our homes with promptness and regularity in pneumatic tubes perhaps, or by whatever means the master mind should decide is the cheapest and the best.

"A Place Where a Way Has Been Found to Cut Down Drudgery and Make Life Easy—Social Science Worked Out Practically by a Connecticut Couple,"
The New York Times, May 7, 1911:

The kitchenette is the last word, Mr. Charles Barnard thinks, in cooking convenience. Things must be carefully arranged so when the mistress of the stove can stand in one place and find ready to her hand all she needs, at a cost of only one or two steps there seems to have been gained a distinct advantage over the "nice roomy kitchen."

Every kitchen, Mr. and Mrs. Barnard declare, should be small, and if there is plenty of space to start, it would be partitioned off and made into a sitting room for the servant. No servant should have to eat in the kitchen. It lessens the appetite and gives her no sense of rest.

It is precisely a sense of rest that the servant needs, says Mr. Barnard, just like the woman who does her own cooking. Fatigue is a poison. Nobody can be "always tired" and keep well. But the body will throw off the poison in a short time if it is given a chance. It must not ever be allowed to accumulate.

For this reason the steps of the housekeeper have to be carefully considered. No exercise is more beneficial than housework if it does not develop into drudgery and bring about a fatigue that cannot be thoroughly recovered from before the next "stint" is undertaken. Hence, the value of the kitchenette, and Mr. Barnard goes even further, and would have much of the simpler meals, like breakfast, cooked over alcohol gas burners, on the table.

Watching the coffee and the toast and the eggs is not a very difficult operation on the face of it, but it has to be done right to the minute or disaster follows. The average maid, getting up with the lark, is pretty tired before she has prepared the meal for the family, even though she sustains herself with the inevitable cup of tea. And when a woman is tired she is liable to let things burn or to take out the eggs before or after they have reached the proper point.

"A woman should get a meal," said Mr. Barnard, "according to the up-to-date methods used in such a trade as bricklaying, for instance. Not long ago the mason picked up his own bricks. Now they find the bricks piled for them at such a height that they do not have to stoop. When a man stoops for a brick he has to pick up not only the brick itself, but about one hundred pounds in addition, the weight of his inclined body.

"So careful managers have done away with that sort of thing. What is more, the bricklayers stop work every hour or two for five or 10 minutes. It is not a long time, but it suffices for rest. Then they go back to their work fresh, and freshness means efficiency. A tired person cannot work well....

"The conservation of energy is the theory of the day, the application of economy of motion to the work that has hitherto been done in a haphazard fashion. There is every reason in the world why this same theory should be applied to the kitchen.

continued

"A Place Where a Way Has Been Found to Cut Down Drudgery and Make Life Easy—Social Science Worked Out Practically by a Connecticut Couple," *(continued)*

Not only should the kitchen be planned so as to save steps, and such things as can comfortably be done on the table transferred there, but the cook should have to sit down and rest at intervals. There shouldn't be minutes here and there stolen perhaps when a careful eye is turned the other way, but regular rest times.

"Another idea we carry out is to cook some meats and vegetables in the dish in which they are to be served. It is possible to buy dishes of good shape and color that will stand great heat. The casserole solves many a difficulty. When the meat or vegetables are cooked, there is nothing to do but set them on the table, and thus the extra washing of pots and pans is saved."

Working along this line, Mr. and Mrs. Barnard got hold of steam cookers, and tried them, with great success. The way in which the steam cooker works is simple enough. The cooker is arranged like a double boiler, with holes in the sides of the inside pot. The steam enters these holes, condenses as it strikes the colder stuff inside, and gives up its heat. This device is admirable for vegetables and stews, and if it is desired, the dish in which the food is to be served may be put in the top and the utensil left perfectly clean. It does not take long, either.

What with the small, scientifically arranged kitchen, with the fireless cooker doing the work for soups and roasts that the gas stove has started, with the steam cooker preparing the other things without danger of their burning, and saving the washing of pots, and the alcohol gas stove doing all that is required of it, the Barnard kitchen is a little wonder. And yet they had not a single "city advantage" to start with, and they are not rich people.

There are a dozen other details that might be described before the kitchenette is left, but there are other parts of the house that must not be forgotten. There is the sweeping and dusting department of housekeeping, always a nuisance, and in these days of automobiles to stir up the dust of country roads, more of a problem than ever.

Of course, the Barnards do not use a broom. That implement does, indeed, belong to the Middle Ages. They have a vacuum cleaner, and twice a month they go over the whole house. Every day it is brushed up lightly with a dustless brusher, but twice a month cleaning with the vacuum apparatus keeps it immaculate.

The cleaner is of fair size. There is a sort of pump arrangement that is carried from one room to the other, with a pipe attachment. The pump could be worked by a child of three and anybody who can lift an eighth of two or three pounds can run the suction end of the thing over the carpet.

One person can do the cleaning alone, but two, one to work the pump and the other to guide the suction pipe, do the work much more quickly. Any woman with a child to help or two hours of somebody's time twice a month can do a spring cleaning that would outdo all rug beating and never feel a moment's fatigue over it.

continued

"A Place Where a Way Has Been Found to Cut Down Drudgery and Make Life Easy—Social Science Worked Out Practically by a Connecticut Couple," *(continued)*

That is not all the vacuum cleaner will do, for it draws the dust out of furniture with a special arrangement and out of clothes with another. One has to be careful, however, about selecting a cleaner, though now there are a number of makes that are really good, in addition to some that are distinctly bad.

The scrubbing of the floor is another obsolete item in the Barnard household. There are several mops that do the work just as well as any woman could. One long mop has a rubber end that acts like the grip of a hand. They put a thick piece of burlap on the floor and rub it back and forth with the long rubber-tipped mop and, behold, the floor is as clean as if some woman had broken her back over it.

Similarly, the mop-handle is used for dusting the floors and walls. Only in this case not burlap but a dustless duster is attached. The dustless duster absorbs the dust. It can't be shaken out, for some occult reason there was not time to inquire into. Every now and then the duster is washed and then the dust leaves it, but it dries out perfectly good and still ready for more work.

"Neighborhood in a Laughing Fit," *The New York Times*, October 1, 1908:

For the last three or four days late sleepers in the houses along Sixty-sixth and Sixty-seventh Streets, between Columbus Avenue and Central Park West, have been awakened by a low, rumbling, raucous sound. There is no resisting it; all hands must get up and laugh.

It has been noted that even 13-year-old girls and boys giggle at the mere thought, apparently, of going to school.

This is the explanation of that low rumbling sound and its effect. The 700 horses in William Durland's stables have been laughing, a hundred of them at a time very often, and the residents nearby have been but yielding to the infection of the horse laugh. Mr. Durland has put in a 12 horsepower tickling machine for his animals. Horses now laugh in his stables that were never known to smile before.

The machine was not designed to make horses laugh. It is a vacuum currier and brusher and cleaner. Up on the second floor of the stable, on the Sixty-seventh Street side, is a new red motor stuck away in a corner. Attached to it is the vacuum machine. Running from the machine at present are four lines of rubber hose, at the end of each of which is a sort of funnel-shaped metal piece with its mouth covered. The metal covering is toothed like a curry comb, and narrow slits are made in the face of the comb that open into the rubber hose.

The motor is started up. It begins to suck in the air. A horse is led up to the neighborhood of a hose, an attendant scrapes him vigorously with the toothed comb, and the suction draws into the hose all the dust that the comb loosens. The hose takes this all to a chest in the basement.

They say at the stable that even Royal laughed at the first application of the machine. Royal is an old white safe and sane animal with a Puritanical Sunday morning expression on his face. As the tickling comb started down his neck the first morning, he braced up. As it passed his shoulders, his lips began twitching. He was trying hard to maintain his sober dignity.

1913 News Feature

"Harnessing Heredity: The New Science of Genetics, Which Has Created New Animals and Plants to Order," Waldemar Kaempffert, *The Outlook: Vol. 103*, **January 25, 1913:**

Far more profitable and surer than panning gold-bearing sand in an icy Alaskan stream…is a new business which commercially applies the principles of genetics. Genetics is a new name coined to designate a new science—the science of so molding germ plasm that it will bring forth a type of organism better adapted to human needs than any similar type the world has ever known.

The average weight of the fleece shorn from an American sheep has been increased 35 percent. Judiciously spent, the sum of $10,000 has given this country a new variety of wheat that has already covered five million acres with crops worth $2.00 an acre more than the variety it displaced.... Sugar beets are raised with a constant sugar content of 21 percent; formerly the sugar content was as low as five percent. These are but a few of a thousand instances in which the principles of the new science, genetics, have been profitably applied.

It must not be supposed that genetics is merely a new name for what was once called "breeding." Its methods may be the same, but its principles are entirely new. The word "breeding" cannot express the scope of this new achievement in biology—it is too indefinite, too narrow. To include all that is implied by the science of consciously artificially improving a strain with the mathematical certainty that the desired organism will be obtained, the word genetics had to be invented.

The new science makes it possible to create a living organism to order, whether it be a better beer-producing microbe or a stronger type of elephant…. Give him an opportunity, and the genetic scientist, at your command, will change the Ethiopian's skin and remove the leopard's spots. He has discovered that hereditary obeys certain laws just as surely as gravitation; that, indeed, hereditary is a great natural force which can be subjugated and made to do useful work.

To the genetic scientist, germ plasm, in which all the potentialities of heredity are locked up, is what bronze is to the sculptor…. By manipulating it knowingly, the lines of a horse can be given the graceful curves of an Arabian charger…. But, mold germ plasm as he will, the scientist has not yet discovered how its immortal substance, confined within a cell so minute that powerful lenses must be used to magnify it into visibility, performs the miracle of unfolding into an oak or a sheep.... Stored up in the germ plasm is a force.... What is this force? Chemical energy, some say; but that does not tell us how the wonder is wrought. After all, we may harness primal forces, but how they originated, how they became endowed almost with a consciousness of their own, we may never know. We light houses and drive machinery with electricity, yet the very definition of electricity changes with each new discovery or its properties.... And we have learned how to control heredity, so that, step by step, we are able to produce organisms that yesterday were unknown. For all that, the nature of the force we call heredity is as veiled to us as the nature of electricity.

The Newton of heredity, the man who discovered its laws, was Gregor Mendel, a monk, who died in 1884, a patient, self-effacing scientist whose work was ignored or overlooked until 1900. In the cloister gardens of Brunn, Mendel conducted experiments with the edible pea—experiments which are now regarded as classic, and which resulted in the discovery of the laws of heredity that now bear his name. Given certain characteristics of two parents, whether they be plants or animals, it is possible by Mendel's laws to state accurately how the offspring will inherit those characteristics.

The Andalusian fowl, for example, may be either pure black or pure white, splashed perhaps here and there. Each variety breeds "true" in breeder's parlance; in other words, black parents invariably produce black offspring, and white parents white offspring. Cross a black and a white fowl, and the result will be grayish-blue chicks, as might be supposed. It might also be supposed that were these grayish-blue fowls inbred we would obtain merely another generation of grayish-blues. Experience teaches otherwise. One-half of the chicks will be grayish-blue, like their parents; one-quarter will be *pure white*, like one of their grandparents; one-quarter will be *pure black*, like the other of their grandparents. Continue the process of inbreeding for another generation—that is, breed the blacks together, the whites together, and the grayish-blues together, and you will find this: the blacks will always produce blacks; the whites will always produce whites; but the hybrid grayish-blues will always produce one-half grayish-blues, one-quarter pure whites, and one-quarter pure blacks. In other words, Mendel discovered that an absolutely pure strain may descend from a hybrid, contrary to general belief, and that a hybrid in which two characteristics are combined will transmit the combination only to a certain proportion of the offspring.

The case of the Andalusian fowl is the simplest that occurs among animals. When a pure black and a pure white guinea-pig are mated, the offspring will not be partly white and partly black, but entirely black. For all their blackness, the hybrid offspring have a white strain, which is masked by the black and which manifests itself in the next generation when they are inbred.... In these hybrids the conspicuous black color is said to be "dominant" and the masked white "recessive."

There must be something in the original germ plasm that caused the pure black Andalusian fowl or the pure black guinea-pig to produce only black offspring— just what we can only surmise. For the time being, the presence or absence in the germ cell of a hypothetical "determiner," as it is called, is supposed to govern the inheritance of simple characteristics.... The hybrids will always be developed from cells one-half lacking the determiner and one-half provided with it. Each characteristic has its special determiner in the cell. Thus, presence or absence of a particular determiner is responsible for length of hair, color of eyes...and many other traits. Whether the experimenter works with guinea-pigs or wheat...hybrids always produce a certain number of individuals absolutely pure in strain; and some characteristics will always be dominant, while others will always be recessive.

The genetic scientist manipulates not simply a single character, but many. Mendel himself handled seven in making his classic experiments with peas—characters such as height...and arrangement of flowers on the stem. Any pair of these opposing characteristics is transmitted to the next generation in definite mathematical ratio without any relation whatever to any other pair of characters. What is still more important, Mendel discovered that if the second generation of a hybrid is sufficiently numerous, there will be found in it every possible grouping or combination of the characters of the original parents. By recombination, it is possible to obtain a pure strain in which those characters are to be found that are desired.

The field in which the genetic scientist may work is almost limitless. Very few of the higher and more useful forms of animal life, in which we must include mammals and birds, have been domesticated. How many of the 5,000 species of mammals classified by zoologists have been tamed to serve man? Only a paltry 25.... Indeed, not in 500 years has any important increase been made to our small list of domestic animals. In the plant world, on the other hand, new useful varieties have been created by the thousands. Now that the laws of heredity are understood, the animal breeder will be able to emulate the plant breeder.

Young as the science of genetics is, it is already of vast economic importance to the world. We have only begun to apply it to increase the amount of food and raiment which we require. More will be demanded of genetic practitioners in the future. The population of the United States is growing at the rate of over 4,300 souls a day and over 51,600 a year.... The task of feeding that host will fall to the lot of 50 million farm people. They will accomplish it, not by opening up new lands, but by harnessing the wonderful, powerful forces of heredity.

1917 Profile

Streetcar advertising was in its infancy when freelance illustrator Grace Wiederseim was first asked to design an ad for Joseph Campbell's Preserve Company.

Life at Home

- Born October 14, 1877, Viola Grace Gebbie was the third daughter of George Gebbie, a lithographer, who was Philadelphia's first art printer and the father of seven.
- Gebbie had emigrated from Scotland in 1862.
- After landing in Quebec and working in upstate New York for a short time, he arrived in Philadelphia, listing his occupation as a bookseller in his immigration papers; he was naturalized in 1869.
- Gebbie was a Scots Presbyterian; Grace's mother, Mary Jane Fitzgerald, was a strict Catholic.
- All six of the Gebbie girls attended Catholic schools.
- Grace grew up in a sophisticated environment of art publishing; her father's library held many belles-lettres and Greek and Roman classics, many illustrated.
- Her sisters and niece, Mary A. Hays Huber, who authored a comic strip of her own, *Kate and Karl*, all had drawing talent.
- Growing up, the sisters learned from each other and from an older relative; drawing cartoon figures was simply another way to amuse each other.
- Early education was in private and church schools, including the Convent of Notre Dame, Philadelphia, and the Convent of Eden Hall, Torresdale, Pennsylvania.
- Grace was 15 years old when her father died in 1892.
- Three years later, Grace began her formal art training from the Philadelphia School of Design for Women, where Robert Henri was a faculty member.

Artist Grace Wiederseim created the "Campbell Kids."

- Grace Gebbie enrolled in Henri's Antiques class, described in the College Catalogue as "Drawing from the antique, artistic anatomy, composition, Crayon portraits."
- The school was founded to prepare women for a successful career in industrial design at a time when "No nice girl should go to art school."
- She married for the first time in 1900 to Theodore Wiederseim, an advertising executive for a Philadelphia streetcar company.

Life at Work

- Grace Gebbie Wiederseim's artistic career began at a young age, with her freelancing as a commercial artist by the time she was 18 years old.
- Often her drawings depicted small-fry characters with round faces, pug noses and full figures that resembled Grace herself.
- Campbell's, founded in 1869 by Joseph A. Campbell and Abraham Anderson, an icebox manufacturer, originally produced a line of canned tomatoes, vegetables, jellies, soups, condiments, and minced meats.
- Rapid industrialization of America's cities had transformed the rural economies; food was now being grown a long distance from its consumers.
- This demanded that less perishable foods be created, capable of surviving the ever-widening distances separating the farm from the urban dinner table.
- Campbell and Anderson believed that canned foods were the answer.
  - Their cannery was located between the fertile fields near Camden, New Jersey, and nearby Philadelphia, a regional transportation hub.
  - Campbell's was especially known for its canned beefsteak tomatoes that exemplified a blending of Anderson's tinsmith skills with Campbell's farming background.
  - The company's big break came in 1897.
  - Dr. John T. Dorrance, a chemist with degrees from MIT and Göttingen University, Germany, developed a commercially viable method for condensing soup by halving the quantity of its heaviest ingredient: water.
  - Dorrance had recently returned from Europe, where he had developed his taste for Continental soups.
  - Franco-American and the Hutchins Company were both making ready-to-eat soups with some success, while Borden had perfected the process for evaporating milk.
  - Dorrance reasoned that if Campbell's was able to create a condensed ready-to-eat soup, the product would be cheaper to ship, take less room in the store and could be sold for less to the busy housewife.
- Within a year of the invention, the Joseph Campbell's Preserve Company was selling five varieties of condensed soups, all easily identified by its can's bright red and white color scheme.
- Herberton Williams, a Campbell's executive, had convinced the company to adopt the look based on the crisp colors of the Cornell University football team's uniforms.
- By 1900, the soups were awarded the Gold Medallion for Excellence from the Paris international Exposition.

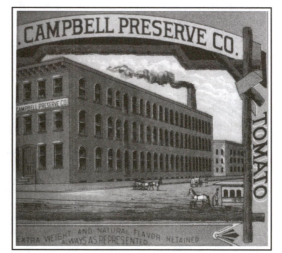

Campbell's began with a few products, including canned tomatoes, jellies, and soups.

- Campbell's wanted to attract the attention of women who had started to become streetcar regulars.
- The National Biscuit Company had its recognizable figure in Zu Zu the ginger snap clown, Sunny Jim hawked the wares of Force Cereal, and Nipper the listening dog was permanently positioned at the horn of a phonograph manufacturer.
- At her husband's urging, Grace Wiederseim designed two plump and adorable little children for a series of streetcar ads in 1904; thus was born the "funny babies" as she called them, known to the world as the Campbell's Kids.
- Her rosy-cheeked, cherub-faced youngsters were an immediate hit for the streetcar line and Campbell's.
- Their first magazine appearance was in the *Ladies' Home Journal* in 1905.
- Before long, the beloved Kids were everywhere—in books, on pajamas, postcards, games, dishes, banks, as dolls, and much more.
- And every American child wanted to be a Campbell's Kid.
- The sales of Campbell's products soared behind the creative marketing force of Grace's unsigned portraits of American life.
- In 1905, the company was advertising "21 kinds of Campbell's Soup—16 million sold in 1904."
- The year 1904 was also when Grace had made her mark on the company known for its $0.10 cans of soup.
- Campbell's had invested heavily in advertising since its inception, a proclivity that only accelerated with the success of the ubiquitous "Campbell's Kids."
- The "Kids" had no individual names, nor were they of any determinative age.
- There was no set number of Campbell's Kids, nor was their relationship to each other ever explained.
- Yet they symbolized the ideal picture of health; intuitively, Grace's pudgy tots proclaimed Campbell's Soup's quality and wholesomeness.
- The company received so many requests for posters of the streetcar ads featuring the Campbell's Kids, it decided to fulfill every request, charging just $0.15 per poster—the cost of postage.
- The first Campbell's Kids doll was issued in 1909, followed quickly by a second doll created by the E.I. Horsman Company in 1910.
- Two years later, both the Sears, Roebuck and Montgomery Ward catalogs featured the cute dolls.
- They were sold by the thousands for $1.00 each.
- That same year, Campbell's added the word "Soup" to its corporate name, an acknowledgement of the role soup products played in the company's profitability.
- Next came pictures of the pudgy toddlers on postcards and bridge tallies and even lapel pins, which declared "I am a Campbell's Kid."
- Under Grace's direction, the Kids began giving etiquette lessons to children and

21 kinds 10c a can

Asparagus   Julienne
Beef   Mock Turtle
Bouillon   Mulligatawny
Celery   Mutton Broth
Chicken   Ox Tail
Chicken Gumbo   Pea
(Okra)   Pepper Pot
Clam Bouillon   Printanier
Clam Chowder   Tomato
Consommé   Tomato-Okra
Vegetable
Vermicelli-Tomato

Just add hot water, bring to a boil, and serve.

Look for the red-and-white label

JOSEPH CAMPBELL COMPANY
Camden N J

I'm on my way
To Camden, N. J.
Where they make the
fine soup
That I eat every day.

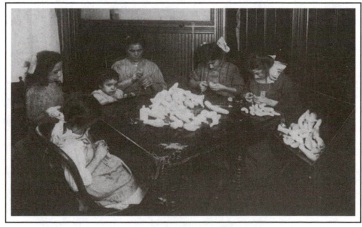

Housewives spent long hours sewing the Campbell dolls.

advised housewives on domestic matters through company-published booklets like *Help for the Hostess*.

- Meanwhile, the Campbell's Kids, as depicted in company-paid advertising, were actively testing early versions of the automobile, the airplane and the telephone.
- Campbell's girls demanded the right to vote; Campbell's boys put on Charlie Chaplin mustaches and pretended to be in the movies.
- Through it all, Grace continued creating.
- Early on, Grace created comics for the *Philadelphia Press* entitled *Bobby Blake* and *Dolly Drake*.
- As her work in cartooning expanded, Grace developed *The Terrible Tales of Captain Kiddo* in collaboration with her sister, Margaret G. Hayes.
- In the midst of this, Grace divorced her first husband in 1911 and married Heyward Drayton III.

The Campbell Kids.

- While the Joseph Campbell Company was busy using Grace's clever illustrations to sell soup to the nation, Grace Drayton continued to illustrate for various magazines.
- In 1913, she created a new character, Dolly Dingle, to appear in the popular publication *Pictorial Review*.
- With her shoe-button eyes and baby curls, Dolly Dingle instantly skipped into the hearts of the American public.
- Soon, Grace would create more than 200 paper dolls in the Dolly Dingle series, printed in full color in the *Pictorial Review*.
- Dolly Dingle's adventures included traveling around the world to visit children of distant lands, including such characters as Beppo and Prince Dalim Kumar.
- These foreign friends came complete with costumes and symbols of their native lands.
- Travel by steamer had never been easier, and even the most stay-at-home Americans were often turned into globetrotters visiting Egypt, Rome, and the Holy Land.
- As 1916 came to a close, with the shadow of American involvement in World War I looming, Grace began to relinquish control of her "funny babies" after 12 years to concentrate on Dolly Dingle.
- By that time, the Campbell's Kids were so critical to the image of the company, Roy Williams of the *Philadelphia Public Ledger* was hired to take over the main drawing duties, leaving Grace more time to create.

Life in the Community: Philadelphia, Pennsylvania

- The history of Philadelphia, Pennsylvania, goes back to 1682, when the city was founded by William Penn.
- Philadelphia quickly grew into an important colonial city, and during the American Revolution was the site of the First and Second Continental Congresses.
- At the beginning of the nineteenth century, Philadelphia was one of the first U.S. industrial centers boasting a variety of industries.

Philadelphia was an important colonial city, and one of the first U.S. industrial centers.

- Following the Civil War, Philadelphia's population grew from 565,529 in 1860 to 674,022 in 1870.
- By 1876, the city's population stood at 817,000.
- A large portion of the growth came from immigrants, mostly German and Irish.
- In 1870, 27 percent of Philadelphia's population had been born outside the United States.
- By the 1880s, immigration from Russia, Eastern Europe, and Italy started rivaling immigration from Western Europe.
- Philadelphia's major industries of that era were the Baldwin Locomotive Works, William Cramp and Sons Ship & Engine Building Company, and the Pennsylvania Railroad.
- There were numerous iron- and steel-related manufacturers, including Philadelphia-owned iron and steel works outside the city, most notably the Bethlehem Iron Company.
- The largest industry in Philadelphia was textiles.
- Philadelphia produced more textiles than any other U.S. city, and in 1904, textiles employed more than 35 percent of the city's workers.
- The cigar, sugar, and oil industries also had an economic impact on the city.

Major department stores lined the city's Market Street.

- During this time, the major department stores—Wanamaker's, Gimbel's, Strawbridge and Clothier, and Lit Brothers—sprang up along Market Street.
- In the beginning of the twentieth century, Philadelphia had taken on a poor reputation.
- *Harper's Magazine* commented: "The one thing unforgivable in Philadelphia is to be new, to be different from what has been."
- Along with the city's "dullness," Philadelphia was known for its corruption.
- The Republican-controlled political machine, run by Israel Durham, permeated all parts of city government.

HISTORICAL SNAPSHOT
1917

- The University of Oregon defeated the University of Pennsylvania 14–0 in college football's 3rd Annual Rose Bowl
- German saboteurs set off the Kingsland Explosion at Kingsland, New Jersey, leading to U.S. involvement in World War I
- President Woodrow Wilson called for "peace without victory" in Europe before America entered World War I
- An anti-prostitution drive in San Francisco attracted 27,000 people to a public meeting; 200 houses of prostitution were closed
- The World War I Allies intercepted the Zimmermann Telegram, in which Germany offered to give the American Southwest back to Mexico if Mexico declared war on the United States; America declared war on Germany
- The Original Dixieland Jazz Band recorded their first commercial record, which included the "Dixie Jazz Band One Step"
- The Jones Act granted Puerto Ricans United States citizenship
- The U.S. paid $25 million for the Danish West Indies, which became the U.S. Virgin Islands
- The first Pulitzer Prizes were awarded to Laura E. Richards, Maud Howe Elliott, and Florence Hall for their biography, *Julia Ward Howe*; Jean Jules Jusserand received the first Pulitzer for history for his work *With Americans of Past and Present Days*; and Herbert Bayard Swope received the first Pulitzer for journalism for his work for the *New York World*

- The Silent Protest was organized by the NAACP in New York to protest the East St. Louis Riot as well as lynchings in Texas and Tennessee
- An uprising by several hundred farmers against the newly created World War I draft erupted in central Oklahoma and came to be known as the Green Corn Rebellion
- At Vincennes outside of Paris, Dutch dancer Mata Hari was falsely accused by the French of spying for Germany and executed by firing squad
- President Woodrow Wilson used the Federal Possession and Control Act to place most U.S. railroads under the United States Railroad Administration, hoping to more efficiently transport troops and materiel for the war effort

Selected Prices

Campbell's Condensed Soup, Can $0.12
Campbell's Tomato Soup, Can $0.10
Cookware, Aluminum, 25 Pieces $10.95
Doll $0.98
Doublemint Gum, 25 Pkgs $0.73
Food Jar, One Gallon $10.00
Hershey's Chocolate Bars, 24 .... $0.98
Instant Coffee $0.10
Pep-O-Mint Life Savers, Roll $0.05
Victrola $125.00

"Have Modern Children Lost Knack of Play, as Famous Artist Claims?" *Pennsylvania Daily News*, June 30, 1930:

Grace Drayton, world-famous artist of *Child Life*, says the sophistication of modern life has crept into even the tiniest tots until they're missing the fun that's due them, in other words, the children of today don't know how to play.

"The good 20th century slogan of 'Give them what they want' is spoiling American's childhood," Mrs. Drayton, creator of Dolly Dimples and Bobby Bounce, declared recently.

"And in the case of children as well as grown-ups the slogan should be changed, to 'Give them what they THINK they want.' For most of us think we want something when all we need is better ideas.

"Years ago toys began to get realistic and lose their play charm. Dolls stopped having great big eyes and pinky complexions. Baby dolls that used to be cunning little dimpled darlings began to look like real newborn babies. Their heads are flat, their bodies are red, and most of them have faces screwed up in an expression of disgust, dismay, and despair that should be reflected in their little girl mothers' faces when they see the trick Santa Claus played on them."

Commercial Canning Timeline

1795
Napoleon offered 12,000 francs to anyone who could devise a way of preserving food for his army and navy.

1809
Nicolas Appert of France devised an idea of packing food into special "bottles," like wine.

1810
Nicolas Appert was awarded the 12,000-franc prize from the French Government after he invented the method of preserving food through sterilization; Appert published the *Book for all Households*, which was translated into English and published in New York.

Peter Durand of England received a patent from King George III that included pottery, glass and tinplated iron for use as food containers.

1812
Thomas Kensett of England established a small packing plant in New York to can oysters, meats, fruits and vegetables in hermetically sealed containers.

1818
Peter Durand introduced his tinplated iron can to America.

1819
Thomas Kensett and Ezra Gagett started selling their products in tinplate cans.

1825
Kensett received an American patent for tinplated cans.

1830
Huntley and Palmer of England began selling biscuits and cakes in decorated cans.

1846
Henry Evans introduced dies to increase production speeds tenfold.

1847
Allan Taylor patented a machine for stamping cylindrical can ends.

1849
Henry Evans was granted a patent for the pendulum press, capable of making a can end in a single operation; production speeds improved from five or six cans per hour to 50-60 per hour.

1856
Gail Borden was granted a patent on canned condensed milk.

continued

Commercial Canning Timeline *(continued)*

1858
Ezra J. Warner of Waterbury, Connecticut, patented the first can opener

1866
E.M. Lang of Maine was granted a patent for sealing tin cans by dropping bar solder in measured drops on can ends.

J. Osterhoudt patented the tin can with a key opener.

1870
William Lyman patented a can opener with a rotating wheel, which cut along the top rim of the can.

Hinged-lid tin cans were introduced.

1875
Arthur A. Libby and William J. Wilson of Chicago developed the tapered can for canning corned beef.

Sardines were first packed in cans.

1877
The simplified "side seamer" for cans came into use.

1880-1890
Automatic can-making machinery debuted.

1892
Tobacco cans were introduced.

1894
AMS Machine Company began manufacturing locked double-seam cans.

1898
George W. Cobb Preserving Company perfected the sanitary can.

1901
The American Can Company was formed.

1909
Tuna canning began in California.

1914
Continuous ovens, used to dry inked tinplate, were introduced.

1917
The Bayer Company introduced pocket-sized cans for aspirin.

Key-opening collar-cans for coffee were introduced.

Food Brand and Product Introductions

1872
- Blackjack chewing gum

1876
- Premium soda crackers (later Saltines)

1881
- Pillsbury Flour

1885
- Dr Pepper

1886
- Coca-Cola

1887
- Ball-Mason jars

1888
- Log Cabin Syrup

1889
- Aunt Jemima pancake mix
- Calumet Baking Powder
- McCormick spices
- Pabst Brewing Company

1890
- Knox Gelatine
- Libby introduces keys on its cans of meat
- Lipton tea

1891
- Del Monte
- Fig Newtons
- Quaker Oats Company

1893
- Cream of Wheat
- Good & Plenty
- Juicy Fruit gum

1894
- Chili powder

1895
- Shredded coconut
- Triscuit

1896
- Cracker Jack
- Michelob beer
- S&W canned foods
- Tootsie Roll

1897
- Campbell's Condensed Soup

- Campbell's Tomato Soup
- Grape-Nuts
- Jell-O

1898
- Nabisco
- Nabisco graham crackers
- Shredded Wheat1899
- Wesson oil

1900
- Chiclets
- Cotton candy
- Hershey's chocolate bar

1901
- Instant coffee

1902
- Barnum's Animal Crackers
- Karo corn syrup

1903
- Pepsi
- Best Foods
- Canned tuna
- Sanka
- Sunshine Biscuits

1904
- Banana split
- Campbell's Kids
- Campbell's pork and beans
- Canada Dry ginger ale
- Peanut butter
- Popcorn

1905
- Epsicle (later Popsicle)
- Holly Sugar
- Royal Crown Cola

1906
- A1 Sauce
- Bouillon cube
- Kellogg's Corn Flakes
- 1907
- Hershey's Kisses

1908
- Dixie cup
- Hydrox
- Monosodium glutamate

continued

Food Brand and Product Introductions *(continued)*

1909
- Quaker puffed wheat and rice
- Tillamook Cheese

1910
- Tea bag

1911
- Crisco
- Mazola Corn Oil

1912
- Cracker Jack prize
- Hamburger buns
- Hellmann's Mayonnaise
- Life Savers
- Lorna Doone Shortbread Cookies
- Morton Salt
- Ocean Spray Cranberry Sauce
- Vitamin pills
- Whitman's Sampler
- Oreos

1913
- Campbell's Cream of Celery Soup
- Peppermint Life Savers

1914
- Doublemint gum
- Fruit cocktail
- Morton Salt girl

1915
- Processed cheese
- Pyrex bakeware

1916
- Fortune cookie
- Kellogg's All-Bran Cereal
- Mr. Peanut
- Orange Crush

1917
- Clark Bar
- Moon Pie

1918
- Campbell's Vegetable Beef Soup
- Contadina Tomato Sauce
- French dip sandwich
- Welch's first jam, Grapelade

"Liner *Cymric* Is Torpedoed off Irish Coast, Great White Star Vessel Was Bound to Liverpool from New York," *The New York Times*, May 9, 1916:

LONDON, May 8—The 13,000-ton White Star Line steamship *Cymric*, which for some time has been engaged in freight service, has been torpedoed by a German submarine, according to advices received here.

The *Cymric* left New York April 29 with an enormous cargo of war munitions. As she usually makes the voyage from New York to Liverpool in ten days, she was therefore within a day or two of her destination. It is considered probable, in the absence of definite details, that the disaster to the *Cymric* occurred off the west coast of Ireland, but whether on the northerly or southerly route cannot be stated.

The fate of the steamship is not yet known, although an early message received in London reported that the *Cymric* was sinking. The crew aboard numbered about 100 men, but the steamer carried no passengers.

The dispatch filed at Queenstown would seem to indicate that the *Cymric* had been attacked off the southwest or south coast of Ireland, possibly not far from where the *Lusitania* went down.

When the *Cymric* sailed from this port on April 29 she carried a crew of 110 officers and men and one of the largest cargoes of munitions of war yet shipped. None of these men is definitely known to be an American, although it was said unofficially yesterday that there were probably twenty Americans among them. J. J. MacPherson, the British Vice Consul in charge of shipping, said that eight new men were shipped on the *Cymric* for her last voyage, and that none of these was American. During the vessel's stay here twelve of her crew deserted and these eight were shipped to replace them.

In addition to the regular crew, three officers and two seamen of other British vessels, who had been stranded in this port, were being sent home.

According to the line's officials, the *Cymric* was in their service, denial being made that she had been taken over by the British Government. There was a very small amount of commercial goods shipped on the vessel, practically the entire cargo consisting of more than 18,000 tons of munitions and other war materiel. While no intimate details of the munitions could be obtained yesterday, the manifest showed that the *Cymric* carried:

continued

"Liner *Cymric* Is Torpedoed off Irish Coast, Great White Star Vessel Was Bound to Liverpool from New York," *(continued)*

8 cases of firearms.

13 cases of guns.

80 cases of rifles.

820 cases of Gaines (gun covers).

590 cases of primers.

2,163 pieces of forgings.

11,049 cases of empty shells.

300 cases of cartridge cases.

40 cases of aeroplanes and parts.

81 cases of tractors and parts.

62 cases of lathes.

7,554 barrels of lubricating oil.

60 cases of steel tubes.

107 cases of copper tubes.

1,768 plates of spelter.

20 cases of gun parts.

6 cases of bayonets.

624 cases of rubber boots and shoes.

220 cases of fuse heads.

7 cases of empty projectiles.

122 cases of forgings.

8,600 cases of cartridges.

6,720 cases of fuses.

18 cases of automobiles.

1,247 cases of agricultural machinery.

1,231 bundles of shovels.

831 bales of leather.

400 reels of barbed wire.

21,908 bars of copper.

1,056 cases of brass rods.

Captain F. E. Beadnell, who has been in the service of the White Star Line for more than twenty years and who was formerly commander of the *Baltic*, was in command of the *Cymric*.

The vessel was built by Harland & Wolff, Ltd., in Belfast, and was launched in 1898. She has a gross tonnage of 13,370 and is 585 feet long, with a beam of 64 feet and a depth of about 38 feet.

Never a fast vessel, the *Cymric* is rated as a ten- or eleven-day ship, and was one day from port at the time it was reported that she was sinking. For the last six weeks she has not carried passengers, and when in that service, only had accommodations for one class. The *Cymric* has had several narrow escapes from submarines during her previous voyages. On March 28, 1915, she was less than twenty miles away from the *Falaba* when the latter was torpedoed, having sailed a short time before that vessel. Captain Beadnell received the *Falaba*'s call for help, but was forced to obey the Admiralty instructions and refrain from going to her assistance.

On Sept 26, 1915, when the *Cymric* reached here, members of her crew said that she was escorted into Liverpool by a cruiser and two torpedo boats, and announced that they believed that the Hesperian was torpedoed in mistake for their vessel, as both looked alike.

When the Cymric arrived here on Jan. 23, 1916, carrying $100,000 in gold and $26,250,000 in American securities, Captain Beadnell said that he had received a wireless warning shortly after clearing from Liverpool, that there were German submarines about and warning him to be on the lookout. This warning came from the Admiral at Queenstown, and the Cymric was met by three heavily armed patrol boats, which escorted her for more than fifty miles, or to the end of the danger zone. On that trip she carried a number of passengers.

"Milledgeville Citizens Take Part in Funeral of Aged Negress," *Atlanta Constitution*, January 12, 1910:

Milledgeville, Ga., January 11 (Special). For the second time in the recent history of Milledgeville has a negro been buried with some of our most prominent white citizens acting as pallbearers. In both instances, it was the funeral of an old colored mammy; this time it was Aunt Amy Latimer. The pallbearers were Judge G. T. Whilden, recorder; Dr. J. E. Kidd, W. W. Stembridge, George H. Brantley, L. H. Andrews, C I. Morris. Last Sunday, Dr. B. J. Simmons, one of the most successful negroes of this state, was buried in this city. He had accumulated some $20,000 in the last 15 years from the practice of medicine. He represented all the most that a progressive man of his race had accomplished in this community. The white people of this city did not ignore his success. He received considerable consideration in many ways as an evidence that his ability was recognized. Quite a number of our citizens attended his funeral, but it safe to say that there is no comparison to be made of the feelings of the white people over the passing away of these two members of another race. Aunt Amy had accumulated little or nothing. It was not what she had, but what she was and what she had been that opened the hearts of her white friends and made them mindful of her even after death. Aunt Amy had been in the valley and shadow with many a good mother in this community. Her tender, humble sympathy and gentle services were not to be forgotten. Her voice had first announced the arrival of many a bouncing boy or girl. The white women sent wreaths and roses.

1919 Profile

Madam C.J. Walker learned early how to survive tough situations—a necessary skill for an African-American pioneer entrepreneur and inventor of a hair-straighting product.

Life at Home

- Sarah Breedlove McWilliams Walker was 37 years old before she launched her hair care business that made her one of the richest black women in America.
- She was born on the Burney plantation in Delta, Louisiana, in 1867 to Owen and Minerva Anderson Walker, former slaves who worked as sharecroppers on the cotton plantation.
- Sarah was the first in her family to be born outside of slavery.
- The shack in which the family lived had no windows, no water, no toilet, one door and a dirt floor.
- Built from cottonwood logs gathered on the plantation, the cabin had a fireplace used for cooking and warmth that dominated one wall of the one-room structure.
- The shanty's other prominent feature was the bedstead topped with a homespun mattress sack stuffed with Spanish moss, gathered from trees in the area.
- Though now sharecroppers and no longer slaves, the Breedloves and young Sarah still lived in a dangerous and hostile environment.
- Venomous snakes and mosquitoes, the latter of which caused diseases such as malaria and yellow fever, were always lurking in the sweltering, swampy climate of the Delta.
- From the day she was born, Sarah Breedlove spent nearly every moment with her parents.
- As a baby, she was strapped to her mother's back while the latter worked in the fields.
- At the age of four, Sarah had learned to work alongside her parents drilling holes in the field where she carefully dropped cotton seeds.

Sarah Walker founded a successful hair care business.

- Each year she received material for her one sackcloth dress from the plantation owner.
- Sarah had no time to attend school even if one existed; instead, she learned to pick cotton and pick it well.
- An orphan at age seven, she had few options and was moved across the Mississippi River to Vicksburg, Mississippi, with her sister Louvenia and her sister's abusive husband Jesse Powell in 1876.
- Life in Vicksburg was hard for the Breedlove sisters; work was scarce and the shanty in which they lived was crowded.
- After the birth of Louvenia's son Willie, her husband became increasingly hostile; there was never enough money or food to sustain the growing family.
- To escape the volatile situation in her sister's home, Sarah became a live-in domestic worker for a white family who provided her with meals, lodging and a small salary.
- Too young to cook, she laid fires, dusted, mopped, washed dishes, scoured pots and pans, changed bed linens, polished boots and took in washing and ironing.
- In 1882, at age 14, she married Moses McWilliams and left her domestic position to work as a laundress.
- "I married at the age of 14 in order to get a home of my own," Sarah explained years later.
- In the 1880s, machines were taking over the laundry business even in Vicksburg, where a new Chinese laundry advertised the newest vacuum-type washing machines.
- Sarah realized she could not compete with the speed and productivity of the steam laundries, so she found other ways to please her customers: reliability and professionalism.
- Sarah Breedlove McWilliams gave birth to a daughter she named Lelia on June 6, 1885; just two years later she found herself a widow and a single parent.
- After the sudden death of her husband, who was rumored to be one of 95 black men lynched nationwide in 1888, she left Vicksburg for St. Louis, Missouri, where her brother Alexander was a barber who lived in the mostly black Mill Creek Valley section of the city.
- The steamboat trip up the Mississippi River consumed a week and cost $4.00 for a mother and child.
- St. Louis was a city filled with black entrepreneurs, including nearly 300 black barbers who shaved their white customers daily.
- Within a decade, the barbering business would dramatically change after King Gillette introduced the easy-to-use safety razor, designed for home use.
- The two-story tenement apartment in which she lived with her brother and her young daughter was a one-room affair which served as a kitchen and sleeping room.
- She soon took a job as a laundress.
- A survey by the St. Louis public schools showed that of 5,076 black parents, 22.6 percent worked as laundresses and 42.6 percent were laborers.
- White steam laundry owners considered blacks particularly suited to the task, given their legendary tolerance for heat and sweltering conditions.

Sarah was married at 14 years old.

- The work required Sarah to stand over hot tubs of boiling water all day stirring the laundry with a long stick, a task demanding great strength and stamina.
- Sarah was making a $1.50 a day when she began her new career in hair care products at age 35; she was living on $468 a year.
- After she deducted $8.00 a month for rent and $3.00 a week for food, she was left with $216 a year for fuel, medicine, transportation, clothing, church donations and incidentals.

Life at Work

- Sarah Breedlove McWilliams was on the edge of becoming entirely bald when she was introduced to Annie Turnbo hair care products for black women.
- Annie Turnbo's agents sold her brand of hair straightener door-to-door.
- For years, like many African-American women, Sarah had shampooed her hair only monthly, less often in the wintertime, and suffered from acute dandruff, lice, eczema and psoriasis.
- In addition, she had used harsh lye soaps, goose fat and meat drippings to straighten her hair; the use of lye and sulfur had burned her skin and destroyed her hair follicles, resulting in hair loss.
- To hide her condition, Sarah often wore a scarf in the fashion she had learned on the farm.

Sarah's job as a laundress was physically demanding.

- As a woman with African features, Sarah was reminded regularly that white skin and shiny straight hair were far more prized than black skin and coiled, kinky hair.

- Even within the black community, long, straight hair denoted prosperity and beauty, while poor hair care marked a woman as coming from the country, unsophisticated and uneducated.
- Eager to cure her baldness, Sarah had tried a variety of concoctions, including several that promised to simultaneously grow and straighten her hair.
- Most failed miserably.
- But after using the Pope-Turnbo Wonderful Hair Grower made by Annie Turnbo and experiencing miraculous results, Sarah joined the army of women selling Pope-Turnbo products door-to-door and quickly became their leading saleswoman.
- As part of her front-porch sales pitch, Sarah told the story of how the Wonderful Hair Grower had changed her life.
- The Pope-Turnbo promotional literature made the connection between beautiful hair and prosperity very clear.
- "Clean scalps mean clean bodies. Better appearance means greater business opportunities, higher social standing, cleaner living and beautiful homes," the brochure said.
- Turnbo's competitors hawked hair straighteners and shampoos with names such as "Kinkilla," "Kink-No-More" and "Straightine."
- The Boston-based Ozono promised in its advertisements to take the "Kinks out of Knotty, Kinky, Harsh, Curly, Refractory, Troublesome Hair."
- Some products were so patently dangerous or useless that black-owned newspapers refused to carry their advertising.
- Most black intellectuals, including Booker T. Washington, disdained most of the hair straightening products sold to Negro women.
- But that had little impact on Sarah's success in St. Louis or Denver, when she took her sales operation farther west.
- In July 1905, with $1.50 in savings, 37-year-old Sarah moved to Denver, where she worked as a cook for druggist E.L. Scholtz and moonlighted selling Turnbo's products.

Women had the freedom to vote.

- Even though the state of Colorado's entire population of 540,000 people was smaller than the city of St. Louis, Sarah smelled opportunity in the mining town..
- She used $0.25 of her $1.50 savings to buy business cards advertising Pope-Turnbo Wonderful Hair Grower, now available in Denver; as orders arrived, Sarah reinvested the profits in more advertising.
- She also found the city welcoming: women could vote and there was less racial animosity toward African-Americans, although the Chinese, whose population was increasing dramatically, were despised.
- Then Scholtz suggested that she provide him with a sample of the product so that it might be analyzed.

- Sarah was soon mixing chemicals for a formula of her own and a new company was launched, featuring a wide variety of hair care products.
- Later she would say that the magical concoction came to her in a series of dreams brought by a man with very specific instructions; competitor Annie Turnbo thought otherwise.
- In 1906, Sarah married C.J. Walker and soon developed her own line of hair care products under the name Madam C.J. Walker; that year she tripled her income to $3,652.
- For the next 18 months, Sarah and her husband demonstrated and sold their products throughout the South, systematically canvassing the region where 90 percent of the nation's African-Americans still lived.
- In each city they would contact the Baptist or African Methodist Episcopal (AME) Church, rent the best house they could afford, introduce themselves to the local black fraternal organizations, arrange a demonstration at the church or lodge, hold classes to train agents, take orders for Madam C.J. Walker's Wonderful Hair Grower and then travel to the next place.
- "All the people who know me are just wild about my hair," Sarah was told by one customer; "I have to take it down and let them see and feel it for themselves. I tell you, I am quite an advertisement here for your goods."
- In the summer of 1907, the volume of orders had become so great Sarah decided to relocate the business to Pittsburgh, whose 16 rail lines offered convenient shipping nationwide—a critical component of her mail-order business.
- In 1908 Madam Walker earned $6,672, nearly twice the previous year's earnings; one year later she took home $8,782, attracting the attention of the Pennsylvanian Negro Business Directory, which called her "one of the most successful businesswomen of the race in this community."
- When women saw her photo and heard her life story, they clamored to take her course and sit for treatments; for thousands of maids and laundresses, Sarah symbolized the progress possible even for black women without a formal education.
- After two and a half years in Pittsburgh, the peripatetic Madam Walker was ready to relocate again, this time to Indianapolis, where a small article in the *Indianapolis Recorder* described her as "the noted Hair Culturalist."
- Advertisements placed by Sarah advised women "calling for treatments will kindly bring comb, brush and two towels"; consultations were free, while scalp treatments cost $1.00 and tins of her Wonderful Hair Grower sold for $0.50 each.
- There she built a manufacturing facility, employed three dozen women and constructed a beautiful six-bedroom house for herself; her income exceeded $10,000.
- Indianapolis was the nation's largest inland manufacturing center, with banks willing to finance startup companies.
- The city's central location also gave Sarah access to Chicago and Cincinnati as well as to her Southern and Eastern markets.
- Press notices preceded her arrival in Indianapolis as she toured the city in her chauffeur-driven $1,500 Pope-Waverly electric runabout that captured lots of attention.

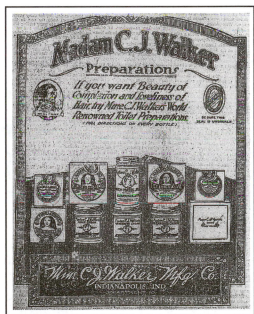

Success of Madam C.J. Walker led her to larger cities.

- Following the opening of her factory, her sales soared to $250,000 annually and Sarah could legitimately claim to have the largest black-owned company in the United States.
- And still she hustled for more business, attending dozens of black-sponsored conventions and gatherings to lecture on hair care.

Sarah donated $1,000.00 to build a YMCA in Indianapolis.

- The restless Madam Walker stayed on the prowl for new customers, always adding to her commissioned workforce of 950 saleswomen.
- She personally trained agents throughout the South and designed their own advertising, even as her marriage to C.J. Walker was disintegrating.
- She also discovered the power and pleasure of philanthropy.
- In 1911, when the concept of building YMCAs for black youth was in its infancy, Sarah stepped forward to accept the challenge laid down by Sears and Roebuck executive Julius Rosenwald to build a YMCA in Indianapolis.
- Sarah made a pledge of $1,000, setting the standard for others, especially in the white community, to match.
- *The Indianapolis Freeman* declared her to be "The First Colored Woman in the United States to Give $1,000 to Colored YMCA Building" and featured her in an article that was read throughout the nation.

- Next, she became involved with the National Association of Colored Women, where she met and helped support Mary McLeod Bethune, a proponent of the need for the education of black girls.
- Sarah's $5,000 donation to the NAACP Anti-Lynching Campaign was the largest in the Campaign's history.
- She also joined a delegation that traveled to Washington to protest the blight of lynching and President Woodrow Wilson's silence on the matter.
- Moved by men and women willing to better themselves, Sarah promoted a Valentine's Day charity benefit for Indianapolis's only black harpist—a 15-year-old girl who had lost her mother at the age of nine.
- In addition, she supported family members, including her daughter who worked in the business, a sister-in-law, four nieces, as well as her elder sister.
- But despite her best efforts, including her continuing business success and her philanthropic donations, African-American thought leader Booker T. Washington continued to ignore her and her company—largely because of his disdain for hair straightening products.
- As a diversion from business, Sarah often attended movies to watch silent romances, Westerns and comedies often featuring entrepreneurs who had found success.
- The movie theaters also propelled her to leave Indianapolis for New York after the owner of the Isis Theatre arbitrarily increased ticket prices from $0.10 to a quarter "for colored people"; Sarah was insulted by the racism and vowed to move.
- During 1914 and 1915, she traveled extensively, especially out West, giving lectures on hair care and making donations, particularly scholarships to worthy students.
- Often, especially in California, Sarah had more invitations for speaking engagements than she had time; everywhere she went she trained new agents, sold Wonderful Hair Grower and laid the groundwork for new business.
- By the time Sarah moved her operation to Harlem in New York City, she employed 10,000 commissioned agents, making her the largest employer of black women in America.
- They were organized into Walker Clubs that rewarded their members based on who raised the most money for charities well as the highest total sales.
- By 1916, she had real estate investments in Indiana, Michigan, Los Angeles and Oklahoma; her federal tax returns reflected that her business and real estate interests provided a net worth of $600,000.
- Even though Sarah moved into a beautifully refinished brownstone on 136 Street W. and Lenox Ave., she saw the flood of poor, undereducated women in need of her services throughout Harlem.
- For women seeking something other than domestic or factory work, Madam C.J. Walker offered an alternative: selling Walker's Scientific Scalp Treatment for the chance to earn between $15 and $40 per week.
- And for working women, making the most money of their lives, Sarah offered an urban, modern look for $1.75 per tin.
- Her goal, she said repeatedly, was to grow hair and confidence.
- Potential agents were tempted by written testimonials: "It is a Godsend to unfortunate women who are walking in the rank-and-file that I had walked. It's helped me financially since 1910. We have to been able to purchase a home and overmeet our obligations."

- Despite the luxury she had created for herself in New York City, Sarah spent the last three years of her life traveling for the war effort to encourage the patriotic service of Negro men and train additional agents.
- On several occasions her travels were halted by nervous exhaustion and failing health.
- For her final crusade, Sarah returned to the question of lynching, armed with a report that said 3,200 people had been lynched in America between 1889 and 1918; the vast majority were black men, and almost all were in the South.
- In 1918 alone, 63 African-Americans, including five women, as well as four white men, had been lynched.
- To that cause alone she pledged $5,000, one of many charitable gifts she made "to help my race."

Harlem, New York.

Life in the Community: Harlem, New York
- Until the early 1870s, Harlem had been a distant rural village of mostly poor farmers in the northern end of Manhattan Island.
- But at the end of that decade, with the launching of the city's first elevated train, Harlem became the city's first suburb.
- Soon thereafter, contractors built opulent brownstones, and Harlem became known for its many mansions.
- An expansion of the Interborough Rapid Transit Line brought a second wave of growth, principally fueled by Irish and Jewish families.
- But when the overheated real estate market collapsed in 1905, West Harlem was saturated with vacant apartments, which became the home of middle-class blacks eager to escape the tenements of the Tenderloin and the San Juan Hill districts.
- In 1911, the prosperous St. Philip's Episcopal Church, an all-black congregation, engineered a million-dollar real estate transaction in Harlem that became the symbolic beachhead for the black presence.
- Three years later, when Sarah gave her first serious thoughts to a New York move, Harlem was home to 50,000 African-Americans.
- A National Urban League report said, "Negroes as a whole are...better housed in Harlem than any other part of the country."
- At the same time, a large influx of African-Americans were being pushed from the South by the floods of 1915 and the boll weevil infestations in 1916.
- Many were pulled to Northern cities, including New York City, where they found employment at factory jobs left vacant when the two-decade-long flood of European immigrants was halted by the beginning of World War I.

- Many African-Americans found they could make as much as $8.00 a day in a Northern city after a lifetime of making only $0.40 a day farming in the South.
- Churches, black newspapers, YMCAs and groups like the National League on Urban Conditions sprang up.
- Manhattan's population topped two million and claimed bragging rights to the world's tallest buildings, from the 60-story terra-cotta Woolworth building on Broadway and Park to the 50-story Metropolitan Life Insurance Building.

African Americans found decent factory jobs in New York City.

HISTORICAL SNAPSHOT
1919

- The Eighteenth Amendment to the United States Constitution, authorizing Prohibition, went into effect despite a presidential veto
- The World War I peace conference opened in Versailles, France
- Bentley Motors was founded in England
- The League of Nations was founded in Paris
- The Seattle General Strike involving over 65,000 workers ended when federal troops were summoned by the State of Washington's Attorney General
- Oregon placed a $0.01 per gallon tax on gasoline, becoming the first state to levy a gasoline tax
- Congress established most of the Grand Canyon as a National Park
- The American Legion was formed in Paris
- Eugene V. Debs entered the Atlanta Federal Penitentiary in Georgia for speaking out against the draft during World War I
- Edsel Ford succeeded his father as head of the Ford Motor Company
- The University of California opened its second campus in Los Angeles, initially called the Southern Branch of the University of California (SBUC); it was eventually renamed the University of California, Los Angeles (UCLA)
- Albert Einstein's theory of general relativity was tested and confirmed by Arthur Eddington's observation of a total solar eclipse in Principe, and by Andrew Crommelin in Sobral, Ceará, Brazil
- Congress approved the Nineteenth Amendment to the United States Constitution, which would guarantee suffrage to women
- The U.S. Army sent an expedition across the continental United States to assess the condition of the Interstate Highway System
- Race riots occurred in 26 cities
- The first NFL team for Wisconsin—the Green Bay Packers—was founded by Curly Lambeau
- Hit songs included "Swanee," "Baby, Won't You Please Come Home?" and "When the Moon Shines on the Moonshine"
- President Woodrow Wilson suffered a massive stroke, leaving him partially paralyzed
- Robert Goddard proposed using rockets to send a vehicle to the moon
- Conrad Hilton spent his $5,000 life savings on the Mobley Hotel in Frisco, Texas
- The first Palmer Raids were conducted on the second anniversary of the Russian Revolution; over 10,000 suspected communists and anarchists were arrested in 23 U.S. cities

Selected Prices

Dress Pattern	$0.10
Farmland, per Acre	$20.00
Gin, Fifth	$2.15
Hair Color	$0.25
Hair Curlers	$0.25
Hair Pins	$0.05
Phonograph Record	$0.65
Radium Water, 50 24-Ounce Bottles	$25.00
Shampoo	$0.33
Travelers' Checks	$0.50

BEAUTY IS AN ASSET CULTIVATE IT

Advertisement, "Asbestos—the only rock on which plants thrive,"
***Leslie's Weekly*, November 15, 1919:**

Industry thrives most where waste is least. And since the development of Asbestos has gone hand in hand with the saving of heat, power and friction, this mineral of wonderful qualities has played an important part in Industrial Conservation.

It is the base of all efficient heat insulation—the necessary *other* 15% in 85% magnesia.

It is, as well, the basic material in the most efficient of friction reducing packings.

As roofings it has qualities of durability and fire-resistance that no other material can approach.

And in innumerable other forms it works miracles of industrial economy that a decade ago would have seemed impossible.

For more than half a century the Johns-Manville Company has steadily grown with the growth of industrial demand for Asbestos.

The Johns-Manville asbestos mines are the largest in the world. In the Johns-Manville plants every Asbestos product is produced under super advantages both of experience and equipment. The Johns-Manville sales-organization, operating through branches in all large cities, is an engineering organization as well, carrying a helpful practical Service, that varies to meet each new requirement but always has for its object—Conservation.

"He Deposits $500 a Month!"

The wisest among my race understand that the agitation of questions of social equality is the greatest folly, and that progress in the enjoyment of all the privileges that will come to us must be the result of severe and constant struggle rather than of artificial forcing.

—Booker T. Washington, speech, 1895 Atlanta Cotton States and International Exposition

"Ragtime Millionaire," popular at the 1904 St. Louis World's Fair:

I'm a ragtime millionaire,
I've got nothing but money to spend;
Automobiles floating in the breeze,
I am afraid I may die of money disease,
Don't bother a minute about what those white folks care;
I am a ragtime millionaire.

"Not Color but Character," Nannie Helen Burroughs, *Voice of the Negro*, 1904:

What every woman who bleaches and straightens out needs, is not her appearance changed, but her mind changed. If Negro women would use half the time they spend on trying to get white, to get better, the race would move forward apace.

"Whisky Sold as Hair Tonic. Detectives in Sailors' Uniforms Arrest Bronx Barber," *The New York Times*, **March 14, 1918:**

Detectives Ferguson and Albrecht of the newly created Division of National Defense of the New York Police Department put on naval uniforms yesterday and visited the barbershop of Nicholas Serra at 1019 East 170th street, the Bronx, where they found several blue-jackets having bottles filled with "hair tonic" from a large-sized demijohn.

In their turn, Ferguson and Albrecht both presented bottles and asked for "hair tonic." After making sure by sampling it that the "hair tonic" was cheap whiskey, the two detectives drew automatic revolvers and told Serra that he was under arrest. Five barbers in the shop had razors in their hands, but made no effort to interfere with the detectives. Serra was later arraigned before United States Commissioner Hitchcock and released on bail of $500.

"I wonder if he's going to be ill"

"Wealthiest Negress Dead. Mrs. C.J. Walker, Real Estate Operator, Made Fortune in Few Years," *The New York Times*, May 26, 1919:

Mrs. C.J. Walker, known as New York's wealthiest negress, having accumulated a fortune from the sale of so-called anti-kink hair tonic and from real estate investments in the last 14 years, died yesterday morning at her country estate at Irvington-on-Hudson. She was proprietor of the Madam Walker hair dressing parlors at 108 West 136th Street and other places in the city. Her death recalled the unusual story of how she rose in 12 years from a washerwoman making only $1.50 a day to a position of wealth and influence among members of her race.

Estimates of Mrs. Walker's fortune have run up to $1,000,000. She said herself two years ago that she was not yet a millionaire, but hoped to be some time, not that she wanted the money for herself, but for the good she could do with it. She spent $10,000 every year for the education of young negro men and women in Southern colleges and sent six youths to Tuskegee Institute every year. She recently gave $5,000 to the National Conference on Lynching.

Born 51 years ago, she was married at 14, and was left a widow at 20 with a little girl to support. She worked as a cook, washerwoman, and the like until she had reached the age of about 37. One morning while bending over her wash she suddenly realized that there was no prospect on her meager wage of laying away anything for old age.

She had often said that one night shortly afterward she had a dream and something told her to start a hair tonic business, which she did, in Denver, Col., on a capital of $1.25.

In a few years she had accumulated a large sum, and invested in real estate in the West and South and in New York State, nearly all the property greatly increasing in value. She then owned a $50,000 home in the northern part of this city, which some years ago she gave to her daughter, Mrs. Lelia Walker Robinson, associated with her in business.

In 1917 Madam Walker completed at Irvington, on the banks of the Hudson, a mansion which cost $250,000, and since then had made her home there. The house, which is one of the showplaces in the vicinity, is three stories high and consists of 30 or more rooms. She had installed in this home an $8,000 organ with furnishings, including bronze and marble statuary, cut glass candelabra, tapestries, and paintings, said to be of intrinsic beauty and value.

"$25 for 'Gouging' Soldier. Barber Fined for Charging $4.60 for a Haircut and Shave," *The New York Times*, May 15, 1919:

It cost Arthur Stading, a barber employed in a shop at 138 West 34th Street, $25 yesterday for the various operations he performed on the unsuspecting head of Cecil Bell, a former member of the Third Anti-Aircraft Machine Gun Battalion, who has just returned from overseas.

Bell entered the barber shop last Monday morning for a haircut, shave "and trimmings." When the barber got through he got a check for $4.60. Bell paid it without a murmur, being unfamiliar with the ways of metropolitan barbers, but his comrades told him that he had been overcharged, so he obtained a summons and Stading was arraigned in Jefferson Market Court before Magistrate Corrigan yesterday morning.

Stading protested that he was only carrying out the instructions of the proprietor, and showed an itemized bill, which included $2 for a "peroxide steaming" and $1 for "mange treatment."

"Have you got the mange?" inquired Magistrate Corrigan of Bell.

"No," replied the soldier. "I didn't ask for the treatment. I didn't know what they were putting on my head."

"This is an outrage," said the court. "That mange cure can be bought for 20 cents a gallon. We have frequent complaints of overcharging from the barber shops and it appears that they have one price for civilians and another for soldiers. If I had the proprietor here I would fine him $100. As it is, I will fine you only $25. That shave and haircut and a lot of superfluous treatment will cost you just $20.40."

Thereupon the magistrate complimented Bell on his initiative in having the barber brought to court.

"Art in Eyebrows," *The New York Times*, May 11, 1919:

Lovers in these days might well write sonnets to their ladies' eyebrows—supposing sonnets were a twentieth-century form of love-making—the eyebrows of the girl of today are works of art. The delicately arched eyebrow, which physiognomists might consider to stand for delicacy of character, means nothing now, for its owner may be naturally a beetled-browed damsel. The round-eyed expression of innocence it gives her is not the work of nature but of her hairdresser.

For the last five or six years there has been more or less experimentation with the eyebrows, but it has not been until this year that the practice of toning down eyebrows that are too heavy or giving the girl who wishes it an eyebrow which appears delicately penciled has become comparatively general. A shampoo, a hair wave and treatment of the eyebrows are now all in a single day's work. Shaving is sometimes practiced, but that is not considered as desirable as the use of a pair of tweezers. A little cold cream is put on before the operation and a simple astringent after it and it can be classed as a minor operation. Where the eyebrows are heavy and scattering, trimming up in this way gives a trim, clean look to the face without altering the expression. The delicately arched eyebrow, where it does not belong, turns the wearer into a different person. There may be a general doubt as to its being an improvement, but there are enough people who like it to make it a regular business for the hairdresser. It does not require doing very frequently; the time differs with different people. Ordinarily, eyebrows pulled with tweezers make their appearance again in about two months.

"Asks $5,000 for Red Hair. Miss Gottdank Sues When Peroxide Fails to Make Tresses Golden," *The New York Times*, January 4, 1917:

The efficacy of peroxide as a hair bleach was brought into question before Supreme Court Justice Erlanger and a jury yesterday when Miss Katie Gottdank, 16 years old, of 230 Second Street, asked $5,000 damages from Julius Kalish Inc., Grand Street druggists. Miss Gottdank complained that, in trying to transform herself from a maiden with hair of chestnut hue into a blonde, she lost part of her hair, and what she had left became brick red.

The plaintiff testified that, when she used one bottle of peroxide without seeing evidence of blondness, the manager of the drug concern advised her to try more, and she kept on doing it until she had poured the contents of five bottles over her locks. She exhibited a shoebox full of hair which, she said, had fallen out during the treatment.

The defendant contended that the plaintiff had failed to prove that the injury to her hair was due to the peroxide and offered to prove that peroxide alone could not cause the hair to become brittle and break off. Miss Gottdank's grandfather, Carl Weisshar, a barber and wig-maker, was called as an expert witness for the young woman, but he was unable to qualify because he admitted that he knew nothing about the effect of peroxide on hair. Justice Erlanger took under consideration a motion to dismiss the complaint because of lack of proof that the young woman's loss of hair was due to the peroxide.

1920 – 1929

The years following the Great War were marked by a new nationalism symbolized by frenzied consumerism. By 1920, urban Americans had begun to define themselves—for their neighbors and for the world—in terms of what they consumed. The car was becoming universal—at least in its appeal. At the dawn of the century, only 4,192 automobiles were registered nationwide; in 1920, the number of cars had reached 1.9 million. Simultaneously, aggressive new advertising methods began appearing, designed to fuel the new consumer needs of the buying public. And buy, it did. From 1921 to 1929, Americans bought and America boomed. With expanded wages and buying power came increased leisure time for recreation, travel, or even self-improvement. And the advertising reinforced the idea that the conveniences and status symbols of the wealthy were attainable to everyone. The well -to-do and the wage earner began to look a lot more alike.

Following the Great War, America enjoyed a period of great expansion and expectation. The attitude of many Americans was expressed by President Calvin Coolidge's famous remark, "The chief business of American people is business." The role of the federal government remained small during the period and federal expenditures actually declined following the war effort. Harry Donaldson's song "How Ya Gonna Keep 'Em Down on the Farm after They've Seen Paree?" described another basic shift in American society. The 1920 census reported that more than 50 percent of the population—54 million people—lived in urban areas. The move to the cities was the result of changed expectations, increased industrialization, and the migration of millions of Southern blacks to the urban North.

The availability of electricity expanded the universe of goods that could be manufactured and sold. The expanded use of radios, electric lights, telephones, and powered vacuum cleaners was possible for the first time, and they quickly became essential household items. Construction boomed as—for the first time—half of all Americans now lived in urban areas. Industry, too, benefited from the wider use of electric power. At the turn of the century, electricity ran only five percent of all machinery, and by 1925, 73 percent. Large-scale electric power also made possible electrolytic processes in the rapidly developing heavy chemical industry. With increasing sophistication came higher costs; wages for skilled workers continued to rise during the 1920s, putting further distance between the blue-collar worker and the emerging middle class.

Following the war years, women who had worked men's jobs in the late 'teens usually remained in the work force, although at lower wages. Women, now allowed to vote nationally, were also encouraged to consider college and options other than marriage. Average family earnings increased slightly during the first half of the period, while prices and hours worked actually declined.

The 48-hour week became standard, providing more leisure time. At least 40 million people went to the movies each week, and college football became a national obsession.

Unlike previous decades, national prosperity was not fueled by the cheap labor of new immigrants, but by increased factory efficiencies, innovation and more sophisticated methods of managing time and material. Starting in the 'teens, the flow of new immigrants began to slow, culminating in the restrictive immigration legislation of 1924 when new workers from Europe were reduced to a trickle. The efforts were largely designed to protect the wages of American workers—many of whom were only one generation from their native land. As a result, wages for unskilled labor remained stable, union membership declined and strikes, on average, decreased. American exports more than doubled during the decade and heavy imports of European goods virtually halted, a reversal of the Progressive Movement's flirtation with free trade.

These national shifts were not without powerful resistance. A bill was proposed in Utah to imprison any woman who wore her skirt higher than three inches above the ankle. Cigarette consumption reached 43 billion annually, despite smoking being illegal in 14 states and the threat of expulsion from college if caught with a cigarette. A film code limiting sexual material in silent films was created to prevent "loose" morals, and the membership of the KKK expanded to repress Catholics, Jews, open immigration, make-up on women, and the prospect of relenting change.

The decade ushered in Trojan contraceptives, the Pitney Bowes postage meter, the Baby Ruth Candy bar, Wise potato chips, Drano, self-winding watches, State Farm Mutual auto insurance, Kleenex, and the Macy's Thanksgiving Day Parade down Central Park West in New York. Despite the growing middle class, the share of disposable income going to the top five percent of the population continued to increase. Fifty percent of the people, by one estimate, still lived in poverty . Coal and textile workers, Southern farmers, unorganized labor, single women, the elderly, and most blacks were excluded from the economic giddiness of the period.

In 1929, America appeared to be in an era of unending prosperity, U.S. goods and services reached all-time highs. Industrial production rose 50 percent during the decade as the concepts of mass production were refined and broadly applied. The sale of electrical appliances from radios to refrigerators skyrocketed. Consumers were able to purchase newly produced goods through the extended use of credit. Debt accumulated. By 1930, personal debt had increased to one third of personal wealth. The nightmare on Wall Street in October 1929 brought to an end to the economic festivities, setting the stage for a more proactive government and an increasingly cautious worker.

1921 News Feature

"Using the Vacuum Tube So That the Deaf May Hear,"
Scientific American, March 26, 1921:

The problem of developing an electrical instrument that will be an aid to the partially deaf, as glasses aid those whose vision is defective, has engaged the attention of some of the world's greatest scientists and physicians.

Considerable progress has been made in the development of telephonic hearing aids for the deaf, but due to the inherent limitations of the telephone transmitter and receiver, development along this line had apparently reached its limit when what is nowadays known as the "vacuum tube amplifier" opened a new field for research and development. Due to the fact that it is a distortionless amplifier of minute electrical impulses, it is adaptable for use in an electric circuit between the telephone transmitter and receiver. In other words, it conveys and reproduces human speech more clearly and loudly than any electrical hearing aid so far produced.

It has remained for Earl C. Hanson of Washington, D.C., to apply the vacuum tube amplifier as a hearing aid for the deaf. The result of his extensive work with vacuum tube amplifiers is represented in the highly compact set shown in the accompanying illustration, which is intended for the use of persons more or less deaf. This set may be used anywhere, being quite portable and entirely self-contained.

One of the great difficulties encountered heretofore has been that in the effort to obtain volume, the transmitter has been overloaded, causing a roaring or undertone in the receiver. Telephone engineers and those familiar with the characteristics of the vacuum tube agree that it amplifies feeble currents without distortion. This permits the use of a telephone transmitter without overloading and thereby retains the clear speech received over line wire telephony. Persons with normal hearing, and even those who hear poorly, hear distinctly on the standard wire telephone. Many persons afflicted with deafness use the telephone satisfactorily, even though they have difficulty in distinguishing ordinary conversation. The reason for this is that the telephone apparatus concentrates the sound in the ear.

Mr. Hanson's device consists of a more or less insensitive microphone or transmitter, as distinguished from a highly sensitive instrument which would pick up all kinds of parasitic sounds; a small vacuum tube, transformer, filament rheostat, filament battery consisting of a standard dry cell, a high-voltage battery comprising 16 cells with a potential of 24 volts, and a pair of telephone receivers. The volume of sound is governed at will by regulating filament rheostat. Despite the employment of an insensitive microphone, the device is extremely sensitive and amplifies any desired sounds because of the amplifying properties of the vacuum tube. It is claimed that this device enables persons afflicted with deafness to obtain better results than have heretofore been secured over the ordinary telephone.

No doubt Mr. Hanson will be recalled as the inventor of the radio cable which enables ships to pick their course by intercepting electromagnetic waves emanating from a submarine cable. His present device was developed largely through the facilities extended by the Volta Bureau of Washington, D.C. This institution was endowed by Dr. Alexander Graham Bell for conducting research work to prevent deafness and to aid those who are hard of hearing.

1923 Profile

Since his earliest days growing up outside Chicago, Illinois, Allan Kusse loved the process of harvesting, shaping and distributing ice.

Life at Home

- Allan Kusse saw gold when he handled a block of ice.
- The advent of electricity in homes had only increased consumer demand for the precious resource.
- Some people—including Allan's eldest son—were predicting that the refrigeration of food would one day be accomplished without an ice delivery.
- But people were also predicting that people would one day walk on the moon, leading Allan to believe that "some people" would forecast anything to get attention.
- Allan was convinced that the ice business was a world without end.
- His son was less confident and wanted to diversify the business, or at least abandon horse-drawn delivery wagons for speedier—and much more expensive—delivery trucks.
- Allan believed that employing the new scientific methods of business would allow them to compete more profitably.
- After all, the growing city of Chicago was supporting 16 separate ice delivery companies—all eager to take his business if he stumbled.
- Rumors of workable, artificial refrigeration had been around since American inventor Oliver Evans designed the first refrigeration machine in 1805.
- His design was followed by that of Jacob Perkins in 1834, who used ether in a vapor compression cycle.

Allan Kusse saw success in the ice business.

- Yet, here the American consumer stood two decades into the most progressive era in the history of humanity—the twentieth century—without a reliable cooling machine.
- In fact, the use of toxic gases such as ammonia, methyl chloride, and sulfur dioxide as refrigerants had led to several fatal accidents when methyl chloride leaked out of refrigerators.
- Allan was sure his son should work harder and think less; once or twice weekly ice delivery to every respectable home in Chicago was here to stay.
- Keeping food cold in an icebox properly loaded with a block of ice was as important and unchangeable as the delivery of milk to the doorstep, Allan believed.
- Born downwind from his grandfather's 54-acre lake, Allan grew up on the ice helping his father and grandfather cut, store and deliver the highly perishable product.
- Allan learned from his father how to use the various tools and special methods needed for cutting and removing the ice, including large saws and horse-drawn cutters.
- Allan stayed in school until the ninth grade when his father's back injury threatened the family business.
- As clear as day, Allan remembered his father, mother and two sisters coming together to ask him to quit school and run the family.
- His mother, who spoke English in her native Dutch accent, said simply: "You are a man now and we need you."
- His father died 16 months later of a massive heart attack while sawing a huge block of newborn ice.
- Fifteen years later, in 1900, when Allan was 31 and his son still an infant, motor-driven saws came into popular use, speeding the harvesting process.
- Seasonal ice harvesting began around the first of January.

Ice harvesting was profitable but risky.

- The ice was then taken to the ice house to be stored until summer.
- The ice house was a double-walled brick or wood building where the ice was covered with layers of hay or sawdust to keep it from melting.
- When the weather turned warm, the demand for ice began.
- The ice wagon, delivering ice door to door, was a common sight around every town.
- The large demand for ice made it one of the top commodities handled by the shipping industry.
- While ice harvesting was a very profitable business, it was also risky.
- In addition to the potential for physical danger to employees, there was the chance that not enough ice would be stored to meet the summertime demand—or that a warm winter might produce a limited supply.

Life at Work

- Allan Kusse was very proud the day he announced to his son the reorganization of the company.
- After months of study, Allan had decided his son would be in charge of harvesting, storage, bookkeeping and wholesale sales to saloons, grocery stores and restaurants.
- Allan would take charge of delivery.
- For years the company had functioned under the implied threat that unhappy ice delivery drivers would quit and take the customers to a competitor.
- From then on, all customers of Kusse Ice were going to stay customers of the company.
- Like most ice companies, it had been the custom of Kusse Ice to split up routes in the early spring and give the new man 30 to 40 customers with the expectation that he would increase that number to 250 customers.
- In the process, the company which was taking all the financial risks of harvesting and storing the ice seldom came into direct contact with the customer, who saw only the driver.
- And that's where the customer's loyalty lay.
- That needed to change.
- Allan knew the biggest drawback to installing modern management methods was the opposition of the employees to anything new.
- This was especially true of drivers who ran their routes in a sloppy manner, allowing more ice to melt than necessary, or drivers who regularly pocketed some of the customer payments, lowering company profits.
- Allan was convinced that 90 percent of the drivers had no desire for additional supervision.

Allan increased customer satisfaction by improving delivery.

- But the scientific management of a company demanded that all work patterns become standardized, all processes measured, and every employee supervised.

- Allan knew that his new organizational plan—with three new supervisors and two checkers—sounded crazy, but he was prepared for dissent.
- When one man with 17 years of experience immediately refused to cooperate, Allan fired him and assigned his route to a new man.
- For weeks afterwards, the fired driver solicited his old customers on behalf of his new employer; 297 stayed and only 14 left.
- Allan figured it was a fair price to pay to stop the previous man's complaining and prove a point to the company's other 66 employees.
- It was time for Kusse Ice to be modern.
- The object of scientific management was to limit waste and increase efficiency, thereby increasing productivity, which meant lowering the cost per article produced.
- In 1911, Frederick Winslow Taylor, the father of scientific management, had pioneered standardization and best practice deployment in his book *Principles of Scientific Management.*
- According to Taylor: "Whenever a workman proposes an improvement, it should be the policy of the management to make a careful analysis of the new method, and if necessary conduct a series of experiments to determine accurately the relative merit of the new suggestion and of the old standard. And whenever the new method is found to be markedly superior to the old, it should be adopted as the standard for the whole establishment."
- Automobile manufacturer Henry Ford popularized this obsession with wasted movement with an improved mass assembly manufacturing system that dramatically improved production, lowered costs and improved profits.

Allan was inspired to transfer Henry Ford's scientific method to Kusse Ice .

- In fact, Allan was inspired to transform Kusse Ice based on the scientific method after reading Henry Ford's book *My Life and Work.*
- Ford wrote, "I believe that the average farmer puts to a really useful purpose only about 5 percent of the energy he expends.... Not only is everything done by hand, but seldom is a thought given to a logical arrangement. A farmer

doing his chores will walk up and down a rickety ladder a dozen times. He will carry water for years instead of putting in a few lengths of pipe. His whole idea, when there is extra work to do, is to hire extra men. He thinks of putting money into improvements as an expense.... It is waste motion—waste effort—that makes farm prices high and profits low."

- Allan knew from experience that similar waste and inefficiency predominated in the delivery department of most ice companies.

- His goal was to eliminate wasted time on routes, making it possible to load more tonnage per wagon, which meant a decreased cost per ton of delivered ice.

- The application of scientific management also would allow managers to measure the exact time required for various operations and establish routes that were more efficient.

- He was determined to cut out the unnecessary motions that drivers performed from the time they commenced to cut a piece of ice to when it was delivered.

- While riding the routes with his drivers—something he hadn't done in years—he overheard the driver saying to his helper, "I think she needs a 10-pounder today."

- The helper then walked, empty-handed, to the house to confirm that the housewife needed 10 pounds of ice to stock her icebox, and returned to tell the driver to saw a 10-pound block of ice, take it to the kitchen, and return.

- The entire operation could have been handled much more efficiently, Allan believed, and he was prepared to make changes.

- Improper routing was also on his list of scientific management issues.

- Since most of the ice was sold for cash, only the drivers really knew how many customers were on a route and who paid what amount.

- Allan believed an exact routing pattern would give the company more control and the ability to make each route more precise.

- That would logically allow more ice to be delivered in a shorter time, leading to more revenues per wagon and possibly less ice melting—which was lost income.

- Next, he wanted to focus on an efficient accounting system capable of tracking the daily transactions that also could be used to summarize the entire operation on a weekly or monthly basis.

- The scientific management system dictated that an organization was only as strong as its leaders.

- Special attention must be lavished on the work of superintendents and foremen; checkers should be hired to review the work of even the most experienced supervisors.

Melting ice was lost income.

- The book *Ice Delivery* advised, "The work of superintendents and foremen should be constantly checked. Daily visits and inspection by the Superintendent of Delivery will keep station superintendents on edge."
- The book even broke down the finances: "As an illustration of the cost and the increase in income as a result of the proper supervision of routes, we will assume a company operates 36 single wagons and has two foremen in charge of them at $7 per day; drivers are paid $5 per day. It will require 40 horses to operate the 36 wagons. With feed and stable expenses of, say, $0.97 a day per horse, the expense will be $38.80; 36 drivers at $5, $180; a total of $232.80.
- "Assume these wagons average 2.3 tons per day, for a total of 83.0 tons, but this will give an average cost of $2.805 per ton. Suppose we change to the more efficient plan of having a foreman for each six wagons, which will increase the total cost to $260.80. As a result of this closer supervision we increase tonnage per wagon to 2.8 tons, or a total of 101 tons a day, which reduces the cost per ton to $2.584.
- "With two foremen above, the cost per ton for a foreman's wage is 16.8 cents per ton; with six foremen it is increased to 41.6 cents, a difference of 24.8 cents per ton. Assume that the average price received per ton is $9.50. On a daily output of 83 tons ,it would amount to $788.50; on a daily output of 101 tons the amount is $959.50, an increase in income of $171. The only additional expense for this increased revenue is the cost of 18 tons of ice at $4 a ton, $72; and the wages of the four additional foremen, $28; a total of $100, leaving the net gain of $71 daily."
- Before he imposed the scientific management system on Kusse Ice, Allan told his son, the family's first child, to finish high school.
- And there was a thundering silence.
- The typically talkative boy, who had chided his father for his old-fashioned ways, finally said, "We are not Ford Motor Company."

Life in the Community: Chicago, Illinois

- Allan Kusse had every reason to be optimistic about the ice business in a city growing as rapidly as was Chicago.
- Incorporated in 1833, Chicago grew at a rate that ranked among the fastest growing in the world during its first 90 years.
- By the close of the nineteenth century, Chicago was the fifth-largest city in the world, and the largest city that did not exist at the dawn of the century.
- Within 50 years of the Great Chicago Fire of 1871, the population had nearly tripled to over 2.7 million.
- Chicago's flourishing economy attracted new residents from rural communities and immigrants from Europe.
- Almost one-third of Chicago's residents were foreign-born; more than one million were Catholics and another 125,000 were Jews.

Immigrants from Poland, Greece, Germany and Russia were settling in Chicago.

- Immigrant groups consistently clustered to preserve the Old World culture of patrimony while learning to become Americans.
- Polish, Greek, German and Russian neighborhoods were clearly defined.
- The growth in Chicago's manufacturing and retail sectors flourished in the Midwest and greatly influence the nation's economy.
- The Chicago Union Stock Yards dominated the packing trade.
- Chicago had become the world's largest rail hub, and one of its busiest ports.
- All of which helped Chicago attract thousands of African-Americans coming north in the Great Migration starting in 1910.
- With new populations competing for limited housing and jobs, especially on the South Side, social tensions rose in the city.
- The post-World War I years were ripe with unrest as black veterans demanded more respect for having served their nation, and some whites resented it.
- In 1919, the Chicago Race Riot, led by members of Irish athletic clubs determined to defend their "territory" against the growing presence of African-Americans, resulted in the death of 23 blacks, 15 whites, and the injury of 537 people.
- The 1920s brought international notoriety to Chicago as gangsters such as Al Capone battled each other and the law during the Prohibition era.

HISTORICAL SNAPSHOT
1923

- *Time* magazine hit newsstands for the first time
- Popular movies included *The Ten Commandments*, *The Hunchback of Notre Dame*, *The White Sister*, and *A Woman of Paris*
- Lee De Forest devised a method of recording sound on film, called fonofilm
- Warren G. Harding, twenty-ninth president of the United States, died in office and was succeeded by Calvin Coolidge
- Roy and Walt Disney founded The Walt Disney Company
- Ida Rosenthal popularized the Maidenform bra by giving one away to each woman who visited her dress store
- Montana and Nevada became the first states to introduce old-age pensions
- "The House That Ruth Built"—Yankee Stadium—opened
- Pan American World Airlines, the Milky Way candy bar, Sanka coffee, Pet Milk, Libby's tomato soup, the name "popsicle" and the oven thermostat all made their first appearance

- A German shepherd rescued by an American soldier in World War I named Rin Tin Tin became a movie star
- Bestsellers included *Babbitt* by Sinclair Lewis, *Etiquette* by Emily Post, *The Outline of History* by H.G. Wells, and *The Ego and the Id* by Sigmund Freud
- Harry Steenbock discovered that radiating food with ultraviolet light added vitamin D
- A sign reading Hollywoodland was erected in Los Angeles, with each letter measuring 30 feet wide by 50 feet tall
- The King *Tutankhamun* discovery set off a rage in women's fashion for oriental fringed scarves, slave bangles and long earrings
- Golfer Bobby Jones won his first USGA Open
- In the aftermath of World War I, hyperinflation in Germany soared; one United States dollar was worth 4.2 quadrillion Papiermarks
- The Moderation League of New York became part of the movement for the repeal of Prohibition in the United States

Selected Prices

Bath Salts, Jar $1.50
Bathtub $29.95
Cigarette Case $11.72
Dress, Crepe $49.50
House Paint, Gallon.. $2.15
Incense and Burner.. $1.00
Iron $4.45
Oil Heater $4.95
Refrigerator, Ice Capacity 100 Pounds...............................$56.95
Toilet.. $6.95

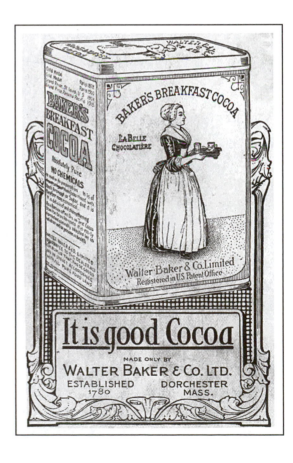

"New Ice Cutting Machine," *Scientific American*, July 22, 1882:

The enormous and very general consumption of ice for manufacturing and domestic purposes has made ice harvesting one of our great industries. Important as the ice crop is, it is extremely precarious, being controlled not only by the variable forces of nature, but also by a great army of men who cut, gather, and store the ice for distribution and use. The ice harvesters, like men employed in many other kinds of business, are liable to disaffection, and it has at times occurred that the best ice this season has been wasted in consequence of want of a force of men necessary to secure it.

In view of the great amount of labor required to harvest ice, and in view of the necessity for accomplishing it at the most favorable time, Mr. Chauncey A. Sager, of Valparaiso, Indiana, has devised a very ingenious and effective steam ice cutter, which makes a longitudinal cut while the machine is advancing and at the same time making transverse cuts, thus forming cakes of suitable size for handling.

The machine propels itself forward slowly, the engine at the same time driving the saws. The saw making the longitudinal cut is suspended on a long arm pivoted to the rear end of the machine on the axial line of the driving shaft, and extending some little distance rearward, and is driven by a cord or belt from the sheave of the driving shaft....

The motion of the saws is controlled by levers at the forward end of the machine. The driving wheels are provided with spikes to give them a firm hold on the ice, and the forward axle of the machine is movable on the king bolt to permit steering.

The two saws with their supporting frames are capable of being folded over on the machine when they are not in use, or when the cutter is to be moved from one place to another.

SAGER'S ICE CUTTING MACHINE.

"Odd Facts in the World of Science," *Leslie's Weekly,* January 10, 1920:

An Automatic Parachute Attachment: The accompanying illustration shows us a new automatic parachute device, which is attached to the body of the aviator, by straps and hence is always handy and available in case of accident. The parachute folds up into a small space, and is fastened to the back, as shown. The device is worn by the aviator all the time he is in the air, and when he is required to jump, he simply pulls a ring, which releases the silk parachute, and it opens itself during the fall. R. W. Bottriel, army aviator, of Chicago, jumped from a mail-carrying plane 2,000 feet in the air, and landed without difficulty with the aid of the parachute which he was wearing. This is a great improvement over the older method, since it leaves the hands of the "jumper" free.

First Machine to Weave Baskets: From the days when Eve wove her first skirt out of leaves and twigs, man has labored over wicker weaving with his hands. For centuries no man has been able to construct a machine which would weave wicker, although many tried and failed until Mr. Marshall Burns Lloyd, former mayor of Menominee, Michigan, performed the feat. All former inventors attempted to use the Biblical method of attaching the weft to the frame of the desired article, and then interlacing the warp. But Mr. Lloyd started at the other end, and found a means whereby he weaves the wicker independent of the frame and attaches to the frame. Two spools of wicker are attached to the top of the machine. The strands run upward over a tension wheel, and then downward into a stationary shuttle. As the large drums revolve, the wicker is drawn through the shuttle, where it is caught by the arm and drawn inward, until it rests in its proper place. Then the arm returns for duplicating the work. Each arm has a weight attached at the other end, so the wicker is packed uniformly at all times. This gives the weaving an evenness which it is impossible to get by hand weaving. The machine weaves the body of a baby carriage in less than 20 minutes. The best hand weaver cannot perform the work in less than 10 hours.

"Inventions New and Interesting," *Scientific American*, March 26, 1921:

"A Telephone Which Fits in the Ear"

That much abused term, "the smallest in the world," is again being used, this time in connection with the tiny telephone receiver shown in the accompanying photograph. A German concern has developed this small telephone as part of a set for deaf persons, and the idea is to have the small telephones fit inside the ears of the users so as to be as inconspicuous and out-of-the-way as possible. The telephone is a perfect bi-polar receiver, and has a diameter considerably smaller that the 5-pfennig coin shown beside it.

Whether it is the smallest telephone receiver or not, is a question. It seems that the thermal telephone, which was described in these columns several years ago, is still smaller and also fits in the ear of the user. However, the thermal receiver works on the principle of air expansion due to the heating of a small platinum wire. The purity of sound obtained with the thermal telephone receiver is remarkable, and far superior to the general run of telephone apparatus, due to the absence of a diaphragm. In this connection it is very doubtful if the present telephone receiver with its tiny diaphragm can reproduce speech as clearly as the usual telephone receiver of far greater size.

Tiny telephone receiver which is worn

"Playing Safe With High Voltage Circuits"

Wood, from which the safety platform shown in the accompanying photograph was made, is specially treated so that contact with a 25,000-volt circuit will not hurt this workman as long as he is standing on this platform. There will be a discharge to his hand as he makes or breaks contact, due to the capacity of his body, but the platform itself has no capacity so that after contact is made there is no sensation felt.

Similar platforms, provided with railings and suspension members, are now being employed in "live" line work. Such platforms, while ensuring safety, do not handicap the linemen in their work. The linemen can now make repairs without the inconvenience of shutting off the power.

"Mail Bags That Won't Sink"

In a recent test and demonstration, special bags were taken up in airplanes and dropped from a height of 300 feet into the water and then picked up by a small boat. The bags were found entirely satisfactory, and it is claimed that they will float on the water for an indefinite period when thrown from airplanes, sinking ships and so on. The bags may be picked up by a small boat sent out from shore or from a steamer, or again, by a man equipped with a non-sinkable suit such as is shown in the accompanying illustration.

"Turning Pliers Into Self-Opening Shears"

With the attachment for pliers shown in the adjacent photograph, a slip-joint design can be turned into a pair of self-opening shears. It is only necessary to snap on this new shear attachment. The work takes but a few seconds and the convenience of having a tool of such a combination in a garage or workshop is self-evident. The attachment will cut wire and metals not exceeding in thickness a medium gage.

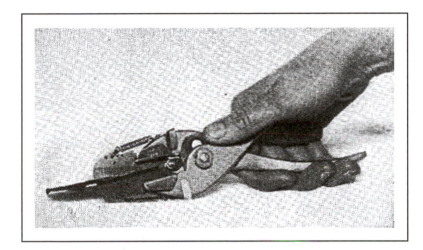

Refrigeration Timeline

1803
The domestic ice box was invented.
Thomas Moore of Baltimore, Maryland. received a patent on refrigeration.

1805
Oliver Evans designed the first closed-circuit refrigeration machine based on the vapor-compression refrigeration cycle.

1809
Jacob Perkins patented the first refrigerating machine.

1810
John Leslie froze water into ice by using an air pump.

1811
Avogadro's law hypothesized that "equal volumes of ideal or perfect gases, at the same temperature and pressure, contain the same number of molecules."

1823
Michael Faraday liquefied ammonia to cause cooling.

1824
Nicolas Léonard Sadi Carnot proposed the Carnot Cycle, the most efficient existing cycle capable of converting a given amount of thermal energy into work or, conversely, for using a given amount of work for refrigeration purposes.

1834
The Ideal gas law was proposed, which gave a good approximation to the behavior of many gases under many conditions.

Jacob Perkins obtained the first patent for a vapor-compression refrigeration system.

Jean-Charles Peltier discovered the Peltier effect, which shows that electricity can cause a heat difference at the junction of two different metals connected together.

1844
Charles Piazzi Smyth proposed comfort cooling.
Circa 1850

Michael Faraday hypothesized that freezing substances increases their dielectric constant, the ratio of the permittivity of a substance to the permittivity of free space.

1851
John Gorrie patented his mechanical refrigeration machine in the U.S. to make ice to cool the air.

continued

Refrigeration Timeline *(continued)*

1856
James Harrison patented an ether liquid-vapor compression refrigeration system and developed the first practical ice-making and refrigeration room for use in the brewing and meat-packing industries.

1859
Ferdinand Carré developed the first gas absorption refrigeration system using gaseous ammonia dissolved in water (referred to as "aqua ammonia").

1862
Alexander Carnegie Kirk invented the air cycle machine, the refrigeration unit of the environmental control system (ECS) used in pressurized gas turbine-powered aircraft.

1864
Charles Tellier patented a refrigeration system using dimethyl ether.

1877
Raoul Pictet and Louis Paul Cailletet, working separately, developed two methods to liquefy oxygen.

1879
The Bell-Coleman compression refrigeration *machine was invented.*

1883
Z.F. Wroblewski condensed experimentally useful quantities of liquid oxygen.

1888
Loftus Perkins developed the "Arktos" cold chamber for preserving food, using an early ammonia absorption system.

1892
James Dewar invented the vacuum-insulated, silver-plated glass Dewar flask.

1895
Carl von Linde filed for patent protection of the Hampson-Linde cycle for liquefaction of atmospheric air or other gases.

1898
James Dewar condensed liquid hydrogen by using regenerative cooling and his invention, the vacuum flask.

1900
Nikola Tesla received U.S. Patent 685,012, *Means for Increasing the Intensity of Electrical Oscillations.* Tesla, also received U.S. Patent RE11,865, *Method of Insulating Electric Conductors.*

continued

Refrigeration Timeline *(continued)*

1906
Willis Carrier patented the basis for modern air conditioning.

1911
Heike Kamerlingh Onnes disclosed his research on the metallic low-temperature phenomenon characterized by no electrical resistance, calling it superconductivity.

1920
Edmund Copeland and Harry Edwards used isobutane in small refrigerators.

1922
Baltzar von Platen and Carl Munters invented the three fluids absorption chiller, exclusively driven by heat.

"Harvesting and Storing Ice on the Farm,"
Farmer's Bulletin, 1928:

Water for the ice supply should be free from contamination or pollution. Ponds and sluggish streams usually have grass and decayed vegetable matter, which is always an objectionable condition and may be injurious to health. These should, therefore, be thoroughly cleared of such growth before cold weather. Green spawn and algae must be destroyed by the use of copper sulfate (blue vitriol). The crystals can be placed in a cloth bag which is hung on the end of a pole and trailed through the water until all the crystals are dissolved. One or two treatments during the summer season at the rate of one pound copper sulfate to 13,000 cubic feet of water will be sufficient to keep down such growths.

Careful investigation should be made to determine whether the source of ice supply is pure and free from contamination or pollution. Streams and lakes are often polluted by sewage or other impurities which it is impossible to eliminate. A pure ice supply is especially important when the ice is to be used directly in beverages or other foods.

Ice Delivery, A Complete Treatise on the Subject, Walter R. Sanders, 1922:

The successful ice companies today are operated according to modern methods. This is especially true in the delivery department, where obsolete methods have been discarded.

It is remarkable how quickly a customer of ice will cease to tolerate the ragged, untidy, coarse ice peddler, when he has once experienced good service by clean, intelligent, uniformed men. He will gladly pay the prevailing price for such service in preference to dealing with the other dealer at a lower price.

Companies will spend thousands of dollars in improved machinery and appliances to reduce the cost of production, and if it is decreased four or five cents a ton, they are highly elated. But when it is proposed to spend money to increase the efficiency of the delivery department, in which cost can be decreased from 25 cents to a dollar more per ton, they will say there it is no use spending money for that purpose, as nothing can be done. While discussing this subject with the manager of the company in a town in Massachusetts, a driver passed the window, and the manager said: "There goes the man I am satisfied has two dollars of my money in his pocket that he took in on his route today, and what can I do about it? He is a good driver, takes good care of his trade, and if I discharge him the trade will suffer. I will have to break in a new man who, in a short time, will be just as bad, if not worse, than he is, so I just try to keep the stealing down to as low a figure as possible and say nothing about it."

"How We Get Our Ice," The Book of Knowledge, 1918:

Ice thick enough to allow skating with perfect safety may be entirely too thin to be cut and stored, for anything less than 12 inches thick cannot be stored profitably, and the icemen prefer to have it even thicker. Cold weather, continued for days, is required to produce ice 12 inches thick....

If snow that has fallen upon the thick ice, it must be removed, and this is done with scrapers. Then follows the marker.... It grooves in the ice about three feet apart as the horse marches up and down the field. Then the horse and man turn and cut lines perpendicular to those already made, and the field takes the appearance of a great checkerboard with squares three feet on a side. Ploughs follow and cut the grooves deeper.

Some of these squares are then separated by means of saws and crowbars, and are either floated through a lane of open water to the icehouse, or else they are loaded on sleds and drawn to the house.

"Brooklyn Students Win Economic Essay Prizes," *Brooklyn Daily Standard Union*, September 10, 1923:

It was announced today that the first and second prizes, $1,000 and $500, respectively, offered by Alvan T. SIMONDS for the best essay on "The Lack of Economic Intelligence" which was open to high school and normal school pupils in the United States and Canada, were won by Brooklynites.

The first prize was awarded to John J. BORCHARDT, 18 years old, a graduate of Commercial High School. He is a first-generation American. His father was born in West Prussia and his mother in Gallicia. They came to the United States in 1901 and his father became a citizen. His father is employed by a furniture factory in Brooklyn and has been there ever since his arrival in this country.

The second prize was given to Morris SALTZMAN, 17, also a graduate of Commercial High. He was born in Russia. His family came to this country in 1909.

Ford's success has startled the country, almost the world, financially, industrially, mechanically. It exhibits in higher degree than most persons would have thought possible the seemingly contradictory requirements of true efficiency, which are: constant increase of quality, great increase of pay to the workers, repeated reduction in cost to the consumer. And with these appears, as at once cause and effect, an absolutely incredible enlargement of output reaching something like one hundredfold in less than 10 years, and an enormous profit to the manufacturer.

—Charles Buxton Going, concerning Henry Ford's use of scientific management, 1915

1926 Profile

Gideon Sundback was working at the Westinghouse Electric and Manufacturing Company when he joined Automatic Hook and Eye to work on a revolutionary invention—the zipper.

Life at Home

- Otto Frederick Gideon Sundback had never heard of the Automatic Hook and Eye Company or its product when he emigrated to America from Sweden in 1905.
- The 24-year-old German-trained engineer quickly made his way to East Pittsburgh, Pennsylvania, where a job as a tracer of engineering drawings awaited him in George Westinghouse's thriving electrical works.
- For a young electrical engineer, Westinghouse was the place to be in the winter of 1905.
- The Westinghouse Electric and Manufacturing Company had been responsible for building the gigantic dynamos installed in the electric power project at Niagara Falls.
- The project and the accompanying publicity placed Westinghouse on the cutting edge of new technology; the world's brightest minds wanted to be a part of the excitement.
- Gideon was well trained for the opportunity before him.
- The son of a prosperous family in southern Sweden, Gideon had completed a thorough technical education in Germany and had received a certificate of electrical engineering in the Polytechnic in Bingen in 1903.
- Wealthy and ambitious, Gideon was drawn to America by opportunity and the glowing stories sent back by friends who had preceded him.
- After six months in Westinghouse, Gideon was promoted to draftsman, a job he held for another year.

Gideon Sundback worked on revolutionizing the zipper.

- During that time, through Swedish social contacts, Gideon was introduced to Automatic Hook and Eye president Frank Russell, who persuaded him to visit the company headquarters in Hoboken, New Jersey.
- There he was offered the opportunity to join a struggling little company with an uncertain future that needed his expertise.
- The company's sliding fasteners were bulky, unreliable and difficult to make.
- Gideon saw a challenge before him.
- It never hurt that he was attracted to—and would eventually marry—the boss's daughter.
- Gideon joined Automatic Hook and Eye at a critical point in its transition in 1906; its founders and discouraged financiers were moving on, refocus was underway, and its newest fastener product was less than a year old.
- The mechanically clever fastener, later renamed the zipper, had experienced a tortured history.

  - Elias Howe, who invented the sewing machine, received a patent In 1851 for an "Automatic, Continuous Clothing Closure."
  - Perhaps because of the overwhelming success of the sewing machine, Howe did not pursue marketing his clothing closure.
  - Forty years later, Whitcomb Judson invented the "Clasp Locker," one of 30 patents he would earn during the last 20 years of his life.
  - The Chicago inventor's "Clasp" was a complicated hook-and-eye fastener that was described as a "locker or unlocker" for shoes.
  - Together with businessman Colonel Lewis Walker, Whitcomb launched the Universal Fastener Company to manufacture the new device.
  - The clasp locker made its public debut at the 1893 Chicago World's Fair and met with little commercial success.
  - Additional patents followed, each seeking to improve the mechanism and make the invention suitable for fastening everything from ladies' fine gloves and corsets to work shoes and heavy-duty mailbags.
  - The patent improvements were among the more than 40,000 applications received by the patent office each year during the 1890s.
  - Undeterred by its limited applicability, its technical uncertainty and the dismal business climate, salesmen were sent out to sell the new technology to shoe manufacturers and housewives who sewed their own clothes.
- Early on, the device worked so sporadically, salesmen learned to avoid towns where they had been successful the previous year.
- Every time a new investor could be found, improvements were made and a new sales effort launched.
- But major changes were underway when Gideon came aboard.

(No Model.)

W. L. JUDSON.
CLASP LOCKER OR UNLOCKER FOR SHOES.

No. 504,038. Patented Aug. 29, 1893.

The "Clasp," also known as a "locker" or "unlocker," for shoes.

Life at Work

- Gideon Sundback was hired just one year after the C-curity fastener was brought to market.
- For the first time in 10 years, the company had a fastener that could be reliably manufactured and sold, even though each one had to be handmade.

- It was believed that no machine was adequate to the task of making the fastener.
- Punch presses were used to cut and shape small pieces of tin sheets of metal and form the hooks and eyes; these tiny pieces were then finished off by smoothing rough edges and applying a protective coating.
- Workers then put them into steel racks and fed them into assembling machines which brought cloth tape to the hooks and eyes that allowed workers to clamp them together with the right spacing.
- The device was promoted as a novelty and sold door-to-door by salesmen trained to convince customers that their purchase would enhance their reputation as modern and efficient women.
- The sales team emphasized the C-curity's ability to prevent skirts from embarrassingly gapping out, and included a personal instruction book on how to install and use the innovative device.
- The instructions included the necessity to remove the fastener before the clothing was washed to prevent rusting.
- Price, too, was an issue in 1906.
- At the time, Sears, Roebuck & Company advertised skirts as cheaply as $0.77 each, and top-of-the-line skirts were less than $2.50.
- Buttons for the skirts were priced at $0.05 a gross, while each fastener cost $0.35 each.
- Gideon Sundback was hired to bring those costs down.
- The Plako fastener was Gideon's first substantial contribution, and was useful in keeping the company's doors open, but its hook-and-eye design suffered from the basic flaws of the past: it was inefficient, stubborn and unreliable.
- Marriage to the plant-manager's daughter Elvira Aronson in 1909 cemented Sundback's desire to make the fastener as ubiquitous as big city trolley cars.
- But it was not easy.
- At one point, to keep the company's metal supplies from being shut off, Gideon took in outside work to keep the company afloat.
- In exchange, the company gave Gideon patent rights to non-American markets, igniting a short-lived effort to peddle the slide fastener to the fashion salons of Paris.
- Then tragedy struck: Gideon's young wife died in 1911 shortly after giving birth to a daughter.
- The grief-stricken young father sent his baby to be raised by his mother in Sweden and then threw himself into his work.
- First, he rejected the hook-and-eye design that he had inherited and improved.
- He explored a new idea that was more flexible and avoided the metallic appearance.
- "One side of the fastener has spring jaw members which clamp around the corded edge of the tape on the opposite side; the slider opens up the jaw members and carries the corded edge in under the jaws.
- "One can see how the cord is inside of the jaw members and held against the crosswise strain which is put on the fastener when it is in active use."

Zippers for skirts were very expensive.

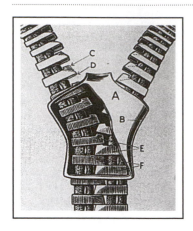

Gideon improves the zipper.

- In the same way that the term "horseless carriage" was a way of referring to automobiles, Gideon referred to his new invention as a "hookless fastener."
- The company even changed its name to the Hookless Fastener Company, but the answer to a truly effective zipper eluded Gideon.
- Then, when this iteration failed to satisfy him, he tried again and applied for another patent.
- This time, Gideon increased the number of fastening elements from four per inch to 10 or 11, had two facing-rows of teeth that pulled into a single piece by the slider, and increased the opening for the teeth guided by the slider.
- The patent for the "Separable Fastener" was applied for in 1916.
- Sundback also created the manufacturing machine for the new zipper, which required no hand work.
- The " S-L" or scrapless machine took a special Y-shaped wire and cut scoops from it, then punched the scoop dimple and nib, and clamped each scoop on a cloth tape to produce a continuous zipper chain.
- Within the first year of operation, Sundback's zipper-making machinery was producing a few hundred feet of fastener per day.
- New life was pumped into the old company and new capital was attracted from old investors; the factory was moved from Hoboken, New Jersey, to Meadville, Pennsylvania.
- A newspaper story covering the factory opening said the company would manufacture "a mechanical fastener for garments, corsets, shoes, curtains, mail patches, partial post packaging, etc."
- The company was particularly desirous of the New York garment industry, where three-quarters of manufactured women's dresses were made every year, employing only buttons or clasps.
- The company's sales force tried flattery, education and anger, but made little progress with the largely German-Jewish owners who were not eager to change.
- Workers unfamiliar with the fasteners wanted more money for putting the new article into dresses, and the unions wanted a say in this change in procedure.
- The Hookless Fastener Company's biggest impediment to additional sales, however, was the abysmal reputation of their previous products; 10 years of selling various unreliable fasteners made new customers hesitant and old customers hostile.
- Then came America's entry into World War I in 1917.
- At first, it appeared to be the beginning of the end; wartime restrictions prohibited new products and limited the availability of metals needed for the fastener's manufacturing.
- The War Industries Board worked hard to diminish what it saw as wasteful competition in many industries; manufacturers of shoes, for example, were forbidden to introduce new styles.
- But aviators had unique needs in their open cockpits, and sailors, who had no pockets in their uniforms, wanted a place to carry cash.
- So at the suggestion of a veteran New York tailor, Gideon and his team created a waistcoat for aviators that incorporated a hookless fastener and a money belt with the unique fastener included.
- The waistcoat languished, but the major New York stores that stocked the money belt sold out immediately.
- From Abercrombie and Fitch to the neighborhood drugstore, the functional virtues of the new product overcame price.

Zippers gave pilots a safe way to carry cash.

- The New York tailor responsible for the innovation became Hookless's biggest customer, and 24,000 men experienced the convenience of a zipper.
- Quickly, other military applications for the zipper were found.
- Gideon was called upon to create a heavier and longer version of the fastener that could be used in sleeping bags, overalls and garment bags.
- Quality control became essential for sliding fasteners in sleeping bags as long as 70 inches; however, this specially created heavier version allowed the zipper to be operated with one hand—another customer selling point.
- Orders came in from the Everfloat Life Preserver Company and the NuBone Corset Company; hookless tennis racket covers and bathing suit bags were also made.
- But it was the Locktite tobacco pouch and B.F. Goodrich galoshes that transformed the hookless fastener from a gimmick to a necessity.
- Locktite bragged about their product: "Once closed, no tobacco will leak out in your pocket. No buttons or strings to fasten."
- By 1922, Gideon's factory was producing 25 gross per week to meet the needs of the Locktite tobacco pouches alone, or 187,200 zippers per year.
- To meet these needs, the factory used Gideon's unique S-L (scrapless) machine that used a preformed wire rather than a flat metal tape as the feed.
- With patents on both the scrapless machine and fastener it produced, Gideon could hold back emerging competitors who had not invested a decade in its development.
- In 1920 the Hookless Fastener Company made 110,005 fasteners; in 1923, the tiny Meadville factory created more than two million units and their biggest order was just around the corner.
- B.F. Goodrich Rubber Company in Akron, Ohio, first ordered $5.00 of fasteners in April 1921; they wanted to look at the novel closure.

- Serious negotiations followed, including a demonstration that the fastener could withstand the stress generated by rubber galoshes, and also discussion of the right of exclusivity.
- In 1922, a satisfied Goodrich Rubber Company unveiled plans for rubber galoshes featuring the sliding fastener, which they dubbed the "zipper" in major magazine ads.
- It was a huge hit, and thanks to their exclusive arrangement with Hookless, Goodrich dominated foul weather shoe sales.
- Goodrich's share of the galoshes market went from 5 to 16 percent in two years, often at the expense of other companies that could not obtain reliable zippers.
- Hookless aggressively pursued imitators in the courts, suing for patent infringement in both America and Canada.
- To balance the impact of the Goodrich account, which consumed 70 percent of the zipper factory's output, Hookless sought new customers in 1926.
- In Kansas City, the H.D. Lee Mercantile Company purchased more than one million zippers for use in firefighter clothing that included five zippers in each jacket.
- And the Hookless Fastener Company began advertising in *The Saturday Evening Post*, featuring its products in quarter-page ads with black-and-white depictions of luggage, sweaters, and children's pencil cases, all linked by the venerable zipper.
- After 21 years, Gideon was an "overnight" success.

Life in the Community: Meadville, Pennsylvania

- Meadville was founded on May 12, 1788, by a party of settlers led by David Mead, at the confluence of Cussewago Creek and French Creek.
- Around 1800, settlers began flocking to the Meadville area after receiving land bounties for service in the Revolutionary War.
- Allegheny College, the second-oldest college west of the Allegheny Mountains, was founded in Meadville in 1815.

Allegheny College.

- Meadville became an important transportation center after construction of the French Creek Feeder Canal in 1837, and of the Beaver and Erie Canal it connected to at Conneaut Lake, as well as subsequent railroad development.
- The Meadville Theological School was established in 1844 by a wealthy businessman and Unitarian named Harm Jan Huidekoper.
- It moved to Chicago in 1926.
- In the late 1700s and early 1800s, Meadville played a small part in the Underground Railroad, helping escaping slaves to freedom.
- An event in September 1880 led to the end of segregation by race in the state's public schools.
- At the South Ward schools, Elias Allen tried unsuccessfully to enroll his two children.
- He appealed to the Crawford County Court of Common Pleas, and Judge Pearson Church declared unconstitutional the 1854 state law mandating separate schools for Negro children.
- This law was amended, effective July 4, 1881, to prohibit such segregation.
- By the late nineteenth century, Meadville's economy was also driven by logging, agriculture, and iron production.

Meadville's economy expanded during the late nineteenth century.

HISTORICAL SNAPSHOT
1926

- Freeman Gosden and Charles Correll premiered their radio program *Sam 'n' Henry*, in which the two white performers portrayed two black characters from Harlem looking to strike it rich in the big city
- Eugene O'Neill's *The Great God Brown* opened at the Greenwich Theatre
- Land on Broadway and Wall Street in New York City was sold at a record $7 per square inch
- The Shakespeare Memorial Theatre in Stratford-upon-Avon was destroyed by fire

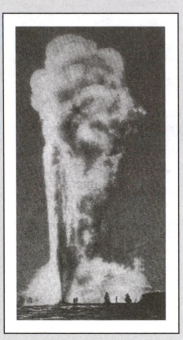

- Robert Goddard launched the first liquid-fuel rocket, at Auburn, Massachusetts
- In the Treaty of Berlin, Germany and the Soviet Union each pledged neutrality in the event of an attack on the other by a third party for the next five years
- Admiral Richard E. Byrd and Floyd Bennett claimed to have flown over the North Pole
- Congress passed the Air Commerce Act, licensing pilots and planes
- Fox Film bought the patents of the Movietone sound system for recording sound onto film
- The National Bar Association incorporated in the United States
- The Warner Brothers' Vitaphone system premiered with the movie *Don Juan* starring John Barrymore
- The League of Nations Slavery Convention abolished all types of slavery
- Gene Tunney defeated Jack Dempsey and became Heavyweight Champion of the World, a battle broadcast nationwide by radio
- Alan Alexander Milne's book *Winnie-the-Pooh* was published
- The NBC Radio Network (formed by Westinghouse, General Electric and RCA) opened with 24 stations
- In Williamsburg, Virginia, the restoration of Colonial Williamsburg began
- Phencyclidine (PCP, angel dust) was first synthesized
- U.S. Marines intervened in Nicaragua to bolster the conservative government

Selected Prices

Alarm Clock $3.25
Ax $1.65
Baseball Bat $2.00
Ceiling Fan $52.00
Clothespins, Five Gross $3.50
Grave Marker...$1.50
Mousetrap $1.80
Safety Razor and Case...$5.00
Sewing Machine..$33.95
Wall Street Journal, Annual Subscription $15.00

"No Thanks, Mr. Bell," *Uncle Joe Cannon*, L. White Busbey, 1927:

I met a learned Justice Supreme Court who had looked into (an invention for converting base metal into gold)…he assured me that a man who had $1,000 to invest would become a millionaire in a few years…I had been a man of frugal ways and had saved $1,000. I had the money in the bank and I took the advice of the jurist and the scientist and got in on the ground floor. The scientist and other less scientific dreamers, including myself, are no longer looking for millions but would be quite happy to get back our thousands.

A few years later I was on Newspaper Row, on 14th St., where the newspaper men had their offices, and I met Uriah Painter, one of the veteran Washington correspondents. He was also a good businessman. Painter asked me if I had ever seen a telephone and I confessed that I had not. We went into his office and he walked over to a little box on the wall. He put a little instrument to his ear, rang a bell and spoke to the box. He said, "Hey, Puss, how are you? I want you to speak to Mr. Cannon, who is here in my office." He handed me the receiver and putting it to my ear, as I had seen him do, I heard Mrs. Painter's voice distinctly. It was amazing. Then he told her to play on the piano and I heard the music. It was magic. I was very much impressed, and Mr. Painter told me about the young Scotchman Bell, how they were organizing a company and insisted the men who invested their money could not lose. He said if I had a thousand to invest, I would be sure to double, perhaps quadruple my money in a few years; and might even make ten thousand by getting in on the ground floor. I had been much impressed by hearing a human voice that I recognized come out of that little piece of metal… but I was even more impressed by the proposition to get in on the ground floor. I remembered my experience with a wonderful discovery to make gold out of an old thing, and I said, "Nay, nay, Brother Painter, I've tried these get-rich-quick inventions and I am done."

Not long afterwards I went down to the office of the Superintendent of Railway Mails to get a young man approved to that service. The superintendent, Theodore Vail, was a bright young fellow, accommodating and always ready to help me when he could. That morning Mr. Vail was not there. His assistant told me that Vail had suddenly become moonstruck and resigned to be the manager of the telephone company that had been foisted on the market. Vail had saved up about four thousand dollars, and in a crazy moment had blown it all on telephone stock and resigned from the government service.

Worse than that, he had persuaded every friend in the office who had a dollar to let him have it for investment. We all liked Vail and were much concerned about his sudden madness, for he was a good Superintendent of Railway Mails and we thought he had a future in the service. We condemned him for the reckless use of his influence over young men in the service who had saved a little money, and he we did not know what would become of them when the magic bubble burst and the telephone stock went like that of a company that was to make gold out of junk.

continued

"No Thanks, Mr. Bell," *Uncle Joe Cannon*, **L. White Busbey, 1927:**
(continued)

Some years later, I was in Boston and I met Theodore Vail. He was round and jolly and looked prosperous. He was the president of the American Telephone Company and the Western Union Telegraph Company. I asked a mutual friend how much Vail was worth, and he said at least twenty-five million. All those fool friends who had let Vail have their savings 30 years ago had made money. They accepted the offer to get in on the ground floor on telephone stock and I refused. I had been a member of Congress and Vail and his friends had been poor devils working in the treadmill. I had the same opportunity as Vail but guessed on the wrong card.

Telephone service, a public trust

New Words That Entered Popular Language Since 1900:

hijacker, Bolshevik, fundamentalism, flapper, jazz, cafeteria, automat, ice cream sundae, Kiwanis, mah-jong, crossword puzzle, no man's land, propaganda, camouflage

---

"The Spirit of the Freeholder," G. W. Westmoreland, *Southern Agriculturist*, August 15, 1928:

The best citizenry has been, in ages past, on the farm. There has always been developed a nobility of spirit in owning and enjoying a piece of land. By the possession of land there has been produced not only a desire to own the land, but a freer spirit in the owner, who has become a freeholder and an independent citizen. In such an environment, future citizens can be reared.

The right to own and enjoy a piece of property will instill into any man that love for country and home without which no country could exist. It's like the birds protecting their nests, and the animals their holes; because man loves that which is his own and is willing, if need be, to die for it. Cincinnatus left his oxen in the field that he might hasten to defend the field against the enemy. Israeli did the same thing in the Revolutionary War. As long as man can own his home he will continue to die for it and no order of conscripting will be necessary. To suffer, he must have something to suffer for.

The Inventor's Universal Educator, Fred G. Dieterich, 1899:

To be sure, thousands of patents have been granted whose merits have never been tested, and no doubt many patents have caused their owners disaster, as it will be found to be the case in any business: but as a general thing, a large portion of patents granted are productive of handsome profits upon a very trifling financial outlay. Compare the cost of all the patents issued up to date with the known worth of a phenomenal invention. Reckoning the average cost of a patent at $60, the amount invested would be $36,000,000; whereas, among the earliest patents issued by this government, the sewing machine has yielded the owners and inventors more than $100,000,000. These are facts which cannot be disputed.

1928 Profile

Joseph Ridgeway left his family's failed farm in Wichita, Kansas, to become a stock pool manager on Wall Street.

Life at Home

- Joseph Ridgeway didn't mind being condemned in the press for being rich.
- He loved being so rich he didn't always remember what he owned.
- Like the time while vacationing in Cuba when he bought a car and then left it behind.
- Or the night he picked up the tab for an entire restaurant.
- He had known poor and had no desire to make its acquaintance again.
- Born during the Panic of 1893, Joseph grew up hearing stories of how his parents lost the farm in Wichita, Kansas, to the bankers and the railroad barons.
- First, they had been victims of the railroads who squeezed the profit out of the wheat crop every year when it came time to ship the harvest eastward.
- Then the bankers, all dressed in clean suits, used a piece of legal paper to take away three generations of hope and hard work.
- His grandfather, using his Civil War-issued Springfield rifle, committed suicide beneath a cottonwood tree after one particularly devastating harvest.
- His father grew more and more bitter every year, and didn't object when his eldest son announced one day that farming was not part of his future.
- His goal, Joseph announced that same day, was to go East and see where the money was hiding.
- Obviously, it wasn't being allowed to travel westward to Kansas.

Joseph Ridgeway left the family farm to make his fortune on Wall Street.

- Educated in the public schools, where hunting season routinely took precedence over a history test, Joseph possessed enough charm and mathematical abilities to catch the attention of well-established rancher Kevin Hatcher.
- Hatcher had long harbored a need to control his own destiny, and he figured that meant controlling a piece of Wall Street.
- Hatcher understood that he was too old to learn the ways of the big city, but the combination of his money and Joseph's personality might give them both a chance.
- Joseph became Hatcher's pupil—and willing participant—in 1911 when the former turned 18.
- Together they learned how to legally manipulate the stock market so America's wealth could start flowing westward again.
- When Hatcher was a young man, cattle ranching paid well for those who worked hard and had inherited vast stretches of land.

Joseph partnered with a rancher to help the farming industry of the west.

- Entrepreneurialism was alive and well until the railroad began fixing prices for the regular farmer and dropping prices for the few.
- The railroads were the key to economic growth in the second half of the nineteenth century, and at first everyone prospered.
- For the first time in America's history, agricultural and manufactured goods could be shipped cheaply and efficiently throughout the country.
- Total rail mileage in the United States grew from 53,000 miles in 1870 to just under 200,000 miles at the turn of the twentieth century.
- Along with the railroad boom came solutions to problems that had plagued the industry in the past.
- Cross-country scheduling, for instance, became easier in 1883 when the railroads established the Eastern, Central, Mountain, and Pacific time zones across the United States, and shipping delays caused by railroads using different gauge track were resolved in 1886 when almost all the companies adopted a 4-foot-8 11/42 inch standard.
- But intense competition among railroads led some into bankruptcy, sank others heavily into debt, and ignited bitter rate wars.
- To limit competition, lines operating in the same region sometimes worked out an agreement to share the territory or divide the profit equally at the end of the year.
- Known as pooling, this process kept rates artificially high and ranchers like Hatcher enraged.
- Lacking cooperation, the companies competed against each other by paying kickbacks or rebates to large customers while making up any losses by charging small shippers more.
- Because of such practices, rates were often lower for a long haul than for a short one; shipping goods from Chicago to New York, for example, where several companies had routes, was cheaper than sending the same shipment from Buffalo to Pittsburgh, where only one railroad had a monopoly.

- The unfairness of such rate-setting practices led to passage of the Interstate Commerce Act of 1887, which required that rates must be "reasonable" and prohibited pooling, rebates, and long/short haul rate differentials.
- To Hatcher's way of thinking—law or no law—the railroad men got fatter every year while the farmers lost weight.
- And his secret weapon was a smart, charming Joseph Ridgeway, future stock pool manager and a loyal son of the West.
- To finance his scheme, Hatcher sold some of his best land—ironically to the railroad men—and leveraged the rest of his land to borrow more.
- When Joseph was 24, Hatcher decided that the younger man's education was complete and financed a trip to New York City.
- It was time to challenge the big boys at their own game.
- Joseph started out as a ticket broker, scalping aisle seats to Broadway hits for partners and executives with the big banks such as Morgan, Lehman, and Goldman Sachs.
- The men of Wall Street loved the eagerness of the Westerner and soon helped him set himself up as a curb broker, where he stayed for two years before moving to the stock exchange—the seat of wealth and power worldwide.

Curb brokers on New York City's Wall Street.

- Wall Street had become the world's money center only recently—in 1914—by default; until then, London, England, had been the unquestioned king for decades.
- But when London money managers suspended gold payments against the pound sterling in the opening weeks of World War I, the financial center of the world quickly shifted to New York.
- When Joseph began trading, the market was highly vulnerable.
- The aftermath of World War I had caused uncertainty, inflation, shifting alliances and overproduction.
- In 1921, when the average price of all farm products was cut in half, Joseph learned the fine art of the bear raid, making money in a falling market.

- Then, in 1922, he learned to be a bull when it came to hot automobile products.
- After all, between 1921 and 1923, the annual factory sales of passenger cars rose from $1.5 million to $3.6 million, and the total number of motor vehicles on American roads increased from 10.5 million to 15.1 million.
- Most of all, Joseph learned the art of market volatility; there was money to be made within huge swings in the market.
- But the real money was waiting to be made in legal stock manipulation—the engineering of a rapid rise in a specific stock followed by a rapid, controlled decline.
- That was the business Joseph for which had been trained; that's how Eastern money was going to move West.

Life at Work

- Joseph Ridgeway was elated, when he was invited to be part of a small group prepared to manipulate the price of Radio Corporation, one of the hottest issues on the market.

Radio Corporation's stock, controlled by Joseph and his partners, made them rich.

- Under a formal partnership agreement approved by their lawyers, the nine men in the room agreed to purchase one million shares with a value of $90 million.
- They had also engaged the services of the stock exchange member who acted as the floor specialist for radio stock.
- At the start of the manipulation, the price of the stock was $90.
- Using a series of carefully contrived maneuvers, deliberately calculated to deceive the investing public, the stock pool manager quickly drove the price to $109 a share.
- The rapid rise caught the attention of the regular investors, who jumped at the chance to ride the wave of this new hot stock, not understanding the price rise was artificial and controlled by nine wealthy men.
- That's when Joseph and his partners began unloading the stock, taking a profit on every share.
- The entire operation took a little over a week; the stock specialist received a $500,000 fee and the nine men split $5 million.
- Joseph kept $150,000 and banked $400,000 for his backer, Kevin Hatcher.
- It was all a perfectly legal and common practice on Wall Street; often, the companies themselves whose stock was being manipulated participated in the profit-taking.
- Only the "rubes" from the street took a loss, many of whom bought on margin, borrowing most of the money to buy a hot stock in expectation of a big payout.
- But when the hot stock lost too much value, the broker would have to sell it; thus, the stock investor would be without the stock but would still owe money for it.

- The radio was the perfect vehicle for creating a hot stock: the medium was new, mysterious, and it was difficult to fathom its real money-making potential.

- Radio enabled listeners to experience an event as it happened; rather than read about aviator Charles Lindbergh meeting President Calvin Coolidge after his flight to Paris, people experienced it with their ears and imaginations.

- The radio, which knew no geographic boundaries, drew people together as never before; millions who listened to a live prize fight via the radio felt a special kinship.

- Soon, people wanted more of everything—music, talk, advice, drama.

- They wanted bigger and more powerful sets, and they wanted greater sound fidelity.

- After KDKA broadcast election results in 1920, radio swiftly became a craze.

- By the end of 1923, 556 stations dotted the nation's map in large cities as well as in places like Nunah, Wisconsin; Paducah, Kentucky; and Yankton, South Dakota.

- An estimated 400,000 households had a radio, a jump from 60,000 just the year before, and in that year's spring catalog, the Sears, Roebuck Company offered its first line of radios, while Montgomery Ward was preparing a special 52-page catalog of radio sets and parts.

- Included was "a complete tube set having a range of five hundred miles and more" for $23.50.

- Overnight, it seemed, everyone went into broadcasting: newspapers, banks, public utilities, department stores, universities and colleges, cities and towns, pharmacies, creameries, and hospitals.

- At first, people's awe at hearing sounds through the air was so great, they would listen to almost anything.

- Broadcasters decided to give them a mix of culture, education, information, and some entertainment.

- Wall Street insiders, with stock exchange approval, regularly shared gullible public lambs tying the stock pool to popular stock.

- To Joseph running a stock pool was simplicity itself—using the stock exchange ticker tape to tell a story that was essentially false, he could lure an all-volunteer army of investors into the pool just as the price was peaking.

- The first time Joseph ran his own pool, he spent almost 60 days quietly acquiring a large block of shares of Hudson Motor Car Company for himself and three other investors.

- This was made easier when the company agreed to participate in the pool manipulation and gave Joseph an option to buy company shares at a fixed price.

Wall Street, New York City.

- On behalf of the pool, Joseph as pool manager began buying and selling shares of the stock at frequent intervals in no apparent pattern.

- Sometimes he would even buy and sell stock between members of the pool to generate activity for tape watchers eager to run with the next wave.

- The constant appearance of the stock symbol on the tape as each transaction was recorded served as an advertisement, drawing in more investors.

- At some point, the manipulation became self-sustaining as public buying pushed the price higher and higher with no help from the pool manager.
- That's when Joseph's skills were tested: how and when he "pulled the plug" would determine his investors' profits.
- Cautiously he fed stock into the market, attempting to keep the price high as long as possible before dumping thousands of shares.
- During the roller coaster ride, his investors who bought at the bottom and sold at the top experienced a rise of $41 per share, while the investing public received everything from small profits to large losses.
- Joseph managed to make $1.2 million; America's money was flowing westward.
- Everyone on Wall Street considered the work of a pool manager a high art; even the investing public did not object because they thought that one day they, too, would hit the big time.
- But some of the New York newspapers were less optimistic; they began publishing Joseph's activities when a pool buy was first developing, robbing it of its secrecy.
- They even called it fraud and Joseph a scoundrel.
- Early in 1928, Joseph solved most of his publicity problems by allowing select reporters to participate in the pool; their silence was considered "sweat equity," he told them.
- Only *The Wall Street Journal* declined the opportunity and managed to provide a day-to-day accounting of Joseph's current stock pool.
- Thanks to the publicity and the eagerness of the public to win on the rise of stock, the pool was a huge success, but Joseph's reputation—a loyal son of the West—was tarnished.
- After an exchange of letters with his mentor, Kevin Hatcher, Joseph decided there was only one thing to do: sell all of his stock on Wall Street and return home a multimillionaire.
- As Joseph boarded the train to Kansas, he couldn't help but wonder what excitement he would be missing in 1929.

Bad publicity in New York papers tarnished Joseph's reputation.

Life in the Community: Wall Street, New York

- Wall Street is located in Lower Manhattan; it runs east from Broadway to South Street on the East River, through the historical center of the Financial District.
- As the first permanent home of the New York Stock Exchange, the name Wall Street became shorthand for the American financial industry.

- Wall Street was also the physical location of the New York Stock Exchange.
- The name of the street was handed down from the seventeenth century, when Wall Street formed the northern boundary of the New Amsterdam settlement, where a barrier was constructed to protect against English colonial encroachment.
- By the late eighteenth century, a buttonwood tree at the foot of Wall Street became the daily gathering place for traders and speculators; in 1792, the traders formalized their association through the Buttonwood Agreement, the origin of the New York Stock Exchange.
- Wall Street's architecture was generally rooted in the Gilded Age, while Wall Street itself represents financial and economic power, elitism and America's symbol of an economic system.
- The business of business was highly pleasurable for many Americans in the second half of the 1920s.
- America was producing five million automobiles a year; overall corporate earnings were rising rapidly, and it was a good time to be in business.
- Predictions that millions of vacationers would soon flock to Florida had ignited a speculative land bubble in that state.
- Wall Street was attracting an army of investors, eager to live the American dream; everyone knew someone who had done well in the market.
- The broad market rise begin in the last six months of 1924.
- In May 1924, *The New York Times* average prices for 25 industrial stocks was 106; in December 1926, the *Times* industrial average had more than doubled to 245, a gain of 69 points for that year alone.
- In June 1928, trading was so heavy five million shares changed hands.
- The year ended with the *Times* industrial average up 86 points for the year to stand at 331, with a dramatic increase in brokers' loans, or stocks purchased on margin with little or no money down.
- In 1928, brokered loans totaled $1.5 billion; by the end of the year, the volume was up to $6 billion.
- Speculative fever had been intensified by the decision of the Federal Reserve System to lower the rediscount rate from 4 percent to 3.5 percent in August 1927, and to allow the purchase of government securities in the open market.
- These actions were taken for the most laudable of motives: several of the European nations were having difficulty stabilizing their currencies, European exchanges were weak, and the easing of American money rates might aid in the recovery of Europe and thus benefit American foreign trade.
- Furthermore, the lowering of money rates might stimulate American exports.
- The lowering of money rates also stimulated the stock market.
- In January 1928, President Coolidge publicly stated that he did not consider the volume of brokers' loans too high, giving White House sponsorship to the very inflation that was worrying the sober minds of the financial community.
- While stock prices had been climbing, business activity was subsiding.

- By February 1928, the director of the Charity Organization Society in New York reported that unemployment was more serious than at any time since immediately after the Great War.

Unemployment lines in New York City.

- Moody's Investors Service said that stock prices had "over-discounted anticipated progress" and wondered "how much of a readjustment may be required to place the stock market in a sound position."
- The financial editor of *The New York Times* described the picture of current conditions presented by the mercantile agencies as one of "hesitation."
- The newspaper advertisements of investment services asked, "Will You 'Overstay' This Bull Market?" and "Is the Process of Deflation Under Way?"
- The air was fogged with uncertainty when Joseph boarded the train to Kansas.

HISTORICAL SNAPSHOT
1928

- The first regular schedule of television programming began in Schenectady, New York, by General Electric's television station W2XB
- Aviator Amelia Earhart became the first woman to successfully cross the Atlantic Ocean
- At the Democratic National Convention in Houston, New York Governor Alfred E. Smith became the first Catholic nominated by a major political party for president of the United States
- The Kellogg-Briand Pact was signed in Paris, the first treaty to outlaw aggressive war
- Paul Galvin and his brother Joseph incorporated the Galvin Manufacturing Corporation, later known as Motorola
- Alexander Fleming discovered a bacteria-fighting substance named penicillin
- Radio premieres included the drama *Real Folks, Main Street*; *The Chase and Sanborn Hour* with Maurice Chevalier; and *The Voice of Firestone* and *Shell Château* with Al Jolson
- An iron lung respirator was used for the first time at Children's Hospital in Boston, Massachusetts
- Box office movie stars included Clara Bow, Lon Chaney Sr., and Greta Garbo
- The International Red Cross and Red Crescent Movement (ICRM) was formally established with the adoption of "Statutes of the International Red Cross"
- Mickey Mouse appeared in *Steamboat Willie*, the third Mickey Mouse cartoon released, but the first sound film
- On Broadway, Eugene O'Neill captured the Pulitzer Prize for *Strange Interlude*
- Johnny Weissmuller retired from swimming, having set 67 world records and won three Olympic gold medals
- Peter Pan Peanut Butter, Rice Krispies, Nehi, adhesive tape, shredded wheat and the quartz clock all made their first appearance
- Personal loans were initiated by the National City Bank of New York
- The U.S. Congress approved the construction of Boulder Dam, later renamed Hoover Dam
- Coca Cola entered the European market through the Amsterdam Olympics
- Frederick Griffith indirectly proved the existence of DNA
- The Episcopal Church in the United States of America ratified a new revision of the *Book of Common Prayer*
- The first patent for the transistor principle was registered in Germany to Julius Edgar Lilienfeld

Selected Prices

Automobile, Willys-Knight	$1,450.00
Bathing Suit	$8.50
Birdhouse	$60.00
Camisole	$0.79
Game, Mahjong	$22.95
Pocket Watch	$63.50
Railroad Ticket, Chicago to San Francisco	$89.00
Stationery, 24 Sheets and Envelopes	$0.50
Train, Chicago to Yellowstone, Round Trip	$56.50
Traveling Bag	$10.50

OLDSMOBILE SIX

GENERAL MOTORS PRODUCT

BUILT-IN MAIL CHUTES

Your Mail
Delivered Outside
Received Inside

ATTRACTIVE
PRACTICAL
CONVENIENT

Send For Folder

American Device Mfg. Co.
Red Bud, Ill.

"Church and Politics: Political Discussions in the Pulpit Grossly Unfair," Dr. Gus W. Dyer, *Southern Agriculturist*, August 15, 1928:

Most people go to church for devotional and religious purposes. It is grossly unfair to these people for the preacher to arbitrarily convert a religious service into a political powwow. Again the law gives special protection to all church services—a protection that is not given to any other service. This special protection is given on the basis that the services are religious. Members of a church congregation are not permitted under the law to take issue with the speaker. Any sort of disturbance here is against the law. Men are fined and put in prison for disturbing church meetings. When the preacher from the pulpit advocates one side of a political question, he uses the special protection given by the law in the interest of religion to take unwarranted and unfair advantage of his political opponents who are not permitted to answer or make any sort of protest, although they are in the pews of their own church. When a preacher uses the pulpit to antagonize a position taken in politics by a portion of the church membership, he hits men whose mouths are locked and whose hands are tied.

"Flatbush Man Is Named Winner in Martinson Coffee Slogan Contest," *Brooklyn Standard Union*, June 16, 1928:

Hyman C. Ferber, of 2177 East Twenty-first Street, Flatbush, is the winner of the Martinson coffee slogan contest, according to an announcement to-day.

"You put in less—and it tastes like more," the slogan submitted by Ferber, was the one the judges deemed best. Ferber gets the $500 first prize.

The $300 second prize goes to P.E. Moreton, of 100 Columbia Heights, for the slogan, "Measures up great!—from the ground to the sealing."

"Commended by those qualified to judge," won the $100 third prize for E. Simonson, of 3373 Twelfth Avenue. Ten other slogans drew $10 each for those submitting them. They follow:

"The blend all chefs recommend," Bertram Ellis, 185 Ralph avenue; "One swallow calls for its mate," by David M. Londoner, 784 Eastern Parkway; "Why debate? Percolate," by Robert G. Smith, 377 Fifth Avenue, Manhattan; "The blend's the thing," by Charles A. Delapierre, 345 Stratford Road; "The aroma won its diploma," by Mrs. Claude Outlaw, 240 Fifty-first Street; "The blend of millions," by Jessie H. DeLong, 255 Prospect Street; "A rhapsody in coffee harmony," by Archie Tarr, 567 West 149th Street, Manhattan; "Once tested, always requested," by Mrs. John W. Bonnett, 3601 Avenue J; "A surprise at first, a pleasure ever after," by Pauline Von Moser, 1201 Bushwick Avenue; "Worth a taste, to taste its worth," by Mae T. Keenan, 2085 Lexington Avenue, Manhattan.

The prizes were offered by Joseph Martinson, head of the coffee importing house, at 85 Water Street, Manhattan. Four judges made the winning selections.

The stock exchange is the stage whereon is focused world's most intelligent and best informed judgment of the values of the enterprises which serve men's needs. It is probable that upon this stage can be discovered the aristocracy of American intelligence.

—Joseph Stagg Lawrence, Princeton economist

The game of speculation is played by some three or four thousand insiders and some half a million outsiders in terms of complete inequality." The outsiders "are permitted to see only a part of their own cards while their professional adversaries have access to the cards of all the players as well as their own.

—Journalist John T. Flynn

No Congress of the United States ever assembled, on surveying the State of the Union, has met with a more pleasing prospect than that which appears at the present time. In the domestic field there is tranquility and contentment...and the highest record of years of prosperity.

—President Calvin Coolidge, December 4, 1928

"Huge Appreciation in General Motors, $10,000 Invested 10 Years Ago Worth $1,600,000 Now Through Extra Stock," *The New York Times*, March 11, 1928:

Wall Street was busy with pad and pencil yesterday figuring the profits that have been made in General Motors and the current advance and by those few fortunate investors in the stock who have held the stock since the original purchase nearly 20 years ago.

It is easy to calculate what profits have been made in any particular move, but much harder to determine what the appreciation has been in an "original investment" because of the many changes that have been made in the capital structure of the company, the extra cash disbursements that have been made, and the generous regular dividends that have been added enormously to holders' profits.

It was figured yesterday that the purchase of 100 shares at $100 a share at the origination of the company in 1908 would, if the stock had been held until the present time, represent for the holder today 10,033 shares. In other words, the purchaser would have seen an investment of $10,000 mount within 10 years to a market value of $1,600,000. Few instances of such an appreciation have taken place in American financial history.

"Rules Are Suggested to Make Radio Installment Sales Safe,"
The New York Times, June 17, 1928:

Radio installment sales were discussed last week by H. P. Lewis, Vice President of Commercial Credit Company, who spoke at the meeting of the National Electrical Manufacturer's Association. Factors that make installment selling safe, according to Mr. Lewis, are: (1) A sufficient down payment to give the buyer a sense of ownership and to penalize him heavily in case of default. (2) A sufficiently rapid rate of payment for the balance to build up his equity to complete ownership and decrease the seller's equity to nothing faster than the resale value the merchandise depreciates. (3) The title retaining instrument on which the goods are sold, which makes complete forfeiture the penalty of delinquency at any stage of the contract. (4) Careful credit work of the well-established finance companies. (5) Alert but discriminating collection work. (6) The spread of risk between thousands or millions of buyers, depending on the industry under consideration. There is no concentrated hazard or any condition approaching the frozen inventory in the installment sales picture

1930 – 1939

Few Americans—including the very rich—escaped the devastating impact of America's longest and most severe depression in the nation's history. Banks failed, railways became insolvent, unemployment rose, factories closed and the upper class moved out of the biggest houses in town. Economic paralysis gripped the nation. Promising businesses and new inventions stagnated for lack of capital and customers. By 1932, one in four Americans was jobless. One in every four farms was sold for taxes. Five thousand banks closed their doors, wiping out the lifetime savings of millions of Americans—rich and poor.

The stock market sank into the doldrums. In urban areas, apple sellers appeared on street corners. Bread lines became common sights. The unemployed wandered from city to city seeking work, only to discover the pervasive nature of the economic collapse. In some circles the American Depression was viewed as the fulfillment of Marxist prophecy—the inevitable demise of capitalism.

President Franklin D. Roosevelt thought otherwise. Backed by his New Deal promises and a focus on the "forgotten man," the president produced a swirl of government programs designed to lift the country out of its paralytic gloom.

Roosevelt's early social experiments were characterized by relief, recovery, and a reform. Believing that the expansion of the United States economy was temporarily over, Roosevelt paid attention to better distribution of resources and planned production. The Civilian Conservation Corps (CCC), for example, put 250,000 jobless young men to work in the forests for $1.00 a day. By 1935, government deficit spending was spurring economic change. By 1937, total manufacturing output exceeded that of 1929; unfortunately, prices and wages rose too quickly and the economy dipped again in 1937, driven by inflation fears and restrictions on bank lending. Nonetheless, many roads, bridges, public buildings, dams, and trees became part of the landscape thanks to federally funded employed workers. The Federal Theatre Project, for example, employed 1,300 people during the period, reaching 25 million attendees with more than 1,200 productions. Despite progress, 10 million workers were still unemployed in 1938 and farm prices lagged behind manufacturing progress. Full recovery would not occur until the United States mobilized for World War II.

During the decade, United Airlines hired its first airline stewardess to a allay passengers' fears of flying. The circulation of Reader's Digest climbed from 250,000 to eight million before the decade ended and Esquire, the first magazine for men, was launched. The early days of the decade gave birth to Hostess Twinkies, Bird's Eye frozen vegetables, windshield wipers, photoflash bulbs, and pinball machines. By the time the Depression and the 1930s drew to a close, Zippo lighters, Frito's corn chips, talking books for the blind, beer in cans, and the Richter scale for measuring earthquakes had all been introduced. Despite the ever-increasing role of the automobile in the mid 1930s, Americans still spent $1,000 a day on buggy whips.

The people of the 1930s excelled in escape. Radio matured as a mass medium, creating stars such as Jack Benny, Bob Hope, and Fibber McGee and Molly. For a time it seemed that every child was copying the catch phrase of radio's Walter Winchell, "Good evening, Mr. and Mrs. America, and all the ships at sea," or pretending to be Jack Benny when shouting, "Now, cut that out!" Soap operas captured large followings and sales of magazines like *Screenland* and *True Story* skyrocketed. Each edition of *True Confessions* sold 7.5 million copies. Nationwide, movie theaters prospered as 90 million Americans attended the "talkies" every week, finding comfort in the uplifting excitement of movies and movie stars. Big bands made swing the king of the decade, while jazz came into its own. And the social experiment known as Prohibition died in December 1933, when the Twenty-first Amendment swept away the restrictions against alcohol ushered in more than a decade earlier.

Attendance at a professional athletic events declined during the decade, but softball became more popular than ever and golf began its drive to become a national passion as private courses went public. Millions listened to boxing on the radio, especially the exploits of the "Brown Bomber," Joe Louis. As average people coped with the difficult times, they married later, had fewer children, and divorced less. Extended families often lived under one roof; opportunities for women and minorities were particularly limited. Survival, not affluence, was often the practical goal of the family. A disillusioned nation, which had worshipped the power of business, looked instead toward a more caring government.

While the nation suffered from economic blows, the West was being whipped by nature. Gigantic billowing clouds of dust up to 10,000 feet high swept across the parched Western Plains throughout the 'thirties. Sometimes the blows came with lightning and booming thunder, but often they were described as being "eerily slight, blackening everything in their path." All human activity halted. Planes were grounded. Buses and trains stalled, unable to race clouds that could move at speeds of more than 100 miles per hour. On the morning of May 9, 1934, the wind began to blow up the topsoil of Montana and Wyoming, and soon some 350 million tons were sweeping eastward. By late afternoon, 12 million tons had been deposited in Chicago. By noon the next day, Buffalo, New York, was dark with dust. Even the Atlantic Ocean was no barrier. Ships 300 miles out to sea found dust on their decks. During the remainder of 1935, there were more than 40 dust storms that reduced visibility to less than one mile. There were 68 more storms in 1936, 72 in 1937, and 61 in 1938. On the High Plains, 10,000 houses were simply abandoned, and nine million acres of farm turned back to nature. Banks offered mortgaged properties for as little as $25.00 for 160 acres and found no takers.

1931 Profile

George Mecherle's experience with farming proved a valuable asset when he decided to establish a farmer automobile insurance company in Illinois which would sell good insurance at the lowest possible price.

Life at Home

- Insurance executive George J. Mecherle grew up on a farm; it was the best education he could receive in the prairielands of Illinois.
- Between his cherished *McGuffey Readers*, the mainstay of educational textbooks in the Midwest, and his ability to understand the moods and needs of farmers, George used his personal experience to reinvent the field of car insurance.
- The son of a German Lutheran immigrant and a devout Quaker mother, George spent his first 40 years farming and raising children.
- Gregarious, extroverted and talkative, he walked, talked and acted like a farmer; he was never happier than when discussing farming problems with his fellow farmers.
- Determined to maximize his yield and share his knowledge, he studied the most advanced scientific farm literature, such as *The Prairie Farmer*.
- But the winter of 1917-1918 was bitter for several reasons: the wind that swept across the prairie was particularly cold and the declining health of his wife Mae worried the entire family.
- Desperate for a solution, the family decided to give up on farming, sell their cattle and equipment and take Mae to a winter sanitarium in Florida.
- At the time, the couple owned 480 acres of fine, prosperous land; the farm was well equipped with the latest machinery and stocked with good shorthorn cattle and Poland China hogs.
- Also, as a result of war preparations, farm prices were rising.

George Mecherle sold insurance at the lowest price possible.

- They sold it all, except the land, which could be leased to a neighbor.
- In 1918, the family discovered the joys of seeing the ocean, surf fishing and the fabulous warm climate, but Mae's progressive rheumatism was undeterred by the change of location.
- So two years later, they returned to Illinois and purchased a home near Bloomington, near the center of the state; at 42, George was not ready to retire.
- First, he accepted a job selling insurance policies for the Union Automobile Indemnity Association of Bloomington, which wrote liability, property damage, fire, theft, and collision insurance on automobiles.
- He also became a regular at the card room of the Bloomington Club where he mingled with the merchants, storekeepers, thinkers, and professional men in the community, as well as the retired farmers.
- He discovered that he was an excellent salesman, but after a falling out with the owners of the insurance company, George signed on as a "bird dog" for the Illinois Tractor Company.
- There he was responsible finding customers amongst his farmers friends for the gasoline-powered contrivances that were becoming standard equipment on any farm.
- The Illinois Tractor Company was a minor player and did not lack for competition.
- Henry Ford's company controlled three-quarters of the tractor market in the United States and was engaged in a bitter rivalry with International Harvesters and General Motors for control.
- With his farming background and his ability to speak the farmers' language, George quickly became the top salesman.

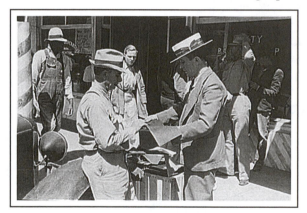

George was a natural salesperson.

- In fact, he found himself selling tractors faster than the company could deliver them, but once again he became dissatisfied with his bosses and quit.
- However, he was still intrigued with selling, especially selling insurance to farmers whose needs he fully understood; besides, 1921 was a tough year for farming.
- In the backwash of World War I, the nation was undergoing its worst economic depression since the 1890s; thousands of bankruptcies were taking place and nearly half a million farmers were losing their land to foreclosure.
- Corn, which fetched $1.88 a bushel in August 1919, had fallen to $0.42.
- At the end of 1921; the price of wheat had shrunk from $2.80 a bushel to $1.00 or less.
- At the same time, Henry Ford had accomplished a lifelong dream of producing cars at the rate of one a minute; automobiles were becoming a major force in the American economy.
- Automobiles that needed insurance—at reasonable prices.

Life at Work

- George Mecherle had slowly come to realize that the only person he liked working for was himself.
- After quitting two jobs following disputes with his boss, George had a plan: establish a farmer automobile insurance company on a statewide basis which would sell good insurance at the lowest possible price.
- Open only to farmers in the state of Illinois, it would be called State Farm Insurance and be headquartered in Bloomington, Illinois.
- George was convinced the insurance rates charged to farmers were too high because they included the risks of city drivers as well; farmers drove less—around fewer cars—and had fewer accidents.

George preferred working for himself.

- Moreover, after 20 years of suffering through the vagaries of the farm economy, it was time that somebody took care of the farmers.
- State Farm was founded in 1922 as a mutual automobile insurance company owned by its policyholders.
- The concept of a "farmers' mutual" was a well-established, democratic form of insurance whose origins dated to the second decade of the nineteenth century.
- Every state in the Midwest had its full share of farmers' mutuals; in Illinois alone there were 216 mutuals that insured 35 percent of the state's farm property.
- George was 45 years old when he launched his new insurance company; there would be few second chances if he failed.
- Using the cardboard insert that supported his starched shirts to write on, George calculated he could insure an automobile for $1.00 per $100 of the physical valuation of the car.
- The prevailing rate was $1.00 per $40 of value.

Farmers desperately needed car insurance.

- He also believed he could overcome the problems that many farm mutuals had experienced with automobile insurance: too much overhead and no organization for the recovery of stolen vehicles.
- George wanted his insurance plan to be as distinct and new "as sunshine is from shadow."
- All members were required to be men of property, and applications would be accepted only from Farm Bureau members and their immediate families.

- George believed that the stability of any insurance company depended on the character of the men and women it insured.
- George told his governing body "you will carry your insurance in a company in which all members are of the same stamp of men as yourself."
- He believed that farmers were a good risk, even if none of the city-oriented, large stock companies, which often treated farmers scornfully, agreed.
- Policies provided insurance protection against loss or damage to an automobile by fire, theft, or by collision with a movable object.
- George believed that anyone who hit a stationary object shouldn't be driving a car.
- Under the terms of the theft and collision policy lurked another new concept: policyholders would bear the first costs, up to $10, the remainder to be paid by State Farm.
- George believed that if the farmer had to pay for minor repairs, he would be more careful with his automobile; besides, the creation of a small deductible would prevent a flood of petty claims each time a member scraped a fender or dented a mudguard.
- Full coverage cost $15 for a life membership fee and $19 for the premium; initially, salesman had to convince farmers to buy a product that cost $34.
- Insurance was a tough sell in 1922-1923, when farm prices were down and few states required it, but George and his team of salesmen believed they were offering something that farmers could appreciate.
- Even the influential *Prairie Farmer* magazine agreed to accept advertising from the upstart company after subjecting George to a stern grilling.
- Initially, State Farm contacted the managers of each of the local farmer's mutuals and convinced them to take the State Farm man on a tour.
- The goals were simple: to sell automobile insurance policies to farmers and to train the farm mutual representative to become a permanent agent once the initial sales drive was over.
- Within six months there were 1,300 policies in force and the hard-charging George and his team had gained an intimate knowledge of the best and worst restaurants and bed-and-breakfasts in rural Illinois.
- After the first year, the company had placed policies in 46 counties through 90 mutual companies; the gross income totaled $45,000 with losses and adjustments of only $8,000.
- Expenses for the year included salaries of $1,600, rent for $520, and then a $25,000 certificate of deposit as required by the state of Illinois.
- But early on, the young company became embroiled in a controversy concerning how to value the automobiles it was insuring.
- On the road, George and his sales team, anxious to please a prospective customer, said the valuation of the farmer's vehicle should be 80 percent of the cost of the car; the policy team back at the home office thought 80 percent of the list price was a more accurate valuation.
- The issue would not go away, and resulted in the resignation of one key employee and several of the founding board members.
- Being a pioneer was not easy.
- By 1926, State Farm began insuring accidents involving stationary objects, and in 1927, its policies included features such as wind coverage, loaned car protection and insurance for buses or private cars used for transporting children to school.
- Growth was tremendous; the home office staff of State Farm expanded from five employees in 1924 to 183 in 1929.

- To secure the right kind of sales force—men who were more than "order takers"—George began recruiting high school principals in small towns.
- They had a need for additional income, a keen knowledge of potential customers and the integrity to do it right.
- As State Farm's insurance business grew, so did the demand for the company to write policies for city dwellers and small-town merchants.
- In 1926, a subsidiary was created to meet the needs of those who were not eligible as farmers; in the same year, the company accepted an invitation to begin selling policies in neighboring Indiana.
- By 1928, State Farm invested $55,000 in a tract of land in downtown Bloomington to build a suitable headquarters; the eight-story building cost a little more than $400,000, but within a short time it was fully occupied by the expanding insurance company.
- On the company's tenth anniversary in 1931, income had reached $7.5 million, assets were $6.6 million, with a surplus of $5.6 million.
- The company had 370,045 policies in force, with 334 employees.
- Although competitors were baffled, George was not.
- Before State Farm entered the market, capital stock insurance companies all set similar prices for insurance and were essentially immune to price competition.
- Also, most companies required the full payment annually, paying an average 25 percent of cash premiums in commissioned wages—keeping the cost of sales high.
- Plus, new policies were issued annually, which meant that every year the agent received his 25 percent commission.
- To further help farmers, George developed semi-annual premiums—instead of yearly—as an important selling point for farmers, who also needed their payments to coincide with the money they would receive from the harvest.
- In addition, State Farm issued policies from its home office instead of the field office, saving the company the cost of clerical staffing in multiple offices.
- The home office was also tasked with the responsibility of billing and collecting renewal premiums; this allowed the salesman in the field to focus on new sales and relieve the company of compensating him for collections.
- This savings was passed on to customers.
- The most unique feature of the State Farm plan was its membership fee system; any person who joined State Farm did so for life as long as they remained "a good risk."
- Many companies included the cost of acquiring customers in their fee structure; State Farm charged a fee only once, reducing the overall cost of the insurance policy every year that it was renewed.
- Finally, farmers were a good investment; during its first 10 years, State Farm would do business at nearly 40 percent less than the stock companies.
- Even the decision to expand beyond the borders of Illinois had been successful; America was a big country with many more cities to conquer.

George recruited high school principals as salespersons.

Life in the Community: Bloomington, Illinois

Some immigrants were skeptical about life in America.

- Between 1850 and 1860, two and a half million immigrants arrived in the United States; 951,667 were German.
- Many came, carried by a tide of optimism they could not put into words, that life would be different in America.
- A steady stream of Germans flowed toward Wisconsin and southern Ohio; thousands more, including Chris and Fred Mecherle, sought the comparative emptiness of Illinois.
- Miraculously, they had been able to run unscathed through the gauntlet of runners, ticket agents, boarding house scams and outright thieves who lived to strip new immigrants of their every possession the minute they arrived onshore.
- After five years of wandering, the couple settled near Bloomington, Illinois, a growing spot in the prairie, thanks to the Illinois Central Railway.
- Their decision coincided with the development of an improved plow that was designed to cut the prairie sod in great swaths.
- It was so large, 16 to 30 oxen were needed to pull it through the rich swampland, rendering the prairie useful for agriculture.
- When the County of McLean was incorporated, a county seat was established wherein the site of Bloomington "would be located later."
- James Allin, who was one of the promoters of the new county, offered to donate 60 acres of his own land for the new town, resulting in a noisy auction on the Fourth of July, 1831.
- People came from all over to trade and do business at the town's center, known today as Downtown Bloomington, including Abraham Lincoln, who was working as a lawyer in nearby Springfield.
- In 1900, a fire destroyed the majority of the downtown, especially the areas north and east of the courthouse.
- However, the burnt area was quickly rebuilt from the designs of local architects George Miller, Paul O. Moratz, and A.L. Pillsbury.
- During the first three decades of the twentieth century, Bloomington continued to grow.
- Agriculture, the construction of highways and railroads, and the growth of the insurance business—mainly State Farm Insurance—all influenced the growth of Bloomington and its downtown area.

Abraham Lincoln worked as a lawyer in nearby Springfield.

HISTORICAL SNAPSHOT
1931

- The film version of *Dracula* starring Bela Lugosi was released as gangster and horror films increased in popularity

- California received the go-ahead by the U.S. Congress to build the San Francisco-Oakland Bay Bridge
- "The Star-Spangled Banner" was adopted as the United States' national anthem
- To generate income, Nevada legalized both gambling and the six-month divorce

- The Scottsboro Boys were arrested in Alabama and falsely charged with rape
- Lucky Strike cigarettes outsold its rival, Camel, for the first time
- Construction of the Empire State Building was completed in New York City
- South Dakota native Ernest Lawrence invented the cyclotron, used to accelerate particles, to study nuclear physics
- Thomas Edison submitted his last patent application
- The National Education Association reported that 75 percent of all cities banned the employment of married women to protect jobs for men
- The Emerson iron lung was perfected as the polio epidemic grew; 6,000 cases of infantile paralysis were reported in New York alone
- Baseball player Pepper Martin of the St. Louis Cardinals batted .500 to lead the "Gashouse Gang" to a World Series championship over Philadelphia
- The comic strip detective character Dick Tracy was created by cartoonist Chester Gould and made its debut appearance in the *Detroit Mirror* newspaper
- Gangster Al Capone was sentenced to 11 years in prison for tax evasion in Chicago, Illinois
- Popular books included *The Good Earth* by Pearle S. Buck, *Only Yesterday* by William Lewis Allen, *Sanctuary* by William Faulkner and *Dear Lovely Death* by Langston Hughes
- The Chinese Soviet Republic was proclaimed by Mao Zedong
- Jane Addams became the first American woman to be awarded the Nobel Peace Prize
- The National Committee for Modification of the Volstead Act was formed to work for the repeal of Prohibition in the United States
- Radio premieres included *The Ed Sullivan Show*, *The March of Time* and *The Eddie Cantor Show*

Selected Prices

Cream Separator $69.95
Field Tiller...$94.50
Hen $25.00
Milker $42.50
Mixer $21.00
Pitchfork... $1.35
Radio $20.00
Screwdriver $1.00
Seed, per Bushel $1.00
Tractor Tires..$35.15

2 for $1
OTHERS ASK $1.29

Durable Chambray
WORK SHIRTS
Men! Here's Real News

35 U 627—Blue. 35 U 628—Gray. Half Sizes: 14½ to 17-inch neck. State size. Postage, 9c. 2 for............................$1.00
Don't imagine for a minute these are the usual 50c Shirts. You'd have to pay at least 69c each in other stores right now. But for our 60th Anniversary Sale we've slashed prices right and left to bring you **Bargains!**
Look at these features—see why these work shirts are so good:
 Durable tough Chambray
 Double thickness across back
 Double thickness at front
   Triple stitched seams
    Roomy cut armholes and cuffs
    Two big pockets with button-down flaps. Good strong buttons put on to stay.

Beau-Arch

$3.29

Formerly $3.69

Style—
Without
Foot-Aches

FOOD MIXER   JUICE EXTRACTOR

★ *STAR-Rite* ★
MAGIC MAID
Food Mixer and Juice Extractor combined **$19.50**

"States Still Experimenting With Automobile Insurance,"
C. L. Mosher, *The New York Times*, January 4, 1931:

If the authorities of the various states throughout the country advocated compulsory automobile insurance—or, as they are called, "fiscal responsibility laws"—in the belief that the enactment of such legislation would decrease the number of motor car accidents, their hope has undoubtedly been banished by the ever-increasing number of the fatalities and injuries in almost every state of the union.

The joy riders and the jaywalkers, like the poor, we have always with us. Insurance does palliate but it has not cured; it does, however, make it easier for everyone after the crash has occurred, but no one yet has put forth a method which legislators can adopt to prevent, or even curb, the number of unnecessary or avoidable motor car mishaps.

But the lawmakers have not been idle during the past three or four years; their efforts to improve road conditions have been earnest and frequent. Many theories have been and are being tried out, and new ones are now proposed, but of them all there is no one measure in sight which promises to be conspicuously better than the measures now in force....

In the New York legislature were introduced 11 bills for resolutions for the adoption of, or for commissions to consider, compulsory compensation insurance in connection with motor car accident. Bills for the creation of "state funds" were introduced in Massachusetts and New York. Bills for the adoption of indiscriminate "compulsory liability insurance" on the Massachusetts plan...were induced in New York, Rhode Island and Virginia; and bills along the line of the "AAA Bill" in whole or in part were introduced in Kentucky, Massachusetts, South Carolina and Virginia.

In addition to these, there were many proposed resolutions and a few exceptional proposals. The federal government, too, did not permit the year to pass without its contribution to interest in motor car protection, with the result that there are pending in Congress, for the District of Columbia, a measure following closely the lines of the "AAA Bill" and one for compulsory compensation insurance in a "state fund."

"Auto Insurance by State Dealt a Heavy Blow,"
Wisconsin Daily Rapids Tribune, March 30, 1927:

Compulsory automobile insurance was dealt a heavy blow in the Corporations Committee of the Senate Tuesday afternoon when several bills providing methods compelling all motorists to take out insurance were under consideration. Bernard Genttleman, Milwaukee, appeared in favor of his bill which would compel every person taking out an automobile license to take a policy of insurance with the state at the same time. Mr. Genttleman said that there were so many accidents in Wisconsin, it was time that the state stepped in to compel every owner of a car to take out a license. Several other bills providing different forms of compulsory insurance are also under consideration.

Edward J. Groves, Milwaukee, representing the fire underwriters, declared that compulsory insurance laws would not reduce the number of automobile accidents in Wisconsin. He said that the only way to reduce accidents was by passing a driver's license bill which would compel every operator of a car to take out a license after satisfactorily passing an examination.

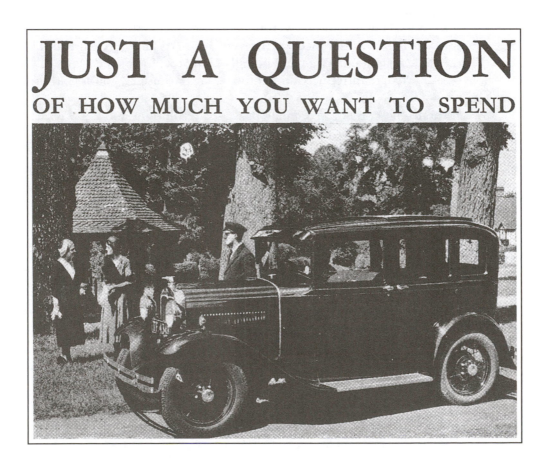

Letter written by George Mecherle concerning State Farm Insurance, 1923:

I find there are many so-called salesmen who are little more than order takers, and as you know, the selling of our insurance requires the man to have the ability to create a demand, sell the insurance, take the application, and complete the whole deal in one call if he expects to make a success of the business. These men seem to be a rare article, but with the standing we have with the Mutual Fire Companies, it seems as though the average salesman could qualify.

As a result of our last week's work in Cass County, we wrote 96 applications on cars in four and one half days, also an amount between $75,000 and $100,000 of fire insurance for their local mutual. I'm satisfied that we wrote 70 percent of our calls for automobile insurance; at least I know that Mr. McDonald and myself wrote a higher percentage than this, but I have no means of checking up on the other boys to find out just what percentage of calls they wrote; but I believe at least 40 or 50 per cent. This was of course well planned and the territory well developed by circulatizing the members of the Farm Bureau for the drive. Everyone was acquainted with the fact that the drive for mutual insurance was the most valuable asset we had.

"Chicago Employment Gains, Auto Sales and Manufacturing Activities to Show Improvement," *The New York Times*, February 22, 1931:

Automobile sales, manufacturing and employment are showing an improvement, which is in part due to seasonal influences. Although automobile sales were below the level two years ago, they are very much higher than for November and December.

Indications are that the decline in employment struck bottom in the period from December 15 to January 15, The State Department of Labor reporting a decline of 2.3 per cent for the period in the number of workers in 1,369 establishments.

This is the same percentage of the decline as the period ended January 15, 1930. Since then companies have been adding workers, and unofficial reports that a large manufacturer of electrical appliance apparatus plans to step up production sharply soon.

Continued price declines in hides, cattle, butter and eggs have caused at least temporary inventory losses for large packing companies.

Wholesale and retail trades are a little slower, with volume about equal to that of February last year. Mail-order houses and city store sales are fairly good, but the farmer buying by mail is sparing.

Have you seen the latest development in visible records?

1934 News Feature

"Off the Record: Snuff," *Fortune*, March 1934:

When the late James Buchanan Duke, some 25 years ago, wanted to give his wife a stock she wouldn't have to worry about, he gave her $100,000 worth of his American Snuff Co. Snuff stock, said Mr. Duke, was a good woman's stock. At the end of last year, all three of America's great snuff makers were paying extra dividends on their stock. U.S. Tobacco Co. paid a dividend of $5.00, which made its dividend $9.40; George W. Helme Co. paid two dollars extra (for the fourth year in a row), making its dividend $7.00; American Snuff paid $0.25 extra, bringing its rate up to $3.25.

The stock Mr. Duke gave his wife was stock in the old American Snuff Company, which was a subsidiary of the old American Tobacco Company, an even more complete monopoly than its parent company. In 1911, when the courts broke up American Tobacco for anti-trust law violation, American Snuff was broken up, too—into three competing units which today are American Snuff, G. W. Helme, and U.S. Tobacco (which makes pipe and chewing tobaccos). The business was divided equally among them, and today, each of the companies still has about a third of the U.S. snuff business. Not more than 5 percent goes to all other makers.

Most people still think that snuff is taken in delicate pinches from enamel boxes and twisted painterly upon the nostril. But very little snuff today is used to induce sneezes. Most snuff is still taken in pinches but stored in the mouth where it is stored for hours, squeezed between gum and cheek. Snuff is a lot more compact, neater and less noticeable than chewing tobacco. Sixty percent of U.S. snuff sales are made in the South, but the Northwest and middle West and New England are good markets, too. Factory hands, lumberjacks, ship workers, farmhands, college professors, baseball players, and church dignitaries, who can't smoke at their work, are important snuff users. U.S. senators used to be great snuff users. In the Senate chamber there are still two snuff boxes—one on the Democratic side of the rostrum and the other on the Republican side. No senator uses snuff anymore—the last snuff chewer was the late Lee Overman—but Senator Harrison rolls it nervously around between his fingers and a senator's secretary dips into the box quite frequently. The Senate, jealous of tradition, replenishes its supply regularly. The boxes have to be replaced almost as often, since visitors are always stealing them. Italian snuff boxes were once used, but when Tom Heflin was on an anti-papist rampage, someone noticed that the boxes bore a distinctly papal design. Before Senator Heflin could catch up with the fact, Japanese boxes were hurriedly substituted and have been used ever since.

The best kind of snuff tobacco is called "dark fired"—a rich, heavy leaf that gets its peculiar, strong flavor from long fermenting. It generally costs more than the cigarette leaf and comes mostly from Kentucky, Tennessee, and Virginia. Half of the 4,000,000 pounds of snuff tobacco used annually in the U.S. (330,000,000 pounds go into cigarettes) is dark fired. Milder, lighter tobaccos are blended into most brands. Snuff users are quick to notice and resent any change in their blends, but are very faithful to a brand once they start using it. Most advertising for that reason is of little use. The most glamorous pictured ladies of the most scientific of reasons couldn't woo, say, a user of Helme's "Buttercup Sweet" over American Tobacco's "Dental" or U.S. Tobacco's "Copenhagen."

1935 Profile

Donald Davis's deep knowledge of the American consumer allowed him to blend Wheaties, radio and athletes into a successful package.

Life at Home

- Donald Davis helped raise the visibility of both ready-to-eat Wheaties and the fledgling business of radio advertising.
- Wheaties started product life in 1921 as the scattered droppings on a hot stove.
- A Minneapolis health clinician had stirred a batch of bran gruel a little too vigorously, resulting in the spill.
- The result was thin wafers of wheat bran with the potential to become a healthy, tasty breakfast food.
- But success was not immediate: 36 varieties of wheat were tried before the Washburn-Crosby Company, the forerunner to General Mills, discovered a flake that would not crumble in the box—a two-year process.
- Yet the discovery came at the same time bran was being touted as the ideal disciplinarian of the digestive tract and an increasingly urban America was showing an interest in breakfast cereal that demanded less preparation.
- The wife of a Washburn-Crosby Company executive, who won a company-sponsored contest to name the new product, suggested Wheaties because "there's nothing as endearing as a nickname."
- Only then did Wheaties appear on grocery shelves in 1924, and was quickly termed "a slow mover."
- Donald Davis believed that the customer was not simply a sales report; the customer was a human being with needs to be satisfied and tastes to be pleased.
- With an engineer's faith in numbers, Davis rejected the idea that consumer tastes were unknowable or mysterious.

Donald Davis made Wheaties visible through the media.

- His method was simple: ask thousands of customers in every geographic area what they wished to eat, what products they liked best and what newspapers and magazines they read.
- All human needs were quantifiable.
- His researchers were constantly ringing doorbells, making phone calls and mailing out questionnaires; his sales force was constantly on the prowl for data on the American housewife.
- What he discovered on these excursions into the minds of American women was that they liked to be spoken to directly, frequently and intimately where matters of food were concerned.
- These preferences spawned the delightfully knowledgeable—albeit fictitious—answer lady, Betty Crocker.
- The name was first created in 1921 as a way to give a personalized response to consumer product questions; the name Betty was selected because it was viewed as a cheery, all-American name.
- Under the supervision of home economist and businesswoman Marjorie Child Husted, the image of Betty Crocker was transformed into an icon for General Mills.
- She received thousands of letters daily.
- In the midst of this atmosphere, Donald laid out a proposal in 1924 that seemed outlandish in its dimensions: to operate the company's own radio station to promote Minneapolis-St. Paul and General Mills's products.
- "Let's walk around the idea," Donald told his staff.
- Radio was still in its crystal set infancy, viewed by most as a toy to hypnotize teenage boys, not a business game changer.
- Donald saw this toy as a major force of communications.
- He was determined to make his company a pioneer in this new medium.
- After all, an electrical engineer at the University of Minnesota had been a leader in radio development, and its menu lists journal operated station WLAG, known for its slogan "the call of the North."
- The stations owned by manufacturers and department stores were established to sell radios, and those owned by newspapers to sell papers and express the opinions of the owners.
- But WLAG was on its last legs when Donald pulled together a group of Minneapolis-St. Paul businessmen to buy half the station and its equipment, on the condition the Twin Cities would assume responsibility for the other half.
- In the deal, the stations call letters were changed to WCCO for Washburn-Crosby Company.
- Seven months later, WCCO made history in the Midwest by using its 5,000-watt voice to broadcast the inauguration of President Calvin Coolidge.
- Thus, the stage was set for Wheaties and radio to execute a decade-long two-step that benefited both.
- In the mid-1920s, the market for ready-to-eat cereal was small—almost as small as the market for the fledgling but emerging radio.
- The answer was inventive: join the two.

Life at Work

- Donald Davis helped breathe new life into the flagging cereal brand Wheaties when Minnesota radio station WCCO formed a male quartet named The Gold Medal Four composed of a municipal court bailiff, printer, businessman, and undertaker, who were paid $24 a week for their work.
- Together, they produced the world's first singing commercial, sung to the tune of the popular song, "She's a Jazz Baby."

The first singing commercials were used to promote Wheaties.

- "Have you tried Wheaties?/They're whole wheat with all the bran/Won't you try Wheaties?/For wheat is the best food of man."
- Two years later, in 1929, as pressure mounted to dump the lagging Wheaties brand at the newly named General Mills Company, research showed that of the 53,000 cases of Wheaties shipped annually, 30,000 cases were going to the Minneapolis-St. Paul area, where the commercials were being broadcast.
- The advertising was working, but a new national approach was needed; a campaign to attain the company's goal to "develop services worthy of the American people."
- The management of General Mills, even before Donald became its president, believed that advertising copy must be "truthful, based on the concept of service, and must be designed to expand the market and not simply take business from the competitors."
- The answer to saving Wheaties was nationwide radio.
- If Wheaties was to be a national brand, Donald fully understood that radio advertising, featuring the Wheaties quartet on national hook-up, was a necessary gamble.
- The vehicle would be the sponsorship of half-hour music programs being created by an upstart company known as Columbia Broadcasting Company.
- The next step was to tailor the message to the right audience.

Wheaties offered special membership for kids.

- The answer came in the form of *Skippy*, a popular comic strip with both the public and Donald personally, who could be transformed into a radio character.
- Finally, General Mills had a way to talk directly to children, instead of through their parents; an advertisement in *The Saturday Evening Post* reading "Make Your Child Love Whole Wheat" was clearly not working.
- Teamed with *Skippy*, Wheaties could offer special treats like membership in a secret-society-of-the-air, unfiltered by parents, for the price of several box tops.
- Then, to make sure mothers were not alienated by this rarified "avenue to the house," Donald's team worked with *Skippy* creator Percy Crosby to organize "no more arguments at breakfast" campaigns.
- When *Skippy*'s power to persuade began to fade and the concerns of child experts were on the rise, Jack Armstrong, the All-American Boy, became the next radio phenomenon under the control of General Mills.
- The storylines centered around the globe-trotting adventures of Armstrong, a popular athlete at Hudson High School, his friends Billy Fairfield and Billy's sister Betty, and their "Uncle Jim," James Fairfield, an industrialist.
- "Uncle Jim" Fairfield's need to visit exotic parts of the world in connection with his business gave Jack Armstrong plenty of adventures.
- Sponsored throughout its run by Wheaties, the 15-minute serial often offered radio premiums, "souvenirs" of the various shows that usually related to Jack's adventures.
- The campaign to push ham and eggs off the breakfast table was further advanced when Donald was persuaded to launch the company into major radio sponsorship of baseball—the domain of men.
- Since 1927, Wheaties advertising had appeared on a billboard at Nicollet Park, home of the Minneapolis Millers minor league baseball team.
- The slogan for the cereal, "Wheaties—The Breakfast of Champions," was created to meet the needs of billboard advertising, and then became as familiar as the famous athletes that gave testimonials for the cereal.
- Wheaties-sponsored baseball broadcasts began from one radio station in Minneapolis, Minnesota, initially covering the minor league Minneapolis Millers on station WCCO.
- This radio sponsorship of baseball games soon expanded to 95 other radio stations and professional teams throughout the country.

"The Breakfast of Champions" slogan was first used by the Minneapolis Millers.

- And as the number of sponsorships grew, the sale of Wheaties followed, topping 1.5 million cases.
- By 1934, the General Mills Company began including pictures of athletes on its Wheaties boxes to help sell the cereal and establish Wheaties as a brand name.
- The first sports figures to appear on the Wheaties cereal box were baseball stars—Lou Gehrig of the New York Yankees and Jimmie Foxx of the Philadelphia Athletics.
- They were followed that year by aviator Elinor Smith and tennis star Ellsworth Vines.
- Within a few years, the slogan "Breakfast of Champions" was so ingrained in the sports culture that athletes who struck out or missed an easy fly ball were accused of failing to "eat their Wheaties" that day.

Life in the Community: Minneapolis-Saint Paul, Minnesota

- Minneapolis-Saint Paul, the most populous urban area in the state of Minnesota, was built around the Mississippi, Minnesota and St. Croix rivers.
- Growth in the 1800s was fueled by agriculture; by 1880, the region was the acknowledged leader in the production of breadstuffs.
- Farmers found that hard red spring wheat was the answer to the harsh, physical conditions of the north central states; in addition, the wheat's hardness resulted from a higher proportion of gluten to starch, giving it a special value as a bread flour.
- The area was nicknamed The Twin Cities for its two largest cities, Minneapolis and Saint Paul, the former the larger and the latter the state capital.
- As early as 1872, publications started using the phrase Dual Cities to describe the cities, which evolved into Twin Cities.
- Despite the Twin moniker, the two cities had independent municipalities with defined borders and were quite distinct from each other; Minneapolis was influenced by its early Scandinavian/Lutheran heritage, while St. Paul was characterized by its early French, Irish and German Catholic roots.

Growth in the 1880s was fueled by agriculture.

- Minneapolis and St. Paul have competed against each other since they were founded.
- Both cities built campuses of the University of Minnesota, and after St. Paul completed its elaborate cathedral in 1915, Minneapolis quickly built the equally ornate Basilica of St. Mary in 1926.
- In the late nineteenth and early twentieth centuries, the competition became so intense that an architect practicing in one city was refused business in the other.
- The rivalry even led to the two cities arresting and kidnapping each other's census takers during the 1890 United States Census in an attempt to keep either city from outgrowing the other.
- The situation could occasionally erupt into inter-city violence, as happened at a 1923 game between the Minneapolis Millers and the St. Paul Saints, both baseball teams of the American Association.

HISTORICAL SNAPSHOT
1935

- Dry Tortugas National Park was established in Florida
- Italian Premier Benito Mussolini and French Foreign Minister Pierre Laval concluded an agreement in which each power agreed not to oppose the other's colonial claims
- Amelia Earhart became the first person to fly solo from Hawaii to California
- The FBI killed the Barker Gang, including Ma Barker, in a shootout
- Coopers Inc. sold the world's first briefs
- Iceland became the first country to legalize abortion on medical grounds
- Bruno Richard Hauptmann was convicted and sentenced to death for the kidnapping and murder of Charles Lindbergh, Jr.
- Airplanes were banned from flying over the White House
- Porky Pig debuted in the Looney Tunes movie, *I Haven't Got a Hat*
- Adolf Hitler announced plans for German rearmament in violation of the Versailles Treaty
- Persia was renamed Iran
- Great dust storms hit eastern New Mexico and Colorado; western Oklahoma suffered the worst of the storms
- *Fibber McGee and Molly* debuted on NBC Radio
- Executive Order 7034 created the Works Progress Administration, known as the WPA, to reduce the number of unemployed in America
- The first nighttime Major League baseball game was played between the Cincinnati Reds and Philadelphia Phillies at Crosley Field in Cincinnati, Ohio
- Baseball star Babe Ruth appeared in his last career game, playing for the Boston Braves in Philadelphia against the Phillies
- Alcoholics Anonymous was founded in Akron, Ohio, by William G. Wilson and Dr. Robert Smith, who at first banned women from attending meetings, creating an all-male fellowship
- James J. Braddock defeated Max Baer at Madison Square Garden to win the Heavyweight Boxing Championship of the World
- The Leo Burnett Advertising Agency opened in Chicago, Illinois
- President Franklin D. Roosevelt signed the Social Security Act into law
- Howard Hughes, flying the Hughes H-1 Racer, set an airspeed record of 352 mph
- Parker Brothers created the board game Monopoly
- Mary McLeod Bethune founded the National Council of Negro Women

Selected Prices

Cereal, Large Box.. $0.27
House Kit $493.00
Kitchen Range $76.95
Pedestal Lavatory $15.00
Pocket Knife.. $0.95
Radio $38.95
Smoking Tobacco, Can.. $0.15
Spark Plug $0.60
Sunglasses.. $1.98
Toothbrushes, Pair $0.50

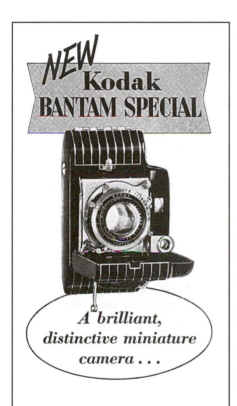

NEW **Kodak BANTAM SPECIAL**

A brilliant, distinctive miniature camera . . .

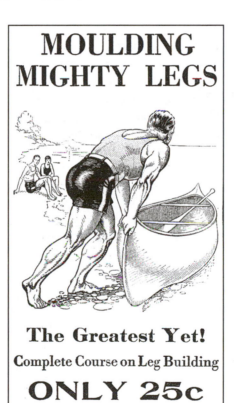

MOULDING MIGHTY LEGS

The Greatest Yet!

Complete Course on Leg Building

ONLY 25c

This compact, ready-prepared soap will wash all your dishes for a month for 25¢

"Rise of Radio Creates New Church Problem, Some Ministers Fear Broadcasting the Church Services Will Decrease Attendance, Most Observers Think Radio 'Sells' Religion," *The New York Times*, August 3, 1924:

Every churchgoer with a radio set has a practical choice to make when Sunday comes around. "Shall I put on my best clothes and go to church or shall I keep my slippers on and attend service in my easy chair?"

Now that a considerable section of every congregation in the country has a radio set, the question of the effect on the Church commands the attention of religious leaders all over the country. That the effect of radio on religion will be profound is deemed certain, but just what the effect will ultimately be is still a matter of conjecture.

For the Catholic Church the question has no immediate importance because church discipline compels physical attendance at Mass. But for the Protestant denominations it has become an outstanding issue. Some ministers have met it one way, others in another, some have not met it at all.

There has been, naturally, considerable apprehension among Protestant leaders about the radio. If the congregations of the future can get a sermon, music, in fact, all the audible parts of the whole religious service simply by turning a button in their homes, will they make the physical exertion of going to church anymore? That small oval, perched on a pulpit like a darkened reading lamp, which has brought hundreds of thousands of listeners into the range of the speaker's voice, might reduce church ritual to a mere talking into an instrument in a church full of empty pews, or even talking into a radio disc among the upholsterings of some broadcasting studio. Furthermore, what effect might radio have on the rural chapel if all the facilities of the powerful metropolitan church were thus placed at the easy disposal of people in the outlying parish?

The more progressive elements in New York's Protestant churches have taken the bull by the horns, and during the past year or so have incorporated radio into their program of action. This same decision has been made in other cities throughout the country, of course, but it is in New York and vicinity the outstanding experiment has been made.

In New York, two distinct methods have been employed: one, that of broadcasting sermons directly from churches during the regular Sunday morning service; the other, broadcasting an ancillary religious program, held specifically in a broadcasting studio, or in a Y.M.C.A. in the afternoon, so as not to conflict with Sunday morning services. This distinction is worth bearing in mind, for reflexive difference of opinion in the subject of radio even among those who favor its use....

An inquiry into the results of this use of the radio has brought to light interesting facts and opinions from persons who are in close touch with the situation. Two questions were asked:

First, how has the radio affected interest in religion?

Second, how has radio reacted on church attendance?

continued

"Rise of Radio Creates New Church Problem, Some Ministers Fear Broadcasting the Church Services Will Decrease Attendance, Most Observers Think Radio 'Sells' Religion," *(continued)*

The response to the first question has been affirmative. In the words of those interviewed, the radio has "sold" religion to the community on a broader scale than ever before.

Radio has sold religion by bringing it to hundreds of thousands of people that otherwise would not have been reached at all. Upon this, all the clergymen agreed. It has forced religion upon the attention of many who never go to church, both those who could not and those who would not. In the latter case, it is largely a matter of the line of least resistance. The broadcasting stations have cooperated fully with the churches to avoid any competitory feature at the time. Fans who tuned up on Sunday morning and afternoon had to get religion, if they got anything.

In the latter case, it has sometimes made a revolutionary change in the immediate background of the theme. As Heyward Broun expressed it once, it was the "first time in his life that he had been able to go to church, smoke a cigarette while listening to a sermon and throw in an occasional cuss word when the minister said something he didn't like."

This is certainly different from the old conventional setting for religion, but many of the clergy don't seem particularly worried. They prefer to have people listen to sermons, even flavored with tobacco smoke, than not at all. In fact, it was an Episcopalian rector, a representative of a church supposed to be the acme of traditionalism, that mentioned this incident as an example of the advantages of radio.

"The radio has shown itself to be a beneficial factor in religious life," said the Rev. William B. Miller, Secretariat in New York Federation of churches. As the central organization of Protestant Christian Churches in New York, the foundation has had charge of the broadcasting of religious programs from station WEAF since the feature was introduced a year ago. "There has been a marked increase in interest in religion recently. True, there has been contributing causes, such as the modernist-fundamentalist controversy. But radio undoubtedly had a large share.

"The function of radio, as I see it, is to supplement the churches, to get to an element in society which they cannot reach. It has possibilities within the church, of course; our radio 'normal school' course for Sunday school teachers illustrates this point. But its chief value, I believe, is to bring religion to people who either cannot or will not attend church."

"Harvard Palates Provide Problem, College Authorities Have Constant Task to Meet Food Likes and Dislikes," *The New York Times*, October 14, 1934:

One of the big problems of Harvard College authorities is that of satisfying more than 3,000 healthy but widely varied student appetites. Harvard undergraduates, it appears, have very definite likes and dislikes when they sit down to meals in the undergraduate dining halls.

For example, they don't care for "New England boiled dinners" or "New England fish dinners," although a large percentage comes from homes in the section where these dishes were made famous, and curiously, they like spinach and eat plenty of it, but never have pie or doughnuts for breakfast.

Among the meals, steak ranks first in popularity, with chicken, lamb chops and roast beef following in that order.

A visiting committee of 20 women, mothers of students, is appointed by the Harvard Board of Overseers each year. These women inspect the menus, talk to the students, and eat in the dining halls about once a week, and offer suggestions to the management.

Menus are so diversified that there is no sense of sameness.

Typical menus are:

Breakfast: Sliced banana or preserved peaches; oatmeal, Wheat Krumbles, cornflakes, Post Toasties, puffed wheat, Shredded Wheat biscuits, Wheaties, Post bran flakes, Pep, puffed rice, rice flakes, Rice Krispies, All Bran, scrambled eggs with bacon, or boiled eggs; toast, rolls, muffins and grilled cakes, tea, coffee, cocoa, milk or buttermilk.

Luncheon: Hamburger steak with mushroom sauce, poached eggs, sautéed potatoes, buttered new cabbage, lettuce hearts with French dressing, cinnamon buns, sliced pineapple, apple pie, cherry cookie; coffee, cocoa, milk, buttermilk; choice of dry cereals, crackers and milk; ice cream or fruit served in the place of meat or dessert.

Dinner: Bisque of tomato; grilled lamb chop, sausage and bacon, French fried sweet potatoes, green string beans, Parker House rolls; pineapple and cream cheese salad; fudge spumoni ice cream, assorted cake and coffee.

Radio Timeline

1916
The first regular broadcasts on 9XM featured Wisconsin state weather, delivered in Morse Code.

1919
The first clear transmission of human speech occurred on 9XM after experiments with voice (1918) and music (1917).

1920
Regular wireless broadcasts for entertainment began in Argentina, pioneered by the group around Enrique Telémaco Susini.

E.W. Scripps's WWJ in Detroit received its commercial broadcasting license and carried a regular schedule of programming.

August 31, 1920
The first known radio news program was broadcast by station 8MK, the unlicensed predecessor of WWJ (AM) in Detroit, Michigan.

October 1920
Westinghouse in Pittsburgh, Pennsylvania, became the first U.S. commercial broadcasting station to be licensed when it was granted call letters KDKA.

Mid-1920s
Amplifying vacuum tubes developed by Westinghouse engineers dramatically improved radio receivers and transmitters, replacing the crystal set receivers.

Inventions of the triode amplifier, generator, and detector improved audio.

Early 1930s
Single sideband (SSB) and frequency modulation (FM) were invented by amateur radio operators.

Westinghouse was brought into the patent allies group, General Electric, American Telephone and Telegraph, and Radio Corporation of America, and became a part owner of RCA.

1933
FM radio, which Edwin H. Armstrong invented, was patented; FM used frequency modulation of the radio wave to minimize static and interference from electrical equipment and the atmosphere in the audio program.

Wheaties advertisement featuring baseball great Lou Gehrig:

I believe any man who wants to go places in any sport has to keep in good physical shape. I always watch my eating pretty closely and make it a point to put away a good breakfast in the morning. But I want my food to taste good, too. And there's nothing better than a big bowl of Wheaties with plenty of milk or cream and sugar. That's a "Breakfast of Champions" you want to try. You'll be glad you did. Because Wheaties sure taste great!

General Mills Timeline

1866
Cadwallader Washburn, owner of Minneapolis Milling Company, opened the first flour mill in Minneapolis.

1877
John Crosby entered into partnership with Washburn, whose company was then renamed the Washburn-Crosby Company.

1880
The Washburn-Crosby Company won a gold medal at the first International Millers' Exhibition, leading to the later creation of the Gold Medal brand.

1888
James S. Bell took over leadership of the Washburn-Crosby Company.

1921
The fictional Betty Crocker was created by Washburn-Crosby.

1924
Wheaties ready-to-eat cereal debuted.

1928
James S. Bell's son, James Ford, led the creation of General Mills through the merger of Washburn-Crosby with several other regional millers.

1931
Bisquick, the first baking mix, was introduced.

1939 Profile

In a journey that took more than two decades, inventor Herbert Thomas Kalmus knew he had made Technicolor a success when he correctly captured the color of his wife's red hair and blue eyes.

Life at Home

- When Herbert Thomas Kalmus enrolled at Massachusetts Institute of Technology in 1900, he was a serious-minded youngster determined to make himself an authority in the new field of electrochemistry.
- Two years later, he met red-haired Natalie Dunfee from Norfolk, Virginia, who was studying art and drama in Boston.
- After he received his bachelor's degree from MIT in 1904 married Natalie, Herbert earned his doctorate at the University of Zurich, then taught physics, electrochemistry, and metallurgy at MIT and Queen's University, Kingston, Ontario, Canada.
- In 1912, Herbert and fellow MIT graduate Daniel Comstock formed Kalmus, Comstock, and Wescott, an industrial research and development firm, with mechanic W. Burton Wescott.
- When the firm was hired to analyze an inventor's flicker-free motion picture system, they became intrigued with the art and science of filmmaking, particularly the color motion picture processes.
- Movie studios were already experimenting with how to add splashes of color to their black-and-white feature films using film tinting; yellow indicated daytime, blue designated night scenes.
- The technique was crude and cumbersome.
- Ultimately, the newly invented device for making motion pictures, called Vanascope, proved to be unworkable, but excited Herbert and his partners.
- But when Vanascope's financial backers agreed to fund further experiments through Kalmus, Comstock, and Wescott, Herbert

Herbert Thomas Kalmus invented Technicolor.

quickly established a standard whenever a new color dye was being tested: his wife Natalie's red hair and blue eyes.

- In 1915, when they decided to test the possibilities of movies as full of color as the real world, the landscape was already littered with companies that had tried and failed to bring full color to picture shows.
- Two years were consumed in the pursuit until 1917, when they hit on a satisfactory process that Herbert called Technicolor—Tech in honor of his alma mater, Massachusetts Institute of Technology.
- The first Technicolor process, a two-color system, utilized a special projector to superimpose red and green filters on the film.
- But the process was cumbersome and needed major funding.
- To make the invention practical, they built a complete photochemical laboratory on a railway car with plans to roll it anywhere a picture company was working and deliver processed film on the spot.
- The railway car's only trip was to Florida to film the first Technicolor movie, *The Gulf Between*, in which Natalie played a leading role.
- But at the preview before a scientific gathering in New York, something went wrong as the film sped through the projector.
- Horses appeared on the screen with two tails, one red, the other one green.
- After a few tries at regular theaters, further showings were canceled.
- Three years later the trio was ready with a new camera that shot two exposures simultaneously, after which the colors were transferred to the master film.
- The results were so impressive that several movie magnates invested considerable capital in the future of Technicolor; Nicholas Schenek even contracted for a full-length picture, *The Toll of the Sea*.
- Its screening in 1922 brought enthusiastic approval; unfortunately, it took almost a year to turn out enough prints to release the picture all over the country, seriously limiting its profitability.
- Producers were impressed, but distributors thought it was too expensive; prints for the movie cost $0.27 a foot to make.
- Herbert met this objection by raising even more money from his friends and backers to build larger laboratories in Boston and Hollywood to crank down the ballooning costs.
- At the same time, Natalie and Herbert divorced, but continued to work together and live in the same house for the next two decades.
- Together, they perfected the process, and in 1926 saw Technicolor used it in parts of the Douglas Fairbanks movie *The Black Pirate*, but the film suffered from technical issues that left the industry skeptical.
- A few more color films followed before the tide turned.
- In 1929, the movie industry, flush with cash and intrigued by the emergence of talkies, turned to color with enthusiasm; efficient processing had cut the price to $0.07 a foot and reduced the unnatural intensity of the final product.
- The success of films such as *Gold Diggers of Broadway* had given Technicolor more contracts to its plant than it could produce in two years.
- Then the Great Depression hit.
- Just as the film pioneers were prepared to reap their own rewards for 15 years of experimentation, studio after studio removed color from their budgets.
- By 1931, Herbert's carefully trained staff of 1,200 had been sliced to 230.

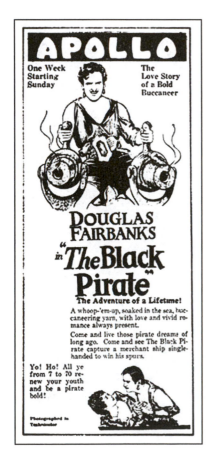

One of the first films to use Technicolor was "The Black Pirate."

Life at Work

- Herbert Kalmus knew he was in the catbird seat when he watched the final screening of *Gone With the Wind* in 1939.
- Everything was perfect, especially for Technicolor.
- After 25 years of experimentation, the movie world had finally discovered the power of color.
- There were only 30 Technicolor cameras in existence and Herbert owned them all.
- Four were in England and 26 in the United States; the price of admission was a $25,000 check, the customary deposit for rental of a Technicolor camera.
- As protective as a new father, Herbert doled them out to the studios most likely to use his invention properly.
- The Walt Disney Studios was among the first to truly grasp Technicolor's potential.
- Even if it demanded two-year exclusivity rights, the payoff came when the world watched *Snow White and the Seven Dwarfs* in color—Herbert's color.
- To ensure quality, Natalie followed the cameras onto the film set to see that color was not used simply to attract attention, but woven into the fabric of the picture show.
- Twenty-six Technicolor cameras, working around the clock, enabled producers to turn out a dozen major features in color and twice that many shorts.
- In exchange, these studios paid Herbert and his associates more than $5 million; a full-length motion picture in Technicolor cost from $100,000 to $250,000 extra to make.
- Making a film in Technicolor was complex.
- Along with each of the jumbo cameras that shot three films simultaneously using three different color filters—the key to Technicolor's sharp, true tones— went a team of technicians whose know-how had been accumulated during more than two decades of painful experiments and near-misses.

Cartoons came to life with the aid of color.

- Filming in Technicolor required more production time, demanded more electrical power and prevented studios from using stock footage from the film library as a way to drive down costs.
- The company's big break came when Walt Disney used the new Technicolor film in his cartoon shorts, particularly the Oscar-winning *Flowers and Trees* in 1932 and *The Three Little Pigs* in 1933.
- After Disney demonstrated that the scripts could be written for color, other studios followed suit; producers, directors and writers incorporated the cost of color into their films.
- The first full-length picture shot in Technicolor was *Becky Sharp*, produced by Pioneer Pictures in association with Technicolor Corporation and released by RKO in 1935.
- In 1936, the Technicolor plant was turning out three million feet per month.
- The use of dramatic color was bolstered by the production of *The Trail of the Lonesome Pine*, which featured rich scenes of natural scenery in full color.

- But progress towards a wider adoption of Technicolor was slow in contrast to the acceptance of sound, which had pushed aside silent movies in under a decade.
- Herbert was so focused on color quality, he instituted controls in 1935 to the use of Technicolor that added to its costs.
- Studios using his innovation were required to employ his technicians, Technicolor's makeup and Technicolor's processing.
- The producer also had to hire a Technicolor consultant who had authority over how color was used in each scene.
- And because threading the firm was a slow, cumbersome process, directors rented two cameras to save time and keep the production rolling.
- After a few moderate successes, Fox Studios embarked on a full slate of Technicolor films, featuring Westerns and musicals.
- The industry remained split: black-and-white was traditional and gritty; color was glossy and eye-popping.
- Top stars such as Claudette Colbert and Joan Crawford were concerned they didn't photograph well in color.
- Then came a stream of spectacular hits: *Snow White and the Seven Dwarfs*, *The Wizard of Oz* and *Gone With the Wind*—all in Technicolor.
- To meet the needs of *Gone With the Wind*, Herbert produced a film that was more light sensitive and similar to monochrome film capable of rendering a tight grain critical to final production.
- Also, the use of prisms to split colors naturally and better lighting techniques had erased the gaudiness of earlier film productions.
- The showing of *Gone With the Wind* in December 1939 was a huge, widely anticipated event.
- Margaret Mitchell's 1936 novel was produced by David O. Selznick in the American South around the time of the Civil War, and shot in Hollywood.
- *Gone With the Wind* starred Clark Gable, Vivien Leigh, Leslie Howard, Olivia de Havilland, and Hattie McDaniel.
- Natalie described the entire process of using Technicolor to being "a ring master to a rainbow."
- Herbert was simply elated.

Life in the Community: Hollywood, California

- Hollywood, California, was a neighborhood in Los Angeles, California—situated west-northwest of downtown Los Angeles.

Hollywood, California.

- Thanks to its fame as the historical center of movie studios and movie stars, the word "Hollywood" was often used as a metonymy of American cinema.
- The name Hollywood was coined by H.J. Whitley while honeymooning with his wife, Gigi, in 1886.
- By 1900, the area had a post office, newspaper, hotel and two markets.
- A single-track streetcar line ran down the middle of Prospect Avenue, but service was infrequent and the trip took two hours.
- The old citrus fruit-packing house was converted into a livery stable, improving transportation for the inhabitants of Hollywood.
- Los Angeles, with a population of 100,000, lay 10 miles east through the vineyards, barley fields, and citrus groves.
- Hollywood was incorporated as a municipality in 1903, and three months later the voters in Hollywood decided, by a vote of 113 to 96, to ban liquor from the city, except when it was being sold for medicinal purposes.
- By 1910, struggling to secure an adequate water supply, town officials voted for Hollywood to be annexed into the City of Los Angeles, whose water system was piping water down from the Owens River.
- That same year, director D.W. Griffith was sent by the Biograph Company to the West Coast with his acting troupe, consisting of actors Blanche Sweet, Lillian Gish, Mary Pickford, Lionel Barrymore, and others.
- While there, the company decided to explore new territories, traveling several miles north to Hollywood, which was friendly and enjoyed the movie company filming there.
- Griffith then filmed the first movie ever shot in Hollywood, *In Old California*, a melodrama about California in the 1800s.
- After hearing about Biograph's success in Hollywood, many movie-makers headed west to avoid the fees imposed by Thomas Edison, who owned patents on the movie-making process.
- Before World War I, movies were made in several U.S. cities, but filmmakers gravitated to Southern California, attracted by the mild climate and reliable sunlight, which made it possible to film movies outdoors year-round, and by the varied scenery that was available.
- *The Jazz Singer*, the first film with synchronized voices, was successfully released as a Vitaphone talkie in 1927.
- In 1929, when the bottom fell out of the global economy, bankrupting millions of people and prompting mass unemployment, Hollywood entered a Golden Age.
- The advent of talking pictures helped re-energize the medium, and people, no doubt desperate for diversion, began flocking to the cinemas in unprecedented numbers.
- Between 60 and 80 million Americans went to the movies once a week or more.
- In the early 1930s, an American movie ticket bought a cartoon, a newsreel, a B-feature and the main film, all of which amounted to four hours' entertainment for a nickel.
- Columbia and Warner Brothers packed theaters across America with films dragged directly from the grim pages of daily newspapers.

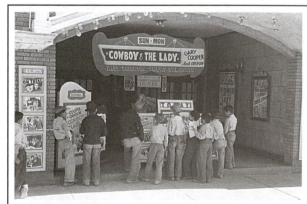

Millions of Americans went to the movies once a week.

- Typical of this tide of social realism was *I Am a Fugitive From a Chain Gang*, a Warner Brothers film in which Paul Muni played a desperate man who is fooled into taking part in a heist and ends up escaping from a vicious Southern chain gang.
- Films were packed with wronged heroes, who seemed as overwhelmed by forces outside their control as the down-at-heel audience watching them.
- Even more popular were the rogues who refused to be cowed by the Depression; audiences reveled in the adventures of organized criminals Edward G. Robinson and James Cagney, who became stars overnight by appearing as vicious thugs.
- Even the most popular comedies of the time were mocking and angry; the Marx Brothers made the transition from Vaudeville to Hollywood in time to gleefully attack the sacred cows of patriotism, monogamy and marriage.
- Hollywood managed to thrive while the rest of the world was collapsing, until the Depression lasted too long.
- All the studios had borrowed heavily to finance the mass purchase of movie theaters and their conversion to sound, leaving the studios heavily in debt.
- By 1933, as mass unemployment took hold of America, cinema attendance began to fall—in that year by a massive 40 percent—and did not recover until the late 1930s.
- MGM dominated the film screen with the top stars in Hollywood, and was also credited for creating the Hollywood star system.
- In 1938, Walt Disney's *Snow White and the Seven Dwarfs* was released during a run of lackluster films from the major studios, and quickly became the highest-grossing film released up to that point.
- A year later, MGM would create the most successful film up to that time and for decades afterwards, *Gone With the Wind*.
- Both *Snow White and the Seven Dwarfs* and *Gone With the Wind* used Technicolor to its best advantage.

Hollywood managed to survive during the Depression.

HISTORICAL SNAPSHOT
1939

- The Hewlett-Packard Company was founded
- Flier Amelia Earhart was officially declared dead after her disappearance during a flight two years earlier
- Adolf Hitler ordered Plan Z, a five-year naval expansion program intended to provide for a huge German fleet capable of crushing the Royal Navy by 1944
- British Prime Minister Neville Chamberlain told the House of Commons that any German attack on France would be automatically considered an attack on Britain
- Sit-down strikes were outlawed by the Supreme Court
- Students at Harvard University demonstrated the new fad of swallowing goldfish to reporters
- African-American singer Marian Anderson performed before 75,000 people at the Lincoln Memorial in Washington, DC, after having been denied the use of both Constitution Hall by the Daughters of the American Revolution, and a public high school by the federally controlled District of Columbia
- John Steinbeck's novel *The Grapes of Wrath* was first published
- Billie Holiday recorded "Strange Fruit," an anti-lynching song
- *Batman*, created by Bob Kane, made his first appearance in a comic book
- Major League Baseball's Lou Gehrig, the legendary Yankee first baseman known as "The Iron Horse," ended his 2,130-consecutive-game streak after contracting amyotrophic lateral sclerosis
- Pan-American Airways began trans-Atlantic mail service with the inaugural flight of its *Yankee Clipper* from Port Washington, New York
- The *St. Louis*, a ship carrying a cargo of 907 Jewish refugees, was denied permission to land in Florida and forced to return to Europe, where many of its passengers later died in Nazi death camps during the Holocaust
- The National Baseball Hall of Fame and Museum was officially dedicated in Cooperstown, New York

- The First World Science Fiction Convention opened in New York City
- Albert Einstein wrote to President Franklin Roosevelt about developing the atomic bomb using uranium, which led to the creation of the Manhattan Project
- MGM's classic musical film *The Wizard of Oz*, based on L. Frank Baum's famous novel, premiered at Grauman's Chinese Theatre in Hollywood

Selected Prices

Camera, Kodak	$20.00
Coca-Cola	$0.25
Home Movie, 16 mm	$8.75
Movie Camera	$49.50
Movie Ticket	$0.25
Nylons	$1.95
Pocket Telescope	$1.00
Seat Covers, Sedan	$5.85
Toothpaste	$0.25
Wall Clock	$6.98

Memorable Movies: 1939

Gone With the Wind	Gunga Din
The Wizard of Oz	Ninotchka
Goodbye, Mr. Chips	Mr. Smith Goes to Washington
Stagecoach	Dark Victory
Wuthering Heights	The Women
Midnight	The Old Maid

"Couldn't you shoot the wedding scenes before the honeymoon sequence? My mother's on the set."

"*Becky Sharp* in Color to Revolutionize Industry, Black-and-White Pictures to Be the Rarity in 10 Years," *The Charleston Gazette* (West Virginia), February 3, 1935:

Jock Whitney's little excursion into the movies is being watched with eager eyes. *Becky Sharp*, the Whitney movie, is all in color. Miriam Hopkins' blonde hair will be as fair as it is in real life, and her deep blue eyes will have their natural tint. And Dr. Herbert Kalmus, as head of Technicolor, said *Becky Sharp* will be the forerunner of other all-color feature films, simply because it will be the first all-color drama.

"In 10 years," said Dr. Kalmus, "black-and-white pictures will be a rarity. Our three-color process has made it possible for every tint to be so distinct and beautiful that the motion picture stars will demand color. We feel that *Becky Sharp* will do for the feature-length pictures what Walter Disney did for cartoons.

"Up to the time Disney made his Silly Symphonies in color, we couldn't get a cartoonist to so much as consider color. Then came *The Three Little Pigs* and other Disney cartoons, which opened up new vistas to other cartoonists who suddenly realized that color was a decided asset to their product."

Luxuries have no place in this college girl's budget

. . . but she can afford a movie record of her undergraduate days

"New Color Technique Marks Film Innovation, Hollywood Plans 13 Technicolor Features," *The Charleston Gazette* (West Virginia), March 1, 1936:

Why is *The Trail of the Lonesome Pine* so much better than any color film yet produced?

At the Wanger Studios, they claim it was made without regard for the color technicians—that Henry Hathaway, the director, put his outdoor epic on the film just as he might have photographed a black-and-white spectacle, and paid no attention to the "dos" and "don'ts" laid down so emphatically in the past by the color experts.

Dr. Herbert Kalmus, just back from a trip abroad, says Walter Wanger is intelligent and that he did have technical advice, but that he didn't let it interfere with his own ideas....

If Technicolor is really as strongly entrenched as everyone says, and it must be since 13 pictures are planned in Hollywood as against the two made last year, then what will be the effect on the motion picture stars of today? Will color have the same effect as sound and eliminate certain favorites, or will it really help those who have facial defects and blemishes to overcome these?

Dr. Kalmus says that beauty of face, hair and character is intensified, and that lack of beauty will not suffer in the flattering tints which make an unattractive woman more attractive, and an ordinary male an Adonis.

"Movie Shorts," *The San Diego Light*, **February 22, 1937:**

Mickey Mouse is going to continue to lead the parade of film stars in Hollywood, and he will continue to be seen in Technicolor. Walt Disney, his proud papa, has just signed a contract with Dr. Herbert Kalmus for 18 shorts including Mickey, Silly Symphonies, and one feature. This feature is *Snow White and the Seven Dwarfs*, and Disney has been working on the famous fairytale for over a year. At the rate he turns out features, it is safe to promise that one will be all he can manage in 12 months.

Photographic Film Timeline

1822
Nicéphore Niépce took the first fixed, permanent photograph, of an engraving of Pope Pius VII, using a non-lens contact-printing "heliographic process."

1826
Nicéphore Niépce took the first fixed, permanent photograph from nature, a landscape that required an eight-hour exposure.

1839
Louis Daguerre patented the daguerreotype.

William Fox Talbot invented the positive/negative process widely used in photography.

1851
Frederick Scott Archer introduced the collodion process, which involved using wet plates.

1854
André-Adolphe-Eugène Disdéri was credited with the introduction of the *carte de visite*, a type of small photograph.

1861
James Clerk Maxwell showed the first color photograph, an additive projected image of a tartan ribbon.

1868
Louis Ducos du Hauron patented a method of subtractive color photography.

1871
Richard Maddox invented the gelatin emulsion.

1878
Eadweard Muybridge made a high-speed photographic demonstration of a moving horse, airborne during a trot, using a trip-wire system.

1887
The celluloid film base was introduced.

Gabriel Lippmann invented a "method of reproducing colors photographically based on the phenomenon of interference."

1888
The Kodak No. 1 box camera was mass marketed as the first easy-to-use camera.

1891
Thomas Edison patented the "kinetoscopic camera" (motion pictures).

continued

Photographic Film Timeline *(continued)*

1895
Auguste and Louis Lumière invented the cinématographe.

1898
Kodak introduced the Folding Pocket Kodak.

1900
Kodak introduced the first Brownie.

1901
Kodak introduced the 120 film format.

1902
Arthur Korn devised a practical phototelegraphy technology used by national wire services.

1907
The Autochrome Lumière became the first color photography process marketed.

1908
Kinemacolor, a two-color process that was the first commercial "natural color" system for movies, was introduced.

1909
Kodak introduced a 35 mm "safety" motion picture film on an acetate base as an alternative to the highly flammable nitrate base. The motion picture industry discontinued its use after 1911 due to technical imperfections.

1912
The Vest Pocket Kodak used 127 film.

Kodak introduced the 22 mm amateur motion picture format, a "safety" stock on acetate base.

1913
Kodak made 35 mm panchromatic motion picture film available on a bulk special order basis.

1914
Kodak introduced the Autographic film system.

The World, the Flesh and the Devil, the first dramatic feature film in color (Kinemacolor), was released.

1920s
Yasujiro Niwa invented a device for phototelegraphic transmission through cable and later via radio.

continued

Photographic Film Timeline *(continued)*

1922
Kodak made 35 mm panchromatic motion picture film available as a regular stock.

Kodak introduced 16 mm reversal film, on a cellulose acetate (safety) base.

1923
Doc Harold Edgerton invented the xenon flash lamp and strobe photography.

1925
Leica introduced the 35 mm format to still photography.

1926
Kodak introduced its 35 mm Motion Picture Duplicating Film for duplicate negatives. Previously, motion picture studios used a second camera alongside the primary camera to create a duplicate negative.

1932
Disney made the first full-color movie, the cartoon *Flowers and Trees*, in Technicolor.

Kodak introduced the first 8 mm amateur motion-picture film, cameras, and projectors.

1934
The 135 film cartridge was introduced, making 35 mm easy to use.

1935
Becky Sharp, the first feature film made in full color (Technicolor), was released.

1936
IHAGEE introduced the Ihagee Kine Exakta 1, the first 35 mm single lens reflex camera.

Kodachrome multi-layered reversal color film was developed.

1937
Agfacolor-Neu reversal color film was introduced.

1939
Agfacolor negative-positive color material, the first modern "print" film, was introduced.

The View-Master stereo viewer was invented.

"Plea for Boycott," *Daily Colonist*, Victoria, Canada, February 5, 1939:

Boycott of Germany and Japan as a means of impressing upon them civilization's disapproval of their actions at the present time, is advocated by Mrs. Lenore D. Underwood, San Francisco attorney-at-law, grand president of the international Jewish organization, B'nai Brith, who addressed a big gathering of women here yesterday afternoon....

The tragedy of the Jewish people in Germany today was not only the tragedy of the Jews. Civilization itself was challenged. No people, no nation, could hope to stand when it was built on hate, said the speaker. Suicides were a daily occurrence in Germany, hopeless victims of ruthless persecution seeing no other way out of their misery. Secret police spied on the Jews' every movement.

A young German refugee in California had told her a story of how his family was seized and hustled off to one of the dreaded concentration camps because he had been one of a small group that met weekly to play cards. Jews in Germany were not allowed to congregate in groups of more than four without reporting to police.

"*The Wizard of Oz* Brings to Screen Something New," *Belton Journal* (Texas), October 12, 1939:

Presenting what is heralded as the most ideal combination of color, music, dancing, spectacle, pageantry, laughs and thrills, *The Wizard of Oz* filmization of the celebrated story by L. Frank Baum comes Sunday and Monday and Tuesday to the Beltonian Theaters, as the most sensational musical to come out of the annals of Hollywood screen entertainment. Successfully combining for the first time adult and juvenile appeal in a motion picture, Technicolor is used for the first time on a sound psychological basis.

1940-1949

The dramatic, all-encompassing nature of World War II dominated the lives and economies of Americans. As Americans became consumed by the national war effort and the need for rapid production of more materials, inventors and entrepreneurs stepped to the front. America quickly shifted from the role of passive observer to fierce warrior following the bombing of Pearl Harbor in December 1941.

People from every social stratum either signed up for the military or went to work supplying the military machine. Even children, eager to do their share, collected scrap metal and helped plant the victory gardens that symbolized America's willingness to do anything to defeat the "bullies." In addition, large amounts of money and food were sent abroad as Americans observed meatless Tuesdays, gas rationing and other shortages to help the starving children of Europe.

Business worked in partnership with government; strikes were reduced, but key New Deal labor concessions were expanded, including a 40-hour week and time and a half for overtime. As manufacturing demands increased, the labor pool shrank, and wages and union membership rose. Unemployment, which stood as high as 14 percent in 1940, all but disappeared. By 1944, the U.S. was producing twice the total war output of the Axis powers combined. The wartime demand for production workers rose more rapidly than for skilled workers, reducing the wage gap between the two to the lowest level in the twentieth century.

From 1940 to 1945, the gross national product more than doubled, from $100 billion to $211 billion, despite rationing and the unavailability of many consumer goods such as cars, gasoline, and washing machines. Interest rates remained low, and the upward pressure on prices remained high, yet from 1943 to the end of the war, the cost of living rose less than 1.5 percent. Following the war, as controls were removed, inflation peaked in 1948; union demands for high wages accelerated. Between 1945 and 1952, confident Americans—and their growing families—increased consumer credit by 800 percent.

To fight inflation, government agencies regulated wages, prices, and the kind of jobs people could take. The Office of Price Administration was entrusted with the complicated task of setting price ceilings for almost all consumer goods and distributing ration books for items in short supply. The Selective Service and the War Manpower Commission largely determined who would serve in the military, whose work was vital to the war effort, and when a worker could transfer from one job to another. When the war ended and regulations were lifted, workers demanded higher wages; the relations between labor and management became strained. Massive strikes and inflation followed in the closing days of the decade and many consumer goods were easier to find on the black market than on the store shelves until America retooled for a peacetime economy.

The decade of the 1940s made America a world power and Americans more worldly. Millions served overseas; millions more listened to broadcasts concerning the war in London, Rome, and Tokyo. Newsreels brought the war home to moviegoers, who numbered in the millions. The war effort also redistributed the population and the demand for labor; the Pacific Coast gained wealth and power, and the South was able to supply its people with much-needed war jobs and provide blacks with opportunities previously closed to them. Women entered the work force in unprecedented numbers, reaching 18 million. The net cash income of the American farmer soared 400 percent.

But the Second World War extracted a price. Those who experienced combat entered a nightmarish world. Both sides possessed far greater firepower than ever before, and within those units actually fighting the enemy, the incidence of death was high, sometimes one in three. In all, the United States lost 405,000 men and women to combat deaths; many suffered in the war's final year, when the American army spearheaded the assault against Germany and Japan. The cost in dollars was $350 billion. But the cost was not only in American lives. Following Germany's unconditional surrender on May 4, 1945, Japan continued fighting. To prevent the loss of thousands of American lives defeating the Japanese, President Truman dropped atomic bombs on the Japanese cities of Hiroshima and Nagasaki, ending the war and ushering in the threat of "the bomb" as a key element of the Cold War during the 1950s and 1960s.

Throughout the war, soldiers from all corners of the nation fought side by side and refined nationalism and what it meant to America through this government-imposed mixing process. This newfound identity of American GIs was further cemented by the vivid descriptions of war correspondent Ernie Pyle, who spent a considerable time talking and living with the average soldier to present a "worm's eye view" of war. Yet, despite the closeness many men and women developed toward their fellow soldiers, spawning a wider view of the world, discrimination continued. African-American servicemen were excluded from the marines, the Coast Guard, and the Army Corps. The regular army accepted blacks into the military—700,000 in all—only on a segregated basis. Only in the closing years of the decade would President Harry Truman lead the way toward a more integrated America by integrating the military.

Sports attendance in the 1940s soared beyond record levels of the 1920s; in football the T-formation moved in prominence, Joe DiMaggio, Ted Williams, and Stan Musial dominated baseball. In 1946, Dr. Benjamin Spock's work, *Common Sense Baby and Child Care*, was published to guide newcomers in the booming business of raising babies. The decade also discovered the joys of fully air-conditioned stores for the first time, cellophane wrap, Morton salt, daylight-saving time, Dannon yogurt, Everglades National Park, the Cannes Film Festival, Michelin radial tires, Dial soap, and Nikon 35mm film.

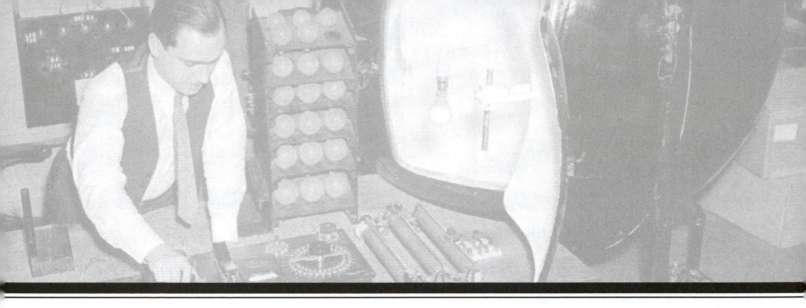

1940 Profile

Thomas Alva Edison and William J. Woods became linked in the history books as the one who invented the electric light bulb, and the other who made it affordable.

Life at Home

- Glassblower William J. Woods was born in 1879, the same year Thomas Alva Edison invented the first commercially successful incandescent electric light bulb.
- Will first arrived in Corning, New York, when he was 19 and newly employed as a glassblower at the Corning Glass Works in 1898.
- A newcomer to Corning, he was raised in Martinsburg, Pennsylvania, the off-spring of an Irish mother and Scottish father who raised three glassblowers.
- As a boy he had learned the art of blowing glass at the Westinghouse Glass Works in western Pennsylvania, but Corning was known to be an innovator; Edison had chosen to work with Corning for 20 years for the same reason.
- Edison's invention of the tinfoil phonograph had already made him famous and garnered him a national tour and an invitation to visit President Rutherford B. Hayes at the White House in April 1878.
- While working to improve the efficiency of a tele-graph transmitter, Edison noted that the tape of the machine gave off a noise resembling spoken words when played at a high speed.

William J. Woods' ribbon machine made electricity affordable.

- This caused him to wonder if he could record a telephone message, and he began experimenting with the diaphragm of a telephone receiver by attaching a needle to it.

By the time Woods was born, Thomas Edison was already a noted inventor.

- His experiments led him to try a stylus on a tinfoil cylinder, which, to his great surprise, played back the short message he recorded: "Mary had a little lamb."
- But his attempts to create a long-lasting electric lamp were stalled by his inability to find a suitable glass bulb, until a message arrived from upstate New York: "We have a glass that may do the job for you."
- The inventor dispatched an assistant to the glass factory for samples, and glassblowers made 165 bulbs the first day.
- The samples were successful, and Corning Glass Works began producing bulbs for Edison's amazing electric lamp.
- As the factory's gaffers—glassblowers—mastered the technique, the production of bulbs rose swiftly.
- When Will arrived at Corning in 1898, a team of four glassworkers using molds turned out more than 1,200 bulbs a day so far behind demand that Edison's much-heralded Age of Universal Light was in danger of not dawning.
- Glassblowers served long apprenticeships, were considered master craftsmen, and were few in number.
- Hand-blown bulbs were so expensive that, even if enough could be produced, electric light would still be outside the financial reach of many people.

- There was also the fear at Corning that major customers such as Westinghouse would begin their own light bulb manufacturing operation.
- By the time Corning's research laboratory was established in 1908, bulbs accounted for over 50 percent of the factory's business.
- Even this huge commitment would not be enough to meet the demands generated by the popularity of electric lighting.

The "E" machine.

- Engineers began the development of a machine to speed bulb production.
- It required a gatherer to supply a glob of glass on a blowpipe, a boy to close the mold and remove the blowpipe, and then close the mold and remove the blowpipe with its finished bulb.
- In 1913, the "E" machine began the world's first automated process for mass light bulb production.
- With four bulb-blowing positions operating, the "solid steel gaffer" was able to produce 10 bulbs per minute.

- The Great War had proved to be a huge stimulus the American industry; in 1914 the U.S. was a large importer of goods.
- But as trade with the Allies rose from $285 million in 1914 to $3.2 billion in 1916, America became an exporter nation for a wide variety of products, including glass.
- In addition, World War I was the first major war powered by electricity; the availability of reliable lighting permitted factories to run around the clock, increasing the demand for light bulbs.
- Corning's sale of bulb glass alone rocketed from $949,000 in 1914 to $1.7 million in 1916; Corning's other major product, Pyrex baking dishes, sold 4.5 million pieces a year as the war drew to a close.
- The more fully automatic bulb blowing "F" machines ended the need for human assistants and achieved production of 42 bulbs a minute.
- It was still not enough.

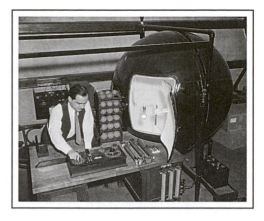

The government was one of the largest users of electricity, and constantly tested light bulbs.

Life at Work

- In 1922, Will Woods was a young Corning Glass Works production superintendent assigned to the Wellsboro, Pennsylvania, facility, with a restless, creative mind, and an idea for a new machine.

The Corning Ribbon Machine.

- The former boxer's inspiration was an ordinary shovel used to collect glass, which had developed a hole in its blade.
- Attached to the shovel's hole was a still-molten glob of glass that looked like a light bulb blank—sparking the revolutionary idea of blowing light bulb blanks through a hole in a metal plate.
- Will reasoned that bulbs could be blown automatically by sagging a ribbon of glass through holes in a continuously moving belt of steel, then shape the glass with a puff of compressed air as molds came up from below.
- Like most ideas that contemplate radical change, the notion was greeted with skepticism and laughter by his fellow glassblowers.
- Working with the company's chief engineer in complete secrecy, Will obtained a piece of boiler plate with a hole in it from the machine shop.

- A compressed air blowhead and a bulb mold completed the experimental equipment; when company officials gathered to view the experiment, a glob of glass was spread over the hole.

Woods helped develop the machine that would soon churn out 250 light bulbs per minute.

- As it sagged through, the blowhead and mold were applied and the bulb was formed.
- From a technical point of view, Will's idea was revolutionary.
- Bulbs and bottles had always been anchored by blowing rods or retaining rings as the hot glass took shape; the use of the plate and gravity was a complete departure.
- Like human glassblowers, early machines had blown upward into the bubble to keep the top thin; Will's idea discarded the approach of imitating the gaffer.
- Will was assigned to work with the chief engineer in designing a machine based on the new principles; over time they would spend $197,000 in development.
- While still working in secret in the company's Wellsboro plant, Will invested several years of patient and inspired effort; in 1926 the first ribbon machine was put into commercial production.
- It was a huge financial success; the ribbon machine was soon producing 250 bulbs per minute.
- By the early 1930s, the machine that Will had conceived was popping out millions of bulbs annually; even though the production of items requiring light bulbs had been slowed by the Great Depression, homes and factories still needed replacement bulbs.
- Light bulbs in a 10-year period had moved from being a luxury item to a necessity, and the versatile ribbon machine still had one more leap to perform.
- For decades, Germany had supplied the world with exquisitely crafted glass Christmas ornaments, a task that was relegated to a low priority when Adolph Hitler invaded Poland in 1939, igniting World War II.
- Corning and the ribbon machine invented by Will leapt into the breach, and in 1940 Corning was making 300,000 ornaments per day; a typical skilled German glassblower was capable of creating about 600 a day in the prewar years.
- Corning sent the Christmas ornament bulbs to a variety of companies.
- The largest customer in 1940 was Max Eckhart, who ran a company known as Shiny Brite; plans to have the ornaments silvered on the inside were shelved by wartime material shortages.
- America, on the brink of war, could still light the house, turn on the Christmas tree and savor the beauty of its ornaments, thanks to the ribbon machine.

Life in the Community: Corning, New York

One of Corning's plants in Pennsylvania.

- Corning, New York was a business-oriented town named for Erastus Corning, an Albany, New York, financier and railroad executive who was an investor in the company that developed the community.
- The Corning area's first real industry was lumber.
- The first settlers in the late 1700s used the area's river systems to transport logs and finished lumber in fleets downstream to buyers.
- This gave rise to large mills which helped develop the area; after the lumber was depleted the great mills moved north to new forests.
- The Chemung River and canal systems also provided employment; in 1850, a newspaper reported that 1,116 boats left the port of Corning and tolls for the year totaled $54,060.39.
- Among the items shipped were 46,572,400 pounds of coal.
- After the Civil War, an industrial boom occurred in the region as Corning became a railroad town in the 1880s.
- Corning Glass Works was originally founded in the Williamsburg section of Brooklyn, New York, but later moved its operations by barge to the city of Corning.
- Corning was one of several glass-cutting firms working in the area.
- The first light bulb blanks used by Thomas Edison were blown up to form in 1880, and the plant installed electric lights as early as 1886.
- In 1887, John Hoare patented the "electric light radiator" of cut glass designed to be a cover for a light bulb.

HISTORICAL SNAPSHOT
1940

- Luftwaffe General Hermann Göring assumed control of all war industries in Germany
- Food rationing began in war-torn Great Britain
- RKO released Walt Disney's second full-length animated film, Pinocchio; Tom and Jerry make their debut in Puss Gets the Boot
- Martin Kamen and Sam Ruben discovered Carbon-14, the basis of the radiocarbon dating method used to determine the age of archaeological and geological finds
- Truth or Consequences debuted on NBC Radio

- Booker T. Washington became the first African-American to be depicted on a U.S. postage stamp
- Following the resignation of Neville Chamberlain, Winston Churchill became prime minister of the Great Britain
- The first McDonald's restaurant opened in San Bernardino, California
- The Dutch and Norway armies surrendered to German forces as France fell
- President Franklin D. Roosevelt asked Congress for approximately $900 million to construct 50,000 airplanes per year
- The Auschwitz-Birkenau concentration and death camp opened in Poland
- World War I General John J. Pershing, in a nationwide radio broadcast, urged all-out aid to Britain in order to defend America, while national hero Charles Lindbergh led an isolationist rally at Soldier Field in Chicago
- The U.S. told Great Britain that 50 U.S. destroyers needed for escort work would be transferred to Great Britain in return for 99-year leases on British bases in the North Atlantic, West Indies, and Bermuda
- Nazi Germany rained bombs on London for 57 consecutive nights
- In Lascaux, France, 17,000-year-old cave paintings were discovered by a group of young Frenchmen hiking through Southern France
- The Selective Training and Service Act of 1940 created the first peacetime draft in U.S. history
- The United States imposed a total embargo on all scrap metal shipments to Japan
- Franklin D. Roosevelt defeated Republican challenger Wendell Willkie to become the first and only third-term president
- Agatha Christie's mystery novel And Then There Were None was published

Selected Prices

Alka Seltzer, Eight Tablets $0.24
Cheese Slicer $0.10
Coffee, Pound $0.33
Lincoln Continental Coupe $2,783.00
Lipstick $1.00
Paper Shelving, Nine Feet $0.05
Radio/Phonograph Cabinet $185.00
Tattoo $0.25
Tea Kettle, Copper $3.49
Varnish, Quart $1.43

Electric Light Bulb Timeline

1809
Humphry Davy, an English chemist, invented the first electric light by connecting two wires to a battery and attaching a charcoal strip between the other ends of the wires; the charged carbon glowed, making the first arc lamp.

1820
Warren De la Rue enclosed a platinum coil in an evacuated tube and passed an electric current through it; the cost of the precious metal platinum made this innovation impractical for widespread use.

1835
James Bowman Lindsay demonstrated a constant electric lighting system using a prototype light bulb.

1850
Edward Shepard invented an electrical incandescent arc lamp using a charcoal filament; Joseph Wilson Swan started working with carbonized paper filaments the same year.

1854
Henricg Global, a German watchmaker, invented the first true light bulb using a carbonized bamboo filament placed inside a glass bulb.

1875
Herman Sprengel invented the mercury vacuum pump, making it possible to develop a practical electric light bulb..

Henry Woodward and Matthew Evans patented a light bulb.

continued

Electric Light Bulb Timeline *(continued)*

1878

Sir Joseph Wilson Swan, an English physicist, was the first person to invent a practical and longer-lasting electric light bulb (13.5 hours); Swan used a carbon fiber filament derived from cotton.

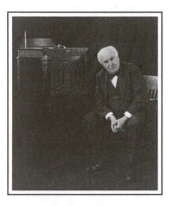

Thomas Alva Edison.

1879

Thomas Alva Edison invented a carbon filament that burned for 40 hours by placing his filament in an oxygenless bulb.

1880

Edison continued to improve his light bulb until it could last for over 1,200 hours using a bamboo-derived filament.

1903

Willis Whitney invented a metal-coated carbon filament that would not make the inside of a light bulb turn dark.

1906

The General Electric Company was the first to patent a method of making Tungsten filaments for use in incandescent light bulbs, though the filaments were costly.

1910

William David Coolidge invented an improved method of making Tungsten filaments, which outlasted all other types of filaments, and Coolidge made the cost practical.

1925

The first frosted light bulbs were produced.

1926

William Woods of Corning Glass Works invented the Ribbon Machine, which automated the process of creating a light bulb sleeve, dramatically reducing the cost of light bulbs.

1940

Corning Glass Works used the Ribbon Machine to create Christmas ornaments.

"Edison Memorial Bulb," *Northern Gazette*, Alberta Canada, December 10, 1937:

The giant electric light bulb, 14 feet tall, which glows as a land beacon atop the $100,000 Edison Memorial Tower at Menlo Park, New Jersey, was completed by the Corning Glass Works.

It took a crew of expert glass workers eight months to complete this emblematic diadem for the tower, the task of laying the model out into curved "orange peel like" sections consuming the greater part of the elapsed time.

The 150-foot beacon will commemorate the invention of the incandescent electric light by Thomas Alva Edison, who in 1879 sent a rough sketch of his idea to Corning, asking that a bulb of glass of definite dimensions be blown.

This original glass bulb, enclosing Edison's carbon filament, became the world's first practical electric light. Corning's contribution to the Memorial commemorating the event is likewise notable since the 14-foot bulb is the first globular cast job in the history of the glass industry.

In preparing the bulb for shipment, more than 6,000 pounds of amber-tinted Pyrex glass were fitted over steel skeleton fashioned in a Bronx iron works and shipped to Corning. The bulb itself consists of 164 pieces of cast glass in a two-inch diamond pattern and is nine feet, six inches in diameter. The combined bulb and steel skeleton weighs six tons.

When finally set up, the giant bulb was transformed into a gleaming tower at night, casting its rays for miles about the surrounding Jersey countryside.

"Patent Approved," *The Wellsboro Agitator* **(Pennsylvania),
November 15, 1916:**

Frank J. Maloney, of Corning, has received word from the U.S. Patent Office at Washington that he has been granted a patent on a machine designed to make a screw-on electric light bulb, in the glass itself, which will save the operation of fastening a brass screw to the bulb. Many have tried to invent such a device but Mr. Maloney is the first to make a screw possible in the glass itself and at the same time have the surface of the bulb perfectly smooth. Mr. Maloney says this will prove a great labor-saving device, as it will be possible for anyone to refill the bulbs when they have been burned out, instead of smashing them up as useless or having them refilled at the factory.

"Regulations Designed for Protection of Motorists," *Logansport Press* (Indiana), December 13, 1921:

Primarily a measure for the protection of motorists using the highways at night, the new automobile light regulations, issued by Secretary of State Jackson, which will be placed in effect December 20, marks another milestone in the progress of the automobile toward perfection.

In the early days of the motor car, neither the type of light used nor the speed of the automobiles necessitated any special regulation governing the illumination of the car at night. Originally, no lights were used on motor cars of any kind, but later, for the protection of the public and other motorists, lights were placed in the car, not to illuminate the road for the benefit of the driver, but to illuminate the car for the benefit of others.

With the development of the electric storage battery and its subsequent use for lighting automobiles, engineers, law enforcement officers and others interested in automobiles were faced with the problem of controlling the blinding glare menace. Headlights, through the use of electricity, became stronger and stronger. Highways became unsafe at night. Accidents became frequent.

It has only been in the last four or five years, however, that the states have begun to take seriously the matter eliminating this blinding glare. It is true that in some localities, failure to use "dimmers" when passing another car would put a driver in a bad light in case of a lawsuit resulting from a subsequent collision, but in Indiana it was not until last winter that the state legislature took up this matter and empowered the Secretary of State to adopt a set of rules and regulations with reference to light control for use in the state of Indiana.

These regulations were announced recently by the Secretary of State, and copies of the rules, together with complete instructions for complying with the Indiana law, may be had from his office upon application.

The light laws of Indiana have been compiled with but one view in mind, namely, to establish a set of uniform light conditions, which will give protection to the motorists using the highways at night. To comply with these orders, motorists must give their attention to the following items:

Equip headlights with proper device.

Install lamps with proper candlepower rating for the device used.

Adjust lamps to proper focus in reflectors.

Adjust or equip headlights to give light beam proper tilt to the road.

"Testimonial Dinner Given in Honor of Corning Glass Works," *The Wellsboro Agitator* (Pennsylvania), September 18, 1940:

Wellsboro spokesmen expressed the appreciation of the community at a testimonial dinner of the Chamber of Commerce and service club members Monday evening at the Penn-Wells Hotel, "thanking" the Corning Glass Works for the establishment of its Christmas tree ornaments manufacturing department in Wellsboro, which has more than doubled the number of persons employed by the Wellsboro division.

Not since the height of the Tioga natural gas drilling at Moon Lake 10 years ago had a Chamber of Commerce meeting generated such enthusiasm in hundreds of persons gathered in the hotel dining room to hear the felicitations exchanged by Wellsboro citizens and Glass Works officials....

The Chamber of Commerce banquet was a "Christmas dinner," and the Corning Glass Works was "Santa Claus," Larry Woodin, official spokesman for the chamber, told the company officials. "Fourteen years ago," Mr. Woodin said, "when I came to Wellsboro, we had hundreds of people walking the streets, with no work, and wondering what they would do when Christmas time came. Now 1,000 people are working for Santa Claus, making Christmas ornaments; everybody has a job, and the town is booming. When Christmas comes around this year, it will be a real Christmas."

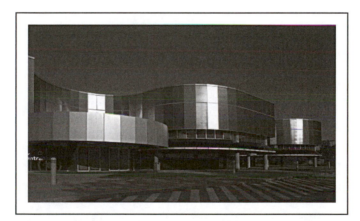

Corning Museum of Glass, Corning, New York.

1945 Profile

Dr. Mary Sears's knowledge of marine tides, which was critical when invading enemy-held islands, allowed the traditionally all-male Navy to overcome its prejudices—at least temporarily.

Life at Home

- In the opening months of the Second World War, U.S. Naval commanders had to overcome two well-established traditions: a distrust of academic types and women in the Navy, especially on ships.
- Born in 1905 and raised in rural Wayland, Massachusetts, outside Boston, Mary took responsibility for raising her two younger siblings in the years after her mother died in 1911.
- When she graduated from Windsor School in Boston in 1923, her classmates believed she was destined for a political career representing the farm bloc in Congress, since she knew everything there was to know about farming, especially raising Guernsey cows.
- At Radcliffe College, Mary planned to study Greek before she was encouraged by her stepmother, a Radcliffe graduate, to explore other subjects.
- A class in biology led to two summers in Bermuda studying corals that triggered a lifetime pursuit of collecting specimens.
- Her pursuit of marine invertebrates channeled her towards a major in zoology, traditionally a male-only path, symbolized by the absence of any women's bathrooms in Harvard's Museum of Comparative Zoology where she spent most of her study time.

Lt. (Dr.) Mary Sears overcame prejudices in the U.S. Navy.

- In 1927, Mary received a bachelor's degree, graduating magna cum laude, and was elected to Phi Beta Kappa; a master's from Radcliffe followed in 1929.
- Her thesis, "The Deep-Seated Melanophones of the Lower Vertebrates," earned her a doctorate in 1933 and served as the foundation for her career in biological oceanography.
- Her next step was employment at the recently opened Woods Hole Oceanographic Institute, where she worked until the early years of the war.
- By then the Navy was eager to embrace new technology; the first few years of the war had been costly and sometimes disastrous.

As a student, Sears enjoyed the study of biology.

- Several island invasions had gone badly, thanks to out-of-date tidal charts and too little knowledge, the result of which was thousands of American soldiers killed.
- Defeating the Germans and the Japanese was going to be difficult.
- World War II, which was clearly shaping up to be a truly technological battle, needed advanced and exact scientific knowledge.
- In addition, the demands of a two-ocean campaign placed enormous pressure on the Navy to rapidly develop new scientific capability.
- Throughout the 1930s, the U.S. Congress had refused to approve funds for oceanographic research by the Navy while the Japanese had assiduously charted the waters of the Pacific Ocean.
- When in early 1942 the War Manpower Commission found itself unable to supply a sufficient number of men, it turned to unorthodox personnel—women.
- Barnard College Dean Virginia C. Gildersleeve remarked, "If the Navy could possibly use dogs or ducks or monkeys, the admirals would probably prefer them to women."
- American women with scientific skills had little incentive to join the Navy or the other services.
- Unlike women in Britain and the Soviet Union, U.S. women were not subject to compulsory military service.
- In fact, the creation of the U.S. draft in September 1940 had taken many young male scientists and mathematicians away from their positions in industry and academia, which opened the way for women in the jobs left behind.
- Not that the list of highly trained women was large.
- Before the war, few women graduated with technical degrees of any sort; fewer than a dozen a year graduated in engineering during the late 1930s.
- Even the Navy's name for the women's organization expressed its ambivalence: WAVES—Women Accepted for Volunteer Emergency Service.

Life at Work

- Shortly after the Japanese attack on Pearl Harbor in December 1941, Dr. Mary Sears made her scientific skills available to the United States Navy.
- Based on the needs—and the financing—of the Navy, the Woods Hole Oceanographic Institute was alive with new projects.
- The collaboration of the Navy and Woods Hole Oceanographic Institute was initially a marriage of convenience that brought money, new equipment and the opportunity to explore untraditional topics.
- Often, different scientifically oriented organizations worked on only parts of any given project, with the Navy itself pulling the final project together.

Sears was determined to make a good impression when she enlisted for WAVES.

- Mary's first assignment was investigating ways to reduce the level of marine life fouling on ships' bottoms, a natural phenomenon that reduced the overall speed of warships—potentially endangering the crew.
- To satisfy the needs of the Navy, Mary created a catalog on barnacles and other organisms that played a part in fouling; this was the first step towards inventing a solution.
- By then Mary was an accomplished oceanographer with little actual experience at sea; even Woods Hole prohibited women from sailing on research vessels because of a lack of "facilities" for women.
- While a graduate student, she had worked at Harvard University with Dr. Henry Bigelow, a founder and the first director of the Woods Hole Oceanographic Institute.
- She began working summers as a planktonologist in 1932, one of the first 10 research assistants to be appointed to the staff at the Institute.
- Although Woods Hole had been a mostly summer-only operation through the 1930s, Mary was named in 1940 as a planktonologist on a year-round basis.
- During this time, she also served as a research assistant at Harvard, a tutor at Radcliffe and an instructor at Wellesley College.
- In 1941, she served at Pisco Bay in Peru as Grant and Faculty Fellow for Wellesley College's Committee on Inter-American Cultural and Artistic Relations.
- When Mary felt called to leave the Institute and join the WAVES, initially the shy, small woman failed a medical exam because of an earlier bout with arthritis.
- But the Old Boy network that she understood so well, and her scientific skills, overcame the bureaucratic hurdles, and she was offered a position as a first lieutenant, junior grade.

- Her first assignment was to head the Oceanographic Unit of the newly formed U.S. Navy Hydrographic Office, whose chief responsibility was the making of navigational charts for use on combat ships.
- The data produced by the Hydro unit were considered "an essential instrument of war" when provided to fleet and shore-based aircraft "in direct combat operations."
  - The need was tremendous.
  - When Mary arrived in June 1943, there were already 43 enlisted WAVES at Hydro with 85 due in July and a projected goal of 250 by September.
  - The need for data was so great, the Hydro unit operated three shifts a day, seven days a week.
  - Mary's team of 12 women and three men included an expert on barnacles, an oceanographic research librarian, the former curator of crustaceans at Harvard University's Museum of Comparative Zoology, an algologist, an limnologist, and Mary served as the planktonologist.
  - The Naval Hydrographic Office was created in 1854 with a focus on ocean bottom mapping for more accurate navigational charts.
  - By the 1930s, the Navy's interest was primarily around submarine warfare and the newly developed sonar technology.
  - Understanding ocean properties such as temperature distribution, pressure, salinity, and bottom characteristics was essential to predicting how sound would travel in the water.
  - Mary's work led to the publication of *Submarine Supplements to the Sailing Directions*, which predicted the presence of thermoclines in certain waters, areas of rapid temperature change in the water column which cause refraction and bending of sound waves.

Sears joined a growing number of enlisted women.

- Thus, the Navy learned that submarines could effectively hide under thermoclines, avoiding detection by ship-mounted sonar devices.
- Naval oceanography was also interested in such diverse subjects as current drift for search and rescue operations and floating mines, surf predictions for amphibious landings, and the turbulent effects of sea and swell waves on moored mines.

The Hydro team worked around the clock laying out navigational charts.

- Marine biology was also an interest, since bioluminescent plankton activated by ship wakes could be used to locate ships in the dark, certain organisms contributed to ambient marine noise that inhibited sonar operations, large kelp growths fouled amphibious landing craft, and certain marine organisms degraded mine mechanisms.

- During the course of the war, the Oceanographic Unit was expanded into a division, and Mary was promoted to lieutenant commander.
- Mary also worked on improving tidal predictions and inventing new ways to mathematically forecast conditions.
- The Navy became ruefully aware of its shortcomings after the battle of Tarawa, when an inaccurate tidal prediction stranded an amphibious group of Marines on a reef, where they were cut to pieces by shore-based Japanese machine gunners.
- Mary further refined her tidal predictions and wave refraction charts to recommend an alternate attack route for the planned amphibious assaults on Luzon and various islands around Okinawa.
- The most taxing of her responsibilities, which were centered primarily in the Pacific and Indian Oceans, was the constant demand for intelligence reports concerning hydrographic factors affecting a possible invasion.
- The reports were always urgently needed for immediate strategic and tactical planning for amphibious operations in the Pacific.
- Her reports, she understood, would impact the lives of thousands; often her best available information on sea and swell in the Indian Ocean came from a Dutch publication written in 1896.
- Time pressure was particularly acute "whenever Roosevelt and Churchill got together," Mary said.
- Often the "pursuit of impossible perfection" had to be abandoned in favor of "quickies" that required her to work all night.
- Her best source of information was provided by the Japanese, who surveyed the ocean and published extensive tracts about Asian waters in the years leading up to the war.
- She also received intelligence by reading the logs of military ships and the gathering of tidal data by sailors.
- Ultimately, Mary's assignment was to draw information from many sources to form an intricate mosaic from which the planners in Washington could form their battle plans.
- During the first months of 1944, the Oceanographic Unit was asked for reports on Sakhalin, the Kuriles and northern Hokkaido, while at the same time the Unit was developing ocean current charts for "certain Pacific areas" as well as bottom settlement charts for Java, the Makassar Strait, Cam Ranh Bay to Cape Varella, and Singapore Strait to the Banka Straits.
- The success of the Oceanographic Unit's work was best illustrated by the Allied landings on Luzon in the Philippines.

American troops were in need of new intelligence.

- The surf was low in the western part of the Gulf in Western Luzon, making it the most attractive location for an invasion; for that reason it was also most heavily fortified by the Japanese.

Better charts enabled the Navy to make safe and tactically successful landings ashore.

- Employing weather data and wave refraction charts, Mary and her team recommended that the invasion take place in the eastern part of the Gulf where it was also safe to come ashore.
- Her recommendations launched the successful Philippine invasion, which had been captured 37 months earlier by the Japanese.
- Ironically, the closer the Americans got to the Japanese homelands, the easier Mary's work became—"as we are able to use the very complete data published by Japanese scientists before Pearl Harbor."

Life in the Community: Woods Hole, Falmouth, Massachusetts

- In 1927, a National Academy of Sciences committee concluded that it was time to "consider the share of the United States of America in a worldwide program of oceanographic research."
- The committee's recommendation for establishing a permanent independent research laboratory on the East Coast to "prosecute oceanography in all its branches" led to the founding in 1930 of the Woods Hole Oceanographic Institute.
- A $3 million grant from the Rockefeller Foundation supported the summer work of a dozen scientists, construction of a laboratory building and commissioning of a research vessel, the 142-foot ketch *Atlantis*, whose profile forms the Institute's logo.
- The Institute was located at Woods Hole, located in the town of Falmouth, Massachusetts, at the extreme southwest corner of Cape Cod, where scientific research had been conducted since 1871.

- The term "Woods Hole" referred to a passage for ships between Vineyard Sound and Buzzards Bay known for its extremely strong current, approaching four knots.
- Historically, Woods Hole's harbor had allowed the area to emerge as a center for whaling, shipping, and fishing during the eighteenth century.
- At the end of the nineteenth century, Woods Hole was the home of the Pacific Guano Company, which produced fertilizer from bird dung imported from islands in the Pacific Ocean, the Caribbean, and the coast of South Carolina.
- After the firm went bankrupt in 1889, Long Neck—the peninsula on which its factory was located—was renamed Penzance Point and was developed with shingle-style summer homes for bankers and lawyers from New York and Boston.
- Woods Hole Oceanographic Institute grew substantially in the late 1930s to support defense-related research, and during World War II expanded dramatically in staff and scientific stature.
- Over the years, Woods Hole scientists have been credited with seminal discoveries about the ocean.

HISTORICAL SNAPSHOT
1945

- The Red Army liberated the Auschwitz and Birkenau death camps
- American soldiers and Filipino guerrillas freed 813 American POWs from the Japanese-held camp at Cabanatuan City, Philippines, following the invasion of the islands
- Eddie Slovik was the first American soldier since the Civil War to be executed by firing squad for desertion
- Thirty thousand U.S. Marines successfully invaded Iwo Jima and raised the American flag
- Dutch teenager Anne Frank died of typhus in the Bergen-Belsen concentration camp, Lower Saxony, Germany
- American B-29 bombers attacked Japan with incendiary bombs; Tokyo was fire-bombed, killing 100,000 citizens

- The Seventeenth Academy Awards ceremony was broadcast via radio for the first time; Going My Way won the award for Best Picture
- Berlin was attacked by 1,250 American bombers; Adolf Hitler ordered that all military installations, machine shops, and transportation and communications facilities in Germany be destroyed
- President Franklin D. Roosevelt, while serving his fourth term, died suddenly at Warm Springs, Georgia; Vice President Harry S. Truman became the thirty-third president of the United States
- The American war correspondent Ernie Pyle was killed by Japanese machine gun fire on the island of Ie Shima off Okinawa
- Rodgers and Hammerstein's Carousel, a musical play based on Ferenc Molnár's Liliom, opened on Broadway
- Heinrich Himmler offered a German surrender to the Western Allies, but not to the Soviet Union; Western Allies rejected any offer of surrender by Germany other than an unconditional one
- British Lancaster bombers dropped food into the Netherlands to prevent the starvation of the civilian population
- Adolf Hitler and his wife of one day, Eva Braun, committed suicide as the Red Army approached the Führerbunker in Berlin
- Poet Ezra Pound was arrested by American soldiers in Italy for treason

continued

HISTORICAL SNAPSHOT (continued)
1945

- A Japanese balloon bomb killed five children and a woman near Bly, Oregon, the only people killed by an enemy attack on the American mainland during World War II
- Winston Churchill resigned as the United Kingdom's prime minister after his Conservative Party was soundly defeated by the Labour Party
- The U.S. B-29 Superfortress Enola Gay dropped an atomic bomb, code-named "Little Boy," on Hiroshima, Japan, and the B-29 Bomber Bockscar dropped another, code-named "Fat Man," on Nagasaki, Japan
- The Zionist World Congress approached the British government to discuss the founding of the country of Israel
- The final official surrender by Japan was accepted by Supreme Allied Commander General Douglas MacArthur and Fleet Admiral Chester Nimitz
- Mohandas Gandhi and Jawaharlal Nehru demanded that all British troops leave India
- Arthur C. Clarke advanced the idea of a communications satellite in *Wireless World* magazine
- The first ballpoint pens went on sale at Gimbels Department Store in New York City for $12.50 each
- John H. Johnson published the first issue of the magazine Ebony
- Telechron introduced the "Musalarm," the first clock radio.
- War trials against 24 Nazi war criminals began at the Nuremberg Palace of Justice
- Assembly of the world's first general purpose electronic computer, the Electronic Numerical Integrator and Computer (ENIAC), was completed
- At the Mayo Clinic, streptomycin was first used to treat tuberculosis

Selected Prices

Ashtray	$8.50
Automobile, De Soto	$2,200.00
Barbell	$8.95
Electric Food Liquidizer	$35.00
Home Permanent Kit	$1.40
Manicure Set	$15.00
Mattress	$54.50
Radio Phonograph	$199.95
Record Cabinet	$13.50
Wrenches, Set of Six	$2.85

Pre-War Full
Swing Skirt

Wartime Soft
and Slim Line

Pre-War Full
Waist Silhouette

Wartime Fitted
Waist Silhouette

"Navy Redoubles Effort In WAVE Enlistments," *Long Beach Independent* (California), November 16, 1943:

Fearing that Italy's capitulation and successful aggressive action on many fronts may cause complacency and letdown in volunteers for the Women's Reserve, the Navy Department issued instructions to the Office of Naval Officer Procurement to redouble efforts to effect enlistment of more WAVES.

Rear Admiral I.C. Johnson, in charge of the WAVE program for the 11th Naval district, called upon his staff and members of the Navy recruiting services to give wide dissemination to the need for women in the Navy now.

"The Navy's war has just begun. Additional men will be needed to man ships taken from the enemy. Shore-stationed blue jackets will be called upon to go into the combat duty at sea, and WAVES must replace these men in vital jobs ashore," Gen. Johnson said.

"Inventions Can Win the War: Have You an Idea That Might Help?" *Popular Science*, October 1942:

In the summer of 1940 Goering's airmen, flushed with their victories in Norway, Belgium, Holland, and France, swept over Britain. There they were met and thrown back by some 3,000 R.A.F. flyers. Several factors played a decisive part in that historic defeat. The heroism of the young men in the Hurricanes and Spitfires was one of them. But heroism does not enable a flyer to see that attacking plane in the dark. There was also a technological factor—the British were equipped with a radio location device by which, in effect, they could see their enemies at night. Without it they would have been unable to bring them down in such vast numbers as to make Goering hesitate—and when he hesitated he was lost.

This is a sample of the part invention is playing in the war. Until recently the radio locator could not even be mentioned in print; even now it can be no more than mentioned. But it is a fact that without this particular unpublicized invention, the British might well have gone down to defeat. Dr. Vannevar Bush, speaking recently on "Science and National Defense," said the "radio detection, developed by a group of devoted British scientist working from 1935 on, at times without much encouragement, offset the element of surprise. This one development may have saved the Isle of Britain."

Dr. Bush should know; besides being president of the Carnegie Institute of Washington, he is director of the Office of Scientific Research and Development, our chief coordinator in the field of organized worktime invention. It takes some coordination. Before the war, out of 170,000 manufacturing companies in the United States, only 1,800 maintained research laboratories, and of those, only a few hundred were big ones. The number of industrial research workers did not exceed 33,000. As Herbert Hoover never tired of pointing out, we were not doing enough research. As a result, now that we are at war, we do not have nearly enough trained scientists to work on the problems which the Army and Navy are pressing for an immediate solution. Needless duplication must be avoided, and that is one responsibility of the Office of Scientific Research and Development and its subsidiary, the National Defense Research Committee, headed by Dr. J.B. Corrigan, who sidelined as the president of Harvard University. Another is to make sure that the most urgent things are done first, and the results of research in one field are articulated with those in the others.

The NDRC officials are responsible for the bulk of the non-medical scientific work required in connection with the war effort. Yet it has no laboratories and does no research of its own. Research projects go to existing laboratories—a model of 100 percent subcontracting. At last advisories, it had over 450 research projects operating under contract, involving the technical facilities for some of the most important university and industrial laboratories in the country.

continued

"Inventions Can Win the War: Have You an Idea That Might Help?" *(continued)*

Every one of these 450 projects is highly confidential. The men working on various problems, although all of them have been investigated and approved by the Federal Bureau of Investigation, are not told of other problems that were allocated to other groups, unless these are so closely related as to be effectively one. Scientific candor, the free exchange of information, are all washed up during the war. A few key officials at the top necessarily know everything that is going on.

"COME OUT OF THAR, WILLIE! YOU'VE PLAYED AIR RAID SHELTER LONG ENOUGH FOR ONE DAY!"

"Germany Sees Us in a Grotesque Distortion Mirror," Thomas Kernan, *Reader's Digest*, August 1944:

When the war is finished, when we have flown our flags above bomb-wrecked Unter den Linden, we shall still face a real problem: the penetration of the German mind.

Goebbels' Propaganda Ministry has so indoctrinated the German mind that the German people do not see with their eyes, or hear with their ears, or even consider it worthwhile bothering to listen to anything the outside world has to say.

I spent 13 months interned at Baden-Baden in Germany. My opportunities for news were exactly those of a German citizen. I was permitted to subscribe to newspapers from Germany and German-occupied places—France, Belgium, Holland, and Italy. I listened to radio broadcasts prepared for Germans and the German-dominated peoples. I was free to compare notes and hold discussions with my fellow internees, many of them newspaperman and diplomats.

By profession a publishing and advertising man, I made it my business to follow the course of German interior propaganda, and to observe the functioning of the machine Dr. Goebbels has brought to sinister perfection.

Goebbels has kept Germans well-informed on favorable military news and misinformed about America. Day by day, bit by bit, we pieced together the image of America in the German mind, and it was rather like looking at oneself in a distortion mirror. The Germans think our liberty a joke. They want no part of our Republican ideas. Everything we are, everything we stand for, has been misrepresented to them with such a plausible twist that, while it is recognizably American in fact, it is completely false in its conclusions.

Goebbels made the most of the opportunity to churn out violent hatred with the stepped-up bombings of German cities by English and American planes. European cities are closely built. Whenever we wish to destroy a railroad junction or a bridge or a plant, we are sure to hit also the homes of the vicinity and a church or two. Goebbels began to teach the Germans that our planes aimed only at non-military targets, and that their job was to do away with the cultural and charitable institutions in Germany. Repeated a hundred times, photographed thousands of times, the theme of an Anglo-American assault on Europe's ancient culture has finally sunk deep into the thoughts of the German people.

In March 12, 1943, an Allied armada passed over us on the way to Stuttgart, released one bomb over Baden and burned up a Catholic church. This was the only bomb dropped on the Baden Valley during our 13-month stay. Because the church was a large one, prominent on a hill, no one will ever be able to persuade the local people the bomb was an accident. Again, a great 6,000-bed hospital in Frankfurt is out in the country, removed from any other buildings. It was totally destroyed by a recent raid, undoubtedly mistaken for some other target. Among the important buildings entirely destroyed or badly damaged are the cathedrals at Cologne, Trier, Aachen and Munster, and all the leading churches and museums of Munich.

When one tells a German that, after all, the Germans did the same thing to London in the winter of 1940-41, he looks at you with blank astonishment, for

continued

"Germany Sees Us in a Grotesque Distortion Mirror," *(continued)*

he never heard of it. He seems honestly ignorant of the Luftwaffe's tragic toll in England, and he actually believes that it was England, not Germany, that began the bombing of cities.

Unfortunately, German control over the press of occupied countries is so complete that even France accepts this propaganda scheme to some extent. Perhaps the most unfortunate incident of all involved the bringing down of an American plane which had been nicknamed by its crew "Murder, Inc." We know that American plane crews christen their ship with whatever name strikes their fancy—Hot Mama, Leaping Lizzie, Fancy Pants, or the like. Such a thing is unthinkable to the literal-minded Germans. To them "Murder, Inc." was an official designation for an American bomb, destined to kill German women and children....

More dangerous is what I might call the "black propaganda" against America, in the form of vicious books and photographs. These play up anything that is in bad taste or scabrous in our vast land, and sell very inexpensively.

One book reproduces a handsome series of OWI posters called "The Highest Standard of Living in the World" and "The American Way," and opposite them are authentic photos showing bums loitering under the Chicago elevated, destitute old men at soup kitchens in New York, the living quarters of sharecropper Negroes. In Germany, where low-cost housing is a fetish and where the psychopathic bum is kept in a concentration camp out of the public sight, these photos give a sad impression of America....

Liberal friends of mine in the United States often say, "Oh, if only our message could get through to the Germans! If only they knew about the Atlantic Charter and the Four Freedoms!"

I regret to report that the German public knows all about the Atlantic Charter and has heard many times about Mr. Roosevelt's Four Freedoms. It is part of Goebbels' technique to reveal our idealistic documents to the Germans, in full and immediately, but with the counterblast of ridicule that disposes of them at once in the German mind.

The Atlantic Charter was dismissed as vague, impractical idealism, a "seaborn rehash," of President Wilson's points. Goebbels blared, "You caught us once in 1918 with your fine phrases; you can't catch us again.

1945 News Feature

"Here Is Something Really New—and Strange—in Plastics,"
Rotarian International, February 1945:

About a year ago a General Electric Company publicist tore open a pack of cigarettes and threw them into a bowl of water.

"Have a smoke, boys," he said to the assembled reporters. When they fished out the cigarettes, the water rolled off of them in little beads and they weren't even damp.

A few months later, Westinghouse engineers took apart a three horsepower electric motor and rewound it with a secret new type of installation. The motor then delivered 10 horsepower.

Soon afterward, our B-29s swarmed over Tokyo equipped with a rubberlike gasket which stood up under intense heat like no other material would.

Then a few weeks ago, some fascinating putty-like stuff made its appearance. It looks like modeling clay, but if you roll it into a wad and drop it on the floor, it bounces like tennis ball.

These achievements, and many others equally amazing, are the work of silicones, a new family of synthetic resins—the greatest sensation in plastics in the last 30 years. Research men of the Dow Chemical Company, the Corning Glass Works and General Electric are responsible for developing the versatile newcomer.

All the silicones are made from the same basic materials—petroleum, brine and ordinary sand. The new material comes in forms all the way from a gas which will vanish in thin air to a solid substance hard as rock. It is a watery liquid, thick oil, pliable rubber. And each shape it takes has unexpected and priceless merits.

The cigarettes, both paper and tobacco, were waterproofed with silicone vapor. Dr. A.L. Marshall, a pioneer in the development of silicones, gave me a demonstration. He held a paper towel over a jar containing a transparent silicone fluid. Then he squirted some water on the paper. Each drop retained its round identity. When he tilted the paper the droplets rolled off intact, leaving the paper without a trace of moisture. Exposure to silicone paper, Dr. Marshall explained, imparts to the fibers of the paper a coating so thin it cannot be seen under a microscope, yet so durable that drops of water will roll off samples treated three years ago.

This simple trick of the new resin opens up numerous possibilities: water-proof grocery bags, for example, and water-repellent paper raincoats to be sold at football games for the price of a hot dog. The vapor treatment can be used also on lightweight summer clothing, even shoes. Someday people may stroll serenely through rainstorms while the drops bounce off their clothes, leaving them as dry as ever. Garments can be washed or dry cleaned without losing their invisible protection.

The vapor treatment is now preventing communications blackouts in many fighting planes. When a plane dives into a rain cloud, moisture is often sucked up by the porcelain insulators of the radio set; the terminals are short-circuited, and the radio goes dead. If the insulators are treated with silicone vapor, they shed moisture like a duck.

An electric motor's power and length of life depends to a great degree upon the amount of heat the insulation will stand without charring. Engineers of Dow Corning, a Michigan firm founded in 1943 solely for the production of the new resin, cooperated with Westinghouse engineers in testing the resin insulation. A trolley car motor, limited normally to the temperature of 266°F, was rewound with silicone insulation until the thermometer showed 482°. It was still in fine condition after 3,000 hours—equivalent to running the motor 400 years under the old conditions. The new insulation means smaller, lighter and more reliable motors for all sorts of jobs.

The exciting new synthetic can also be made into Vaseline-like grease, which will not harden at 40° below zero or melt at 400° above. Lubricating oil made from it pours freely at 100° below. Use in airplanes, which often climb in a few minutes from a sweltering tropical airfield to the frigid stratosphere, is clearly indicated.

Behind the most valuable attribute of the silicones—their indifference to the thermometer—lies the story of a molecule's backbone. In all plastics, and in natural and synthetic rubbers as well, carbon is the principal building block of the long, chainlike molecules. Carbon is indispensable in a plastic, but carbon compounds are susceptible to heat. For many years, scientists have been trying to insert a heat-resistant backbone in these molecules. Silicon, found in sand and quartz, and one of the most abundant elements on Earth, is far less sensitive to temperature and would give this new merit to a plastic. Finally, they succeeded. By a kind of chemical crossbreeding, a completely new molecule was produced, which had a backbone composed of atoms of silicon and oxygen instead of carbon. In this chemical marriage between two groups of elements never before fruitfully united, the sand partner contributes the convenient versatility which permits the formulation of silicones into the wide variety of liquid and solid products....

The development of silicon has been so rapid that the possibilities for future use still lie in the realm of speculation. Research men are enthusiastic. All signs indicate that it is much more than a new plastic—that a new industry has been born.

1947 Profile

Percy Lebraon Spencer—the man who put the quick pop into popcorn and speed into everyday cooking—used his machining skills to invent the microwave.

Life at Home

- Percy Lebraon Spencer was born in 1894 in the tiny town of Howland, Maine.
- His father died when Percy was only three years old, and his mother, who never showed any interest in having a child, left him behind shortly thereafter.
- An aunt and uncle took him in even though money was tight; life was tough and toys were few.
- He learned mathematics from his wooden toy blocks, and he learned about survival from his uncle, with whom he quickly bonded.
- His uncle was a machinist at the mill where six-year-old Percy would follow him around observing the machinery from every angle; Percy was small enough that he would get inside some larger machines and examine their structure.
- His uncle died when Percy was only seven.
- For the second time in his short life, his father figure was gone; Percy helped his aunt out at home doing chores and was a good helper.
- He became particularly adept with tools and working in the garden—traits that would accompany him into adulthood.
- In fact, it was his ability to address problems in an unorthodox, but practical manner that led to some of his greatest inventions, including the microwave oven.
- When the economy struggled, Percy realized that chores at home would not be enough to support the family; at age 12, he stopped attending school and became an apprentice in a spool mill.
- Like most workers in 1906, he rose at dawn for work and was at the mill until after sundown, including on Saturdays.
- Maintaining the machines became a natural fit for Percy; he felt at home among moving parts, wires and grease.
- He even assisted in the transition of the mill from steam power to electricity.

Percy Spencer invented the microwave oven.

279

- When the company wanted to switch to electricity, Percy volunteered to work on the complex conversion, even though he had no experience with the emerging new energy force.
- Possessing only a sixth-grade education, he had little technical data to draw upon, so he "problem-solved" as he went along, basically teaching himself to be an electrician.
- A few hair-raising jolts along the way did not deter him; in fact, with electricity as his tutor, Percy learned very quickly about what went where and what didn't.
- Like many Mainers, Percy enjoyed the outdoors, with fishing and hunting as his preferred hobbies; the meat from the game was much appreciated.
- Wild meat and home-grown vegetables could also be bartered with neighbors for fresh fruit and other goods that the family could not afford to purchase.
- At age 18, the Navy was a logical choice for a northern New Englander who wanted an opportunity to travel and learn wireless telegraphy.
- His electronic and radio experience in the Navy aided Percy in getting a job with Raytheon, a new electronics company in Waltham, Massachusetts.

The newly formed company, Raytheon, located just west of Boston, was a perfect fit for Spencer.

Life at Work

- In 1922, upon returning from his Navy experience, Percy Spencer embarked on a journey of discovery at the small start-up company of Raytheon.
- A friend of Percy's was among the founders of Raytheon in Waltham, a town west of Boston, Massachusetts, and fully understood Percy's capabilities and potential.
- Percy was the fifth employee hired, brought in as an engineer even though he had no formal training.
- The electronics company grew quickly in the expanding economy of the 1920s and survived the downturn of the 1930; Percy supplied the curiosity, and Raytheon provided the structure that would lead to over 220 patents in his lifetime.
- Percy worked long hours, seven day a week, to keep production up.
- He also took an interest in his employees, in particular, the night shift—men and women who often felt ignored or forgotten.
- When Percy discovered that a Raytheon worker wore a hat all the time because he was balding, Percy led him to the office of Charles Adams, the president of Raytheon, who was himself bald.
- Percy told the man, "See, this man, a descendant of two U.S. presidents, isn't ashamed of not having hair."

During WWII new innovations were encouraged and embraced throughout the country.

- During the opening days of World War II in Europe, Raytheon's focus on military electronics resulted in a much-coveted invitation from several British scientists who wanted to make improvements to the recently invented magnetron, at the heart of their newly developed radar tracking system.
- England was under attack from the air and sea and desperately needed to mass-produce the magnetron so more radar units could be manufactured; the German assault on their island nation was relentless.
- During a confidential meeting with British experts, Percy told them that their proposed methods of improvement were "impractical and awkward."
- Then he asked for time over the weekend to examine the device and suggest better ways to manufacture it; typically, in 1941, it took one week for a master machinist to produce one tube.
- Magnetrons were being produced at a total rate of 17 per day when the need was in the thousands; Percy set out to create a simpler magnetron that could be mass produced.
- The result was a magnetron that replaced precision copper bars that had laminated and soldered internal wires with a simple solid ring—an improvement that allowed for faster production.
- His solution also meant that the highly prized magnetron could be made by any semi-skilled worker, allowing production to climb to 2,600 magnetron tubes a day.

England was desperate for a faster way to manufacture magnetrons for their radar tracking systems.

- As a result, the English army and navy could dramatically expand the use of radar to detect and defeat German attacks, and Raytheon became the supplier of 80 percent of the world's magnetrons by the end of the war.
- In 1945, while touring a Raytheon laboratory, Percy continued to tinker with his invention and paused in front of a magnetron.
- While standing near the electronic tube, Percy realized that the chocolate peanut bar in his pocket was getting warm, and when he opened it, the chocolate had melted.
- Percy's brain went into overdrive, and he rushed to get a bag of popcorn kernels.
- He held the bag near the magnetron and felt a quake within the bag.
- Soon the kernels began to pop and the fluffy white snack burst open.
- His nascent thoughts of using the radar technology for cooking food were reforming, and Percy couldn't wait to experiment more with his discovery.

- He would next try an egg, which exploded in the face of a fellow experimenter.
- To be assured that the radar technology worked properly, he contained it all within a box, creating the Radarange.
- Percy was not the first person to notice this phenomenon; he was simply the first to explore the idea.
- Engineers went to work on Spencer's hot new idea, developing and refining it for practical use.
- By late 1946, the Raytheon Company had filed a patent proposing that microwaves produced by an electronic tube, or magnetron, would bounce back and forth in the metal container until they were absorbed by food and the energy was converted to heat, thus cooking the food.
- The company loved the idea of a fast-cooking machine, and the patent office agreed; Percy received U.S. patent 2,495,429.
- With women working during World War II and many not wanting to fully return to their housewife duties, fast and simple cooking of meals was in demand.
- Working all day in the kitchen could be replaced with the Radarange, it was assumed.
- The researchers determined that food was cooked when energy was absorbed by water molecules in the first inside inch of the food, and heat was transferred inward as molecules collided with each other.
- Microwaves could pass through air and materials such as paper, glass and plastic before penetrating food and being absorbed by the water molecules.

An early microwave oven.

- They also confirmed that microwaves were converted entirely into heat and did not cause radioactive contamination; numerous stories had been bruited about microwaves causing cataracts, burns, sterility and blood poisoning.
- An oven that heated food using microwave energy was then placed in a Boston restaurant for testing; it was fast, as promised, but did not heat evenly or always brown food as a conventional oven might.
- A year later, in 1947, the first commercial microwave oven hit the market; standing nearly six feet high and weighing almost 750 pounds, the first microwave ovens sold for $5,000 each, not including the cost of plumbing.
- The magnetron tube had to be water-cooled, so plumbing installations were also required.
- Raytheon ads boasted that it could cook a steak in a minute, a Thanksgiving turkey in 30 minutes.
- Percy believed the new invention would be widely used on trains and ocean liners; initially, only the military and major catering enterprises showed any interest.
- One of the Raytheon executives was so thrilled by his company's new discovery that he insisted his personal chef cook every meal in the microwave.
- When the chef complained that not every food item was cooking properly, or flavor was being lost, the executive would hear none of it.

- The chef quit in disgust, while the rest of the culinary community agreed.
- Many foods did not taste as good in the microwave when compared to traditional cooking methods.
- Percy begrudgingly realized that his new patent was not yet ready to become the most important appliance in the commercial or home kitchen.
- But as the food industry began to recognize the potential and versatility of the microwave oven, its usefulness was put to new tests.
- Industries began using microwaves to dry potato chips and roast coffee beans and peanuts; even the shucking of oysters was made easier by microwaves.
- In time, microwaves were being used to dry cork, ceramics, paper, leather, tobacco, textiles, pencils, flowers, wet books and match heads.

Life in the Community: Waltham, Massachusetts

- Waltham, Massachusetts, about 12 miles west of historic Boston, is home to Brandeis University.
- The school was intended to be named after Albert Einstein, but he clashed with the founders, withdrew his support, and the university was named after Louis Brandeis, the first Jewish member of the U.S. Supreme Court.
- Raytheon was mainly a defense contractor, primarily using radar and missile technology.
- The company produced about 80 percent of magnetron tubes during World War II.
- The division would expand from 15 to 5,000 workers during the war.
- For a person with only an elementary school education, Percy lived and worked among America's most intellectually gifted.
- The universities of Harvard, Tufts, and MIT were just a few miles away.
- MIT was closely allied with Raytheon, and one contemporary scientist said of Percy's success, "Scientists are taught what won't work. No one ever taught Percy what wouldn't work, so he tries and tries again for himself."
- Waltham is sometimes referred to as "Watch City" because of the Waltham Watch Company, which opened its factory in 1854.
- It was the first company to produce watches on an assembly line.

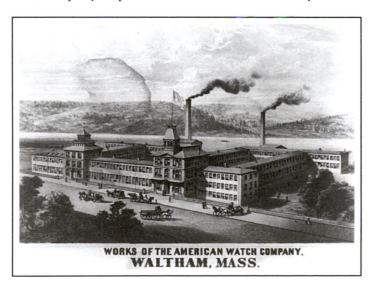

The Waltham Watch Company.

- In 1876, it would win the gold medal at the Philadelphia Centennial Exposition.
- The company produced over 40 million watches, clocks, and instruments before shutting down in 1957.
- Waltham is considered, at least by the local Chamber of Commerce, to be the birthplace of the American Industrial Revolution.

Waltham, Mass is considered by some to be the birthplace of the American Industrial Revolution.

HISTORICAL SNAPSHOT
1947

- The popular spinning platters that year included "Time After Time," "Old Devil Moon," "Nature Boy," and "Everybody Loves Somebody"
- *The Voice of America* radio program began airing in Communist countries
- In New York City, Edwin Land demonstrated the Polaroid Land camera, the first instant camera
- The USS *Newport News* was the first completely air-conditioned warship
- The Truman Doctrine was proclaimed to help stem the spread of Communism
- A World War II Japanese booby trap exploded on Corregidor Island, killing 28
- Jackie Robinson, the first African-American Major-Leaguer, signed with the Brooklyn Dodgers
- Movies included *Miracle on 34th Street, Great Expectations, The Bachelor and the Bobby-Soxer* and *The Bishop's Wife*
- UFO sightings in Washington State were widely reported, as was the first encounter with "Men in Black"
- Captain Chuck Yeager flew the Bell-X1 rocket plane faster than the speed of sound, the first time this had been accomplished
- The program *Meet the Press* debuted on NBC-TV
- Notable insomniac Al Herpin died at age 94; he did not own a bed and claimed he had gone 10 years without sleep
- The Tennessee Williams play *A Streetcar Named Desire* opened on Broadway
- Several tall jars of pottery containing leather scrolls—which became known as the Dead Sea Scrolls—were discovered in a cave near Wadi Qumrun
- The U.S. House of Representatives voted 346-17 to approve citations against the Hollywood 10, after 10 men refused to cooperate with the House Un-American Activities Committee regarding allegations of Communist influences in the motion picture industry
- The UN voted to partition land that would create the state of Israel
- An explosion at O'Connor Electro-Plating Company in Los Angeles resulted in 17 deaths, 100 damaged buildings, and a 22-foot-deep crater

Selected Prices

Bath Towel	$0.62
Boxer Shorts	$0.65
Car Seat	$1.98
Jaguar Sedan	$4,600.00
Portable Phonograph	$27.50
Record of Handel's *Messiah*	$1.25
Red Wagon	$3.29
Scooter With Rubber Tires	$1.59
Toaster	$15.05
Veal, per Pound	$0.90

First–every year for 31 years

GOODYEAR

More people ride on Goodyear tires than on any other kind

ARROW SHORTS

AMERICA'S FAVORITE
CHAMPION
SPARK PLUGS

"Twelve Things That the War Will Do to America," *Predictions of Things to Come*, February 1943:

Quincy Howe, author, editor and CBS news commentator, predicts in an article in *Harper's Magazine* the following 12 things the war will do to America:

1. The war will abolish mass unemployment in America.

2. The war will make it necessary for America to feed and re-quip much of Europe and some of Asia.

3. After this war, no American will be allowed to receive more than $25,000 a year, and every American family will be assured an annual income of at least $2,500.

4. The war will reduce the power and income of the small businessman and of the unorganized middle-class.

5. The war will whittle away some of the recent gains of organized labor.

6. The war will reduce the power of the American farm bloc.

7. The war will give the United States a self-sufficient, continental economy.

8. The war will increase the power of the administrator at the expense of the professional politician.

9. Our new Army, in peace as in war, will remain the most powerful pressure group and the reservoir from which our next generation of leaders will come.

10. The war has brought universal compulsory military training here to stay.

11. The war will give American air power control of the skies of the world.

12. The war will create a new spirit of nationalism in our people.

"Not Enough Jobs Here for Returning Men, P.D. Mazyck Says," *The Index-Journal* (Greenwood), South Carolina, August 14, 1946:

P.D. Mazyck, local manager the United States Employment Service, announced today that employers in Greenwood and Greenwood County will be solicited for at least 500 job openings to be filled by veterans, former war plant workers and others. Mr. Mazyck further states:

"This job development campaign parallels the state and national campaign to promote the listing of all jobs for all classes of workers.

"There is a widening gap between the number of returning veterans and other workers, and the jobs listed in the public employment offices.

"At the present time, there are approximately 600 veterans in Greenwood County either looking for work or waiting for schools to open to resume their education. During the war we felt it was our duty to back up our service men in every way, and our obligation to them will not be fulfilled until these veterans are again employed in useful occupations.

"Many of the veterans have had some work experience, and many of those who have not had work experience received some form of training while in the service that can be applied to civilian work," said Mr. Mazyck. "These men are the potential business leaders of the future. They have been through the hardships of war and are physically able to work.

"We do not have enough job openings in which to refer these workers, and all employers are urged, when in need of workers of any kind, to place orders with the employment service," he continued.

"The employment service will then refer the best qualified men, and the employer can choose the worker he prefers. Many employers have found it advantageous to place orders with employment services, and with so many veterans registered for work, the employment services would like the opportunity to refer these unemployed veterans, and give them a start back to civilian life."

"News of Food, Radarange Among Future Home Marvels, It Cooks a Chicken in Only Two Minutes," *The New York Times*, March 14, 1949:

Margaret Fairchild has been concerned with meal preparation in the ship's galley rather than a home kitchen in the experiments on electronic cooking she has been conducting at Columbia University. But in her work on the Radarange as possible equipment for the United States Navy, the technician has discovered many advantages that housewives will enjoy in the future in this fastest device for preparing food for the table.

It will take several years, according to Mrs. Fairchild, before the Radarange is made by the Raytheon Manufacturing Company in sizes suitable for home use. Production costs are exceedingly high. For one thing, the magnetron that supplies the heat costs about $500 to make, so one can imagine what the selling price would be. When the electronic ovens are available, though, housewives will be able to cook oatmeal in 15 minutes, half a chicken in two minutes and fresh corn on the cob in 45 seconds.

We watched some of this split-second cooking recently when we visited Mrs. Fairchild in her kitchen laboratory at Teachers College. She was working there under the supervision of Dr. Mary de Garmo Brian, professor of institutional management at Columbia.

"Taste this lemon meringue pie," she said. "I made the filling in the Radarange in two minutes."

Though it's called a stove or oven, the Radarange doesn't look like any stove we've ever seen. It is a little more than five feet high, two feet wide and two feet deep. Designed of stainless steel, it has a screened oven door so that foods may be watched as they cook.

During the 20 seconds it took Mrs. Fairchild to bake gingerbread cup cakes (you can actually see them rise), she told us about some of the other things she's found the oven will do.

"The Radarange is going to be particularly useful for preparing frozen foods," she said. "I've put fried chicken that was frozen solid in the oven, and in 2 1/2 minutes it was defrosted and hot enough to serve."

The range also does an excellent job of warming over foods that have been cooked before. This Fairchild demonstrated this for us with a dish of Spanish rice that had been baked the previous day. She reheated it in the oven for 10 minutes and it came out "as good as new."

"Specialist Corps Formed," *Popular Science*, October 1942:

Possibly you are a metallurgical engineer, a businessman skilled in personal management, a transportation expert, or perhaps you are trained and experienced in any of a number of other professions. If so, the chances are the Army may have a place for you in its recently formed Specialist Corps.

This is an organization of uniformed civilians which will play an active part in winning the war. It is for men skilled in science, engineering, technical work, or business administration, but unlikely to be called for military service because of family dependence or minor physical defects. The most important qualification for members is proved ability.

While most of the men taken in the Corps will have duty with the services of supply, many will be assigned to tactical organizations in the United States and in the overseas theaters of operations. They are not doing the actual fighting, but some of them are likely to see service close to the fighting fronts.

The Corps is a branch of the War Department headed by Director General Dwight F. Davis, former Secretary of War and former governor general of the Philippines. Its job is the procuring of the most skilled men available to fill thousands of Army jobs which do not require military training and experience, but which do demand outstanding ability in varied fields of civilian activity. It is highly probable that Specialist Corps members will soon relieve, and release for purely military duties, many officers now filling administrative or technical positions in Washington DC and elsewhere....

The initiative for using specialists in any of the special jobs will come from the Army itself. While rosters of qualified men are being built for the purpose of filling future requisitions, no appointments are being made or enlistments accepted, except at the request of the Army, to fill definite vacancies.

1950-1959

As the 1950s began, the average American enjoyed an income of 15 times greater than that of the average foreigner. Optimism and opportunity were everywhere. The vast majority of families considered themselves middle class; many were enjoying benefits of health insurance for the first time. Air travel for the upper class was common, and the world was their oyster. America was manufacturing half of the world's products, 57 percent of the steel, 43 percent of the electricity, and 62 percent of the oil. The economies of Europe and Asia lay in ruins, while America's industrial and agricultural structure were untouched and well-oiled to supply the needs of a war-weary world.

In addition, the war years' high employment and optimism spurred the longest sustained period of peacetime prosperity in the nation's history. A decade full of employment and pent-up desire produced demands for all types of consumer goods. Businesses of all sizes prospered. Rapidly swelling families, new suburban homes, televisions, and most of all, big, powerful, shiny automobiles symbolized the hopes of the era. During the 1950s, an average of seven million cars and trucks were sold annually. By 1952, two thirds of all families owned a television set; home freezers and high-fidelity stereo phonographs were considered necessities. Specialized markets developed to meet the demand of consumers such as amateur photographers, pet lovers, and backpackers. At the same time, shopping malls, supermarkets, and credit cards emerged as temporary economic forces.

Veterans, using the GI Bill of Rights, flung open the doors of colleges nationwide, attending in record numbers. Inflation was the only pressing economic issue, fueled in large part by the Korean War (in which 54,000 American lives were lost) and the federal expenditures for Cold War defense. As the decade opened, federal spending represented 15.6 percent of the nation's gross national product. Thanks largely to the Cold War, by 1957, defense consumed half of the federal government's $165 billion budget.

This economic prosperity also ushered in conservative politics and social conformity. Tidy lawns, bedrooms that were "neat and trim," and suburban homes that were "proper" were certainly "in" throughout the decade as Americans adjusted to the post-war years. Properly buttoned-down attitudes concerning sexual mores brought stern undergarments for women like bonded girdles and stiff, pointed, or padded bras to confine the body. The planned community of Levittown, New York, mandated that grass be cut at least once a week and laundry washed on specific days. A virtual revival of Victorian respectability and domesticity reigned; divorce rates and female college attendance fell while birth rates and the sales of Bibles rose. Corporate America promoted the benefits of respectable men in gray flannel suits whose wives remained at home to tend house and raise children. Suburban life included ladies' club memberships, chauffeuring children to piano and ballet classes, and lots of a newly marketed product known as tranquilizers, whose sales were astounding.

The average wage earner benefited more from the booming industrial system than at any time in American history. The 40-hour work week became standard in manufacturing. In offices many workers were becoming accustomed to a 35-hour week. Health benefits for workers became more common and paid vacations were standard in most industries. In 1950, 25 percent of American wives worked outside the home; by the end of the decade the number had risen to 40 percent. Communications technology, expanding roads, inexpensive airline tickets, and a spirit of unboundedness meant that people and commerce were no longer prisoners of distance. Unfortunately, up to one third of the population lived below the government's poverty level, largely overlooked in the midst of prosperity.

The Civil Rights movement was propelled by two momentous events in the 1950s. The first was a decree on May 17, 1954 by the U.S. Supreme Court which ruled "that in the field of public education the doctrine of 'separate but equal' has no place. Separate educational facilities are inherently unequal." The message was electric but the pace was slow. Few schools would be integrated for another decade. The second event established the place of the Civil Rights movement. On December 1, 1955, African-American activist Rosa Parks declined to vacate the White-only front section of the Montgomery, Alabama, bus, leading to her arrest and a citywide bus boycott by blacks. Their spokesman became Martin Luther King, Jr., the 26-year-old pastor of the Dexter Avenue Baptist Church. The year-long boycott was the first step toward the passage of the Civil Rights Act of 1964.

America's youths were enchanted by the TV adventures of "Leave It to Beaver," westerns, and "Father Knows Best," allowing them to accumulate more time watching television during the week (at least 27 hours) than attending school. TV dinners were invented; pink ties and felt skirts with sequined poodle appliqués were worn; Elvis Presley was worshipped and the new phenomena of *Playboy* and Mickey Spillane fiction were created only to be read behind closed doors. The ever glowing eye of television killed the "March of Time" news-reels after 16 years at the movies. Sexual jargon such as "first base" and "home run" entered the language. Learned-When-Sleeping machines appeared, along with Smokey the Bear, Sony tape recorders, adjustable shower heads, Mad Comics, newspaper vending machines, Levi's faded blue denims, pocket size transistor radios, and transparent plastic bags for clothing. Ultimately, the real stars of the era were the Salk and Sabin vaccines, which vanquished the siege of polio.

1954 Profile

When many scientists still struggled to comprehend the fundamentals, Edwin Howard Armstrong grasped the intricate nuances of electronics and invented FM radio.

Life at Home

- When Edwin Howard Armstrong jumped from the thirteenth-floor window of River House in New York City in 1954, his thoughts were not on a lifetime of innovation, but on the patent disputes that haunted his work.
- The architect of FM and the three basic circuits upon which rested the whole of modern radio communications had lost the will to fight anymore.
- To him, the actions of tubes, coils, and condensers were like the unfolding of a drama—and he was the author.
- Born in New York City in 1890, he was the son of John Armstrong, U.S. representative to the Oxford University Press.
- In this comfortable, bookish household, Ed grew up absorbing stories about inventors Watt, Volta, Hertz, Tesla, Marconi, and his hero, Michael Faraday.
- At nine years old, he suffered an attack of St. Vitus's Dance, or rheumatic fever, that kept him out of school for two years and left him with a tic in his shoulder and jaw for the rest of his life.
- A serious child, he soon caught up with his classmates and displayed a fascination for Marconi's inventions.
- He soon learned all there was to know about wireless devices.
- When he enrolled in electrical engineering in 1909, he commuted to Columbia University, riding a red Indian motorcycle.

Edwin Howard Armstrong invented FM radio, but was plagued by patent disputes.

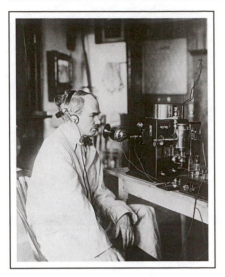

Armstrong was able to improve upon De Forest's electrical work.

- While still an undergrad, he made his first great discovery, regeneration, and ignited his first patent fight.
- At that time, inventor Lee De Forest's audion tube, the first triode vacuum tube, had been around for several years, but was not well understood.
- Edwin discovered that the voltage gain of a triode amplifier could be dramatically increased by using positive feedback—by feeding some of the amplifier output back into the input.
- Given enough feedback, the amplifier became a stable and powerful oscillator, perfect for driving radio transmitters.
- Supplied a little less feedback, the amplifier became a more sensitive radio receiver than anything else at the time.
- Titled a "wireless receiving system," and later as "regenerative radio," the invention improved the amplification of radio signals.
- Edwin sold his red motorcycle in 1913 to finance the patent fees.
- After De Forest heard of Edwin's work, he immediately directed his own research into regenerative techniques and quickly filed patents on variants of the technique.
- Then he started attacking Edwin's patents.
- De Forest was infuriated that such a young man had used his own tubes better than he himself had; he was determined to control their use.
- De Forest was backed up by American Telephone & Telegraph (AT&T), which stood to receive enormous financial gains if it could control a fundamental circuit of radio.
- The patent fight lasted 14 years, cost over $1 million, and was presented to the Supreme Court several times.
- De Forest's evidence of priority was a 1912 note in a lab book that a particular circuit emitted a howl when tuned a certain way.
- Eventually, De Forest and AT&T won in a widely criticized verdict, leaving Edwin bitter.
- Edwin's second invention came while he was still in his twenties, serving as an Army Signal Corps Major in World War I in France.
- The super heterodyne was a subtle and elegant technique for improving reception and tuning at the same time.
- Manufacturers had found it difficult to build an amplifier that would work at high frequencies, and at the same time construct a tuning filter than could select a narrow band of frequencies.
- The filter must tune in to one station and reject all others, but then be capable of tuning in to other stations.
- It was far easier to build a tunable oscillator, Edwin decided.
- Edwin's early inventions, vital to the new radio industry, brought him almost instant wealth and a professorship at Columbia.
- After World War I ended, Westinghouse Electric and Manufacturing Company paid him $530,000 over 10 years for his first two patents.
- In 1922, he sold a less important invention, the super regenerative circuit, to Radio Corporation of America (RCA) for $200,000 and 60,000 shares of RCA stock.

- Then, at age 32, the now wealthy inventor went to Europe and came home with a Hispano-Suiza sports car to impress his girlfriend.

- They were married in 1923, and on their honeymoon in Palm Beach, he carried along the first portable radio ever built—a present created for the occasion.

- Like his hero Faraday, whose discoveries founded the electrical industry, Ed was an original non-mathematical thinker in electric magnetic waves.

Armstrong bought a new shiny sports car to impress his girlfriend.

- Too many discoveries, he believed, had been put off by math calculations that said they were impossible and thus were never attempted.

- His forte was the acute analysis of ambiguous physical phenomena, and he relished debating accepted theories about the laws of nature.

- In his whole career, Edwin never became an employee.

- Instead, he was on the faculty of Columbia for a salary of $1.00 a year, since his patents paid him much more than the university could.

- He never taught classes, he never incorporated, and he did all his work with only a few assistants, some of whom went on to do significant work of their own.

Life at Work

AT&T executives and De Forest prevailed over Armstrong in the courts.

- The 14-year patent fight with Lee De Forest and AT&T had left Edwin Armstrong exhausted and humiliated.

- When the courts turned against Edwin and the newspapers referred to him as "that discredited inventor" in 1934, he resolved to show them all.

- Edwin was in his early forties, past the creative prime for most engineers, when he came up with his greatest invention of all, frequency modulation (FM).

- At the time, amplitude modulation (AM) dominated radio broadcasts, based on the idea that the strength of a radio signal was proportional to the strength of the audio signal being transmitted.

- Unfortunately, the natural world was full of similarly modulated signals, often heard as static.

- In FM, the frequency of the main signal varied instead of its amplitude.

- FM had been tried in the 1920s and was rejected.

- Detailed mathematical analyses had showed that a narrow-band FM signal would always sound worse than an AM signal of the same power.

- Edwin's insight was that an FM signal didn't have to have a narrow range of frequencies, but could vary over a wide range, and have a far better signal-to-noise ratio.

- By relying on experimentation and physical reasoning, Edwin got beyond the equations.

- Edwin offered the FM patents only for licensing, not for sale; he was determined to control the quality of FM.
- To Edwin's way of thinking, AM was producing inferior sound because of its fundamental technology and the overcrowding of radio stations in limited frequencies transmitted to inferior receivers.
- He showed the innovation to RCA, but they were unimpressed; RCA had made vast investments in AM radio and was not interested in a competitive change.
- All of their transmitters and all of the millions of radios they had sold used AM, and the investment had not depreciated.
- The industry giant informed Edwin that the public was not interested in high fidelity, and moreover, with television just on the horizon, FM had arrived too late.
- RCA said that consumers didn't care what the music sounded like from their radios; they just wanted to get it as cheaply as possible.
- Edwin never forgot their insult.
- He then licensed FM to smaller companies, including in the package a transmitter, antennas, and receivers, and set up pilot broadcasting services in New York and New England in 1939.
- The world was mesmerized by the quality of the music.
- RCA immediately struck back by petitioning the Federal Communications Commission to give FM's frequency assignments to upstart television, but this was rejected.
- RCA next offered Edwin $1 million for his patents, but no subsequent royalties.
- Edwin refused.
- If every other licensee paid royalties, RCA could, too.
- Then America's priorities shifted with the start of World War II, when FM was extensively used for military purposes.
- Edwin allowed the military to use his patents royalty-free; mobile FM communications proved their value by saving thousands of lives across Europe and the Pacific.

- When the Germans and Japanese were defeated, Edwin still had corporations like RCA and Columbia Broadcasting System (CBS) as powerful foes.
- In 1945, RCA and a bloc of other radio companies successfully lobbied the FCC to move the FM band from 44-50 MHz to 88-108 MHz, which made obsolete all the transmitters and receivers that had been built.
- The FCC also voted to severely limit FM's broadcasting power, and disallow radio relays from central stations to mountaintop antennas.
- FM broadcasting was crippled by the decisions; AM continued to have a regulatory advantage.
- Edwin redesigned and reworked his invention at the higher frequencies, and by 1948 he was ready to move forward, even though his patents only had two years left until their expiration.
- RCA had been building FM receivers using his patents for the previous eight years without paying him, so he brought a patent infringement suit against them in 1949.

Armstrong's discoveries were used royalty-free by the military during WW II.

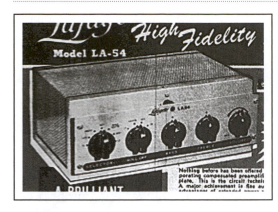

High fidelity amplifier.

- At the trial, Edwin was called to be the first witness, and RCA's lawyers kept him on the witness stand for an entire year with questions.
- Another two years were consumed while RCA laid out the research it had done on FM in the 1930s, including the claim that RCA had invented FM all by itself without any help from Edwin.
- Edwin lost his ability to compromise or settle after that was said.
- By 1953, Edwin's licenses and patents had all expired.
- His crushing legal bills and research expenses brought him to near bankruptcy; in addition, a bitter argument with his wife on Thanksgiving day caused her to leave him.
- On January 31, 1954, he wrote a two-page letter to her and left it on his apartment desk.
- He dressed neatly in an overcoat, hat, scarf and gloves, and walked out a thirteenth-story window.
- He hit a third-story overhang, so his body wasn't discovered until the next day.
- His wife Marion continued his suits and, unlike her husband, she was willing to compromise.
- She settled with RCA for over $1 million, then went after other companies like Sylvania and CBS that had also infringed on his patents.

Life in the Community: New York City

- The modern city of New York—with its five boroughs—was created in 1898 with the consolidation of the cities of New York, including Manhattan, the Bronx, Brooklyn, and the largely rural areas of Queens and Staten Island.
- The consolidation precipitated greater physical connections among the boroughs and facilitated the building of the New York City subway.
- The Williamsburg Bridge in 1903 and the Manhattan Bridge in 1909 further connected Manhattan to the rapidly expanding bedroom community in Brooklyn.
- Grand Central Terminal opened as the world's largest train station on February 1, 1913.
- New York City was the main point of embarkation for U.S. troops traveling to Europe during World War I.
- The 1920 Census showed Brooklyn for the first time overtaking Manhattan as the most populous borough, just as the Immigration Act of 1924 severely limited further immigrants from Southern and Eastern Europe.
- Instead, New York experienced growth as a result of the Great Migration of African-Americans from the South, resulting in a flowering of African-American culture in the Harlem Renaissance.
- Tin Pan Alley developed towards Broadway, and the first modern musical, Jerome Kern's *Show Boat* opened in 1927 as the theater district moved north of 42nd Street.

- New York City became known for its skyscrapers that transformed the skyline, epitomized by the dueling spires of the Chrysler Building and the Empire State Building.
- Then came the Great Depression, and the recently completed Empire State Building would be known as the "Empty State Building."
- New York, long a city of immigrants, became a culturally international city with the influx of intellectual, musical and artistic European refugees that started in the late 1930s.
- The 1939 New York World's Fair marked the 150th anniversary of George Washington's inauguration in Federal Hall and carried the theme "Building the World of Tomorrow," until the outbreak of World War II in Europe, when the focus shifted to "For Peace and Freedom."

New high-powered public address system.

- The city was significantly affected by the war; shipping was hurt by the German U-boats, windows were blacked out for fear of German bombing, and the Brooklyn Navy Yard again increased its production of warships.
- For the duration of the war, the Port of New York handled 25 percent of the nation's trade.
- With 75,000 workers, the Navy Yard was the world's largest shipyard.
- The only major world city unscathed by the war, New York emerged as the leading world city, with Wall Street contributing to America's ascendancy and, in 1951, with the United Nations relocating from its first headquarters in Flushing Meadows Park, Queens, to the East Side of Manhattan.

HISTORICAL SNAPSHOT
1954

- The Soviet Union stopped demanding war reparations from East Germany
- Marilyn Monroe married baseball great Joe DiMaggio
- The National Negro Network was established with 40 charter member radio stations
- The first nuclear-powered submarine, the USS *Nautilus*, was launched in Groton, Connecticut
- President Dwight Eisenhower warned against United States' intervention in Vietnam
- The first mass vaccination of children against polio began in Pittsburgh, Pennsylvania
- The U.S. conducted a hydrogen bomb test on Bikini Atoll in the Pacific Ocean
- American journalists Edward R. Murrow and Fred W. Friendly produced a 30-minute *See It Now* documentary, entitled *A Report on Senator Joseph McCarthy*
- Boxer Joey Giardello knocked out Willie Tory at Madison Square Garden, in the first televised boxing prize fight to be shown in color
- RCA manufactured the first color television set featuring a 12-inch screen and costing $1,000
- Congress authorized the founding of the United States Air Force Academy in Colorado
- Fifty-four percent of Americans owned a television set
- Senator Joseph McCarthy began hearings investigating the United States Army for being "soft" on Communism
- Roger Bannister ran the first four-minute mile
- The U.S. Supreme Court ruled that segregated schools were unconstitutional
- The words "under God" were added to the Pledge of Allegiance
- Food rationing in Great Britain ended with the lifting of restrictions on the sale and purchase of meat, 14 years after it began early in World War II and nearly a decade after the war's end
- The first issue of *Sports Illustrated* magazine was published in the United States
- The last new episode of *The Lone Ranger* was aired on radio, after 2,956 episodes over a period of 21 years
- The first *Godzilla* movie premiered in Tokyo, Japan
- The transistor radio was developed
- The U.S. Supreme Court decided the landmark case *Berman v. Parker*, upholding the federal slum clearance and urban renewal program
- For the first time, the Dow surpassed its 1929 peak level reached just before that year's crash
- The U.S. Senate voted 67–22 to condemn Joseph McCarthy for "conduct that tends to bring the Senate into dishonor and disrepute"
- The first Burger King opened in Miami, Florida
- The TV dinner was introduced by the American entrepreneur Gerry Thomas

Selected Prices

Adding Machine Tape	$1.79
Cake Mix	$0.35
Carbon Paper	$1.19
Card Table and Chairs	$49.75
Coffee, One Pound	$0.83
Gun Rack	$17.95
Home Freezer	$399.95
Monopoly Game	$4.00
Pocket Radio	$44.00
Television	$200.00

Events in New York City: 1954

The Caine Mutiny by Herman Wouk premiered.

After 1,928 performances, *South Pacific* closed at Majestic Theater.

The musical *The Pajama Game* opened on Broadway for 1,063 performances.

The King and I closed at St. James Theater after 1,246 performances.

Bill Haley & the Comets recorded "Rock Around the Clock" at Pythian Temple.

Bell Labs announced the first solar battery.

Opera singer Edith Mason performs on the first radio program of operas.

The New York Giants beat the Cleveland Indians in the World Series; Willie Mays made a spectacular catch and throw in the eighth inning of the first game.

Marian Anderson.

The Boy Friend opened at the Royale Theater for 483 performances.

Marian Anderson became the first black singer hired by the Metropolitan Opera.

The Broadway show *Fanny* opened at the Majestic Theater for 888 performances.

Ellis Island closed after having processed more than 20 million immigrants since opening in New York Harbor in 1892.

Gian Carlo Menotti's opera *Saint of Bleecker Street* premiered.

Joseph Papp founded the outdoor New York Shakespeare Festival.

"FM Inventor Improves His System, Putting Three Programs on Single Wave," Jack Gould, *The New York Times*, March 17, 1953:

A frequency modulation radio station can transmit simultaneously two or three different programs on a single channel under a new transmission system announced yesterday by Dr. Edwin H. Armstrong, Professor of Electrical Engineering at Columbia University and inventor of FM radio.

Under the system, a set owner would tune his FM set once as at present and receive the first program. Then he can flip the switch and receive a second program. Flip the switch again and he would receive a third program.

Under the new system, the existing 13 FM stations in New York City could offer a total of 39 programs at the same time.

Present FM transmitters could be modified for the new system at the cost of "a few thousand dollars," according to Dr. Armstrong, but listeners at home will have to buy new FM receivers. The system, the inventor said, does not work with AM, or amplitude modulation, radio. AM stations broadcast in the so-called standard between 550 and 1,600 kilocycles.

Dr. Armstrong, whose inventions have played a major role in shaping the technical course of modern broadcasting, said one station could offer simultaneously a classical music program, a popular music program and a news program.

"Economically, the broadcaster could sell twice or three times as much advertising," he observed....

Announcement of the new system promised to pose a new problem for the Federal Communications Commission, which prohibits ownership of more than one radio station in the same city.

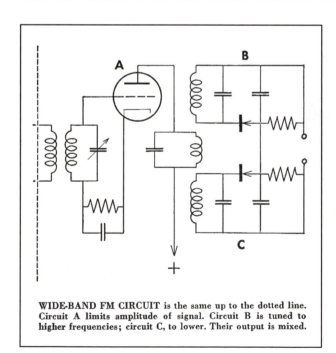

WIDE-BAND FM CIRCUIT is the same up to the dotted line. Circuit A limits amplitude of signal. Circuit B is tuned to higher frequencies; circuit C, to lower. Their output is mixed.

"Radio Show Brings Activity in Stocks," *The New York Times*, September 24, 1924:

Radio men, brokerage offices that handle their stocks, and those who speculate in them or buy them for investment are taking a leaf from the book of leaders of the automobile industry. During the Automobile Show in New York each year, it has become a habit for motor shares to "get a whirl" in the stock market. Just now, with the Radio World's Fair on, radio shares quoted on the New York Curb are getting "a whirl," and some of them have advanced rapidly in the last few days.

There are 14 radio stocks quoted on the Curb market, of which 10 are active, and this activity is confined in most cases to common shares. At yesterday's quotations, the shares were selling in the open market at an aggregate valuation of $29 million, based on the entire capitalization of the 14 companies.

"Radio Aids Enforcement," *Troy Tribune* (Illinois), February 14, 1952:

Modernization of the Illinois State Police radio system by installation of frequency modulation for all transmitting and receiving stations has been completed. The change to FM on all 50 permanent stations, 400 squad cars and three airplanes understates police supervision.

Radio first became an adjunct of the Illinois State Police in 1936 with the establishment of seven stations which could transmit to squad cars within a 25-mile radius. The vehicles could not return calls in those early days. Five years later, a two-way system was installed and the distance for reception was more than doubled by construction of booster stations.

In January 1950, the Federal Communications Commission granted its first police experimental FM license to Illinois. Two years of testing equipment and methods and waiting for completely satisfactory equipment followed before adoption of the static-free system.

The new state police network consists of 11 5,000-watt stations for the radius of 85 miles, 22 transmitters at 50 watts installed in truck weighing stations, three 250-watt stations and 14 booster stations. This system enables radio voice coverage of the entire state.

The present network permits three-way conversation. Each squad car now is equipped to talk with the permanent stations and other cars in its area. Each vehicle is a moving radio transmitting and receiving station.

1954 News Feature

"Computers in Business, The Large Electronic Machines, Heretofore Found Only in the Computation Laboratory, Are Now Being Applied to the Automatic Handling of Entire Office Procedures," *Scientific American*, January 1954:

When the first giant, all-electric digital computer went into operation in 1945, fantastic predictions about its capacity were heard. Such "giant brains," it was said, would speedily take over all the paper functions of business and the running of entire automatic factories. Actually, these impressive monsters have proven harder to tame and put to work than was first thought. But their domestication is underway, and it is possible to report how some of them have begun to function in everyday business tasks.

The machines are a different genus from the smaller electronic computers or data processing machines that evolved out of them in some profusion after 1945. The small case scale electronic computers that are widely used in business are employed only for limited routine tasks for special purposes; for example, one electronic computer handles all seat reservations at New York for a major airline, and another collates flight schedules for the Civil Aeronautics Authority. The jobs to be given to the new giants are of a higher order of magnitude: increased inventory control, general accounting, factory management and even the human equation.

Essentially, these machines operate in the same way as the smaller ones: they add, subtract, multiply and divide, and they work with "bits" of information represented by pulsed electrical signals based on the binary number system. They have the same basic organs as any electronic computer: an arithmetical unit for computation, a control unit to direct the sequence of operations, a memory unit to store numbers and instructions, and several input-output devices for putting data and instructions into the machine and getting answers out. But they have many more of them, and the greater complexity enables them to work on very large problems, or groups of problems, without human intervention.

The giant computers still inspire the same awe that the first of the genus, ENIAC, did when its thousands of vacuum tubes began winking eerily in the basement of the Moore School of Engineering at the University of Pennsylvania nine years ago. There is something a bit frightening about them. An operator demonstrates their incredible speed in a problem involving some 780 arithmetical steps: before he has lifted his finger from the starting button, the machine is typing out the answer. Another machine reads and translates Russian documents at the rate of 100 words a minute. Another takes in masses of personal data on college freshmen and predicts with better than 90 percent accuracy which students will flunk out of a college course. (The same technique can be applied to the hiring of employees.)

ENIAC was designed to calculate ballistic tables and work on other complex equations in science and engineering. Scientific problems are still the main occupation of these machines, of which there are now more than 30 in the U.S. The reason their adaptation to business problems has been slow is not merely their cost ($1 million for a machine installed), but the fact that the kind of operation required for a business task is very different. A scientific problem usually involves a great deal of computation on relatively small amounts of data within a few fixed rules. Most business problems, on the other hand, are characterized by masses of data, relatively little computation, and multitudes of variables. Attempts to translate these problems into large programs are just beginning.

The business possibilities are well illustrated, on a limited scale, by an inventory control machine called Distribution, which was built by the Chicago mail-order house of John Plain & Co. by Engineering Research Associates, a division of Remington Rand. While the machine is by no means a "giant brain," it is the first major application of its kind and a simple approach to the larger type of problem. It is so simple that one of its designers says depreciatingly: "This machine does practically nothing, but it does nothing extremely well." Its first successful work out came in the Christmas rush just ended.

The problem was this. John Plain sells some 8,000 gift and houseware items by catalogue through about 1,000 retail merchants, mostly rural. Its business is highly seasonal, ranging from less than 2,000 orders per day in the off-season to more than 15,000 per day in the Christmas period. The company must follow inventories closely and ship items fast when they are needed. For checking inventories, it employed a battery of women clerks, who recorded each order with a checkmark against the catalogue number on a tally card and registered the totals from hundreds of these cards each week in a master tally. Since the work was tedious and seasonal, it did not attract a high grade of workers. During the rush season, the reports fell a week or two behind, and there were many errors.

Last season, the company replaced the 60 tally clerks with the Distribution machine and 10 operators. The machine is about the size of an office locker. It contains a magnetic drum memory and a small arithmetical control unit for simple addition and subtraction, to which are attached 10 input units like small desk adding machines. The orders are recorded on the revolving magnetic drum, whose sensitized surface is divided into 130 invisible tracks capable of holding 39,000 digits or "bits" of information. The quantity of each item in stock is imprinted as tiny magnetized spots at a place designating the catalogue number, and the spots already at intervals on the tracks. When an order is received for a dozen, say, of some item, the operator taps out the quantity and the catalogue number on her keyboard. If she types a wrong catalogue number, the machine flashes a signal and tells her to try again. The machine then searches the drum surface, traveling at 100 mph, finds the catalogue number, plucks off the stock total or the day's sales total, transmits it to holding relays, subtracts 12 from one total or adds 12 to the other and returns a new total to the proper place in the drum—all in 2/5 of a second.

The machine can handle 90,000 tallies a day. To get out the sales total on any one item, an operator simply types out O plus the catalogue number; the total instantly appears in illuminated numbers on the panel above her keyboard. For sales embracing more than one item, the machine has a separate output unit to which is punched the required catalogue numbers and causes it to type out those numbers in their store sales totals on a paper strip. Each night, the machine is set up to run off automatically a complete report on all of the 8,000 items in the catalogue. To compile a daily stock report by the old tally card method would have required some 150 clerks. Moreover, the Distribution does its work far more accurately than tally clerks could.

With modifications in size and in the type of input-output, the same machine can handle many other kinds of inventory problems, materials scheduling and so on. It belongs to a class of moderately fast magnetic drum machines which are now offered by a number of manufacturers. A neat, medium-sized model capable of a large variety of office jobs has reached quantity production by the Computer Research Corporation of California, recently acquired by the National Cash Register Company. The latest is the International Business Machines Corporations Magnetic Drum Calculator. Somewhat more versatile than others, it stores up to 20,000 digits and up to 2,000 separate operating instructions. It can hold entire rate tables for calculating insurance policies, freight invoices, inventory bills and the like, or entire production programs for scheduling the flow of parts and materials. The price range of the magnetic drum machines is $50,000-$100,000, or if they are rented, from $500-$1,000 a month. On a small scale, they introduce into the business machine field the important principle of the internal stored program....

The Monsanto Chemical Company recently took to IBM's computer center a problem in cost distribution. The task was to figure out how overhead charges, such as utility services, steam and the like, should be apportioned to calculate the cost of producing a certain chemical product. In multi-product industries, such as chemicals and oil, cost distribution becomes exceedingly complicated, and in many simpler industries they are so obscured that managers never get to know the actual cost per product in time for the information to have any significance. The problem that Monsanto presented to the 701 computer involved a large set of simultaneous equations and about 400,000 arithmetic operations. The machine worked out a cost sheet for the product in a few hours. Monsanto has ordered an advanced version of the 701 to prepare such cost sheets on about 1,200 items and to compute quarterly reports and do other accounting jobs which it has been doing for two years on much smaller IBM electronic computers.

1955 Profile

Jack Simplot was called a gambler and reckless wheeler-dealer before his hard work created a fortune from French Fries, recognizing him as an "entrepreneurial genius."

Life at Home

- John Richard "Jack" Simplot's success story was built on potatoes.
- Jack and the humble spud were linked from the moment a flip of a silver dollar in 1928 gave him his partner's half of an electric potato sorter, to the Second World War when his company became the largest shipper of potatoes in the nation, to the creation of the first commercial French fry.
- The $254 electric potato sorter he won on a coin toss speeded up work enough that Jack's Declo, Idaho, neighbors eagerly sought its services.
- One electric portable sorter led to four, one potato shed to 33, and an empire was born.
- Born on January 4, 1909, to Charles and Dorothy Simplot on an Iowa homestead, Jack was one of six children.
- He was still in diapers when the family moved to Declo, where his father built a log cabin and cleared land with a team of horses.
- Like most farm children, J.R. got up at five o'clock every morning and milked the cows before walking to school, only to run home to do more chores in the afternoon.
- It was an unsentimental life.
- When young Jack lost a fingertip in an accident and a doctor admonished his parents for not bringing it to be reattached, they told him the chickens had eaten it.
- At 14, when his father refused to let him attend a basketball game, Jack left home, quit school and moved to the Enyeart Hotel in Declo.
- With money he made raising orphaned lambs, he purchased interest-bearing scrip at $0.50 on the dollar from teachers living at the hotel and used it as collateral to buy 600 hogs at $1.00 a head, a rifle, and a pick-up truck.

Jack Simplot commercialized French Fries.

- He used the rifle to shoot wild horses, and—after stripping the hides for future sale at $2.00 each—he mixed their meat with potatoes cooked on sagebrush-fueled flames.
- The hogs ate the result during the winter of 1923.
- When he sold the fattened pigs the next summer for $12.50 each during a nationwide pork shortage, Jack made more than $7,800 profit.
- That gave him capital to buy farm machinery and six horses and become a farmer.
- First, he leased 120 acres to grow potatoes, beans and hay.
  - After three years, he sold the horses and the machinery and stayed in the potato business, an industry that was still developing.
  - Idaho's altitude, warm days, cool nights, light volcanic soil and abundance of irrigation made it an ideal setting for growing Russet Burbank potatoes.
  - Next, he acquired half of an electric potato sorter with a partner.
  - After they argued about its use, they flipped a coin for full ownership; Jack won, and expanded to all phases of the potato industry.
  - Determined to have the entire region known for its quality, he decided that cull potatoes as seed stock weren't good enough to meet his goals, so he furnished certified seed to the growers, buying by the carloads.
  - "I told 'em, 'You keep the sprouts off that damn stuff somehow or 'nother, keep 'em cool, turn 'em over, and plant 'em on the tenth of June. If you do, you'll raise yourself some good seed.'"
  - In 1931, he married Ruby Rosevear whom he had met on a blind date; he proposed to her in his Model A Ford.
  - She was quiet and introverted, and wanted a simple life; she hated anything that was showy.
  - Nine years after marrying her, Jack owned 30,000 acres of farm and ranch land and was shipping 10,000 boxcars of potatoes a year.
  - While other Idahoans took their families to the mountains on vacation, Jack took his to Grand View, where the company farmed and fed up to 150,000 head of cattle.

Simplot sold his fattened pigs at a premium during a pork shortage.

A potato sorter was the beginning of Simplot's success in the potato industry.

Ruby Rosevear married Simplot after meeting on a blind date.

Life at Work

- To Jack Simplot, the outbreak of World War II presented a special opportunity: hungry soldiers in America and overseas.
- The answer was dehydrated and fresh potatoes.
- Already wealthy by 1941 because of a prune drying machine he bought in Southern California that he used to dry onions in Idaho, Jack understood the meaning of the word opportunity.
- Before the war, he had used the prune drying machine to create dehydrated products for onion powder and onion flakes.
- One customer wanted 300,000 pounds of onion powder and 200,000 pounds of flakes, which netted Jack $600,000 the first year.
- Relying on a contract scrawled on the back of an envelope, Jack leveraged that order for 500,000 pounds of dried onions into an immediate need for a plant to process them.
- He wanted to build the manufacturing facility at Parma, Idaho, but a man with a deed to the land sicced his dogs on Jack and he settled on Caldwell, Idaho, instead.
- The Caldwell plant, equipped with the world's largest food dehydrator, was key to his becoming the largest supplier of potatoes to the military during World War II.
- Under contract to the federal government during World War II, Jack shipped 33 million pounds of dehydrated potatoes to the U.S. Armed Forces from 1942 through 1945.
- By 1945, more than 50 million pounds of spuds were being used by the military and, of 156 companies supplying dried food, Simplot had one-third of the action.
- When war shipments started in 1942, Jack employed 100 workers in his Caldwell plant; by 1944, he had 1,200 employees and the largest dehydrating plant in the world.
- That activity supplied a lot of potato waste from the dehydration plant, so Jack established a 2,000-hog feedlot next door.
- When wartime shortages made it difficult to buy fertilizer, Jack built a manufacturing plant in Pocatello, Idaho, and produced his own.
- That kind of ingenuity continued during the early 1950s as the Simplot Company created and marketed the first commercially viable frozen French fries in the world.
- In 1945, a chemist at the Simplot lab in Caldwell asked Jack to give him a freeze box so that he could practice freezing vegetables.
- "Hell," Jack told him, "you freeze spuds and they will go to mush."
- But he bought the guy a 10-foot box anyway and after a few months, Jack was tasting hot French fries that had been previously frozen.
- "I ate some and said, 'My God, good product.'"
- Within six months, he had bought a 10,000-ton cold storage facility and a 60-ton-per-day ice manufacturing plant.
- They also made potato granules, which became instant mashed potatoes.
- It was the golden age of food processing.
- After World War II, millions of Americans bought refrigerators which, for the first time, included a freezer.

The potato in three forms - dehydrated, natural and sliced.

- Within a few years, one marvelous innovation after another promised to simplify the lives of American housewives: frozen orange juice, frozen TV dinners, Cheez Whiz, Jell-O salads, and Miracle Whip.
- Depression-era scarcity gave way to a cornucopia of new foods; ad campaigns made space-age processed foods appear more attractive than fresh.
- Restaurants even featured frozen dinners on their menus.
- Jack began selling frozen French fries in 1953 just as the budding fast food industry was searching for its identity and menu.
- They could be eaten informally without a fork and they tasted great—especially when cooked in beef tallow.
- For the emerging fast food industry, frozen French fries offered uniformity and reduced labor costs; French fries quickly became the most profitable item on the menu.
- And Jack's company held all the relevant patents.
- Sales began slowly in 1953, then skyrocketed.
- By 1955, the year the company incorporated all of its operations under the name "J.R. Simplot Co.," annual French fry production exceeded 10 million pounds.
- The future looked bright.
- A medium-size 5.3-ounce potato with the skin provided 27 mg of vitamin C, 620 mg of potassium, 0.2 mg vitamin B6 and trace amounts of thiamin, riboflavin, folate, niacin, magnesium, phosphorus, iron and zinc.
- The fiber content of a potato was equivalent to that of many whole grain breads, pastas and cereals.

Life in the Community: The State of Idaho

- Idaho was named as the result of a hoax.
- In the early 1860s, when the U.S. Congress was considering organizing a new territory in the Rocky Mountains, eccentric lobbyist George M. Willing suggested the name "Idaho," which he claimed was derived from a Shoshone language term meaning "the sun comes from the mountains" or "gem of the mountains."
- Willing later claimed that he had made up the name himself.
- Congress ultimately decided to name the area Colorado Territory when it was created in February 1861.
- Idaho, as part of the Oregon Country, had been claimed by both the United States and Great Britain until the United States gained undisputed jurisdiction in 1846.

Shoshone Falls, Snake River, Idaho.

- Idaho achieved statehood in 1890 when its population was 88,000; its economy, which had been primarily supported by metal mining, shifted towards agriculture and lumbering.
- Sixty percent of Idaho's land is held by the National Forest Service or the Bureau of Land Management, and boasts a perfect climate for growing potatoes.
- The landscape is rugged, with some of the largest unspoiled natural areas in the United States; the 2.3 million-acre River of No Return Wilderness Area is the largest contiguous region of protected wilderness in the continental United States.
- Potatoes were planted in Idaho as early as 1838; by 1900, the state's production exceeded a million bushels.
- Prior to 1910, the crops were stored in barns or root cellars, but by the 1920s, potato cellars came into use.
- U.S. potato production increased steadily; by 1955, two-thirds of the potato crop came from Idaho, Washington, Oregon, Colorado, and Maine.
- In the 1950s, the growth of the French fry industry led to a focus on developing varieties for the industry.
- The 1950 U.S. Census recorded Idaho's population as 588,000 residents.

Lumber was important to Idaho's economy.

HISTORICAL SNAPSHOT
1955

- The Pentagon announced a plan to develop ICBMs (intercontinental ballistic missiles) armed with nuclear weapons
- Congress authorized President Dwight D. Eisenhower to use force to protect Formosa from the People's Republic of China
- Eisenhower sent the first U.S. advisors to South Vietnam
- Evan Hunter's movie adaptation of the novel *Blackboard Jungle* premiered, featuring the single "Rock Around the Clock" by Bill Haley and His Comets
- The Salk polio vaccine, having passed large-scale trials, received full approval by the Food and Drug Administration
- The TV quiz program *The $64,000 Question* premiered on CBS-TV in the United States, with Hal March as the host
- *The Lady and the Tramp*, the Walt Disney Company's fifteenth animated film, premiered in Chicago
- The Disneyland Theme Park opened in Anaheim, California
- The first edition of *The Guinness Book of Records* was published in London
- The long-running program *Gunsmoke* debuted on the CBS-TV network
- Vladimir Nabokov's controversial novel *Lolita* was published in Paris by Olympia Press
- *Alfred Hitchcock Presents* and *The Mickey Mouse Club* both debuted on television
- The Brooklyn Dodgers finally won the World Series, defeating the New York Yankees 2-0 in game 7 of the 1955 baseball playoff
- Seventy-mm film for projection was introduced with the release of Rodgers and Hammerstein's musical *Oklahoma!*
- Rosa Parks was arrested for refusing to give up her seat on a bus to a white person, a defining event in the national Civil Rights Movement
- The American Federation of Labor and the Congress of Industrial Organizations merged to form the AFL-CIO
- American cytogeneticist Joe Hin Tjio discovered the correct number of human chromosomes: 46
- General Motors Corporation became the first American company to make a profit of over $1 billion in one year

Selected Prices

Cake Mix	$1.00
Dance Lessons	$25.00
Drink Powder, Nestle's Quik	$0.66
Girdle, Playtex	$4.95
Potato Chips, Pound	$0.49
Potatoes, Burbank Russet, 20 Pounds	$0.49
Sofabed	$69.95
Soup, Campbell's, Can	$0.16
Television, Zenith	$550.00
Typewriter, Smith Corona	$164.50

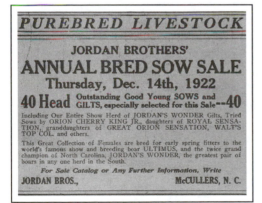

Potato Growing and Dehydration

- Potatoes were first domesticated in Peru between 3000 BC and 2000 BC.
- In the Altiplano, potatoes provided the principal energy source for the Inca Empire, its predecessors, and its Spanish successor.
- Processing potatoes for storage has a long history; the Incas used climate to produce the first dehydrated potatoes.
- Their method entailed an overnight freezing and thawing cycle plus low humidity.

Potato cellar.

- The ice crystals that formed forced openings in the cell tissue, allowing liquid to escape; the Incas also employed foot power to expel the liquid.
- The cycle was repeated several times to lower the moisture content, and then the marble-sized potatoes were dried for storage.
- The Incas called it chuño, and it was a staple used by soldiers.
- Sufficient quantities of chuño were dehydrated as well to guard against shortages.
- Potatoes yield abundantly with little effort as long as the climate is cool and moist enough for the plants to gather sufficient water from the soil to form the starchy tubers.
- There are about 5,000 potato varieties worldwide; 3,000 of them are found in the Andes alone, mainly in Peru, Bolivia, Ecuador, Chile and Colombia.
- Europeans first used potatoes for provisioning ships in the sixteenth century.
- By the eighteenth century, the potato had become the major food source in a large part of the Europe.
- Introduced to Europe by Spain in 1536, the potato was subsequently conveyed by European mariners to territories and ports throughout the world.
- Throughout Europe, the most important new food in the nineteenth century was the potato, which had three major advantages over other foods for the consumer: its lower rate of spoilage, its ability to easily satisfy hunger, and its low cost.
- By 1845, the potato crop occupied one-third of Irish arable land and potatoes comprised about 10 percent of the caloric intake of Europeans.
- In England, the potato promoted economic development by underpinning the Industrial Revolution in the nineteenth century.

continued

Potato Growing and Dehydration *(continued)*

- It served as a cheap source of calories and nutrients that was easy for urban workers to cultivate on small backyard plots.
- Potatoes became popular in the north of England, where coal was readily available, so a potato-driven population boom provided ample workers for the new factories.
- In Ireland, the expansion of potato cultivation was due entirely to the landless laborers, renting tiny plots from predominantly English landowners, who were interested only in raising cattle or in producing grain for market.
- A single acre of potatoes and the milk of a single cow was enough to feed a whole Irish family a monotonous but nutritionally adequate diet for a healthy, vigorous, and desperately poor rural population.
- Often, even poor families grew enough extra potatoes to feed a pig that they could sell for cash.
- A lack of genetic diversity left the crop vulnerable to disease.
- In 1845, a plant disease known as late blight, caused by the fungus-like oomycete *Phytophthora infestans*, spread rapidly through the poorer communities of western Ireland, resulting in the crop failures that led to the Great Irish Famine.
- But the potato had two major drawbacks: it was bulky and it had a short shelf life in comparison to grains.
- Potato flour was prepared in 1786, and experiments were conducted to find processes for drying potatoes.
- In the end, potato flour and potato starch—first produced in the United States in 1831—were the main examples of potato processing.
- Potato chips—first called Saratoga chips—appeared in the middle of the nineteenth century.
- At first, chips were prepared in the home, accompanied by some small-scale commercial production.
- Major commercial applications had to await improved peeling and frying techniques.
- Potato chip production did not become a big business until after World War II.

- Increased consumer demand for convenience foods prompted a renewed search for ways of extending the shelf life of potatoes, with emphasis on developing instant mashed potatoes.
- Ultimately, two processes emerged for producing dehydrated mashed potatoes: granules and flakes.
- Fixing on a quick-drying process using a single-drum drier was a major breakthrough following research focused on the appearance and flavor of the reconstituted flakes.
- Idaho's Russet Burbank potatoes were used commercially in making dehydrated mashed potatoes because of their high solid content necessary to obtain good texture when reconstituted.

"Army Says Dehydrated Food Saves Space, 'Builds Ships',"
Wisconsin State Journal, June 25, 1942:

The general tucked away mashed potatoes, beets, potato salad, bacon and eggs, and a thick wedge of apple pie, then told his 47 listeners that the Army was "building ships" by serving similar dehydrated meals to soldiers in the field.

"We are making history here," said Brig. Gen. Joseph F. Barzynski, looking down the row of empty plates. "It is almost as if we are building ships, since we have found that dehydrated foods take up only one third as much shipping space as ordinary foods."

The meal was the first of its kind ever served to civilians. It had variety, taste and color. Nine commandants of the Army's bakers' and cooks' schools and the invited guests said the "chow" was the "best meal of its kind" they'd ever eaten.

The Army subsistence laboratory of the Chicago quartermaster depot, of which Barzynski is the commanding general, developed the dehydrated foods that were served. Barzynski showed his guess how a large apple when dehydrated shrinks to the size of a $0.50 piece. Other foods whose water content has been removed were reduced proportionally in size and weight.

"A package the size of an ordinary loaf of bread will serve 100 portions of bacon and eggs to the men in the field," Barzynski said. "Not only do we save shipping space, but we save time, equipment, and man-power cooking dehydrated foods."

Dehydrated potatoes provide one of the best examples of how shipping space can be saved. A shipment of 27,000,000 pounds of potatoes can be reduced to 3,000,000 pounds, which will save at least 500,000 cubic feet of cargo space. This amounts to more than the capacity of cargo ships, or about 1,000 ships' tons.

"What's the percentage of shipping water abroad," said one of the officers at the Army meal, "when the hydrated food will produce chow like this?"

The Army has also found that frozen, boneless meat makes for similar shipping space savings. It can be sent at a 30 percent savings in weight and a 60 percent savings in bulk.

"Dehydrated Potatoes Get Government Praise," *The Greeley Tribune* (Colorado), June 24, 1943:

Quality of dehydrated potatoes being turned out at the plant of Dehydrated Food Products Company of Colorado has been praised by government inspectors who have inspected the product and accepted delivery on about half a carload of the dehydrated product, according to Orville Ruler, general manager of the company....

The plant is now employing about 150 people; 100 more women workers are needed. The plant operates three eight-hour shifts. Shifts are from 4 p.m. to midnight, from midnight to 8 a.m., and from 8 a.m. to 4 p.m. Workers are on a shift for a month and then transferred to another shift. Basic wages $0.40 an hour, and time and a half for overtime over 40 hours. Most workers get about 42 hours a week, Ruler said.

"Jack Simplot Builds It!" *The Salt Lake Tribune,* January 16, 1949:

Simplot is a magic name in intermountain West. In towns up and down Idaho's Snake River Valley are signs reading "J. R. Simplot Co.," signs of a new empire founded on the agricultural economy of the Gem State and its contiguous territory.

J. R. Simplot is the guiding genius of this empire, which reaches into Utah with the acquisition of the wartime Kalnite plant at Salt Lake City, now being converted to produce phosphate fertilizer to augment the supply pouring from his Pocatello plant.

Jack Simplot's interests are wide, but his chief holdings are concerned with agriculture. Besides his string of warehouses which make him Idaho's biggest shipper of potatoes and fresh vegetables, and his Pocatello and Salt Lake plants, he operates the world's largest dehydrating plant, a string of Snake River Valley farms, hog ranches, a box factory, a real estate firm, an insurance firm, hotels. He is a director of the Idaho Power Company and has interests in gold, silver and lead mines.

Just turning 40, Jack Simplot is a multimillionaire of boundless energy and acute business acumen. He left school at the age of 14, and at 16 was farming on his own. At 20, he became a produce dealer when he shipped his first car of potatoes. During the Depression years, he acquired 18 warehouses and shipped as high as 8,000 boxcars of potatoes annually to 41 states. He bought more farms and raised onions, among other things. It was while inspecting an onion dehydrating plant in California that the idea for dehydrating potatoes was born. He constructed his own plant in Caldwell, equipped with six drying kilns. This was increased to 30 kilns during the war years and employed 1,200 workers. It produced some 65 percent of the Army's dehydrated potato consumption.

continued

"Jack Simplot Builds It!" *(continued)*

It was to supply his own farms with commercial fertilizer that got Simplot in the super phosphate manufacturing business, but the outside demand was so immediate and so great that the Pocatello plant has been under constant expansion since it began operating in December of 1944. Much of its output has gone to Japan and other Pacific Islands.

The organization Simplot has built, and is continuing to build, has a great deal to do with the success of his enterprises. His executives are young men all with that Simplot enthusiasm for the job at hand, no matter what it is. There are, as one of his aides remarked, no "old fogies" running the Simplot machinery, no institutional taboos to retard initiative. His executive force is, in the main, pretty free to make individual decisions and exercise sound judgment in matters of their own bailiwicks. This has built an intense loyalty for the "boss" throughout the entire organization.

1959 Profile

Jack Kilby, while working at Texas Instruments in Dallas, invented a version of the integrated circuit that revolutionized the electronics industry.

Life at Home

- When Jack Kilby began chasing the alchemist's dream of turning ordinary sand into an electronic brain, he was one of several dozen scientists struggling with the complexities of the integrated circuit.
- Already vales, relays and wires had given way to transistors, diodes and interconnects, dramatically improving reliability, but the challenge that loomed was how to use solid block materials such as silicon to connect all the key components needed for electronic systems.
- Jack was well prepared for the challenge.
- Born in 1923, Jack grew up in Great Bend, Kansas, which got its name because the town was built at the spot where the Arkansas River bends in the middle of the state.
- His father ran a small electric company that provided power to customers scattered across the rural western part of Kansas.
- During the summertime, Jack accompanied his father on trips, often crawling through generating stations looking for faulty equipment; there he got an education in the power of electricity to transform rural America.
- While Jack was in high school, a huge ice storm knocked down most of the poles that carried the telephone and electric power lines, so his father worked with amateur radio operators to communicate with customers who had lost their electricity and phone service.
- That experience with amateur radio sparked Jack's interest in electronics, and "that's when I decided that this field was something I wanted to pursue," he said years later.

Jack Kilby revolutionized the electronics industry with his integrated circuit.

- After high school, Jack planned to attend MIT but failed to get a passing mark on the entrance exam; instead, he entered the University of Illinois, where most of his classes were in electrical power.

  - Four months after he entered college, the Japanese attack on Pearl Harbor compelled Jack to enlist; his wartime service was partially served in India, where he was assigned to radio repair.
  - When he returned home from the war, he re-entered college and took some vacuum tube engineering and physics classes.
  - He graduated in 1947, just one year before Bell Labs announced the invention of the transistor, an innovation that rendered vacuum tubes obsolete.
  - His first job was with an electronics manufacturer in Milwaukee, Wisconsin, that made parts for radios, televisions and hearing aids.
  - There he worked on silk-screening techniques for printing a substrate onto which germanium transistors could be soldered; it was an important introduction into the integration of circuits.
  - While still working in Milwaukee, Jack took evening classes at the University of Wisconsin towards a master's degree in electrical engineering—a schedule that presented its own set of challenges.

- In 1958, he and his wife moved to Dallas, Texas, where Jack took a job with Texas Instruments, the only company willing to let him work full-time on electronic component miniaturization.

- Texas Instruments, widely known as TI, was founded to manufacture the newly invented transistor, but its roots stretched back to 1930 when Dr. J. Clarence Karcher and Eugene McDermott founded Geophysical Service, a pioneering provider of seismic exploration services to the petroleum industry.

- In 1939, the company reorganized as Coronado Corporation, with Geophysical Service Inc. (GSI) as a subsidiary.

  - Two years later, on the day before the attack on Pearl Harbor, McDermott along with three other GSI employees—J. Erik Jonsson, Cecil H. Green, and H.B. Peacock—purchased GSI.
  - During World War II, GSI built submarine detection equipment for the U.S. Navy, discovering that the rugged nature of the equipment they built for the oil industry was similar to the military's equipment needs.
  - In 1951, the company changed its name to Texas Instruments.
  - Early in 1952, Texas Instruments purchased a patent license to produce germanium transistors from Western Electric Company, the manufacturing arm of AT&T, for $25,000 and hired Gordon K. Teal away from Bell Labs as research director.
  - Teal brought expertise in semiconductor crystals that attracted talented scientists and engineers who were fascinated by the new and rapidly expanding semiconductor industry.
  - Among his new hires was Willis Adcock, who focused on the task of fabricating "grown-junction *silicon* single-crystal small-signal transistors."

Kilby witnessed first-hand the transforming power of electricity in rural America.

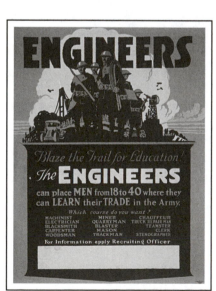

Life at Work

- During his first summer at Texas Instruments, Jack Kilby, as a new employee, had no vacation time coming and was left alone to work in the lab.
- Articulating the current problem was simple: how to cut the distance that electrical impulses traveled so that computers could be smaller, more reliable, and faster.
- The solution, however, was more complex.
- After the launch of the *Sputnik* satellite in 1957, Americans became obsessed with "catching up" with the Russians; the space race was underway and Jack was on the front lines of the technological battle.
- Slow-talking Jack considered himself an engineer, not a scientist.
- Engineers, he believed, were practical-minded people who made things work better, cheaper and more easily; he felt that too many scientists liked to think big thoughts that never went anywhere.
- Since no school in America taught one how to be an inventor, to Jack's way of thinking, creating something new was simply hard work.
- The first issue that summer was how to get to the core of the problem as quickly as possible.
- The second issue was to search for the unexpected and ignore the obvious, even when doing so violated scientific convention.
- The third issue was the creation of an affordable solution; costs had to be factored in if the product was ever to be useful.
- Jack knew it was possible to make diodes and transistors out of silicon if properly doped with the right impurities to conduct an electrical charge.
- So on July 24, 1958, he wrote in his lab notebook, "The following circuit elements could be made on a single slice: resisters, capacitors, distributed capacitors and transistors."
- After all, designing a complex electronic machine normally increased the number of components involved in order to make technical advances, unless there was a way to form a monolithic, single-crystal integrated circuit.
- When his new boss, Willis Adcock, returned from vacation, Jack explained his concept and requested funds to construct a model around his idea.
- That's when a deal was struck.

The space race with Russia was an important issue to most Americans.

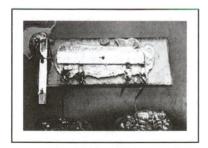

Kilby needed to develop a working capacitator and transistor.

- If Jack could construct a working capacitor and a working transistor on separate pieces of silicon, funds would be found for an integrated circuit on a chip.
- The commercial race to financial success was also underway.
- In January 1954, Bell Labs created the first workable silicon transistor; working independently, TI unveiled the first commercial silicon transistor four months later.
- Then, the breakthrough that began the "Silicon Age" occurred in early 1955, when Bell Labs invented the diffused-base silicon transistor created by solid-state diffusion of impurities—work critical to Jack's later discoveries.

- To increase the consumer demand for transistors, TI manufactured the first transistor radio using germanium transistors because silicon transistors were so expensive.
- Even though Texas Instruments had invested millions to develop equipment capable of purifying silicon and to build silicon transistors, few were suggesting that components be manufactured out of semiconductor material—before Jack went to work for TI.
- Jack created a circuit known as a phase-shift oscillator to complete his part of the deal and get his funding.
- Working with borrowed and improvised equipment, Jack then built the first electronic circuit in which all of the components, both active and passive, were fabricated in a single piece of semiconductor material half the size of a paper clip.
- Though the device he showed colleagues was relatively simple—only a transistor and other components on a slice of germanium—few realized that he was about to revolutionize the electronics industry.
- "Humankind eventually would have solved the matter, but I had the fortunate experience of being the first person with the right idea and the right resources available at the right time in history," Jack said.
- "What we didn't realize then was that the integrated circuit would reduce the cost of electronic functions by a factor of a million to one; nothing had ever done that for anything before."
- Six months later, Robert Noyce of Fairchild Semiconductor independently developed the integrated circuit with integrated interconnect.
- Both men filed for patents in 1959, igniting a battle that would last another decade.

Life in the Community: Dallas, Texas

- Dallas prided itself on being a city that liked to do business.
- In 1949, *Fortune* magazine remarked that Dallas was "a monument to sheer determination."
- City fathers bragged that "people do not come to Dallas looking for history but for progress."
- Located in North Texas, Dallas lacked the port facilities that defined most major cities, but sustained its growth as a center for the oil and cotton industries, thanks to its numerous railroad lines.
- Founded in 1841 and formally incorporated as a city in February 1856, Dallas primarily based its early economy on railroad transportation, publishing, lumbering and saddle manufacturing.
- By the turn of the twentieth century, Dallas was the leading drug, book, jewelry, and wholesale liquor market in the Southwestern United States.
- As the century progressed, Dallas transformed from an agricultural center to a center of banking, insurance, fashion retailing and other businesses, including the founding of Neiman Marcus.
- In 1911, Dallas became the location of the Eleventh Regional Branch of the Federal Reserve Bank, and millionaire Dr. William Worthington Samuell purchased the first ambulance for the city.
- In 1915, the Southern Methodist University opened.

- Aviation became a major industry in the city in World War I, when Love Field was established as an aviation training ground.

Love Field, Dallas, Texas.

- Despite the onset of the Great Depression for most of the nation, construction flourished in Dallas in 1930, and Columbus Marion "Dad" Joiner struck oil 100 miles east of Dallas in Kilgore, spawning the East Texas oil boom.
- Dallas quickly assumed the role of financial center for the oil industry in Texas and Oklahoma, and its banks made loans to develop the oil fields.
- In 1936, Texas chose Dallas as the site of the Texas Centennial Exposition, attracting 10 million visitors.
- During World War II, Dallas served as a manufacturing center for the war effort; the Ford Motor plant in Dallas converted to wartime production.
- In 1957, developers Trammell Crow and John M. Stemmons opened a Home Furnishings Mart that grew into the Dallas Market Center, the largest wholesale trade complex in the world.
- The integrated circuit invented by Jack Kilby of Texas Instruments punctuated the Dallas area's development as a center for high-technology manufacturing.
- The city soon became the nation's third-largest technology center, with the growth of such companies as LTV Corporation and Texas Instruments.

Texas Centennial Exposition, Dallas, TX: Federal exhibit building.

A Texas Instruments assembly line.

Historical Snapshot
1959

- Fulgencio Batista fled Havana, Cuba, when the forces of Fidel Castro advanced

- The Soviet Union successfully launched the *Luna 1* spacecraft
- Alaska and Hawaii became the forty-ninth and fiftieth states
- Motown Records was founded by Berry Gordy, Jr.
- Walt Disney released his sixteenth animated film, *Sleeping Beauty*
- A chartered plane transporting musicians Buddy Holly, Ritchie Valens, Roger Peterson and The Big Bopper (Jiles Perry "JP" Richardson, Jr.) crashed in foggy conditions near Clear Lake, Iowa, killing all four occupants on board
- At Cape Canaveral, Florida, a Titan intercontinental ballistic missile was successfully test-fired
- The United States launched the *Vanguard II* weather satellite
- Recording sessions for the album *Kind of Blue* by Miles Davis took place at Columbia's 30th Street Studio in New York City
- The Barbie doll debuted
- *A Raisin in the Sun* by Lorraine Hansberry opened on Broadway
- NASA announced the first U.S. astronauts
- The USS *George Washington* was launched as the first submarine to carry ballistic missiles
- The film *The Nun's Story*, based on the best-selling novel, was released, with Audrey Hepburn starring as the title character
- Charles Ovnand and Dale R. Buis became the first Americans killed in action in Vietnam
- The first skull of Australopithecus was discovered by Mary Leakey in the Olduvai Gorge of Tanzania
- Rod Serling's anthology series *The Twilight Zone* premiered on CBS
- The U.S.S.R. probe *Luna 3* sent back the first photos of the far side of the moon
- MGM's widescreen, multimillion-dollar Technicolor version of *Ben-Hur*, starring Charlton Heston, was released and became the studio's greatest hit
- Pantyhose were introduced by Glen Raven Mills

Selected Prices

Automobile, Cadillac $13,075
Cat Food, Three Cans $0.39
Cough Syrup.. $0.49
Eyelash Curler.. $1.00
Grill $79.95
Hamburger, Burger King $0.37
Ironing Table $13.95
Lawn Sprinkler $16.95
Milk, Quart $0.60
Sofa Bed $69.99

"Transistorized Sets Are Economical, Too," *The Brownsville Herald* (Texas), August 5, 1958:

A Texas company has perfected the television receiver that all but does away with vacuum tubes, the main source of trouble in TV set breakdowns.

The company is Texas Instruments, which makes transistors. It has substituted transistors for vacuum tubes. The only tubes in a transistorized Texas Instruments receiver are the picture and a high-voltage rectifier.

"The only reason we haven't got a transistor where we used the high-voltage rectifier is because the cost would be prohibitive," Cecil Lightfoot of Texas Instruments said. "We have the transistor."

Texas Instruments' transistor TV set was shown last week at the Texas Electronic Association meeting in Dallas. It has a nine-inch picture tube and weighs a total of 39 pounds, including battery.

The transistors require so little current—a little over eight watts, in this case, as opposed to 90 watts for an ordinary television set—that a battery will operate the set. The battery will operate the set for about four hours and it can be recharged by attaching it to the house current.

The set receives stations on a par with a vacuum tube set. Lightfoot said the difference in cost between it and the vacuum tube set is about the same as it is between a radio receiver with vacuum tubes and one with a transistorized circuit, if the set were in production.

Transistorized radios cost about three times more. Actually, Texas Instruments' TV is not for sale. It was built by the company's engineers to show TV manufacturers that it can be done. The set will not be put into production by Texas Instruments.

Transistorized television receivers should reduce television repair cost dramatically, since transistors last 20 to 25 years.

William G. Stroud (NASA project manager) shows satellite circuitry to Lyndon B. Johnson.

"Lyndon Pledges Satellite Probe," *The Paris News* (Texas), October 18, 1957:

Sen. Lyndon Johnson said yesterday the only reason the successful Earth satellite was labeled "made in Moscow" was lack of intelligent, united effort in the United States. He promised to lead efforts in Congress to find out why and what can be done about this "man-made object whizzing through the air over our heads."

The Senate majority leader spoke at the Tyler Rose Festival.

"We have got to admit frankly without evasion the Soviets have beaten us at our own game: daring scientific advances in the atomic age," Johnson said.

"This is obviously a situation which requires a careful study by Congress. The reports are conflicting. Official sources are long on warm optimism, short on cold facts...."

Johnson said his subcommittee's preliminary work would try to get answers to such questions as: "Could we have matched Soviet achievement? Would it have been worthwhile to match the Soviet achievement? Does the Soviet satellite indicate that this country has slipped behind in the development of its defense? If so, what do we have to do to catch up?"

"We may discover that the alarms are false; that there is no great cause for concern," Johnson said. "But we may also find out that our whole defense structure needs a thorough overhaul top to bottom."

"*Sputnik* Rocket to Be Seen by Texans Early Today," *The Paris News* (Texas), October 18, 1957:

Early-rising Texans got a good look Friday at the rocket trailing the Russian Earth satellite across the dawn skies.

Sightings were reported throughout the state. Most reports said the bright orange object is clearly visible without telescopic aid.

It coursed across the skies between 5:20 a.m. and 5:25 a.m. The satellite *Sputnik* itself was about 15 minutes behind the rocket which launched it into the space orbit. The satellite was not visible to unaided vision.

Don Clark, a Dallas truck driver, described the rocket as a bright, flashing object. He spotted it while driving between Three Rivers and Mathis on Highway 281.

Capt. Henry C. Walburn of Fort Worth, an American Airlines pilot, radioed at 5:22 a.m. that he spotted the rocket over Lordsburg, New Mexico.

He said the rocket appeared underneath the handle of the Big Dipper just over the plane's right wing. He said it was an intermittent flashing light, making a vast sweeping arc to the Southwest.

At College Station, Jack Kent of Texas A&M headed the official moon watch team which saw the rocket cross the dawn sky. Many other persons in the Bryan area saw the rocket, but apparently none saw the satellite itself.

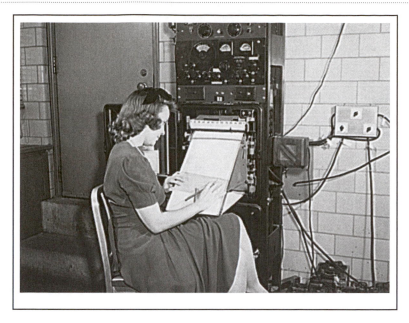

To forecast weather, high frequency radio signals are recorded from small transmitters attached to aloft balloons.

"Forecasting of Weather Tough Task," *Denton Record-Chronicle* (Texas), July 26, 1957:

The weatherman, even with modern electronic computers, cannot accurately forecast day-by-day variations in the weather more than one week in advance, University of Texas meteorologist K. H. John says.

"Many people tend to believe that the computer is the final achievement in weather forecasting. They think the present weather conditions can be fit into the computer, which would then produce a perfect forecast," John says. That is not the case. Computers may be expected to be more professional, but they are not necessarily more accurate than man," John explains.

Detailed weather forecasts are possible for two or three days in advance, but the reliability of the prediction decreases progressively after the first day, John says in explaining just what the public might expect from a professional meteorologist.

"Forecasts of the weather expected three to seven days in advance must be issued in less specific terms than the shorter range of projections and are ordinarily restricted to a statement that the temperature will be higher or lower than general for that time of year."

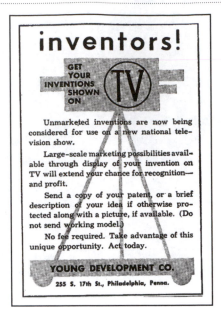

Inventions: 1950 to 1959

1950
Ralph Schneider invented the credit card.

1951
Super Glue was invented.

Francis W. Davis invented power steering.

Charles Ginsburg invented the first video tape recorder (VTR).

1952
Mr. Potato Head was patented.

The first patent for bar code was issued to inventors Joseph Woodland and Bernard Silver.

The first diet soft drink, a sugar-free ginger ale intended for diabetics, was sold.

Edward Teller and his team built the hydrogen bomb.

1953
Radial tires were invented.

RCA invented the first musical synthesizer.

David Warren invented the black box flight recorder.

Texas Instruments invented the transistor radio.

---

continued

Inventions: 1950 to 1959 *(continued)*

1954

An oral contraceptive for women (the "pill") was invented.

The first nonstick Teflon pan was produced.

Chaplin, Fuller and Pearson invented the solar cell.

1955

Tetracycline was invented.

Optical fiber was invented.

1956

The first computer hard disk was used.

Christopher Cockerell invented the hovercraft.

Bette Nesmith Graham invented "Mistake Out," later renamed Liquid Paper, to paint over mistakes made with a typewriter.

1957

The Fortran computer language was invented.

1958

The computer modem was invented.

Gordon Gould invented the laser.

Richard Knerr and Arthur "Spud" Melin invented the Hula Hoop.

Jack Kilby and Robert Noyce invented the integrated circuit.

1959

Wilson Greatbatch invented the internal pacemaker.

Ruth Handler (the co-founder of Mattel) invented the Barbie Doll, named after her own daughter Barbara.

Jack Kilby and Robert Noyce both invented the microchip.

"Teenomania," Marion Walker, *Alcaro*, September 1952:

I want to make it perfectly plain that I have nothing whatsoever against teenagers. Some of my favorite people are teenagers, including my oldest son. But I can't help wondering if there isn't currently much too much commotion about them.

I wonder if the teens haven't come to be considered too much an age apart, an age completely different from any other. I wonder if the teenager isn't too continually in both the public and the family lime-lights. And, at the risk of being put summarily in my place by the experts, I wonder if parents, those long-suffering clay pigeons in How-To-Bring–Up-Your-Children propaganda, haven't been given a good deal of slightly hysterical and extremely unsound advice about how to cope with this particular stage in their offspring's development.

The teenager is a fairly recent discovery. Twenty years or so ago, if you were between 12 and 17, you were referred to rather vaguely as being "at that age" or "in between." There were no clothes designed especially for you; you wore little girl dresses until the waistlines were under your armpits. And then you graduated abruptly into your mother's kind of clothes. If you were a boy, you were promoted to pants when your legs got long enough. No one considered your patois amusing. No one considered your antics diverting. And no one considered your problems important. You were low man on the social totem pole.

This was a deplorable state of affairs and clearly needed improvement. But now the pendulum seems to have swung as far the other way. Today the teenager, also known as teenster, the teener, the subdeb, the prep, and the junior miss—is a national celebrity. He, or she, is society's most publicized and pampered pet. Newspapers headline his doing. Magazines feature his problem. Novels, plays, comic strips, movies, radio serials, and television programs are based on his escapades and his wit. Fashion experts vie to design his clothes. And the general public views him with the flattering mixture of affection and alarm that used to be reserved for collegians in raccoon coats.

At home, the teenager used to be treated like an ordinary member of the family. Today it is considered de rigueur to treat him like visiting royalty. The family kitchen and the family living room should be at his instant disposal, the experts tell us. Some authorities suggest that we remodel an entire section of the family residence for his exclusive use.

According to the experts, it is a teenager's privilege to monopolize the family radio and the family telephone. It is considered his privilege to monopolize practically all his parents' time, effort, patience, energy and attention....

continued

"Teenomania," *(continued)*

This vogue of lionizing the teenager is based on good intentions. Its purpose is to give him a fair share of social prominence, to help him avoid some well-known pitfalls, and help him solve the problems of growing up. But does it really accomplish what it sets out to? In my opinion, it is being carried to such extremes that it creates new problems instead of solving old ones. In my opinion, it is unfair to everyone concerned.

Let's try a novel experiment. Let's take a look at the parent's side of the question. For parents are people, too, a fact that often seems to escape the experts. Parents, a well as growing boys and girls, have emotional difficulties to overcome, romances to keep alive and glowing, friendships to maintain, and personal enthusiasms to pursue. Can they accomplish any of these feats of balanced and successful living if they are required quite literally to knock themselves out for their teenage children?....

Few teenagers grow up to find society quick to make allowances for them. Instead, they are expected to be adult, mature, responsible, cooperative. Is it fair to expect them to develop these qualities if we make them the lodestar of their parents' whole existence?

1960-1969

The 1960s were tumultuous. Following the placid era of the 1950s, the seventh decade of the twentieth century contained tragic assassinations, momentous social movements, remarkable space achievements, and the longest war in American history. Civil Rights leader Martin Luther King, Jr., would deliver his "I have a dream" speech in 1963, the same year President John F. Kennedy was killed. Five years later in 1968, King, along with John Kennedy's influential brother Bobby, would be shot. And violent protests against American involvement in Vietnam would be led and heavily supported by the educated middle class, which had grown and prospered enormously in the American economy.

From 1960 to 1964, the economy expanded; unemployment was low and disposable income for music, vacations, art or simply having fun grew rapidly. Internationally, the power of the United States was immense. Congress gave the young President John F. Kennedy the defense and space-related programs Americans wanted, but few of the welfare programs he proposed. Then, inflation arrived, along with the Vietnam War. Between 1950 and 1965, inflation soared from an annual average of less than two percent (ranging from six percent to 14 percent a year) to a budget-popping average of 9.5 percent. Upper class investors, once content with the consistency and stability of banks, sought better returns in the stock market and real estate.

The Cold War became hotter during conflicts over Cuba and Berlin in the early 1960s. Fears over the international spread of communism let to America's intervention in a foreign conflict that would become a defining event of the decade: Vietnam. Military involvement in this small Asian country grew from advisory status to full-scale war. By 1968, Vietnam had become a national obsession leading to President Lyndon Johnson's decision not to run for another term and fueling not only debate over our role in Vietnam, but more inflation and division nationally. The antiwar movement grew rapidly. Antiwar marches, which had drawn but a few thousand in 1965, grew in size until millions of marchers filled the streets of New York, San Francisco, and Washington, DC, only a few years later. By spring 1970, students on 448 college campuses made ROTC voluntary or abolished it.

The struggle to bring economic equality to blacks during the period produced massive spending for school integration. By 1963, the peaceful phase of the Civil Rights movement was ending; street violence, assassinations, and bombings defined the period. In 1967, 41 cities experienced major disturbances. At the same time, charismatic labor organizer Cesar Chavez's United Farm Workers led a Civil Rights-style movement for Mexican-Americans, gaining national support which challenged the growers of the West with a five-year agricultural strike.

As a sign of increasing affluence and changing times, American consumers bought 73 percent fewer potatoes and 25 percent more fish, poultry, and meat and 50 percent more citrus products and tomatoes than in 1940. California passed New York as the most populous state. Factory workers earned more than $100 per week, their highest wages in history. From 1960 to 1965, the amount of money spent for prescription drugs to lose weight doubled, while the per capita consumption of processed potato chips rose from 6.3 pounds in 1958 to 14.2 pounds eight years later. In 1960, approximately 40 percent of American adult women had paying jobs; 30 years later, the number would grow to 57.5 percent. Their emergence into the work force would transform marriage, child rearing, and the economy. In 1960, women were also liberated by the FDA's approval of the birth-control pill, giving both women and men a degree of control over their bodies that had never existed before.

During the decade, anti-establishment sentiments grew; men's hair was longer and wilder, beards and mustaches became popular, women's skirts rose to mid-thigh, and bras were discarded. Hippies advocated alternative lifestyles, drug use increased, especially marijuana and LSD; the Beatles, the Rolling Stones, Jimi Hendrix, and Janis Joplin became popular music figures; college campuses became major sites for demonstrations against the war and for Civil Rights. The Supreme Court prohibited prayer, assured legal counsel to the poor, limited censorship of sexual material, and increased the rights of the accused.

Extraordinary space achievements also marked the decade. Ten years after President Kennedy announced he would place a man on the moon, 600 million people around the world watched as Neil Armstrong gingerly lowered his left foot into the soft dust of the moon's surface. In a tumultuous time of division and conflict, the landing was one of America's greatest triumphs and an exhilarating demonstration of American genius. Its cost was $25 billion and set the stage for 10 other men to walk on the surface of the moon during the next three years.

The 1960s saw the birth of Enovid 10, the first oral contraceptive (cost $.55 each), the start of Berry Gordy's Motown Records, felt-tip pens, Diet-Rite cola, Polaroid color film, Weight Watchers, and Automated Teller Machines. It's the decade when lyrics began appearing on record albums, Jackie and Aristotle Onassis reportedly spent $20 million during their first year together, and the Gay Liberation Front participated in the Hiroshima Day March—the first homosexual participation as a separate constituency in a peace march.

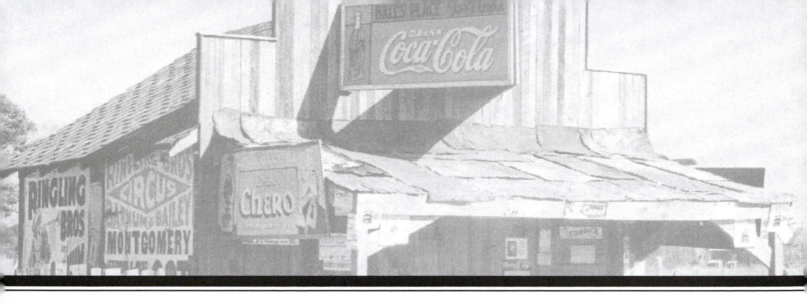

1960 News Feature

"This Is Coca-Cola?" *Business Week*, October 8, 1960:

Last week, Coca-Cola Company made a brief announcement that it was test-marketing a new soft drink called Sprite. From many companies, such a new product announcement would pass as routine. But with Coke, the announcement has more than usual significance, especially for the soft drink industry and its suppliers.

Sprite is the latest sign of Coke's expansionist mode. Earlier signs include going to market with new soft drink products, diversifying into other kinds of beverages, and introducing new packaging to add to its familiar bottle.

Clearly, the industry giant (with 1959 sales of $342 million) is ending its long dependence on a single product—even one that is world-famous. To stay at the head of its industry, Coca-Cola Company is broadening its coverage of a market its executives described expansively as "liquid refreshments."

Along with announcing Sprite, Coca-Cola is now pushing domestic distribution of its Fanta line of flavored soft drinks, which it began selling overseas years ago. News of Sprite and Fanta follows Coke's proposal of a merger with Minute Maid Corp., which would mean diversification out of the carbonated beverage field into frozen juices and instant coffee and tea.

A few months ago, too, the company confirmed that it is reluctantly making Coke nationally available in cans. Now the company reportedly is thinking about putting the drink in a new throwaway bottle.

For the first 70 years or so of its history, Coca-Cola maintained a successful "one product in one size" policy, so these developments indicate a decided shift in management attitude. Coke executives will say little about it—they stress "evolution" and "continued progress"—but Coke bottlers and industry competitors are more vocal.

"I've never seen a company change its policies as drastically as Coca-Cola has done," said a leading distributor.

Coke's flavored soda drinks, Sprite and Fanta, illustrate the new directions in which the company is moving. Sprite, a lemon-like flavor, can be drunk either alone or as a mixer. Coke bottlers are testing it in two markets: Sandusky, Ohio, and Lansing, Michigan. The company says tests may continue for six months before the product is put into general distribution. Fanta is the label for a full line of soft drink flavors, plus ginger ale and club soda. The line, developed in Germany many years ago, is sold in 36 countries. Coke began testing Fanta in the U.S. in late 1958. According to the company, about 190 bottlers have taken steps to offer it.

With these drinks, Coca-Cola is going after a share of the soft-drink market that it has never exploited before. Flavored soda drinks account for about a third of the total soft-drink business, with cola-type drinks taking two-thirds. Pepsi-Cola Company, second biggest in the industry, which introduced the Patio line of flavored drinks last February in Kentucky on a regional basis, is now adding more regions, with 57 bottlers signed up.

Sprite, coming along as a separate product from the broad Fanta line of flavors, reveals Coke's determination to penetrate deeply in the non-cola market.

According to industry members, the demand for lemon-lime soda, such as Sprite, is distinct from that of flavored beverages generally. Consumers tend to ask for flavored sodas more or less by the flavor they want—such as orange or grape—but they ask for the lemon-lime soda by a brand name. The industry credits this habit to the success of 7-Up, probably the third leading soft drink, establishing a brand identity for its lemon-lime soda.

Most soft-drink companies sell a similar drink, such as Pepsi's Team and Royal Crown's Upper 10. Pepsi introduced Team in April 1959, in both bottles and cans, and now has 152 franchise bottlers.

Despite Coke's entry into this new field, company officials see no sharp departure from the past. They point out that Coke has always followed the policy of slow but steady evolution. It took Coke 25 years, for example, to move from fountain sales to the bottles.

"We've done many things in the past 75 years," says the vice president. "They haven't been years of status quo."

For the past few years, he continues, Coke has been occupied with establishing its larger 10- and 26-ounce bottles, after long holding fast to its six-ounce bottle—"Little Gem," as Coke men call it. Now, in the fullness of time, the company is ready for new moves forward....

Many observers say Coke's expansion into new products lies in large part in Coke's relations with its independent bottlers.

The economics of bottling increasingly demanded full product lines and packages.

Many bottlers, particularly those in Eastern states where the peak hot weather selling season for soft drinks is short, need additional lines to maintain their production facilities and help take care of overhead. Also, a lot of bottlers service vending machines, many of which now dispense several varieties of soda drinks. It makes sense for the bottler to be able to stock the machine completely.

For such reasons, many Coke bottlers have taken on product lines from other companies. Coke has now decided it ought to start selling its bottlers these products.

One bottler points out that, compared with the company's tremendous volume in Coke itself, the new products won't add much to the total volume, and not for a long time. He believes handling the new product right now is chiefly to keep bottlers happy. However, he goes on to say, many bottlers' "investment in glass may keep them from switching to the Fanta flavors," which come in a different container.

1965 Profile

Entrepreneur and art collector Norton Simon believed that life was controlled by the three P's: power, paranoia and publicity, and he used all three to parlay $7,000 into a multimillion-dollar empire, largely by taking over mismanaged companies and making them more profitable, starting with Hunt's.

Life at Home

- Norton Simon was born into a moderately successful Jewish family in Portland, Oregon; his father ran a family-owned department store and dabbled in real estate and a steel products company.
- When Norton was 14, his mother died, and Norton's father moved the family, including Norton's two younger sisters, to San Francisco to live with relatives.
- In school, Norton was an indifferent pupil who rejected rote learning and arrogantly read novels during class.
- Both father and son possessed a photographic memory and the ability to add or multiply several figures at once rapidly in their heads.
- Norton joined a group of boys who called themselves "The Nocturnes," whose primary expertise was playing craps.
- Already an entrepreneur, Norton bought bags, towels and tissues from paper manufacturers after school and sold them to San Francisco stores.
- Then, at 16, he leased a vaudeville theater and was on the road to profitability when his father persuaded him to pull out of show business.
- His money then went into the stock market, where he developed an effective system of hedging; later, he would emerge from the 1929 stock market crash with $35,000 when others had lost everything.
- At his father's insistence, he enrolled in the University of California at Berkeley, but withdrew from his prelaw studies within the first six weeks to run a sheet metal distribution company.

Norton Simon's unconventional path, led to a multi-million dollar empire that included the Hunt brand.

- With three uncles who were lawyers, it was assumed in the Simon family that a talkative, persuasive, argumentative Jewish boy would enjoy the law.
- "The University," Norton said years later, "was involved with requirements, and I was interested in learning only what I wanted to learn."
- In 1927, he invested $7,000 in an orange juice bottling plant in Fullerton, California; it was insolvent and he renamed it Val Vita Food Products Company.
- Using a business formula he would continue to refine throughout his life, Norton cut costs, switched from bottles to cheaper cans, undersold competitors, and eventually switched the plant from orange juice to tomatoes.
- During the next decade, Val Vita sales rose from $43,000 to $9 million; then, abruptly, Norton sold the business to Hunt Brothers Packing, a moderately sized canner in the San Francisco area.
- For some time he had been buying Hunt stock; with the money he made off the sale of Val Vita—almost $4 million—he bought even more and made a play for control.
- After a considerable struggle, he won control of Hunt Brothers in 1943 and changed the name to Hunt Foods.
- Its most dominant products were prepared tomato sauce and ketchup.
- The term "ketchup" first entered the English language at the end of the seventeenth century when tomatoes were an expensive rarity.
- Ketchups were long-keeping, often vinegar-based sauces flavored with mushrooms, anchovies, onions, lemons, oysters, pickled walnuts, etc.
- British explorers, colonists and traders came into contact with the sauce in Southeast Asia, but most attempts to duplicate it failed since soybeans were not grown in Europe.
- In America, experimentation continued with a variety of additional ingredients, including beans and apples.
- Tomato ketchup was widely used throughout the United States in the early nineteenth century, and small quantities of it were first bottled in the 1850s.
- After the Civil War, commercial production of ketchup rapidly increased, and tomato ketchup became the most important version.
- By 1896 the *New York Tribune* was reporting that tomato ketchup was America's national condiment.
- Up until 1900, ketchup was mainly used as an ingredient for savory pies and sauces, and to enhance the flavor of meat, poultry and fish.
- In the twentieth century, ketchup became popular following the appearance of hamburgers, hot dogs, and French fries.

Ketchup would soon become one of America's favorite condiment.

Life at Work

- At Hunt Foods, Norton Simon immediately displayed a combination of toughness and imagination that would foster controversy.
- To cut costs, he bought his own can-making company and installed it next to the factory; to promote his brand name he spent 7 percent of revenue on advertising—almost triple the industry average—including 52 full-page ads in *Life* magazine in one year.
- To make his package more attractive, he insisted on printing the labels directly onto the cans; to move his goods more efficiently, he bought his own trucks.
- Then, in a move that would unsettle the industry, he broke one of the hallowed rules.
- After decades of canning "private-label" products for grocery store chains like A&P, which were then sold under the store name, Norton declared that Hunt was eliminating the marginally profitable private packaging operation and the competition it created on the store shelf.
- This antagonized the big distributors.
- Unshaken, Norton simply bought up several small canneries which had done private-label packaging and converted them to handling Hunt products, also.
- The entire conflict came to a head after the Second World War when the demand for consumer food goods was great and distributors need for products high.
- Many distributors vowed to boycott Hunt products once their contracts had run, but Norton's heavy advertising campaign was so successful that most stores were required to stock Hunt's ketchup whether they wanted to or not.
- With Hunt tomato products as his base, Norton expanded.
- First came the Ohio Match Company, which was churning out millions of matchbooks with Hunt recipes on the covers.
- Norton began buying in, and by 1946, held a controlling interest.
- Using the profits of Ohio Match, Norton purchased a huge interest in Northern Pacific Railroad; when skyrocketing stock prices preventing him from gaining a controlling interest, he sold out for a $2.8 million profit and started buying into cottonseed oil.
- Then he acquired New Orleans-based Wesson Oil for $76 million; he quickly doubled its size and strengthened its marketing.
- Next, he noticed that publishing stocks were undervalued because of the potential competition posed by television; in this adventure he won *McCall's* magazine, but lost most of the staff when they walked out in protest.
- Norton's new team then produced a magazine that increased the company's circulation by 60 percent and the company's profitability by 550 percent.

Norton used the Ohio Match Company for advertising Hunt recipes.

Canada Dry and Wheeling Steel were among the companies Norton bought and improved.

- He then made aggressive overtures to companies as diverse as Wheeling Steel, Canada Dry, and Knox Glass, earning him the slur of being a corporate raider.
- It was a charge he rejected because he typically kept and improved the companies he bought.
- Norton generally looked for companies whose stock was undervalued in the market, widely held by investors, and most important, whose profits were restricted by unimaginative management.
- Typically he would buy stock either personally or through one of his companies, but always on the sly.
- When he had a sizable chunk, Norton would come charging into a stockholders' meeting firing questions at directors, demanding to know why performance was not better, waving charts and graphics statistics to back up his points.
- He was never conventional—but always interesting.
- *Fortune Magazine* called him the least popular businessman in California.
- Even his most loyal employees said he was not easy work for: "He demands your best all the time," said one.
- But he did have the ability to listen to everyone and acquired a reputation for hiring and promoting talented women.
- "I was always breaking up the cartel-like combinations in the business world" he said. "I was always coming in and cutting the price to the point where it busted up their combination most, while still making my profit."
- His other passion was art—exquisite, historic paintings by the world's finest artists: Picasso, Monet, van Gogh, Cézanne, Gauguin, and Rembrandt.

Norton and his wife had an eye for fine art and a wallet to match.

- The leap from ketchup to culture, and the money spent, attracted considerable attention for the secretive and cautious Los Angeles-based businessman.
- And despite his $100 million wealth, Norton made a point of studying the quality and pedigree of every art purchase as intensely as he had done with any company he had ever acquired.
- After Norton Simon purchased Rembrandt's portrait of his son Titus for $2.2 million in 1965, they both appeared on the cover of *Time* magazine.
- Even *Time* was unable to discern whether Norton was an art connoisseur who engaged in business or a businessman who collected art.
- Franklin Murphy, chancellor of the University of California at Los Angeles and Norton's closest friend, said, "Most businessmen tend to be rather traditional and representational in their approach to business. But I think of Norton as a Cézanne or Picasso—unconventional, constantly probing and testing, constantly dissatisfied."

Life in the Community: Los Angeles, California

- Los Angeles was founded on September 4, 1781, by Spanish Governor Felipe de Neve as *El Pueblo de Nuestra Señora la Reina de los Angeles del Río de Porciúncula* (The Village of Our Lady, the Queen of the Angels of the River of Porziuncola).
- It became a part of Mexico in 1821, following its independence from Spain.
- In 1848, at the end of the Mexican-American War, Los Angeles and the rest of California were purchased as part of the Treaty of Guadalupe Hidalgo, thereby becoming part of the United States.
- Los Angeles was incorporated as a municipality on April 4, 1850, five months before California achieved statehood.
- Often known by its initials, L.A., and nicknamed the City of Angels, Los Angeles constituted one of the nation's most substantial economic engines excelling in agricultural processing, manufacturing and entertainment.
- One portion of Los Angeles—Hollywood—was known as the "Entertainment Capital of the World," leading the world in the creation of motion pictures, television production, and recorded music.

Los Angeles, CA in 1869.

- Railroads arrived when the Southern Pacific completed its line to Los Angeles in 1876.
- Oil was discovered in 1892, and by 1923, Los Angeles was producing one-quarter of the world's petroleum.
- By 1900, the population had grown to more than 102,000.
- In the 1920s, the motion picture and aviation industries kept the area's growth rising, ensuring that the city suffered less than other areas during the Great Depression.
- In 1932, with the population surpassing one million, the city hosted the Summer Olympics.
- The postwar years saw an even greater boom, as urban sprawl expanded the city into the San Fernando Valley, known for it agriculture.
- California had a long history in the fruit- and vegetable-packing business, with many companies dating their origin to the 1860s.
- Demand was so high that, starting in the 1880s, women of Mexican descent were recruited as workers.
- But fruit-canning tended to be highly seasonal work, with most of the peaks in the summer and the lows in the winter.
- Previously dominated by mom-and-pop canners, who suffered most from the Depression, fruit-canning became the domain of the big money corporations.
- During the period from 1939 to 1950, California produced more canned fruits and vegetables than any other state.
- Canneries processed apricots, peaches, blackberries, pears, tomatoes, eggs, apples, cherries and salad fruit.
- In 1946, the state's share of the U.S. fruit-packing market was approximately 50 percent.

The weather in California made the area surrounding Los Angeles ideal for growing fruits and vegetables.

Historical Snapshot
1965

- President Lyndon B. Johnson proclaimed his plans for the "Great Society" during his State of the Union Address
- Black leader Malcolm X was assassinated in Manhattan
- *The Sound of Music* premiered at the Rivoli Theater in New York City
- Approximately 3,500 United States Marines arrived in South Vietnam, becoming the first official American combat troops there
- The wreck of the *SS Georgiana*, reputed to have been the most powerful Confederate cruiser ever built and owned by the real Rhett Butler, was discovered off the Isle of Palms, • South Carolina, by teenage diver E. Lee Spence, exactly 102 years after it was sunk with a million-dollar cargo while attempting to run past the Union blockade into Charleston

- NASA successfully launched *Gemini 3*, America's first two-person spacecraft, into Earth's orbit
- Despite repeated acts of violence, Martin Luther King, Jr. and 25,000 Civil Rights activists marched from Selma, Alabama, to the Capitol Building in Montgomery
- At the Academy Awards, *My Fair Lady* won Best Picture and Best Director; Julie Andrews won an Academy Award for Best Actress in *Mary Poppins*
- The West German parliament extended the statute of limitations on Nazi war crimes
- Charlie Brown and the *Peanuts* gang were featured on the cover of *Time* magazine
- *In Cold Blood* killers Richard Hickock and Perry Smith, convicted of murdering four members of the Herbert Clutter family of Holcomb, Kansas, were executed
- The first Students for a Democratic Society (SDS)-sponsored march against the Vietnam War attracted 25,000 protestors to Washington, DC
- U.S. troops were sent to the Dominican Republic by President Johnson, "for the stated purpose of protecting U.S. citizens and preventing an alleged Communist takeover of the country," thus thwarting the possibility of "another Cuba"
- President Johnson signed the Social Security Act of 1965 into law, establishing Medicare and Medicaid

continued

HISTORICAL SNAPSHOT *(continued)*
1965

- The Watts Riots erupted in Los Angeles

- The Beatles performed the first stadium concert in the history of rock, playing at Shea Stadium in New York

- Jonathan Myrick Daniels, an Episcopal seminarian from Keene, New Hampshire, was murdered in Hayneville, Alabama, while working for the Civil Rights Movement

- The *Tom & Jerry* cartoon series made its world broadcast premiere on CBS

- President Johnson signed an immigration bill which abolished quotas based on national origin

- The student-run National Coordinating Committee to End the War in Vietnam staged the first public burning of a draft card in the United States to result in arrest under the new law

- The New York World's Fair at Flushing Meadows closed after experiencing financial losses

- Pope Paul VI announced that the Ecumenical Council had decided that Jews were not collectively responsible for the killing of Christ

- In St. Louis, Missouri, the 630-foot-tall parabolic steel Gateway Arch was completed

- Pillsbury's mascot, the Pillsbury Doughboy, was created

- The soap opera *Days of our Lives* debuted on NBC

Selected Prices

Air Conditioner	$455.00
Beer, Schlitz, -Pack	$0.99
Calculator, Remington	$189.50
Camera, Kodak Instamatic	$240.00
Girdle	$11.00
Record Album	$5.98
Refrigerator-Freezer	$300.00
Shoes, Men's Leather	$13.80
Slide Projector	$149.50
Ticket, Newport Jazz Festival	$6.50

Norton Simon Quotes:

"I am inclined to believe that much of our economy is based upon the feelings of people rather than upon reality. And, therefore, the primary belief I have is never to be too sure about anything."

"Picasso says that creativity is a series of destructions. You really don't create anything until you knock something else out of the way. You have to tear down homes before you put in freeway. But in professional management, and in the investment process, you recognize that you should tear down only so much before it is time to build anew, for excessive tearing down takes a destructive process beyond the realm of creativity. The question is, How much destruction can be tolerated?"

"I believe in a paradoxical form of life. I don't believe anything is wholly right, but both right and wrong. There is a thin line in between. There's a Chinese proverb that 'Life is the search for truth and there is no truth.' It is important to know that truth carried too far becomes destructive."

"My hostilities are usually showing but I do get rid of anger. Some people are born with peace of mind. I was not. In the Dostoevskian sense, I am the suffering man. I know this about myself. I know now that working my way out of it is a very gratifying experience."

"Stockholders to Vote on Proposed Merger,"
Oakland Tribune, **November 9, 1945:**

Stockholders Hunt Foods, Inc., will meet in Hayward, November 19, to vote on the proposed merger of California Conserving Company Inc. with Hunt, it was announced today by Norton Simon, Chairman of the Board of Hunt Foods.

M. E. Wangenhelm, president of California Conserving Company, is to become president of Hunt Foods, Inc., following the merger, with Norton Simon continuing as Chairman of the Board....

California Conserving Company's six plants bring to 15 the number of plants controlled or wholly owned by Hunt throughout the West, and the merged company is expected to produce sales exceeding $30 million per year.

The History of Hunt Foods

- Hunt Foods was founded by Joseph and William Hunt in 1888 in Sebastopol, California, as the Hunt Brothers Fruit Packing Company
- The brothers relocated to nearby Santa Rosa in 1890, and then to Hayward in 1895.
- Their canning operation grew rapidly, focused on canning the products of California's booming fruit and vegetable industries.
- In 1943, Hunt was taken over by Norton Simon's Val Vita Food Products, founded in the early 1930s.
- The merged firm kept the Hunt name and was incorporated as Hunt Foods, Inc.
- The new management decided to focus the company on canned tomato products, particularly prepared tomato sauce.
- Besides canned tomato sauce, the Hunt brand appeared on tomato paste; diced, whole, stewed, and crushed tomatoes; spaghetti sauce; ketchup; barbecue sauce; and canned potatoes.

WHEELING STEEL

CANADA DRY

OHIO MATCH

HUNT'S

"Our Biggest Single Industry Is Hunt's," *Hayward Daily Review* (California), June 30, 1948:

- A million teeming square feet of valuable factory land, sprawling on both sides of B Street, supports the men, machinery and raw materials which together form the biggest plant of Hunt Foods, Inc., and the biggest single industry in all Hayward.

- Here at the peak of the canning season, 3,600 people convert a steady stream of the products of California's fertile fields into canned and packaged goods, which are distributed into the markets throughout America and overseas in many foreign lands. In the process of that conversion, millions of dollars of new wealth are created for Hayward workers and the farmers of surrounding counties....

- Two strong lines of the Pacific Coast food industry came together in 1943 to form Hunt Foods, Inc.: Hunt Brothers Packing Company of San Francisco and Val Vita Food Products Company of Fullerton. Since that time, many smaller organizations have been absorbed as branches in this sturdy trunk, which today is a national distributor of over 90 products whose sales total more than $46 million annually. Today Hunt ranks fourth in the nation among all companies packing and distributing a general line of fruits and vegetables under their own labels, and second on the Pacific Coast....

- Hunt's first year's pack was 30,000 cases of cherries, apricots, peaches, pears, prunes, grapes and tomatoes—a far cry from the millions of cases which bore the Hunt name in 1948

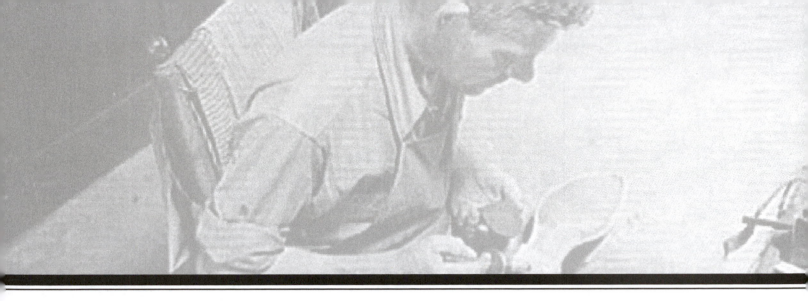

1967 Profile

Dr. Harry Coover was part of the research team that discovered, quite by accident, Super Glue. Ted Grant was the soldier whose life was saved by the invention.

Life at Home

- Drunk or sober, Ted Grant always sang the praises Dr. Harry Coover—the man he credited with saving his life.
- The two men, born 30 years apart, had never met; indeed, Dr. Coover did not even know Ted existed.
- They were brought together by glue; Dr. Coover was an accidental glue guru, and Ted was a man in need of his services.
- Born in Newark, Delaware, on March 6, 1919, Dr. Coover received his B.S. from Hobart College and continued his studies at Cornell University, where he earned an M.S. in chemistry in 1942 and a Ph.D. in 1944.
- Shortly thereafter, he began working for Eastman Kodak's chemical division in Rochester, New York.
- Ted was born in Lancaster, South Carolina, where both his parents worked third shift at the Springs Textile Mill.
- His parents assumed that Ted would join them when he turned 16 and no longer had to attend school.
- However, Ted had other ideas; he loved how he looked in a football uniform and especially cherished the attention lavished on an aggressive linebacker eager to make the tackle on every play.
- Coaches whispered that college football might be in his future.
- And 1965, Ted's junior year in high school, was the perfect time to showcase his athletic skills, they said, particularly in a town where football was a religion.

Dr. Coover accidentally made a "super" discovery—the Super Glue that saved Ted Grant's (below) life.

Ted Grant, his family, and the rest of Lancaster, SC loved football.

- The year 1965 was also when an incredibly stable adhesive known as Super Glue, previously invented by Dr. Coover, was to become a medical treatment in the bloody battlefields of Vietnam—a place Ted could not locate on a world map.
- For most of human history, research into adhesive glues focused on joining two pieces of wood or other cellulose products using another natural substance; gluing skin back together was not a consideration.
- The first adhesive was probably blood, which formed a strong bond in hair while congealing.
- The earliest record of the use of glue comes from Egypt, where 3,300 years ago a piece of veneer was glued to a plank of sycamore for a coffin; later the Phoenicians sealed their ships with bitumen.
- Both civilizations were conquered by the Romans, whose technology included tar and beeswax for shipbuilding.
- The role of natural adhesives, such as hides, starch, dextrin and gum, remained important because of their tendency to cost less than synthetics.
- The most critical advance of the early twentieth century came with the patenting of Bakelite, the first synthetic polymer resin.
- This invention by Leo Baekeland led to polymer science, which also stimulated research into new adhesives.
- During World War II, Dr. Coover was part of a team conducting research with chemicals known as cyanoacrylates in an effort to make a clear plastic that could be used for precision gun sights for soldiers.
- While working with the chemicals, the researchers discovered that they were extremely sticky, a property that made them very difficult to work with.
- Moisture caused the chemicals to polymerize, and since nearly all objects have a thin layer of moisture on them, bonding would occur in virtually every testing instance.
- The research team rejected cyanoacrylates and moved on; a war was underway and there was no time for distractions.
- "Serendipity had knocked, but I didn't hear it," Coover commented years later.

Life at Work

- Linebacker Ted Grant had been waiting the whole game on the fleet tailback from Rock Hill High to run a naked reverse in a close game between traditional rivals.
- Ted was sure he could hit the little scat-back hard enough to take him out of the game; a helmet to the hip was the perfect plan.
- The only thing Ted had not calculated was the fumble caused by his sensational wallop.
- In the resulting scramble for the loose ball, Ted's teammates drove viciously to recover the fumble, breaking Ted's leg in two places.
- Ted clearly remembered the standing ovation he received when he was carried off the field; the trip to the hospital and the next two days were less clear.
- What he realized after two months in a cast was that his football career was over.
- Ted's father wasted no time securing him a job at the mill; in fact, Ted was just going to work on the second shift the day his draft notice arrived.
- After 18 months in the mill, Ted was ready for a change; he was very familiar with the location of Vietnam now that 540,000 U.S. troops were committed to the fight and the death toll had reached 33,000 American soldiers.
- History would show it was only two years after Ted was born that the lines linking Ted Grant and Dr. Harry Coover began to cross.
- In 1951, Dr. Coover was transferred to Kodak's chemical plant in Kingsport, Tennessee, where he rediscovered the cyanoacrylates and recognized in them a new potential.
- He had been overseeing the work of a group of Kodak chemists who were researching heat-resistant polymers for jet airplane canopies.
- When one of the compounds was applied between the lenses to test its effect on light, the lenses would not come apart.
- The researcher became upset at the potential loss of expensive lenses, but Dr. Coover saw things differently.
- They did further tests on the cyanoacrylate monomers, and this time, Dr. Coover realized these sticky adhesives had unique properties—they required no heat or pressure to bond.
- He and his team tried the substance on various items in the lab, and each time, the items became permanently bonded together.
- Dr. Coover—and his employer—knew they were on to something; Coover received patent number 2,768,109 for his "Alcohol-Catalyzed Cyanoacrylate Adhesive Compositions/Superglue" and began refining the product for commercialization.

Grant's football career was over before it even started.

Grant joined the hundreds of thousands of soldiers already in Vietnam.

- His company packaged the all-purpose adhesive as "Eastman 910" and began marketing it in 1958; it was named Eastman 910, as Dr. Coover explained, because "You could count 1, 2, 3, 4, 5, 6, 7, 8, 9, 10 and it was bonded."
- During the 1960s, Eastman Kodak sold cyanoacrylate to **Loctite**, which in turn repackaged and distributed it under a different brand name "Loctite Quick Set 404."
- By the mid-1960s, Dr. Coover became somewhat of a celebrity, appearing on television in the show *I've Got a Secret*, where he lifted the host, Garry Moore, off the ground using a single drop of Super Glue.
- During the Vietnam War, Dr. Coover developed a cyanoacrylate spray based on the same compound, which was sprayed onto soldiers' serious wounds to quickly halt bleeding so the injured could be transported to medical facilities instead of morgues.
- Cyanoacrylates were then used for sealing dental repairs, lesions, and bleeding ulcers, and for suture-free surgery.
- Meanwhile, Army Pvt. Ted Grant had discovered that the steaming jungle of Vietnam was unpredictable and dangerous.
- While walking point on a routine patrol, he realized that an ambush lay ahead.
- Acting on finely tuned survival instincts, he signaled the squad to halt and was silently moving his fellow soldiers back when the shooting began.
- Three Americans were killed immediately, while Ted was wounded in three places: his shoulder, leg and hand.
- He was bleeding profusely.
- When the medic arrived, he bandaged some of Ted's wounds and then glued several other wounds shut with a spray-on Super Glue not yet authorized for medical use.

Grant's quick reflexes had managed to save most of his platoon.

- The crude system worked temporarily and gave medics time to move the critically wounded soldiers to the safety of a hospital; the glue saved Ted's life, and became his badge of honor.
- Back home, drinking beer at the Dixie Tavern in Lancaster, South Carolina, Ted always drank a toast to the man who saved his life: Dr. Super Glue.

Life in the Community: Tennessee Eastman, Kingsport, Tennessee

- Tennessee Eastman in Kingsport, Tennessee, got its start thanks to World War I and the scarcity it caused.
- Raw materials such as photographic paper, optical glass, gelatin and many chemicals, including methanol, acetic acid and acetone, were unavailable to the powerful Eastman Kodak Company.
- At the close of the war, Eastman Kodak founder George Eastman decided to insure that he always had an independent supply of chemicals for his photographic processes.
- In his search for suitable quantities of methanol and acetone, Eastman turned his attention to the Southern United States and its forests, as well as to Kingsport, Tennessee.
- In 1920, Tennessee Eastman was founded with two major platforms—organic chemicals and acetyls.
- From the primary feedstock of pyroligneous acid, many of Eastman's basic chemical building blocks were manufactured, studied and perfected.
- Products such as calcium acetate, sodium acetate, acetic acid and acetic anhydride became the bases for other major company platforms.
- During World War II, RDX, a powerful explosive, was manufactured for the U.S. government at Holston Ordnance Works at Tennessee Eastman sites.
- At the peak of production, the ordnance plant was producing a million and a half pounds of explosives each day.
- Eastman's portfolio of products continued to expand, and by the 1960s, Tennessee Eastman Company was manufacturing products that became familiar features of everyday life: polyester fibers for apparel and home furnishings, plastics for the automobile industry, and a growing number of industrial chemicals.
- Kingsport Tennessee itself was first chartered in 1822, and over time became an important shipping port on the Holston River.
- Goods originating for many miles from the surrounding countryside were loaded onto barges for the journey downriver to the Tennessee River at Knoxville.
- The town lost its charter after a downturn in its fortunes precipitated by the Civil War.
- Re-chartered in 1917, Kingsport was an early example of a "garden city," designed by city planner and landscape architect John Nolen of Cambridge, Massachusetts.
- It carries the nickname The Model City from this plan, which organized the town into areas for commerce, churches, housing and industry.
- The result included some of the earlier uses of traffic circles, or roundabouts, in the U.S.
- Kingsport was among the first municipalities with a city manager form of government and a school system built on a model developed at Columbia University.
- Most of the land on the river was devoted to industry.
- Indeed, most of Long Island was occupied by Eastman Chemical Company.

George Eastman, founder of Eastman Kodak.

- Lancaster, South Carolina, on the other hand, was established in the mid-1700s by Scots-Irish and English settlers from Lancaster, Pennsylvania.

Employees at the Lancaster Cotton Mills, 1908.

- The newcomers named the area for their homelands in England, the region of the famous House of Lancaster that opposed the House of York in the legendary War of the Roses.
- During the Civil War, troops under General William Tecumseh Sherman occupied the town after the Southern campaign in 1865.
- Following the war, Col. Leroy Springs founded Springs Cotton Mill in 1895, an industrial enterprise that grew to become one of the largest textile plants in the world.
- For most the twentieth century, Springs Industries shaped the fortunes of Lancaster and its citizens.

It was not unusual for children to work at the mills.

HISTORICAL SNAPSHOT
1967

- The Doors' self-titled debut album was released
- Dr. James Bedford became the first person to be cryonically preserved with the intent of future resuscitation
- Louis Leakey announced the discovery of pre-human fossils in Kenya; he named the species *Kenyapithecus africanus*
- The Green Bay Packers defeated the Kansas City Chiefs 35-10 at the Super Bowl
- In Munich, Wilhelm Harster, accused of the murder of 82,856 Jews (including Anne Frank) when he led German security police during the German occupation of The Netherlands, was sentenced to 15 years in prison
- Astronauts Gus Grissom, Edward Higgins White, and Roger Chaffee were killed when a fire broke out in their *Apollo* spacecraft during a launch pad test
- The American Basketball Association was formed
- The Twenty-fifth Amendment to the Constitution concerning presidential succession and disability was ratified
- American researchers discovered the Madrid Codices by Leonardo da Vinci in the National Library of Spain
- The song "Respect" was recorded by Aretha Franklin
- Civil Rights leader Martin Luther King, Jr. denounced the Vietnam War during a religious service in New York City
- *A Man for All Seasons* was named Best Picture at the Academy Awards
- Heavyweight boxing champion Muhammad Ali refused military service on religious grounds and was stripped of his title
- The Soviet Union ratified a treaty with the United States and the United Kingdom, banning nuclear weapons in outer space
- The Beatles released *Sgt. Pepper's Lonely Hearts Club Band*, nicknamed "The Soundtrack of the Summer of Love"

- Israel occupied the West Bank, Gaza Strip, Sinai peninsula and the Golan Heights after defeating its Arab neighbors in the Six-Day War
- The Supreme Court declared unconstitutional all laws prohibiting interracial marriage

continued

HISTORICAL SNAPSHOT *(continued)*
1967

- Solicitor General Thurgood Marshall was named the first African-American Justice of the Supreme Court
- In Detroit, Michigan, one of the worst riots in United States history began on 12th Street in the predominantly African-American inner city; 43 were killed
- The Doors defied CBS censors on *The Ed Sullivan Show* when Jim Morrison sang the word "higher" from their Number One hit "Light My Fire"
- Guerrilla leader Che Guevara and his men were captured in Bolivia and executed
- Thirty-nine people, including singer-activist Joan Baez, were arrested in Oakland, California, for blocking the entrance of the city's military induction center
- The musical *Hair* opened off-Broadway
- Walt Disney's nineteenth full-length animated feature, *The Jungle Book*, was released, and was the last animated film personally supervised by Disney
- Tens of thousands of Vietnam War protesters marched in Washington, DC, where poet Allen Ginsberg symbolically called upon the protestors to "levitate" the Pentagon
- President Lyndon B. Johnson signed legislation establishing the Corporation for Public Broadcasting

Selected Prices

Acne Medicine, Clearasil	$0.98
Baby Walker	$5.99
Blazer, Women's	$25.95
Boy Scout Uniform	$10.75
Car Battery, Installed	$7.88
Chain Saw	$149.95
Cigarette Table	$28.95
Margarine, Pound	$0.15
Permanent Wave	$7.50
Theater Ticket	$6.60

"Patent Protects Inventor Rights," *Charleston Daily Mail*, November 16, 1967:

Suppose you invent something that you think can make a lot of money for you. You don't want anyone to "steal" your idea, that is, have the right to copy it exactly.

The government protects you from having this happen by granting you a "patent." A patent is an agreement between the government, representing the public, and the inventor.

The government agrees that no one but the inventor will be allowed to manufacture, use, or sell his invention for 17 years without the inventor's permission. In return, the inventor files his new discovery in the patent office so that everyone will profit from it when the 17 years are over.

Any person who has invented or discovered a new and useful art, machine, manufacture, or composition of matter may obtain a patent for it. This also includes any new or useful improvement.

Application for a patent must be made by the inventor, but he is usually represented by a patent lawyer or agent. A written description and drawings of the invention, together with an application fee, must be submitted to the Patent Office.

If the patent examiners (experts who work for the government's Patent Office) find the invention is actually new, a patent is granted after the payment of an additional fee. The patent now becomes the inventor's own property, and he may sell or assign it.

If anyone disregards a patent, the inventor can force him to stop using it or sue him for the profits made.

The present U.S. Patent system was started in 1836. It laid down the principle, then new, that patents should be given only after inventions had been carefully examined and compared with earlier ones. Two questions were asked: "Is the invention useful?" and "Is it new?" This system was copied by the rest of the civilized world.

"King Charges U.S. Stifled War Dissent," *Delaware County Daily Times* (Chester, Pennsylvania), June 1, 1967:

Dr. Martin Luther King has accused the Johnson administration of bringing the U.S. commander in Vietnam back to the United States to stifle antiwar dissent.

"It's a dark day in our nation when high-level authorities will seek to use every method to silence dissent," King declared Sunday.

Gen. William C. Westmoreland spoke before a joint session of Congress Friday.

In his sermon at the Ebenezer Baptist Church, where he is co-pastor with his father, the Rev. Martin Luther King, Sr., the civil rights leader said some "equate dissent with disloyalty."

King told the packed congregation he chose to preach in Vietnam "because conscience gives me no other choice."

Reiterating passages in a recent New York address, King deplored the downgrading of antipoverty programs which has coincided with increasing war expenditures, and charged that "a nation that continues year after year to spend more money on military defense than on programs of social uplift is approaching spiritual death."

In his impassioned sermon, King said America must repent from a "tragic, reckless adventure in Vietnam. This madness must stop. We must admit we've been wrong from the beginning of our adventure in Vietnam."

The Nobel Prize winner urged every young man who finds the war objectionable and unjust to file as a conscientious objector.

"It matters what you think of Mohammed Ali (heavyweight champion Cassius Clay's black Muslim name). You certainly have to admire his courage," King told the congregation, which included "Black Power" advocate Stokely Carmichael.

Cries of "Amen" greeted the mention of Clay, who refused to be inducted into the Army last week and was stripped of his heavyweight title.

"Here is a young man willing to give up millions of dollars to do what conscience tells him is right," King said.

"Smelter Suit Wins $400,000 Award," *Arizona Republic,*
February 17, 1967:

A Superior Court jury yesterday awarded a $400,000 judgment to a Douglas man who charged his melting process invention was used illegally by two copper companies.

Plaintiff Eugene R. Redmond had named in his "unjust enrichment" suit the Magma Copper Company of Superior and the San Manuel Copper Company, a subsidiary of Magma, now dissolved.

Redmond complained that both companies had used his blister copper invention from June 1957 through October 1958 without his permission and without giving him compensation.

He asked the jury to award him $600,000 which, he said, is the amount the companies were enriched by his invention.

Redmond's counsel, Donald R. Kunz and William Drummond, said Redmond disclosed his invention to the San Manuel company in writing when he was employed there as a converter foreman. According to Kunz, the company fired Redmond when he patented the invention.

An intricately detailed model of a smelting plant, measuring about 20 feet long and five feet high, was used during the three-week trial to familiarize the jury with the smelting process.

Notable Inventions: 1960 to 1967

1960
- The halogen lamp

1961
- Valium
- Nondairy creamer

1962
- The audio cassette
- The fiber-tip pen
- Spacewar, the first computer video game
- Silicone breast implants

1963
- The video disc

1964
- Acrylic paint
- Permanent-press fabric
- BASIC (an early computer language)

1965
- Astroturf
- Soft contact lenses
- NutraSweet
- The compact disc
- Kevlar

1966
- Electronic fuel injection for cars

1967
- The first handheld calculator

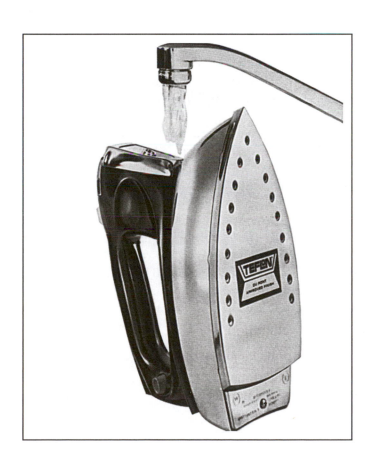

Broken Glass Marks Namath Success Trail," *Evening Independent* (Massillon, Ohio), January 7, 1965:

MOBILE, Alabama. The windows of the neighborhood laundry on Fourth Ave. in Beaver Falls, Pennsylvania, are carefully guarded by strong steel wire.

The wiring is Beaver Falls's monument to Joe Namath, who spent a good part of his errant youth smashing glass panes with well-aimed footballs, but went on to become the town's most famous and one of its richest citizens.

Now the townspeople, and the proprietors of the laundry most of all, look at the wired windows with pride and say:

"Little Joe, he was a card, wasn't he?"

"When Joe was a boy he busted every window in the place," recalls Joe's mother, Mrs. Rose Sznolnoki, who divorced Namath's steelworker father and remarried several years ago.

"The laundry people were very mad and they kept coming around to make us pay damages. Finally, they put up the steel wiring, and it's still there."

Today Joe is not only in a position to pay for all the broken windows, but could buy the laundry and half the town. Star quarterback of the national champion Alabama football team, he signed a week ago the largest contract ever offered a football rookie: a $400,000 salary and bonuses for three years with the New York Jets in the American Football League. He plays his last college game Saturday in the Senior Bowl here.

The contract, which also reportedly included a $5,000 a year pension for life, staggered the professional football world. Only Beaver Falls, a bustling little steel community of 30,000 30 miles from Pittsburgh, took the news in stride.

"Everything here is just the same," said Mrs. Sznolnoki. "Everyone knew Joe would make it good."

Joe, whose parents are Hungarian, was the youngest of five children: John, now 33, career soldier in Germany; Robert, 30, a mill hand; Frank, 27, a life insurance salesman, and Rita, 26, a sister living in Philadelphia.

"Joe was throwing the football when he was big enough to walk," the mother recalled.

"Bobby and Franklin always got up football games in the front yard. Joe was just five and too little to play, but the boys needed a quarterback. So Joe was it.

"Bobby and Franklin taught Joe to throw the ball over the telephone wires. They agreed he shouldn't be tackled. Joe got so he could throw the ball out of sight and he could hit a stump from 40 yards away."

Namath was outstanding as a high school athlete, playing football, basketball and baseball. When he finished high school, the Baltimore Orioles tried to sign him to a baseball contract.

Joe liked football and wanted to go to college. Scores of big schools sent scouts to court him. His first choice was Notre Dame.

"Joe was flying out so much, I found myself washing and packing him out the door every day," Mrs. Sznolnoki said.

continued

Broken Glass Marks Namath Success Trail," *(continued)*

Namath failed to get into Notre Dame and finally chose Alabama. "I was responsible for that," his mother said. "I made him go to Alabama, and he never quit thanking me...."

Paul (Bear) Bryant, head coach of the Crimson Tide, said he hardly got to see Namath as a freshman.

"It was 1961 when we had our championship unbeaten team, and I was kept pretty busy," Bryant recall. "But the coaching staff kept telling me we had a fine prospect in Namath."

This was borne out the next year when, as a sophomore, Namath completed 76 of 146 passes for 1,192 yards and 12 touchdowns. In 1963, he hit 63 of 128 for 765 yards, although he was booted off the team for the last game of the season for breaking training.

"I knew Joe wasn't a bad boy," Bryant said. "I talked to him and he admitted he had broken training. He promised never to do it again, and he has been perfect—an inspirational leader ever since."

"Computers May Enable Men to Farm by Phone," *The Greenville News* **(South Carolina), November 25, 1963:**

"Farming by phone" may be the next big innovation in agriculture, says a national farm magazine.

The phone would be used by farmers to take advantage of centralized computer installations, according to an article, "Livestock Feeding of the Future," in the November issue of *Electricity on the Farm* magazine.

The computers can help the farmer make the many business decisions he has to, such as how much of which ingredients to feed his animals for the best meat and milk, or production at the lowest cost. It's being done on a limited scale right now in Washington State, and the idea is expected to spread.

Here's the way it would work: the farmer could pick up the phone, call a number, and read off the type of animal he wants to feed, types of feed ingredients available, and other such information. This information would be fed into a computer at the state university or other centralized computer location.

The farmer would then be instructed to take a certain computer-type punch card from a file on his desk. He would place this card into an electronic "brain" in his office or in the barn, which would automatically instruct feed-making machinery how much of which ingredients to use for the most efficient feeding ration.

Automatic equipment could then easily convey the feed to the cows, chickens, hogs, etc., in feeding areas around the farmstead.

Automation and computerization are fast becoming common to most large industries in the U.S., and agriculture, America's largest industry, will be no exception.

Computers May Enable Men To Farm By Phone

NEW YORK — "Farming by phone" may be the next big | "brain" in his office or in the barn, which would automatically

1969 Profile

Just when Benjamin Eisenstadt was convinced that the government's ban on cycla-mates would bankrupt his company, a nimble response and high customer loyalty came to the rescue.

Life at Home

- The dining public cherished its right to pour Sweet'N Low from pink packets into their drinks and—governmental ban or not—they were going to have a sugar substitute.
- As a result of adversity and excellent timing, Ben Eisenstadt's artificial sweetener once again dominated the U.S. market.
- Ben was born in New York City on the Lower East Side of Manhattan on December 7, 1906.
- His parents, Rose and Morris Eisenstadt, emigrated to the United States from Poland; Morris worked on the waterfront unloading the ships.
- When Ben was seven years old, his father tripped on a scaffold and fell several stories before being saved by a hook that caught his pants.
- A year later, his father was rushed to the hospital after suffering a massive heart attack.
- When eight-year-old Jewish Ben arrived at the hospital, he was told "Your father is with Jesus," signaling the start of a tumultuous childhood.
- Because his mother Rose couldn't afford to raise three children, Ben was sent to live with his uncles, where he was moved from apartment to apartment, often sleeping on floors and couches in the industrial wasteland of northern New Jersey.
- He lost contact with his mother and siblings when they fled to California follow-ing a gang fight that resulted in death threats against his brother Robert.
- Ben attended school and worked in his uncle's teabag factory until 1927, when he was given an apprenticeship by a Manhattan lawyer.
- Soon after, he enrolled in St. John's University School of Law and graduated in 1929 as class valedictorian.

Benjamin Eisenstadt made a fortune with his individually packaged sugar substitute.

During the war, workers at the Brooklyn Navy Yard always ate at Eisenstadt's cafeteria.

Eisenstadt turned the old cafeteria into the Cumberland Packing factory.

- After graduation, Ben rented an office on Broadway, but because of the Great Depression, there were no clients.
- Taking a job at a cafeteria his father-in-law operated in Brooklyn, Ben later ran a couple of cafeterias of his own, eventually finding a measure of success by opening one in 1940 on Cumberland Street, in the Fort Greene section, just across from the Navy Yard in Brooklyn, which became a boomtown in World War II.
- In 1944, there were 900,000 military personnel in NYC.
- When the end of the war turned the Navy Yard into a ghost town and left Ben bereft of customers, he recalled that his uncle had once operated a company that filled tea bags, so he removed the lunch counter and stools and turned the Cumberland Cafeteria into the Cumberland Packing Company, a tea bag factory.
- Ben's wife Betty had often complained about the messy and unsanitary sugar dispensers that filled nearly every restaurant.
- As his tea bag venture limped toward oblivion in 1947, Ben had the brainstorm that changed the way Americans dispensed sugar: the same equipment that injected tea into tea bags, he realized, could be used to put sugar into little paper packets.
- Why not make sugar clean and personal—one person, one time.
- At a time when restaurants only used open sugar bowls or heavy glass dispensers, the idea of individual sanitary sugar packets was so revolutionary—and Ben was so naïve—that when he proudly showed his sugar operations to executives of a giant sugar company, they simply set up their own sugar-packet operations.
- His proposal to Domino Sugar resulted in them calling to say they had duplicated his machine and would not need his services.
- When his son Marvin came to work, a contract with the small Jack Frost Sugar Company was keeping Cumberland alive, but without a branded line of its own, it was a marginal operation.
- Cumberland Packing also produced packaged duck sauce, perfume, and tokens, and grossed approximately $100,000 a year, most of which was invested in new machines and workers.
- Ben bestowed half of the factory to his son, teaching him accountability of ownership.

Life at Work

- The father-son partnership of Ben and Marvin Eisenstadt was tested in 1956 when the two men were approached by executives of a pharmaceutical company seeking a sugar substitute that could be individually packaged.
- They wanted a medical product that could be sold to diabetics; in return, the Eisenstadts would control the packaging.
- To meet the challenge, they hired Dr. Paul Kracaver, a chemist, to help them develop a mixture that would imitate the look and feel of sugar.
- Faced with a new opportunity, they mixed saccharin, a derivative of coal tar, with cyclamate, searching for the proper tastes—especially as a sweetener for coffee.
- Saccharin had been around since the nineteenth century, had suffered scandal concerning its inventor, had been used by President Theodore Roosevelt, and was then banned for a short period by President Howard Taft—only to be redeemed when World War I dramatically reduced the worldwide supply of sugar.
- Considered a medicine for diabetics, saccharin was generally available only as a liquid or in pill form, and its use was restricted to diabetics and the obese despite a growing demand for diet foods.

A call went out during WWI for less consumption of sugar.

- Saccharin's bitter aftertaste was of particular concern.
- Initially, the various combinations had failed to eliminate the bitterness of the saccharin or create enough bulk for the mixture to fill an entire package.
- Marvin found the answer in an old cookbook.
- With the addition of lactose, which bulked up food and leached out taste, they perfected the formula that would become Sweet'N Low.
- When they returned to the pharmaceutical company executives, they no longer had an interest in an individually packaged sugar substitute because they believed the market was too small.
- Taking care to patent the first granulated low-calorie sugar substitute, Ben named the product Sweet'N Low after the Tennyson poem and distinguished it from white sugar packets with a pink packet printed with a treble-clef musical logo.
- Now, his timing was perfect.
- The man who had made spooning sugar passé with his first idea had created a sugar substitute just as the American health craze was in its infancy.
- With a claim of fewer than three calories per serving, Cumberland launched Sweet'N Low in 1957 as a product for anyone—and everyone—watching his or her weight.

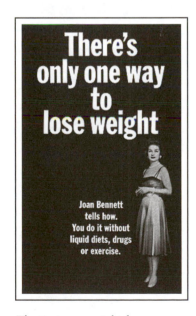

The timing was right for Eisenstadt's product—everyone was watching their weight.

- A&P, one of the nation's leading grocery chains, contacted Cumberland and asked if it could distribute Sweet'N Low nationally.
- Very quickly, Cumberland's sugar substitute became the most popular brand of its type on the market.
- Sweet'N Low was a hit—a successful new product that swept to the top of a booming niche in the 1960s.
- The sugar substitute market picked up further with the debut of diet sodas in 1962.
- Demand for Sweet'N Low rose accordingly; competitive products quickly appeared to cut into their market share.
- However, the federal government decided that the chemicals in Sweet'N Low had not been thoroughly studied.

The federal government deemed all cyclamates unsafe for human consumption.

- Some testing had indicated that cyclamates might cause cancer or birth defects in chickens and rats, and in 1969, the Food and Drug Administration decided to run more definitive tests on the chemical.
- After just three weeks of testing, the government abruptly declared a ban on cyclamate sweeteners.
- Preliminary results had shown the growth of cancerous tumors in rats, and consequently, cyclamates were deemed unsafe for humans.
- The ban was announced in late October, and all cyclamates were to be off the shelf by February 1.
- This might well have been the end of Cumberland Packing and Sweet'N Low.
- But Ben and Marvin were prepared, having anticipated a possible ban.

- Marvin was able to use his chemical expertise and devise a new formula for Sweet'N Low, made with saccharin but without the addition of cyclamates.
- As the ban loomed, the Eisenstadts went to their bank and borrowed $1 million as loyal dieters bought Sweet'N Low by the case—concerned that the product would disappear.
- While their competitors held a strategy committee meeting, Ben and Marvin publicly removed all their old inventory off shelves across the country and buried it in landfills—in the glare of national television news cameras.
- Then, Cumberland supplied its distributors with its reformulated product, judged safe to use.
- Their competitors had failed to react as quickly, and several disappeared.
- Sales of Sweet'N Low tripled to dominate the market.

Life in the Community: New York City

- In the mid-nineteenth century, the German Jews of New York City were well established and often assimilated into New York society as the flood of uneducated poor poured into the city from Poland and Russia.

- In 1836, just 10,000 Jews lived in New York; 75 years later, half a million lived in the Lower East Side alone.

- Entire towns dropped off the map of Eastern Europe, only to reappear in the streets of New York.

- Because so many of the newcomers' names ended with the "ki" of the Russian and Polish peasantry, the German Jews branded their poor cousins "kikes."

- The 1920 Census showed Brooklyn for the first time overtaking Manhattan as the most populous borough.

- By 1924, two million Jews had arrived from Eastern Europe.

- Growing anti-immigration sentiment in the United States at this time resulted in the National Origins Quota of 1924, which severely restricted immigration from Eastern Europe after that time.

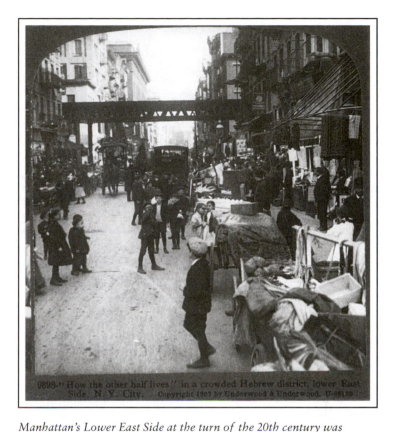

Manhattan's Lower East Side at the turn of the 20th century was known as the "Hebrew district."

- The Jewish community took the lead in opposing immigration restrictions, which remained in effect until 1965.

- This period instead saw a major domestic movement to the city, as the influx of blacks from the South resulted in a flowering of African-American culture in the Harlem Renaissance.

- For most of his term, Tammany Mayor Jimmy Walker enjoyed a period of prosperity for the city, with the proliferation of the "speakeasy" during Prohibition.

- Tin Pan Alley developed toward Broadway, and the first modern musical, Jerome Kern's *Show Boat*, opened in 1927 as the theater district moved north of 42nd Street.

- The Great Depression, which was to affect the rest of the world, began with the Stock Market Crash of 1929.

- The Depression was a time of unemployment and poverty, and a period of increased government involvement in the economy.

- In 1931, the recently completed Empire State Building would be known as the "Empty State Building" for many years because it could not attract a sufficient number of tenants in the bleak business climate.

- In 1933, Republican reformer Fiorello La Guardia was elected mayor.

- La Guardia was of both Italian and Jewish descent, and acted as an exuberant populist with a multi-ethnic sensibility.

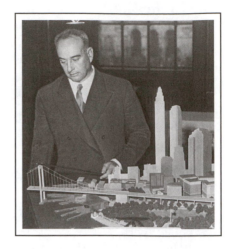

- La Guardia's term also saw the rise of the long-careered planner Robert Moses—bridges, parks and parkways coordinator and great proponent of automobile-centered modernism—whose legacy of massive construction projects is controversial today.
- The last large expansion of the subway system and municipal ownership of the previously privately owned subway companies gave the system its final shape.
- New York became a culturally international city with the influx of intellectual, musical and artistic European refugees that started in the late 1930s.

Robert Moses with a model of the proposed Battery Bridge.

- The 1939 New York World's Fair, marking the 150th anniversary of George Washington's inauguration in Federal Hall, was a high point of technological optimism, meant to mark the end of the Depression.
- After the start of World War II, though, the theme was changed from "Building the World of Tomorrow" to "For Peace and Freedom."
- The city was significantly affected by the war.
- For the duration of World War II, the Port of New York handled 25 percent of the nation's trade.
- Much of this passed through the Brooklyn Army Terminal and the Brooklyn Navy Yard.
- By the war's end, the Navy Yard was the world's largest shipyard, with 75,000 workers.

Skilled workers and the machine shop at the eastern Navy Yard, Brooklyn, NY.

Selected Prices

Blender	$13.49
Camera, 8 mm	$129.95
Car Battery	$12.88
Dishwasher	$119.25
Drill, Electric	$10.99
Dryer	$178.00
Lawn Mower	$79.95
Pepsi, Six 10-Ounce Bottles	$0.59
Razor Blades, 10	$0.99
Slide Viewer	$2.45

"Lawyer Doubles in Cafeteria Job," *The New York Times*, May 1, 1935:

The versatility of Benjamin Eisenstadt, a young attorney, became known in the Tombs Court yesterday when it was related that only a few hours before he had doffed his white linen coat as a counterman at a Flatbush cafeteria to become counsel for a man accused of forgery.

"This counterman matter is just a side racket," Eisenstadt explained to reporters in the presence of Detective James McDonnell of the Old Slip Station and client Lewis Barash, 24 years old, the detective's prisoner. "You see, I have a law office at 1440 Broadway, but I've been filling in as a counter man at the Flatbush Cafeteria at 1016 Nostrand Avenue because I am practically the owner of the place now, although it is in the name of my father-in-law."

Then Eisenstadt entered a not-guilty plea for Barash and waived examination for a grand jury inquiry on the charge of David Wallace, secretary of the Hall Jewelers, Inc., 35 Maiden Lane, that Barash had defrauded his company of a watch worth $42.50 through forging a name as that of a buyer.

McDonnell had arrested Barash shortly before 9 a.m. in his home at 467 Empire Boulevard, Brooklyn. Mr. Wallace was with him to make certain that the right man was arrested. As they started for the Tombs Court, Barash complained that he had not had time to eat breakfast, and the detective agreed to go into the nearby Flatbush Cafeteria with him.

Eisenstadt served the three men at the counter and immediately became engrossed in their conversation, during which Mr. Wallace outlined the charge against Barash.

"Will I have to have a lawyer in a case like this?" Barash asked the detective.

Before he could reply, Eisenstadt spoke up.

"Sure you'll need a lawyer," he said, "and I'm the lawyer who will defend you."

As he spoke, Eisenstadt took off his linen jacket, and, donning a black fedora hat and well-pressed sack coat, accompanied the client, the detective and the complainant to court.

"Suggested Dinner Party Menus," *Silver Jubilee Super Market Cook Book*, **Edith Barber, 1955:**

- Chilled Melon, Lobster Newberg in Croustades, Crown Roast of Lamb, Potatoes with Parsley Butter, Peas with Mint Cream, Chestnut Cream, Coffee
- Hors d'oeuvres Tray, Relishes, Roast Turkey, Cranberry Jelly, Potato Puff, Spinach Ring with Baby Lima Beans, Grapefruit and Endive Salad, Vanilla Ice Cream with Tutti Frutti, Small Cakes, Coffee
- Consommé Bellevue, Relishes, Filet Mignon, Bordelaise Sauce, Chestnut Purée, String Bean Celery, Mixed Green Salad, Chocolate Soufflé, Coffee
- Littleneck Clams, Relishes, Roast Duck, Orange Sauce, Wild Rice with Mushrooms, Buttered Asparagus, Bombe of Raspberry Ice and Vanilla Ice Cream, Small Cakes, Coffee
- Oysters in the Half Shell, Roast Chicken, Whole Hominy with Sherry, Broccoli with Brown Crumbs, Macaroon Cream with Sliced Peaches, Coffee
- Fish Fillets with Normandie Sauce, Roast Beef, Yorkshire Pudding, Braised Celery, Mixed Vegetable Salad, Mincemeat Turnovers, Coffee
- Consommé Madrilene, Relishes, Baked Virginia Ham, Grilled Sweet Potatoes, Cauliflower with Lemon Butter, Romaine with Roquefort Dressing, Wine Jelly with Whipped Cream, Coffee

"Crackdown on Food Additives Challenges Good Cooks," Harriet Van Horne, *Tucson Daily Citizen*, November 24, 1969:

Unexpected blessings—some of them delicious—may soon be gracing our bill of fare.

It was high time the government cracked down on cyclamates, monosodium glutamate, and all those dubious additives described in squinty little letters on the label. Now good cooks have been challenged.

To the average housewife, HEW's subtracting of an additive leaves her with the uneasy feeling that she ought to go find a substitute additive.

If synthetic sweeteners produce cancer of the bladder of laboratory rats, why not be daring and try some other sweetener? Sugar is non-toxic but boring. Why not honey?

Honey in hot tea is delicious. Honey stirred into warm milk at bedtime makes a lovely posset. John the Baptist found wild honey dandy with a locust.

The Elizabethans put honey on everything, including their toothpaste, which explains why everybody from Queen Bess down had terrible teeth. But no rats have ever expired from a surfeit of honey. (A surfeit of locusts, well, maybe.)

The innocuous white powder called MSG gives convulsions to rats and migraine headaches to people who overeat in Chinese restaurants. (It was, in fact, this "Chinese restaurant syndrome" which led to further research on MSG.) As all cooks know, MSG is not so much a seasoning as a stimulant. It opens the taste buds and makes them say "Mmmm...."

Deprived of MSG, a housewife may have to revise her table of flavorings. Honest, black powder straight from the pepper mill should enjoy a new vogue. It has always worked more efficiently than MSG.

A whiff of curry powder may enliven the blended sauces nobody likes. Who knows? Fresh herbs may reassert their good green tang in roast meat and casseroles.

While food packagers suffer the agonizing reappraisal that always follows government bans, I wish some chemist with a decent respect for good food would invent an MSG that works in reverse. That is, an inexpensive white powder to close the taste buds. Close them firmly and politely when the food on the plate is inedible.

What embarrassment, what digestive distress we'd all be spared on those nights of horror when we must dine where the cuisine is not the glory of the house. Please, can I have a little GSM in my pillbox?

The government's new firm stand on pesticides should sweeten our lives, too.

Now, at last, we can eat an apple, skin and all, and not worry about when the twitching may start. (The classic pattern of DDT poisoning is random excitement, twitching, convulsions, death. Now you know.)

A ban on DDT, when it comes, may mean that raw carrots no longer taste of gasoline. And baked potatoes will be served in preference to the noodles in the add-water-and-mix sauce which, naturally will be chock-a-block with MSG, cyclamates, and if I may voice my own dark suspicions, sawdust and bone dust.

continued

"Crackdown on Food Additives Challenges Good Cooks," *(continued)*

We spend enormous amounts of money on food in this country, but too many people have forgotten how to eat. And too many women, beguiled by jiffy mixes and frozen prefixed feasts, have never learned to cook.

We've come a long way, perhaps too far, from our seventeenth-century ancestors who knew how to pot a swan, preserve flowers in syrup and make "kissing comfits" to sweeten the breath.

"What's That Funny Taste? The Never-Ending Quest for Fake Sugar," Benjamin Siegel, *American Heritage*, June, 2006:

Just as diet soda's multibillion-dollar industry stems from the unassuming Russian Jewish émigré Hyman Kirsch, so the history of artificial sweeteners is an immigrant story, one that begins in a Johns Hopkins University laboratory in 1879. Constantine Fahlberg, a "well-built, handsome, German-American," according to an article *Scientific American* published years later, was working there examining the properties of coal tar. Quite by accident, he stumbled upon a chemical that would forever sweeten the course of history.

One evening I was so interested in my laboratory," Fahlberg told *Scientific American*, "that I forgot about supper until quite late, and then rushed off for a meal without stopping to wash my hands. I sat down, broke a piece of bread, and put it to my lips. It tasted unspeakably sweet. I did not ask why it was so, probably because I thought it was some cake or sweetmeat. I rinsed my mouth with water, and dried my mustache with my napkin, when, to my surprise, the napkin tasted sweeter than the bread. Then I was puzzled."

Fahlberg quickly realized what he had stumbled upon, a byproduct of coal tar that, strangely enough, "out-sugared sugar." After running back to the lab, he proceeded to violate several principles of scientific safety, tasting each and every chemical in order to figure out which one had accidentally found its way into his food. Stumbling upon saccharin, Fahlberg began secretly to study the compound, and in time went back to Germany to set up his own manufacturing company. Soon he was selling his product worldwide.

Diet soda was certainly the furthest thing from Fahlberg's mind; medicine was where saccharin would prove most useful, he thought, and suggested that the chemical be used in "fine wafers and other foods for invalids," hoping it would prove "invaluable in disguising and destroying all the bitter and sour tastes in medicine without changing the character or action of the drugs."

Fahlberg wasn't concerned with side effects. Saccharin "has no injurious effect on the human system," he said; "what effect has been noticed is rather beneficial than otherwise." And soon he was looking beyond medical applications: "In the future, the new sugar will be used by druggists, physicians, bakers, confectioners, candy makers, preserve and pickle makers, liquor distillers, wine makers, and dealers in bottlers' supplies."

However, saccharin was always viewed a bit suspiciously; from the earliest days of its marketing and even during the First World War's intense sugar rationing, some Americans saw the substance as a poor substitute for energy-rich sugar and perhaps even as something hazardous.

In 1937, Michael Sveda, the son of Czech immigrants and an amateur violinist and woodworker, stepped out for a cigarette after a long day of working toward his chemistry Ph.D. at the University of Illinois. Like Constantine Fahlberg before him, Sveda realized that what he was putting in his mouth was unusually sweet. He walked back in the lab for another groundbreaking chemical taste test. He had stumbled upon cyclamate.

continued

"What's That Funny Taste? The Never-Ending Quest for Fake Sugar," *(continued)*

Cyclamates were everything that saccharin was not: They lacked the metallic aftertaste that plagued saccharin, and there were no initial concerns about safety. Hyman Kirsch used them to sweeten No-Cal, Royal Crown to sweeten Diet Rite Cola. For close to two decades, cyclamates went into everything from toothpaste to canned fruit.

Then came 1969 and the alarm about cyclamates causing cancer in rats. In the years that followed, aspartame would have its day, though that chemical, too, has been plagued by reports linking it with cancer.

While most technologies have changed dramatically in the last hundred years, artificial sweeteners aren't much more advanced than they were in Constantine Fahlberg's time, and the regular association of them with cancer may help explain why the diet-soda industry changes formulas every 20 years or so. Splenda, the brand name for sucralose, is the latest in the line of new artificial sweeteners. Like its predecessors, it was born when a researcher happened to taste a chemical he had merely been asked to "test."

Dieting in America

One of the earliest dieting programs was developed in the early nineteenth century by Presbyterian minister Sylvester Graham. Graham's diet involved ingesting fruits, vegetables, and other high-fiber foods while abstaining from spices and meats. The staple of Graham's diet was his own recipe called "Graham Bread," later known as the graham cracker.

Yet, rather than simply weight loss, Graham's diet was originally intended to curb gluttony and to prevent impure thoughts. Another early dieting fad of the late nineteenth century involved rules on chewing.

Dubbed "The Great Masticator," Horace Fletcher was the most famous proponent of such chewing diets.

Fletcher's maxim was that food ought to be chewed 32 times before being swallowed, claiming "Nature will castigate those who don't masticate."

These fads were followed by "diet pills" in the early twentieth century that claimed to contain tapeworms or tapeworm eggs.

One advertisement poster depicted a woman pensively standing before a mountain of food. The text reads, "Fat. The enemy that is shortening your life banished! How? With sanitized tapeworms. Jar packed. 'Friends for a fair form.' Easy to swallow." There are even reassuring phrases in this ad that note that sanitized tapeworms are "guaranteed harmless" and have "no ill effects."

During the 1950s, doctors prescribed diet pills to patients that contained amphetamines, which were used extensively during World War II to help soldiers overcome fatigue.

One of the side effects of amphetamine use was appetite suppression, but the use of amphetamines also led to substance abuse problems.

Doctors eventually stopped prescribing amphetamines for weight loss in the 1960s.

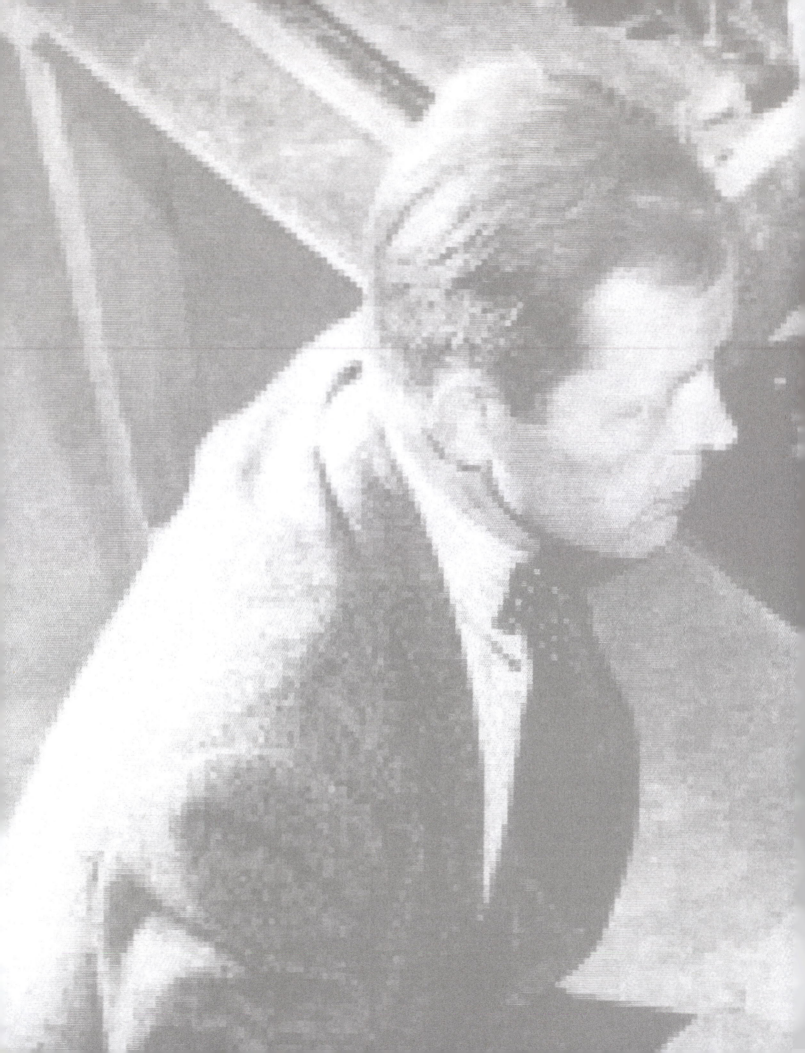

1970-1979

Despite considerable economic and political turbulence, America's inventors and entrepreneurs made the 1970s the age of the practical computer. Their creations included the floppy disk, microprocessors, the laser printer and Pong, the first computer game. The era also gave rise to the video cassette recorder, magnetic resonance imaging, and a period of spiraling costs, spawned by the Vietnam War. The result was an America stripped of its ability to dominate the world economy and a nation on the defensive. In 1971, President Richard Nixon was forced to devalue the U.S. dollar against foreign currencies and allow its previously fixed value to "float" according to changing economic conditions. By year's end, the money paid for foreign goods exceeded that spent on U.S. exports for the first time in the century. Two years later, during the "Yom Kippur" War between Israel and its Arab neighbors, Arab oil producers declared an oil embargo on oil shipments to the United States, setting off gas shortages, a dramatic rise in the price of oil, and rationing for the first time in 30 years. The sale of automobiles plummeted, unemployment and inflation nearly doubled, and the buying power of Americans fell dramatically.

The economy handicapped by the devaluation of the dollar and inflation, did not fully recover for more than a decade, while the fast-growing economics of Japan and western Europe, especially West Germany, mounted direct competitive challenges to American manufacturers. The value of imported manufactured goods skyrocked from 14 percent of U.S. domestic production in 1970 to 40 percent in 1979. The inflationary cycle and recession returned in 1979 to disrupt markets, throw thousands out of work, and prompt massive downsizing of companies—awakening many once-secure workers to the reality of the changing economic market. A symbol of the era was the pending bankruptcy of Chrysler Corporation, whose cars were so outmoded and plants so inefficient they could not compete against Japanese imports. The federal government was forced to extend loan guarantees to the company to prevent bankruptcy and the loss of thousands of jobs.

The appointment of Paul Volcker as the chairman of the Federal Reserve Board late in the decade gave the economy the distasteful medicine it needed. To cope with inflation, Volcker slammed on the economic brakes, restricted the growth of the money supply, and curbed inflation. As a result, he pushed interest rates to nearly 20 percent—the highest level since the Civil War. Almost immediately the sale of automobiles and expensive items stopped.

The decade also was marred by deep division caused by the Vietnam War. For more than 10 years the war had been fought on two fronts; at home and abroad. As a result, U.S. policy makers conducted the war with one eye always focused on national opinion. When it ended, the Vietnam War had been the longest war in American history, having cost $118 billion and resulted in 56,000 dead, 300,000 wounded, and the loss of American prestige abroad.

The decade was a time not only of movements, but of moving. In the 1970s, the shift of manufacturing facilities to the South from New England the Midwest accelerated. The Sunbelt became the new darling of corporate America. By the 1970s, the South, including Texas, had gained more than a million manufacturing jobs, while the Northeast and the Midwest, lost nearly two million. Rural North Carolina had the highest percentage of manufacturing of any state in the nation, along with the lowest blue collar wages and the lowest unionization rate n the country. The Northeast lost more than traditional manufacturing jobs. Computerization of clerical work also made it possible for big firms such as Merrill Lynch, American Express, and Citibank to shift many of their operations to the South and West.

The largest and most striking of all the social actions of the early 1970s was the women's liberation movement; it fundamentally reshaped American society. Since the late 1950s, a small group of well-placed American women had attempted to convince Congress and the courts to bring about equality between the sexes. By the 1970s, the National Organization for Women (NOW) multiplied in size, the first issue of *Ms. Magazine* sold out in a week, and women began demanding economic equality, the legalization of abortion, and the improvement of women's role in society. "All authority in our society is being challenged," said a Department of Health, Education, and Welfare report. "Professional athletes challenge owners, journalist challenge editors, consumers challenge manufacturers…and young blue-collar workers, who have grown up in an environment in which equality is called for in all institutions, are demanding the same rights and expressing the same values as university graduates."

The decade also included the flowering of the National Welfare Rights Organization (NWRO), founded in 1966, which resulted in millions of urban poor demanding additional rights. The environmental movement gained recognition and momentum during the decade starting with the first Earth Day celebration in 1970 and the subsequent passage of the Federal Clean Air and Clean Water acts. And the growing opposition to the use of nuclear power peaked after the near calamity at Three Mile Island in Pennsylvania in 1979. As the formal barriers to racial equality came down, racist attitudes became unacceptable and the black middle class began to grow. By 1972, half of all Southern black children sat in integrated classrooms, and about one third of all black families had risen economically into the ranks of the middle class.

The changes recorded for the decade included a doubling in the amount of garbage created per capita from 2.5 pounds in 1920 to five pounds. California created a no-fault divorce law, Massachusetts introduced no-fault insurance, and health food sales reached $3 billion. By mid-decade, the so-called typical nuclear family, with working father, housewife, and two children, represented only seven percent of the population and the family size was falling. The average family size was 3.4 persons compared with 4.3 in 1920.

1975 Profile

Roy and Dotty Eargle plunged into the ever-changing world of antiques, learning on the fly how to bid at auctions, where to make the best deals, and how to transform an abandoned Victorian house into a showplace.

Life at Home

- On a blistering hot morning in August 1973, the jet-lagged, exhausted Eargle family poured from a taxi onto the curb of a working-class neighborhood in Northern Virginia and stood silently appraising their new home, an aging 1950s cookie-cutter bungalow akin to all on the block.
- Tiredness was no match for the disappointment that clouded the faces of Roy and Dotty Eargle that day.
- A casual observer might well have dismissed the scene as that of just another down-and-out family migrating from Europe.
- Broke they were, yet flush with six successful years in Germany where Dotty was an understudy of Elizabeth Gruemer of the Berlin Opera and earned her degree in Concert Singing from the University of Heidelberg-Manheim.
- The bungalow was a world away from Germany where Dotty had sharpened her college-German to near fluency, performed her exceptional voice in a number of settings, and learned quickly to stand her ground in shopping and bus lines with strong, resolute German Putzfrauen.
- Roy got his foot in the door as a civilian employee of the Department of the Army, worked hard, and gained promotions to higher-level positions at the U.S. Army Headquarters, Berlin, and later at European Headquarters, Heidelberg.
- Roy's six-year tour of overseas Civil Service employment expired in August 1973.

Roy and Dotty Eargle created a successful antique business.

- Fortunately, the Department offered to continue Roy's civilian employment upon his agreement to serve a minimum of one year at the Pentagon.
- They were also offered the incentive of expense-paid transportation home to America for the family, and temporary housing in the DC area: thus, arrival at the little bungalow in Virginia Hills.
- The move to DC proved to be its own nightmarish culture-shock.
- Without a single workday break from Germany to DC, Roy was initiated into the world's fastest-paced work environment, the Pentagon.
- He was thrown that first work day among the masses to negotiate the city's Great Bus and Transit Puzzle and, most traumatically, was awakened to the fact that survival in the world's second-most expensive city would require funds in excess of his meager Civil Service salary.

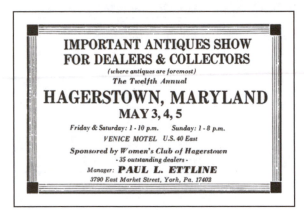

Dotty looked forward to their weekend "wicker hunts."

- Once again, necessity was the breeding ground of an entrepreneur.
- Since government apartments in Berlin and Heidelberg were completely furnished, the Eargles needed living room furniture, and Dotty decided that they should decorate with original Victorian wicker.
- The DC area was well populated with antique dealers who were in easy reach of abundant supplies of old furniture from New York and Pennsylvania.
- With a ready local source from which to select, they began to acquire some beautiful pieces of wicker over the first several months.
- But the buying didn't seem to come to an end; on each new shopping trip, Dotty found a piece or two more desirable than the ones she had previously purchased.

- In this fashion, as the living room was filled, the less favored pieces were moved to the basement.
- By the end of the year, they both admitted that the buying had to cease, or there would be no money for food, rent or utility bills.
- Their small, two-line newspaper advertisement, "Original Victorian wicker for sale by private owner," in Sunday's *Washington Post* in late January 1974 drew over 60 telephone calls, and their unwanted inventory was gone within just a few days.
- Without further debate, they took up the initiative to become antique dealers.
- Dotty spent several weeks in March 1974 investigating the availability of rental spaces in various flea markets in the area before settling on an ancient brick and timber warehouse in Old Town Alexandria.
- Having developed a pleasant acquaintance with the manager during their wicker-buying days, Dotty was able to wheedle from him, outside the long waiting list, a coveted 10 foot by 10 foot space, albeit at the breathtaking rent of $20 per weekend.
- In anticipation, Roy began to clean up the remaining pieces of unwanted wicker and sketching a layout of their meager inventory onto the 100 square foot plan of the flea market space.

The Eargles also sold smaller items with a big mark up.

- It quickly became painfully obvious that they didn't have nearly enough bait to go fishing and had to ask coworkers at the Pentagon to place antique items on consignment.
- Roy and Dotty then spent time pricing their goods and displaying them attractively so as to provide for convenient customer flow and inspection.
- They opened on the weekend of May 11, 1974, with glowing enthusiasm and smiley-faced sales tactics, but nothing helped to bring about the blow-out sales they had so naively hoped for.
- They settled for total weekend sales of $230.
- The letdown did, however, provide the self-examination they needed.
- Concluding that small, rustic items, both useful and decorative, were bestsellers, they realized that if they were to be successful, their inventory needed to change.
- That's when they discovered the world of auctioneering at Thorp's Country Auction on Routes 29 and 211, near Gainesville, Virginia.
- Old "Ed," the 1971 Volkswagen bus they brought back from Germany, became their "truck"; the rear seat folded down flat to make a fair-sized carrying space, although with only $150 seed money they didn't expect the need of a trailer.
- The low, squatty auction house, sided with split and knotted planks bleached white over the years by the hot Virginia sun, oozed from the dark soil just high enough to overshadow the tall, smothering hostas.
- When Roy and Dotty arrived, dozens of dusty pickups and vans were already squeezed into every available space.
- The large crowd was intimidating, adding to their already nervous concerns about the whole process of bidding.
- Roy signed in, obtained a bid card, and found seats to observe both the body language of the auctioneers and the bid-by-bid reactions of the audience.
- As the evening waned, they gingerly bid $5.00 on an old floor lamp, raised their bid to $7.00, and in doing so, had become antique dealers.

Life at Work

- Attempting to stay within their $150 "bank" that first night, Dotty and Roy Eargle bought a few lamps, old tools, and other small, rustic items believed to have crowd appeal.
- Their bidding system was elementary: Dotty nudged Roy lightly with her elbow when she thought they should bid or raise, and more forcefully when she thought they should quit or when she suspected that Roy was about to bid on something she didn't want.
- Afterwards, Dotty cleaned the purchases and Roy made any necessary repairs to get them ready for sale in the flea market booth—including the stated price.
- Competitive pricing was a challenge.
- They experimented in the beginning by marking items up 300 percent; that is, a 10-dollar cost on the

Dotty refinished the bigger items.

stump, requiring only minor cleaning or repairs, became a 30-dollar sales item.

- The resulting end-prices seemed competitive and left the couple with room to bargain, as the public was certainly wont to do.
- They generally held to this method of pricing, even after refinishing high-quality golden oak became a major part of their business.
- As their little bank of seed money began to grow, they became experts at stuffing, cramming, and tying antique pieces on top of the bus until old Ed sometimes resembled a monster porcupine.
- This limited hauling capacity also taught Roy a lesson in both logistics and the sound intelligence that comes from the mouths of children.
- The Eargles were buying lots of oak "pressed back" chairs, which they refinished for resale by simply knocking them apart, cleaning the parts, and gluing them back together.
- Towards the end of an excellent buying night at Thorp's, when Roy suspected that Old Ed was already overloaded, a magnificent set of six carved oak chairs was brought out by the auctioneer.

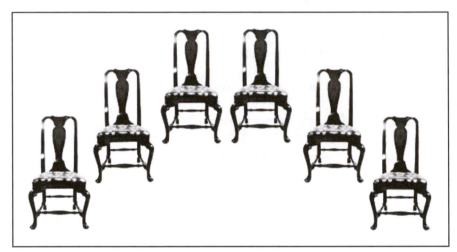

- When Dotty whispered that they must get them, Roy whispered back that they had no room left in the bus.
- Their nine-year-old son elbowed Roy instantly and whispered, "Let's knock 'em apart, Dad. We gonna do it anyway to get 'em refinished."
- They never lost the purchase of a fine set of chairs after learning that closely held "corporate trade-secret."
- Buying was always a priority, so on the way back from his son's summer camp, Roy noticed a cluster of rundown, plank-sided farm buildings that seemed to reek of antiquity.
- After shooing aside a flock of Rhode Island Reds, several beagles, and a calico cat stretched across the freshly swept dirt pathway, Roy climbed a rickety pair of steps onto a wide front porch, slanting dangerously in several directions.
- An old cow bell served as a doorknocker, the sound of which, after a long wait, brought to the door a thin, erect woman of indiscriminate age.
- A strong smell of shoe polish and the freshness of Octagon soap drifted from the doorway as clear, cloud-grey eyes searched Roy's face without speaking.
- Roy had struck the equivalent of an antique gold mine.
- The owner was a second-generation German who was born on the land and whose family had lost their wealth during the Great Depression.
- She was on her way to work in St. George's Kitchens as a dietician when Roy met her that Sunday.
- Roy learned that she was financially able to move to a little cottage in the town but was determined to save the land, which held a small tobacco allotment, for her children.

- Over the next few months, she led Roy into each snake-infested barn, from which he pulled handmade farm tables, jelly cupboards, linen presses, walnut and pine Empire-style pie safes, a wealth of Gone With the Wind, Aladdin, and other oil lamps, embroidery pieces and samplers, quilts, and boxes of Depression glass and old crockery.

- She explained that the stuff was moved from the original home place; intent on saving the furnishings for the children, her husband had stored them in the scattered barns around the compound.

- Now that her husband was dead, she had not known how to dispose of the large and diverse volume of furnishings.

- Because she was living in so remote an area, and since no previous inquiries presented themselves, she was eager to bargain with Roy, provided he bought everything.

- Their combined efforts during those long months in the summer of 1974 paid handsomely, and the Eargles quickly expanded at the Old Town Flea Market to several more sales spaces as they became available.

The old farm was full of handmade furniture and antique gems.

- Dotty refinished during the day, with Roy helping at night after his day job at the Pentagon.

- If necessary, Dotty would put in a full evening as well.

- Since further expansion space at the Old Town Market was severely limited, and the expiration of the lease on their rental house in Virginia Hills was approaching, they needed to find new quarters for both the family and the growing business.

Roy looked past the long grass and disrepair to see Victorian diamonds in the rough.

- Luckily, Roy had spotted an elegant three-story Victorian mansion in Old Alexandria that sat abandoned at the corner of Madison and North Washington streets.

- There were no signs on the property and the grass was always knee-high in the side yard.

- To the north of the mansion, with a narrow alley between, lay a modern motel and parking lot, and across the street stood an always-crowded Howard Johnson's restaurant.

- The property was strategically located on a major link between DC and Mount Vernon, making it a highly desirable spot for retail sales.

- Low-rent public housing occupied a number of city blocks to the west, which tended to detract from the property's comfortable and safe living accommodations.

- The mansion's location and potential as both living quarters and shop, however, outweighed the negative aspects of industry and public housing.

Life in the Community: Alexandria, Virginia

- Alexandria, Virginia, was shaped by its proximity to the nation's capital and was largely populated by civil servants and professional contractors.
- Major employers included the U.S. Department of Defense and the Center for Naval Analyses.
- In 1791, Alexandria was included in the area chosen by George Washington to become the District of Columbia.
- A portion of the City of Alexandria—known as "Old Town"—was originally in Virginia, ceded to the U.S. Government to form the District of Columbia, and later retro-ceded to Virginia by the federal government in 1846, when the District was reduced in size.
- Its history and look made Alexandria the perfect place for an antique store.
- So Roy Eargle took the first opportunity in July 1974 to investigate the abandoned mansion he had spotted, stopping first at the adjoining motel where he learned that the house was part of the motel property held under lease by a property management firm in DC.
- With the manager's assistance, Roy contacted the senior partner of the family firm and they agreed to meet that afternoon.
- The senior partner explained that his family's interest was only in motel management, but that, under the terms of his lease, it had been necessary to take on the unwanted responsibility of the old home as well.

The Furniture Mill's kitchen was the perfect showroom.

- The property, he informed Roy, was in an estate of 18 relatives who were unable to agree on any fair disposition of the property.
- Thus, it had lain dormant for over a decade.
- He told Roy quite frankly that he had never received much interest in the old house, and that the strict historical preservation ordinance in Old Alexandria prevented razing or altering the structure.
- The size, location and historic character of the property, however, was ideal for Roy and Dotty's antique business, and offered the interesting and efficient old-country custom of living over one's shop.
- The old gentlemen was delighted with their plans to restore the elegant rooms and architectural appurtenances of the home, and upgrade the infrastructure—all without violating the ordinances of the city.
- They negotiated a 10-year lease based on little more than the monthly pro rata share of the total property taxes and insurance that was favorably one-sided because it relieved that burden from the management company's master lease.
- The historic old mansion was an architectural gem, but basic care and maintenance had suffered greatly for two decades until the home was condemned by the city due to unsafe, out-of-date electrical and plumbing systems.
- The Eargles began their plans for restoration the minute they signed the long-term lease on September 15, 1974.
- They found the interior of the old home horribly defaced: the hardwood floors all were covered with sheet linoleum, and paneled heart pine doors and moldings lost their delicacy under multiple coats of cheap oil paint, as did the smoothly plastered walls, splattered with a plethora of garish colors.

HISTORICAL SNAPSHOT
1975

- Altair 8800 was released, sparking the era of the microcomputer
- John N. Mitchell, H. R. Haldeman and John Ehrlichman were found guilty of the Watergate cover-up
- *Wheel of Fortune* premiered on NBC
- Ella Grasso became Governor of Connecticut—the first female U.S. governor who did not succeed her husband
- In Super Bowl IX, The Pittsburgh Steelers defeated the Minnesota Vikings 16–6 at Tulane Stadium in New Orleans, Louisiana
- In response to the energy crisis, daylight saving time commenced nearly two months early
- Actor Charlie Chaplin was knighted by Queen Elizabeth II
- *The Rocky Horror Show* opened on Broadway in New York City
- Bill Gates founded Microsoft in Albuquerque, New Mexico
- The Vietnam War ended as North Vietnamese forces captured Saigon, resulting in mass evacuations of Americans and South Vietnamese
- Cambodian forces seized the United States merchant ship SS *Mayaguez* in international waters
- The Suez Canal was reopened for the first time since the Six-Day War in 1967
- An American *Apollo* and Soviet *Soyuz* spacecraft docked in orbit, marking the first such linkup between spacecraft from the two nations
- Teamsters Union president Jimmy Hoffa was reported missing and presumed dead
- President Gerald Ford posthumously pardoned Confederate General Robert E. Lee, restoring to him full rights of citizenship
- In Sacramento, California, Lynette Fromme, a follower of jailed cult leader Charles Manson, attempted to assassinate President Ford, but was thwarted by a Secret Service agent

- Muhammad Ali defeated Joe Frazier in a boxing match in Manila, The Philippines
- NBC aired the first episode of *Saturday Night Live* with George Carlin as the first host; Billy Preston and Janis Ian were the first musical guests
- An independent audit of Mattel, one of the United States' largest toy manufacturers, revealed that company officials fabricated press releases and financial information to "maintain the appearance of continued corporate growth"

Selected Prices

Antique Cupboard, circa 1790 ....$690.00
Bandages, Curad, 30.. $0.69
Basketball $4.80
Car Set, Matchbox $4.47
Card Table, circa 1760..$1,950.00
Casserole Dish $58.00
Clock, Nineteenth Century French..............................$2,800.00
Pressure Cooker $10.88
Stereo Cassette System $400.00
Tire, Steel Belted...$42.00

The Helpers, Roy Eargle, 2010:

A most timely and fortunate milestone in the history of our business enterprise was reached with the introduction into our lives of two young people of quite disparate personalities. The event occurred shortly after our taking possession of the old house and at the time we had brought over a moving van with some equipment and supplies preparatory to restoration. Within moments, the van was surrounded by a dozen young black men quietly gathered for the chance to make a few dollars helping with the unloading. A sea of pleading yet sorrowful faces was reaching out as I stepped from the truck, and it pained me that I could use only several for the few items to be unloaded.

I was reluctant at first glance to make an arbitrary selection, and as I looked again there appeared more prominently than the rest one physically erect fellow at least a head above the crowd. He stood a little alone from the others, seemingly without emotion, except for a spark of hope that shone warmly in the midnight of his eyes. His slim, well-formed face with high cheekbones, straight nose and smallish lips suggested a Caucasian influence, while his polished ebony skin left no doubt of his pure African heritage. I didn't have to point; he moved toward me as our eyes met, without pushing, slowly through the crowd of young men who seemed to give sway to his presence, and I asked his name. A shorter, less physical yet interestingly friendly youth moving along behind shouted, "He Pee Wee and I'm his cutty, Leroy," and as they moved to the back of the truck, the crowd began to melt away. Lee "Pee Wee" Wilkerson and his brother, Leroy, were each in their mid-teens and living in the Public Housing Complex behind our new home and shop. I have always believed that it was very much an act of Divine Providence, because it brought into our lives a young man whose life to that point had been a useless struggle to survive and whose future offered only destitution and the likelihood of perhaps wasteful years in prison. Because of his gentle nature, he was just naturally "Pee Wee" to us, in spite of his huge size. Over the 10 years Lee worked for us full-time in our refinishing shop, his personal confidence grew steadily from the shyness of not being able to look us in the eye to a highly talented craftsman whose outgoing personality and high character made him an enjoyable acquaintance and a productive human being.

continued

The Helpers, Roy Eargle, 2010: *(continued)*

The style and magnificence of the interior wood craftsmanship of the old mansion, though blighted with disinterested abuse over the years, is worthy of mentioning. Architecturally its design echoed the narrow floor plan so common in Charleston and New Orleans. Rooms were laid out one behind the other in domino fashion with a long covered porch along the windowed side, within a narrow court-yard, for privacy from a neighbor or the busy side street. The time-worn stone steps of a broad entrance stoop led to deeply paneled double pine doors through which one entered a shallow vestibule opening directly into an inviting foyer. A large living room led off to the left through tall in-the-wall sliding pine-paneled doors. The high-ceilinged room was crowned with wide concave-molded pine trim and lighted with the brilliancy of the morning sun, through enormous double hung windows, set in both the north and east walls. An imposing carved oak over-mantel along the east wall surrounded a deep-set tile-faced fireplace and tended to overwhelm one's attention on entering from the foyer. The narrow-milled tongue-and-groove floors were of the clearest heart pine, adorned around the perimeter with a tall three-piece molded heart pine baseboard. Returning to the foyer, itself a deep hallway leading to the basement stairs at its rear, there rose from its far side the wide, elegantly carved stairway to the second floor.

On leaving the living room toward the rear of the house, one entered into an equally large dining room whose long series of tall windows along the east wall invited the brightness of the noonday sun. Sheltered by the wide covered porch alongside, the sharp rays fell in subtle shadows across the soft glow of the old pine floor. The wide square room was complemented by a delicately carved fireplace mantel-surround and embellished with the same warm, rich grains of pine floor-ing and molding enjoyed throughout the great old house. A spacious, well-lighted kitchen brought up the rear and enjoyed the convenience of a large pantry and laundry closet. The kitchen was floored with wide-plank pine, and Dotty decided on sight that she would scrub the old floor each night with lye-entrenched hot water. Treated such over the years, the old floor began to glow with a white luster that emanated cleanliness and a primitive character. The kitchen was entered from the dining room through and just beyond a wide landing at the foot of the rear service steps, which provided a private entrance to the our second-floor personal quarters. The wide landing also served as a mud room entrance from the covered porch and the large fenced-in courtyard beyond.

continued

The Helpers, Roy Eargle, 2010: *(continued)*

The job of restoring the old Victorian house was, indeed, a heavy undertaking, but a delight to behold as the work progressed. The great old pine floors throughout were covered with linoleum, which had to be scraped off and hauled away. The heavily carved window and door moldings, most of the wide baseboards, and a number of the paneled pine doors were covered with thick coats of paint. Pee Wee, with a wonderfully willing attitude, demonstrated immediately such natural skill at refinishing the fine old pine moldings and architectural appurtenances that we set him full time, with Dotty's guidance, to that singular task. He accomplished the work of removing the old paint and cracked, yellowed varnish with such a delicate touch that each refinished piece of work brought forth the rich grains and warm patina of heart pine, leaving no evidence of gouging or surface scratches. Leroy, whose personality was more open and active, brought a sense of indifference to his work and was reprimanded by Pee Wee several times in the beginning for gouging too deeply with his floor scraper. Nevertheless, he seemed delighted with the more elementary, physical work, and complained little when brought up at times by Pee Wee's sharp instructions. We learned later that the term "cutty" signified one who is, by nature or submission, obligated to another for a favor granted and to whom he must share part of the reward. That is, Leroy was Pee Wee's cutty, and in recognition of what he believed to be some mystical influence Pee Wee may have had in getting him the job, he owed a "cut" of his pay working for us to Pee Wee.

Old Ed, Roy Eargle, 2010:

The distance and speed necessary to make a timely trip was too much of a burden for our Volkswagen bus, and, although we had recently traded some antiques for a two-horse trailer, the combination was inefficient and slow. Like so many trying, on-the-road stories in my memory, there was a time in Danbury, Connecticut, one Sunday morning, both Old Ed and the horse trailer were loaded to the gills, after I had been on the road collecting antiques from my pickers since Friday. Exhausted and ready to go home, I pulled away from the pumps of a filling station I had frequented on past trips, and the overloaded trailer snatched Old Ed's rear bumper to the ground with a blood-curdling screech. I had to be back at my job at the Pentagon at six-thirty the next morning, and, being Sunday and six to seven hours away, had no immediate solution. The station owner sauntered leisurely from his position at the wide plate glass of his station, restraining himself, no doubt, at the sight of my unfortunate plight. I shall never forget that broad grin on his round, red-stubbled face as he laughingly informed me that his brother was already on the way with his portable welder. In all my trips, I never met a New Englander who was not one step ahead of his fellow man in efficiency and helpful friendliness, despite their irritating conservatism. I was back on the road by early afternoon, but having to negotiate the heavy Sunday afternoon traffic on the Connecticut and New Jersey Turnpikes, crawl through New York, and take the long bypass around Philadelphia and Baltimore, I wasn't able to reach Alexandria and home until after midnight.

"Antique Shops Report Booming Sales," Dan Gordon, *Nevada State Journal*, July 13, 1975:

A washing machine that does not wash or a straight-back wooden bench do not sound like hot selling items in this world of plush sofas and rapid-action washers.

However, these items, if they happen to be antiques, not only sell, but are commanding high prices.

Antiques are not collecting dust in shops these days.

Instead, the demand for antique items has been steadily increasing, and one Reno dealer described the current interest among consumers as a "mania."

The Yankee Trader antique store on Highway 395 south of Reno has been in business for 23 years, and the owner Harold Andrews said the market has remained healthy throughout. However, in recent years, consumer interest has reached even greater heights.

Many of the items have lost their function in the modern world, but that has not diminished their value.

"The function of the furniture is secondary," Andrews said. "It's the appearance and the history that counts."

Andrews, himself, has a keen appreciation of the furniture he sells. While pointing to an ornate grandfather clock, he can rattle off who built the clock and when.

This type of knowledge is indispensable, because a dealer purchases the items for his store, and consequently must be able to spot quality goods.

Because these quality items are often hidden in remote places, like attics or under piles of used furniture, the dealer must have a sharp eye.

Andrews said there is a lively traffic for antique items in Nevada, but the strongest interest still exists in the East.

"Most antiques are back East," Andrews said.

The definition of an antique is an object of beauty or rarity that is at least 100 years old, and for that reason the East has a head start on the Western states as far as being a center for antiques.

Each year, to renew his supply of antiques, Andrews returns back to the East on a buying trip. He also buys locally and in California.

Andrews said through his 23 years in business in Nevada, he has developed a reputation that attracts many customers throughout the United States. He also said there is a healthy local trade.

Tastes differ across the country.

"This is Victorian country," Andrews said. "Most of the people are interested in Victorian furniture because that was the type used when the state was first settled."

Andrews himself is most interested in eighteenth-century American furniture....

Janet Thompson of the Old Timer store on West 2nd Street said both collectibles and antiques are good investments because they appreciate in value.

At the same time, consumers are increasingly attracted to antiques and collectibles because of the personal flavor of owning old furniture and decorations.

"When you buy an antique, it is something that no one else owns," Thompson said. "People can create their own personal atmosphere with antiques."

Selling antique or collectible items is not so difficult, she said. However, buying good furniture is becoming more and more difficult.

"It is becoming very hard to find good antiques," she said.

"'Ibis': Wading Through Antiques,"
The Pocono Record, June 7, 1975:

Linda DeRussy and Paul Fuhrman, antique lovers both, sought to escape the urban pressures of New York City, so they found an apartment in Stroudsburg and began furnishing it with antiques that they found scouting auctions and flea markets.

Soon the apartment was cluttered and furniture items were piled on top of each other. The problem was solved when the two decided to open an antique store, though they never were in business before.

The store is unusual because it is stocked only with merchandise that the owners have had in their own home. It's not simply an antique store, either. Antiques are combined with clothing, jewelry, gifts, cosmetics, prints and toys.

"Ibis, a General Store and Antiques," is located on Main Street in Stroudsburg across from the Sherman theaters. It opened this spring, and the owners report that the idea of blending antiques with other types of merchandise was successful.

Antiques are acquired from rural areas in western Pennsylvania, and much of the other merchandise is imported from Europe, South America and Asia.

"So far, we are still buying from us," DeRussy said, though other local merchants warned them that the practice can be bad for business. Another unusual guideline is nothing made from plastic is sold.

The toys, many imported from the Soviet Union, are made from wood, which DeRussy prefers because they are attractive and fun to play with, but they are relatively indestructible.

1976 Profile

Bette Nesmith Graham's artistic bent came from her mother, her entrepreneurial drive and her invention, Liquid Paper, grew out of necessity.

Life at Home
- Born in 1924 in Dallas, Texas, but raised in San Antonio, Bette Claire McMurray was strong willed, talkative and sometimes considered a discipline problem at school.
- Her artist mother owned a knitting shop and her father ran an auto parts store.
- When only 17 years old, she dropped out of Alamo Heights High School to marry her high school sweetheart, Warren Nesmith, just before he went off to war.
- Ten months later, their son Michael, who would be famous in the 1960s as a member of the music group the Monkees, was born in 1943.
- When her husband returned from war, their marriage rapidly fell apart, and by 1946 Bette found herself divorced and the single mother of a three-year-old.
- Putting aside her love of art, Bette talked her way into a job as a secretary even though she didn't know how to type.
- The firm liked her energetic spirit and agreed to send her to secretarial school to learn typing.
- By 1951, Bette had moved to Dallas and worked her way up to the role of executive secretary at Dallas Bank and Trust, when the company introduced new IBM electric typewriters.
- Bette, who still struggled to type an entire page without a single mistake, found that the new carbon film ribbons on the machines made matters worse; they did not erase well and corrections simply made a mess.
- Electric typewriters had come into widespread use after World War II, and even though the new machines made typing easier, making corrections with a pencil eraser was nearly impossible.

Bette Nesmith Graham combined craftiness, business know-how, and necessity to invent Liquid Paper.

- Betty grew tired of having to retype the entire page because of a single error or typo.

Bette was tired of retyping a whole page to fix one mistake.

- That's when she drew inspiration from the artists decorating the bank's front windows at Christmastime.
- To earn extra money, Bette was helping to dress the bank window when she noticed that the artists painting the glass corrected their imperfections by painting another layer over them.
- If erasures were unnecessary on glass, why should they be required on paper?
- Bette then went home and attempted to mimic the artists' techniques by mixing up a white, water-based template paint which she applied with a thin paintbrush to cover her typing errors.
- It worked beautifully.
- Experimenting in her kitchen, she learned how to mix her special formula to match the exact shade of stationery.
- Her boss never noticed the correction paint on his documents, and for five years she kept her invention largely to herself.
- Eventually, word spread throughout the bank; other secretaries were willing to pay for a bottle of the mistake fixer.
- Working over her kitchen sink, Bette prepared the first batch of "Mistake Out" in 1956, which she had bottled with the help of her son and his friends.
- The reaction was enthusiastic, and the recipe for Bette Nesmith's Mistake Out continued to evolve; customers wanted the liquid to be thicker and dry faster.
- Unable to afford a chemist, she recruited a person who worked in the office supply store, her son's high school chemistry teacher, and a friend from a paint-manufacturing company to help her perfect her product.
- Experiments were conducted using an aging mixer on her kitchen counter.
- Nightly she mixed, bottled and shipped the product, now called Liquid Paper, after a full day at the office.
- She struggled to keep up with orders totaling hundreds of bottles per month from her garage.

Life at Work

- Being a full-time secretary and part-time entrepreneur was both exciting and exhausting for Bette Nesmith Graham.

Liquid Paper went from part-time job to family breadwinner.

- At one point, she attempted unsuccessfully to persuade IBM to market her invention.
- Knowing that women were not viewed as capable entrepreneurs, she signed her letters to the company "B. Nesmith" to disguise her gender.
- In her spare hours, she visited office supply stores to interest them in her correction fluid.
- Then, in 1958, Bette unexpectedly received an opportunity to market her product full-time after she had made a serious mistake on a letter she typed and sent out.

- She was fired on the spot.
- Suddenly, Liquid Paper was her only means of support; her $300-a-month salary, which had been used to support the family and develop the correction fluid, was gone.
- Luckily, a brief but glowing description of her product in an office trade magazine produced 500 orders from across the United States.
- *The Secretary* magazine followed up with a favorable report and more orders poured in.
- General Electric Company placed the first single large order for over 400 bottles in three colors—four times her monthly production.
- Despite these successes, in 1960 her company's expenses exceeded its income.
- But the increase in sales for IBM electric typewriters worldwide—and superb word of mouth advertising—were spurring the need for liquid paper correcting fluid.
- In 1961, a decade after she had invented liquid paper, Bette hired her first full-time employee.
- Help also came from a new husband, Robert Graham, who joined her in the business in 1962.
- Together they traveled throughout the South and West demonstrating their magic product.
- In 1963, Liquid Paper increased its weekly production tenfold from 500 to 5,000 bottles.
- Three years later, the company was selling 40,000 bottles per week, and moved its operations into a 10 by 26-foot metal shed Bette had built in her backyard.
- There the bottles were filled, labels attached and distribution handled.
- By 1968, the company was grossing $1 million annually and constructing its own automated factory.
- Bette's kitchen sink was no longer large enough to keep up with demand.
- The new factory, designed by Bette, included a daycare center for her employees to accommodate the needs of working mothers.
- Raised in the Methodist Church but having converted to Christian Science in 1942, Bette gave credit to her religion for her success.
- To that end, her corporate statement of policy emphasized egalitarian thinking and proclaimed that the company was built to foster the cultural, educational and spiritual development of its employees.
- Company committees comprised a cross-section of employees.
- Every aspect of the new factory was designed to encourage communication between those who worked in the office complex and those in the plant.
- Her belief that women brought a more caring culture to the male-dominated business world was demonstrated by the fish pond included in the company greenway and the company library.
- In 1971, the number of bottles sold surpassed five million.
- By 1975, Liquid Paper Corporation had built an international headquarters in Dallas capable of producing 500 bottles a minute.
- But the sweet taste of success was tempered by her deteriorating relationship with her husband, Robert Graham.
- With their marriage ending and their messy divorce, Bette decided to retire in 1975, leaving her husband to run the company she had built.

Bette's business was growing, while her home life was deteriorating.

- Shrewdly, Bette remained the majority stockholder.
- Almost immediately, she regretted her decision to retire.
- Her ex-husband eliminated the cherished Statement of Policy and changed the format for Liquid Paper to deprive her of many of her royalties.
- Bette then launched a fight for control of the company.
- A self-proclaimed feminist, Bette also established in 1976 a foundation designed to educate "mature" women in business practices.

Life in the Community: San Antonio, Texas

- San Antonio, the second-largest city in Texas, was famous for Spanish missions and the Alamo.
- San Antonio's economy depended upon attracting thousands of tourists annually and the strong military presence, including Fort Sam Houston, Lackland Air Force Base, and Randolph Air Force Base.
- Early Spanish settlement of San Antonio began as a means to reassert Spanish dominance over Texas from the nearby French in Louisiana.
- In 1719, the Marqués de San Miguel de Aguayo made a report to the king of Spain proposing that 400 families be transported from the Canary Islands, Galicia, or Havana to populate the province of Texas.
- San Antonio grew to become the largest Spanish settlement in Texas, and for most of its history, the capital of the Spanish—later Mexican—province of Tejas.

You no longer have to choose between tape dictation and belt dictation.

- The Battle of the Alamo took place from February 23 to March 6, 1836.
- The outnumbered Texian force was ultimately defeated, with all of the Alamo defenders seen as "martyrs" for the cause of Texas' freedom.
- "Remember the Alamo" became a rallying cry in the Texian Army's eventual success at defeating Santa Anna's army.
- In 1845, the United States annexed Texas and included it as a state in the Union, which led to the Mexican-American War.
- During the war, the population of San Antonio was reduced by almost two-thirds, or 800 inhabitants; by 1860, at the start of the Civil War, San Antonio had grown to a city of 15,000 people.
- In 1877, the first railroad reached San Antonio and the city was no longer on the frontier.
- At the beginning of the twentieth century, the streets of San Antonio's downtown section were widened to accommodate streetcars and modern traffic, with many historic buildings destroyed in the process.
- The city continued to experience steady population growth, and boasted a population of just over 650,000 in the 1970 Census.

HISTORICAL SNAPSHOT
1976

- The Cray-1, the first commercially developed supercomputer, was released by Seymour Cray's Cray Research.
- Super Bowl X: The Pittsburgh Steelers defeated the Dallas Cowboys 21-17 at the Orange Bowl in Miami, Florida
- The United States vetoed a United Nations resolution that called for an independent Palestinian state
- *Live from Lincoln Center* debuted on PBS
- The New Jersey Supreme Court ruled that coma patient Karen Ann Quinlan could be disconnected from her ventilator; she remained comatose and died in 1985
- Apple Computer Company was formed by Steve Jobs and Steve Wozniak
- The Jovian-Plutonian gravitational effect was reported by astronomer Patrick Moore
- The U.S. Treasury Department reintroduced the two-dollar bill as part of the Bicentennial celebration
- The punk rock group the Ramones released their first self-titled album
- In the Indianapolis 500, Johnny Rutherford won the rain-shortened race
- A car bomb fatally injured *Arizona Republic* reporter Don Bolles, who was investigating the mafia
- The Boston Celtics defeated the Phoenix Suns 128-126 in triple overtime in the NBA Finals at the Boston Garden
- The National Basketball Association and the American Basketball Association agreed to merge
- In *Gregg v. Georgia,* the U.S. Supreme Court ruled that the death penalty was not inherently cruel or unusual and constitutionally acceptable
- U.S. cities celebrated the 200th anniversary of the Declaration of Independence
- The first class of women were inducted at the United States Naval Academy
- The *Viking 2* spacecraft landed at Utopia Planitia on Mars, taking the first close-up color photos of the planet's surface
- The Copyright Act of 1976 extended copyright duration for an additional 20 years in the United States
- The Cincinnati Reds swept the New York Yankees to win the 1976 World Series
- *Hotel California* by the Eagles was released
- The first laser printer was introduced by IBM, the IBM 3800

Selected Prices

Apron	$12.00
Baby Walker	$10.88
Blazer, Woman's	$50.00
Computer, IBM	$1,795.00
Copier	$2,995.00
Desk, Executive	$139.95
Food Processor	$99.99
Tobacco Pipe	$18.75
Typewriter, Manual	$89.95
Wrinkle Cream	$15.00

History of Office Equipment

By 1900, nearly 100,000 people in the U.S. were working as secretaries, stenographers, and typists in an office. The average worker was employed for 60 hours per six-day work week. Specialized training was available for people who wished to study office skills.

Copiers

The mimeograph machine of the 1890s increased the number of copies that could be made from a few to a hundred, using a "master." But the only way to copy an original after it had been made was to retype, redraw, or re-photograph it.

The first photostat machine was developed before World War I, but it was too expensive, too big, and required a trained operator.

After World War II, 3M and Eastman Kodak introduced the Thermo-Fax and Verifax copiers into the workplace. The office models were relatively inexpensive and easy to use, but their special paper was expensive and turned dark over time.

Chester Carlton's discovery of the effect of light in photoconductivity led to the success of the Haloid Xerox 914 machine in 1960.

Typewriters

The first typewriter to be commercially successful was invented in 1867 by C. Latham Sholes, Carlos Glidden, and Samuel W. Soule in Milwaukee, Wisconsin.

The patent was sold for $12,000 to Densmore and Yost, who made an agreement with E. Remington and Sons to commercialize the machine as the Sholes and Glidden Type-Writer.

Remington began production of its first typewriter in 1873, in Ilion, New York, using the QWERTY keyboard layout, which was slowly adopted by other typewriter manufacturers.

Unfortunately, the typist could not see the characters as they were typed, giving life to the "visible typewriters" such as the Oliver typewriters, which were introduced in 1895.

continued

History of Office Equipment *(continued)*

By 1910, the manual typewriter had achieved a standardized design, including the invention of the Shift key, which reduced the number of required keys by half.

In 1941, IBM announced the Electromatic Model 04 electric typewriter, featuring the concept of proportional spacing. By assigning varied rather than uniform spacing to different-sized characters, the Type 04 recreated the appearance of a printed page, an effect that was further enhanced by a typewriter ribbon innovation that produced clearer, sharper characters on the page.

IBM introduced the IBM Selectric typewriter in 1961, which replaced the typebars with a spherical element (or typeball), slightly smaller than a golf ball, with reverse-image letters molded into its surface. The Selectric used a system of latches, metal tapes, and pulleys driven by an electric motor to rotate the ball into the correct position and then strike it against the ribbon and platen. The typeball moved laterally in front of the paper instead of the former platen-carrying carriage moving the paper across a stationary print position.

Dictating Equipment

Early attempts to transform Thomas Edison's early phonograph equipment into a dictation machine were a dismal failure in the late 1800s.

But practitioners of Scientific Management believed that dictating letters into a machine would cut the cost of producing a letter and make the executive more creative. Numerous attempts were made to popularize dictaphones, which were cumbersome to use.

It took magnetic tape in the 1950s to make dictating practical. Then letters, memos and bright ideas could be captured by tape recorders and played back easily.

Ballpoint Pen

The first patent on a ballpoint pen was issued on October 30, 1888, to John Loud, a leather tanner, who made a writing implement to write on the leather he tanned. Although the pen could be used to mark rough surfaces such as leather, it proved to be too coarse for letter writing and was not commercially exploited.

In the period between 1904 and 1946, there was intense interest in improving writing instruments. In the early inventions, the ink was placed in a thin tube whose end was blocked by a tiny revolving ball that did not always deliver the ink evenly and often smeared.

László Bíró, a Hungarian newspaper editor, frustrated by the amount of time wasted in filling up fountain pens and cleaning up smudged pages, designed in 1938 a new type of pen that used fast-drying printer's ink in a pressurized cartridge.

During World War II, U.S. businessman Milton Reynolds saw a Biro pen in a store in Buenos Aires and began producing the Biro design without a license as the Reynolds Rocket. The first ballpoint pens went on sale at Gimbels department store in New York City on October 29, 1945, for $12.50 each.

"A Tale of the Monkees," *Pacific Stars & Stripes*, September 26, 1968:

Between skirmishes, I chatted with Mike Nesmith and learned that the Monkees consider it "a moral victory" that their television series wasn't renewed for next season.

The Monkees will appear in Tokyo October 3-4 at the Budokan Hall.

"We couldn't have gone through another season with the series," he said. "We were in the middle of a political struggle and, although we didn't precipitate any of it, we got a bad press. Now we've instituted an open-door policy to talk to anyone, anytime. This is a moral victory for us," Mr. Nesmith said

They will continue together as a group, of course.

"Now we'll be able to do the things the way we want to," Nesmith says. We each have our own style. Peter is understatement, quieter, melodic; Mickey is ragtime, old-fashioned; Davy is Broadway, mohair tuxedo, and I'm hard-driving West Coast rock, and our albums will have a bit of each."

He says the "pop music establishment" is down on them, possibly out of jealousy, and that they haven't received the recognition they deserve as musicians. But he believes, with time, that will change and they will be appreciated.

"People think we are tools of the establishment," he says, "but we're not. We're really the truest expression of iconoclastic youth today."

Their personal lives have, naturally, changed considerably since the lightning struck. Nesmith has adjusted beautifully to the problems of fame and fortune.

"The solution," he says, "is to realize what you can and cannot do. I learned early that I can go into Denny's for a hamburger. But I've found quiet, out-of-the-way places where I can go. It may cost me $50 to get in, but I have privacy.

"Paper Restoring: A Scary Business,"
The New York Times, May 3, 1975:

When Margo Feiden is scared, she shares her fears with her clients. As she talks, "somehow things come together," and, as in the fairytales, everything turns out happily in the end.

Well, you may ask, just what does Margo Feiden do that inspires such foreboding? Now that you've asked, here's the answer. She's a paper restorer and preserver, a profession not usually thought of as scary, probably because it's a profession not usually thought of it all.

The scary part of her work comes when it's necessary to reduce paper almost to its liquid state, and although the work isn't always suspenseful, it is frequently strange.

"Would you believe it is easier to fix something that's ripped than something that has been creased?" Miss Feiden asked somewhat rhetorically.

Miss Feiden, who is also Mrs. Stanley R. Goldmark, began her unusual work almost by accident. She was an art collector and art dealer (and still is), and noticed that, although age was being blamed for stains and discoloration, Rembrandt etchings were often in better condition than modern works.

"I began noticing that more drawing and etchings were stained when they were covered by a mat and framed, than those that remained unframed, and the theory that age was accountable for damage just didn't make sense to me," she said.

After reading everything available on the subject, experimenting and finally making her own paper in a bathtub, Feiden reached the conclusion that a hefty percentage of artwork requiring restoration had been damaged by improper framing. Now, with almost 12 years of experience behind her, her conclusions have solidified.

"Mats made of cardboard contain acids that attack paper," she said. "And some adhesives for holding mats or pictures in place promote the growth of damaging molds and fungi."

Feiden, who has done work for the graphics department of Sotheby Parke Bernet and a number of well-known collectors, restores documents, marriage licenses, works of art and books. She just finished working on a document (a receipt for their pay) signed by five of the men who signed the Declaration of Independence.

1977 News Feature

"CBS Inventor Recalled First Color Telecast," *Naples Daily News*, December 8, 1977:

"Boy, they were good pictures," Dr. Peter C. Goldmark said, referring to photographs of the Jones Beach beauties he beamed from New York for man's first successful color telecast in 1940.

The pictures were taken at the Long Island resort and were transmitted from New York City's Chrysler Building.

Goldmark, 71, whose color television process began on Earth and soared to the moon, was killed in a Harrison, New York, automobile accident Wednesday. His many inventions did not bring him great wealth, however.

He was a "working man, a salaried employee," Leo Murray, a spokesman, said of Goldmark, a retired president of Columbia Broadcasting System Laboratories in Stamford, and vice president of CBS.

Almost as soon as the pictures of the girls were transmitted in 1940, the Radio Corporation of America locked legal horns with Goldmark's firm, CBS Laboratories, over the technological form of color.

RCA's chairman David Sarnoff rejected Goldmark's system, which was called the "field sequential system."

Sarnoff advocated an all-electric compatible system under which both black-and-white and color could be transmitted simultaneously. Such a system was adopted and is the one now in general use.

RCA in 1971 obtained the prestigious assignment of providing the National Aeronautics and Space Administration (NASA) with the camera to record the 12-day moon mission for *Apollo 15*.

But the only method that could have been used to relay the RCA pictures, due to the moon's low light levels, was Goldmark's, the same one RCA fought all the way to the Supreme Court in the 1960s.

The Hungarian-born Goldmark was asked how it felt to have his old corporate adversary use his system in its moon pictures.

"I watch television using their system, so they can use mine on the moon. It's a fair exchange. I think it was an engineering decision, really. I don't think the engineers gave the old fight any thought, "he said.

1979 Profile

Born in a rural section of Georgia, Hank Selman escaped the shadow of the neighborhood textile mill and became a financial junkie who lived for risk.

Life at Home

- As the 1970s came to an end, Hank Selman was making $600,000 a year and paying his 30-year-old wunderkinds at MVL, Inc. straight salaries of $100,000 each, plus stock plans worth nearly as much.
- A never-ending supply of Perrier in the corporate refrigerators was a company trademark.
- Sales were so spectacular in 1977 that MVL staged a seven-day extravaganza cruise to celebrate the previous year's sales, which cost the company $1.5 million.
- In 1978, the cost was even higher: 1,200 people earned the right to go to Acapulco, Mexico—all expenses paid.
- Although his San Francisco-based leasing company was only 12 years old, projections for the coming year, 1979, envisioned earnings of $61 million on $1.1 billion in revenue.
- Hank never dreamed MVL would come apart so quickly or crash so hard.
- Summers were spent at the country club in Dalton, Georgia, serving as a caddie for his father's bosses; winters, Hank worked part-time in Dalton's finest men's clothing store where he rubbed shoulders with the city's elite and bought the "right" clothing on discount.
- He attended Georgia Tech on a scholarship, and then fled to San Francisco the same night he received his degree in finance.
- First, he worked as an accountant and then as a business consultant, determined to be on an airplane two or three times a week.

Hank Selman lived large and fell hard as a financial wheeler dealer.

- He regularly dropped a dozen picture postcards in the mail before boarding a return flight from London or Rome or Hong Kong.
- His high school friends thought he was a show-off, but his mother was very proud.
- Within a few years, he become very comfortable with complex, highly leveraged transactions that took advantage of federal tax laws to achieve higher-than-normal earnings.
- Inert "1979-2" and "1979-3" to go around here – space for caption #2
- Making money was the point of every deal, of course, but Hank loved the high that resulted from looking over the "edge."
- Hank always thought of himself as the smartest person in the room and was rarely shy about proving this belief.
- In fact, while matching wits with a recent Noble Prize winner in economics that Hank conceived the framework for his company MVL—named after his three daughters: Martha, Veronica and Lucy.
- Since IBM dominated the world of top-of-the-line mainframe computers, why not form a company to lease the giant mechanical brains to companies intimidated by the $100,000 to $1 million-plus price tag and the fear of the equipment becoming obsolete overnight?
- Hank decided that with a little creative financing, he could lease the System 370 Mainframe for less than IBM itself was charging, still take a substantial fee, and then make a killing on the residual value of the highly dependable computers at the back end of the lease.

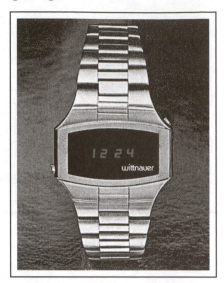

Selman and his peers bought the latest and greatest, thinking their money would last forever.

Life at Work

- MVL, Inc. was founded in 1967 by Hank Selman and Robert Crutz, a former IBM San Francisco branch manager.
- The two also shared a birthday, July 1, 1947, and a vision for making money—lots of money—leasing mainframe computers to businesses ready to join the computer age.
- Using only $72,000 of their own money, the two men raised $10 million in equity from the Fireman's Fund Insurance Company and $90 million in debt to buy IBM System/360 computers, which they put on lease.
- By the early 1970s, MVL became one of the first companies to write tax-leveraged leases for IBM System/370 computers.

Companies leased expensive IBM computers from Selman and MVL, Inc.

- The entrepreneurial upstarts were able to cut the cost on their mainframe computer leases by reducing their effective cost of capital.
- MVL did this by offering investors willing to put up 20 percent of the cost of the computer as a tax advantage depreciation and investment tax credit, plus a share the computer residual value; lenders put up the rest.
- As a result, the company leasing the computer got the needed equipment for prices below what they would have paid IBM for the same product.
- Adding a middleman who was armed with creative financing to the transaction actually reduced the cost of the product.
- MVL took a minimum risk; the leasing contract required lessees to pay lenders and equity investors for the machine, while MVL took a fee for putting the deal together and retained a financial interest in the residual value of the computer at the end of the lease.

MVL wrote expensive leases for IBM equipment.

- The idea was expanded in 1976 to include leasing bundles that comprised IBM mainframe and compatible peripheral computers which MVL bought from independent manufacturers as a single package.
- Using aggressive selling strategies, MVL wrote $1.7 billion in leases on IBM equipment—second only to IBM—in the 1970s.
- And since Hank believed in an authoritarian top-down planning system, typically sales managers were told annually to achieve a 35 percent growth rate over the previous year.
- The original IBM System/360 family was announced in 1964, followed in the summer of 1970 by a family of machines called System/370.

- Big, fast disk drives were one of the strengths of IBM; in 1973, the big mainframe disk drive with 400 megabytes cost $111,600, or $279 per megabyte.
- With that leasing experience came further expansion: an airplane division was embraced by the market after it realized pretax profit of $13 million; another division handled less expensive types of equipment such as machine tools and microcomputers, and was grossing $80 million with wide profit margins.
- After that came the leasing of railroad cars and heavy equipment; anything seemed possible.
- As sales grew, so did MVL's flair for good living; Mercedes and Porsches filled the parking lot, Samadhi tanks large enough for floating meditation sessions became the rage.
- At the same time, stories about inflation and an unstable economy dominated the headlines of the business sections of the newspapers.

Some at MVL never saw the downturn coming.

- Although the company was already heavily leveraged in 1979, MVL was still able to borrow $1.25 billion—a record for a company of its size in a single year—to expand into plug-compatible computers that used IBM software but cost less than IBM hardware.
- Hank remained convinced that 1979 was going to be another spectacular year, even when the sales started slow.
- Most of the young staff had never experienced a downturn and could not imagine anything but growth.
- Then, within a six-month period, it all fell apart.
- The company reported losses of $60 million per quarter as its stock fell from a high of $28 to below $10; portfolio managers admitted for the first time "to my knowledge no analyst ever really knew what the company did."
- What made the company so mysterious was MVL's team of young entrepreneurs, who had pioneered leasing methods complicated enough to produce huge profits.
- For years, Hank had made outrageous profit demands, and over time, the company had come to see itself as invincible.
- The downfall started in 1978 when the company gave its sales force permission to write leases for plug-compatible computers purchased from Hitachi and National Semiconductor Corp., both of which used IBM software but less expensive hardware.
- It was an immediate success, especially after IBM was unable to deliver some of its hottest new machines in quantity.
- In anticipation of an even bigger year in 1979, the company signed long-term contracts with its two new suppliers and increased its sales force by 80 percent.

- That's when IBM announced it would launch a new line of aggressively priced machines in the first quarter of 1979; the market believed customers would hold off buying until the new machines became available.
- MVL plowed ahead.
- To compete with IBM's new pricing structure, Hank negotiated more favorable pricing from National Semiconductor, but in exchange had to buy more computers.
- In May, sales continued to be down, but the inventory of returned, obsolete IBM System/370s was growing rapidly; with IBM's new introduction, the old equipment had little to no residual value.
- Losses continued to grow while expenses continued unabated.
- By mid-summer, MVL withdrew a $50 million financing package when outside lenders, alarmed by the falling sales numbers, began to demand a premium interest rate for loans.
- By midyear, a showdown during a raucous board meeting resulted in changes in the corporate management structure, but left Hank still in charge.
- The computer group was cut back from 3,000 people to 2,000.
- When word spread throughout the industry that MVL's financial problems could impact its technical support going forward, buyers became wary of long-term leases.
- Fights developed with MVL's suppliers.
- Scrambling for cash, MVL grew desperate and again disposed of its assets: first a railcar manufacturing plant, then eight ships, and even the corporate airplane.
- That raised $175 million—not enough to meet severance payments to salespeople and to maintain the operation of the company.
- Retained earnings that had been built up over a decade fell from $107 million to $43 million within months.
- Major executives, in charge of the divisions still doing well, threatened to resign—further undercutting the profitability of the organization.
- Overnight, it seemed, the company lost a quarter of its 6,400 employees and 18 of its 32 divisions; its forays into manufacturing stopped and its highflying ways were cut back.
- In October, when Hank refused to resign, the Board of Directors summarily fired him.
- The next day, headlines speculated that the San Francisco-based leasing company could fail.

IBM's new line of affordable computers threatened Selman's business.

Life in the Community: San Francisco, California
- San Francisco was the fourth most populous city in California and the twelfth most populous city in the United States.
- As the only consolidated city-county in California, it encompassed a land area of 46.7 square miles and claimed the title of being the second-most densely populated large city in the United States.
- In 1776, the Spanish established a mission named for Francis of Assisi on the site, but it was the California Gold Rush in 1848 that propelled the city into a period of rapid growth.
- San Francisco increased its population in one year from 1,000 to 25,000, making it the largest city on the West Coast.

San Francisco, CA in 1877.

- San Francisco entrepreneurs sought to capitalize on the Gold Rush, founding Wells Fargo in 1852 and the Bank of California in 1864.
- The development of the Port of San Francisco established the city as a center of trade; Levi Strauss opened a dry goods business and Domingo Ghirardelli began making chocolate.
- Immigrant laborers, including Chinese railroad workers who created the city's Chinatown quarter, made the city a polyglot culture.
- The first cable cars carried San Franciscans up Clay Street in 1873.
- By the turn of the twentieth century, San Francisco was known for its flamboyant style, stately hotels, ostentatious mansions on Nob Hill, and a thriving arts scene.
- On April 18, 1906, a major earthquake struck San Francisco and northern California; more than half the city's population of 400,000 were left homeless.
- Rejecting calls to completely remake the street grid, San Franciscans opted for speed, aided by loans from Amadeo Giannini's Bank of Italy, later to become Bank of America.
- In ensuing years, the city solidified its standing as a financial capital; during the Great Depression San Francisco undertook two great civil engineering projects, simultaneously constructing the San Francisco-Oakland Bay Bridge and the Golden Gate Bridge, completing them in 1936 and 1937, respectively.
- During World War II, the Hunters Point Naval Shipyard became a hub of activity, and Fort Mason became the primary port of embarkation for service members shipping out to the Pacific Theater of Operations.
- The U.N. Charter creating the United Nations was drafted and signed in San Francisco in 1945 and, in 1951, the Treaty of San Francisco officially ended the war with Japan.
- Urban planning projects in the 1950s and 1960s saw widespread destruction and redevelopment of west side neighborhoods and the construction of new freeways, of which only a series of short segments were built before being halted by citizen-led opposition.
- By the late 1970s, port activity moved to Oakland, San Francisco began to lose industrial jobs, and the city turned to tourism as the most important segment of its economy.

HISTORICAL SNAPSHOT
1979

- The U.S. and the People's Republic of China established full diplomatic relations
- Ohio agreed to pay $675,000 to victim's families in the Kent State shootings
- In Super Bowl XIII, the Pittsburgh Steelers defeated the Dallas Cowboys 35-31 at the Miami Orange Bowl
- Ayatollah Ruhollah Khomeini returned to Iran after nearly 15 years in exile and seized power; Iranian radicals then invaded the U.S. Embassy in Tehran and took 90 people hostage
- The radio news program *Morning Edition* premiered on National Public Radio
- The U.S. *Voyager I* space probe photos revealed Jupiter's rings
- Philips unveiled the compact disc
- America's most serious nuclear power plant accident, at Three Mile Island, Pennsylvania, halted nuclear power expansion
- The Pinwheel Network changed its name to Nickelodeon and began airing on various Warner Cable systems
- After Dan White received a light sentence for killing San Francisco Mayor George Moscone and Supervisor Harvey Milk, gays in the city rioted
- John Spenkelink was executed in Florida, in the first use of the electric chair in America after the reintroduction of the death penalty in 1976
- A blowout at the Ixtoc I oil well in the southern Gulf of Mexico resulted in the worst oil spill in history
- Jimmy Carter and Leonid Brezhnev signed the SALT II agreement in Vienna
- Michael Jackson released his first breakthrough album *Off the Wall,* which sold seven million copies in the United States alone
- The Entertainment Sports Programming Network, known as ESPN, debuted
- The comic strip *For Better or For Worse* began
- The Federal Reserve System changed from an interest rate target policy to a money supply target policy, causing interest rate fluctuations and economic recession
- The Pittsburgh Pirates defeated the Baltimore Orioles in Game 7 of the World Series
- Eleven fans were killed during a stampede for seats before The Who concert at the Riverfront Coliseum in Cincinnati, Ohio
- The world premiere for *Star Trek: The Motion Picture* was held at the Smithsonian Institution in Washington, DC
- The eradication of the smallpox virus was certified; it was the first human disease driven to extinction
- The first Usenet experiments were conducted by Tom Truscott and Jim Ellis of Duke University
- McDonald's introduced the Happy Meal

Selected Prices

Automobile, Toyota Corolla	$2,788.00
Circular Saw	$22.88
Compact	$4.50
Microwave Oven	$168.00
Punch Bowl	$35.00
Sno-Cone Maker	$5.66
Spinning Top	$4.49
Stationery, 100 Sheets	$6.95
Turntable	$199.95
Vodka, 1.75 Liters	$8.59

NCR systems are
a big factor in factories!

Notable Inventions: 1970-1979

1970
- The daisy-wheel printer
- The floppy disk

1971
- The dot-matrix printer
- The food processor
- The liquid-crystal display (LCD)
- The microprocessor
- VCR (video cassette recorder)

1972
- The word processor
- Pong, first video game
- Hacky sack

1973
- Gene splicing
- The Ethernet (local computer network)
- Bic disposable lighter

1974
- Post-it notes
- Liposuction

1975
- The laser printer
- The push-through tab on drink cans

1976
- The ink-jet printer

1977
- Magnetic resonance imaging (MRI)

1978
- The VisiCalc spreadsheet
- The artificial heart, Jarvik-7

1979
- Cell phones
- The Cray supercomputer
- The Walkman
- Roller blades

"Computer Feeds Crop of Chickens," *Clovis News Journal* (New Mexico), March 23, 1975:

How would you like to prepare breakfast, lunch and dinner for a million plus egg-laying hens every day?

No big deal, right? All you have to do is take one ton of corn and blend in one ton of millet; add a combined ton of soybeans and meat by-products for body; stir well; and season to taste with a variety of vitamins and minerals. Blend well and pour into the troughs.

Wrong. Today preparing chicken feed requires all the nutritional expertise which goes into feeding an astronaut in space or a professional athlete in training.

"The nutritional value of eggs is a direct result of the hens' diet—the quality of the blends they receive," said John Prohoroff Jr., general manager of Prohoroff Poultry Farms, Santa Marcos, California.

Prohoroff Farms produces an average of one million marketable eggs a day on a 600-acre site north of San Diego.

To make sure the hens are receiving the most nutritious diet possible, two IBM computers were installed at the farm a year ago. An IBM 1130 computing system helps determine recipes used in blending feed for the firm's 1.2 million White Leghorn hens.

Another computer, an IBM System-7, controls the actual feed mixing operation to make sure the amounts of ingredients used correspond to the formulas prescribed by the first computer.

Prohoroff blends his own seed mixes and changes them frequently. Formulas are recalculated as often as six times a week for each flock of 70,000 hens.

The best diet for each flock varies constantly. As weather changes and the hens grow, their dietary needs change, Prohoroff explained.

"IBM Feels Bite of Growing Computer Leasing Industry,"
Lebanon Daily News (Pennsylvania), August 14, 1972:

The independent computer leasing industry is starting to bite the hand that feeds it.

Giant international Business Machines Corp., which has 70 percent of the world's computer business, owns the paw that's getting bit. Companies like Leasco Corp., IBM's biggest single customer, are doing the biting. Nor is IBM at all likely to retaliate. Any retaliatory measure might hurt IBM more than it would help.

Asked about the matter, IBM said it doesn't care to comment.

To be specific, Leasco has taken some of the IBM 360 computers it owns and added more memory capacity so they compete rather well with the Model 150 series for the new IBM 370 computers. This is working out so well for Leasco that Executive Vice President Jack Leatham said he's not sure that Leasco will be interested in buying IBM's today's computers with "virtual storage" capacity just announced. Leasco rents these souped-up 360s for less than IBM charges for its 370s.

Of course, that's the essence of the independent computer leasing game—the ability to rent IBM's computers for less than IBM is willing to rent them.

"The reason we can do so is that all the IBM hardware will last much longer than IBM's depreciation policies prescribe," Leatham explained. Because it needs a high cash flow and because its global dominance of mainframe computer manufacturing industry enables it to do so, IBM sets its rental prices and comparatively short lifespans. Yet, said Leatham, one-third of IBM's 1401 computers, sold back in the late 1950s and early 1960s, are still in use.

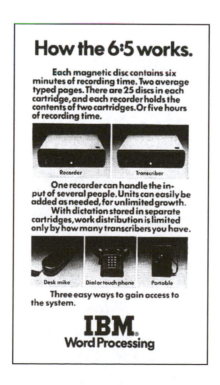

1980-1989

The economic turbulence of the 1970s continued during the early years of the 1980s. Rates for both interest and inflation were at a staggering 18 percent. With the economy at a standstill, unemployment was rising. By 1982, America was in its deepest depression since the Great Depression of the 1930s. One in 10 Americans was out of work. Yet, by the end of the decade, thanks in part to the productivity gains provided by computers and new technology, more and more Americans were entering the ranks of the millionaire and feeling better off than they had in a decade.

Convinced that inflation was the primary enemy of long-term economic growth, the Federal Reserve Board brought the economy to a standstill in the early days of the decade. It was a shock treatment that worked. By 1984, the tight money policies of the government, stabilizing world oil prices, and labor's declining bargaining power brought inflation to four percent, the lowest level since 1967. Despite the pain it caused, the plan to strangle inflation succeeded; Americans not only prospered, but many believed it was their right to be successful. The decade came to be symbolized by self-indulgence.

At the same time, defense and deficit spending roared into high gear, the economy continued to grow, and the stock market rocketed to record levels (the Dow Jones Industrial Average tripled from 1,000 in 1980 to nearly 3,000 a decade later). In the center of recovery was Mr. Optimism, President Ronald Reagan. During his presidential campaign he promised a "morning in America" and during the eight years, his good nature helped transform the national mood. The Reagan era, which spanned most of the 1980s, fostered a new conservative agenda of good feeling. During the presidential election against incumbent President Jimmy Carter,

Reagan joked, "A recession is when your neighbor loses his job. A depression is when you lose yours. And recovery is when Jimmy Carter loses his."

The economic wave of the 1980s was also driven by globalization, improvements in technology, and willingness of consumers to assume higher and higher levels of personal debt. By the 1980s, the two-career family became the norm. Forty-two percent of all American workers were female, and more than half of all married women and 90 percent of male college graduates worked outside the home. Yet, their median wage was 60 percent of that of men. The rapid rise of women in the labor force, which had been accelerating since the 1960s, brought great social change, affecting married life, child rearing, family income, office culture, and the growth of the national economy.

The rising economy brought greater control o personal lives; home ownership accelerated, choices seemed limitless, debt grew, and divorce became commonplace. The collapse of communism at the end of the 1980s brought an end to the old world order and set the stage for realignment of power. America was regarded as the strongest nation in the world and the only real superpower, thanks to its economic strength. As a democracy swept across Eastern Europe, the U.S. economy began to feel the impact of a "peace dividend" generated by a reduced military budget and a desire by corporations to participate in global markets—including Russia and China. Globalization was having another impact. At the end of World War II, the U.S. economy accounted for almost 50 percent of the global economic product; by 1987, the U.S. share was less than 25 percent as American companies moved plants offshore and countries such as Japan emerged as major competitors. This need for a global reach inspired several rounds of corporate mergers as companies searched for efficiency, market share, new products, or emerging technology to survive in the rapidly shifting business environment.

The 1980s were the age of the conservative Yuppie. Business schools, investment banks, and Wall Street firms overflowed with eager baby boomers who placed gourmet cuisine, health clubs, supersneakers, suspenders, wine spritzers, high-performance autos, and sushi high on their agendas. Low-fat and fiber cereals and Jane Fonda workout books symbolized much of the decade. As self-indulgence rose, concerns about the environment, including nuclear waste, acid rain, and the greenhouse effect declined. Homelessness increased and racial tensions fostered a renewed call for a more caring government. During the decade, genetic engineering came of age, including early attempts at transplanting and gene mapping. Personal computers, which were transforming America, were still in their infancy.

The sexual revolution, undaunted by a conservative prescription of chastity, ran head-on into a powerful adversary during the 1980s with the discovery and spread of AIDS, a frequently fatal, sexually transmitted disease. The right of women to have an abortion, confirmed by the Supreme Court in 1973, was hotly contested during the decade as politicians fought over both the actual moment of conception and the right of a woman to control her body. Cocaine also make it reappearance, bringing drug addiction and a rapid increase in violent crime. The Center on Addiction and Substance Abuse at Columbia University found alcohol and drug abuse implicated in three fourths of all murders, rapes, child molestations, and deaths of babies suffering from parental neglect.

For the first time in history, the Naval Academy's graduating class included women, digital clocks and cordless telephones appeared, and 24-hour-a-day news coverage captivated television viewers. Compact disks began replacing records, and Smurf and E.T. paraphernalia was everywhere. New York became the first state to require seat belts, Pillsbury introduced microwave pizza, and Playtex used live lingerie models in its ads for the "Cross Your Heart" bra. The Supreme Court ruled that states may require all-male private clubs to admit women, and 50,000 people gathered at Graceland in Memphis, Tennessee, on the tenth anniversary of Elvis Presley's death.

1984 Profile

Stephen Hassenfeld joined his father's company, Hasbro, in 1964, and became president in 1974 when toy sales topped $73 million, spurred by the popularity of G.I. Joe.

Life at Home

- When Stephen Hassenfeld was a boy, there were toys all over the house.
- That's how it is when your father runs a toy factory.
- The toys not only came from the family factory, but included gifts of salesmen's samples from other companies, such as all the Lionel trains being made.
- Moreover, Stephen was enthralled by Daddy's factory, where everything was interesting: the injection molders, the sewing machines, the assembly line—even the creaky old elevators and the grease-stained floors where Mr. Potato Head had been made.
- By the time Stephen was in his forties and president and chairman of Hasbro Industries, the family company in Pawtucket, Rhode Island, he believed that success would grow out of tradition.
- That's why Hasbro reintroduced its G.I. Joe in 1982 and concentrated on action toys, preschool toys like Mr. Potato Head and action games including Hungry Hungry Hippos—while chasing the video game market.
- The Hassenfeld family fled Poland in 1903 to escape the Jewish pogrom, and settled—like many eastern European Jews—in Manhattan's crowded Lower East Side.
- In 1923, two brothers—Henry and Helal Hassenfeld—founded Hassenfeld Brothers, a textile remnant company in Hasbrouck Heights, New Jersey.
- Over the next two decades, the company expanded to produce pencil cases and school supplies and resettled in Pawtucket, Rhode Island.

Stephen Hassenfeld fine-tuned his family's company, Hasbro, with savvy acquisitions and the help of G.I. Joe.

- The brothers discovered that filling the empty pencil boxes with rulers, compasses, notebooks, erasers, and things purchased from outside suppliers brought further success.

Mr. Potato Head was a long-lasting hit in the world of toys.

- Several expansions later, with revenues soaring, Hassenfeld Brothers produced doctor-and-nurse kits—its first toys—in 1940.
- Hassenfeld Brothers' first toy hit was Mr. Potato Head, which the company purchased from inventor George Lerner in 1952.
- The concept of attaching plastic noses, ears, eyes, eyeglasses, mustaches and hats to fruit had already been rejected by a slew of other toy manufacturers.
- Stephen's father Merrill thought the funny-looking toy was a good candidate for an advertising campaign on television—a new medium which was being neglected by most toy companies.
- The company paid a $500 advance against a five percent royalty, and in 1952, Mr. Potato Head debuted in newspaper and TV commercials.
- Thanks to its pure silliness, Mr. Potato Head wound up on TV with comedian Jackie Gleason and in favorable newspaper stories nationwide.

- Because the toy was such a success, the company could not keep up with the orders.
- But the toy industry was a difficult place to claim consistency.
- The next big hit came in 1964.
- By then Stephen had graduated from Moses Brown School, a private academy founded by Quakers in 1784 in Providence, Rhode Island, and attended Johns Hopkins University, where he majored in political science, joined a fraternity and was the only student among his peers to have a credit card.
- Early in his senior year, in the fall of 1962, Stephen left Johns Hopkins without graduating.
- At his father's insistence, Stephen worked at a Providence advertising agency before rejoining his father's company, Hasbro, in 1964.
- By then the company had created G.I. Joe, which they termed an "action figure" in order to market the toy to boys who wouldn't want to play with "dolls."
- Toy competitor Mattel had taken the toy world by storm in the late 1950s with its Barbie dolls, and Hasbro wanted to introduce a similar product for boys.

Hasbro's "action figures" appealed to boys.

- In 1963, Hasbro began development of a military-themed line of dolls that, like Barbie, could be accessorized with different outfits and equipment.
- The original strategy called for a different figure for each branch of the military, but Hasbro seized on the universality of the kind of soldier depicted in a 1945 film called The Story of G.I. Joe.
- The term "G.I. Joe" itself came from World War II, where it was used as a shorthand symbol for the typical serviceman, or "Government-Issue Joe."

- G.I. Joe was initially a massive success, and Hasbro expanded the line throughout the 1960s, reimagining Joe as an astronaut, a deep-sea diver and a Green Beret.
- What made G.I. Joe unique was its 21 moving parts for interactive play, which helped ignite the imagination of young boys.
- The company's promotional efforts included the catchphrase "Boy Oh Boy! It's A Hasbro Toy!" in television commercials and print ads.
- While orders and cash flowed in, Stephen introduced tighter controls and information systems that helped restore order to the factory.
- Within two years, he restructured Hasbro's national sales force, improved its distribution network, and experimented with the company's marketing profile.
- Stephen was named executive vice president in 1968, the year Hasbro went public, and president in 1974 when toy sales topped $73 million but cash flow was so poor that his father had to use personal collateral to borrow operating capital.
- Until then, Hasbro had been run on the philosophy that great products will drive great sales and everything else will resolve itself.
- Stephen focused on inventory control, the collection of receivables, improving cash flow, and the establishment of working capital.
- He often worked 18-hour days, seven days a week to make sure that the company founded by his grandfather was not vulnerable to outside forces, competitors or capricious bankers.
- By the early 1970s, the G.I. Joe brand was doing quite well and Hasbro came up with innovative ways to keep it thriving.
- As the 1970s continued to evolve, so did G.I. Joe: the figure received lifelike hair, moveable eyes and a "kung-fu" grip, enabling him to hold on to objects for the first time.
- But some of the changes proved to be gimmicks, taken even further by Hasbro with the development of a space-traveling "Super Joe" in 1976.
- The reception was lukewarm to "Super Joe," and by 1978, Hasbro gave G.I. Joe an honorable discharge.

Hassenfeld worked hard to improve the company and the G.I. Joe brand.

Life at Work

- In 1982, G.I. Joe and Stephen Hassenfeld discovered an unlikely savior in *Star Wars*.
- The sci-fi flick and the collectables it spawned had rekindled America's appetite for action figures, so Hasbro reintroduced a line of smaller-sized G.I. Joes to capitalize on the trend.
- Instead of a single character, there was an entire battalion of G.I. Joes, each given signature weapons, back stories, and code names like Scarlett and Snake Eyes.
- Joe also got a new enemy, Cobra—"a ruthless terrorist organization determined to rule the world," as described in the intro to the 1980s TV cartoon *G.I. Joe: A Real American Hero*.

- Stephen had taken over as the company's president four years earlier when Hasbro posted a loss of $2.5 million on sales of $73 million.

The 1982 film Star Wars created a renewed interest in collectable action figures.

Hassenfeld's partnership with Marvel Comics was well-calculated and netted millions in sales.

- Hasbro had avoided the fate of some other mid-sized toy companies whose fortunes soured in the late 1970s in the face of rising oil prices and runaway inflation.
- Indeed, Hasbro had increased sales and earnings steadily; it estimated that 1982 revenues would reach $135 million and the company would obtain a net income of $6.5 million.
- It was also in 1982 that G.I. Joe was licensed with Marvel Comics, a partnership critical to selling $51 million worth of the Real American Heroes line that Christmas.
- Television's voluntary guidelines limited extensive information in toy commercials, but there was no rule concerning TV commercials for comics, creating a spectator opportunity to reach children as their Christmas lists were being formed.
- By that time, there were uniforms, weapons, vehicles and comic books rounding out the G.I. Joe brand, along with a marketing plan that included fan clubs, posters for grammar school classrooms, and the out-licensing of G.I. Joe's image on breakfast cereals, lunch boxes, trading cards, sneakers, sleeping bags and swimming fins.
- In 1983, Hasbro produced another successful toy franchise, My Little Pony, a toy for girls.
- But the greatest opportunity in 1984 was not more toy products, but the potential acquisition of competitor Milton Bradley, whose legacy dated back to the Civil War and whose portfolio of products included The Game of Life, Candyland, Twister, Chutes and Ladders and Yahtzee.
- Twenty-three-year-old Milton Bradley was a struggling lithographer looking for new uses for his underutilized press when, in the summer of 1860, he invented The Checkered Game of Life.
- The board game sold 40,000 copies that first winter, launching a new business.
- By the early 1900s, Milton Bradley sold games such as Ring Off, a wireless telephone game; The Auto Game, and Air King Game featuring a zephyr.
- Then, in the early 1980s, Milton Bradley Company, twice the size of Hasbro and still a leader in educational games for children, plunged into video games.
- U.S. video hardware sales had reached $950 million annually—more than three times the level just two years earlier—and software sales were growing at a rate of 500 percent a year to $1 billion.
- Mattel and Coleco had already joined Commodore, Atari, and Texas Instruments in a competitive battle for the video game dollar; Milton Bradley did not want to be left behind.
- It was a total disaster.

- Retailers who didn't want ColecoVision or Mattel Intellivision had even less interest in Milton Bradley's Vectrex.
- Collective losses were in the millions.
- Hasbro, which had been tempted to jump into the video game competition that year, had not found the right product and stuck with old-fashioned plastic.
- As a result, Stephen's Hasbro was able to buy the venerable Milton Bradley Company despite competition from Ronald O. Perelman, who was backed by junk bond king Michael Milken.
- Many investors on Wall Street greeted the Bradley deal with derision, but as 1984 came to a close, Stephen found himself chairman of the largest toy company in the world, ahead of archrival Mattel, and owner of the Milton Bradley catalog of games.
- He was even finding some early success with the toy introduction known as transformers.
- And most of it because of sound business practices, good timing, and the popularity of a boy's doll who seemed to have many lives.

Life in the Community: Pawtucket, Rhode Island

- Pawtucket, Rhode Island, was a major contributor of cotton textiles during the Industrial Revolution.
- Slater Mill, built in 1793 by Samuel Slater on the Blackstone River Falls in downtown Pawtucket, was the first commercially successful cotton-spinning mill with a fully mechanized power system in America.
- Other manufacturers followed, transforming Pawtucket into a center for textiles, iron working and other industries.
- The textile business in New England declined during the Great Depression, when manufacturers moved their facilities South where operations and labor were cheaper.
- But unlike numerous older mill towns in the region, Pawtucket retained much of its industrial base.
- Goods produced in the city included lace, non-woven and elastic woven materials, jewelry, silverware, metals and textiles.

Slater Mill, downtown Pawtucket.

- Hasbro, one of the world's largest manufacturers of toys and games, was also headquartered in Pawtucket.
- Twenty percent of Pawtucket residents were French or French-Canadian.
- Similar to nearby cities such as Providence and East Providence in Rhode Island, and Fall River and New Bedford in Massachusetts, Pawtucket hosted a significant population from across the Portuguese Empire, as well as an extremely significant Cape Verdean population.
- Pawtucket was also one of the few areas of the United States with a significant Liberian population, mostly refugees from Charles Taylor's regime.

Pawtucket Falls, RI.

HISTORICAL SNAPSHOT
1984

- Dr. John Buster and the research team at Harbor-UCLA Medical Center announced the first embryo transfer, from one woman to another, resulting in a live birth
- The Apple Macintosh was introduced
- Astronauts Bruce McCandless II and Robert L. Stewart made the first untethered space walk
- President Ronald Reagan called for an international ban on chemical weapons
- The Soviet Union boycotted the 1984 Summer Olympics in Los Angeles, California
- Virgin Atlantic Airways made its inaugural flight
- Beverly Lynn Burns became the first woman Boeing 747 captain in the world
- Vanessa Lynn Williams became the first Miss America to resign when she surrendered her crown after nude photos of her appeared in Penthouse magazine
- President Reagan, during a voice check for a radio broadcast, remarked, "My fellow Americans, I'm pleased to tell you today that I've signed legislation that will outlaw Russia forever. We begin bombing in five minutes"
- The Space Shuttle Discovery made its maiden voyage

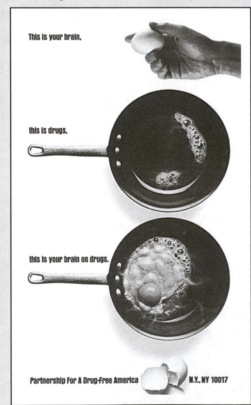

- Crack, a cheap, smokable form of cocaine, was first introduced into the Los Angeles area and soon spread across the United States in what became known as the Crack Epidemic
- Incumbent President Reagan defeated Walter F. Mondale with 59 percent of the popular vote, the highest percentage since Richard Nixon's 61 percent victory in 1972; President Reagan carried 49 states in the electoral college
- César Chávez delivered his speech, "What the Future Holds for Farm Workers and Hispanics" at the Commonwealth Club in San Francisco
- A methyl isocyanate leak from a Union Carbide pesticide plant in Bhopal, Madhya Pradesh, India, killed more than 8,000 people outright and injured over half a million in the worst industrial disaster in history

Selected Prices

Alphabet Blocks	$4.95
Beef Jerky	$1.99
Briefcase	$89.99
Caftan	$22.00
Chisel Set	$51.95
Fishing Tackle Box	$89.95
Game, Fisher Price	$9.97
Hunting Suit	$74.95
Playskool Doll	$24.97
Video Game Home Arcade	$299.95

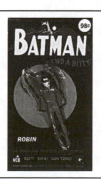
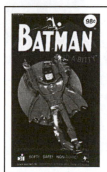

"Toy Fair Unwraps the Latest Offerings," Ron Alexander, *The New York Times*, February 17, 1982:

The American Toy Fair, the annual Christmas-like event when toy manufacturers unwrap their newest, shiniest creations for the nation's wide-eyed toy buyers, is back in town and the message is clear: a great many of the new toys are pro-fashion, antiterrorist and good to smell.

When it comes to fashion, toyland's familiar faces were still very much in evidence at the fair at the Toy Center building on 23d Street and at other locations in Manhattan. It would be difficult, for example, not to notice Barbie, who this year is seated at the keyboard of an electronic baby grand piano dressed in an outfit that Liberace might envy, but such old standbys are about to get some keen competition from heavyweight newcomers.

Brooke Shields herself introduced her 11 1/2-inch-tall fashion lookalike, plus enough designer accessories to cram the closets of a dozen doll houses, at a party on Monday evening given by LJN, the licensee for toys bearing the name of "the world's most glamorous teen-ager" (it says so on the box). Although the doll can fit into Barbie's clothes, in the long run the upkeep is probably cheaper on the Brooke Shields Glamour Center, which consists only of a life-size model of her head, lots of hair and an assortment of pink plastic rollers.

Fashion is the raison d'être for the new Sergio Valente and Miss Sergio Valente dolls, which may be the first dolls in history to be named after a nonexistent fashion designer. But never mind: Their endless assortment of outfits, said Murray Pottick, president of Toy Time, are exact copies in the exact fabrics as Sergio Valente's fashions. Shirley Temple, who took her first toyland bow almost 50 years ago, is making a comeback with a retro wardrobe: Ideal Toys is bringing her back dressed as she was in six of her films.

Even Little Orphan Annie, who once had but one dress to her name, is getting star treatment and a half-dozen new costumes from the Knickerbocker Toy Company. With Columbia Pictures' version of the comic-strip-turned-show *Annie* coming out soon, Annie's face is about to be seen on everything from license plates (for bicycles) to lip gloss (it comes with bubble gum). Youngsters who like to pretend they're orphans can also crave Annie dolls, Sandy dolls, models of Annie's blue Duesenberg convertible and Daddy Warbucks's mansion, or play an Annie board game and wear Annie stretch wigs.

Dolls have also gone to sea and vacated yesterday's doll house for a much-more-with-it cruise ship. A replica of the Love Boat comes with either two or six staterooms of furniture and a crew of three; the Glamour Gals Ocean Queen Cruise Ship with seven cabins and a heart-shaped swimming pool can hold 24 not-included glamour dolls.

Should the ships be pirated by terrorists, the glamorous guests need not worry. The Eagle Force is an elite group designed to protect the American way of life, according to the Mego Corporation, which is bringing out the 18 metal pliable action figures.

continued

"Toy Fair Unwraps the Latest Offerings," *(continued)*

"The Eagle Force is a miniaturization into toys of an age of terrorism, a feeling that this country isn't going to be pushed around anymore," a Mego spokesman said.

If the Eagle Force ever needs assistance, G.I. Joe is back. He's been on furlough since 1976, when, according to Hasbro Industries, his manufacturer, he was getting heavy sales opposition from Evel Knievel. Smaller-size (3 3/4 instead of 11 1/2 inches) Joe is now part of a 13-member rapid deployment force.

As for the smells, there's Kisses, Ideal Toys' teddy bear, which wears a T-shirt with a Hershey bar logo and is guaranteed to keep its chocolate aroma for two years, and Jelly Belly Dolls, also from Ideal, which come scented in one's choice of lemon drop, purple punch or bubble gum.

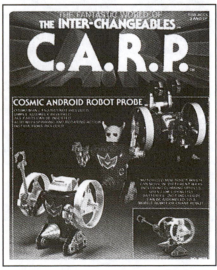

"Toys Hold Their Own at Christmas," *The Paris News (Texas)*, December 25, 1974:

Although sales of cards, major appliances and more expensive items were down this Christmas, toys hold their own during a period of economic uncertainty.

A Parris News survey revealed area toy stores reporting good to record years. But the larger, more expensive toys were lagging far behind, with the less expensive toys making up the difference in sales.

It looked as if Santa's sleigh was pretty well loaded this year with a good supply of Evel Knievel toys ranging from Evel himself, to his motorcycle, to a ramp for him to jump his make-believe "Canyon." And dolls, as usual, made Christmas happier for many little girls, according to Paris merchants, while G.I. Joe dolls are welcome additions to many boys' toy collections.

Sammy Cunningham, owner of "Sammy's Place," a store with toys as its specialty, reported its overall sales down but not in the main toy lines. And, he said, the Creative Playthings Magazine, a national industry magazine for toy distributors, has reported that national toy sales are not at the level expected.

The Barbie Town House, a multilevel dollhouse made especially for the famous "Barbie" doll, was a good seller, according to Cunningham and fellow toy dealers. Cunningham said he ran out of the playhouses, which sell for about $20, long before Christmas. And, he added, "I could've sold a truckload."

Although the more expensive toys are not selling as well, customers, most merchants agreed, were looking for more sturdy playthings. Many, Cunningham explained, would rather buy two or three sturdier toys than a number of the cheaper, short-lived toys.

Important American Toy Creations

1900
- Lionel trains

1903
- Crayola crayons
- Teddy bear

1906
- Model T. Ford die cast cars

1913
- Erector set
- Tinker toys

1915
- Raggedy Ann doll

1916
- Lincoln Logs

1929
- Mme. Alexander collectible dolls
- Yo-yo

1934
- Sorry board game

1935
- Monopoly

1937
- Betsy Wetsy doll

1938
- Viewmaster 3-D viewer

1947
- Tonka trucks
- Magic Eight Ball

1948
- Scrabble
- Slinky

1949
- Candyland board game
- Clue board game

1950
- Silly Putty

1952
- Mr. Potato Head

1953
- LEGO

1954
- Matchbox cars

1956
- Play-Doh
- Yahtzee

1957
- Frisbee

1958
- Hula Hoop

1959
- Barbie

1960
- Etch-a-Sketch

1961
- Troll dolls

continued

Important American Toy Creations *(continued)*

1963

- Easy-Bake Oven

1964

- G.I. Joe

1966

- Twister

1967

- Battleship

1968

- Hot Wheels

1970

- Nerf ball

1972

- Uno

1974

- Dungeons & Dragons
- Playmobil

1977

- Star Wars action figures

1978

- Rubik's Cube

1979

- Strawberry Shortcake

1982

- Trivial Pursuit

1983

- Cabbage Patch Kids
- My Little Pony

1984

- Transformers

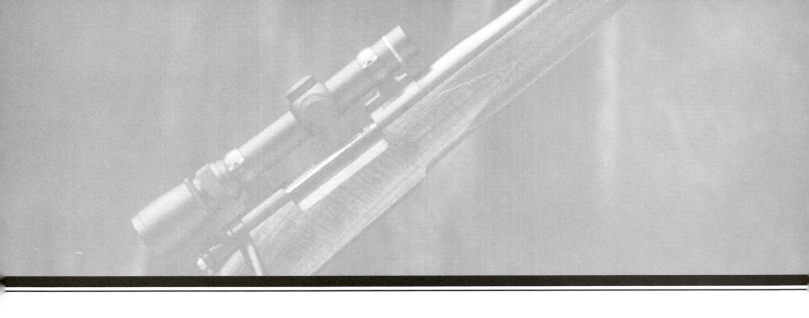

1986 Profile

Kenny Jarrett's farm machinery know-how helped him build rifles with accuracy never seen before.

Life at Home

- James Kennedy Jarrett was obsessed with achieving the kind of pinpoint rifle accuracy most hunters never considered possible.
- Kenny's precision standard revolved around the ability to fire three bullets through the same hole at a distance of 300 yards.
- Or, at the very least, to consistently hit a penny from a distance of three football fields.
- He already personally held six world records for competitive shooting and his rifles had established nine more.
- But since his first love was hunting, Kenny's real passion was for the development of super accurate hunting rifles and hand-loaded cartridges that delivered in the field.
- His inventive dedication to accuracy had already earned the bearded, tobacco-chewing "good ol' boy" from rural South Carolina a local following of Southern hunters eager to take down a big buck at 400 yards.
- Now it was time to expand his market to include a national audience.
- Kenny grew up a soybean farmer on his uncle's 10,000-acre Cowden Plantation, situated on a secondary road near Jackson, South Carolina.
- By the age of 12, he had a farm boy's familiarity with machinery, matched by a natural ability to create and fabricate with his hands what his brain envisioned.
- His days were consumed by farming problems and deer hunting pleasures on the expansive property of Cowden Plantation, bordered by the Savannah River to the west and the government-con-

James Kennedy Jarrett's handcrafted precision rifles were a hunter's dream.

trolled Savannah River Site to the south, where plutonium had been manufactured since the 1950s.

- But Kenny eventually grew frustrated that off-the-rack hunting rifles rarely delivered the accuracy he needed to bag the shy bucks who warily stayed on the fringes of the soybean fields 400 yards away—and out of range.

- He decided to do something about it: he bought a metal lathe and began building precision big-game rifles as a hobby.

- Like most one-man operations, Kenny started out making rifles using customer-supplied actions which he retuned to fit with an outsourced barrel and stock.

- His results were inconsistent.

- The performance of the rifle, after all, depended on the quality of the components as much as the skill with which they've been put together.

- It was a time of learning, listening, and absorbing the accuracy lessons of the hyper-competitive benchrest shooting crowd.

Jarrett was not satisfied with a "good enough for hunting" rifle.

- He came to hate the phrase "good enough," as in "good enough for hunting," as he formed a vision of inventing a precision rifle that exceeded expectations for accuracy.

- Then, in 1979, after farming most of his life, Kenny turned to gunsmithing full-time.

- For the next seven years, Kenny stayed busy building hunting rifles to his exacting specifications—often exceeding the expectations of his customers, who bragged about their Jarrett rifle at every hunt camp in the South.

- His own field exploits added to the mystique after Kenny fired one memorable shot that took down a gemsbok in Africa at 557 yards.

- At the same time, he continued pursuing another passion—collecting the artifacts left on the river banks of the Savannah River or in the fields by multiple generations of Native Americans.

- The flowing waters of the Savannah River had attracted some of the earliest inhabitants to the region, most of whom left some evidence of their lives: from scrapers, to projectile points, to nutting rocks.

- Nearly every year's plowing exposed new "points" and even delicately carved gorgets, which were worn around the neck.

- Each was appropriately preserved and mounted in glass cases that dominated an entire room in Kenny's home.

- Like most things in his life, there was an exacting artistry to the display.

- In addition, to accommodate the needs of a growing family, Kenny built a swimming pool and fishing ponds, and purchased trampoline sets for the children.

- A fourth-generation soybean farmer, Kenny was determined to keep his kids on the farm.

Life at Work

- Kenny Jarrett realized early on there was a niche in the gun market for an accurate game rifle that was built the right way—even when experts predicted that hunters would not pay top-drawer prices for a hunting rifle.
- Traditionally, the highest-priced rifles sported highly carved walnut stocks that added artistry and weight to the rifle, but not dependability.
- Kenny abstained from using walnut stocks—in fact, any wood stocks at all—convinced that wood movement was a handicap to accuracy.
- To attract the elite hunter willing to spend triple the ordinary price for a one-of-a-kind hunting experience, he needed to be the best.
- To be the entrepreneur he envisioned, he also had to capture the title of inventor and find a mentor.
- The most influential accuracy expert was Texas gunmaker and benchrest shooter Harold Broughton, who took the time to set Kenny on the right path to making accurate rifles.
- But it was hundreds of hours in the shop and more than a few sleepless nights that gave Kenny the insights he needed to be a pioneer.
- His first year building rifles he grossed $17,000—enough to encourage expansion.
- By 1985, the sale of Jarrett rifles topped $300,000 and 13 people were working in his 2,200-square-foot shop built of cypress wood milled by Kenny using trees cut from his property.
- The basic price for a Jarrett rifle was about $2,800; extensive options could hike the price up to as much as $4,500.
- "If your rifle ain't accurate, you might as well have a pocket full of fire-crackers, 'cause all you'll have is a noisemaker," he told the nation's top sports writers when they journeyed to remote Jackson, 40 minutes from Aiken, South Carolina.
- There he entertained the nation's most widely read hunting experts with long-range shooting demonstrations, fried catfish dinners and lots of homespun wisdom.
- "There's no magic in what I do. It ties correctly education, trial and error, and beating my head against the wall until it's right."
- He talked his Bubba talk, spat his chewing tobacco, and dazzled the writers with his long-range weapons, soon dubbed the "beanfield rifle"—an ultra-deadly rifle/cartridge combination for taking whitetail deer at long distances, typically 300 to 400 yards.
- In appreciation, the nation's most respected hunting and fishing magazines featured Kenny's country-wise quotes, constant suspenders and expensive rifles on their pages.
- He understood that the number of hunters willing to risk a marital fight to own a Jarrett was small and scattered, and he had to find that market by becoming a national name.
- So he traveled to gun shows and national meetings where he talked, promoted and demonstrated.

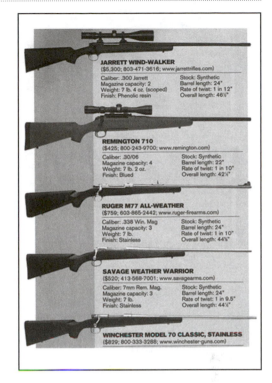

A Jarrett rifle, although more expensive than most, was well worth the money.

Crafting a Jarrett rifle took many hours and each customer waited a long time to own one.

The specifications for a Jarrett rifle were so exact that many supplier parts had to be refitted.

Jarrett's words of wisdom were almost as famous as his standards for accuracy.

- Eventually, the cult of accuracy and the personality of Kenny Jarrett were intertwined.
- Sales increased, his delivery time on a custom gun stretched to one year, and competitors scrambled out of the woodwork—each claiming to be an accuracy guru.
- "I never wanted to be rich; I just wanted to be the best," he explained.
- So he continued to listen, innovate and promote.
- But building a Jarrett rifle was a very labor-intensive process, limiting the number of guns that could be made to his exacting standards.
- He was encouraged to borrow more money and double the size of his shop, so the nine- to 12-month backlog of orders could be reduced.
- He was encouraged to move to a city where he'd have more exposure to customers, and advised to make less expensive rifles, even if it meant compromising quality.
- He listened, but took his own path.
- "When you get one of my rifles, the other rifles will gather dust 'cause you won't want to shoot them anymore."
- "It isn't that you need a half minute rifle to shoot deer; you pay the extra because accurate is what a rifle should be, and you can't abide a rifle that doesn't measure up."
- Of the one million-plus rifles sold each year, less than 5,000 were custom-built.
- "We are not everything to everybody and we don't try to be" Kenny said.
- But challenges remained.
- He found that one-third of the barrels he bought from the best supplier in the business would not shoot to his standard of sub one minute.
- These barrels were well built and achieved the benchrest standard of the day with a bore diameter with a consistency of three 10-thousands of an inch from the breech to the muzzle.
- Kenny decided that to get better performance, a barrel must have a deviation of no more than one-tenth of a thousandth.
- No one manufactured a barrel with that standard, so Kenny decided he would do it himself.

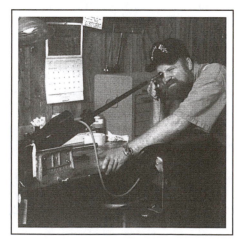

Jarrett tested each rifle before it was sent to the customer.

- Most Jarrett rifles began with a Remington 700 action, but so much time was devoted to refitting; he was moving toward custom actions for all his rifles—a project that could take years.
- For testing his new rifles, Kenny established a state-of-the-art 100-, 200- and even 600-yard firing range; that way he didn't have to guess what his guns and cartridges would do at these distances—he knew.
- And he tested every rifle before it was sent to a customer.

- But most of all, the accuracy guru who loved to promote his inventions listened.
- He asked questions, made adjustments and studied the trends.
- "You can't get educated in a day," Kenny said, "I learn something everyday."

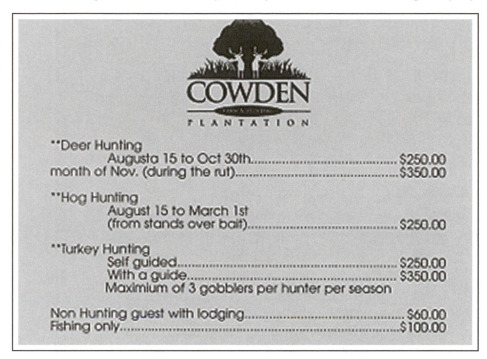

COWDEN
PLANTATION

**Deer Hunting
Augusta 15 to Oct 30th........................ $250.00
month of Nov. (during the rut)....................$350.00

**Hog Hunting
August 15 to March 1st
(from stands over bait)........................ $250.00

**Turkey Hunting
Self guided................................ $250.00
With a guide............................... $350.00
Maximium of 3 gobblers per hunter per season

Non Hunting guest with lodging....................$60.00
Fishing only...................................$100.00

Life in the Community: Cowden Plantation, Jackson, South Carolina

- Cowden Plantation in tiny Jackson, South Carolina snuggled up to the broad shoulders of the Savannah River for more than a mile.
- For 4,000 years, hunters had roamed the fields, oxbows and cypress swamps.
- Ancient artifacts, left behind thousands of years ago, tell the tale of tribes of hunters who relied on this land for their survival.
- Antebellum days brought King Cotton to Cowden under the ownership of James Henry Hammond, a South Carolina governor whose home, Redcliffe, still proudly stands.
- The sprawling Savannah River Site near Cowden Plantation was constructed during the early 1950s to produce the basic materials used in the fabrication of nuclear weapons, primarily tritium and plutonium-239.
- These materials were used in support of our nation's defense programs, a result of the Cold War.
- The communist Soviet Union had recently tested a nuclear weapon of its own, and America's brief tenure as the lone holder of nuclear weapons in the world was at an end.
- In the immediate aftermath of the American bombing of Nagasaki and Hiroshima, scientists worldwide were horrified by the power that had been unleashed.
- But the emergence of the Soviet Union as a nuclear power happened in the midst of scientific and political debate; retaliation, it was felt, was the only defense, and a remote corner of South Carolina was a necessary tool in that battle.

HISTORICAL SNAPSHOT
1986

- After losing a patent battle with Polaroid, Kodak left the instant camera business
- The Space Shuttle *Columbia* was launched with the first Hispanic-American astronaut, Dr. Franklin Chang-Diaz
- The first PC virus, Brain, spread
- The United Kingdom and France announced plans to construct the Channel Tunnel
- The first federal Martin Luther King, Jr. Day was observed
- The *Voyager 2* space probe made its first encounter with Uranus
- Space Shuttle *Challenger* disintegrated 73 seconds after launch, killing the crew of seven astronauts, including schoolteacher Christa McAuliffe
- Pixar Animation Studios opened
- After waiting 37 years, the U.S. Senate approved a treaty outlawing genocide
- The Senate allowed its debates to be televised
- *Out of Africa* won Best Picture at the 58th Annual Academy Awards
- A mishandled safety test at the Chernobyl Nuclear Power Plant in Pripyat, Ukraine, Soviet Union, killed 4,056 people and damaged almost $7 billion of property; radioactive fallout from the accident forced at least 350,000 people to be forcibly resettled
- Approximately five million people formed a human chain from New York City to Long Beach, California, to raise money to fight hunger and homelessness
- Eric Thomas developed LISTSERV, the first e-mail list management software
- Two weeks after it was stolen, the Picasso painting *Weeping Woman* was found in a locker at the Spencer Street Station in Melbourne, Australia
- Desmond Tutu became the first black Anglican Church bishop in South Africa
- News Corporation completed its acquisition of the Metromedia group of companies, thereby launching the Fox Broadcasting Company
- The centennial of the Statue of Liberty's dedication was celebrated in New York Harbor
- The Lebanese magazine *Ash-Shiraa* reported that the United States was selling weapons to Iran in secret, in order to secure the release of seven American hostages held by pro-Iranian groups in Lebanon

- Sperry Rand and Burroughs merged to form Unisys, becoming the second-largest computer company
- Mike Tyson won his first world boxing title by defeating Trevor Berbick
- After 35 years on the airwaves and holding the title of longest-running non-news program on network television, the daytime drama *Search for Tomorrow* ended

Selected Prices

Bicycle Helmet $19.99
Carving Set $625.00
Clogs $19.99
Jumpsuit, Woman's $34.99
Printer, Epson $429.00
Rifle, Beeman Feinwerkbau .177 Caliber............................$299.50
Scanner...$299.99
Shotgun, Winchester $1,200.00
Sushi Buffet...$15.00
Television, 41-Inch $1,995.00

THE NAME SAYS IT ALL.

A name that says here's a tool drop forged of highest grade steel. Precision machined. Beautiful high polish finish. CHANNELLOCK BLUE™ plastic comfort grips. A name that assures you top quality in every detail. CHANNELLOCK.

CHAN NEL LOCK
FOR YOU WHO WANT THE BEST

MAN USES TEETH TO FINISH BATHROOM.

There was still some PVC pipe and Romex wire left to cut before the bathroom was done. And since the kids snapped the hacksaw blade and lost the pliers, there was only one thing to do. Rely on the cutting power of a RoughCut™ knife with the serrated-tooth blade. The stainless-steel teeth easily handled the PVC and Romex, finishing the job and saving the day.

The RoughCut™ knife can do the same for you – on everything from heavy rope to sheet metal.

But don't take our word for it. Ask your hardware or sporting goods dealer about RoughCut™ knives. The double lock-back knives with razor-sharp teeth.

Coleman by WESTERN
1800 Pike Rd., Longmont, CO 80501

SAKRETE.

You Jane, Me Gund.

Gotta Getta GUND.

Kenny Jarrett has explored exciting new territory in the development of long-range hunting rifles. His blend of cartridge performance know-how and rifle-building skills have made him a leader in state-of-the-art accuracy. With a Jarrett rifle, long-range hunting is not a theory, but a reality.

—Jim Carmichael, shooting editor of *Outdoor Life*

I own five Jarrett rifles and have shot probably six times that many. They are capable of impossible accuracy not in the realm of discussion 10 years ago. Jarrett rifles are absolutely the most accurate in the world.

—Dave Petzal, executive editor and co-shooting editor of *Field & Stream*

A truly accurate rifle impresses you the same way a truly fast, quick-footed sports car impresses you, or a truly great musician leaves you speechless. It imposes a responsibility, too. Knowing the rifle will shoot into one hole, you put your marksmanship on the line. Triggering a Jarrett with Kenny watching, you feel compelled to perform as well as the rifle.

—Author Wayne Van Zwoll, *Deer Rifles and Cartridges*

Savannah River Site Timeline

1950

E. I. du Pont de Nemours and Company was asked by the Atomic Energy Commission to design, construct and manage the Savannah River Plant, a nuclear facility.

1951

The Savannah River Ecology Laboratory began ecological studies of Savannah River Site plants and animals.

Construction began for the Savannah River Plant.

1952

Production of heavy water for site reactors began in the Heavy Water Rework Facility.

1953

The R-Reactor, the first production reactor, went critical.

1954

The P-Reactor, L-Reactor, and K-Reactor went critical; the first irradiated fuel was discharged.

1955

The first plutonium shipment left the site; H-Canyon, a chemical separation facility, began radioactive operations.

1956

Construction of the basic plant was completed.

1963

The Receiving Basin for Off-Site Fuels received its first shipment of off-site spent nuclear fuel.

1964

The R-Reactor was shut down.

1971

The K-Reactor became the first production reactor automatically controlled by computer.

continued

Savannah River Site Timeline *(continued)*

1972

The site was designated as the first National Environmental Research Park.

1981

M-Area Settling Basin cleanup began under the Resource Conservation and Recovery Act.

1982

The Heavy Water Rework Facility was closed.

1983

Ground was broken for construction of the Defense Waste Processing Facility.

1985

The HB-Line began producing plutonium-238 for NASA's deep-space exploration program.

The L-Reactor was restarted and the C-Reactor was shut down.

A full-scale groundwater remediation system was constructed in M-Area.

1986

Construction of Saltstone began, as did construction of the Replacement Tritium Facility.

"Telephony With Pictures," Stephen A. Booth, *Popular Mechanics*, February 1988:

Some concepts have staying power. No matter how fantastic and far-off they seem at first, there's something about them that captivates the imagination and holds it hostage till the real thing comes along. This lasting appeal is what separates fad from future.

Like 3-D imaging in the flat-panel television, which is virtually on our door-steps, the concept of a telephone with pictures is long-lived and persistent. AT&T offered a glimpse of the future nearly a quarter of a century ago, when it's Picturephone shared the limelight with Miss Rheingold at the New York World's Fair. Now the videophone is here, ready and waiting to take its place beside the VCR, microwave and other household appliances.

The first practical videophone for the home hails from Mitsubishi, and carries a $399 price tag and the name VisiTel. In reality, it's the little brother of Mitsubishi's $1,500 Luma 1000 videophone, the first such device that could send and receive black-and-white still images over ordinary phone lines.

Until then, video teleconferencing was limited to entities wealthy enough to afford the hardware and the special 56-kilobyte Accunet phone lines necessary to send images and sound.

As reported here in 1986, the Luma 1000 was designed for commercial and institutional use—by police departments, for instance. In fact, the Mitsubishi videophone made a cameo appearance in TVs *Miami Vice* that season. Part of the Luma 1000's $1,500 figure was a pretty sophisticated spare-no-expense telephone. That's the part Mitsubishi stripped away to make its VisiTel affordable for home use.

The new product assumes you own your own phone, to which the VisiTel connects via the standard, modular jack. Despite its lower price, VisiTel actually projects a larger picture than its commercial predecessor.

"The Field & Stream Guide to Jarrett Custom Rifles," David Petzal, *Field & Stream*, November 2004:

In 1986, I was visiting with knife-making great George Herron in South Carolina when he mentioned there was a gunmaker named Kenny Jarrett in nearby Jackson whose rifles were more accurate than anything he'd ever seen. Herron then showed me some targets he'd shot with a Jarrett rifle, and the effort of not wetting myself caused me to turn several alarming colors. Kenny Jarrett, farmer and a self-taught gunsmith, had brought a whole new standard of accuracy to big-game rifles.

Jarrett started building guns as a hobby, and in 1979 went into the business using factory actions, custom barrels, and the very first synthetic stocks. His aim was to produce big-game rifles that would shoot under a minute angle, which, in those days was absurd idea. No one could make such a gun, and no one expected it. Any centerfire hunting rifle that would put three shots in less than an inch, all the time, was a one-in-a-million freak.

Jarrett had considerable experience building benchrest rifles, and had set accuracy records with them. He reasoned that if he applied the standards involved in the sport to big-game rifles, he could achieve his goal. Other gunsmiths had doubts. Some thought the precision you could get with benchrest rifles, firing small caliber cartridges with small powder charges, would be unattainable with big-game rounds. Others believed that hunters would never pay the price. Benchrest competitors, who are basically crazy, will pay any amount money for their rifles—as long as they're perfect.

continued

"The Field & Stream Guide to Jarrett Custom Rifles," *(continued)*

The naysayers were wrong. Jarrett was able to build rifles in all calibers, and even though they were roughly finished (once in a while he gets these old rifles back for rebarrelling and thinks, My god, did I build that?), they shot to a standard that no one had seen before.

As it turned out, South Carolina was the ideal place to build such a rifle because it's the home of hunters who shoot whitetails over beanfields and make a specialty of long, long shots from tower blinds. And when you shoot at a 100-pound deer from 400 to 600 yards, super accuracy becomes very important.

So people heard about the gunmaker in Jackson, and they pay his prices. But there were problems. Jarrett was forced to take factory bolt actions and "blue-print" them—remachine them to be virtually perfect. It was time-consuming, but there is no other way to get the results he wanted.

Barrels were also problems. Even those that were made to benchrest specifications (interior dimensions that varied no more than three 10-thousands of an inch for the length of the bore) would not shoot to his standard, and he was rejecting a third of the barrels he bought. What he needed was a tolerance of no more than 10-thousandth of a inch, and to get it he would have to make his own barrels. It took a year and a half to learn how, but he did it.

"Scouting Is the Key to Trophy Block Hunting Every Year," Pat Robertson, *Buckshot*, 2001:

"The American Indians had great reputations as hunters because they lived in nature. We (modern hunters) are of the opinion we can go to Wal-Mart and buy a camo suit and a gun and a bottle of Tink's 69 scent and go deer hunting," says one of South Carolina's top deer hunters.

Kenny Jarrett, creator of the super accurate custom Jarrett Hunting Rifle, grew up deer hunting in South Carolina, and he has taken more than 700 deer in his lifetime—none in the manner he just described.

The first key to successful deer hunting, he said, is scouting .

"Most people want to hunt, not scout. But the guy with the trophy spreads on his wall will spend four hours scouting for every hour of hunting. You're just not going to kill that big buck unless you know where he is."

The second key is location of the hunter—and that depends on the wind direction.

"You want to hunt with the wind coming to you because no cover scent is as good as the deer can smell," he said. Jarrett uses smoke bombs from the firecracker store to determine the prevailing wind direction, and when he settles in to wait, he checks the wind again with a cigarette lighter.

"If the wind changes, I move," he said.

The deer's super scenting ability must also be addressed in scouting and walking to a hunting spot, he noted. The feet may be the smelliest part of the human, and regular hunting boots do little to contain that scent, so Jarrett recommends rubber boots for deer hunting and scouting.

Noise is another factor. For that reason he disdains climbing stands because of all the clanging and banging sounds they create when a hunter scales a tree in one.

He also cares little for permanent stands because the deer are smart enough to know where they are located.

"You need to get where you can watch a corner coming into the field. I kill a lot of deer sitting on a bucket, down in the creek bottom where two paths cross."

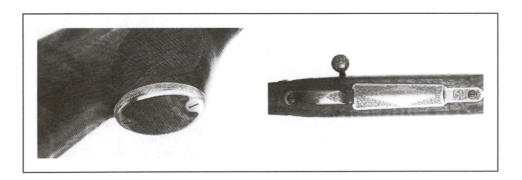

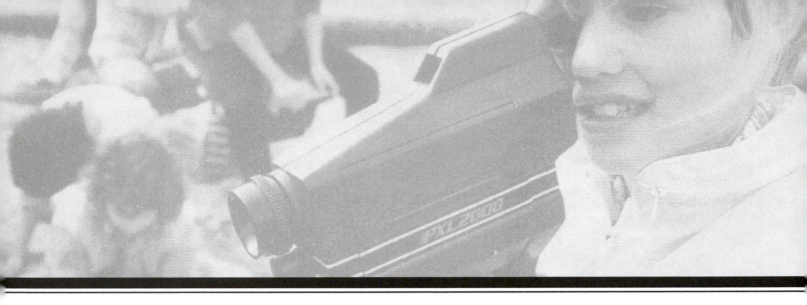

1987 News Feature

"Kidcorder: Sold as a Toy, It's Actually a Functioning Camcorder," William J. Hawkins, *Popular Science*, August 1987:

"Adults know this camcorder is for kids," says Bob Fisher, senior product design manager for Fisher-Price. "But they say 'I wouldn't mind having one myself anyway.'"

The plastic prototype I hold in my hand weights under two pounds, runs for five hours on AA batteries, records on an audio cassette, plays back on any TV set, and is so simple an eight-year-old can use it. And its price—$150—is about one-tenth of many other camcorders. Toy? Yes, but to make it work, Fisher-Price didn't play games. The company successfully updated a 25-year-old design.

To capture the enormous amount of information contained in video signal, all video recorders operate at a high head-to-tape speed. Conventional camcorders and VCRs spin the recording head at high speeds across slow-moving tape. The Fisher-Price camcorder takes the opposite approach. "It uses a fixed head," says Fisher, "and the tape speed is increased." That eliminates the cost, bulk, loading mechanism, and tolerances of the spinning head system. "It's basically an audio deck," says Fisher.

Used in early video recorders, the system was abandoned because of excessive headwear and its appetite for tape. Fisher claims that the company beat the wear problem by using a special wear-resistant head. But cutting the amount of tape being used required a trade-off. Instead of taking gulps of tape that would zip through a cassette in seconds, the camcorder's speed—15.3 inches per second, or about the same as fast forward—is set to take tape in more conservative bites. "You can shoot from 5.5 minutes on each side of the C-90 cassette," says Fisher. But being conservative has a penalty: lower picture quality. "I'd describe the playback as near black-and-white-TV quality," Fisher says, "but it depends on the TV you use." Fisher recommends viewing the playback on a 13-inch TV or smaller. "On larger sets, you'll see the pixels produced by the CCD," he says.

Pixels—individual dots, or picture elements—are created by the camcorders' charge- coupled-device. The greater the number of pixels, the finer the picture detail. However, Fisher discovered something else.

"When we first looked at computer simulations of 90 by 120 pixels, the picture looked fine," Fisher says, "but when we tried it in the camera, the picture wasn't good at all." What was the difference? "The computer created a picture using an unlimited number of gray scales," Fisher explains. "The original camera had eight. We found that the higher number of gray scales gave a better transition— a smoother-looking picture. We now use 64, and your eye almost blends them together."

The resolution of 90 by 120 pixels is half (or less) than that of other black-and-white video gear, but Fisher doesn't mind. "This is a toy in the sense that it's fun, but it opens up a technological and creative world to children," he says. "It's like the first time you heard your voice on a tape recorder. It's kind of a magical thing."

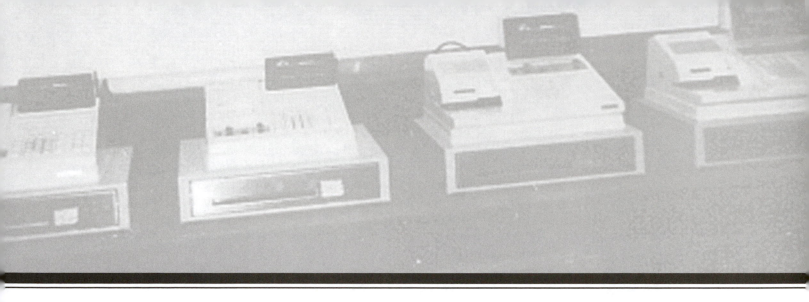

1989 Profile

A heart attack at 34-years-old transformed Bill Reindollar, creator of Cash Register Service, from a caring cop to a moneywise entrepreneur.

Life at Home

- Born in 1939 in Hollidaysburg, Pennsylvania, near Altoona, the middle child of Paul and Isabel Reindollar, Bill was born into world that was economically struggling and politically divided over concerns on how to handle the burgeoning militaristic nation of Germany and its leader, Adolph Hitler.
- Early on, Bill developed a curiosity for how things worked, and at age six took apart his elder sister's talking doll so he could see how it worked, removing the record cylinders in the doll's torso from which emanated songs and nursery rhymes.
- When he attempted to put the doll back together, he was left with extra parts and a doll that no longer worked.
- Over time, as his skills at taking apart and putting them back together again improved, family members came to believe that his interest in tools came from his paternal grandfather, a worker on the Pennsylvania Railroad, whose hobby was woodworking.
- Bill was very close to his grandparents, Mervin and Agnes, and cherished the time spent building furniture in his grandfather's woodshop.
- Bill also worked a paper route to help the family during some lean financial years.
- Kind and trusting, he sometimes went home without money because his customers couldn't pay him on time.
- This angered his father, who once threw a hot iron at him when he learned that Bill didn't collect from a customer who had fallen on hard times.

Bill Reindollar turned a life-threatening event into an opportunity to create Cash Register Service.

Reindollar reluctantly followed in his father's footsteps, taking a position at National Cash Register (NCR).

- Bill preferred to stay with his grandparents, where his grandfather would go into his woodshop after work, smoke his pipe, and work on a project to relax—habits that Bill would use later in his own life.
- When Bill was 14, his grandfather died.
- He moved in with his grandmother to become the man of the house.
- At the same time, Bill worked at the local hardware store, saving his money to buy a Schwinn bicycle that came with one year of free theft protection.
- Schwinn was quickly becoming the favorite bike of Americans, selling 500,000 a year; one out of every four bicycles in the U.S. was a Schwinn.
- After graduating from high school in 1957, Bill got a job at National Cash Register (NCR).
- He had little choice in the matter.
- His father, once a janitor at NCR, had seen how well the company cared for its service technicians and wanted his son to have that opportunity.
- So, after church one Sunday, his parents drove him to the NCR headquarters in Dayton, Ohio, and dropped him off outside to wait—in his wool suit in the humid summer weather—for the office to open on Monday morning.
- Shy by nature, Bill was encouraged by NCR to take a 14-week correspondence course offered by Dale Carnegie, called "How to Win Friends and Influence People."
- The book, first published in 1937, was one of the first bestselling self-help books on the market, selling millions of copies.
- However, despite his talent and the excellent company, NCR was not his dream job, but his father's, though, out of loyalty, Bill worked more than a decade for the company.

Life at Work

- At age 29, Bill Reindollar decided to leave NCR to pursue his dream job and become a state trooper.
- Just coming in under the age limit, Bill trained at the police academy in Hershey, Pennsylvania, where he learned to swim, enhance his observation skills and improve his problem solving.
- The only downside was working in the stables, something every cadet was required to master since the police still relied on horses for patrolling and exhibitions.
- Upon graduation, he was sent "to serve and to protect" in the western part of the state, where he focused on helping people, often giving breaks to youths he believed had simply fallen in with the wrong crowd or had a rough home life.
- He spent time talking with the kids and even fed them, learning sometimes that it was their first meal in days.

TANNERY SCHOOL SAFETY PATROL

Shown are members of the safety patrol at Tannery school in Allegheny township, two miles west of Duncansville. They are (left to right): Lynn Johnston, Judy Diehl, Billy Reindollar, Polly Hoover, Betty Yeckley and Ralph Pounds.

Young Reindollar had always wanted to help people and be a state trooper.

- The other officers called him "the Social Worker."
- Life was not only changing professionally, but personally after he met and began dating Sharon Nulph at her parent's family restaurant.
- Having lived a sheltered life, Sharon thought that when Bill suggested eating at McDonald's, he was referring to the home of one of his friends.
- Even though the Big Mac was founded by Pittsburgh McDonald's owner/operator Jim Delligatti one year earlier in 1967, the small towns were devoid of franchises.
- On their first date, they saw *Midnight Cowboy*, the first X-rated motion picture to win the Academy Award for Best Picture.
- They were married within a year and had four children in seven years.
- Bill became a detective and handled homicide cases and a kidnapping.
- Going to the family of a young woman who had drowned was the most difficult thing he had ever had to do.
- Though grieved by the news, the family was grateful for his compassion during this horrific period in their lives, and added him to their Christmas card list.
- The siblings of the girl bought him a children's book called *Sam Sunday and the Strange Disappearance of Chester Cats* that told of a compassionate detective aggressively on the case, and gave it to Bill as a "thank you" gift, addressing him as Sam Sunday.
- The odors of a homicide and difficult moments led him to take up smoking at age 34, initially to help him through dealing with crime scenes; it would later became a crutch for stressful moments.
- Only air traffic controllers and dentists were believed to have more stressful occupations than law enforcement officials, who were also renowned for not seeking help with their stress.
- Officers who committed suicide rarely had a record of discussing the problems they dealt with: continual danger, a difficult boss and public, and shift work that disrupted family life.
- In 1982, Bill began having chest pains and insisted on being admitted to the hospital, where he collapsed in the hall and had to be shocked back to life.

Reindollar played an active role in his community.

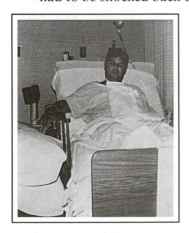

The stress of being a police officer took its toll on Reindollar's health.

- Having had a heart attack meant he had to retire from police work; for a time his senses and memory were affected.
- Afterwards, Bill coached his son's little league baseball team as he recuperated and relied on his woodworking and electrical skills for several years to help out the family financially.
- The national unemployment rate was more than 10 percent, and the economically depressed small town didn't offer many opportunities.
- Uncertain of what to do, Bill recalled his NCR training.
- In the 18 years he had been away from that line of work, business machines had become more technological; however, he decided to take a risk repairing old machines.

Reindollar bought a VCR with the money he made repairing old cash registers.

- In 1985, he filled up the gas tank in the car and drove to Butler, the closest city, where he cold-called on businesses that owned old wood and iron NCR cash registers no one was willing to service.
  - NCR was encouraging the use of smaller, easier to use electronic cash registers, and no longer trained service techs to repair aging machines.
  - Bill did several repairs and made $350 that first day.
  - With the windfall, Bill and Sharon bought a Zenith VCR, and though cable TV was not an option in the rural areas, they passed on a satellite dish, which would cost $1,995 to receive 100 channels.
  - Since the turn of the twentieth century, NCR had been the dominant company for business machines.
  - Founded in 1879 as National Manufacturing Company in Dayton, Ohio, to sell the cash register invented by James Ritty, the firm was renamed in 1894.
- A training school was established in 1893, along with a social welfare program for the employees.
- By 1911, the company had sold one million machines and had 6,000 employees.
- NCR controlled 95 percent of the market.
- In 1922, the company went public and issued $55 million in stock; at the time it was the largest public company ever in the United States.
- Since the company treated its employees so well, they were loyal, refusing to do business with restaurants or stores that used a competitor's cash register.
- Another established, but smaller company, also known by its initials, claimed it would compete with NCR; Bill and his coworkers at NCR quipped that the company's initials stood for, Itty Bitty Machines.
- Bill's repair business blossomed as he worked a wider and wider territory comprising, almost exclusively, small towns.
- One day, Bill picked up a register to take back to the office for repair work.
- He drove two hours to pick up the machine and two hours to the office, only to discover that the client had left money in the cash drawer of the machine.
- He elected to drive two hours back to give them their money and then back to the office, spending an entire workday essentially traveling for one machine.
- After that, Bill always checked for himself to make sure the money had been removed before taking a cash register.
- After getting his feet wet in the field again, he decided to accept a job with an established company; after working for the company for a month, without pay, he and the other employees realized they needed to go elsewhere.
- The experience helped Bill find suppliers and additional clientele who needed a new service company when the dysfunctional company folded.
- As an entrepreneur, Bill maintained a repair shop in the basement of his family's home.

This home office and workshop was soon a thriving and profitable business.

- Monday through Friday, he would fill up his large thermos of coffee and drive 45 minutes to and from Butler, where he had his business office.
- He called the company Cash Register Service.
- Like many children of the Depression, Bill distrusted banks and the stock market, and was uncomfortable borrowing money.
- He always believed the money could disappear, so rather than seek loans for his business needs, he saved up the money for purchases.
- He built an office in the basement of the house and purchased an Apple II home computer for $795.00 (he still couldn't bring himself to buy an IBM), a non-rotary telephone that remembered three phone numbers and had a speaker, and a separate answering machine.
- The 5¼-inch floppy disks that the computer required sold for $9.95 a box.
- Bill also discovered there was money to be made in antique machines, which he refurbished and sold to stores and collectors.
- He enjoyed being out in the field and working with the machines, but soon grew weary of sitting in the office returning phone calls and handling the paperwork.
- The company grew and its value eventually became $50,000.
- In need of money to support a family of six and wanting to have fewer office details to deal with, Bill decided to sell the company.

Reindollar did not want to be tied to a desk or the paperwork.

- There were not many takers in the small town who could pay that sum, so he offered the company for $30,000, with the condition that he be employed as a service tech, relieving him of office work.
- The company was purchased by a local restaurant owner looking for a business investment, who had relied extensively on get-rich-quick books and was determined to apply those techniques to a small company.
- The new owner placed no emphasis on employee happiness, but considerable focus on fast and high profits.
- Bill believed that if you did your job right and took care of the customer, the money would come; the new owner's approach, plus increased prices, caused many customers to look elsewhere for service.
- As stress built up for Bill, a patch of hair fell out of the back of his head from what he considered execrable business practices.
- Part of each week was consumed with meetings, where Bill would get bored and angry at the direction the company was taking.
- Bill didn't believe in the big-business approach to his once home-based business operation, and made his feelings known; he thought the business had become unnecessarily complicated.
- The owner did not like Bill's questioning him and fired him, adding him to the 5.3 percent unemployed in the U.S.
- The patch of hair grew back shortly thereafter.

Life in Community: Butler, Pennsylvania

- Butler, Pennsylvania, where Bill Reindollar established his business, was named after American Revolutionary War General Richard Butler in 1800.
- The 2.7-square-mile city of 15,000 was 35 miles north of Pittsburgh and was known for its trolley cars.
- The Army's Jeep prototype was produced in Butler by American Bantam Car Company, and was called the BRC (Bantam Reconnaissance Car) 40.
- The company's 1938 model was the inspiration for Donald Duck's car.
- Butler was also known for Moraine State Park, named for its moraine glaciers, which attracted over a million visitors each year.
- The park covered 16,725 acres; hunting, a popular pastime in the area, was allowed on 13,000 acres.
- The North Country Trail, which goes from Lake Champlain in New York to Lake Sakakawea in North Dakota, passes through Moraine State Park.
- The famous low-budget black-and-white horror movie *Night of the Living Dead* was filmed in Butler County; made for $114,000, the film grossed $30 million internationally.

HISTORICAL SNAPSHOT
1989

- The World Health Organization estimated the number of AIDS cases would increase from 450,000 to five million by the year 2000
- The Louvre Museum in Paris reopened with a glass entrance designed by I.M. Pei
- Panamanians voted out General Manuel Noriega, but he refused to step down, causing the use of military force to oust him

- Kenya called for a worldwide ban on trading ivory
- Books published included *Billy Bathgate* by E.L. Doctrow, *Midnight* by Dean Koontz, *A Time to Kill* by John Grisham, and *A Prayer For Owen Meany* by John Irving
- The Exxon *Valdez* hit a reef off the coast of Prince William Sound in Alaska, spilling nearly 10 million gallons of oil
- Chinese government fired on pro-democracy protesters in Tiananmen Square
- New South African President F.W. de Klerk, permitted apartheid marches and released some political prisoners
- West German citizens were permitted to visit East Germany without visas
- Cinemagoers saw *Batman, Dead Poets Society, Driving Miss Daisy, Field of Dreams,* and *Indiana Jones and the Last Crusade*
- The original script for the movie *Citizen Kane* was sold at auction for $210,000
- The national debt was $2.684 trillion, more than 26 times the figure in 1980
- The first increase in the minimum wage since 1980 was announced, from $3.15 to $3.80 per hour
- Research studies showed that children from smaller families attained a better education than did children from larger families
- Lt. Col. Oliver North was found guilty of felony in the Iran-Contra affair
- The 1901 Pablo Picasso self-portrait, *Yo Picasso,* was sold for $47,850,000, the highest price paid for artwork from the twentieth century
- Popular songs included The B-52s' "Love Shack," Billy Joel's "We Didn't Start the Fire," and Fine Young Cannibals' "She Drives Me Crazy"
- *The Simpsons* television show debuted as a Christmas special; it was the first successful primetime animated series since the syndicated *Wait Till Your Father Gets Home* ended in 1974
- Rev. Barbara Harris became the first female bishop of the Episcopal Church
- Jerry Jones bought the NFL Dallas Cowboys for $143 million
- HBO's Comedy Channel (soon to be Comedy Central) debuted

Selected Prices

Adirondack Chair and Ottoman	$119.95
Bicycle, Boy's 20" -Inch Challenger BMX Bike	$59.99
Camcorder, Sharp 8x	$1799.99
Cash Register	$179.99
Cereal, per 18 Ounces	$1.55
Coffee, per Pound	$2.92
Glue Gun	$24.99
Hammer	$10.99
Microwave Oven	$219.99
Sweater, Men's Long Sleeve	$29.25

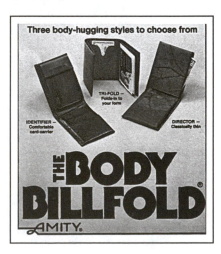

Business Machines Timeline

1888
William S. Burroughs received a patent for the adding machine.

1902
The first electric typewriter was produced by Blickensderfer Manufacturing Company of Stamford, Connecticut.

1904
For the World's Fair in St. Louis, NCR built a replica of the Ritty Model 1, a cash register designed for businesses that had non-family members performing business transactions. The Ritty brothers dubbed the machine, "Ritty's Incorruptible Cashier."

1906
Xerox was founded in Rochester, New York, as Haloid Photographic Company.

Inventor Charles Kettering of NCR added an electric motor to a cash register.

1910
The typewriter, invented in 1870, received its standardized design.

1917
Wellington Parker Kidder made the "noiseless" typewriter, which failed to sell well; people prefered the "clickety-clack" sound of the keyboard.

1937
George Stibitz invented a relay-based calculator he called "Model K" (the K stood for kitchen table, on which he assembled the machine). It was considered the first digital computer.

1939
The Hewlett-Packard Company was founded.

1949
The Bar Code Reader was patented.

1959
Xerox introduced its 914 Model photocopy machine; by 1965, the revenues from the photocopier was more than $500 million.

1969
Gary Starkweather of Xerox invented the laser printer.

1978
The solar-powered calculator was introduced. 1979

Visa developed the first dial-up credit card machine.

"Acid Rain Killing World's Forests," *Chicago Daily Herald*, April 1, 1984:

Millions of acres of forests in the United States and Europe show signs of dead, dying and damaged trees, apparently caused by acid rain and other airborne pollutants, the Worldwatch Institute reported Saturday.

The increasing damage, probably linked to the long-term effects of industrial air pollution, could cause multimillion-dollar timber losses and eventually destroy large regions of forests on both continents, the study by the Washington-based private research Institute declared.

The report comes just two days after Environmental Protection Agency Administrator William Ruckelshaus warned Congress that scientists have found a wide area of eastern U.S. forest suffering a "pronounced decline" in tree growth, possibly stemming from airborne chemicals.

"At least nine million acres of forests in Europe and broad areas of the eastern United States now show damage linked to air pollutants," Worldwatch included in the study, "Air Pollution: Acid Rain and the Future of Forests."

"A comprehensive look at worldwide forest damage reveals multiple pollutants—including acid-forming sulfates and nitrates, gaseous sulfur dioxide, ozone and heavy metals that acting alone or together place forests under severe stress," said the report.

Although scientists cannot explain how the destruction is occurring, "Air pollutants in acid rain are apparently stressing sensitive forests beyond their ability to cope," said author Sandra Postal, Worldwatch senior researcher.

"Electronics News Front: Data Card," William J. Hawkins, *Popular Science*, July 1987:

"That card holds 200 megabytes of data," says Jim Russell, inventor of the Hi-Lite optical card. "And you can access any of them in half a second."

The card I'm holding looks like a pocket mirror: flat, reflective, the size of a credit card. But Russell's invention is akin to a read-only memory compact disc. Data are recorded as tiny, laser-made microscopic pits just one micron in diameter. However, unlike a CD-ROM and player which is a read-only system, the Hi-Lite card can be used to save and write data, too.

Inserted in a special PC-compatible reader, the card is scanned with a laser for reading or writing data. "The card remains stationary," says Russell. "This would be a marvelous backup device for a computer's hard disk."

But it can be used for much more.

Because the card can hold huge amounts of data, it can be used on large computers as a backup to WORM (write once read many) optical discs. "If you've got a gigabyte optical disk on your machine, the cards become a quick and easy way to back it up," Russell says. To back up that amount of data, Russell has developed a carousel reader. "It's about the size of a refrigerator," he says, "and it contains 10,000 cards."

The carousel holds up to a terabyte (one million megabytes) of data and finds any single piece of information in less than three seconds, twice as fast as comparable optical disc changers. "With the disc changer, you must stop the spinning, change the disk, and start it again," says Russell. "With ours, the scanner runs continuously."

Russell envisions non-computer uses for the Hi-Lite cards, too. Used in a car, the cards could become the basis of an electronic map. "Six cards could cover all of North America," he says. In your home, the cards could become part of the future entertainment system. "The card can hold 145 minutes of compact disc-quality stereo music or a video single," says Russell. And in your pocket, it could be a credit card-sized personal information bank containing "everything from identification codes to digitized pictures."

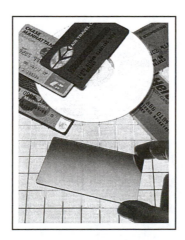

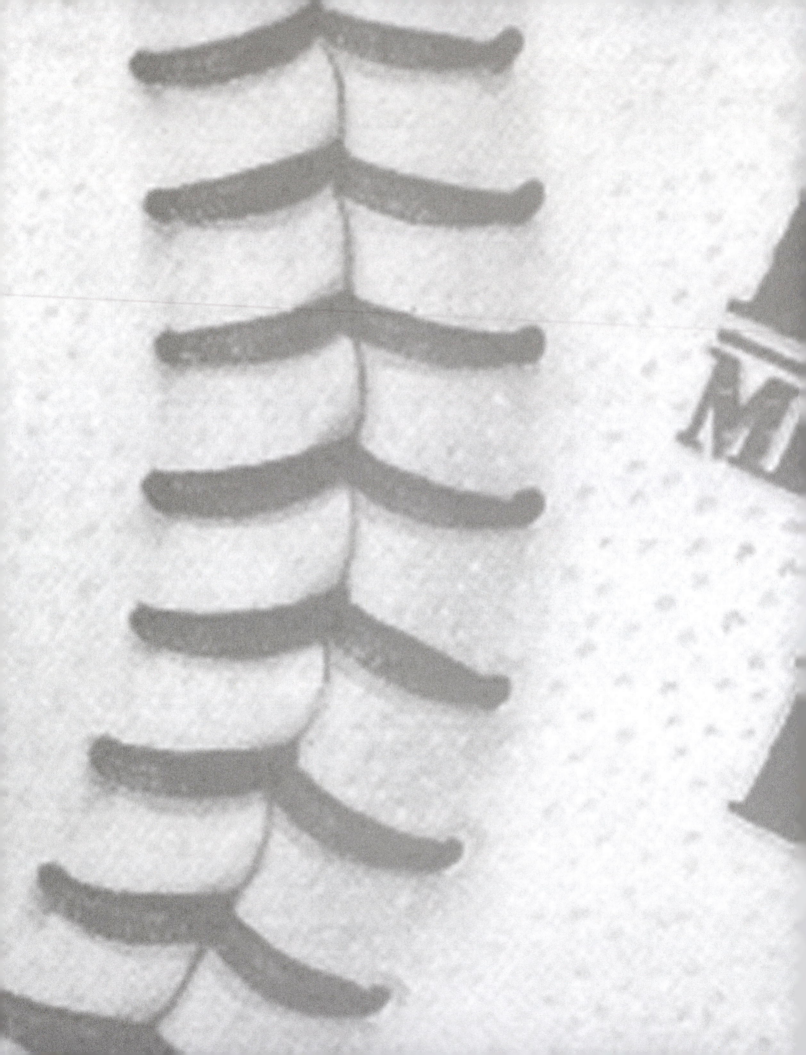

1990-1999

The 1990s, called the "Era of Possibilities" by *Fortune* magazine, were dominated by an economic expansion that became the longest in the nation's history. Characterized by steady growth, low inflation, low unemployment and dramatic gains in technology-based productivity, the expansion was particularly meaningful to computer companies and the emerging concept known as the Internet. This economy swelled the ranks of the upper class as Americans of all backgrounds invested in the soaring stock market and dreamed of capturing a dot-com fortune.

The '90s gave birth to $150 tennis shoes, condom boutiques, pre-ripped jeans, Motorola 7.7 ounce cellular telephones, rollerblading, TV home shopping, the Java computer language, digital cameras, DVD players, and Internet shopping. And in fashion, a revival of the 1960s' style brought back miniskirts, pop art prints, pants suits, and the A-line. Black became a color worn at any time of day and for every purpose. The increasing role of consumer debt in driving the American economy also produced an increase in personal bankruptcy and a reduction in overall savings rate. At the same time, mortgage interest rates hit 30-year lows during the decade, creating refinancing booms that pumped millions of dollars into the economy, further fueling a decade of consumerism.

The decade opened in an economic recession, a ballooning national debt, and the economic hangover of the collapse of much of the savings and loan industry. The automobile industry produced record losses; household names like Bloomingdale's and Pan Am declared bankruptcy. Housing values plummeted and factory orders fell. Media headlines were dominated by issues such as rising drug use, crime in the cities, racial-tensions, and the rise of personal bankruptcies. Family values ranked high on the conservative agenda, and despite efforts to limit Democrat Bill Clinton to one term as president, the strength of the economy played a critical role in his re-election in 1996.

Guided by Federal Reserve Chair Alan Greenspan's focus on inflation control and Clinton's early efforts to control the federal budget, the U.S. economy soared, producing its best economic indicators in three decades. By 1999, the stock market produced record returns, job creation was at a 10-year high, and the federal deficit was falling. Businesses nationwide hung "Help Wanted" signs outside their doors and even paid signing bonuses to acquire new workers. Crime rates, especially in urban areas, plummeted to levels unseen in three decades, illegitimacy rates fell, and every year business magazines marvelled at the length of the recovery, asking, "Can it last another year?"

The stock market set a succession of records throughout the period, attracting thousand of investors to stocks for the first time, including the so-called glamour offerings of high technology companies. From 1990 to the dawn of the twenty-first century, the Dow Jones Industrial Average rose 318 percent. Growth stocks were the rage; of Standard and Poor's 500 tracked stocks, almost 100 did not pay dividends. This market boom eventually spawned unprecedented new wealth, encouraging early retirement to legions of aging baby boomers. The dramatic change in the cultural structure of corporations continued to threaten the job security of American workers, who had to be more willing to learn new skills, try new jobs, and move from project to project. Profit sharing, which allowed workers to benefit from increased productivity, became more common. Retirement programs and pension plans became more flexible and transferable, serving the needs of a highly mobile work force. The emerging gap of the 1990s was not always between the rich and the poor, but the computer literate and the technically deficient. To symbolize the changing role of women in the work force, cartoon character Blondie, wife of Dagwood Bumstead, opened her own catering business which, like so many small businesses in the 1990s, did extremely well. For the first time, a study of family household income concluded that 55 percent of women provided half or more of the household income.

In a media-obsessed decade, the star attraction was the long-running scandal of President Bill Clinton and his affair with a White House intern. At its climax, while American forces were attacking Iraq, the full House of Representatives voted to impeach the president. For only the second time in American history, the Senate conducted an impeachment hearing before voting to acquit the president of perjury and obstruction of justice.

During the decade, America debated limiting abortion, strengthening punishment for criminals, replacing welfare for work, ending Affirmative Action, dissolving bilingual education, elevating educational standards, curtailing the right of legal immigrants, and imposing warning on unsuitable material for children on the Internet. Nationwide, an estimated 15 million people, including smokers, cross-dressers, alcoholics, sexual compulsives, and gamblers, attended weekly self-help support groups; dieting became a $33 billion industry as Americans struggled with obesity.

The impact of the GI Bill's focus on education, rooted in the decade following World War II, flowered in the generation that followed. The number of adult Americans with a four-year college education rose from 6.2 percent in 1950 to 24 percent in 1997. Despite this impressive rise, the need for a more educated population, and the rapidly rising expectations of the technology sector, the century ended with a perception that the decline in public education was one of the most pressing problems of the decade. Throughout the decade, school violence escalated, capturing headline year after year in widely dispersed locations across the nation.

1 Hydrogen

1994 Profile

Marie Moffett grew up in Atlanta, Georgia, attracted to theater and puppetry, never dreaming she would become a twenty-first-century hydrogen fuel cell visionary and investor.

Life at Home

- During Marie Moffett's sophomore year at Oglethorpe University in Atlanta, she applied for a summer job building theater sets; the only other position open required her to repair cars.
- Necessity followed form and function, and she soon became a mechanic who spent as much time as possible under the hood of a car, wistfully dreaming of how to make automobiles as efficient as possible.
- She imagined a car that didn't use vanishing fossil fuels to function, but was capable of fast starts, long-distance travel and high style.
- The car of the future should be both smart and sexy, she believed.
- A decade later—in 1990—she decided the answer was hydrogen fuel cells that emitted only vapor out the tailpipe.
- Hydrogen fuel cells made possible a car that was largely pollution-free, was not dependent on fossil fuels, was cheap to run, and most important—because it had no engine or traditional transmission—could be designed a million new and different ways.
- The car she envisioned wasn't exactly a car but the underpinnings of one, sort of a skateboard that encased the car's power and control system, which could be kept for decades while customers shuffled car bodies as tastes changed.
- And the bodies, too, would be radically different, with the windshield extending all the way down to the floor, if desired, because the car's essential systems are kept underfoot.
- The brake pedal and accelerator could be replaced with electronically controlled steering using hand grips on the wheel.

Marie Moffett invested her time and money in her vision of a hydrogen-fueled car.

- But it was not going to be easy: similar to the early days of autos in 1900, there was a race among France, Germany, and the United States; Japan had its own $11 billion initiative called New Sunshine to be the leader in hydrogen power.

- Marie fully expected that the blending of technologies would result in a hybrid using both hydrogen and electricity initially.

- She knew, taken together, the technologies would move the automobile from the machine age to the digital age and result in a car that emitted no carbon dioxide.

- By then, she had earned a master's degree in engineering and gone to work designing the car of the future—and repairing cars for her mechanically challenged brothers.

- Marie was the last of seven children; her older sister was 26 years old when she was born.

- She was so much younger, Marie was treated like a talkative house pet who could be dragged to every adult event without a thought; hers was a resource-filled childhood jammed with events and adventures that required Marie to grow up quickly if she wanted to keep up.

The car of the future would have interchangeable bodies, and a power source that could last for decades.

- As a result, she knew few children her age and joined an adult theater group when she was 12; at 16 she entered college, and at 26, she was convinced she was being called to help solve the world's energy crisis.

- Four years later, reports of acid rain, dying forests and global warming all cried out for a carbonless solution to America's energy needs.

- She first dabbled with the potential of solar energy, then thermal, then wind, before discovering the potential of hydrogen fuel cells.

- Hydrogen—an invisible, tasteless, colorless gas—is the most abundant element in the universe, and when combined with a fuel cell, highly efficient.

- Fuel cells are electrochemical engines that combine hydrogen and oxygen in a flameless process to produce electricity, heat and pure, distilled water.

- The hydrogen fuel cell operated similarly to a battery: it had two electrodes, an anode and a cathode, separated by a membrane; oxygen passed over one electrode and hydrogen over the other.

- The hydrogen reacted to a catalyst on the electrode anode that converted the hydrogen gas into negatively charged electrons (e-) and positively charged ions (H+).

- The electrons flowed out of the cell to be used as electrical energy.

The challenge was to efficiently and economically harness hydrogen as a fuel source.

- The hydrogen ions moved through the electrolyte membrane to the cathode electrode where they combined with oxygen and the electrons to produce water; unlike batteries, fuel cells never run out.

- The problem with hydrogen as an energy source was devising an economical way of making the fuel and how to efficiently store it in a tightly controlled container.

- The first fuel cell was conceived in 1839 by Sir William Robert Grove, a Welsh judge, inventor and physicist who mixed hydrogen and oxygen in the presence of an electrolyte and produced electricity and water.

- The invention, which later became known as a fuel cell, didn't produce enough electricity to be useful.

- In 1889, the term "fuel cell" was first coined by Ludwig Mond and Charles Langer, who attempted to build a working fuel cell using air and industrial coal gas.
- In the 1920s, fuel cell research in Germany paved the way to the development of the carbonate cycle and solid oxide fuel cells of today.
- In 1932, engineer Francis T. Bacon began his vital research into fuel cells.
- Early cell designers used porous platinum electrodes and sulfuric acid as the electrolyte bath.
- Using platinum was expansive, and sulfuric acid was corrosive.
- Bacon improved on the expensive platinum catalysts with a hydrogen and oxygen cell using a less corrosive alkaline electrolyte and inexpensive nickel electrodes.
- It took Bacon until 1959 to perfect his design, when he demonstrated a five-kilowatt fuel cell that could power a welding machine.
- In October of 1959, Harry Karl Ihrig, an engineer for the Allis-Chalmers Manufacturing Company, demonstrated a 20-horsepower tractor that was the first vehicle ever powered by a fuel cell.
- During the early 1960s, General Electric produced the fuel cell-based electrical power system for NASA's *Gemini* and *Apollo* space capsules.
- The Space Shuttle's electricity was provided by fuel cells, and the same fuel cells provided drinking water for the crew.
- NASA funded more than 200 research contracts exploring fuel cell technology, bringing the technology to a level now viable for the private sector.
- The first bus powered by a fuel cell was completed in 1993, and several fuel cell cars were being built in Europe and in the United States.

Life at Work

- For Marie Moffett, hydrogen represented the space-age fuel of the future, so drawing upon her theater experience and her passion for a new energy policy, she traveled the nation telling the hydrogen energy story and personally investing in ideas that excited her.
- "The Space Shuttle already used hydrogen fuel cells to provide onboard electricity and drinking water; BMW operated experimental buses using fuel cells.
- And one of the leading firms working on hydrogen-powered cars had developed its technology to provide energy underwater.
- Energy Partners, based in West Palm Beach, Florida, was founded by John H. Perry, Jr., a former newspaper and cable television owner who introduced computerized typesetting into the newsroom.
- In the 1960s, Perry began producing small manned submarines for the offshore oil industry, eventually cornering 90 percent of the market.
- He also built the hydrogen fuel cell-powered Hydrolab, in which astronauts trained underwater for the weightlessness of space, and began to experiment with fuel cells in submarines.
- "The fuel cell," he told Marie, "is the silicon chip of the hydrogen age."
- Speaking to college groups, business forums and economic developer conclaves on behalf of Energy Partners and hydrogen fuel cells became an all-consuming job.

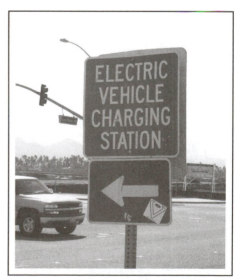

An electric car could be quickly recharged at stations across the country.

- America needed to understand the potential of this energy source, she told her brothers and sisters when she moved back to Atlanta to take advantage of the city's airport, rail and road transportation.
- She quickly learned that the explosion of the *Hindenburg* cast a pall over hydrogen, and the words "fuel cell" caused considerable confusion.
  - Fuel cells were bulky and very expensive, until the development of proton exchange membranes, or PEMs for short.
  - A PEM was a type of Teflon that looked like a regular sheet of transparent plastic.
  - When treated with platinum as a catalyst, it split hydrogen and separated out its electrons to form electricity.
  - A series of PEM's stacked one on top of another like layers of meat in a sandwich produced a fuel cell that was light, small and potentially cheap enough to use in a car.
  - After all, hydrogen can be burned in an internal-combustion engine.
  - BMW, Mercedes-Benz, and Mazda all had prototype internal-combustion cars working on hydrogen fuel, but when used instead to produce electricity in a fuel cell, it will take that same car twice as far.
  - A fuel cell in an electric car could increase its range to about 400 miles, and reduce its recharge time to two or three minutes.
  - Energy Partners planned to build a "proof of concept" car, rather than a production prototype, running on two hydrogen fuel cells.
  - With it, Marie hoped to demonstrate that such cars can be ready for the mass market by the end of the decade, rather than 20 years from then, as most experts predicted.
  - One of the many advantages of hydrogen as an energy carrier was fuel flexibility: hydrogen can be made from just about anything.
  - It could be reformed either aboard the car or at the service station from methanol, ethanol or natural gas.
- It could even be produced by using solar power to electrolyze water.
- It seemed the perfect fantasy: a car running basically on sun and water.
- But outside Munich, Germany, an experimental power plant was already producing hydrogen from solar power and water.
- Solar technology may have been nowhere near the stage where it could power a family car directly, but its potential to power the car indirectly, by producing hydrogen, had now been established.
  - The problem was building a market—at the right price—that was big enough to justify the large production runs that would make electric cars more economical.
  - Marie came to realize it was economics, not science, that dominated this whole issue.
  - The hydrogen-powered cars had to be affordable, which was even trickier when gasoline was cheaper than bottled water.
  - Department of Energy studies indicated that fuel cells cost $141 per kilowatt; the car industry believed fuel cell engines couldn't compete with conventional ones until they cost less than $50 a kilowatt.
  - Ford Motor Company said it could mass-produce hydrogen cars once 10,000 natural gas-reforming pumps at $250,000 to $1.5 million each were installed at filling stations around the country.

Unfortunately, hydrogen often was thought of in connection with the 1937 Hindenburg disaster.

Marie realized technology was not standing in her way, but marketing and economics were.

Marie's dream is that everyone would own a vehicle with a fuel cell engine.

- Marie continued to bet on the future, making 50 speeches a year while investing $1.6 million of her own money.

Life in the Community: Atlanta, Georgia

- Atlanta, Georgia, the capital and most populous city in the state, with a metropolitan population approaching six million.
- Like many areas in the Sun Belt, the Atlanta region had experienced explosive growth since the 1970s, thanks to its role as a primary transportation hub of the Southeastern United States, including highways, railroads, and airports.
- It was an industrial legacy dating back to the Civil War, when Atlanta served as a vital nexus of the railroads and hence a hub for the distribution of military supplies.
- On September 7, 1864, Union General William T. Sherman ordered the city's civilian population to evacuate, then torched the buildings of Atlanta to the ground, sparing only the city's churches and hospitals.
- In 1868, the Georgia State Capital was moved from Milledgeville to Atlanta because of the latter's superior rail transportation network; it was the fifth location of the capital of the State of Georgia.
- On December 15, 1939, Atlanta hosted the film premiere of *Gone with the Wind*, the epic film based on Atlanta's Margaret Mitchell's best-selling novel *Gone with the Wind*.
- "Several stars of the film, including Clark Gable, Vivien Leigh, Olivia de Havilland, and its legendary producer, David O. Selznick, attended the gala event, which was held at Loew's Grand Theatre.
- When the date of the Atlanta premiere of *Gone with the Wind* approached, Hattie McDaniel, who had played Mammy, told director Victor Fleming she would not be able to go, when in actuality she did not want to cause trouble because of the violent racism in Atlanta at the time.

- During World War II, companies such as the Bell Aircraft Company and the manufacture of railroad cars were dedicated to the war effort.
- Shortly after the war, the Federal Centers for Disease Control and Prevention was founded in Atlanta.
- During the 1960s, Atlanta was a major organizing center of the Civil Rights Movement, with Dr. Martin Luther King, Jr., Ralph David Abernathy, and students from Atlanta's historically Black colleges and universities played major roles in the movement's leadership.
- Two of the most important civil rights organizations, the Southern Christian Leadership Conference and the Student Nonviolent Coordinating Committee, had their national headquarters in Atlanta.
- Despite racial tension during the Civil Rights era, Atlanta's political and business leaders labored to foster Atlanta's image as "the city too busy to hate."
- In 1961, Atlanta Mayor Ivan Allen, Jr., became one of the few Southern white mayors to support desegregation of his city's public schools.
- African-American Atlantans demonstrated their growing political influence with the election of the first African-American mayor, Maynard Jackson, in 1973.

- In 1990, Atlanta was selected as the site for the 1996 Summer Olympic Games, and undertook several major construction projects to improve the city's parks, sports facilities, and transportation.
- By the 1990s, Atlanta was so unruly it was considered to be an archetype for cities experiencing rapid growth and urban sprawl.
- Unlike most major cities, metropolitan Atlanta does not have any natural boundaries, such as an ocean, lakes, or mountains, that might constrain growth.

HISTORICAL SNAPSHOT
1994

- The North American Free Trade Agreement (NAFTA) was established
- In Detroit, Michigan, Nancy Kerrigan was clubbed on the right leg by an assailant, under orders from figure skating rival Tonya Harding's ex-husband
- The Superhighway Summit was held at UCLA, the first conference to discuss the growing information superhighway
- President Bill Clinton and Russian President Boris Yeltsin signed the Kremlin Accords, which stopped the preprogrammed aiming of nuclear missiles toward each country's targets, and also provided for the dismantling of the nuclear arsenal in Ukraine
- In South Carolina, Shannon Faulkner became the first female cadet to attend The Citadel, but soon dropped out
- Byron De La Beckwith was convicted of the 1963 murder of Civil Rights leader Medgar Evers
- Edvard Munch's painting *The Scream* was stolen in Oslo
- Aldrich Ames and his wife were charged with spying for the Soviet Union by the U.S. Department of Justice
- In *Campbell v. Acuff-Rose Music, Inc.*, the Supreme Court ruled that parodies of an original work are generally covered by the doctrine of fair use
- *Schindler's List* won seven Oscars including Best Picture and Best Director at the 66th Academy Awards, hosted by Whoopi Goldberg
- The journal *Nature* reported the finding in Ethiopia of the first complete *Australopithecus afarensis* skull
- Kurt Cobain, songwriter and front man for the band Nirvana, was found dead, apparently of a single, self-inflicted gunshot wound
- The Red Cross estimated that hundreds of thousands of Tutsis had been killed in the Rwanda massacre
- Nelson Mandela was inaugurated as South Africa's first black president
- Nicole Brown Simpson and Ronald Goldman were murdered outside the Simpson home in Los Angeles, California; O.J. Simpson was charged in the killings
- The 1994–1995 Major League Baseball strike ended the 1994 MLB season
- President Clinton signed the Assault Weapons Ban, which banned the manufacture of new weapons with certain features for a period of 10 years
- The first version of Web browser Netscape Navigator was released

Selected Prices

Alarm Clock	$9.99
Car Seat	$65.00
Christmas Tree, Artificial	$124.99
Comforter	$26.88
Lawn Mower	$289.00
Leggings	$15.00
Light Bulb, Halogen	$8.96
Microwave Oven	$99.00
Shower Curtain	$19.77
Videotape, Three Blank	$8.49

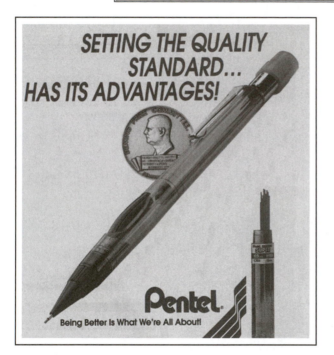

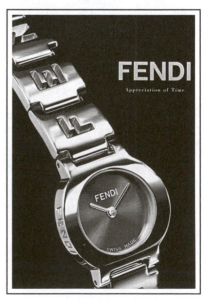

"Next in Car Fuel: Hydrogen," *Cedar Rapids Gazette*, February 8, 1993:

Hydrogen power is the Holy Grail of clean energy; it doesn't pollute and it's universally available. But until recently, it's been too expensive for widespread use.

Now, a Florida company has invented a simplified fuel cell that can eliminate the internal combustion engine and run a car on hydrogen, and Energy Partners, Inc., says it's just the beginning.

"We think we can have an economically competitive car by the end of the century," says owner John Perry, Jr., who runs Perry Oceanographics. "Eventually this could replace all fossil fuels." The company's experimental hydrogen-fueled "Green Car" is scheduled to be unveiled in March.

Company vice president Mitch Ewan briefed this staff of environmentally oriented Vice President Al Gore before the election, he said, and the company has also worked closely with Sen. Tom Harkin, (D-Iowa), a strong supporter of hydrogen as a nonpolluting power source.

A fuel cell, although it sounds like some type of battery, is actually an electrochemical engine. It takes a fuel, hydrogen in this case, and pumps it through a chemically impregnated plate, generating an electrical current and the system's only waste product—water vapor.

And unlike internal combustion engines, it has no moving parts.

Energy Partners has supplied NASA with material for its Space Shuttle fuel cells, but the technology used in space is too cumbersome for widespread use on Earth, Perry says.

So the company set out to design a fuel cell that could be mass-produced in a factory. The company's fuel cell eliminates heat and hard-to-handle chemicals that make fuel cells unsuitable for most mundane uses, replacing them with a simple plastic sheet impregnated with chemical chains and platinum.

By the year 2000, Perry believes, the price of a fuel cell car engine could be down to about $3,000 and would last twice as long as gasoline engines. And cars are not the only use. Eventually, a television-sized hydrogen fuel cell can supply all the power needed by an average home.

There are several problems, Ewan says. To further reduce the size and weight, the company is working with the California designer to install fuel cells in a flying wing. The aircraft would use solar power to produce the hydrogen and could theoretically stay in the air for two years.

Fuel cell production requires far tighter tolerances than current engines, which means the manufacturing process must have very high precision.

Another problem is storing the hydrogen. The Green Car gets a respectable 120 miles per tank, but that's not enough for most consumers. So the company is working on techniques of absorption—adhesion to a surface that would bind the hydrogen gas to solid materials in the tank.

If it works, a full-sized van could eventually get 1,500 miles per tank, says Ewan.

"Gasoline Pollution Is Serious, Too," Marvin Legator and Amanda Daniel, *Galveston Daily News*, June 8, 1996:

Question: How safe is our gasoline? It is my understanding that one of the major sources of pollution is gasoline. How dangerous is gasoline, and what can we do about it?

Answer: Gasoline is a complex chemical mixture containing more than 1,000 possible substances. Gasoline vapors are released at bulking installations, refineries, during tank and barge transportation and when refueling automobiles at service stations.

According to the U.S. Environmental Protection Agency, approximately 40 percent of all gasoline releases occur during refueling. Gasoline represents a major source of exposure to the general population of toxic substances, including several known carcinogens such as benzene and butadiene.

Most experts agree that it's likely gasoline will be the dominant motor vehicle fuel well into the next century, although General Motors has developed an electric vehicle that is currently showing at select stops throughout the country.

This automobile uses no gasoline, no water and no spark plugs. It runs on a battery which remains charged for approximately 70 miles. This is a step in the right direction, and with further development may be the automobile of the future.

"EPA Unveils Plan to Reduce Acid Rain," *Salina Journal*, October 30, 1991:

The Environmental Protection Agency on Tuesday unveiled its plan to curb acid rain by forcing utilities to cut sulfur oxide emissions by 40 percent this decade.

EPA Administrator William Reilly estimated that the proposed rules would cost $4 billion annually by the year 2000. They will lead to sharp increases in electricity rates in the areas of the country that have the dirtiest coal-burning power plants, he said.

The new rules are expected to push up electricity rates about 1.5 percent nationwide, but much higher in some areas, Reilly said. He maintained the higher cost "will be more than offset" by the environmental benefits from controlling acid rain.

The proposed regulations, which are expected to be made final early next year, implement the Clean Air Act passed by Congress last year.

Acid rain is the name given to the industrial pollution that may be carried long distances in the atmosphere before returning to the earth as rain, snow, or soot, killing aquatic life. Sulfur dioxide emissions, mainly from coal-burning power plants in the Midwest, are a major cause of acid rain.

1995 Profile

Jerry D. Neal's childhood interest in telephone communications had positioned him to be in the forefront of the cell phone revolution—if he could only find the capital to launch his company, RF Micro Devices, and keep it funded.

Life at Home

- Jerry D. Neal's fascination with telephone and radio began in elementary school when he checked out of the school library a book on inventor Alexander Graham Bell.
- The story of how the Scotsman, whose initial focus was on the deaf, transformed American communications inspired Jerry to build his own functioning telephone using coffee can lids.
- By the time he was 11, Jerry reconstructed Guglielmo Marconi's original experiments with the wireless telegraph and later built a primitive microphone transmitter that allowed him to create his own radio station in Greensboro, North Carolina, where he grew up.
- With his father's help, Jerry would load his high-stack 45 RPM record player with Conway Twitty, Brenda Lee, and the Everly Brothers, put a microphone beside the speaker and drive around the country roads to see how far the signal was reaching.
- He also devoured a radio repair correspondence course his father had ordered, which deepened his technical understanding.
- Bill Pratt was the general manager of Analog Devices, Jerry was a regional marketing manager reporting to Bill, and Powell Seymour was in charge of the team making the prototype parts.

Jerry D. Neal longed to be a vanguard in the emerging cell phone and wireless telephone communications market.

- In 1991, in the midst of a management change, Bill and Powell left Analog Devices to form their own company, RF Micro Devices, with Jerry following a short time later.
- As part of the separation, Analog Devices agreed to give Bill the rights to the radio frequency chips he'd already developed, agreed to continue paying the rent on the lab until the lease expired, and offered to sell the equipment that Bill and Powell were using at the bargain price of $70,000, and then made Bill a loan for that amount with generous repayment provisions.
- The plan was for Bill and Powell to take care of design, testing, and manufacturing while Jerry took care of marketing.
- But first, they had to raise money to launch the company.
- Before the new company was formed, several friends and business associates had indicated they were interested in investing in the startup, but when it came time to write checks, Jerry quickly encountered a plethora of creative reasons why "now" was not the right time to invest.
- The entire list of potential investors yielded not a single dollar, even though Analog Devices had spent $1.5 million developing the products RF Micro Devices planned to manufacture and sell.
- Many people had recently lost money on tech stocks and were loath to consider diving into the deep end again.
- Besides, few investors fully understood the potential commercial value of radio frequency integrated circuits.
- Even though RF Micro Devices held the rights to chips unlike anything the market had seen, people were reluctant to invest in unexplored new technology.
- Using his personal frequent flier points, in 1992 Jerry booked flights to California where he pitched the potential of the company, demonstrated the chips and talked numbers—potential revenues, rate of growth, size of the potential market and possible investor return.
- Months later, still with no clear signs of success, RF Micro Devices turned to venture capital firms despite their reputations for demanding too much control, too much ownership and too little flexibility.
- After numerous grueling sessions with venture capital firms nationwide, the three partners were told they lacked passion, needed to live in a more exciting place than Greensboro, North Carolina, to get funding, and must give up 60 percent of the company to receive $1.5 million—most of which was conditioned on hitting very aggressive benchmarks.
- For Jerry, it was a bitter pill to swallow.
- When a manufacturer made a better offer, Jerry turned down the venture capital offer, but then had to beg that the deal be put in place when the "white knight" financing literally disappeared into Mexico.
- After more than a year of work, RF Micro Devices was just getting started.
- The three partners had not taken a paycheck from RF Micro Devices in 12 months.
- The new investors owned almost two-thirds of the company; Jerry and his two partners combined held 36 percent of the company they had conceived, built and grown.

Life at Work

- With money in hand, a sales team was recruited and a catalog of products set.
- Jerry Neal and RF Micro Devices had only one problem—making the chips work as promised.
- Even though Jerry had been taught by his father to "run toward problems," not away from them, the challenges at times appeared overwhelming.
- RF Micro Devices had signed two customers interested in radio frequency technology—only neither wanted existing products.
- The first, a Canadian company, wanted to manufacture wireless motion and smoke detectors and asked Jerry's firm to provide transmitter and receiver chips.
- They had been looking for a solution for two years and were willing to pay $185,000 in engineering fees to find a solution.
- The second was a Japanese company based in California which needed a power amplifier for an upscale phone.
- However, no power amplifier had never been designed as an integrated circuit, and they were willing to pay $200,000 in engineering fees to make it happen.
- Suddenly, company projections of $1 million in first-year revenues looked promising.
- In reality, the path to making cell phones ubiquitous was littered with dozens of hard-fought failures alongside a handful of victories.
- In 1978, AT&T set up the first cellular phone system in Chicago with 2,000 subscribers; three years later Motorola established a trial system in Washington and Baltimore.
- By 1982, the Federal Communications Commission was ready to authorize commercial cellular service, mostly restricted to large cities where the huge, cumbersome "bag phones" could be serviced with towers.
- Despite the inconveniences, by 1987 a million subscribers had signed up for the service, outstripping capacity and transmission technology.
- Clearly, the future of wireless devices rested in digital technology in which the code of zeros and ones—which also operated computers—would convert and condense the voice signal to binary code, allowing a far greater number of calls to be transmitted over the same frequencies.
- RF Micro Devices believed that the semiconductor gallium arsenide, which conducts electricity six times faster than silicon, represented the future of power amplifiers even though the technology had never been used in a mass-market product.
- With one manufacturer, the price quotes were astronomically high; with another the chips failed to work.
- Customers were becoming impatient with the little startup from North Carolina that couldn't produce a workable prototype.
- Meanwhile, the venture-capital firm providing $1.5 million was demanding that the company hire a chief executive officer of their choosing.
- The staff had grown to 16—five times the size of the prior year—while revenues reached $212,000 in 1993, almost $800,000 short of the goal.

Two good-sized contracts helped Neal launch RF Micro Devices.

As Neal's company expanded, investors wanted more say in the decision-making.

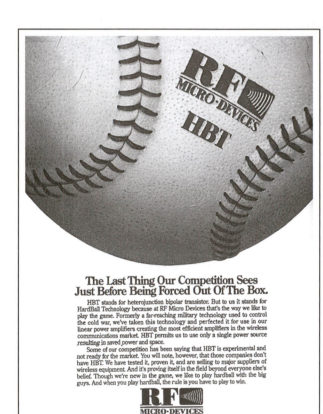

Neal's creative marketing approach brought in the sales.

- Just when RF Micro Devices needed new money, the company produced a working prototype that met all the criteria.
- Success was in the air: the chip was a powerhouse with a great potential for success—a real breakthrough in technology.
- It was Jerry's job to tell the world through advertisements in trade magazines, speeches and hundreds of presentations.
- Quickly it became clear that the industry didn't believe that gallium arsenide heterojunction bipolar transistor (HBT) could be reliable or produced at a reasonable cost.
- Most in the industry still saw it as flawed technology that only the government could afford to make work, and impractical for an integrated circuit power amplifier.
- So Jerry began giving chip samples to everyone who inquired.

- At the same time, the company had to return to its venture capital firm and ask for more money; the seed round of $1.5 million was spent.
- They asked for an extra $1.75 million and got it.
- The partners all gave up more equity in their creation, but they had little choice; they were dead in the water without new funding.
- To tell their success story, Jerry designed an advertising campaign featuring a levitating football field around the slogan "Optimum Technology Matching," with two-page advertisements that were headlined, "Unfortunately for Our Competition, We've Just Unleveled the Playing Field."
- The company then designed a second advertisement featuring a baseball that appeared to be coming straight at the reader, accompanied by the words, "The Last Thing Our Competition Sees Just Before Being Forced Out of the Box."
- Jerry then mailed hundreds of specially designed baseballs to prospective customers with a letter that described RF Micro Devices' revolutionary new product.
- And it worked.
- AT&T signed on, ordered more than 150,000 chips, and even appeared at a press conference in Washington to promote the new technology.
- The company was jubilant.
- Then, just as Jerry was anticipating millions of dollars in new revenues, AT&T canceled the order, along with the phone they had planned to introduce.

- Next up was Motorola, which was selling one million emergency two-way radios worldwide every year and eventually redesigned their phone around the little company's microchip and saved $10 million a year.
- Then came Qualcomm/Sony with its next-generation cell phone, which offered call waiting, caller identification, and call answering.
- Qualcomm had a reputation for being tough; they proved tougher and signed a letter of intent.
- At the same time, RF Micro Devices was running out of money—again.
- The company's capital needs had grown from $3 million to $5.75 million; more investors were brought in, while more equity in the company was forfeited.
- Twelve-hour days had allowed Jerry to see his dreams coming into focus, while watching his ownership interest get smaller and smaller.
- By October 1994, RF Micro Devices had grown to 36 employees, 45 standard products, extensive quality monitoring program boundaries, and a greatly expanded lab.
- As the year progressed, Motorola downsized its order, Nokia showed increased interest, Qualcomm/Sony was willing to be part of a joint advertisement, and the cell phone business was beginning to boom.
- Business was growing at 40-50 percent a year.
- Although few people had cell phones, most who knew about them were keen to have one.
- System providers could not set up systems fast enough; the demand for phones, base stations and other equipment was overwhelming.
- A maker of high-quality radar detectors, which had ordered 22,500 parts in the previous year, ordered 300,000 parts in 1995.

RF Micro Devices continued to grow and to meet their own standards for quality products.

- That's when Jerry got a phone call from Motorola: the chips were failing in emergency radios that required a zero failure rate.
- Then, another complaint: a small company in Maryland that made tiny transmitters for tracking migratory birds had also received faulty chips; trackers' scientific studies, having lost contact with the birds, were ruined.
- A solution had to be found immediately or the company's entire reputation would be lost.
- Working with Motorola, the company frantically searched for a way to troubleshoot faulty chips, only to discover that a-wire-bond was causing the problem.
- Then, in conjunction with a Motorola vendor, RF Micro Devices began testing the chips, rejecting entire batches if a faulty wire was found.
- In all, 40,000 chips—$184,000 worth, or 10 percent of the previous year's sales—ended up in the dumpster.
- As that dilemma abated, Qualcomm began increasing the pressure for delivery of its new product.

- Changing one aspect of a chip could increase one function while lowering another.
- By midsummer, Qualcomm was ready to begin production, but habitually rejected RF Micro Devices' chips as unacceptable.
- Tension was enormously high; both companies had a great deal at stake.
- Some meetings dissolved into screaming sessions.
- Jerry considered working with Qualcomm "one of the most difficult challenges of my career."
- New pricing and new testing procedures were arranged, but frustration remained high when the foundry was unable to meet the production.
- As production issues increased, the venture capitalists agreed to invest further, bringing their total commitment to $23.5 million.
- As a result, the portion of the company owned by Jerry and his two partners was down from 12 percent each at the initial investment to 2.63 percent per partner.
- The original plan, outlined by the venture capitalists, was to sell micro devices within five years and get a return on their money 10 times over.
- But RF Micro Devices' fantastic rate of growth had changed all that; as 1996 loomed, plans were underway to make the company publicly owned.
- RF Micro Devices needed to meet the exploding demands of its customers without losing its reputation for quality.

Life in the Community: Greensboro, North Carolina

- Greensboro, the third-largest city in North Carolina, was home to 223,891 residents one-third of the Piedmont Triad that embraced Greensboro-Winston-Salem-High Point, North Carolina, and counted $1 million residents.
- In 1808, Greensboro was created around a central courthouse square in the geographical center of the county, a location more easily reached by the majority of the county's citizens.
- The city was named for Major General Nathanael Greene, commander of the American forces at the Battle of Guilford Court House on March 15, 1781.
- Although the Americans lost the battle, Greene's forces inflicted such heavy casualties on the British Army that Lord Cornwallis chose to pull his battered army out of North Carolina and into Virginia.

  - This decision allowed a combined force of American and French troops to trap Cornwallis at Yorktown, Virginia, where the British were forced to surrender on October 19, 1781, thus ending the military phase of the American Revolution.
  - In the early 1840s, after Greensboro was linked to a new railroad line, the community grew substantially in size and soon became known as the "Gate City" due to its role as a transportation hub for the state.
  - The railroads transported goods to and from textile mills, which grew up with their own mill villages around the city.
  - In the 1890s, the city continued to attract attention from northern industrialists, including Moses and Ceasar Cone of Baltimore.

White Oak Cotton Mill in Greensboro, N.C.

- The Cone brothers established large-scale textile plants, changing Greensboro from a village to a city within a decade.
- By 1900, Greensboro was considered a center of the Southern textile industry, with large factories producing denim, flannel and overalls.
- During the twentieth century, Greensboro continued to expand in wealth and population.
- The city remained a major textile headquarters with the main offices of Cone, Burlington Industries, Galey & Lord, Unifi, and VF Corporation, which sold Wrangler, Lee, North Face and Nautica.
- Other industries became established in the city, including Vicks Chemical Company, maker of over-the-counter cold remedies such as VapoRub and NyQuil; Carolina Steel Corporation; and Pomona Terra Cotta Works.
- On February 1, 1960, four black college students from North Carolina Agricultural and Technical College sat down at an all-white Woolworth's lunch counter and refused to leave after they were denied service.
- Hundreds of others soon joined in this sit-in, which lasted several months.
- Similar protests quickly spread across the South, ultimately leading to the desegregation of Woolworth's and other chains.

HISTORICAL SNAPSHOT
1995

- The World Trade Organization (WTO) was established
- The most distant galaxy yet discovered (an estimated 15 billion light years away) was found by scientists using the Keck telescope in Hawaii
- The 104th U. S. Congress was the first controlled by Republicans since 1953
- San Francisco 49ers became the first NFL team to win five Super Bowls
- Yahoo! was founded in Santa Clara, California
- Astronaut Norman Thagard became the first American aboard a Russian launch vehicle, the *Soyuz TM-21*
- Mississippi ratified the 13th Amendment, the last state to abolish slavery
- The movie *Forrest Gump* won Best Picture at the 67th Academy Awards
- In Oklahoma City, 168 people were killed in the bombing of the Alfred P. Murrah Federal Building
- A Unabomber bomb killed lobbyist Gilbert Murray in Sacramento, California

- Actor Christopher Reeve was paralyzed from the neck down after falling from his horse in a riding competition
- Ceremonies in Hiroshima, Nagasaki, Washington, DC, and Tokyo marked the fiftieth anniversary of the dropping of the atomic bombs
- Microsoft released Windows 95
- The DVD, an optical disc computer storage media format, was announced
- eBay was founded
- The Million Man March was held in Washington, DC, conceived by Nation of Islam leader Louis Farrakhan
- The Dow Jones Industrial Average closed above 4,000 and 5,000, the first time the Dow surpassed two millennium marks in a single year
- The first full-length computer animated feature film, *Toy Story*, was released by Pixar Animation Studios and Walt Disney Pictures
- President Clinton signed the National Highway Designation Act, which ended the federal 55 mph speed limit
- The final original *Calvin and Hobbes* comic strip was published

Selected Prices

Art Exhibit, New York $8.00
Camcorder.. $2,700.00
Cell Phone $49.99
Chair, Walnut $195.00
Low-Flush Toilet $270.00
Roaster, Calphalon.. $99.99
Rollerblades... $34.97
Shaving Cream $0.99
Soccer Cleats $129.95
Whirlpool Tub $1,660.00

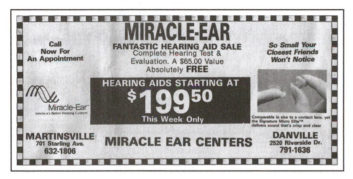

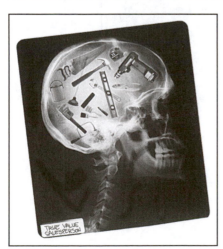

Timeline of Cell Phones and Wireless Communications

1876
Alexander Graham Bell invented the telephone. By the end of 1880, 47,900 telephones were in use in the United States.

1895
Guglielmo Marconi, an Italian inventor, proved the feasibility of radio communications by sending and receiving the first radio signal. Four years later, Marconi flashed the first wireless signal across the English Channel.

1903
The first international wireless conference was held in Berlin.

Guglielmo Marconi.

1906
Reginald Fessenden successfully completed an 11-mile wireless telephone call from his laboratory in Brant Rock, Massachusetts.

1912
The Radio Act was the first domestic legislation to address radio spectrum allocation.

1921
The Detroit Police Department began one-way radio messaging.

1941
A Motorola two-way radio was installed in a police cruiser.

1946
The first commercial mobile radiotelephone service was introduced in St. Louis.

1965
AT&T's Improved Mobile Telephone Service (IMTS) eliminated the need for push-to-talk operation and offered automatic dialing.

1968
The Federal Communications Commission (FCC) opened Docket 18262 to address questions regarding spectrum reallocation.

Students practicing at Marconi wireless school, New York City, 1912.

continued

Timeline of Cell Phones and Wireless Communications
(continued)

1972

Bell Labs received a patent for its Mobile Communications System, which described and enabled handoffs between cells.

1977

Experimental cellular systems were launched in Chicago and the Washington, DC/Baltimore region.

1981

In May, the FCC announced the decision to award two cellular licenses per market—one for a wireline company and one for a non-wireline company.

1983

Advanced Mobile Phone Service (AMPS) was released using the 800 MHz to 900 MHz frequency band and the 30 kHz bandwidth for each channel as a fully automated mobile telephone service. AMPS was the first standardized cellular service in the world.

Motorola introduced the DynaTAC mobile telephone unit, the first truly "mobile" radiotelephone. The phone, dubbed the "brick," had one hour of talk time and eight hours of standby.

On October 13, the first commercial cellular system began operating in Chicago.

In December, the second system was activated in the Baltimore/Washington, DC, corridor.

1984

The Cellular Telecommunications Industry Association was founded.

1985

The 100th cellular system was activated in New Bedford, Massachusetts.

1986

The FCC switched to a lottery system to license cellular markets. At the urging of the industry, the FCC allocated an additional 10 MHz of spectrum for cellular telecommunications; cellular subscribership topped two million with 1,000 cell sites across America.

continued

Timeline of Cell Phones and Wireless Communications
(continued)

1987
The industry topped $1 billion in revenues.

1988
CIBER Record for carriers was created, which allowed nationwide wireless services.

1989
Motorola announced the MicroTAC personal cellular phone, which used a flip-lid mouthpiece and retailed for an estimated $3,000.

1990s
RAM Mobile Data Network was brought online. CDPD packet networks began deployment. GSM cellular systems supported circuit-switched data.

1990
Nextel Communications, Inc., filed a series of waivers with the FCC to set up low-power, multiple transmitter networks in six of the top U.S. markets. Cellular subscribership surpassed five million.

1992
The FCC allocated spectrum in the 2-GHz band for emerging technologies, including Personal Communications Services (PCS). The number of cellular users passed the 10 million milestone, served by 10,000 cell sites across America.

1992
The world's first commercial text message was sent by employees of Logica CMG.

1993
Bell Labs developed the DSP1616 chip, a digital signal processor used in millions of handsets.

1994
iDEN network technology, a packet-data network that integrates paging, data communications, voice dispatch and cellular capabilities, was unveiled.

"Keep a Close Eye on the Deep End," Jerry D. Neal, *Fire in the Belly*, 2005:

Naïveté surely is a common affliction for those starting a new business. So naïve were we that we had no idea that what we were undertaking actually would be revolutionary, that we would end up drastically affecting the way people communicate and the way some huge corporations did business. We did, however, dream of creating a company that would become preeminent in this field....

Of this I feel certain: no pessimist ever could start such a business and bring it to fruition.

A confident, positive, perhaps even occasionally rosy-eyed view, and, yes, inevitable naïveté are necessities to pulling anybody through all these miseries and rare bursts of jubilation that are certain to befall those who enter such perilous depths.

Wireless tower in Nome, Alaska, 1916.

"Cellular Phones Interfering at Hospitals," *Wisconsin State Journal*, June 15, 1995:

Code blue: cardiac arrest! Doctors and nurses sprint into the hospital room and grind to a breathless halt.

The patient is lulling in bed, in the throes of nothing worse than a killer crossword puzzle. His big-shot brother-in-law is chattering away with the home office on a cellular phone.

False alarm. Blame it on cellular interference.

A growing number of hospitals are limiting the use of cellular telephones and other wireless communications for fear of such scenarios or worse.

The industry, meanwhile, is seeking ways to keep phone signals from gumming up the electronics of life-saving equipment. It wants to ensure that electromagnetic interference doesn't threaten doctors' growing use of cell phones.

In a series of interviews, hospital, industry and government officials said they didn't know of any patient injuries from cell phone interference, though many acknowledged the risk. In most cases, they said such interference amounts to a slight false reading here, a false alarm there, without harm to anyone.

"Not very often is it something that's life-threatening. A lot of times it's something that causes someone to raise an eyebrow," said Guy Knickerbocker, chief scientist at ECRI of Plymouth Meeting, Pa., a company that helps hospitals manage their high-tech equipment.

1996 Profile

Entrepreneur Maurice Jennings learned to make the big buttermilk biscuits that launched his restaurant chain, Biscuitville, Inc., from his grandma.

Life at Work

- Maurice Jennings spent summers with his grandmother in middle Tennessee, where she made biscuits, a Southern staple, and set the taste standard Maurice would use when he opened his restaurant.
- According to company legend, before she died, Erma Jennings gave her grandson Maurice a choice: inherit the family farm or her biscuit recipe.
- He took the recipe, using it to launch Biscuitville Inc., a chain of restaurants.
- A needlepoint at company headquarters in Burlington, North Carolina—and in each of the 43 restaurants—said so.
- It was a touching story if only it were true.
- Maurice cribbed the recipe from a flour sack.
- Or maybe it was a cookbook; he wasn't really sure.
- Wherever it came from, he tinkered with it until he found a taste and texture he liked.
- He ran his businesses much the same way—displaying a willingness to tinker with any idea and always remain flexible.
- Maurice started with a bread shop, then moved to pizzas before settling into a breakfast-biscuit niche.
- Maurice's biscuit-making education started when his father bought a bakery in Burlington, North Carolina, in 1941.
- There, the third-grader learned how to bake and set out carryout boxes for the wholesale operation; he also learned that if you eat three dozen doughnuts in one day when no one's looking, you won't want another doughnut for two years.
- As he grew up, Maurice worked in the bakery, played football and baseball and did everything he could to sneak into University North Carolina football games at Chapel Hill when running back Charlie "Choo Choo" Justice was playing.

Maurice Jennings struck it big with biscuits.

- Maurice and his buddies also formed "The Blue Streak Boxing Club" to stage fight exhibitions in his basement; the club was named after the blue streak left by the printer on the event tickets.
- When he was 12 years old, mornings before school were spent delivering the Greensboro newspaper starting at 5:30 a.m. and the Burlington paper in the afternoon.
- In 1950, when Maurice was 15, his father suffered a stroke and was less able to work after that.
- Maurice went to work for a movie theater, clothing store, radio stations and on a farm to help support the family.
- The summer he turned 18, Maurice thumbed a ride to Kansas to work the wheat harvest driving a truck; he slept wherever he could find a place, usually in the wheat truck, and earned $1.50 a hour—$1.00 in cash and $0.50 at the end of the season, if he stayed to the end of the harvest.
- Then, after one semester at Elon College, Maurice joined the Air Force, only to return to Burlington in 1955 to help with the family bakery ingredient business.
- By then, his father, a flour merchant, was no longer able to talk, so Maurice traveled the region developing the wholesale flour part of the business while his mother stayed home and ran the office.
- Maurice found considerable success in the bakery flour business, enough to buy his first airplane, a Beechcraft Bonanza, and use it for business travel.
- During that time, he saved $30,000—enough to start another business.
- One of Maurice's flour customers in Memphis had opened a bread store he admired, so he tried the same concept in Burlington.
- Because there was extra space in the store, Maurice added pizza to the menu, a rare commodity at that time.
- Pizzas proved so popular that the bread concept disappeared and the pizza stayed, forming the basis for a small chain of carry-out places called Pizzaville.
- By the early 1970s, the chain had grown to 12 stores throughout north-central North Carolina.
- This was followed by a steakhouse that specialized in ribeye steaks cut to order.
- In 1972, the 37-year-old Maurice re-enrolled in Elon College and took every business course they offered.

Life at Work

- Maurice Jennings remembers the exact moment he conceived of Biscuitville.
- He was on the way to the company's Chapel Hill, North Carolina, Pizzaville when it occurred to him they could take the salad bar down at night and open the next morning with a jelly bar featuring freshly made buttermilk biscuits.
- "I love sweets and could see people taking their biscuits down the line getting all kinds of jams and jellies," Maurice said.
- So he put in a jelly bar with about 40 types of jams.

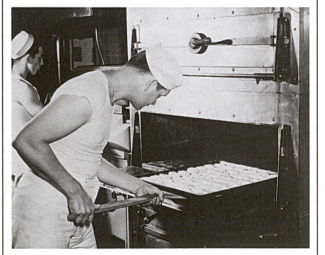

The key to success was fresh, warm biscuits.

- "People would come in and look at the jelly bar and say, 'Now ain't that a cute idea? Gimme two ham biscuits and a cup of coffee,'" Maurice said. "That lasted about two weeks. We threw the jelly bar out and kept the biscuits."
- The first all-biscuit store opened in Danville, Virginia, in 1975 in an old Rich's hamburger building.
- "It was pretty efficient, and the biscuits were always warm."
- The biscuit store in North Asheboro grossed $12,000 a week.
- "I should have dropped everything else and concentrated on Biscuitville; instead, like a true entrepreneur, I tried about a dozen different things. No use listing them: the point is, when you stumble onto something that really works, you should concentrate on that almost single-minded, like you're running a straight line."
- Before long, customers could stuff the biscuits in two dozen ways.
- Within a few years, the company made $30 million annually, just on the biscuits.
- The recipe was simple—flour, buttermilk and shortening; in the early 1990s, shortening became all-vegetable for the health-conscious.
- "The secret in making good biscuits is in handling them right, which is a physical thing, and also in keeping them young. If you let them sit there and dry out, they are not going to be any good."
- Unlike its competitors, Biscuitville doesn't do franchises, stays close to its biscuit theme and doesn't tolerate downtime.
- For a long time, the stores stayed open until 8 p.m., serving up fried chicken, green beans and other Southern dishes to the dinner crowd.
- That brought in customers at night but left a quiet afternoon.
- So the company ditched dinner and closed every day at 2 p.m.
- It also simplified the menu, emphasizing biscuit breakfasts and lunches.
- By limiting its hours, Biscuitville cut its second-largest cost—labor.
- The new schedule needed only one shift of workers.
- It also meant less sales per restaurant compared with other fast food chains.
- Each Biscuitville brought in about $645,000 a year in sales.
- A typical Bojangles' pulled in $900,000, much of it during dinner.
- But since Biscuitville concentrated on carbohydrates rather than protein, its food costs were lower and margins higher.
- In 1991, Biscuitville created a profit-sharing plan to attract the best managerial talent.

Bacon, egg, and cheese on a biscuit soon became a best-seller.

Biscuitville's high-carb, low protein menu kept food costs low.

- Part of each manager's pay was based on profit.
- Many managers didn't like the concept.
- Maurice found that profit-sharing required a different mentality; some managers would much rather know what they are going to make.
- Many of those who stayed turned the plan to their advantage; Biscuitville managers earned on average $70,000 a year.
- Maurice also learned through the years that the mundane aspects of the business such as accounting were critical to understanding the profitability and reacting accordingly.
- "I strongly believe that if you're doing poorly, you want to know why; if you are doing well, you want to know why."
- When Maurice began Biscuitville, he bought and paid for his equipment and leased the land and buildings; with some experience, he learned to do just the opposite: he leased his equipment and bought—with financing—the land and buildings.
- But buy carefully, he learned.
- "Location is the most important decision an entrepreneur can make, and it's the hardest to change."
- In 1996, the Jennings family biscuit recipe and business were passed to a new generation.
- Jennings's son, Burney, took over as president and CEO.
- During the next five years, Burney Jennings wanted to build 27 more Biscuitvilles, a growth rate of more than 60 percent.
- Much of the growth was planned in Winston-Salem, which already had eight Bojangles', and Raleigh, home to 12 Hardee's.

Biscuitville's managers made an average of $70,000 a year.

- The growth carried risks.
- Attracting and keeping good help—always a struggle in the fast-food industry—was even tougher in a tight labor market; expand too fast and you end up with new managers training newer ones, and quality plummets.
- Biscuitville planned to finance its growth internally, without help from franchising, which would spread the investment risk and responsibility for finding good help to franchisees.
- Maurice, whose strong survival instinct built the chain, said his formula for success was simple: "We move like a river. We try to go wherever it is natural to go."

Burlington, N.C., 1943.

Life in the Community: Burlington, North Carolina

- Burlington was born of the railroad, bred on the loom and built on an ability to turn adversity into opportunity.
- Alamance County, where Burlington was located, was settled by several groups of Quakers, German farmers, and Scots-Irish immigrants.
- It was the site of several American Revolutionary War battles, including the War of the Regulation, which took place prior to the actual Revolution, when citizens rebelled against the corrupt British Colonial Government.

- The Holt family was instrumental in building several different textile mills in Burlington and the surrounding towns; these textile mills provided much of the economic base on which the county would grow.
- The need of the North Carolina Railroad Company in the 1850s to locate land where it could build, repair and do maintenance on its track was the genesis of Burlington, North Carolina, which was originally dubbed "Company Shops."
- By the time the shops were completed in 1857, the village had grown to 27 buildings.
- Thirty-nine white men, 20 Negro slaves and two free Negroes were employed in or around the shops.
- In 1887, after the North Carolina Railroad Company transferred its operations to Manchester, Virginia, and the stores at Company Shops were closed, a committee of the town's leading citizens renamed the community "Burlington."
- The City of Burlington was incorporated and a charter was issued by the state legislature on February 14, 1893.
- Textiles, in particular, hosiery, took the place of the railroads and as the century turned, many new jobs were created, making Burlington "The Hosiery Center of the South."
- In the 1920s, with the financial support from the Chamber of Commerce, Burlington Mills was begun—which became the largest textile maker in the world.
- But that company faced adversity immediately.
- The market for its cotton goods fell into depression, so the mill switched to a new and untried manmade fiber—rayon.
- On that product, Burlington Mills would become an industrial giant.
- During World War II, an aircraft factory was opened, adding new citizens to Burlington's work force.
- After the war, Western Electric came, adding electronics to the city's economic base.
- After textiles suffered a severe decline in the 1970s, when unemployment rose to almost 20 percent, the local leadership embarked on a diversification campaign so Burlington would no longer rely on a single industry.
- The city's largest single employer in 1996 was a medical diagnostic company.
- Employing 3,000 people, LabCorp was one of the largest clinical laboratory companies in the world, had its headquarters and several testing facilities in Burlington, and was the county's largest employer.
- Burlington had a population of 40,000 in 1996 and was part of the Piedmont Triad region of the state.
- Biscuitville, a regional fast food chain, and Gold Toe Brands, a manufacturer of socks, were both based in Burlington.

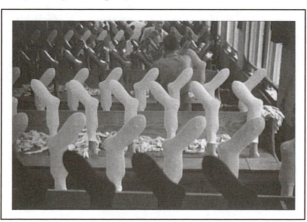

HISTORICAL SNAPSHOT
1996

- Motorola introduced the Motorola StarTAC Wearable Cellular Telephone, the world's smallest and lightest mobile phone
- The first version of the Java programming language was released
- Chess computer "Deep Blue" defeated world chess champion Garry Kasparov for the first time
- Canadian singer Alanis Morissette became the youngest person to win the top honor, Album of the Year, at the 38th Annual Grammy Awards
- *Braveheart* won Best Picture at the 68th Academy Awards, hosted by Whoopi Goldberg
- Suspected "Unabomber" Theodore Kaczynski was arrested at his Montana cabin
- Major League Soccer in America began
- The Keck II telescope was dedicated in Hawaii
- The Supreme Court ruled against a law that prevented cities in the state of Colorado from taking any action to protect the rights of homosexuals
- The Hoover Institution released a report that global warming would reduce mortality in the United States and provide Americans with valuable benefits
- In Philadelphia, Pennsylvania, a panel of federal judges blocked a law against indecency on the internet
- The Nintendo 64 video game system was released in Japan
- Dolly the sheep, the first mammal to be successfully cloned from an adult cell, was born at the Roslin Institute in Midlothian, Scotland
- Martina Hingis became the youngest person in history at age 15 to win at Wimbledon in the Ladies' Doubles event
- Michael Johnson won the 200-meter finals of the 1996 Summer Olympics in Atlanta with a world-record time of 19.32 seconds
- NASA announced that the ALH 84001 meteorite, thought to originate from Mars, contained evidence of primitive life forms
- Osama bin Laden wrote "The Declaration of Jihad on the Americans Occupying the Country of the Two Sacred Places," a call for the removal of American military forces from Saudi Arabia
- President Clinton signed the Comprehensive Nuclear-Test-Ban Treaty at the United Nations

continued

HISTORICAL SNAPSHOT *(continued)*
1996

- In the U.S. presidential election, Democratic incumbent Bill Clinton defeated Republican challenger Bob Dole to win his second term
- Mother Teresa received honorary U.S. citizenship
- Federal Reserve Board Chairman Alan Greenspan gave a speech in which he suggested that "irrational exuberance" may have "unduly escalated asset values"

Selected Prices

Advil, 50 Count $3.99
Bathroom Tissue, 12-Pack $5.49
Cordless Drill $129.00
Cutlery Set $9.99
Fishing Reel $99.99
Gas Grill $259.00
Pizza, Little Caesar's $12.95
Scanner $49.00
Studio Apartment, NY, Month $1,300.00
Tennis Racquet $79.99

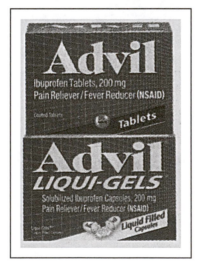

Fast Food and Chain Restaurant Timeline

1916
- Nathan's Famous Hot Dogs

1921
- White Castle Hamburgers
- A&W

1925
- Howard Johnson's
- Orange Julius
- Maid-Rite

1932
- Krystal

1934
- Steak 'n Shake

1936
- Carvel Ice Cream
- Papa Gino's
- Big Boy

1937
- Krispy Kream

1939
- Country Kitchen

1940
- Dairy Queen

1945
- Baskin Robbins

1947
- Shoney's
- Bell's Burger

1948
- McDonalds
- In-N-Out-Burger
- CoCo's

1950
- Whataburger
- Dunkin' Donuts

1951
- Jack-in-the-Box

1952
- Kentucky Fried Chicken
- Church's Chicken
- Fatburger

1953
- Denny's

1954
- Burger King
- Shakey's
- El Tonto
- Taco Tia

1958
- International House of Pancakes (IHOP)
- Sizzler
- Pizza Hut

1959
- Little Caesars
- Taco Time
- Pancake House

1960
- Domino's Pizza
- Hardee's

1962
- Taco Bell

1964
- Arbys
- Blimpie
- Villa Pizza

continued

Fast Food and Chain Restaurant Timeline *(continued)*

1965
- TGI Friday
- Subway

1967
- Chick-fil-A
- Minnie Pearl Chicken

1968
- Red Lobster
- Braum Ice Cream

1969
- Long John Silver
- Capt. D's
- Cracker Barrel
- Wendy's

1971
- Starbucks

1972
- Popeye's
- The Cheesecake Factory
- Ruby Tuesdays
- Godfather's Pizza

1975
- Chili's
- Miguels Jr.
- Chi-Chi's

1978
- Chuck E. Cheese
- Damon's

1980
- Applebees
- Fuddruckers

1981
- Buffalo Wild Wings
- Farmboys
- Papa Aldos

1982
- Olive Garden
- Dave and Busters

1983
- Hooters
- Quizno's
- Miami Subs

1984
- Cafe Express
- American Café

1985
- Boston Market
- Cinnabon

1986
- Carrabba's Italian Grill
- Manhattan Bagel

1987
- Outback Steak House
- Cold Stone Creamery
- Market Broiler

1988
- Zaxby's
- Baja Fresh

1989
- Pretzel Maker

1993
- Texas Roadhouse Grill
- Atlanta Bread Company

1994
- Juice It Up

1996
- Bahama Breeze

"And Now...Biscuit Mania," Craig Webb,
European Stars & Stripes, March 16, 1980:

Not too many years ago, the ham biscuit was to be found only in back-road Southern diners.

It had and has, its devoted fans. Critics, too.

Some call them light as only home-baked biscuits can be. Some said that those home-cooked biscuits weren't always so light.

Brace yourself, Yankees. The fast food industry has hold of the ham biscuit; sausage, too.

In pursuit of the breakfast trade, Wendy's, Hardee's, 7-Eleven, even the golden arches crowd have been testing them, mostly on Southerners.

There is the story of the New York girl who came to Raleigh, North Carolina, hungry. She wanted a bagel. Her Southern friend didn't know bagels. He brought her a sausage biscuit.

It didn't look like a bagel. Biscuits are kind of white and golden with no hard crust, generally. They taste different. And there's the meat—patty or slice. Sometimes it sticks out. Sometimes it stays in.

They cost $0.40 plain, around a dollar stuffed. Size varies. Some are rounded as a telephone dial, a bit thicker. Others are big as a hamburger bun. But what he bought her came close to your average bagel, but no hole.

It is said, after that, that she gave up bagels for biscuits, the sausage kind. Ham, too.

Maybe the fast food chains heard that story. They figured there's a market. Several are moving to the North and West. There's the 7-Elevens. Alicia Martin, of that Dallas-based chain, says they've had sausage biscuits in their artillery for seven years.

continued

"And Now...Biscuit Mania,"(continued)

She boasts they are now in 6,700 7-Elevens in 42 states and the District of Columbia. "One of our best-selling food items," she says.

At Hardee's chains, they began offering biscuits at 900 outlets last year. Now biscuits account for 12 percent of sales.

"It's a resounding success," said Hardee's Ron Werthelm. He said Hardee's Western outlets are offering biscuits now. Northern franchises will be pushing them this spring.

McDonald's is test marketing ham and sausage biscuits in parts of Virginia and the Raleigh area. Wendy's has them in Raleigh and is trying them out in Ohio.

The ultimate in biscuit mania is a 17-store Virginia-based chain called Biscuitville. The store offers 16 kinds of biscuits, including pork tenderloin, cheese, and egg. There's talk of a beefsteak biscuit; fried chicken, too.

The people who speak for the chains say biscuits make sense for commuting breakfasters. They contain neither the gooey filling of doughnuts nor the sticky icing of sweet rolls on which the quickie breakfaster has been hardened. There is only biscuit and filling, a combination that doesn't crumble or spill.

And they're simple to make, consisting mainly of milk, flour and eggs. They're filling.

While a piece of toast has 70 calories, a yeast doughnut 175, the typical sausage biscuit weighs in at nearly 300.

Marjorie Donnelly, a home economist with North Carolina's agricultural extension service, says ham and sausage biscuits probably were invented by poor blacks who used starchy baked goods to fill out a meal.

Wayne Bunning, operational director for the Biscuitville chain, said Biscuitville started in 1971 when he and the other owners of the six-store pizza chain decided to sell biscuits during the hours before the pizza trade began. The flour and ovens they used for pizza crusts were easily adaptable to biscuits. Soon some of the stores were making more money selling biscuits than pizza.

In the late 1977, Hardee's conducted its first test. The company is based in Rocky Mount, North Carolina. Half its stores are in six other states, an area acquainted with biscuits.

"The educational process in the Midwest and the North is more difficult...so your advertising must key in to explain what a biscuit is," Wertheim said.

Speaking for McDonald's, Stephanie Skurdy said their biscuit tests have met with "a certain degree of success" but may not be sold in all of the nation's 4,860 McDonald's.

Wendy's said it has been trying sweet rolls and English muffins along with biscuits in Lancaster and Toledo, Ohio. The company hasn't decided yet which to sell nationwide. One chain in the breakfast trade, Burger King, is staying clear of biscuits for now.

"People throughout the country have a certain expectation for breakfast," said Paul Reinhard, manager of corporate public relations.

"Fast Food Industry Boxing Over Plastic Foam," *Chicago Daily Herald*, November 11, 1990:

Call it the environmental burger war.

Spurred on by a growing number of environmentally conscious customers, the fast food industry is getting into an argument about which company decided to make less trash first.

The latest combatant is Burger King Corp., the Miami-based number two chain.

Burger King burst forth Wednesday with newspaper advertisements implying that archrival McDonald's Corp. is a Johnny-come-lately to the world of environmental consciousness.

"Welcome to the club," said Burger King ad. "We wonder what the planet would be like if you had joined us in 1955."

At issue is a much publicized announcement by McDonald's on November 1 that they will no longer serve sandwiches in convenient but non-biodegradable plastic foam boxes.

Environmentalists have argued for some time that hamburger packaging of this sort is a waste and a hazard because it is used only briefly, then sits around making landfills full.

In announcing the decision, Ed Rensi, president of U.S. operations at McDonald's, said that other fast food companies are likely to follow the lead set by McDonald's.

But Burger King says it never used plastic foam to package its sandwiches. Instead, it packages its hamburger in paper boxes.

Foodmaker Inc.'s Jack-in-the-Box chain, a smaller rival of McDonald's said it had already eliminated foam packaging from 93 percent of its menu items and hopes to drop all of it within the next few months.

1998 News Feature

"Toying With Science," *Chicago Daily Herald*, **October 4, 1998:**

A curious hybrid of math professor and poet, Chuck Hoberman considers himself an accidental toy maker. "I didn't set out to make toys," says Hoberman, a lanky 42-year-old known in the play business as the erudite inventor of the Hoberman Sphere, a collapsible, skeletal ball made of brightly colored plastic. "But it's been a revelation to see the huge variety of relationships that people have with toys. The world of toys is a place where people share whatever is neat and exciting to them."

Hoberman, who has a bachelor of fine arts degree from Cooper Union and a master's degree in engineering from Columbia University, best represents a new breed of start-up toy makers specializing in colorful, versatile, tactile and refreshingly non-digital playthings. Their toys convey a 1990s sensibility, embodying the current buzz-words of "innovation" and "interactivity." Relying on a child's own ingenuity rather than force-fed Hollywood or gender-specific imagery, they are as mysterious to the uninitiated as their names: Chaos, K'nex and Zoob, to name other leaders of the pack. All have been developed by entrepreneurs like Hoberman, who share a passion for art and science. Their toys, which have the appeal of modern abstract sculpture, introduce children to complex mathematical and scientific concepts through the universal language of play.

In the last three years, Hoberman's toy company, Hoberman Designs, has released the full-size ($45 to $55) and mini editions of his sphere ($18 to $23), as well as a fold-up flying disk called the Pocket Flight Ring ($7). (Prices are suggested retail.) All are child-friendly versions of Hoberman's breakthrough engineering feat: the elegant, enigmatic Unfolding Structure.

This design, which has been applauded by architects and industrial designers alike, consists of small, individual pieces connected by pivoting joints. This hinge system allows a geometric form, like a sphere or polyhedron, to mechanically blossom or contract while retaining its original shape. This explains the magical, morphing quality of Hoberman's toys, which children can bounce, roll, throw, wear or just plain analyze and admire.

The design of the Unfolding Structure, Hoberman explains, can be applied to anything from easily retractable surgical instruments to gigantic stadium domes that dilate gracefully like the pupil of an eye—inventions he is currently developing.

"They expand, like we do as creatures," he says, describing his toys as a chorus of ambulance siren wails outside the downtown Manhattan loft where he works. "They echo the movements of clouds, of fireworks."

As if his left brain has suddenly scrambled to keep up with his right, Hoberman adds: "I always wonder what the folks who purchase our products discover. I think what they see in these objects are relationships of a mathematical nature. And what is happening, hopefully, is that people are exposed to the pleasure of mathematics and geometry."

The most versatile of the new, sculptural, science-based toys is Zoob, a system of interlinking plastic pieces. Think of Legos on steroids, Tinkertoys on caffeine, Erector sets with an honorary degree from MIT, and you have a basic idea of what Zoob—an acronym of sorts for the disciplines of zoology, ontology, ontogeny and botany—represents.

The five basic Zoob units, which incorporate patented ball-and-socket, hinge and flexible saddle-joint shapes, can connect in over 20 different ways. Available in sets ranging from $8 to $80, Zoob can create anything from movable models of dinosaurs and spiders to stylish, usable handbags or functional tables.

"Zoob is parallel to a language or an alphabet," says its inventor, Michael Grey, 36, as he sits in a conference room at the San Francisco headquarters of Primordial, the two-year-old toy and media company he started with his business partner Matt Brown, a lawyer. Resembling a youthful, black-clad Santa Claus who sports stubble rather than a beard, Grey is also a respected artist whose work is included in the collection of the Museum of Modern Art in New York.

Primordial's offices are decorated with Zoob creations, ranging from a flamboyant lamp to a bumpy, armorlike dress. Artful Zoob constructions dangle from the ceiling like Alexander Calder mobiles and hang on the wall like Mark Rothko canvases.

"Zoob really is its own medium," says Grey, who, like Hoberman, holds disparate degrees: a bachelor of science in genetics from the University of California at Berkeley and a master of fine arts from Yale University. Fittingly, Grey likes to compare Zoob to the ultimate medium, DNA, the building block of life itself. One of the easiest constructions you can make with Zoob, Grey is quick to point out, is a three-dimensional likeness of DNA's double helix.

Like Zoob, K'nex and Chaos are sophisticated scions of classic construction toys. Both Joel Glickman, the inventor of K'nex, and Jim Rothbarth, the creator of Chaos, describe their products with powerful metaphors. They make it clear, as do Hoberman and Grey, that their toys are far from mere gizmos or gewgaws; they're subtle learning tools and effective channels for creativity.

Glickman, 57, who has a bachelor of fine arts degree from Syracuse University and is based in Hatfield, Pennsylvania, developed K'nex 10 years ago while he was working for the Rodon Group, his family's successful plastic-manufacturing business. He calls K'nex "three-dimensional crayons, an intellectual exercise in problem-solving." This colorful, ever-expanding system of plastic rods, wheels, panels and connectors can be used to build anything from life-size grandfather clocks to bird models with flappable wings to working mini-roller coasters. (Sets range from $2 to $110; the sophisticated versions include motors or, most recently, solar panels.) Through playing with K'nex, children can unwittingly learn about eclectic topics like animal anatomy, environmentally safe energy and centrifugal force.

"I remember how I just turned off in class when I was a kid learning about centrifugal force," Glickman recalls. "What if a kid built a small roller coaster himself and asked, 'Why doesn't the car fall off the tracks?'" Glickman muses. "Now imagine that someone tells him the answer is centrifugal force. Suddenly, physics has a context that the kid can identify with."

Rothbarth, 49, who holds an engineering degree from Washington University and designed electronic and navigation equipment before starting his toy company last year, says any creation built with the Chaos construction system is a "kinetic sculpture." In fact, Rothbarth was inspired by the beauty and dynamism of the kinetic sculptures of George Rhoads, whose work Rothbarth first encountered at the Magic House, St. Louis Children's Museum.

With the Chaos system of plastic tubes and snap-on connectors, children can design vertical structures that almost always resemble Rube Goldberg contraptions. The goal is to roll a ball from the top of the piece to the bottom. (Balls are included in the sets, which range from $60 for the starter version to $135 for the master set.) The ball is to pass smoothly through a series of chutes, trampolines, arcs and other mix-and-match accessories (there is even a motorized elevator of sorts), assembled into a dynamic pathway by the child.

"The ball is a unique illustration that actually teaches kids about physics," explains Rothbarth, who is based in St. Louis. "At the same time, playing with Chaos is always an open-ended exploration. Kids can be creative artists, too."

This new crop of decidedly user-defined toys helps children understand "how to deal with frustration when things don't work," says Paul Doherty, an experimental physicist and senior staff scientist at the Exploratorium, a hands-on museum and teacher-training center in San Francisco. "They challenge kids to discover what fits and what doesn't."

Doherty, a lively, pony-tailed man who demonstrates scientific principles on popular television shows like *Late Show With David Letterman*, says another benefit is an increased familiarity with mathematical, scientific and esthetic patterns. Children retain an understanding of the relationships among geometric forms as they complete their academic careers, says Doherty, whether they're studying design, computer science, art history, medicine or architecture.

2000-2010

The opening decade of the 21st century brought two recessions, two wars, a divided nation armed with a plethora of personal entertainment creations, each sporting unfamiliar names such as iPods, YouTube and Facebook. Hybrid cars, wind farms and solar panels all splashed onto the scene as America struggled to reduce its dependence on foreign oil or simply to avoid rising gas prices. Yet, history will record the century began in the United States on September, 11, 2001, when four American commercial airliners were hijacked and used as weapons of terror. After the tragedies at the World Trade Center in New York, Shanksville, Pennsylvania, and the Pentagon in Washington, DC, Americans felt vulnerable to a foreign invasion for the first time in decades. America's response to the attacks was to dispatch U.S. forces around the world in a "War on Terror." The first stop was Afghanistan, where a new brand of terrorist group known as al-Qaeda had planned and executed the attacks under the protection of the country's Taliban rulers. America's technologically superior weaponry was impressively displayed as the Afghan government was quickly overthrown, although capturing al-Qaeda leader Osama bin Laden and stabilizing a new government proved more vexing. With the shell-shocked economy in overall decline and the national debt increasing at a record pace, the United States rapidly shifted from Afghanistan to Iraq. Despite vocal opposition from traditional allies such as Germany and France, President George W. Bush launched Operation Iraqi Freedom with the goal of eliminating the regime of Saddam Hussein and his cache of weapons of mass destruction. The invasion resulted in worldwide demonstrations, including some of America's largest protest marches since the Vietnam War. As in the invasion of Afghanistan, the

U.S. achieved a rapid military victory, but struggled to secure the peace. When no weapons of mass destruction were found, soldiers continued fighting while an internal, religious civil war erupted; support for the war waned and vocal protest increased.

Despite the cost of the war, the falling value of the dollar and record high oil prices, the American economy began to recover by 2004. Unemployment declined, new home purchases continued to surge, and the full potential of previous computer innovation and investment impacted businesses large and small. Men and women of all ages began to buy and sell their products on the Internet. eBay created the world's largest yard sale; Amazon demonstrated, despite sneering critics, that it could be the bookstore to the world; and we all learned to Google, whether to find the exact wording of a Shakespearian sonnet or the menu at Sarah's Pizza Parlor two blocks away. At the same time, globalization took on a new meaning and political import as jobs—thanks to computerization—moved to India, China or the Philippines, where college-educated workers were both cheap and eager. American manufacturing companies that once were the centerpiece of their community's economy closed their U.S. factories to become distributors of furniture made in China, lawn mowers made in Mexico or skirts from Peru. The resulting structural change that pitted global profits and innovation against aging textile workers unable to support their families resulted in a renewed emphasis in America on education and innovation. If the U.S. was to maintain its economic dominance, the pundits said, innovative ideas and research would lead the way.

As the decade drew to a close, after eight years of the presidency of George W. Bush, America's economy was in recession—the victim of its own excesses: too much consumer borrowing, extensive speculation in the housing market and widespread use of "exotic" financial instruments that failed to reduce risk. In the wake of the economic crash, some of the most respected firms on Wall Street disappeared through mergers or collapse, unemployment topped 10 percent and consumer confidence plummeted. When newly elected President Barack Obama took office in 2009, America was at war in Iraq and Afghanistan, the federal government was spending billions of dollars to save the banking system and the price of oil was on the rise. President Obama made universal health care a key element of his first year in office, igniting controversy and exposing the deep divisions that existed nationwide.

Sports during the first decade of the twenty-first century became a 24/7 obsession for many. With the dramatic expansion of the Internet, cell phones, the addition of new cable channels and a plethora of new sporting events, America was clearly addicted to sports—including many whose lure was tinged with danger. NASCAR expanded its geographic reach and began challenging football for most viewers, the Williams sisters brought new life to professional tennis and Tiger Woods continued his winning ways on the golf course. Despite a decade of falling television ratings, NBC paid an astonishing 2.3 billion for the combined rights to the 2004 and 2008 Summer and the 2006 Winter Olympic Games.

Professional women, who for decades had struggled to rise past the glass ceiling in their companies, began to find bigger opportunities in the 2000s. Significantly, the promotion of a woman to a top slot in a Fortune 500 company ceased to make headlines. Some top female CEOs even began to boldly discuss the need for more balance the workplace. Yet surveys done at mid-decade showed that more Americans were working longer hours than ever before to satisfy the increasing demands of the marketplace and their own desire for more plentiful material goods. In some urban markets the average home price passed $400,000; average credit card debt continued to rise and the price of an average new car, with typical extras, passed $20,000.

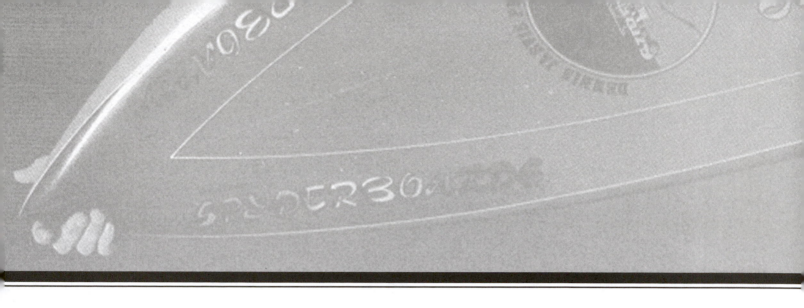

2008 Profile

Rey Banatao believed that the transformation of the surfboard industry was at hand—similar to the virtual world of computers: "Now it's like the dot.com period for surfing," he said.

Life at Home

- Thirty-four-year-old Rey Banatao and his brother Desi wanted to fundamentally change the way surfboards were built.
- The secret, they believed, was sugar beet oil.
- For decades the surfboard industry had been ripping through polyurethane foam cores, known as blanks, coated in petrochemical solvents and polyester resin—all wrapped in fiberglass.
- In most cases, modern surfboard blanks were so heavily packed with chemicals, including volatile organic compounds, they could be deemed carcinogenic by the EPA.
- This gave the impression that surfers, shapers, and glassers were willing participants in the destruction and soiling of the environment their lifestyle depends upon.
- Surfboard manufacturering, which had long been a garage-scale business, was dominated by shapers, who turned out a few hundred surfboards a year, priced at around $700 each, and netted maybe $40,000 a year.
- Rey and his brother, both surfers and materials scientists, were convinced that their semi-natural boards performed as well as those made from fiberglass.
- Now they had to prove it to the surfing community.
- When the two brothers began the project, they were definitely outsiders.
- Rey was finishing up postdoctoral research on nanomaterials at the University of California, Los Angeles.
- Desi had a master's degree in materials science from Berkeley, and had just lost his job at a Portland Oregon engineering company when his projection TV technology became obsolete.

Rey Banatao and his brother Desi, resolved to make a better and greener surfboard.

- Their father, a venture capitalist and semiconductor engineer, proposed that they start a company to make use of their tech degrees.
- Growing up, the brothers fell in love with board sports: snowboarding, skateboarding and surfing.

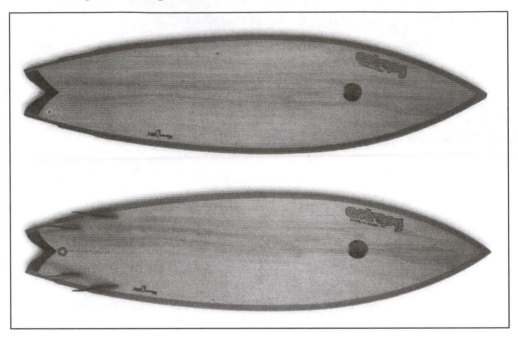

With their father's advice, the Banatao brothers started their own company, Entropy.

- They started Entropy to make equipment for all these sports.
- They also wanted to understand and respect the traditions that had brought board sports like surfing to prominence.
- The ancient Hawaiian people did not consider surfing a mere recreational activity, but something to be integrated into their culture.
- Prior to the surfer entering the ocean, the priest would bless the undertaking with a spiritual ceremony devoted to the construction of the surfboard.
- Hawaiians would carefully select one of three types of trees, including the koa, then dig the tree out and place a fish in the hole as an offering to the gods.
- Selected craftsmen of the community were then hired to shape, stain, and prepare the boards, employing three primary shapes: the *'olo*, *kiko'o*, and *alaia*.
- The *'olo was* thick in the middle and gradually got thinner towards the ends.
- The *kiko'o* ranged in length from 12-18 feet, while the *alaia* board was around nine feet long and required great skill to ride and master.
- Aside from the preparatory stages prior to entering the water, the most skilled surfers were often of the upper class, including chiefs and warriors who surfed the best waves on the island.
- These upper-class Hawaiians gained respect through their enduring ability to master the waves and this art the Hawaiians referred to as surfing.
- In 1907, George Freeth was brought to California from Hawaii to demonstrate surfboard riding as a publicity stunt to promote the opening of the Los Angeles-Redondo-Huntington Railroad owned by Henry Huntington.

Even Jack London had tried surfing on his visit to Hawaii.

- Surfing on the East Coast of the United States began in Virginia Beach, Virginia, in 1912, when James Matthias Jordan, Jr. captivated the locals astride a 110-pound (50 kg), nine-foot Hawaiian redwood.
- Around the same time, Hawaiians living close to Waikiki began to revive surfing, and soon reestablished surfing as a sport.
- Duke Kahanamoku, "Ambassador of Aloha," Olympic medalist, and avid waterman, helped expose surfing to the world.
- Author Jack London, already famous for his adventure books, wrote about the sport after having attempted it on his visit to the islands.
- As surfing progressed, innovations in board design exploded.
- In the 1960s, the release of the film *Gidget* boosted the sport's popularity immensely, moving surfing from an underground culture into a national fad and packing many surf breaks with previously unheard-of crowds.
- B-movies and surf music authored by the Beach Boys and Surfaris formed the world's first ideas of surfing and surfers, while the 1980s included portrayals of surfers represented by characters like Jeff Spicoli from *Fast Times at Ridgemont High*.
- The evolution of the short board in the late 1960s to the performance hotdogging of the 1980s and the epic professional surfing of the 1990s brought more and more exposure.

Movies and bands helped popularize surfing.

Life at Work
- The Banatao brothers began working on bio-boards in 2006, opening a makeshift office in the basement of an office building owned by their father.
- They first focused on snowboards by combining epoxy resins with carbon nanotubes to create materials that would resist cracking.
- The nanotubes acted as barriers to a crack, preventing it from lengthening, but too many nanotubes make some materials unworkable.
- With the help of a Ph.D. student from Berkeley, they found the optimal concentration of tubes and proudly crafted a prototype for a custom snow ski company in Idaho.

Banatao searched for a way to make surf boards environmentally safer and "greener."

- The technology was a success, but the company didn't like the design, so the brothers turned to surfboards created with nanotube technology and then shaped with simple hand tools.
- Again the bio-board was a success, but the grayish boards were a sleeper.
- That's when Rey went green.
- In December 2005, the surfboard blank manufacturing company Clark Foam shut its doors without warning, reportedly due to a mass of workers' compensation lawsuits and strict Environmental Protection Agency regulations.
- The vacuum left by Clark Foam's demise opened a giant door for new innovations in surfboard construction, including the manufacturing of "greener" surfboard materials.
- "It forced the industry to be open-minded," Rey said.
- Innovations included ways to effectively use bamboo in surfboard construction, as well as bio-plastic leash plugs and removable fin systems.
- For the committed, surfing was a spiritual enterprise—a connection with a divine energy unleashed by the interaction of wind, water and ocean-floor geography.
- The fact that the board used to tap into this energy was made from petroleum-based foam, polyester resins and chemically treated fiberglass had long been surfing's quiet contradiction.
- A broken board tossed in a landfill will take generations to biodegrade; the plastic fins probably never will.
- Even the thin strip of wood that runs down the middle to provide strength came at an environmental cost—a minuscule yield from the raw material from which it is milled.

Banatao's boards had to be strong, perform well, and look good.

- A wave of experimentation sought to detoxify surfboards by using materials that suggested the Whole Earth catalog rather than the periodic table of elements: hemp, bamboo, kelp and silk instead of fiberglass; foam made from soy and sugar rather than polyurethane, which is composed of toluene diisocyanate, or TDI, a possible carcinogen that can be inhaled and absorbed through the skin; and adhesive resins made from linseed, pine and vegetable oils.

- But changing the way surfboards were made had proved difficult.
- The few who have sought to go greener have struggled not only with finding just the right materials, but also with overcoming resistance from shapers and professional surfers reluctant to fix what they don't consider broken.
- Making a performance surfboard—one that flexes and maneuvers correctly—was a black art.
- Shapers work quickly; their tools and techniques have been refined by years of working with Clark Foam.
- Rey had chosen to have their foam blanks made from sugar beet oil instead of polyurethane because chemically, the beet polymer was almost identical to polyurethane, but could be processed using much less toxic chemicals.
- Rey then wrapped the blanks in the layer of hemp cloth to fine-tune their flex and feel; the hemp rendered each board a yellowish color.
- Ray learned the craft from a do-it-yourself website and asked his friends to test his early efforts.
- "There have been a couple of boards breaking in bad situations, but everyone is still alive" said Desi.
- They finished developing the bio-board two years later, completing several dozen samples in their Santa Monica garage that doubled as the company headquarters.
- The challenge was then winning the respect of California surfers, who often maintained long-standing relationships with local shapers.

A few broken boards were to be expected.

- The brothers had spent $150,000 on the bio-board, mostly borrowed from their wives; thus far, only two dozen boards had been sold.
- The company needed to move 300 boards to gross $200,000 and break even.
- Rey was hoping that several of the local superstars of the sport would embrace his enviro ethic and help launch the green board revolution.
- After all, Rey knew his philosophy was sound and the quality of his boards excellent; the only thing he didn't know was whether enough surfers would be willing to pay for them.
- Timing, Rey understood, was everything in surfing and in business.

Life in the Community: Santa Monica, California
- Santa Monica, California, situated on Santa Monica Bay and surrounded on three sides by Los Angeles, had always been known as a resort town.
- Named for Saint Monica of Hippo, the area was first visited by Spaniards on her feast day.
- First incorporated in 1886, Santa Monica waged a battle with Los Angeles in the 1890s to be designated as the Southern Pacific Railroad's seaport and lost, thereby preserving the charm of the town.
- In 1895, Ocean Park was developed as an amusement park and residential projects, followed by a race track and a golf course.

- By 1900, amusement piers were becoming enormously popular, stimulated by the Pacific Electric Railroad's ability to transport people from across the Greater Los Angeles area to the beaches of Santa Monica.
- At the same time, Santa Monica experienced a growing population of Asian-Americans, primarily Japanese fishermen and Chinese laborers; white Americans were often well disposed towards the Japanese but condescending to the Chinese.
- After the Ocean Park Pier burned down in 1912, Fraser's Million Dollar amusement pier was built, which claimed to be the largest in the world at 1,250 feet long and 300 feet wide.

Two Piers, 1916.

- The pier housed a spacious dance hall, two carousels, the Crooked House funhouse, the Grand Electric Railroad, the Starland Vaudeville Theater, Breaker's Restaurant and a Panama Canal model exhibit.
- Next came auto racing, culminating in events that by 1919 were attracting 100,000 people, at which point the city halted them.
- In the 1920s, Donald Wills Douglas, Sr. founded the Douglas Aircraft Company and built a factory.
- In 1924, two Douglas-built planes circumnavigated the globe, covering 27,553 miles in 175 days, and were greeted on their return on September 23, 1924, by a crowd of 200,000.
- The prosperity of the 1920s also fueled a population boost from 15,000 to 32,000 and a downtown construction boom.
- Beach volleyball is believed to have been developed in Santa Monica during this time.
- Surfing guru Duke Kahanamoku brought a form of the game with him from Hawaii when he took a job as athletic director at the Beach Club.
- Competitions began in 1924 with six-person teams, and by 1930 the first game with two-person teams took place.

- The La Monica Ballroom, which opened in 1924 on the Santa Monica Pier, was capable of accommodating 10,000 dancers in its over 15,000-square-foot area and hosted many national radio and television broadcasts in the early days of these networks.

- From 1958 to1962, the ballroom became one of the largest roller-skating rinks in the western U.S.

- Comedian Will Rogers bought a substantial ranch in Santa Monica Canyon in 1922, where he played polo with friends Spencer Tracy, Walt Disney and Robert Montgomery.

- Upon his untimely death, it was discovered that he had generously deeded to the public the ranch now known as Will Rogers State Historic Park, Will Rogers State Park, and Will Rogers State Beach.

- The Great Depression hit Santa Monica hard; numerous resort hotels went bankrupt.

Arcadia Bath House.

- Muscle Beach, located just south of the Santa Monica Pier, started to attract gymnasts and body builders who put on free shows for the public, and continues to do so today.

- At the outbreak of World War II, the Douglas plant's business grew astronomically, employing as many as 44,000 people in 1943.

- To defend against air attacks, set designers from the Warner Brothers Studios prepared elaborate camouflage that disguised the factory and airfield.

- Never fully shedding its resort personality, Santa Monica was also home to the rock and roll club, The Cheetah, which featured performers such as the Doors, Alice Cooper, Pink Floyd, Love, the Mothers of Invention, the Seeds, Buffalo Springfield and others.

- The completion of the Santa Monica Freeway in 1966 brought the promise of new prosperity, though at the cost of decimating the Pico neighborhood that had been a leading African-American enclave on the Westside.

- The Douglas plant closed in 1968, depriving Santa Monica of its largest employer.

- During the 1970s, a remarkable number of notable fitness- and health-related businesses started in the city, creating the Supergo bicycle shop chain, the Santa Monica Track Club, which trained Olympians such as Carl Lewis, and Gold's Gym.

- The city's economy began to recover in the 1980s and with it, the resort feel of Santa Monica.

- After a hurricane badly damaged the pier, rundown stores and bars, the pier and shopping areas were extensively renovated.

- The failed Santa Monica Mall was transformed into the Santa Monica Promenade, and between 1988 and 1998, taxable sales in the city grew 440 percent, quadrupling city revenues.

- The increasingly upscale nature of the city was the cause of some tensions between newcomers and longtime residents nostalgic for the more bohemian, countercultural past.
- Nevertheless, with the recent corporate additions of Yahoo! and Google, gentrification continued.

Venice Pier, 1924.

HISTORICAL SNAPSHOT
2008

- During a nearly 40-minute speech, presidential candidate Barack Obama explained the complexities of race in America

- Three men wearing ski masks stole artwork from the Zurich Museum, including a Cezanne, a Degas, a van Gogh, and a Monet, with a combined worth of $163 million

- At a news conference in Baghdad, a reporter for a Cairo-based satellite television network hurled his shoes at President George W. Bush and called him a "dog"

- New York Governor Eliot Spitzer, known as a crusader against white-collar crime, was pressured to resign after he confessed to hiring prostitutes

- Danica Patrick won the Indy Japan 300, becoming the first woman to win an IndyCar race

- The U.S. Supreme Court ruled five to four that prisoners at Guantánamo Bay, Cuba, had a right to challenge their detention in federal court

- American swimmer Michael Phelps won eight gold medals at the Summer Olympics in China to beat a 36-year-old record set by countryman Mark Spitz

- A five-year inquiry by the Intelligence Committee found that President George W. Bush and his staff repeatedly overstated evidence that Saddam Hussein possessed nuclear, chemical, and biological weapons and misled the public about ties between Iraq and al-Qaeda

- Bill Gates ended his day-to-day management of Microsoft, the computer giant he founded

- The Supreme Court ruled five to four that the Constitution protected an individual's right to possess a gun, but insisted that the ruling "is not a right to keep and carry any weapon whatsoever in any manner whatsoever and for whatever purpose."

- Barack Obama won the presidential election against Senator John McCain, taking 365 electoral votes to McCain's 162

- Notable books for the year included *The Appeal* by John Grisham; *The Audacity of Hope* by Barack Obama; *Diary of a Wimpy Kid: Rodrick Rules* by Jeff Kinney; *Eat, Pray, Love* by Elizabeth Gilbert; *The Last Lecture* by Randy Pausch and Jeffrey Zaslow; and *Three Cups of Tea* by Greg Mortenson

- Researchers decoded the genome of a cancer patient and found mutations in the cancer cells that may have either caused the cancer or helped it to progress

- Mortgage giants Freddie Mac and Fannie Mae collapsed just days before investment bank Lehman Brothers declared bankruptcy

- The Iraqi government took command of 54,000 Sunni fighters who turned against al-Qaeda in Mesopotamia in 2007 and began siding with the United States

Selected Prices

Backup Hard Drive $44.71
Book, Paperback $10.20
Business Cards, 250 Count $19.99
Coffeemaker, Krups $90.00
Combination Router/Modem $160.00
Phone Service, Land Line, Monthly $70.00
Printer Ink, Three-Pack $71.00
Surfboard $735.00
Toaster, Krups $90.96
Trimline Corded Telephone $14.72

"How to Shape a Surfboard," Jay DiMartino, *About.com Guide*, 2008:

Watching your surfboard as it's shaped is a bit like watching your baby being born...just a little. If you haven't stood in the shaping room during this wondrous birth and felt foam dust waft up your nostrils as it blank to fully designed, you are missing out on a special moment. It takes the relationship between you and your surfboard to a deeper level, and may just lift your surfing to another level.

For those not familiar with the latest craze to invade the sun-drenched Pacific coast of Southern California, here is a definition of "surfing"—a water sport in which the participant stands on a floating slab of wood, resembling an ironing board in both size and shape, and attempts to remain perpendicular while being hurtled toward the shore at a rather frightening rate of speed on the crest of a huge wave (especially recommended for teen-agers and all others without the slightest regard for either life or limb).

—Sleeve notes on The Beach Boys' 1962 album *Surfin' Safari*

Our goal is to create high-performance resin systems that optimize the sustainability of endproducts by replacing petroleum-based chemicals with bio-based renewable resources. By employing bio-derived materials such as pine oil components sourced as a co-product from wood pulp processing and vegetable oil components sourced from the waste stream of bio-fuel processing, we are able to lower our resins' environmental impact from processing and improve the overall health and safety of our products.

—Entropy website (www.Entropyresins.com)

Walking on Water

"How Surfboards Became Danny Hess' Livelihood,"
Eric Gustafson, Special to *The San Francisco Chronicle*,
November 11, 2009:

Step into the workshops of most surfboard-makers and you'll find a fluffy, snow-like layer of polyurethane foam under your feet. The floor of Danny Hess' Outer Sunset garage is covered with sawdust. As with the ancient Polynesians who invented surfing, Hess builds his surfboards out of wood. However, unlike some shapers who are re-creating wooden boards from the past, mostly for the satisfaction of collectors who hang them on their walls, Hess chose wood to make a better surfboard.

Though they may help a rider peacefully commune with nature, most modern, high-performance surfboards have an environmental dark side. The polyurethane foam "blank" that is sculpted into a finished shape is made using a host of nasty chemicals, and the polyester resin used to cure a surfboard's fiberglass shell is toxic. The propensity of such boards to break in half only heightens their negative impact.

By synthesizing the woodworking techniques of cabinetmakers and boat builders with the standard foam-and-fiberglass approach, Hess creates surfboards that push the boundaries of environmental sustainability, aesthetic beauty and speed generation. They may cost twice as much as conventionally shaped surfboards, but they have the durability to last a lifetime.

The desire to build a better surfboard is not a new goal for Hess, 34. Ever since he started surfing regularly as a teenager in Ventura, he has been searching for superior equipment. As his skills progressed, so did his frustration with the boards available at the time. In the late '80s, surfboard design entered into a period of stagnation; the short, three-finned Thruster became the ubiquitous shape. Hess didn't like the way these boards surfed, and he was particularly unhappy with their short life spans.

By the time he turned 16, he was already making his own surfboards, inspired by older designs that were then seen as outmoded. His materials, however, were the usual fare. Hess' path to wood was a circuitous one. Oddly enough, it started with a straw-bale house. In the late '90s, having graduated from UC Santa Cruz with a double major in fine arts and marine biology, Hess found himself in Colorado, immersed in a sustainable-building project.

"It wasn't until I built that straw-bale house that I started seeing myself as a carpenter," says Hess. He learned another equally profound lesson during this landlocked period: "Living in Colorado made me realize how much I couldn't live away from the ocean."

Hess moved to San Francisco and quickly established himself in the Ocean Beach surfing lineup. It wasn't long before he had a contractor's license and a business doing sustainable remodels.

continued

"How Surfboards Became Danny Hess' Livelihood,"
(continued)

"Working with wood had become a fundamental part of my life at this point, and I wanted to incorporate it into as many parts of my life as possible," Hess says. The time had come for his two passions to merge. Problem was, there was no template for the wooden surfboard he had in mind.

Early hollow wooden surfboards, such as the "kook boxes" of the '30s, which were ostensibly lifeguard paddleboards, had some peripheral influence, but Hess' thinking was more directly shaped by his experience as a woodworker. Mastering techniques utilized for building radius cabinets—lamination, using molds and vacuum bagging, in which air pressure is used to bond glued pieces together—opened him up to the possibilities of wood. Taking courses at the San Francisco Institute of Architecture helped give structure to his thoughts.

"I spent something like a year constantly thinking about an approach, an idea," says Hess.

Then, in late 2000, he had an epiphany. He thought of constructing a surfboard using a molded perimeter frame, with the exterior decks supported by an interior skeleton and encased in a thin layer of fiberglass. Creating this design wasn't easy, however.

"It took me probably 140 hours to build that first board over a period of eight months," he says. During the next two years, he built about 10 experimental wood boards for himself and friends, making incremental improvements along the way.

But the boards didn't perform as well as he had hoped. They were too heavy and stiff. The solution was to ditch the wood skeleton and replace it with foam. This shed a significant amount of mass, taking the board down to the same weight as its conventional equivalent, and allowed it to flex more naturally because the decks were no longer rigidly linked. By using recycled expanded polystyrene foam instead of polyurethane, Hess was able to maintain both environmental and structural integrity. He says the resulting board was a "massive leap forward."

Until that point, he wasn't really thinking about making surfboards for a living—it was more of an artistic outlet. But the word got out, and demand for his boards quickly expanded beyond his circle of friends. In 2005, with 15 orders in hand, Hess finished his last remodel and "jumped into surfboard-making headfirst."

His timing couldn't have been better. Spurred in part by the closure of surf industry giant Clark Foam—which for decades had had a stranglehold on the foam blank business, stymieing innovation through standardization—and by a growing number of adventurous surfers looking for a more expansive range of designs, surfboard making was entering into a creative renaissance.

Hess admits that 10 years ago, there wouldn't have been a business case for selling $2,000 wooden surfboards. Today he has a seven-month backlog of orders.

continued

"How Surfboards Became Danny Hess' Livelihood,"
(continued)

Though he has nine basic surfboard models in varying sizes, several with Ocean Beach-related street names such as Noriega and Quintara, Hess custom-builds each one for a rider's weight and skill level.

Poplar is Hess's go-to material. It has the strength-to-weight ratio he demands, and the trees' fast growth makes the wood more sustainable than slower-growing redwood or cedar. Hess is particularly creative in what he does with his leftovers: He turns them into hand planes for bodysurfing. Designed to support the entire forearm, these boards function like a hydrofoil, elevating the rider's torso out of the water, allowing for higher speed and greater maneuverability.

Hess may not have chosen to use wood on purely aesthetic grounds, but his surfboards are nevertheless works of art. The clear epoxy fiberglass shell allows the viewer to revel in the uninterrupted flow of wood grains, with the intricately laminated rails framing each of these floating canvases. On his Singer model, Hess collaborates with Santa Cruz artist Thomas Campbell to add color and graphics. Still, this short, four-finned board is designed for high performance, not lofts with high ceilings.

In 2008, Hess shaped 170 surfboards; this year he hopes to surpass the 200-board mark. "Compared to a regular surfboard-maker, that's kind of laughable," says Hess. "For a wood surfboard-maker, I feel like it's a real accomplishment."

Given how labor-intensive his boards are to build, how is he able to make a profit?

"I've been able to refine the system down enough so that I can make a decent living," answers Hess, adding that each board takes 10 to 12 hours to build. "Nobody is getting rich building surfboards, and I never got into this to get rich. It's the love of doing it and making a living at the same time. I have time to surf—when I'm not too busy."

OBEY YOUR

BREWMASTER.

SINK THE STATUS QUO.

2009 Profile

It had never occurred to William Thomas Davis that at age 72, he would spend his retirement years wrestling with a start-up business he called Thomas Creek Brewery in Greenville, South Carolina.

Life at Home

- William (Bill) Thomas Davis was familiar with many of life's challenges after 42 years as an architect.
- Often as a young boy, Bill helped his father work as a brick mason laying brick in the hot South Carolina summers.
- It was during one afternoon that an architect visited the site with a set a blueprints.
- Meeting the architect and learning what he did helped Bill realize what he wanted to do for the rest of his adult life—design buildings as an architect.
- In the years after college and earning his degree, Bill Davis joined Craig Gaulden Architects, and within two years, he made partner in 1977.
- The firm changed its name to Craig Gaulden & Davis and went on to design a number of schools, libraries, and churches throughout the Southeast.
- Bill's hand was involved in a number of landmark buildings constructed in Greenville, including the Peace Center for the Performing Arts and the Greenville Art Museum.
- In addition to designing buildings, Bill traveled to committee meetings and conferences with the American Institute of Architects that met throughout the United States.
- It was during these travels that he discovered good brews in Oregon and Washington states.
- In the late 1970s, the craft beer renaissance was just beginning in the United States; start-up breweries were forming to create beers not made by the national distributors.

William Thomas Davis started a microbrewery with his son at age 72.

Bill funded their new venture while son Tom honed his brewing skills.

- "I've never brewed in my life, but I know what good beer tastes like," he told his son Tom.
- The stuff Bill was discovering was nothing like Pabst Blue Ribbon or the European imports found locally.
- Tom, who was then working as a bartender and manager of Henni's Restaurant in Greenville and had access to some of the better brands of beer, realized that his tastes were "slightly off kilter" because the choices his father suggested were limited in South Carolina.
- So 22-year-old Tom started to study home brewing books to learn how to create the craft beers his father was bragging about.
- After educating himself about home brewing, Tom skipped over five-gallon extract brewing, which most beginners used, and started with 10-gallon all-grain batches.
- Discovering that he could make quality craft beer, Tom knew that he wanted to become a professional brewer and sell his own beer.
- Regretfully, he had an obstacle in front of him—the South Carolina law did not allow brewpubs until 1994.
- When the law passed, the owner of Henni's wanted to turn his restaurant in a brewpub and dreamed of creating a franchise of brewpubs throughout the state.
- Tom and Bill realized this was an opportunity and formed a leasing company.

The brewery started off as a three and a half-barrel system.

- Bill financed the operation and agreed to lease the beer brewing systems to the restaurant for this possible franchise opportunity; Tom would be responsible for the restaurant's brewing.
- Bill purchased a tiny three and a half-barrel system that could make over 150 gallons of beer for Henni's.
- Then, for the next couple of years, Tom crafted quality beer while Bill grew concerned about the lack of growth in the franchise.
- When Bill talked with Henni's owner, he learned the owner now wanted out of the franchise beer business and was only interested in operating a restaurant.
- Bill realized that his leasing approach was not going to work due to the limited number of brewpubs in South Carolina.
- Meanwhile, Tom wanted to take advantage of the economies of scale that a brewery could offer and reach a wider audience through a network of distributors.
- Setting up a chain of brewpubs to reach a larger population would be too costly.

- To sell beer in South Carolina, a businessperson had to either form a brewery that sold beer directly to distributors, who in turn sold it to retailers.
- The other option would be to have a brewpub, which required having a restaurant.
- It was one or the other—a company could not do both.
- Since Tom had improved his brewing prowess during the prior few years, both father and son were interested in creating a brewery while still providing product to Henni's.
- It would allow them to maintain revenues for their brewing operations.
- Much of the endeavor was really Tom's idea, and he encouraged his father to partner.
- The final decision required a number of weeks as father and son discussed their business ideas while enjoying Tom's homemade brew.
- In 1997, Bill again provided the financing for the new brewing operation, but finding a lender proved difficult.
- Ultimately, Bill worked with a local bank that appeared to have little interest in the businesses, especially with the risk of lending money to a new company.
- Bill also questioned whether the loan officer had any interest in his product as well.
- To get a loan, Bill was required to mortgage his house to finance the operation and secure a $200,000 letter of credit, even though he was still active in his architecture career and carried no debt.
- Next, they began the search for a good commercial brewing system and an industrial building.
- This proved extremely difficult.
- To be successful, they needed to be in a warehouse facility with high ceilings, access to a lot of water, and have sloped drainage floors.
- The drainage floors are necessary for a brewery because workers constantly squeegee all the water and spilled beer off the floor.
- Unable to find a suitable location, Bill shared his woes with a neighbor during a Christmas party.
- The neighbor—and owner of Huskey Construction Company—was familiar with the Davis men's efforts.
- He agreed to build them a warehouse on the site of an old junkyard on Piedmont Highway on the south side of Greenville.
- The next step was a name for the brewery.
- "Thomas" was an obvious choice for both men, and they decided to focus on a water theme for their beer.
- Thus, Thomas Creek Brewery was created, which also provided a rustic image.

Thomas Creek Brewery's new warehouse was a team effort.

Life at Work

- Starting a new business, Bill Davis knew preserving capital and limiting expenditures were a necessity in the first years of operations.
- When his son Tom discovered a discounted 60-barrel system from a defunct Kernersville, North Carolina, brewery called Woodhouse Brewery, they made a purchase.
- In 1998, Thomas Creek Brewery fired up its brewhouse and began to make two brands of beer: Amber Ale and Multigrain.

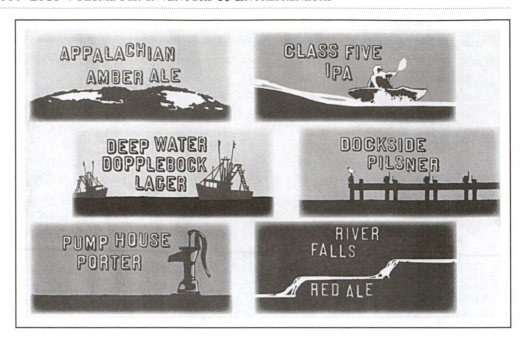

Amber Ale was their first beer and Red Ale became their most popular.

- Six months later, the company started brewing its Red Ale, which became their flagship beer.
- Due to the limited funds, Bill and Tom agreed to focus on a grassroots marketing effort.
- They did this by participating in festivals in the Southeast, such as the Brewgrass Festival in Asheville, North Carolina, and many others.
- They even offered private tastings for business clubs and community associations while sponsoring events in the Greenville community.
- A number of venues included the local chapter of the American Red Cross, Hands On Greenville, the March of Dimes, and the United Way.
- At all of the events, attendees enjoyed the beers produced by Thomas Creek Brewery and wanted to know where to buy more.
- But many had trouble finding Thomas Creek Brewery beer in their stores, even with the strong demand for its product.
- Bill grew frustrated with the limited distribution of the company's products.
- By law in South Carolina, a brewery was classified as a manufacturing operation and could only sell its product to a distributor, who made sales directly to retailers.
- Bill was working with a local distributor, who feared that Thomas Creek Brewery's beer would only be in demand in the Greenville market.
- When Bill requested a statewide distribution, the distributor sold the distributing rights for Thomas Creek Brewery to another company that primarily handled wines.
- Finally, they could achieve statewide distribution.
- As sales improved, the men discovered that they needed to improve their product's image; distributors had noted that their bottle labels "looked homemade."
- So Bill Davis hired a Greenville marketing firm—Bounce—to do a complete makeover.
- Over the weeks, the ad people from Bounce created names for every beer while maintaining the theme of water referenced in the name Thomas Creek Brewery.

- Thomas Creek was brewing eight of their beers year-round; names included Up The Creek Extreme IPA, River Falls Red Ale, Deep Water Dopplebock, and Dockside Pilsner.
- The marketers also presented Bill with the overall theme of "Sink the Status Quo" for his product, and developed witty banners to appeal to a younger generation of drinkers.
- One read, "Yelling 'Play "Free Bird" was funny about 23 years ago…. Come up with something original," referencing the Lynyrd Skynyrd song habitually requested at concerts, no matter the band.

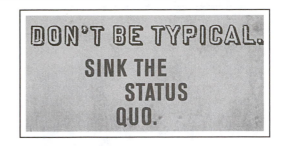

A catchy theme appealed to customers of all ages.

- Bounce won local, regional and national Best in Show awards for the banner ads promoting Thomas Creek Brewery.
- Even with the new distributor and improved sales, however, Thomas Creek was struggling with its cash flow; Bill continued to finance the operations from his personal savings.
- It took five years for Thomas Creek Brewery to make a profit in one of its quarterly reports.
- It took an additional two years for the company to make its first annual profit.
- While many entrepreneurs would have quit, Bill and Tom were dedicated to make this family business a success.
- With sales growing by 2004, Bill realized they needed more equipment to support the new growth.
- At that time, Thomas Creek had a bottling system that took three days and 135 man-hours to empty a 60-barrel tank.
- Employees had to stack, package and label each bottle.
- At age 68, Bill found himself doing physical labor in bottling and stacking his product in this laborious manufacturing process.
- New equipment was needed to keep up with the business growth, and that required finding additional financing.
- Even though Thomas Creek was just becoming profitable, Bill knew that finding additional financing was going to be difficult with their current lender.
- After a number of conversations, Bill decided to change his banking relationship and collaborated with a few new investors.
- With the influx of fresh capital in business, Thomas Creek was able to buy the additional tanks, chillers and a bottling line.
- Finding good prices for the tanks and chillers was easy, but it was Tom's luck in discovering the company's new bottling system.
- Early one morning, Tom was on the Internet visiting a professional brewer's website when he discovered a brewery in Toronto selling its bottling line.
- Tom immediately posted an offer subject to inspection and approval.
- Several other offers followed later that day, but Tom's was first.
- Tom had a friend inspect the equipment a few days later, and he called Tom and told him to buy it.
- It was perfectly designed for a microbrewing operation.

Thomas Creek was gaining national recognition for quality and great taste.

Thomas Creek beers won two awards in five years.

- The bottling system would have traditionally cost as much as $400,000, but Thomas Creek secured it for only $80,000.
- Once installed, the new equipment was highly automated and improved efficiency.
- Thomas Creek could now bottle 60 barrels of beer within six to seven hours and package 50 bottles per minute.
- National brewers that produce established brands, such as Budweiser and Miller, typically bottle 500 to 600 bottles per minute.
- With the new equipment, Bill and Tom started producing more beer and expanding Thomas Creek's market into North Carolina, Georgia, Virginia, Florida and Alabama through a growing number of new distributorships.
- They also began doing contract brewing for a number of companies, including Charleston Brewing and Orange Blossom Brewing.
- Over the next several years, Thomas Creek became a more recognizable name by the various industry publications; they also continued to win regional and national awards.
- One of the most significant awards for Thomas Creek was the Silver Medal in both 2003 and 2008 at the World Beer Championships.
- The brewery won in the German-Style Strong Bock with its Deep Water Dopplebock beer, which was proclaimed to be outside the norm for the style with its prominent roasted malt character and chocolate notes.
- Even with all of the awards and national recognition, a phone call in 2009 caught Bill Davis by surprise.
- An agent representing a European distributorship was interested in Thomas Creek and seeking a regional microbrewery that could export product for the growing demand of quality American beers in Scandinavia.
- Without hesitation, Bill Davis shipped him a number of beers to sample and the agent loved them.
- The agent wanted to use Thomas Creek to introduce Scandinavians to "The microbrew from the United States' Southeast."

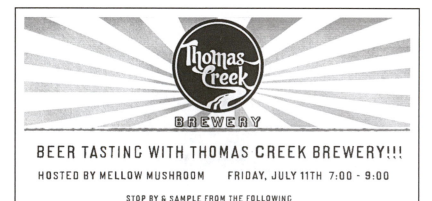

Bill relied on local marketing to get the word out for their handcrafted brews.

- Tom and Bill went to work providing a shipment to Sweden and delivered 50 barrels of Thomas Creek product by the fall of 2009.
- In addition to the quality of the product, many in Sweden liked the microbrews because they were less costly than European beers.
- European brewers must pay a value-added tax throughout their manufacturing costs: a single beer may cost three times as much as a Thomas Creek beer exported to the country.
- Within the first week, the Scandinavian distributor had sold out of all the bottles shipped.

Life in the Community: Greenville, South Carolina

- Greenville, South Carolina, is located in the northwestern corner of the state along Interstate 85, one of the busiest interstate highways in the nation.

- The area is centrally situated between two of the largest cities in the Southeast, Charlotte and Atlanta, and is one of the most rapidly growing areas of the country and the fastest in the state.

- Over the past decade, Greenville has attracted more than $6 billion in new business investments and 43,000 new jobs.

- This growth allowed for more businesses to be created per

Downtown Greenville, S.C.

capita than any other region in the Southeastern United States.

- National and international companies that can be found in Greenville include Michelin, Lockheed Martin, General Electric, Hubble Lighting, Samsung, 3M, and IBM.

- Much of the community's successes began in 1970s, when then Mayor Max Heller spearheaded a massive downtown revitalization project.

- The first and most important step in changing downtown's image was the streetscape plan, narrowing the street's four lanes to two, and installing angled parking, trees, and decorative light fixtures, as well as creating parks and plazas throughout downtown.

- By 2009, the city's Main Street possessed a lofty canopy of trees and shops that attracted a number of visitors annually.

- The pedestrian-friendly atmosphere has been compared to that of a European city.

- One of Greenville's biggest attractions was the Falls Park on the Reedy, featuring two sets of waterfalls visible from the landmark Liberty Bridge.

- The pedestrian suspension bridge served as the community's icon.

- Connecting the various parks within the city are miles of walking and bicycle trails.

- One of the city's longest was the Swamp Rabbit Trail, a former railroad line that ran through the community during its textile days in the late nineteenth and early twentieth centuries.

- Greenville has been rated one of *Bike Magazine's* "Top 5 Best Places to Live and Ride," which has helped it attract the annual USA Pro Cycling Championships and many professional cyclists who live in the area.

- Greenville also boasts year-round arts and entertainment.

- The Greenville County Museum of Art, which specializes in American art, is noted for its collections by Andrew Wyeth and Jasper Johns, as well as a contemporary collection that features such notables as Andy Warhol and Georgia O'Keeffe.

HISTORICAL SNAPSHOT
2009

- Barack Obama was inaugurated as the forty-fourth, and first African-American, president of the United States

- A Russian and an American satellite collided over Siberia, creating a large amount of space debris

- NASA's Kepler Mission, a space photometer which will search for extrasolar planets in the Milky Way Galaxy, was launched from Cape Canaveral Air Force Station, Florida

- UNESCO launched the World Digital Library

- North Korea announced that it had conducted a second successful nuclear test in the province of North Hamgyong

- NASA launched the *Lunar Reconnaissance Orbiter/LCROSS* probes to the moon, the first American lunar mission since *Lunar Prospector* in 1998

- The death of American entertainer Michael Jackson triggered an outpouring of worldwide reaction; online, the event crippled several major websites and services

- At the G-20 Pittsburgh Summit, world leaders announced that the G-20 will assume greater leverage over the world economy, replacing the role of the G-8 in an effort to prevent another financial crisis like that in 2008

- After analyzing the data from the *LCROSS* lunar impact, NASA announced that it had found a "significant" quantity of water in the moon's Cabeus crater

- President Obama signed the Lilly Ledbetter Fair Pay Act, an equal-pay act which expanded workers' rights to sue in pay disputes

- Apple began selling music on iTunes without copyright protection, where digital rights management software and customers were able to move songs freely among computers, MP3 players, and phones

- To stimulate the failing economy, Congress passed an $838 billion stimulus plan designed to create 3.5 million jobs

- Bernard Madoff plead guilty to operating a massive Ponzi scheme, defrauding his many clients out of billions of dollars over the past 20 years

- In the N.C.A.A. men's college basketball tournament final, the North Carolina Tar Heels cruised to victory against the Michigan State Spartans, 89–72

- Vermont and Maine became the fourth and fifth states to legalize same-sex marriage, just days after Iowa became the third

- New York Federal Appeals Judge Sonia Sotomayor was named to the Supreme Court, replacing Justice David Souter

- Chrysler Automotive Company, which filed for bankruptcy, announced plans to shut down a quarter of its dealers across the country in an effort to downsize the company and reduce costs

- The unemployment rate peaked at 10.2 percent as the recession stretched into its second year

Selected Prices

Bookcase $119.00
Bottled Water $1.50
Coffee Grinder $60.53
Concert Ticket, Allman Brothers $159.00
Digital Cordless Phone $119.99
Kindle, 3G + Wi-Fi $189.00
Phone, Camera Flip Phone $99.00
Printer, HP All-in-One $548.88
Sofa $899.00
Toolset, 137 Pieces $99.99

"Thomas Creek's Appalachian Amber Ale," Jake Grove, *Independent Mail Newspaper*, August 20, 2009:

For some strange reason, local breweries have been overlooked in this column of late.

Sure, a few regional brews have been reviewed, like those from the Highland family of beers in Asheville, N.C., or the Terrapin variations from Athens, Ga., but the very local breweries have been largely ignored.

That begins to change starting now.

A couple of weeks back, Greenville's Village Gallery on Pendleton Street threw its monthly First Friday art walk. During that time, the Upstate Visual Arts group was out there providing beer for those who donated to the cause and attended the event. And the beer they aptly put in their coolers was Greenville's own Thomas Creek.

They had four different brews available, but the one that caught this reviewer's eye was none other than the Appalachian Amber Ale.

For months I have been hung up on the amber ales. They typically have a roasted malt flavor with some nutty side tastes and a hint of hops on the back end. They are becoming more popular among brewers of late, much like the IPA of years past.

Since I only drank the Appalachian Amber out of a bottle at the event, I had to buy one on my way home to try from a pint glass to provide the full report. I was happy to do it.

The pour from the Appalachian Amber was just what you might expect. A deep red body followed up by an off-white head that lifted quickly, but vanished just as fast.

The aroma was light, mostly of malts and a slight citrus tone, with a nice grain tone to balance things out.

As for taste, there was more going on with this amber ale than one might expect. It starts off sweet with those roasted malts and nutty flavors coming out to start. As it goes along, things turn a bit bready, but with a light mouthfeel as the beer goes down. But the aftertaste is slightly of hops and a hint of orange.

The lacing is light if anything. The body of the beer doesn't promote anything thick or heavy, but it leaves a quality aftertaste that goes nicely with the crispness of the brew itself. Overall, this beer is a fine addition to a mix-and-six-pack or to try on tap in Greenville, but perhaps not something one would drink one after another with friends.

The nice thing is, Thomas Creek provides many different beers and a mixer of those would be ideal. Thomas Creek is available most everywhere, including specialty stores and grocery stores. They run around $7 per six-pack, and many varieties are available.

Craft Beer—Associated Press Release

Brewers Association Reports Mid-Year Craft Brewing Numbers:
Number of U.S. Breweries the Highest in 100 Years

Boulder, CO. August 17, 2009—The Brewers Association, the trade association representing the majority of U.S. brewing companies, reports America's small and independent craft brewers are still growing despite many challenges, and are continuing to provide jobs to the U.S. economy. Dollar growth from craft brewers during the first half of 2009 increased 9 percent, down from 11 percent growth during the same period in 2008. Volume of craft brewed beer sold grew 5 percent for the first six months in 2009, compared to 6.5 percent growth in the first half of 2008. Barrels sold by craft brewers for the first half of the year is an estimated 4.2 million, compared to four million barrels sold in the first half of 2008.

"At a time when many of the giant beer brands are declining, small and independent craft brewers are organically growing their share and slowly gaining shelf and restaurant menu space one glass of craft beer at a time," said Paul Gatza, Director of the Brewers Association.

The U.S. now boasts 1,525 breweries, the highest number in 100 years when consolidation and the run-up to Prohibition reduced the number of breweries to 1,498 in 1910. "The U.S. has more breweries than any other nation and produces a greater diversity of beer styles than anywhere else, thanks to craft brewer innovation," Gatza added.

"Beer Edges Out Wine, Liquor as Drink of Choice in U.S.,"
Gallup Online, June 29, 2009:

Among the nearly two-thirds of Americans who say they drink alcoholic beverages, 40 percent say they most often drink beer, 34 percent say wine, and 21 percent choose liquor.

"2010 Bright for County Economic Development," Jerry Howard,
Greenville Business Magazine, December 2009:

With more than a dozen announcements through October 2009 generating over 750 new jobs and nearly $170 million in capital investment, Greenville County enjoyed another good year in attracting new and growing existing businesses—despite challenging economic circumstances nationally....

Fundamental economic development principles placed in service in 2001 have spearheaded Greenville's success. The Greenville Area Development Corporation has built and retained a team that is a model for economic development organizations nationwide. Diverse, talented and innovative, your GADC team leverages economic development systems, processes, tools and insight to great advantage for Greenville.

Marshalling the talents and investment of both public and a record 125 private sector investors this year, your GADC delivers cost-effective, coordinated and results-driven efforts to attract and retain top companies, jobs and investment in our community.

And momentum builds as we enter 2010. Despite the downturn, GADC staff continues to meet with a record number of prospects interested in considering relocating or expansion in Greenville County—a stream of leads attributable to several consecutive years of focused marketing, communications and outreach programs.

Many of these companies are key players in our identified target segments of Advanced Materials, Automotive, Aviation/Aerospace Headquarters, Research and Development and Life Sciences. This selective targeting not only focuses precious marketing resources, it also translates into those segment companies cumulatively offering an average hourly wage of $28.06—nearly double historical South Carolina, Greenville County, and national wage averages....

"Anheuser-Busch Introduces Wheat Beer Nationwide,"
St. Louis Business Journal, October 5, 2009:

Anheuser-Busch rolled out Bud Light Golden Wheat nationwide Monday in an effort to tap into the surge in popularity of sweeter beers and wheat beers from craft brewers.

Bud Light Golden Wheat marks the third brand extension under the Bud Light name following launches of Bud Light Chelada and Bud Light Lime in 2008.

The marketing budget for Bud Light Golden Wheat is about $30 million a year, similar to the marketing budget for Bud Light Lime.

St. Louis-based Anheuser-Busch is owned by Belgium-based Anheuser-Busch InBev, the world's largest brewer.

"Opinion: South Carolina's Laws Too Hurtful on Breweries,"
Jaime Tenney of Coast Brewing Company,
The Digital Charleston, May 14, 2009:

So, we've been in the beer industry for over a decade now (and by we I mean David has been professional brewing for 12 years and we've have been operating COAST for over 2). We knew the laws when we started the brewery and ran Pop the Cap SC, which changed the law allowing beer over 6 percent to be made in SC. Fine and Dandy. Except, I am fed up with all the other laws that essentially annihilate small breweries to operate successfully.

We are not allowed to sell direct, self-distribute, or even give a tasting at our own brewery. Down right Ridiculous. With the passage of the Microdistillery Bill, distilleries now join wineries in the fact that they can have tours, do tastings and sell directly to consumers at their place of business. But STILL not beer. What gives?

The SC Beer Wholesalers oppose any legislation that "infringes on the 3-Tier system," that's what gives. Seems to me that this is downright unconstitutional to have these basic rights for wineries and distilleries but not beer. I have never seen such discrimination for a business sector in my entire life. Nor have I seen such absolute political power held by a special interest group (though I am sure it happens all the time).

continued

"Opinion: South Carolina's Laws Too Hurtful on Breweries," Jaime Tenney of Coast Brewing Company, *(continued)*

Which leaves us with what to do from here? I absolutely love owning a brewery. We get to be self-employed, run our business the way we want to (morally and socially responsibly), and we're really proud of the beer we make. I can still say that after all the long hours, frustrations and very little pay (though David may disagree). Right now, though, it's not enough. I just can't rationalize these ridiculous laws and excuses that go with them any longer. SO, we have two choices. Keep going and keep fighting for better beer laws. Or, pack up and move somewhere that appreciates what we do by allowing us to make an honest living and to be able to invest back into our business and community. There are reasons you don't see many new breweries open here; it just isn't worth it. Why open here when North Carolina will welcome you with open arms? Well, that's exactly what has been happening in NC: many new breweries have opened there in the last few years. Maybe we should, too?

South Carolina is literally turning away small businesses (and breweries are one of the few businesses still growing in the current economy!), giving up increased tax revenue and generally not listening to what her citizens want. Is that any way to run a state? It's a damn shame because I love living in Charleston; it's a beautiful, engaging city, and the beaches are second to none.

What does the future hold for South Carolina's craft beer industry? I wish I knew.

The "family" at Thomas Creek Brewery.

2010 Profile

Gorm Bressner's career in industrial design began as a child "test engineer" for Legos years before the famous toy made its mark in the United States.

Life at Home

- Gorm Bressner was born April 8, 1965, in Chargin Falls, Ohio, but moved around a lot as a child with his engineering consultant father.
- One of four brothers—two older and an identical twin, Eric, who was born five minutes later, Gorm was third in the family pecking order.
- Gorm's "build a better mousetrap" mentality came from his father, Stanley Henry Bressner, a first-generation Russian Jew whose parents were from the Black Sea city of Odessa, Ukraine.
- Father Stan attended Rensaellear Polytechnic Institute after World War II on the G.I. Bill and then went to Denmark when American know-how was vogue in Europe.
- There he worked first as an engineering consultant for furniture manufacturers, then for Lego, years before the popular toy was introduced in the U.S.
- Gorm and his brothers grew up surrounded by bags and bags of the latest Lego shapes still in development.
- "We were the luckiest kids in the neighborhood," Gorm remarked.
- The Bressner boys built a variety of structures that spanned beds and dressers, testing the plastic pieces as rigorously as the best Research & Development team.
- Their parents encouraged tinkering, and instead of buying the twins the desired go-cart, they would say: "if you want it so badly, build one," which they did.
- During one invention-adventure, Gorm and his brother Eric fabricated a turbo-charger for their lawn mower using an old vacuum cleaner and car parts.

Gorm Bressner's Industrial designs earned him not only a number of patents, but also a good living.

Gorm's mother's family came from Denmark.

- It worked so powerfully, it blew the lawn mower engine—and impressed Dad.
- A more mischievous creation was a mousetrap altered with a tack, so as to burst a water balloon placed over his brothers' bedroom door.
- During frequent trips to the library, Gorm focused on art books, fascinated by light and shadow, while Eric went straight to the section on airplanes and gliders.
- A sibling competition began as they spent hours seeing who could build the better glider.
- While still in high school, Gorm became interested in chair mechanisms: How does one pull of a handle recline the back of a La-Z-Boy and extend the footrest at the same time?
- Gorm didn't stop tinkering until he re-created this motion with wood and dowels.
- His father encouraged him to take his model to a machine shop operator, where together, they created a mechanical rocking chair without rails.
- The design became Gorm's first patent and his first lesson in the process required for how to protect inventive ideas.
  - After graduating from high school, Gorm and Eric both entered the University of Massachusetts School of Engineering.
  - Their father expected good grades, which would be rewarded with the opportunity and tuition to transfer to Rensaellear Polytechnic Institute, or RPI.
  - Gorm discovered that he wasn't the least interested in Young's modulus, differential equations, Pascal, Fortran or anything to do with numbers; Eric, on the other hand, excelled and left UMass the following year for RPI.
  - "Eric got the smarts and I got the arts," Gorm said, "not to mention having received a polite, but stern letter from the Dean of Engineering earlier that semester, that I was about to fail out of school and should reconsider my major in engineering."
  - After a bit of soul searching, he applied to the Rhode Island School of Design (RISD) and was accepted into the Industrial Design program based on four drawings that included a boot and a bicycle.
  - "It wasn't until RISD, that I *knew* that I wanted to be a designer and I wanted to design everything: buildings, products, cars, systems…anything," Gorm explained.
  - "It became clear to me then that engineering was more about making 'it' accurate, whereas designing was all about how many different ways can you make 'it' and make 'it' look beautiful in the process."

Gorm loved to design, evident in his home and backyard projects.

Life at Work

- Gorm Bressner's first job after graduating from RISD was with a small design firm in Atlanta.
- There, Gorm applied his newly minted skills to projects that entailed restyling or improving the manufacturability of products, and was rewarded with several patents.
- His patents included a mechanical assist device to squeeze a syringe for thick fluids, and urinary catheters with an alternative securing method.
- Missing New England and his girlfriend (and eventually his wife), he moved back to Providence, Rhode Island, where he could rent cheap studio space in a depressed area southwest of the city that was abundant in large old mills and raw space.
- Gorm shared space with metal workers and sculptors, wood and furniture makers, painters, printmakers, and photographers who served as inspiration for anything creative and artistic.
- After a bit of freelancing, Gorm landed the position that would launch his career: industrial designer at Arthur D. Little (ADL)—based in Cambridge, Massachusetts.

Gorm moved back to New England to marry and start a family.

- ADL was one of the largest consulting firms in the world, representing clients from hundreds of diverse industries.
- The company's capabilities reached into dozens of technologies and science-related disciplines.
- As one of only two industrial designers, Gorm enjoyed free rein to explore the boundaries of industrial design, human capabilities and mechanical engineering.
- Gorm's work over the next 10 years earned him over a dozen patents for medical devices, military hardware, food service equipment, heating technologies and others.
- As a member of the ADL, all rights to developments became the property of the company; however, staff who were involved with originating the idea—the inventing—would receive bonuses in the form of cash payments when the patents were commercialized or sold.
- In 2001, Gorm's tenure at ADL came to a bittersweet ending; ADL found itself in Chapter 11 and Gorm found himself without a job.
- Almost worse than no job were his worthless stock options that would have secured him a comfortable retirement.
- After ADL, Gorm joined the Mosely Corporation, a consulting firm specializing in branded food service.
- For five years, he worked on developing food delivery systems for major brands including Nestlé, Unilever, Dunkin' Donuts, Bertucci's and White Castle.

For ten years he worked on dozens of prototypes.

Although a favorite of Gorm's, this coffee roaster system never made it very far.

Gorm and his partners developed, manufactured, and marketed a cooking ring for grilling. .

- One his proudest achievements at Mosely was the creation of an automatic coffee roasting system.
- Unfortunately, this project resulted in the client being sued and the product dying a slow death—another lesson learned on trade-secret infringement
- After leaving Mosely, Gorm began consulting on his own in product and technology development with an emphasis on commercial food equipment—fryers, ovens, ranges, charbroilers, refrigerators, freezers.
- Currently, he heads up industrial design for Manitowoc Food Service, responsible for harmonizing the way the company's 10,000 different products look and feel.
- Recently, his time has been split between working from his home office in Providence and at the offices of Manitowoc in Tampa, Florida, plus traveling among the dozen of its manufacturing operations in the U.S.
- But the urge to invent is never far away.
- One current recent project involves a cooking tool invented by a friend about seven years ago.
- It was Gorm's job to take silversmith Peter Prip's cooking ring for grilling food (Patent No. 6,644,176) and help him commercialize it.
- The invention involved a series of small, medium and large grilling rings, coupled to special tongs, that grilled and caramelized surfaces, providing grilling enthusiasts a new and different way of barbecuing food.
- Initially, Gorm put together a joint venture business agreement on which he would help patent and commercialize the product in exchange for 40 percent of the business.
- Commercialization would entail either owning the manufacture and distribution of the product themselves, which provided higher revenue potential, or licensing the rights of the design to a cooking products type of company, which would result in far fewer revenues.
- But Gorm so overwhelmed his potential partner with all the complexities of commercializing products, he decided to go it alone.
- Another couple of years transpired when they bumped into each other and Gorm learned that the patent process was complete but Peter "hadn't done much" since then.

Various size rings and special tongs result in perfect grill marks.

- But Peter had learned that taking an invention to market could be time consuming and vexing, so he asked Gorm if he was still interested in helping him again.
- This time, they agreed to a joint venture along with a mutual friend and designer, Don Nguyento, to start a business, each with a 33 percent stake.

- The business was based on friendly terms in which the inventor would be primarily responsible for marketing and culinary development, the new partner would provide product development and manufacturing, and Gorm would focus on the business and customer development.
- Gorm's other pending invention involved a children's drawing toy.
- "It was one of these rare instances that inspiration comes to you in a nanosecond, while watching the neighborhood children playing outside with chalk.
- The idea was so simple that Gorm went downstairs to his basement shop and made a working prototype.
- "Within about a half-hour, I brought up a wood and metal model and showed the kids how the idea worked.
- "They all were fighting over who got to play with it first, and each took turns trying it out; I knew I had a winner and am now filing a provisional patent.
- Once complete, the provisional patent will allow Gorm one year of "protection" (provisional patents establish a date of conception) so that he can approach a couple of toy companies to learn if they are interested in licensing the idea.
- His hope and expectation was to license the idea and earn a three- to five percent royalty fee, which would cover the costs of maintaining the patent rights along with a tidy revenue stream.
- If he strikes out with a licensing agreement, he plans to take the harder step of getting the product into the market via infomercials.
- Under that scenario, the challenge would be finding manufacturers to make and distribute the product, plus the initial costs to get started.
- Initial costs of tooling would average $30,000-$40,000 for each injection mold plus an upfront, minimum order commitment that contract manufacturers typically require for an outlay of about $100,000 just to get into the game.
- "But the upshot is potentially huge, in the millions," Gorm said.

Gorm's workshop.

Life in the Community: Providence, Rhode Island

- The coastal city of Providence, Rhode Island, was one of the first cities established in the United States and currently boasts a metropolitan statistical area embracing 1.6 million people.
- Located at the head of Narragansett Bay, Providence was founded in 1636 by Roger Williams, a religious exile from the Massachusetts Bay Colony, who named the area in honor of "God's merciful Providence" for revealing such a haven for him to settle.
- Following the Revolutionary War, Providence was the country's ninth-largest city—with 7,614 people—and an economy that was shifting from maritime endeavors to manufacturing, particularly machinery, tools, silverware, jewelry and textiles.
- The city's industries attracted many immigrants from Ireland, Germany, Sweden, England, Italy, Portugal, Cape Verde, and French Canada.
- By the turn of the twentieth century, Providence boasted some of the largest manufacturing plants in the country, including Brown & Sharpe, Nicholson File, and Gorham Silverware.
- As the home to many casting and stamping companies, Providence became known as the costume jewelry capital of the U.S.
- When the jewelry and textile industries abandoned the city, they left behind brick and stone mill spaces which slowly became renovated and gentrified into studios, lofts and artist spaces.
- The Great Depression hit the city hard, and Providence's downtown was subsequently flooded by the New England Hurricane of 1938.
- Though the city received a boost from World War II, this ended with the war; the population would drop by 38 percent over the next three decades.
- From the 1950s to the 1980s, Providence was a notorious bastion of organized crime, ruled by mafia boss Raymond L. S. Patriarca.
- In the 1990s, Mayor Vincent "Buddy" Cianci, Jr., showcased the city's strength in arts and pushed for further revitalization, ultimately resulting in the uncovering of the city's natural rivers, which had been paved over; the relocation of a large section of railroad underground; the creation of Waterplace Park and river walks along the river's banks; and construction of the Fleet Skating Rink.

Gorham Manufacturing, Providence, RI, 1906.

- As a result, Providence became a walking city and now abounds with students from one of the five surrounding colleges and universities: Brown University, Rhode Island School of Design, Johnson and Wales University, Providence College and the University of Rhode Island.
- Providence also boasts a disproportionate number of excellent restaurants, due largely to Johnson and Wales University and its culinary arts program.
- Once nicknamed the "Beehive of Industry," Providence began re-branding itself as the "Creative Capital" in 2009 to emphasize its educational resources and arts community.

HISTORICAL SNAPSHOT
2010

- As the war in Iraq slowly wound down, additional American troops were assigned to Afghanistan
- The tallest manmade structure, the Burj Khalifa in Dubai, United Arab Emirates, was officially opened
- Dallas Braden of the Oakland Athletics pitched the nineteenth perfect game in Major League Baseball history in a 4–0 home win over the Tampa Bay Rays
- A 7.0-magnitude earthquake in Haiti—one of the deadliest natural disasters on record—devastated the nation's capital, Port-au-Prince, and killed more than 230,000 people
- The sculpture *L'Homme qui Marche I* by Alberto Giacometti sold for $103.7 million, setting a new world record for a work of art sold at auction, only to be surpassed a few months later by *Nude, Green Leaves and Bust* by Pablo Picasso, which sold for $106.5 million
- The New Orleans Saints defeated the Indianapolis Colts 31-17 to win their first Super Bowl in franchise history
- Volcanic ash from one of several eruptions beneath Eyjafjallajökull, an ice cap in Iceland, disrupted air traffic across northern and western Europe for weeks
- The Deepwater Horizon oil platform exploded in the Gulf of Mexico, killing 11 workers and resulting in the largest oil spill in history
- Alabama defeated Texas 37–21 in the 2010 BCS National Championship Game at the Rose Bowl in Pasadena, California
- President Barack Obama presented to Congress his 2011 budget of $3.8 trillion, which included a $1.6 trillion deficit in the next fiscal year
- Scientists conducting the Neanderthal genome project announced that they had sequenced enough of the Neanderthal genome to suggest that Neanderthals and humans may have interbred
- Congress passed President Obama's history-making Health Care Reform Bill
- Scientists announced that they had created a functional synthetic genome
- The 2010 FIFA World Cup, which was held in South Africa, was won by Spain
- The first 24-hour flight by solar-powered plane *Solar Impulse* was completed
- Wikileaks, an online publisher of anonymous, covert, and classified material, leaked to the public over 90,000 internal reports about the United States-led involvement in the War in Afghanistan from 2004 to 2010

Selected Prices

Bathroom Scale, Digital	$49.99
BlackBerry Phone	$649.99
Bluetooth Headset	$99.99
Computer, Toshiba Laptop	$499.99
GPS Navigator, Garmin	$219.99
La-Z-Boy Recliner	$499.99
Pampers, 176 Count	$48.99
Refrigerator/Freezer, Whirlpool	$471.72
Sole F80 Treadmill	$1,999.99
Vacuum, Hoover WindTunnel	$129.99

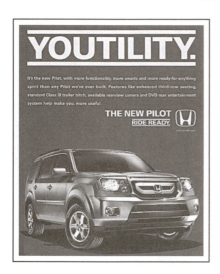

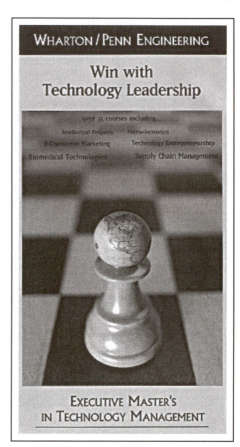

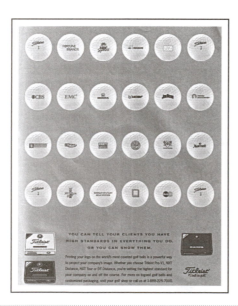

"Engineers, Designers, Inventors, and Artists," Gorm Bressner

Engineering is all about making "it" accurate, whereas designing is all about how many different ways can you make "it," including how to make "it" beautiful.

I really don't see a distinction between designing and inventing. They go hand-in-hand. Designing and inventing are processes. One must design while inventing, and vice versa. In most cases, engineering has to happen before any designing can take place.

I think the classic view of an inventor is a person (mad scientist type) who spends hours in the laboratory tinkering and experimenting to solve a problem. By this definition, the solution of a problem lies in the mechanics and functionality of a product or system, how it works, not so much how it looks.

Like the mad scientist, the artist will spend hours in his or her studio or atelier, struggling to reconcile their emotions with whatever media they are working. Unlike the inventor, the artist's challenge is knowing when the work is "done." It is highly subjective and not everyone will like it or even see the point. Art is primarily for the artist and his or her self-satisfaction. It rarely addresses, let alone solves, the problems of others.

Designing and engineering take into account other people's problems and their solutions. The designer, however artistic, must address the needs of others first before he is free to think of his own artistic needs. The functional aspect of a product or thing—the solution—is quantifiable and easily measured. Art cannot be measured in these terms. This marks a fundamental difference between the goal of an artist versus that of a designer or engineer.

continued

"Engineers, Designers, Inventors, and Artists," *(continued)*

On the other hand, there are similarities between designers and artists. Design, like art, explores the form and aesthetic qualities of a solution, product or thing. Designers, like artists, strive to create, if not the most beautiful, the most expressive, idea, with the goal of turning an otherwise utilitarian thing or mundane solution into a work of art.

This discussion forms the basis of the never-ending debate of whether form follows function, function has form, form is function, etc., etc., etc.

Inventing occurs across the spectrum. Artists "invent" new forms of expression or new processes using media. Engineers "invent" new ways of solving problems mechanically or electronically. Designers (i.e., industrial designers) "invent" ways of integrating the two.

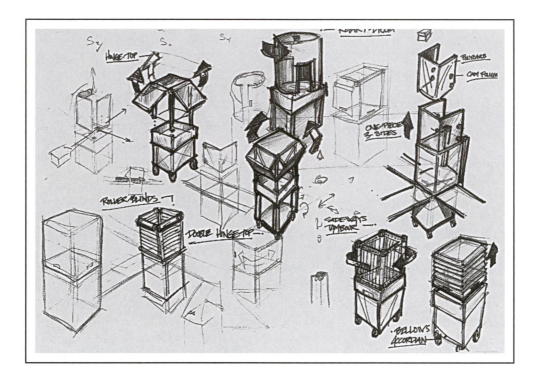

Intellectual property, or IP, is expensive for an individual…you have to have deep pockets to "own" your ideas. It costs about $10,000-$15,000 to retain a patent attorney to go through the formalities of filing patent applications, which doesn't guarantee that you'll ever get a patent. Once the patent is granted, you have to pay maintenance fees according to a schedule (about $2,500 every three years) that can total to $20,000-$30,000 over the 20-year life of the patent. By the end of the life of the patent, one can expect to pay about $50,000 to actually own the patent.

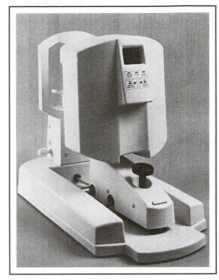

"Reinventing the Suitcase by Adding the Wheel," Joe Sharkey, *The New York Times*, October 4, 2010:

Many thousands of years ago, there were two important inventions, the wheel and the sack. As a traveler, I can't help wondering why it took so long to put rollers on that sack to create wheeled luggage.

"It was one of my best ideas," Bernard D. Sadow said the other day. Mr. Sadow, who owned a Massachusetts company that made luggage and coats, is credited with inventing rolling luggage 40 years ago this month.

First, the background. Mr. Sadow, now 85, had his eureka moment in 1970 as he lugged two heavy suitcases through an airport while returning from a family vacation in Aruba. Waiting at customs, he said, he observed a worker effortlessly rolling a heavy machine on a wheeled skid.

"I said to my wife, 'You know, that's what we need for luggage,'" Mr. Sadow recalled. When he got back to work, he took casters off a wardrobe trunk and mounted them on a big travel suitcase. "I put a strap on the front and pulled it, and it worked," he said.

This invention, for which he holds United States Patent No. 3,653,474, "Rolling Luggage," did not take off immediately, though.

"People do not accept change well," Mr. Sadow said, recalling the many months he spent rolling his prototype bag on sales calls to department stores in New York and elsewhere. Finally, though, Macy's ordered some, and the market grew quickly as Macy's ads began promoting "The Luggage That Glides."

The patent, which Mr. Sadow applied for in 1970 and received in 1972, noted that people were dealing with luggage in a new way, as airplanes decisively replaced trains as the common mode of long-distance travel.

continued

"Reinventing the Suitcase by Adding the Wheel," *(continued)*

The patent stated, "Whereas formerly, luggage would be handled by porters and be loaded or unloaded at points convenient to the street, the large terminals of today, particularly air terminals, have increased the difficulty of baggage-handling." It added, "Baggage-handling has become perhaps the biggest single difficulty encountered by an air passenger."

Until Mr. Sadow's invention, the major recent innovation in luggage toting had been small, fold-up wheeled carts that travelers strapped suitcases to and pulled behind them. By the late 1960s, travel gear shops were selling lots of these as more Americans began flying, especially internationally.

But Mr. Sadow's suitcase was ultimately supplanted by a more popular innovation—the now ubiquitous Rollaboard and its imitators.

The Rollaboard was invented in 1987 by Robert Plath, a Northwest Airlines 747 pilot and avid home workshop tinkerer, who affixed two wheels and a long handle to suitcases that rolled upright, rather than being towed flat like Mr. Sadow's four-wheeled models.

Mr. Plath initially sold his Rollaboards to fellow flight crew members. But when travelers in airports saw flight attendants striding briskly through airports with their Rollaboards in tow, a whole new market was created. Within a few years, Mr. Plath had left flying to start Travelpro International, now a major luggage company. Other luggage makers quickly imitated the Rollaboard.

"Travelpro really popularized the telescoping handle with the two wheels, after Plath got the flight attendants to start carrying them," Richard Krulik, the chief executive of U.S. Luggage, whose subsidiary Briggs & Riley Travelware markets luggage. Mr. Sadow is the former owner of U.S. Luggage.

So why did it take so long for wheeled luggage to emerge? Mr. Sadow recalled the strong resistance he met on those early sales calls, when he was frequently told that men would not accept suitcases with wheels. "It was a very macho thing," he said.

But it was also a time of huge change in the culture of travel, as a growing number of people flew, airports became bigger and far more women began traveling alone, especially on business trips. It had taken a long time, but common sense and the quest for convenience prevailed. The suitcase acquired wheels; travelers no longer routinely needed porters and bellhops.

So here's a toast to the inventors, and especially to Mr. Sadow, on the fortieth anniversary of his rolling luggage. But let's also give three cheers to the flight attendants—the early adopters who showed the rest of us how to carry a suitcase sensibly.

Now if only someone could find a sensible way to stow that bag on an airplane.

United States Patent [19]

Bressner

[11] **Patent Number:** 5,681,063

[45] **Date of Patent:** Oct. 28, 1997

US005681063A

[54] **CONNECTOR ASSEMBLY FOR DOUBLE TUBING**

[75] Inventor: Gorm Bressner, Providence, R.I.

[73] Assignee: E.R. Squibb & Sons, Inc., Princeton, N.J.

[21] Appl. No.: 563,847

[22] Filed: Nov. 28, 1995

[51] Int. Cl.⁶ F16L 39/00

[52] U.S. Cl. 285/360; 285/376; 285/133.1; 285/138

[58] Field of Search 285/360, 376, 285/377, 133.1, 138

[56] **References Cited**

U.S. PATENT DOCUMENTS

448,261	3/1891	Ridge	285/133.1
917,204	4/1909	Walther	285/360
1,221,935	4/1917	White	285/376
1,525,794	2/1925	Blake	285/360
1,541,139	6/1925	Hayden et al.	285/377
1,947,593	2/1934	Hamilton	285/360
2,221,284	11/1940	Folsom	285/376
2,317,729	4/1943	Bruno	285/377
2,823,699	2/1958	Willis	285/376
3,129,993	4/1964	Ross	285/360
5,005,875	4/1991	Hune	28/360

FOREIGN PATENT DOCUMENTS

367363	3/1963	Switzerland	285/360

Primary Examiner—Eric K. Nicholson
Attorney, Agent, or Firm—Stuart E. Krieger

[57] **ABSTRACT**

The connector assembly for double tubing includes a pair of interengageable coupling members that engage when latches on the respective coupling members are aligned in a predetermined nonlatching position. Locking of the coupling members together is accomplished by rotating one of the coupling members with respect to the other coupling member to interengage the respective latches of each coupling member. A latch section of one of the coupling members extends transversely of the coupling member body and a latch section of the other coupling member extends longitudinally of the coupling member body. A locking notch in one of the latch sections receives the other latch section to place the coupling members in a locked position when one of the coupling members is rotated to engage the latches. Further rotation of the coupling members unlatches the respective latch members to permit separation of the coupling members upon imposition of oppositely directed forces on each of the coupling members. Whether the coupling members are engaged in a locked or unlocked condition, fluid flow through the coupling members is maintained because engagement of the coupling members aligns the fluid flow tubes of each coupling member in leak-tight fashion.

23 Claims, 4 Drawing Sheets

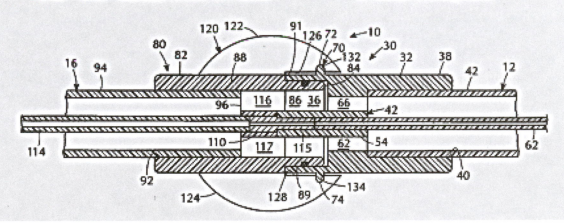

"The Patent Process," Gorm Bressner, 2010:

The patent process remains pretty much the same since I first started getting involved with patents. One has to file a Provisional Patent of the invention, which includes an abstract and detailed description of the invention, submit formulas, calculations, drawings or pictures of prototypes of the invention, and most importantly, be able to articulate the "claims" of the idea. The claims describe the novelty of the idea and how it differs from "prior art," the existing patents in the USPTO or in the public domain.

Once the application is filed, it will take anywhere from 12 months to 18 months before the patent office responds with questions or requests clarity over aspects of the invention…this is called an Office Action (essentially the first rejection by the examiner), and one has to further describe the nuances of the invention and how it differs from prior art…one of the criteria of a patentable idea is for its "non-intuitiveness."

During this time, one can also file for a Continuing Application, Divisional Patent or Continuation-in Part (CIP), which provides expansion of claims or claims to be added to the original patent application—this is frequently done to (literally) buy additional time (more application fees to the USPTO) when the patent first gets rejected.

If everything goes well, you'll receive a letter from the USPTO in about two years that you have been awarded a patent. You'll then have about three years of protection before the first maintenance fee is due and about a year to pay before it lapses.

Bressner family men.

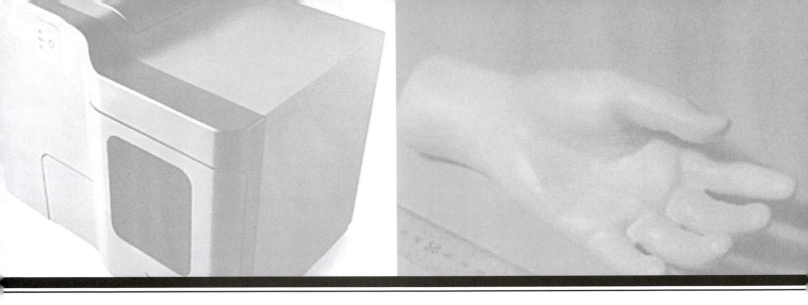

2010 News Feature

"3-D Printing Spurs a Manufacturing Revolution," Ashlee Vance, *The New York Times*, September 13, 2010:

SAN FRANCISCO—Businesses in the South Park district of San Francisco generally sell either Web technology or sandwiches and burritos. Bespoke Innovations plans to sell designer body parts.

Charles Overy, founder of LGM, has a model of a resort in Vail, Colo. "We used to take two months to build $100,000 models," he said, adding that now they cost about $2,000.

The company is using advances in a technology known as 3-D printing to create prosthetic limb casings wrapped in embroidered leather, shimmering metal or whatever else someone might want.

Scott Summit, a co-founder of Bespoke, and his partner, an orthopedic surgeon, are set to open a studio this fall where they will sell the limb coverings and experiment with printing entire customized limbs that could cost a tenth of comparable artificial limbs made using traditional methods. And they will be dishwasher-safe, too.

"I wanted to create a leg that had a level of humanity," Mr. Summit said. "It's unfortunate that people have had a product that's such a major part of their lives that was so underdesigned."

A 3-D printer, which has nothing to do with paper printers, creates an object by stacking one layer of material—typically plastic or metal—on top of another, much the same way a pastry chef makes baklava with sheets of phyllo dough.

The technology has been radically transformed from its origins as a tool used by manufacturers and designers to build prototypes.

These days it is giving rise to a string of never-before-possible businesses that are selling iPhone cases, lamps, doorknobs, jewelry, handbags, perfume bottles, clothing and architectural models. And while some wonder how successfully the technology will make the transition from manufacturing applications to producing consumer goods, its use is exploding.

A California start-up is even working on building houses. Its printer, which would fit on a tractor-trailer, would use patterns delivered by computer, squirt out layers of special concrete and build entire walls that could be connected to form the basis of a house.

It is manufacturing with a mouse click instead of hammers, nails and, well, workers. Advocates of the technology say that by doing away with manual labor, 3-D printing could revamp the economics of manufacturing and revive American industry as creativity and ingenuity replace labor costs as the main concern around a variety of goods.

"There is nothing to be gained by going overseas except for higher shipping charges," Mr. Summit said.

A wealth of design software programs, from free applications to the more sophisticated offerings of companies including Alibre and Autodesk, allows a person to concoct a product at home, then send the design to a company like Shapeways, which will print it and mail it back.

"We are enabling a class of ordinary people to take their ideas and turn those into physical, real products," said J. Paul Grayson, Alibre's chief executive. Mr. Grayson, said his customers had designed parts for antique cars, yo-yos, and even pieces for DNA analysis machines.

"We have a lot of individuals going from personal to commercial," Mr. Grayson said.

Manufacturers and designers have used 3-D printing technology for years, experimenting on the spot rather than sending off designs to be built elsewhere, usually in Asia, and then waiting for a model to return. Boeing, for example, might use the technique to make and test air-duct shapes before committing to a final design.

Depending on the type of job at hand, a typical 3-D printer can cost from $10,000 to more than $100,000. Stratasys and 3D Systems are among the industry leaders. And MakerBot Industries sells a hobbyist kit for under $1,000.

Moving the technology beyond manufacturing does pose challenges. Customized products, for example, may be more expensive than mass-produced ones, and take longer to make. And the concept may seem out of place in a world trained to appreciate the merits of mass consumption.

But as 3-D printing machines have improved and fallen in cost along with the materials used to make products, new businesses have cropped up.

Freedom of Creation, based in Amsterdam, designs and prints exotic furniture and other fixtures for hotels and restaurants. It also makes iPhone cases for Apple, eye cream bottles for L'Oréal, and jewelry and handbags for sale on its Web site.

Various designers have turned to the company for clothing that interlaces plastic to create form-hugging blouses, while others have requested spiky coverings for lights that look as if they could be the offspring of a sea urchin and a lamp shade.

"The aim was always to bring this to consumers instead of keeping it a secret at NASA and big manufacturers," said Janne Kyttanen, 36, who founded Freedom of Creation about 10 years ago. "Everyone thought I was a lunatic when we started."

His company can take risks with "out there" designs since it doesn't need to print an object until it is ordered, Mr. Kyttanen said. Ikea can worry about mass appeal.

LGM, based in Minturn, Colo., uses a 3-D printing machine to create models of buildings and resorts for architectural firms.

"We used to take two months to build $100,000 models," said Charles Overy, the founder of LGM. "Well, that type of work is gone because developers aren't putting up that type of money anymore." Now, he said, he is building $2,000 models using an architect's design and homegrown software for a 3-D printer. He can turn around a model in one night.

Next, the company plans to design and print doorknobs and other fixtures for buildings, creating unique items. "We are moving from handcraft to digital craft," Mr. Overy said.

But Contour Crafting, based in Los Angeles, has pushed 3-D printing technology to its limits.

Based on research done by Dr. Behrokh Khoshnevis, an engineering professor at the University of Southern California, Contour Crafting has created a giant 3-D printing device for building houses. The start-up company is seeking money to commercialize a machine capable of building an entire house in one go using a machine that fits on the back of a tractor-trailer.

The 3-D printing wave has caught the attention of some of the world's biggest technology companies. Hewlett-Packard, the largest paper-printer maker, has started reselling 3-D printing machines made by Stratasys. And Google uses the CADspan software from LGM to help people using its SketchUp design software to turn their creations into 3-D printable objects.

At Bespoke, Mr. Summit has built a scanning contraption to examine limbs using a camera. After the scan, a detailed image is transmitted to a computer, and Mr. Summit can begin sculpting his limb art. He uses a 3-D printer to create plastic shells that fit around the prosthetic limbs, and then wraps the shells in any flexible material the customer desires, be it an old bomber jacket or a trusty boot.

"We can do a mid-century modern or a Harley aesthetic if that's what someone wants," Mr. Summit said. "If we can get to flexible wood, I am totally going to cut my own leg off."

Mr. Summit and his partner, Kenneth B. Trauner, the orthopedic surgeon, have built some test models of full legs that have sophisticated features like body symmetry, locking knees and flexing ankles. One artistic design is metal-plated in some areas and leather-wrapped in others.

"It costs $5,000 to $6,000 to print one of these legs, and it has features that aren't even found in legs that cost $60,000 today," Mr. Summit said.

"We want the people to have input and pick out their options," he added. "It's about going from the Model T to something like a Mini that has 10 million permutations."

CREDITS

INDEX

Bold indicates profile subjects.

Bold indicates profile subjects.

Bold indicates profile subjects.

Bold indicates profile subjects.

Bold indicates profile subjects.

Bold indicates profile subjects.

Bold indicates profile subjects.

Bold indicates profile subjects.

Bold indicates profile subjects.

Bold indicates profile subjects.

Bold indicates profile subjects.

Grey House Publishing
2010 Title List

Visit **www.greyhouse.com** for Product Information, Table of Contents and Sample Pages

General Reference

American Environmental Leaders: From Colonial Times to the Present
An African Biographical Dictionary
Encyclopedia of African-American Writing
Encyclopedia of American Industries
Encyclopedia of Emerging Industries
Encyclopedia of Global Industries
Encyclopedia of Gun Control & Gun Rights
Encyclopedia of Invasions & Conquests
Encyclopedia of Prisoners of War & Internment
Encyclopedia of Religion & Law in America
Encyclopedia of Rural America
Encyclopedia of the United States Cabinet, 1789-2010
Encyclopedia of Warrior Peoples & Fighting Groups
Environmental Resource Handbook
From Suffrage to the Senate: America's Political Women
Global Terror & Political Risk Assessment
Historical Dictionary of War Journalism
Human Rights in the United States
Nations of the World
Political Corruption in America
Speakers of the House of Representatives, 1789-2009
The Environmental Debate: A Documentary History
The Evolution Wars: A Guide to the Debates
The Religious Right: A Reference Handbook
The Value of a Dollar: 1860-2009
The Value of a Dollar: Colonial Era
University & College Museums, Galleries & Related Facilities
Weather America
World Cultural Leaders of the 20th & 21st Centuries
Working Americans 1880-1999 Vol. I: The Working Class
Working Americans 1880-1999 Vol. II: The Middle Class
Working Americans 1880-1999 Vol. III: The Upper Class
Working Americans 1880-1999 Vol. IV: Their Children
Working Americans 1880-2003 Vol. V: At War
Working Americans 1880-2005 Vol. VI: Women at Work
Working Americans 1880-2006 Vol. VII: Social Movements
Working Americans 1880-2007 Vol. VIII: Immigrants
Working Americans 1770-1869 Vol. IX: Revol. War to the Civil War
Working Americans 1880-2009 Vol. X: Sports & Recreation
Working Americans 1880-2010 Vol. XI: Entrepreneurs & Inventors

Bowker's Books In Print®Titles

Books In Print®
Books In Print® Supplement
American Book Publishing Record® Annual
American Book Publishing Record® Monthly
Books Out Loud™
Bowker's Complete Video Directory™
Children's Books In Print®
El-Hi Textbooks & Serials In Print®
Forthcoming Books®
Large Print Books & Serials™
Law Books & Serials In Print™
Medical & Health Care Books In Print™
Publishers, Distributors & Wholesalers of the US™
Subject Guide to Books In Print®
Subject Guide to Children's Books In Print®

Business Information

Directory of Business Information Resources
Directory of Mail Order Catalogs
Directory of Venture Capital & Private Equity Firms
Food & Beverage Market Place
Grey House Homeland Security Directory
Grey House Performing Arts Directory
Hudson's Washington News Media Contacts Directory
New York State Directory
Sports Market Place Directory
The Rauch Guides – Industry Market Research Reports

Statistics & Demographics

America's Top-Rated Cities
America's Top-Rated Small Towns & Cities
America's Top-Rated Smaller Cities
Comparative Guide to American Suburbs
Comparative Guide to Health in America
Profiles of… Series – State Handbooks

Health Information

Comparative Guide to American Hospitals
Comparative Guide to Health in America
Complete Directory for Pediatric Disorders
Complete Directory for People with Chronic Illness
Complete Directory for People with Disabilities
Complete Mental Health Directory
Directory of Health Care Group Purchasing Organizations
Directory of Hospital Personnel
HMO/PPO Directory
Medical Device Register
Older Americans Information Directory

Education Information

Charter School Movement
Comparative Guide to American Elementary & Secondary Schools
Complete Learning Disabilities Directory
Educators Resource Directory
Special Education

TheStreet.com Ratings Guides

TheStreet.com Ratings Consumer Box Set
TheStreet.com Ratings Guide to Bank Fees & Service Charges
TheStreet.com Ratings Guide to Banks & Thrifts
TheStreet.com Ratings Guide to Bond & Money Market Mutual Funds
TheStreet.com Ratings Guide to Common Stocks
TheStreet.com Ratings Guide to Credit Unions
TheStreet.com Ratings Guide to Exchange-Traded Funds
TheStreet.com Ratings Guide to Health Insurers
TheStreet.com Ratings Guide to Life & Annuity Insurers
TheStreet.com Ratings Guide to Property & Casualty Insurers
TheStreet.com Ratings Guide to Stock Mutual Funds
TheStreet.com Ratings Ultimate Guided Tour of Stock Investing

Canadian General Reference

Associations Canada
Canadian Almanac & Directory
Canadian Environmental Resource Guide
Canadian Parliamentary Guide
Financial Services Canada
History of Canada
Libraries Canada

Grey House Publishing
4919 Route 22, PO Box 56, Amenia NY 12501-0056 | (800) 562-2139 | www.greyhouse.com | books@greyhouse.com